Collins

The Shangh Maths Project

For the English National Curriculum

Teacher's Guide 5A

Teacher's Guide Series Editor: Amanda Simpson
Practice Books Series Editor: Professor Lianghuo Fan
Authors: Sarah Eaton, Linda Glithro, Jane Jones, Steph King, Richard Perring, Paul Wrangles

Collins

William Collins' dream of knowledge for all began with the publication of his first book in 1819.

A self-educated mill worker, he not only enriched millions of lives, but also founded a flourishing publishing house. Today, staying true to this spirit, Collins books are packed with inspiration, innovation and practical expertise. They place you at the centre of a world of possibility and give you exactly what you need to explore it.

Collins. Freedom to teach.

Published by Collins
An imprint of HarperCollins*Publishers*
The News Building
1 London Bridge Street
London
SE1 9GF

Browse the complete Collins catalogue at
www.collins.co.uk

© HarperCollins*Publishers* Limited 2018

10 9 8 7 6 5 4 3 2 1

978-0-00-819723-0

The authors assert their moral rights to be identified as the authors of this work.

Teacher's Guide Series Editor: Amanda Simpson

Practice Books Series Editor: Professor Lianghuo Fan

Authors: Sarah Eaton, Linda Glithro, Jane Jones, Steph King, Richard Perring and Paul Wrangles

All rights reserved. No part of this publication may be reproduced, stored in a retrieval system, or transmitted in any form by any means, electronic, mechanical, photocopying, recording or otherwise, without the prior written permission of the Publisher or a licence permitting restricted copying in the United Kingdom issued by the Copyright Licensing Agency Ltd, Barnard's Inn, 86 Fetter Lane, London, EC4A 1EN.

British Library Cataloguing in Publication Data

A catalogue record for this publication is available from the British Library.

Publishing Manager: Fiona McGlade and Lizzie Catford
In-house Editor: Mike Appleton
In-house Editorial Assistant: August Stevens
Project Manager: Karen Williams
Copy Editors: Tanya Solomons and Karen Williams
Proofreader: Gerard Delaney
Cover design: Kevin Robbins and East China Normal University Press Ltd.
Internal design: 2Hoots Publishing Services Ltd
Typesetting: Ken Vail Graphic Design Ltd
Illustrations: Ken Vail Graphic Design Ltd
Production: Sarah Burke

Printed and bound by CPI Group (UK) Ltd, Croydon, CR0 4YY

MIX
Paper from responsible sources
FSC® C007454

This book is produced from independently certified FSC paper to ensure responsible forest management.

For more information visit:
www.harpercollins.co.uk/green

Contents

The Shanghai Maths Project: an overview ... iv

Chapter 1 Revising and improving ... 1
- Unit 1.1 Multiplication and division ... 3
- Unit 1.2 Addition and subtraction of fractions ... 10
- Unit 1.3 Decimals (1) ... 17
- Unit 1.4 Decimals (2) ... 25
- Unit 1.5 Mathematics plaza — which area is larger? ... 32

Chapter 2 Large numbers and measures ... 39
- Unit 2.1 Knowing large numbers (1) ... 40
- Unit 2.2 Knowing large numbers (2) ... 46
- Unit 2.3 Knowing large numbers (3) ... 52
- Unit 2.4 Rounding of large numbers (1) ... 57
- Unit 2.5 Rounding of large numbers (2) ... 62
- Unit 2.6 Converting kilograms and grams ... 66
- Unit 2.7 Litres and millilitres (1) ... 73
- Unit 2.8 Litres and millilitres (2) ... 80

Chapter 3 Dividing by 2-digit numbers ... 87
- Unit 3.1 Speed, time and distance (1) ... 89
- Unit 3.2 Speed, time and distance (2) ... 96
- Unit 3.3 Dividing 2-digit or 3-digit numbers by a 2-digit number (1) ... 103
- Unit 3.4 Dividing 2-digit or 3-digit numbers by a 2-digit number (2) ... 111
- Unit 3.5 Dividing 2-digit or 3-digit numbers by a 2-digit number (3) ... 121
- Unit 3.6 Dividing multi-digit numbers by a 2-digit number (1) ... 128
- Unit 3.7 Dividing multi-digit numbers by a 2-digit number (2) ... 137
- Unit 3.8 Practice and exercise ... 145

Chapter 4 Comparing fractions, improper fractions and mixed numbers ... 153
- Unit 4.1 Comparing fractions (1) ... 154
- Unit 4.2 Comparing fractions (2) ... 161
- Unit 4.3 Comparing fractions (3) ... 167
- Unit 4.4 Comparing fractions (4) ... 174
- Unit 4.5 Improper fractions and mixed numbers ... 181
- Unit 4.6 Adding and subtracting fractions with related denominators (1) ... 189
- Unit 4.7 Adding and subtracting fractions with related denominators (2) ... 198
- Unit 4.8 Multiplying fractions by whole numbers ... 206

Chapter 5 Consolidation and enhancement ... 214
- Unit 5.1 Large numbers and rounding (1) ... 216
- Unit 5.2 Large numbers and rounding (2) ... 222
- Unit 5.3 Four operations of numbers ... 226
- Unit 5.4 Properties of whole number operations (1) ... 233
- Unit 5.5 Properties of whole number operations (2) ... 240
- Unit 5.6 Properties of whole number operations (3) ... 247
- Unit 5.7 Roman numerals including thousands ... 255
- Unit 5.8 Solving problems in statistics ... 262

Resources ... 268

Answers ... 397

The Shanghai Maths Project: an overview

The Shanghai Maths Project is a collaboration between Collins and East China Normal University Press Ltd. adapting their bestselling maths programme, *One Lesson, One Exercise*, for England, using an expert team of authors and reviewers. This carefully crafted programme has been continually reviewed in China over the last 24 years, meaning that the materials have been tried and tested by teachers and children alike. Some new material has been written for The Shanghai Maths Project, but the structure of the original resource has been preserved and as much original material as possible has been retained.

The Shanghai Maths Project is a programme from Shanghai for Years 1–11. Teaching for mastery is at the heart of the entire programme, which, through the guidance and support found in the Teacher's Guides and Practice Books, provides complete coverage of the curriculum objectives for England. Teachers are well supported to deliver a high-quality curriculum using the best teaching methods; pupils are enabled to learn mathematics with understanding and the ability to apply knowledge fluently and flexibly in order to solve problems.

The programme consists of five components: Teacher's Guides (two per year), Practice Books (two per year), Shanghai Learning Book, Homework Guide and Collins Connect digital package.

In this guide, information and support for all teachers of primary maths is set out, unit by unit, so they are able to teach The Shanghai Maths Project coherently and confidently, and with appropriate progression through the whole mathematics curriculum.

The Shanghai Maths Project: an overview

Practice Books

The Practice Books are designed to serve as both teaching and learning resources. With graded arithmetic exercises, plus varied practice of key concepts and summative assessments for each year, each Practice Book offers intelligent practice and consolidation to promote deep learning and develop higher-order thinking.

There are two Practice Books for each year group: A and B. Pupils should have ownership of their copies of the Practice Books so they can engage with relevant exercises every day, integrated with preparatory whole-class and small-group teaching, recording their answers in the books.

The Practice Books contain:
- chapters made up of units, containing small steps of progression, with practice at each stage
- a test at the end of each chapter
- an end-of-year test in Practice Book B.

Each unit in the Practice Books consists of two sections: 'Basic questions' and 'Challenge and extension questions'.

We suggest that the 'Basic questions' be used for all pupils. Many of them, directly or sometimes with a little modification, can be used as starting questions, for motivation or introduction or as examples for clear explanation. They can also be used as in-class exercise questions – most likely for reinforcement and formative assessment, but also for pupils' further exploration. Almost all questions can be given for individual or peer work, especially when used as in-class exercise questions. Some are also suitable for group work or whole-class discussion.

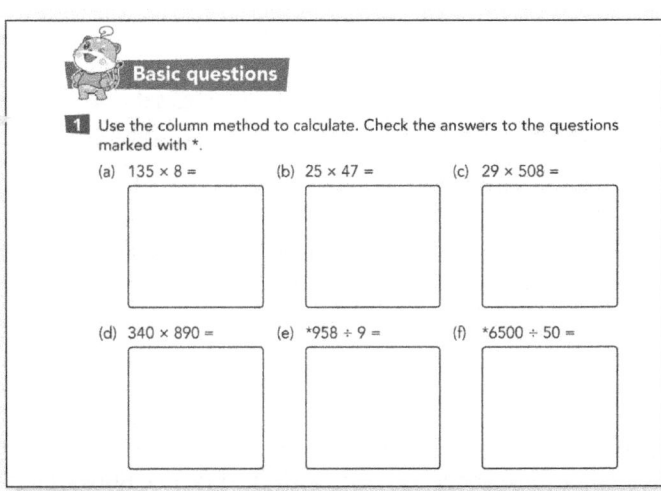

All pupils should be given the opportunity to solve some of the 'Challenge and extension questions', which are good for building confidence, but they should not always be required to solve all of them. A general suggestion is that most pupils try about 40–60 per cent of the 'Challenge and extension questions'.

Unit tests sometimes include questions that relate to content in the 'Challenge and extension questions'. This is clearly shown in the diagnostic assessment grids provided in the Teacher's Guides. Teachers should make their own judgments about how to use this information since not all pupils will have attempted the 'Challenge and extension questions'.

The Shanghai Maths Project: an overview

Teacher's Guides

Theory underpinning the Teacher's Guides

The Teacher's Guides contain everything teachers need in order to provide the highest quality teaching in all areas of mathematics, in line with the English National Curriculum. Core mathematics topics are developed with deep understanding in every year group. Some areas are not visited every year, though curriculum coverage is in line with Key Stage statutory requirements, as set out in the National curriculum in England: mathematics programmes of study (updated 2014).

There are two Teacher's Guides for each year group: one for the first part of the year (Teacher's Guide 5A) and the other for the second (Teacher's Guide 5B).

The Shanghai Maths Project is different from other maths schemes that are available, in that there is no book called a 'textbook'. Lessons are a mixture of teacher-led, peer and independent work. The Teacher's Guides set out subject knowledge that teachers might need, as well as guidance on pedagogical issues – the best ways to organise activities, to ask questions and to increase difficulty in small steps. Most importantly, the Teacher's Guides contain, threaded throughout the whole book, a strong element of professional development for teachers, focusing on the way mathematics concepts can be enabled to develop and connect with each other.

The Shanghai Maths Project Teacher's Guides are a complete reference for teachers working with the Practice Books. Each unit in the Practice Book for each year group is set out in the corresponding Teacher's Guide over a number of pages.

Most units will need to be taught over more than one lesson – some might need three lessons. In the Practice Books, units contain a great deal of learning, densely packed into a few questions. If pupils are to be able to tackle and succeed with the Practice Book questions, they need to have been guided to learn new mathematics and to connect it to their existing knowledge.

This can only be achieved when teachers are able to break down the conceptual learning that is needed and to provide relevant and high-quality teaching. The Teacher's Guides show teachers how to build up pupils' knowledge and experience so they learn with understanding in small steps. This way, learning is secure, robust and not reliant on memorisation.

The small steps that are necessary must be in line with what international research tells us about conceptual growth and development. The Shanghai Maths Project embodies that knowledge about conceptual development and about teaching for mastery of mathematics concepts and skills. The way that difficulty is varied, and the same ideas are presented in different contexts, is based on the notion of 'teaching with variation'. 'Variation' in Chinese mathematics carries particular meaning as it has emerged from a great deal of research in the area of 'variation theory'. Variation theory is based on the view that, 'When a particular aspect varies whilst all other aspects of the phenomenon are kept invariant, the learner will experience variation in the varying aspect and will discern that aspect. For example, when a child is shown three balls of the same size, shape, and material, but each of a different color: red, green and yellow, then it is very likely that the child's attention will be drawn to the color of the balls because it is the only aspect that varies.' (Bowden and Marton 1998, cited in Pang and Ling 2012)

In summary, two types of variation are necessary, each with a different function; both are necessary for the development of conceptual understanding.

Variation

Conceptual
Function – this variation provides pupils with multiple experiences from different perspectives.

↑

'multi-dimensional variation'

Procedural
Function – this variation helps learners:
- aquire knowledge step by step
- develop pupils' experience in problem solving progressively
- form well-structured knowledge.

↑

'developmental variation'

Teachers who are aiming to provide conceptual variation should vary the way the problem is presented without varying the structure of the problem itself.

The problem itself doesn't change but the way it is presented (or represented) does. Incorporation of a Concrete–Pictorial–Abstract (CPA) approach to teaching activities provides conceptual variation since pupils experience the same mathematical situations in parallel concrete, pictorial and abstract ways.

The Shanghai Maths Project: an overview

CPA is integrated in the Teacher's Guides so teachers are providing questions and experiences that incorporate appropriate conceptual variation.

Procedural variation is the process of:
- forming concepts logically and/or chronologically (i.e. scaffolding, transforming)
- arriving at solutions to problems
- forming knowledge structures (generalising across contexts).

In the Practice Book there are numerous examples of procedural variation in which pupils gradually build up knowledge, step by step; often they are exposed to patterns that teachers should guide them to perceive and explore.

It is this embedded variation that means that when The Shanghai Maths Project is at the heart of mathematics teaching throughout the school, teachers can be confident that the curriculum is of the highest order and it will be delivered by teachers who are informed and confident about how to support pupils to develop strong, connected concepts.

Teaching for mastery

There is no single definition of mathematics mastery. The term 'mastery' is used in conjunction with various aspects of education – to describe goals, attainment levels or a type of teaching. In teaching in Shanghai, mastery of concepts is characterised as 'thorough understanding' and is one of the aims of maths teaching in Shanghai.

Thorough understanding is evident in what pupils do and say. A concept can be seen to have been mastered when a pupil:
- is able to interpret and construct multiple representations of aspects of that concept
- can communicate relevant ideas and reason clearly about that concept using appropriate mathematical language
- can solve problems using the knowledge learned in familiar and new situations, collaboratively and independently.

Within The Shanghai Maths Project, mastery is a goal, achievable through high-quality teaching and learning experiences that include opportunities to explore, articulate thinking, conjecture, practise, clarify, apply and integrate new understandings piece by piece. Learning is carefully structured throughout and across the programme, with Teacher's Guides and Practice Books interwoven – chapter by chapter, unit by unit, question by question.

Since so much conceptual learning is to be achieved with each of the questions in any Practice Book unit, teachers are provided with guidance for each question, breaking down the development that will occur and how they should facilitate this – suggestions for teachers' questions, problems for pupils, activities and resources are clearly set out in an appropriate sequence.

In this way, teaching and learning are unified and consolidated. Coherence within and across components of the programme is an important aspect of The Shanghai Maths Project, in which Practice Books and Teacher's Guides, when used together, form a strong, effective teaching programme.

Promoting pupil engagement

The digital package on Collins Connect contains a variety of resources for concept development, problem solving and practice, provided in different ways. Images can be projected and shared with the class from the Image Bank. Other resources, for pupils to work with directly, are provided as photocopiable resource sheets at the back of the Teacher's Guides, and on Collins Connect. These might be practical activities, games, puzzles or investigations, or are sometimes more straightforward practice exercises. Teachers are signposted to these as 'Resources' in the Unit guidance.

Coverage of the curriculum is comprehensive, coherent and consolidated. Ideas are developed meaningfully, through intelligent practice, incorporating skilful questioning that exposes mathematical structures and connections.

Shanghai Year 5 Learning Book

Shanghai Year 5 Learning Books are for pupils to use. They are concise, colourful references that set out all the key ideas taught in the year, using images and explanations pupils will be familiar with from their lessons. Ideally, the books will be available to pupils during their maths lessons and at other times during the school day so they can access them easily if they need support for thinking about maths. The books are set out to correspond to each chapter* as it is taught and provide all the key images and vocabulary pupils will need in order to think things through independently or with a partner, resolving issues for themselves as much as possible. The Year 5 Learning Book might sometimes be taken home and shared with parents: this enables pupils, parents and teachers to form positive relationships around maths teaching that is of great benefit to children's learning.

---

* Note that because Chapter 6 in Year 5 is a Consolidation and Enhancement Chapter, there is no Chapter 6 in the Year 5 Learning Book.

The Shanghai Maths Project: an overview

How to use the Teacher's Guides

Teaching

Units taught in the first half of Year 5:

Contents

Chapter 1 Revising and improving
- 1.1 Multiplication and division.........................1
- 1.2 Addition and subtraction of fractions 4
- 1.3 Decimals (1)....................................7
- 1.4 Decimals (2)....................................9
- 1.5 Mathematics plaza — which area is larger?.......12
- Chapter 1 test....................................16

Chapter 2 Large numbers and measures
- 2.1 Knowing large numbers (1)......................20
- 2.2 Knowing large numbers (2)......................25
- 2.3 Knowing large numbers (3)......................29
- 2.4 Rounding of large numbers (1)..................32
- 2.5 Rounding of large numbers (2)..................36
- 2.6 Converting kilograms and grams.................38
- 2.7 Litres and millilitres (1).....................41
- 2.8 Litres and millilitres (2).....................44
- Chapter 2 test....................................47

Chapter 3 Dividing by 2-digit numbers
- 3.1 Speed, time and distance (1)...................53
- 3.2 Speed, time and distance (2)...................56
- 3.3 Dividing 2-digit or 3-digit numbers by a 2-digit number (1).....................................59
- 3.4 Dividing 2-digit or 3-digit numbers by a 2-digit number (2).....................................63
- 3.5 Dividing 2-digit or 3-digit numbers by a 2-digit number (3).....................................67
- 3.6 Dividing multi-digit numbers by a 2-digit number (1)....71
- 3.7 Dividing multi-digit numbers by a 2-digit number (2)....75
- 3.8 Practice and exercise..........................78
- Chapter 3 test....................................81

Chapter 4 Comparing fractions, improper fractions and mixed numbers
- 4.1 Comparing fractions (1)........................85
- 4.2 Comparing fractions (2)........................88
- 4.3 Comparing fractions (3)........................91
- 4.4 Comparing fractions (4)........................94
- 4.5 Improper fractions and mixed numbers 98
- 4.6 Adding and subtracting fractions with related denominators (1)..............................101
- 4.7 Adding and subtracting fractions with related denominators (2)..............................105
- 4.8 Multiplying fractions by whole numbers 108
- Chapter 4 test...................................112

Chapter 5 Consolidation and enhancement
- 5.1 Large numbers and rounding (1).................116
- 5.2 Large numbers and rounding (2).................120
- 5.3 Four operations of numbers 124
- 5.4 Properties of whole number operations (1).....127
- 5.5 Properties of whole number operations (2).....130
- 5.6 Properties of whole number operations (3).....133
- 5.7 Roman numerals including thousands............138
- 5.8 Solving problems in statistics 140
- Chapter 5 test...................................144

Teacher's Guide 5A sets out, for each chapter and unit in Practice Book 5A, a number of things that teachers will need to know if their teaching is to be effective and their pupils are to achieve mastery of the mathematics contained in the Practice Book.

Each chapter begins with a chapter overview that summarises, in a table, how Practice Book questions and classroom activities suggested in the Teacher's Guide relate to National Curriculum statutory requirements.

Chapter overview

Area of mathematics	National Curriculum statutory requirements for Key Stage 2	Shanghai Maths Project reference
Number – number and place value	Year 5 Programme of study: Pupils should be taught to:	
	■ read, write, order and compare numbers to at least 1 000 000 and determine the value of each digit	Year 5, Units 2.1, 2.2, 2.3
	■ count forwards or backwards in steps of powers of 10 for any given number up to 1 000 000	Year 5, Units 2.1, 2.2, 2.3
	■ round any number up to 1 000 000 to the nearest 10, 100, 1000, 10 000 and 100 000	Year 5, Units 2.4, 2.5
	■ solve number problems and practical problems that involve all of the above.	Year 5, Units 2.4, 2.5
	Year 6 Programme of study: Pupils should be taught to:	
	■ read, write, order and compare numbers up to 10 000 000 and determine the value of each digit	Year 5, Unit 2.1, 2.2, 2.3
	■ round any whole number to a required degree of accuracy	Year 5, Units 2.4, 2.5
	■ solve number and practical problems that involve all of the above.	Year 5, Units 2.1, 2.2, 2.3, 2.4, 2.5
Measurement	Year 5 Programme of study	

The Shanghai Maths Project: an overview

It is important to note that the National Curriculum requirements are statutory at the end of each Key Stage and that The Shanghai Maths Project does fulfil (at least) those end of Key Stage requirements. However, some aspects are not covered in the same year group as they are in the National Curriculum Programme of Study – for example, end of Key Stage 1 requirements for 'Money' are achieved in Year 2 and 'Money' is not taught again in Year 2.

All units will need to be taught over 1–3 lessons. Teachers must use their judgment as to when pupils are ready to move on to new learning within each unit – it is a principle of teaching for mastery that pupils are given opportunities to grasp the learning that is intended before moving to the next variation of the concept or to the next unit.

All units begin with a unit overview, which has four sections:

Conceptual context – a short section summarising the conceptual learning that will be brought about through Practice Book questions and related activities. Links with previous learning and future learning will be noted in this section.

Conceptual context

The first three units in this chapter explain the mathematical magnitudes of millions (and later billions), and how to read and write these very large numbers. Pupils are already familiar with the concept of place value where each new column on the left is 10 times bigger than the column on its right.

(i) A continuous string of numbers would be very difficult to read. To make reading them easier, numbers are separated into groups of three. Each group contains three subgroups: ones, tens and hundreds. This is illustrated in the place value table below.

Millions			Thousands			Ones		
Hundreds	Tens	Ones	Hundreds	Tens	Ones	Hundreds	Tens	Ones

To read numbers without a place value chart, numbers are separated into groups of three, beginning from the right. Numbers are then read from the left, beginning with the largest group. Thus 123456789 is separated from the right to become 123 456 789 and is read from the left as one hundred and twenty-three million, four hundred and fifty-six thousand, seven hundred and eighty-nine.

Learning pupils will have achieved at the end of the unit

- Pupils will have identified the place value of each digit in numbers containing up to nine digits (Q1, Q2, Q3, Q4)
- Pupils will have established that large numbers are written as groups of three digits, separated into groups from the right (Q1)
- Reading and writing numbers containing up to nine digits will have been practised (Q1, Q2, Q3, Q4)
- The use of place value tables will have been extended to include millions (Q1, Q2)
- The use of zero as a placeholder will have been extended so it is understood in numbers containing up to nine digits (Q1, Q2, Q3, Q4)
- Pupils will have explored partitioning numbers containing up to nine digits (Q2)

This list indicates how skills and concepts will have formed and developed during work on particular questions within this unit.

These are resources useful for the lesson, including photocopiable resources supplied in the Teacher's Guide. (Those listed are the ones needed for 'Basic questions' – not for 'Challenge and extension questions'.)

This is a list of vocabulary necessary for teachers and pupils to use in the lesson.

Resources

place value chart; place value arrow cards (to include millions); mini whiteboards; **Resource 5.2.1a** Making 9-digit numbers; **Resource 5.2.1b** Value of the 4 in 9-digit numbers; **Resource 5.2.1c** Population numbers; **Resource 5.2.1d** 9-digit numbers in numerals and words; **Resource 5.2.1e** 9-digit number puzzles

Vocabulary

ten thousands, hundred thousands, millions, ten millions, hundred millions, placeholder

The Shanghai Maths Project: an overview

After the unit overview, the Teacher's Guide goes on to describe how teachers might introduce and develop necessary, relevant ideas and how to integrate them with questions in the Practice Book unit. For each question in the Practice Book, teaching is set out under the following headings:

> **What learning will pupils have achieved at the conclusion of Question X?**
> This list responds to the following questions: Why is this question here? How does this question help pupils' existing concepts to grow? What is happening in this unit to help pupils prepare for a new concept about …? This list of bullet points will give teachers insight into the rationale for the activities and exercises and will help them to hone their pedagogy and questioning.

> **What learning will pupils have achieved at the conclusion of Questions 3 and 4?**
> - Pupils will have identified the place value of each digit in numbers containing up to nine digits.
> - Reading and writing numbers containing up to nine digits will have been practised.
> - The use of zero as a placeholder will have been extended so it is understood in numbers containing up to nine digits.

> **Activities for whole-class instruction**
> - Give pupils mini whiteboards and ask them to draw a place value chart for nine-digit numbers, showing millions, thousands and ones. Check their charts.
>
> | Millions | | | Thousands | | | Ones | | |
> | --- | --- | --- | --- | --- | --- | --- | --- | --- |
> | Hundreds | Tens | Ones | Hundreds | Tens | Ones | Hundreds | Tens | Ones |
>
> - Ask pupils to identify particular columns by pointing to the correct column.
> - Pupils should complete Questions 3 and 4 in the Practice Book.

Activities for whole-class instruction

This is the largest section within each unit. For each question in the Practice Book, suggestions are set out for questions and activities that support pupils to form and develop concepts and deepen understanding. Suggestions are described in some detail and activities are carefully sequenced to enable coherent progression. Procedural fluency and conceptual learning are both valued and developed in tandem and in line with the Practice Book questions. Teachers are prompted to draw pupils' attention to connections and to guide them to perceive links for themselves so mathematical relationships and richly connected concepts are understood and can be applied.

The Concrete–Pictorial–Abstract (CPA) approach underpins suggestions for activities, particularly those intended to provide conceptual variation (varying the way the problem is presented without varying the structure of the problem itself). This contributes to conceptual variation by giving pupils opportunities to experience concepts in multiple representations – the concrete, the pictorial and the abstract. Pupils learn well when they are able to engage with ideas in a practical, concrete way and then go on to represent those ideas as pictures or diagrams, and ultimately as symbols. It is important, however, that a CPA approach is not understood as a one-way journey from concrete to abstract and that pupils do not need to work with concrete materials in practical ways if they can cope with abstract representations – this is a fallacy. Pupils of all ages do need to work with all kinds of representations since it is 'translating' between the concrete, pictorial and abstract that will deepen understanding, by rehearsing the links between them and strengthening conceptual connections. It is these connections that provide pupils with the capacity to solve problems, even in unfamiliar contexts.

In this section, the reasons underlying certain questions and activities are explained, so teachers learn the ways in which pupils' concepts need to develop and how to improve and refine their questioning and provision.

Usually, for each question, the focus will at first be on whole-class and partner work to introduce and develop ideas and understanding relevant to the question. Once the necessary learning has been achieved and practised, pupils will complete the Practice Book question, when it will be further reinforced and developed.

The Shanghai Maths Project: an overview

Same-day intervention

Pupils who have not been able to achieve the learning that was intended must be identified straight away so teachers can try to identify the barriers to their learning and help pupils to build their understanding in another way. (This is a principle of teaching for mastery.) In the Teacher's Guide, suggestions for teaching this group are included for each unit. Ideally, this intervention will take place on the same day as the original teaching. The intervention activity always provides a different experience from that of the main lesson – often the activity itself is different; sometimes the changes are to the approach and the explanations that enable pupils to access a similar activity.

> **Same-day intervention**
> - Give pupil pairs **Resource 5.2.1d** 9-digit numbers in numerals and words.
>
> Answers: two hundred and ten million; two hundred and one million; two hundred million, one hundred thousand; two hundred million and ten thousand; two hundred million and one thousand; two hundred million and one hundred; two hundred million and ten; two hundred million and one; 531 642 999; 100 200 300; 777 777 777; 963 864 210; 404 303 202

> **Same-day enrichment**
> - Give pupil pairs **Resource 5.2.1e** 9-digit number puzzles. They may work individually or in pairs as appropriate. Answers will vary.

Same-day enrichment

For pupils who do manage to achieve all the planned learning, additional activities are described. These are intended to enrich and extend the learning of the unit. This activity is often carried out by most of the class while others are engaged with the intervention activity.

Lessons might also have some of the following elements:

Information point
Inserted at points where it feels important to point something out along the way.

> (i) It is important that pupils know $\frac{7}{9}$ means 'seven one-ninths'; they will need this understanding when comparing fractions with the same denominator.

All say ...
Phrases and sentences to be spoken aloud by pupils in unison and repeated on multiple occasions whenever opportunities present themselves during, within and outside of the maths lesson.

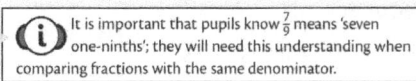
For fractions that have the same denominator, a larger numerator means the fraction is larger.

> Look out for ... pupils who find it tricky to compare fractions that are not organised from smallest to largest or largest to smallest. Encouraging them to select two fractions to compare and identify the correct inequality or equals symbol before moving on to another two may help with this.

Look out for ...
Common errors that pupils make and misconceptions that are often evident in a particular aspect of maths. Do not try to prevent these but recognise them where they occur and take opportunities to raise them in discussion in sensitive ways so pupils can align their conceptual understanding in more appropriate ways.

Within the guidance there are many prompts for teachers to ask pupils to explain their thinking or their answers. The language that pupils use when responding to questions in class is an important aspect of teaching with The Shanghai Maths Project. Pupils should be expected to use full sentences, including correct mathematical terms and language, to clarify the reasoning underpinning their solutions. This articulation of pupils' thinking is a valuable step in developing concepts, and opportunities should be taken wherever possible to encourage pupils to use full sentences when talking about their maths.

Ideas for resources and activities are for guidance; teachers might have better ideas and resources available. The principle guiding elements for each question should be 'What learning will pupils have achieved at the conclusion of Question X?' and the 'Information points'. If teachers can substitute their own questions and tasks and still achieve these learning objectives they should not feel concerned about diverging from the suggestions here.

The Shanghai Maths Project: an overview

Planning

The Teacher's Guides and Practice Books for Year 5 are split into two volumes, 5A and 5B, one for each part of the year.
- Teacher's Guide 5A and Practice Book 5A cover Chapters 1–5.
- Teacher's Guide 5B and Practice Book 5B cover Chapters 6–10.

Each unit in the Practice Book will need 1–3 lessons for effective teaching and learning of the conceptual content in that unit. Teachers will judge precisely how to plan the teaching year, but, as a general guide, they should aim to complete Chapters 1–4 in the autumn term, Chapters 4–8 in the spring term and Chapters 8–10 in the summer term.

The recommended teaching sequence is as set out in the Practice Books.

Statutory requirements of the National Curriculum in England 2013 (updated 2014) are fully met, and often exceeded, by the programme contained in The Shanghai Maths Project. It should be noted that some curriculum objectives are not covered in the same year group as they are in the National Curriculum Programme of Study – however, since it is end of Key Stage requirements that are statutory, schools following The Shanghai Maths Project are meeting legal curriculum requirements.

A chapter overview at the beginning of each chapter shows, in a table, how Practice Book questions and classroom activities suggested in the Teacher's Guide relate to National Curriculum statutory requirements.

Level of detail

Within each unit, a series of whole-class activities is listed, linked to each question. Within these are questions for pupils that will:
- structure and support pupils' learning, and
- aid teachers' assessments during the lesson.

Questions and questioning

Within the guidance for each question are sequences of questions that teachers should ask pupils. Embedded within these is the procedural variation that will help pupils to make connections across their knowledge and experience and support them to 'bridge' to the next level of complexity in the concept being learned.

In preparing for each lesson, teachers will find that, by reading the guidance thoroughly, they will learn for themselves how these sequences of questions very gradually expose more of the maths to be learned, how small those steps of progression need to be, and how carefully crafted the sequence must be. With experience, teachers will find they need to refer to the pupils' questions in the guidance less, as they learn more about how maths concepts need to be nurtured and as they become skilled at 'designing' their own series of questions.

Is it necessary to do everything suggested in the Teacher's Guide?

Activities are described in some detail so teachers understand how to build up the level of challenge and how to vary the contexts and representations used appropriately. These two aspects of teaching mathematics are often called 'intelligent practice'. If pupils are to learn concepts so they are long-lasting and provide learners with the capacity to apply their learning fluently and flexibly in order to solve problems, it is these two aspects of maths teaching that must be achieved to a high standard. The guidance contained in this Teacher's Guide is sufficiently detailed to support teachers to do this.

Teachers who are already expert practitioners in teaching for mastery might use the Teacher's Guide in a different way from those who feel they need more support. The unit overview provides a summary of the concepts and skills learned when pupils work through the activities set out in the guidance and integrated with the Practice Book. Expert mastery teachers might, therefore, select from the activities described and supplement with others from their own resources, confident in their own 'intelligent practice'.

There is more material in the Teachers' Guide than most teachers will need. This is because there are enrichment and intervention activities designed to match each question in the Practice Book. Teachers might find that they are able to deliver the programme, keeping their whole class focused on the same content at all times. This means that all pupils receive teaching input, then complete particular Practice Book questions, before returning for teaching related to the next part of the lesson together. This would look like this:

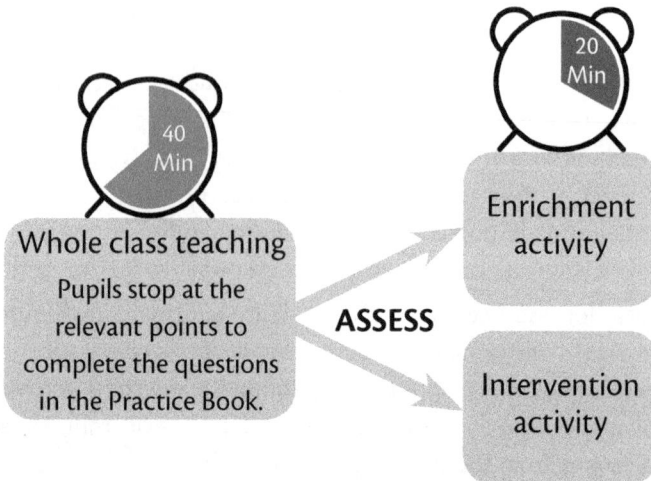

The Shanghai Maths Project: an overview

Following this model, at the end of the first session of the day, teachers will use pupils' attainment, evident in class interactions and Practice Book exercises to assess which pupils require intervention. Teachers then select which of the enrichment and intervention activities, linked to the content taught, are most relevant for their class that day. Usually, more than one question will have been covered during the lesson so some activities will not be used.

There is also scope for teachers to be more flexible if they find it difficult to keep the whole class working at the same pace. If there is a disparity among pupils in the time taken to complete Practice Book questions, teachers can select one enrichment activity for all early finishers to move on to if they complete the Practice Book questions quickly. The enrichment activity might be something that pupils work on in two or three 'bites' following completion of successive Practice Book questions at different stages in the lesson.

All pupils should come together for the second and consecutive teaching inputs. Following the next input, all pupils should complete the relevant practice questions and, if appropriate, return to their enrichment activity.

The enrichment activity selected to be used would be the same for all pupils and would not then be available for use in the second part of the maths input later in the day (or next day).

As with the previous, simpler, model, at the end of the first session of the day, teachers will use pupils' attainment, evident in class interactions and Practice Book exercises to assess which pupils require intervention and which should go on to complete other enrichment activities.

Assessing

Ongoing assessment, during lessons, will need to inform judgments about which pupils need further support. Of course, prompt marking will also inform these decisions, but this should not be the only basis for daily assessments – teachers will learn a lot about what pupils understand through skilful questioning and observation during lessons.

At the end of each chapter, a chapter test will revisit the content of the units within that chapter. Attainment in the text can be mapped to particular questions and units so teachers can diagnose particular needs for individuals and groups. Analysis of results from chapter tests will also reveal questions or units that caused difficulties for a large proportion of the class, indicating that more time is needed on that question/unit when it is next taught.

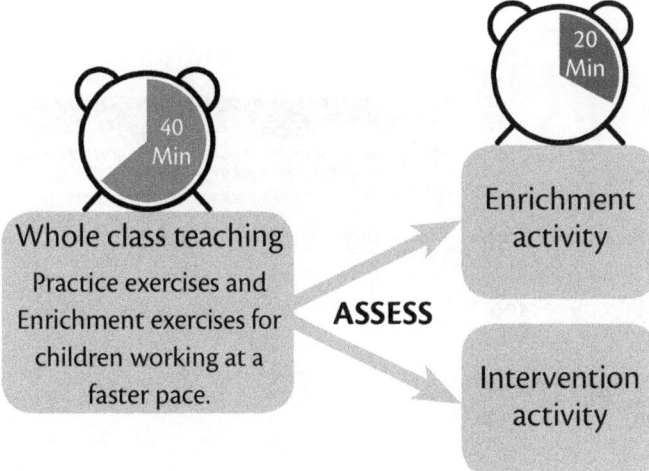

The Shanghai Maths Project: an overview

Shanghai Year 5 Learning Book

As referenced on page vii, The Shanghai Maths Project Year 5 Learning Book is a pupil textbook containing the Year 5 maths facts and full pictorial glossary to enable children to master the Year 5 maths programmes of study for England. It sits alongside the Practice Books to be used as a reference book in class or at home.

Maths facts correspond to the chapters in the Practice Books for ease of use.

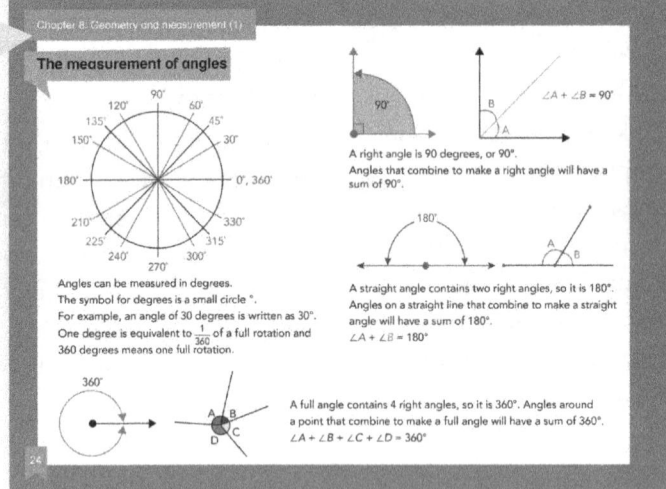

Key models and images are provided for each mathematical concept.

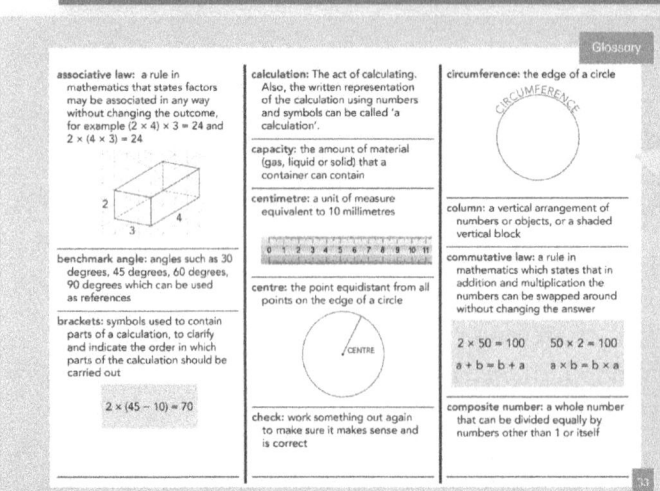

A visual glossary defines the key mathematical vocabulary children need to master.

Homework Guides

The Shanghai Maths Project Homework Guide 5 is a photocopiable master book for the teacher. There is one book per year, containing a homework sheet for every unit, directly related to the maths being covered in the Practice Book unit. There is a 'Learning Together' activity on each page that includes an idea for practical maths the parent or guardian can do with the child.

Homework is directly related to the maths being covered in class.

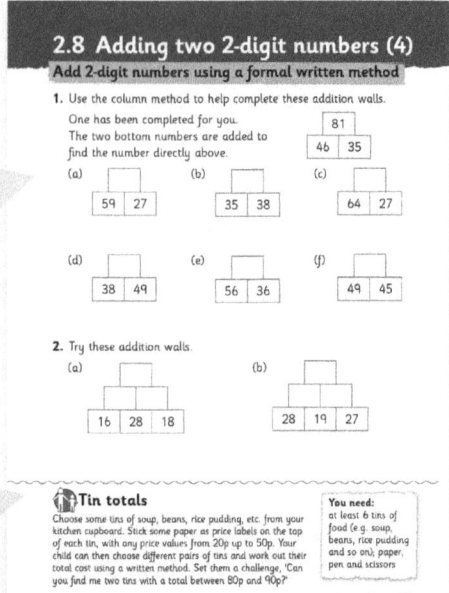

An idea for practical maths the parent or guardian can do with the child

The Shanghai Maths Project: an overview

Collins Connect

Collins Connect is the home for all the digital teaching resources provided by The Shanghai Maths Project.

The Collins Connect pack for The Shanghai Maths Project consists of four sections: Teach, Resources, Record, Support.

Teach

The Teach section contains all the content from the Teacher's Guides and Homework Guides, organised by chapter and unit.
- The entire book can be accessed at the top level so teachers can search and find objectives or key words easily.
- Chapters and units can be re-ordered and customised to match individual teachers' planning.
- Chapters and units can be marked as complete by the teacher.
- All the teaching resources for a chapter are grouped together and easy to locate.
- Each unit has its own page from which the contents of the Teacher's Guide, Homework Guide and any accompanying resources can be accessed.
- Teachers can record teacher judgments against National Curriculum attainment targets for individual pupils or the whole class with the record-keeping tool.
- Units from the Teacher's Guide and Homework Guide are provided in PDF and Microsoft Word versions so teachers can edit and customise the contents.
- Any accompanying resources can be displayed or downloaded from the same page.

Resources

The Resources section contains 35 interactive whiteboard tools and an image bank for front-of-class display.
- The 35 maths tools cover all topics, and can be customised and used flexibly by teachers as part of their lessons.
- The image bank contains the images from the Teacher's Guide, which can support pupils' learning. They can be enlarged and shown on the whiteboard.

Record

The Record section is the home of the record-keeping tool for The Shanghai Maths Project. Each unit is linked to attainment targets in the National Curriculum for England, and teachers can easily make records and judgments for individual pupils, groups of pupils or whole classes using the tool from the 'Teach' section. Records and comments can also be added from the 'Record' section, and reports generated by class, by pupil, by domain or by National Curriculum attainment target.
- View and print reports in different formats for sharing with teachers, senior leaders and parents.
- Delve deeper into the records to check on the progress of individual pupils.
- Instantly check on the progress of the class in each domain.

Support

The Support section contains the Teacher's Guide introduction in PDF and Word formats, along with CPD advice and guidance.

Chapter 1
Revising and improving

Chapter overview

Area of mathematics	National Curriculum statutory requirements for Key Stage 2	Shanghai Maths Project reference
Number – fractions (including decimals)	Year 4 Programme of study: Pupils should be taught to: ■ recognise and show, using diagrams, families of common equivalent fractions	Year 5, Unit 1.2
	■ solve problems involving increasingly harder fractions to calculate quantities, and fractions to divide quantities, including non-unit fractions where the answer is a whole number	Year 5, Unit 1.2
	■ add and subtract fractions with the same denominator	Year 5, Unit 1.2
	■ solve simple measure and money problems involving fractions and decimals to two decimal places	Year 5, Unit 1.3
	■ round decimals with one decimal place to the nearest whole number	Year 5, Unit 1.3
	■ compare numbers with the same number of decimal places up to two decimal places	Year 5, Unit 1.4
	■ recognise and write decimal equivalents of any number of tenths or hundredths.	Year 5, Units 1.3, 1.4
Number – fractions (including decimals and percentages)	Year 5 Programme of study Pupils should be taught to: ■ identify, name and write equivalent fractions of a given fraction, represented visually, including tenths and hundredths	Year 5, Unit 1.2
	■ add and subtract fractions with the same denominator and denominators that are multiples of the same number	Year 5, Unit 1.2
	■ read and write decimal numbers as fractions [for example, $0.71 = \frac{71}{100}$]	Year 5, Units 1.3, 1.4
	■ recognise and use thousandths and relate them to tenths, hundredths and decimal equivalents.	Year 5, Units 1.3, 1.4

Measurement	Year 5 Programme of study Pupils should be taught to: ■ measure and calculate the perimeter of composite rectilinear shapes in centimetres and metres ■ calculate and compare the area of rectangles (including squares), and including using standard units, square centimetres (cm^2) and square metres (m^2) and estimate the area of irregular shapes.	Year 5, Unit 1.5 Year 5, Unit 1.5
Number – multiplication and division	Year 4 Programme of study: Pupils should be taught to: ■ recall multiplication and division facts for multiplication tables up to 12 × 12 ■ use place value, known and derived facts to multiply and divide mentally, including: multiplying by 0 and 1; dividing by 1; multiplying together three numbers ■ recognise and use factor pairs and commutativity in mental calculations ■ multiply two-digit and three-digit numbers by a one-digit number using formal written layout.	Year 5, Unit 1.1 Year 5, Unit 1.1 Year 5, Unit 1.1 Year 5, Unit 1.1

Chapter 1 Revising and improving

Unit 1.1
Multiplication and division

Conceptual context

Pupils will have learned a range of strategies for written and mental calculation. These include using factors to expand multiplication sentences so that pupils can choose to do easy calculations, for example 16 × 25 = 4 × 4 × 25. Pupils also know about the order of operations and understand how to interpret brackets.

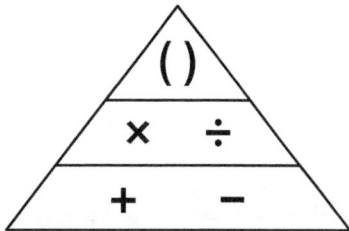

In this unit, pupils will revise these methods and further improve their fluency by making choices about the strategies they are using as well as utilising their reasoning skills to explain and justify.

Learning pupils will have achieved at the end of the unit

- Pupils will have developed fluency when using the column method to multiply and divide numbers with up to four digits (Q1, Q2, Q3)
- Knowledge of the laws of operations will have been applied to calculate efficiently (Q2)
- Pupils will be able to interpret mathematical vocabulary to complete calculations (Q3)
- Pupils will be able to apply knowledge of multiplication and division and use reasoning skills to explain and justify their decisions (Q3)

Resources

mini whiteboards; number cards; operation cards; place value counters; **Resource 5.1.1** Spot the mistake

Vocabulary

multiplication, multiply, times, factor, product, divide, division, divided by, inverse, dividend, divisor, quotient, order of operations, law of operations

Chapter 1 Revising and improving

Unit 1.1 Practice Book 5A, pages 1–3

Question 1

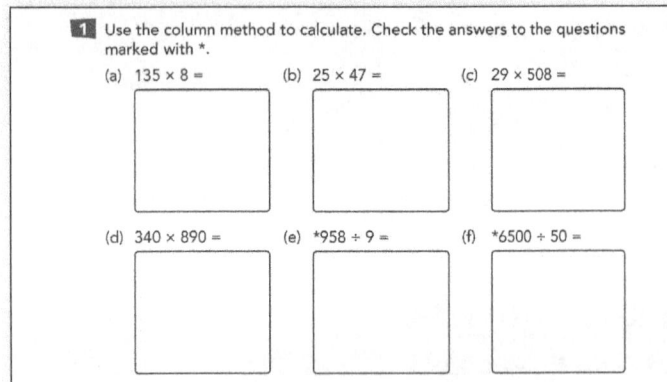

1 Use the column method to calculate. Check the answers to the questions marked with *.
(a) 135 × 8 =
(b) 25 × 47 =
(c) 29 × 508 =
(d) 340 × 890 =
(e) *958 ÷ 9 =
(f) *6500 ÷ 50 =

What learning will pupils have achieved at the conclusion of Question 1?

- Pupils will have developed fluency when using the column method to multiply and divide numbers with up to four digits.

Activities for whole-class instruction

- On the board, write 56 × 37 = ☐. Start by asking pupils to calculate an approximate answer by rounding. Pupils are likely to round both numbers up. Ask: *Will your approximation be greater than or less than the actual product? How do you know?* Draw the overlapped arrays below. Ask pupils what calculation the black array represents and what calculation the grey array represents?

- Pupils should calculate the product on their whiteboards using the column method and then share with a partner to check their answers. When pupils have finished, select a pupil to play the role of the teacher to model to the rest of the class how they calculated the answer. The pupil should try to talk through the process.
- On the board, write 752 ÷ 7 = ☐. Ask pupils to make an approximate answer by rounding and consider how they could partition the dividend to help them do this (700 + 52). Pupils should calculate the quotient on their whiteboards using the column method. Ask pupils to check their answers with a partner. Ask a different pupil from the last calculation to come to the front to model to the rest of the class how they calculated the answer. Once again, they should try to talk through the process.

- On the board, write 4300 ÷ 50 = ☐. Ask pupils what is different about this calculation from the previous division? Agree that the divisor is a two-digit number whereas the previous divisor was a one-digit number. Remind pupils that they divided by multiples of 10 in Year 3. Pupils should discuss in pairs whether they think they will need to use a column method. What facts do they already know that they can use to help them?
- Model dividing by 100 and then doubling the quotient:
  4300 ÷ 100 = 43
  43 × 2 = 86

Look out for ... pupils who try to halve the quotient because 50 is half of 100. It may help pupils to think about facts they know about 10 and 5 to help them understand that the quotient needs to be doubled because 50 is half of 100.

- Pupils should complete Question 1 in the Practice Book.

Same-day intervention

- Base 10 apparatus will be needed.
- **Multiplication:** Pupils will need to review their understanding that each column is multiplied separately to find the product for that 'part', and then the part products are added together.
- Write 163 × 6 = ☐ on the board and model each step with pupils.

```
        1   6   3
    ×           6
    ─────────────
            1   8   (6 × 3 ones)
        3   6   0   (6 × 6 tens)
        6   0   0   (6 × 1 hundred)
    ─────────────
        9   7   8
```

Look out for ... pupils who are finding each part of the multiplication difficult. These pupils will need to use place value counters and regroup when necessary, for example 18 ones for 1 ten and 8 ones.

- Complete the same calculation but without expanding. Ask: *What is the same and what is different?* Can pupils see the relationship between the two methods?

```
        1   6   3
    ×           6
    ─────────────
        9   7   8
            3   1
```

Chapter 1 Revising and improving Unit 1.1 Practice Book 5A, pages 1–3

- **Division:** (Pupils learned how to divide two- and three-digit numbers by a one-digit number in Year 3, Chapter 9.)
- On the board, write 678 ÷ 6 = ☐. Ask: *What is the value of the 6?* (6 hundreds) *What is the value of the 7?* (7 tens) *What is the value of the 8?* (8 ones) Pupils will have learned to divide using place value counters. Give pupils counters to represent 6 × 100, 7 × 10 and 8 × 1. Establish that because the divisor is 6, the counters will need to be shared into six equal groups.
- Give pupils six place value counters that each represent 100.

  (100)(100)(100)(100)(100)(100)

- Pupils should divide the counters into six columns to represent the six equal groups. Agree that they will have 1 ten in each column. Record this as shown below.

  ```
         1
  6 | 6 7 8      (100)(100)(100)(100)(100)(100)
  ```

- Give pupils seven place value counters that each represent 10.

  (10)(10)(10)(10)(10)(10)(10)

- Ask: *Can you share the tens into the six groups?* Pupils should arrange the counters underneath the six columns of 1 ten. Agree that there is 1 ten in each group. There will be 1 ten left over. Give pupils the opportunity to discuss what they could now do with their 1 ten to help them divide it into groups of 6. Agree that the ten should become 10 ones and go into the ones column so there are now 18 ones.

  ```
         1 1
  6 | 6 7 8      (100)(100)(100)(100)(100)(100)
      6 0 0      (10)(10)(10)(10)(10)(10)
        7 8
        6 0
        1 8
  ```

  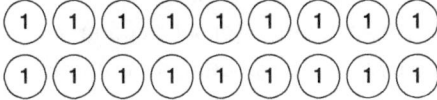

- Ask pupils to divide their 18 ones into the six groups. Agree that there are 3 ones in each column. Record this to complete the written calculation.

  ```
         1 1 3     (100)(100)(100)(100)(100)(100)
  6 | 6 7 8        (10)(10)(10)(10)(10)(10)
      6 0 0        (1)(1)(1)(1)(1)(1)
        7 8        (1)(1)(1)(1)(1)(1)
        6 0        (1)(1)(1)(1)(1)(1)
        1 8
        1 8
          0
  ```

Same-day enrichment

- Give pupils **Resource 5.1.1** Spot the mistake. Pupils should identify the errors in procedures or answers and then recalculate.

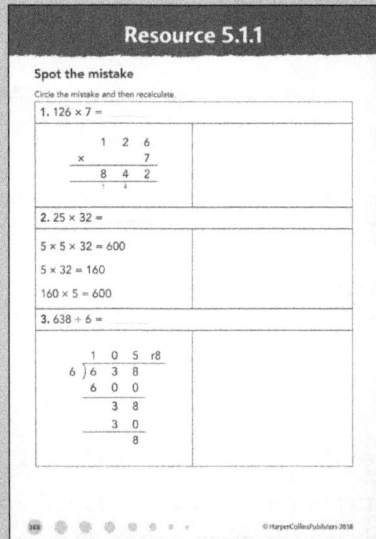

Answers: 1. 882. The 4 tens that have been carried over to the tens column should be circled; 2. 800. The calculation 160 × 5 = 600 should be circled; 3. 106 r 2. The numbers 30 and 8 should be circled.

Chapter 1 Revising and improving

Unit 1.1 Practice Book 5A, pages 1–3

Question 2

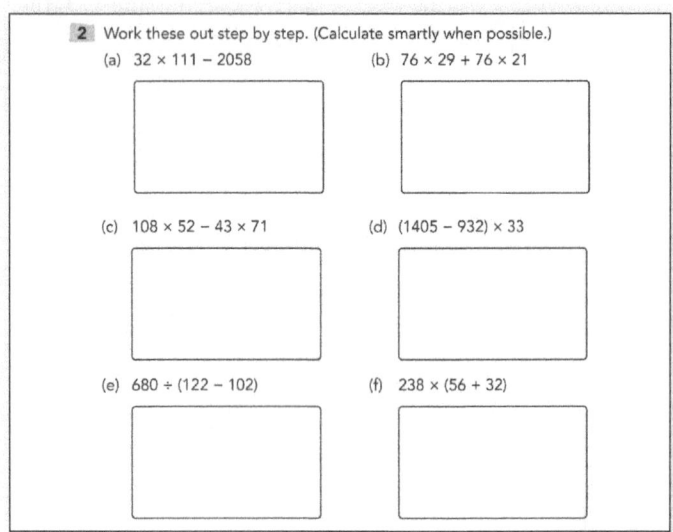

What learning will pupils have achieved at the conclusion of Question 2?

- Pupils will have developed fluency when using the column method to multiply and divide numbers with up to four digits.
- Knowledge of the laws of operations will have been applied to calculate efficiently.

Activities for whole-class instruction

- Give pupils symbols cards:

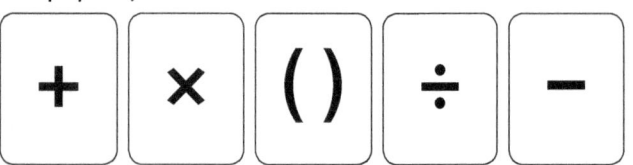

- Ask pupils to put the operation cards in the order that they should calculate when they appear in a calculation.

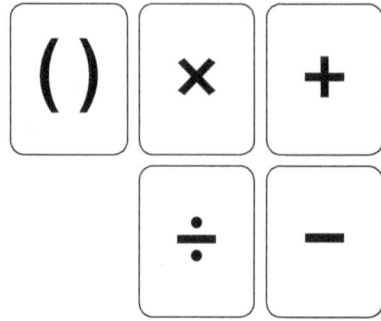

- Pupils should organise their cards in a similar way to those above. This should indicate that the brackets will be completed first, followed by multiplication/division then addition/subtraction.

 *When calculating with more than one operation, we complete the brackets first, multiplication and division second and addition and subtraction third.*

- Give pupils the following number cards:

  | 48 | 73 | 25 | 104 |

- Ask them to use at least three of the number cards and the operations to write a calculation for their partner to solve. Repeat.

- Pupils will be expected to recall what they have learned about the laws of operations from Year 4.

- The distributive law of multiplication over addition states that where an addition in brackets is multiplied by a number, each part of that addition can be written as a separate multiplication without the brackets and then those two products added together. For example, in the calculation 5 × (6 + 2), both the 6 and the 2 are being multiplied by 5. This can then be written as (5 × 6) + (5 × 2). Note that, while it is common in algebra to write a number immediately next to brackets to imply multiplication (without the need for a symbol), at this level, multiplication symbols should be used at all times to avoid confusion.

- The distributive law works in the opposite direction. In the following calculation the number 6 is common: (6 × 23) + (6 × 12). It can therefore be rewritten with brackets as 6 × (23 + 12) to show the 6 being 'distributed' across both parts of the addition. The distributive law of multiplication over subtraction works in the same way. For example, 7 × (10 − 3) is the same as (7 × 10) − (7 × 3), where the 7 is 'distributed' across the subtraction.

- The distributive law is particularly useful in helping pupils to simplify tricky multiplications. For example, if they can see that 73 × 12 is the same as 73 × (10 + 2) then they can use the distributive law to form two easier multiplications to find the total of 73 × 10 and 73 × 2.

- The distributive law could help simplify a calculation where each term in an addition (or subtraction) is being multiplied by the same amount, for example: (45 + 36) × 3 instead of 45 × 3 + 36 × 3.

- The associative law states that the numbers in an addition or multiplication can be grouped in different ways and the answer is unchanged. It only applies to addition and multiplication.

Chapter 1 Revising and improving

Unit 1.1 Practice Book 5A, pages 1–3

- Pupils have used their understanding of the associative law to simplify calculations before solving them so that they can calculate as efficiently as possible. They have learned it is sometimes quicker to expand brackets than to work out the calculation within them. For example, in the calculation (25 + 30) × 4, expanding the brackets gives the calculations 25 × 4 + 30 × 4. Pupils may instantly recognise that 25 × 4 is equal to 100, so all they need to do is to multiply 120 by 100.
- Show pupils these images from Year 4:
- These 'All say …' statements were used in Year 4. Discuss and revise them with pupils.
  - The commutative law means that the numbers in an addition or multiplication can be swapped around and the answer is unchanged.

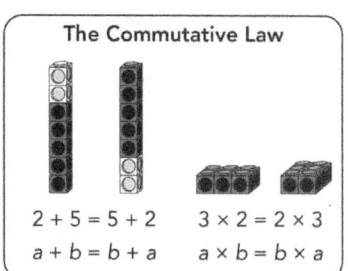

  - The associative law means that it doesn't matter which part of an addition or multiplication we do first.

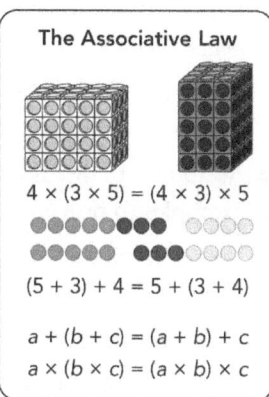

  - The distributive law means that multiplying something by each of the numbers inside the brackets and adding those products together is the same as adding the numbers in the brackets together and then multiplying that by the number outside the brackets.

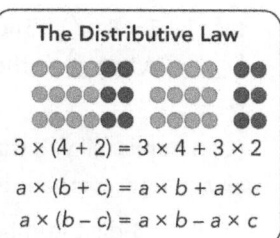

- Write the following calculation on the board:

  23 × 45 + 72 × 24

- Tell pupils that Amanda thinks the answer is 26 568. Ask: *Is she right?*
- Pupils should start by rounding to calculate an approximate answer first. Can they say whether they think Amanda's answer is right? Agree that Amanda's answer is too great to be the correct answer to the calculation. Ask: *What mistake did she make?* Pupils should notice that Amanda calculated from left to right without using her knowledge of the order of operations.

- Pupils should use mini whiteboards and work with a partner to calculate the correct answer to the calculation. When they have an answer, select a pupil to come to the front of the class to model their strategy to solve the calculation.
- On the board, write 23 × 45 + 23 × 25 = ☐. Ask pupils to discuss what they know that will help them to calculate. Do they need to use the same strategy as before? Why not?
- Draw the following image below on the board. Discuss what it represents.

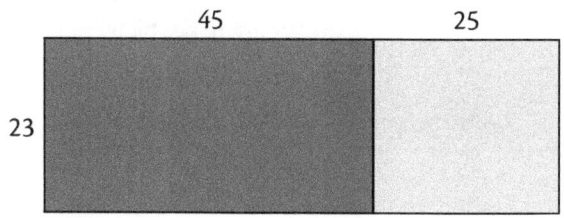

- Pupils should recognise that they do not need to calculate 23 × 45 and 23 × 25 but can calculate 23 × (45 + 25). Give pupils time to calculate the answer. This is an example of the distributive law being applied in order to calculate efficiently.
- Pupils should complete Question 2 in the Practice Book.

Same-day intervention

(i) Check whether the barrier to learning for any pupil struggling with Question 2 is related to understanding of:
- order of operations
- laws of operations
- difficulties with calculating.

- Give pupils the following calculations:

  61 × 84 − 2023
  59 × 100 + 24 × 78
  345 ÷ (276 − 271)
  25 × 62 − 34 × 18

- Ask them to look carefully at each calculation and then to label it to show the order in which they should calculate.

  For example:

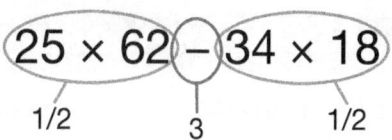

- Then ask them to calculate the answer.

Chapter 1 Revising and improving

Unit 1.1 Practice Book 5A, pages 1–3

Same-day enrichment

- Ask pupils to answer these questions using the cards from the whole-class activity:
  - What is the smallest value you can make?
  - What is the greatest value you can make?
  - Can you write a calculation where the answer is odd/even?
  - Can you write a calculation that has a solution close to …
  - Can you write a calculation that includes two multiplications and an addition in which
    - both multiplications must be worked out?
    - only one multiplication is needed?

Question 3

> **3** Fill in the spaces to make each statement correct.
> (a) The product of the greatest 2-digit number and the smallest 3-digit number is ☐ .
> (b) The product of 780 × 50 is a ☐-digit number with ☐ zero(s) at the end.
> (c) In ☐ ÷ 9 = 12 r △, the greatest number that △ could be is ☐ . When △ is that value, ☐ is ☐ .
> (d) ☐70 is a 3-digit number. In the calculation ☐70 ÷ 50, the quotient is a 1-digit number when the number in the ☐ is _____ . When the number in the ☐ is _____ , the quotient is a 2-digit number.

What learning will pupils have achieved at the conclusion of Question 3?

- Pupils will have developed fluency when using the column method to multiply and divide numbers with up to four digits.
- Pupils will be able to interpret mathematical vocabulary to complete calculations.
- Pupils will be able to apply knowledge of multiplication and division and use reasoning skills to explain and justify their decisions.

Activities for whole-class instruction

- As a starter, ask pupils to answer the following questions on their whiteboards:
  - What's the greatest one-digit number?

   9 is the greatest one-digit number.

  - What's the greatest two-digit number?

   99 is the greatest two-digit number.

  - What's the smallest two-digit number?

   10 is the smallest two-digit number.

  - What's the greatest two-digit number that is also a multiple of 5?

   95 is the greatest two-digit number that is also a multiple of 5.

  - What the smallest three-digit number?

   100 is the smallest three-digit number.

  - What's the greatest three-digit number that has no tens?

   909 is the greatest three-digit number that has no tens.

- Ask: *Is the following statement always, sometimes or never true?*

  When you multiply a two-digit number by a one-digit number, the product will be a three-digit number.

- Ask pupils to discuss the statement. Can they find examples to prove/disprove the statement?

- Show the class the following questions:

  The product of 620 × 50 is a _____-digit number with _____ zero(s) at the end.

  (Can pupils explain that an efficient way to calculate would be 620 × 100 and then halve the product?)

  In ☐ ÷ 7 = 8 r △. The greatest number △ could be is ____. When △ is the greatest number it can be, ☐ is ____.

  (Can pupils tell you that the largest possible remainder is always one less than the divisor?)

  ☐40 is a 3-digit number. In ☐40 ÷ 20, when the missing number is _____, the quotient is a one-digit number.

  (Can pupils tell you that the only possible missing number to give a one-digit quotient is 1 because 240 ÷ 20 = 12?)

- Ask pupils to talk about each question in pairs first. Ask: *What facts do you know that can help you to solve the question?* Emphasise that it is the journey to the answer that is most important.

- After each question, pupils should share what they discussed to find the answer. Ask: *How do you know?*

Chapter 1 Revising and improving

Unit 1.1 Practice Book 5A, pages 1–3

Look out for ... pupils who are using a trial and error approach to find the missing answers rather than using their existing knowledge and reasoning skills. Talk about what they know first and use effective prompts to support them.

- Pupils should complete Question 3 in the Practice Book.

Same-day intervention

- Give pupils the following words. What do they mean? Can they use them in a sentence? For example: 'The product of 8 × 10 is 80.'

| Product | Greatest | Three-digit number | Quotient | Least |

- Pupils should work with an adult to answer each question in Question 3 in the Practice Book together. In each question, there are several prerequisites that are needed, such as:
  – What is the greatest two-digit number?
  – What is the smallest three-digit number?

Same-day enrichment

- Give pupils the following calculations. Can they find the missing numbers?
  – 12☐4 ÷ 214 = 6
  – 65☐☐ × 2☐ = 128☐☐
  – 325 ÷ ☐5 = 13
  – 2☐3 × 24 = 6072
  – 364☐ ÷ 6 = 607 r3

Challenge and extension question

Question 4

4 (a) If you use all four of the digits 2, 3, 4 and 5 once each to form all the possible multiplications of two 2-digit numbers, which gives the greatest product and which gives the smallest product? Write them down and then calculate the products.

(b) Without calculating, say which product is greater: 12 345 × 67 890 or 12 346 × 67 889. Explain your reasoning.

In part (a), pupils are required to find all possibilities when multiplying two-digit numbers. It might help to give them digit cards so they can create the multiplication sentences. Pupils should be encouraged to work systematically. Ask: *How do you know you have found all possibilities?*

In part (b), pupils need to have a secure understanding of place value and multiplication. They should be able to answer this question by reasoning. They should identify key information:

- the second factor ('factor B') is much larger than 'factor A'
- there is one more of 'factor B' in the second calculation.

Pupils can then reason that although the value of 'factor B' is one less in the second calculation, because there is one more of 'factor B' (and it is greater than 'factor A') the product of the second calculation will still be greater than that of the first calculation. Pupils should not complete the calculation.

Chapter 1 Revising and improving

Unit 1.2
Addition and subtraction of fractions

Conceptual context

This second unit in Chapter 1 revises learning about fractions from Years 3 and 4. Pupils begin by revisiting the role of the numerator and denominator when identifying non-unit fractions of shapes and quantities divided into equal parts. Pupils are required to draw on their understanding of equivalence when identifying fractions of a shape or quantity. This understanding will be needed when solving contextualised problems within Unit 1.2 and also when comparing fractions in Chapter 4. Pupils will improve their ability to add and subtract fractions with the same denominator – this was first introduced in Year 4. Within this unit they will be required to solve multi-step calculations involving both addition and subtraction – this will prepare pupils for adding and subtracting fractions with related denominators in Chapter 4.

Learning pupils will have achieved at the end of the unit

- Pupils will be able to recognise a fraction of a shaded shape divided into equal parts and record it using fraction notation (Q1, Q2)
- Pupils will be able to recognise a fraction of a quantity and record it using fraction notation (Q2)
- Understanding of adding and subtracting fractions with the same denominator within one whole will have been reinforced (Q3)
- Pupils will be able to add and subtract fractions with the same denominator to solve contextualised problems (Q4, Q5)

Resources

sticky notes; large sheets of paper; 1–10 dice; a selection of counters in four different colours; mini whiteboards; bananas and a bowl; dice labelled $\frac{1}{20}, \frac{2}{20}, \frac{3}{20}, \frac{4}{20}, \frac{5}{20}, \frac{6}{20}$; strips of paper divided into 10 equal parts; **Resource 5.1.2** Shading fractions of shapes

Vocabulary

equal parts, divided, equivalent, numerator, denominator, hundredths, simplified, consecutive

Chapter 1 Revising and improving

Unit 1.2 Practice Book 5A, pages 4–6

Question 1

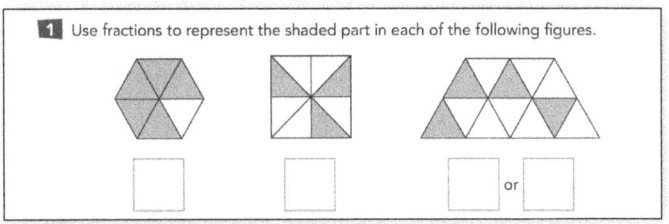

What learning will pupils have achieved at the conclusion of Question 1?

- Pupils will be able to recognise a fraction of a shaded shape divided into equal parts and record it using fraction notation.

Activities for whole-class instruction

- Provide each pupil with a sticky note and ask them to draw a rectangle with $\frac{5}{8}$ shaded. Ask: *What is the same and what is different about the shaded rectangles?* Give pupils time to discuss in small groups before taking responses. Establish that in each rectangle $\frac{5}{8}$ of the whole has been shaded but the size, orientation or proportions of the rectangles may be different.

- Ask: *Have all the rectangles been divided in the same way?* Share examples of rectangles that have been divided in different ways. If pupils have not divided the rectangles in a range of ways, share some possible examples on the board, for example:

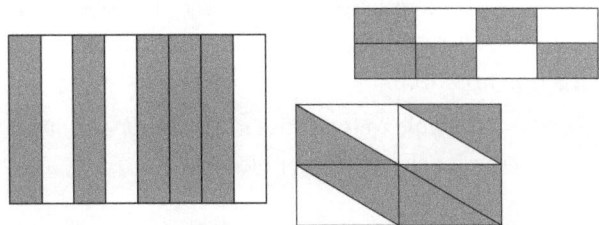

- Ask: *Did anyone draw a rectangle that has not been divided into equal parts?* If so, share responses from these pupils. If not, ask pupils to consider an image of a rectangle with $\frac{5}{8}$ shaded that has not been divided into equal parts. Give pupils time to consider alternative rectangles that have not been divided into equal parts before sharing responses. Examine an example that has not been divided into equal parts but where $\frac{5}{8}$ still remains shaded, for example:

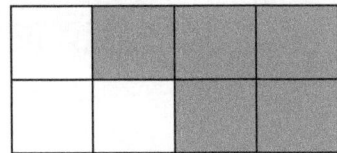

- Ask: *Why is the shaded part of this image equivalent to $\frac{5}{8}$?* Draw lines on the rectangle to divide it into eight equal parts. Establish that $\frac{1}{2}$ is equivalent to $\frac{4}{8}$ and that $\frac{4}{8} + \frac{1}{8} = \frac{5}{8}$.

 *When two fractions represent the same amount they are equivalent.*

- Ask: *Did anyone draw a rectangle that has been divided into more than eight parts?* If so, share responses from these pupils. If not, ask pupils to consider an image of a rectangle with $\frac{5}{8}$ shaded that has been divided into more than eight parts. Give pupils time to consider alternative rectangles that have been divided into more than eight parts before sharing responses. Examine an example that has been divided into more than eight equal parts but where 5/8 still remains shaded, for example:

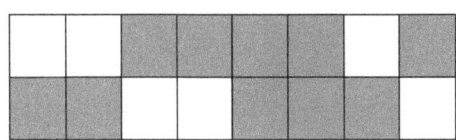

- Ask: *Why is this image equivalent to $\frac{5}{8}$?* Establish that 10 out of 16 parts are shaded and that $\frac{10}{16}$ is equivalent to $\frac{5}{8}$. Next to the shaded rectangle, write: $\frac{5}{8}$ or $\frac{10}{16}$.

Look out for ... pupils who do not identify $\frac{5}{8}$ as equivalent to $\frac{10}{16}$. It may help to reorganise the shaded squares into pairs so they can see $\frac{2}{16} = \frac{1}{8}$, for example:

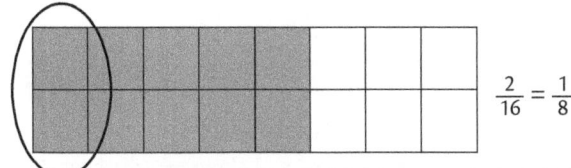

- Arrange pupils into groups of four. Provide them with a large sheet of paper and ask them to work together to draw a variety of different rectangles with $\frac{2}{6}$ shaded. Give pupils time to work on this task before examining responses with the rest of the class. Ask pupils to reflect on what is the same and what is different about each rectangle.

Chapter 1 Revising and improving

Unit 1.2 Practice Book 5A, pages

- Provide pairs of pupils with a copy of **Resource 5.1.2** Shading fractions of shapes and two 1–10 dice.

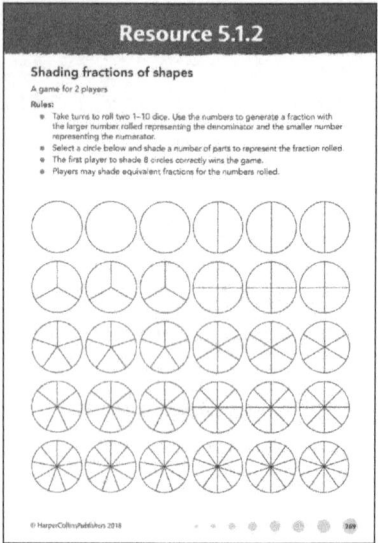

- Pupils should play the game in pairs, focusing on accurate representation of the fractions rolled. Encourage pupils to focus on justification of equivalent fractions, if appropriate.

Look out for … pupils who interpret the fraction as a ratio of shaded parts to not shaded parts rather than a proportion of the total number of parts, for example:

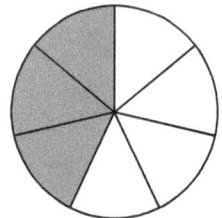

- In response to the question 'What fraction of this shape is shaded?' a pupil might incorrectly identify $\frac{3}{4}$ rather than $\frac{3}{7}$. If this happens, encourage the pupil to count the number of parts and record the denominator. Then count the number of shaded parts and record the numerator to reinforce the role of the numerator and denominator.

- Pupils should complete Question 1 in the Practice Book.

Same-day intervention

- Pupils should explore whether it is always, sometimes or never true that shading $\frac{5}{6}$ of a shape means the shape is divided into six equal parts and five of the parts are shaded. Provide examples to support your justification. Can pupils explain that a shape might be divided into 12 equal parts, with 10 of them shaded, and that this is equivalent to $\frac{5}{6}$? For each example used, pupils should record both ways to describe the fraction, for example: $\frac{5}{6}$ or $\frac{10}{12}$.

Same-day enrichment

- Ask pupils to draw and shade a shape where it is not immediately obvious that $\frac{5}{6}$ is shaded. What about a shape where $\frac{5}{9}$ is shaded? What about $\frac{7}{12}$? Pupils should choose their own fraction and create a shape where it is not immediately obvious what fraction is shaded. They give it to a friend and ask them to identify the shaded fraction.

Question 2

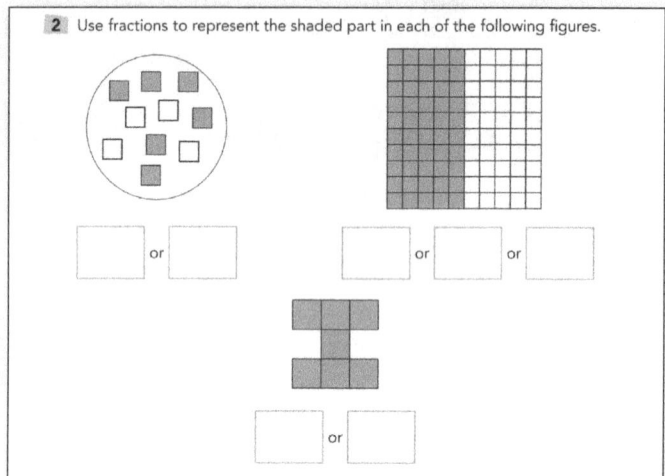

What learning will pupils have achieved at the conclusion of Question 2?

- Pupils will be able to recognise a fraction of a shaded shape divided into equal parts and record it using fraction notation.
- Pupils will be able to recognise a fraction of a quantity and record it using fraction notation.

Activities for whole-class instruction

- Show pupils these grids:

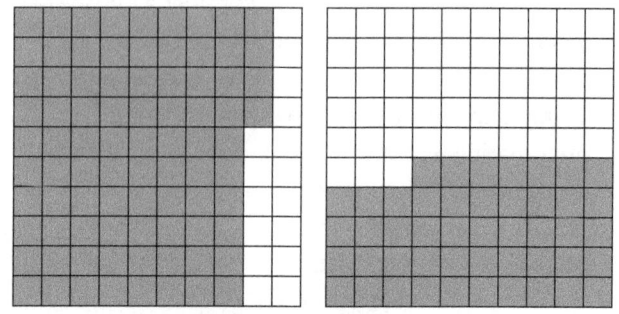

Chapter 1 Revising and improving

Unit 1.2 Practice Book 5A, pages

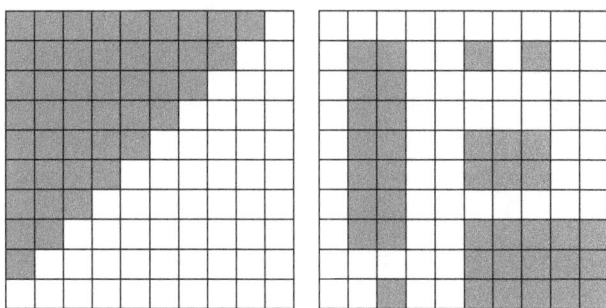

- Examine the first 10 × 10 grid and ask pupils to identify what fraction of the whole is shaded. Give pupils time to identify the answer before sharing responses. Agree that $\frac{84}{100}$ is shaded. Ask: *How did you find out what fraction of the whole is shaded?* Share a range of strategies including: counting in ones; counting in tens and ones; counting how many were unshaded and subtracting this from 100. Ask pupils to consider which strategy was the most efficient for this image.

- Ask: *How many more parts need to be shaded so that $\frac{90}{100}$ is shaded?* Agree that six more parts need to be shaded and, if necessary, count while shading these parts to convince pupils. Record $\frac{90}{100} = $ —— on the board. Ask: *What fraction is equivalent to $\frac{90}{100}$?* Agree that $\frac{90}{100} = \frac{9}{10}$ by counting each column as $\frac{1}{10}$.

- Ask: *How many more hundredths need to be shaded so that $\frac{100}{100}$ is shaded?* Agree that 10 more hundredths need to be shaded and, if necessary, count while shading these parts to convince pupils. Record $\frac{100}{100} = $ —— on the board. Ask: *What fraction is equivalent to $\frac{100}{100}$?* Agree, $\frac{10}{10}$. Also agree, $\frac{100}{100} = \frac{1}{1}$ since the whole square can be considered as one 'thing' and all of it is shaded if all the hundredths are shaded. So, the big square is a whole, which can be recorded as 1.

 *When the numerator and denominator are the same, the fraction is equivalent to 1.*

- Examine the second 10 × 10 grid and ask pupils to identify what fraction of the whole is shaded. Give pupils time to identify the answer before sharing responses. Agree $\frac{47}{100}$. Ask: *How did you find out what fraction of the whole is shaded?* Share a range of strategies as previously. Ask pupils to consider which strategy was the most efficient for this image.

- Ask: *How many more parts need to be shaded so that $\frac{50}{100}$ are shaded?* Agree that three more parts need to be shaded. Record $\frac{50}{100} = $ —— on the board. Ask: *What fraction is equivalent to $\frac{50}{100}$?* Agree, $\frac{5}{10}$. Also agree that $\frac{50}{100}$ is equal to $\frac{1}{2}$ by 'noticing' that $\frac{1}{2}$ the whole has been shaded. Repeat with the third and fourth grids as appropriate.

- Provide pairs of pupils with a pile of counters in four different colours. Ask Pupil A to select a handful of counters and lay them on the table. Pupil B identifies what fraction of the handful of counters are one colour.

- Pupil B records the fraction symbolically (using numerator and denominator) on a mini whiteboard. Pupil A checks.

- Ask: *Can this fraction be simplified to an equivalent fraction?* If so, Pupil B should record the equivalent fraction alongside the original fraction, for example:

$$\frac{5}{15} = \frac{1}{3}$$

- Pupil A then identifies what fraction of the handful of counters are a second colour.

- Pupil A records the fraction symbolically (using numerator and denominator) on a mini whiteboard. Pupil B checks.

- Ask: *Can this fraction be simplified to an equivalent fraction?* If so, Pupil A should record the equivalent fraction alongside the original fraction, for example:

$$\frac{3}{15} = \frac{1}{5}$$

- Pupils take turns to repeat this process for the remaining two colours. Repeat the activity, if appropriate.

 … pupils who record the numerator and denominator the wrong way round. Further

13

Chapter 1 Revising and improving

Unit 1.2 Practice Book 5A, pages 4–6

systematic counting of the total number of parts, recording the denominator before counting the number of one particular colour and recording the numerator may help to overcome this.

- Pupils should complete Question 2 in the Practice Book.

Same-day intervention

- Ask pupils to answer the following question:

  Which is the odd one out in each of these sets of numbers?

  $\frac{2}{6}, \frac{2}{9}, \frac{4}{12}$

  $\frac{25}{50}, \frac{50}{100}, \frac{40}{100}$

  $\frac{6}{15}, \frac{7}{10}, \frac{2}{5}$

- Ask: *Why? Can you think of a reason why each number in the set could be the odd one out?*

Same-day enrichment

- Ask pupils to answer the following questions:

  Can you think of a fraction that is:
  - equivalent to $\frac{4}{5}$
  - and has a numerator that is a multiple of 5
  - and has a denominator that is greater than 40?

  Can you think of a fraction that is:
  - equivalent to $\frac{3}{7}$
  - and has a denominator that is a multiple of 5
  - and has a denominator that is greater than 35?

- Ask pupils to write their own fraction puzzles like these for a friend to solve.

Question 3

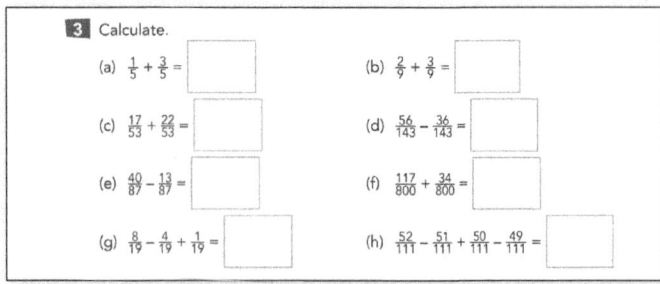

What learning will pupils have achieved at the conclusion of Question 3?

- Understanding of adding and subtracting fractions with the same denominator within one whole will have been reinforced.

Activities for whole-class instruction

- On the board, write: $\frac{2}{7} + \frac{3}{7} = \frac{5}{14}$. Pupil pairs should draw an image that demonstrates why this calculation is incorrect. Each pair should then explain their image to another pair using precise terminology.

- Ask: *What is wrong with the calculation? What should the answer be?* Agree that the answer should be $\frac{5}{7}$. Ask: *What mistake has been made with this calculation?* Pupils should identify that the denominators have been added.

- Present pupils with a bowl containing five bananas. Add four more bananas to the bowl. Ask: *How many bananas are in the bowl altogether?*

 *Five bananas add four bananas equals nine bananas.*

- Repeat, adding different numbers of bananas, each time saying: *... bananas add ... bananas equals ... bananas.*

- Repeat using a different set of objects, each time saying: *... _____s add ... _____s equals ... _____s.*

- Ask: *What is two sevenths add three sevenths?*

 *Two sevenths add three sevenths equals five sevenths.*

- Agree that when adding fractions that have the same denominator, it is the same as adding numbers of any objects that are the same. The result is simply the total number of those things.

 *When adding two fractions with the same denominator, the denominator does not change.*

- Repeat with a subtraction example: $\frac{5}{8} - \frac{3}{8} = \frac{2}{0}$. Pupil pairs should draw an image that demonstrates why this calculation is incorrect. Each pair should then explain their image to another pair using precise terminology.

- Ask: *What is wrong with the calculation? What should the answer be?* Agree that the answer should be $\frac{2}{8}$. Ask: *What mistake has been made with this calculation?* Pupils should identify that the denominators have been subtracted. Ask: *What is 2/8 equivalent to?*

- Present pupils with a bowl containing seven bananas. Remove five bananas from the bowl. Ask: *How many bananas are now in the bowl?* Confirm that there are now two bananas in the bowl and that they are still bananas. Establish that when subtracting fractions this is also true. When subtracting eighths, the difference will also be eighths.

Chapter 1 Revising and improving Unit 1.2 Practice Book 5A, pages 4–6

 *When subtracting fractions with the same denominator, the denominator does not change.*

- Provide pupils with a sticky note and tell them to write down 'the easiest fraction calculation' they can think of involving addition or subtraction. Pupils should work independently for a few minutes before discussing in small groups to evaluate which calculation they collectively feel is the easiest. Encourage pupils to consider a justification as to why this calculation is the easiest. Share ideas. Ask: *Which calculation is the easiest? Why?*
- Repeat for 'the hardest fraction calculation'.
- Write: $\frac{23}{28} + \frac{4}{28} - \frac{5}{28} + \frac{6}{28} = \underline{}$. Ask: *What do you notice?* Give pupils time to discuss their observations with a partner. Ensure pupils identify:
  - the calculation involves the same denominators
  - the calculation involves both the addition and the subtraction of fractions
  - the calculation involves adding and subtracting consecutive fractions.
- Pupil pairs should solve the calculation. Agree the answer is $\frac{28}{28}$. Ask: *What is this equivalent to?* Agree $\frac{28}{28}$ is equal to 1.

 *When the numerator and denominator are the same, the fraction is equivalent to 1.*

- Ask pupil pairs to record a fraction calculation involving addition and subtraction that results in an answer of 1. Share responses.
- Pupils should complete Question 3 in the Practice Book.

Same-day intervention

- Provide pairs of pupils with a dice labelled $\frac{1}{20}, \frac{2}{20}, \frac{3}{20}, \frac{4}{20}, \frac{5}{20}, \frac{6}{20}$. Agree roles.
  - Pupil A will complete addition calculations. Their target number is 1.
  - Pupil B will complete subtraction calculations. Their target number is 0.
- Play commences with a start number of $\frac{10}{20}$. Pupil A rolls the dice and adds the number rolled to $\frac{10}{20}$. They record this calculation on a mini whiteboard. Pupil B rolls the dice and subtracts the number rolled from the number reached by Pupil A. They record this calculation on a mini whiteboard. Play continues until one of the target numbers is reached. Pupils swap roles and repeat as appropriate.

Same-day enrichment

- Ask pupils to answer the following questions: *Which one is the odd one out in each of these sets?*

Set 1	Set 2
$\frac{2}{7} + \frac{5}{7}$	$\frac{9}{12} - \frac{3}{12}$
$\frac{12}{18} + \frac{6}{18}$	$\frac{21}{28} - \frac{7}{28}$
$\frac{1}{9} + \frac{8}{9}$	$\frac{19}{24} - \frac{7}{24}$
$\frac{4}{16} + \frac{11}{16}$	$\frac{47}{60} - \frac{17}{60}$
$\frac{5}{13} + \frac{8}{13}$	$\frac{11}{16} - \frac{3}{16}$

- Ask pupils to add a further statement to each list that would also fit within the group, and then to add a further statement to each list that would not fit within the group.
- Ask pupils to write their own set of addition or subtraction statements involving fractions with an odd one out. A friend should try to identify the odd one out.

Questions 4 and 5

4 There are 30 pupils in a class. $\frac{3}{5}$ of the pupils are girls.
  (a) What fraction of the pupils are boys?
  (b) What is the difference between the number of girls and the number of boys? First write your answer as a fraction of the total number of pupils in the class, and then write the answer identifying the number of pupils.

5 A teacher brought 50 books to his class. $\frac{1}{10}$ of them are fiction books, $\frac{3}{10}$ are science books, $\frac{2}{5}$ are storybooks, and the others are mathematics books.
  (a) What fraction of the books are mathematics books?
  (b) Which type of book were there most of? Which type of book were there least of? Write the four types of books in order, starting from the least.

What learning will pupils have achieved at the conclusion of Questions 4 and 5?

- Pupils will be able to add and subtract fractions with the same denominator to solve contextualised problems.

Chapter 1 Revising and improving

Unit 1.2 Practice Book 5A, pages 4–6

Activities for whole-class instruction

- Draw this table:

What the money was spent on	Fraction of the total
Drink	$\frac{1}{4}$
Food	$\frac{1}{2}$
Hats	$\frac{1}{8}$
Party bags	

- Introduce the scenario that Susie is having a birthday party and has £200 to spend on it. The table outlines how she chose to distribute the £200 to cover the cost of the party.
- Ask: *What fraction of the total money was spent on party bags?* Can pupils tell you that $\frac{1}{8}$ was spent on party bags and provide a robust justification for their answer?
- Ask: *What fraction of the total money was spent on food and drink altogether?* Pupils should work in pairs to record a number sentence on mini whiteboards and agree their answer. They should use their knowledge of $\frac{1}{2}$ being equivalent to $\frac{2}{4}$ to help them find the answer of $\frac{3}{4}$.
- Ask pupils to work with a partner to identify what Susie spent the least money on and what she spent the most money on. Order these starting with the least. Ask: *How much money was spent on each thing?* Share responses and examine any errors that have occurred.
- Pupils should complete Questions 4 and 5 in the Practice Book.

Same-day intervention

- Provide pupils with a strip of paper divided into 10 equal parts. Tell them to imagine they have £100 to spend on a party. Ask pupils to consider an approximate proportion of the £100 they will spend on different items for the party. Tell pupils to shade parts on the strip of paper according to the fraction of the £100 they will spend on each item. They should label the strip to show the fraction of the whole budget that will be spent on each item. Encourage pupils to count in $\frac{1}{10}$ if appropriate.
- Ask: *How much money will be spent on each item?* Ensure pupils can identify the fraction of the whole and also the amount of money. Ask pupils questions relating to the fraction/amount of money spent on two or three items for the party.

Same-day enrichment

- Tell pupils to imagine they have £200 to spend on a party. They should create their own table, which identifies how the money will be distributed to cover the cost of the party. What fraction of the £200 will be spent on each item? How much money will be spent on each item? They should share their table with a partner. The partner asks questions about fractions of the whole budget spent on two or three items for the party.

Challenge and extension questions

Question 6

6 Complete each calculation with a suitable fraction.

(a) $\frac{5}{16} + \boxed{} = \frac{1}{2}$ (b) $\frac{79}{100} - \boxed{} = \frac{3}{10}$

(c) $\frac{19}{22} - \boxed{} = \frac{3}{22}$ (d) $\frac{37}{100} + \boxed{} = \frac{1}{2}$

This question requires pupils to use both addition and subtraction to solve calculations involving fractions. They will need to draw on their knowledge of equivalent fractions and understanding of inverse relationships to calculate efficiently.

Question 7

7 A storybook has 96 pages. Joshua plans to read through the whole book in 3 weeks. If he reads $\frac{1}{8}$ of the book in the first week, and $\frac{3}{8}$ of the book in each of the remaining two weeks, can he complete his plan? If not, how many pages will be left? (Hint: Use addition or subtraction of fractions to find your answer.)

This question presents a contextualised problem that will require pupils to add or subtract fractions to or from one whole and calculate fractions of quantities.

Chapter 1 Revising and improving

Unit 1.3
Decimals (1)

Conceptual context

This unit revisits some of the key ideas from Year 4 where pupils learned to compare, order and round pure decimals and mixed decimals, and generally develop a secure understanding of how decimals are part of the number system. Pupils are familiar with referring to decimals as tenths, hundredths and thousandths and have already learned about equivalence across those.

Pupils have learned that the same value can be expressed in different ways – for example 5.50 m as 550 cm, 1.2 as 1.200 or $\frac{7}{10}$ as 0.7. This will be emphasised in this unit as pupils focus on knowing fraction equivalents of decimals.

(i) Care should be taken to ensure that pupils use the correct vocabulary when saying decimals (for example ensure that 0.15 is read as 'zero point one five' rather than 'zero point fifteen') since this is a key strategy to avoid the common misconception that, for example, 0.15 > 0.2 because 'fifteen is bigger than two'.

Learning pupils will have achieved at the end of the unit

- Pupils will have securely understood the structure of a decimal number and the values of digits in different columns (Q1)
- Pupils will have understood that numbers that look different can have the same value (Q2, Q3, Q4, Q5)
- Pupils will be able to exploit the structure of decimal numbers to identify ways to change the look of a number without changing its value (Q2, Q3)
- Pupils will be able to convert between fractions where the denominator is 10, 100 or 1000 and their decimal equivalents (Q4)
- Pupils will be able to use their understanding of place value to identify the nearest integers to a given decimal number (Q6)

Resources

Gattegno chart; place value chart; place value counters; sticky notes; mini whiteboards; coins; **Resource 5.1.3a** Benny's cards; **Resource 5.1.3b** Numbers and shapes; **Resource 5.1.3c** Less, same, more grid; **Resource 5.1.3d** Place value slider; **Resource 5.1.3e** Rounders

Vocabulary

decimal, fraction, tenths, hundredths, thousandths

Chapter 1 Revising and improving

Unit 1.3 Practice Book 5A, pages 7–8

Question 1

> **1** Think carefully and then fill in the missing numbers.
> (a) 25.792 consists of ☐ tens, ☐ ones, ☐ tenths, ☐ hundredths and ☐ thousandths.
> (b) The number that consists of 2 hundreds, 3 tenths and 4 thousandths is ☐.
> (c) 15.15 = 10 + ☐ + ☐ + ☐
> (d) 318.79 = 300 + ☐ + ☐ + 0.7 + ☐

What learning will pupils have achieved at the conclusion of Question 1?
- Pupils will have securely understood the structure of a decimal number and the values of digits in different columns.

Activities for whole-class instruction

- Use a Gattegno chart. Write a decimal number on the board, for example 25.38, and tap the Gattegno chart, asking pupils to say the number that you have tapped (for example, for 25.38, tap the 20 then the 5 then the 0.3 and finally the 0.08, saying each number as you tap it. You and the class then say together 'twenty five point three eight'.)
- Repeat this, tapping out and saying together the numbers 25.39, 125.39 and 125.3, writing the number on the board then tapping it out.
- Now tap out a number without writing it on the board. Ask pupils to write the number you have tapped out on their mini whiteboards and to hold up their boards.
- When they are able to fluently work with numbers such as 25.38, try introducing some zeros into the number, for example 100.17, and then 100.017 and 125.107.
- Finally, write a decimal number on the board and ask pupils to write on their whiteboards the numbers on the Gattegno chart you would need to tap to make it. For example, if you give them the decimal number 30.501 you would expect them to write 30, 0.5 and 0.001.
- Pupils should complete Question 1 in the Practice Book.

Same-day intervention
- Supplement the Gattegno chart with place value counters.
- Work with pupils to construct the same number using the Gattegno chart (if yours is wiped off they could circle the appropriate value) and the place value counters. Then deconstruct the number by showing pupils a decimal number made using the counters, and working with them to break it into its component parts and identify them on the Gattegno chart. For example, if you make 0.37, pupils identify that this is constructed from 3 × 0.1 counters and 7 × 0.01 counters, and so find 0.3 and 0.07 on the Gattegno chart.
- Now ask pupils to work in pairs – one should use the Gattegno chart and the other counters. As you say a decimal number, challenge them to see who can make that number most quickly using their equipment.
- When they have familiarised themselves with the equipment, write a number on the board, say 23.17, and show them that it can be written as 20 + 3 + 0.1 + 0.07. Ask them to show this using their equipment.
- Now ask them to put the equipment to one side, and to write similar additions for the following:

41.87
86.33
290.26
4567.29

- Work with pupils, only using the equipment where necessary to check, so that they are able to break a decimal number into an addition.
- Pupils should then challenge their partners to write the additions for decimals that they choose.

Same-day enrichment
- Give pupils **Resource 5.1.3a** Benny's cards, in which they arrange digit cards to create different decimal numbers according to given rules.

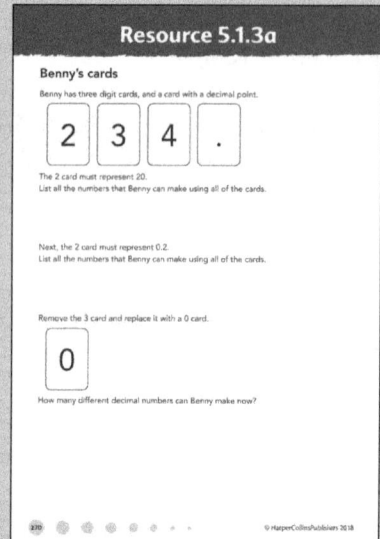

Answers: 23.4 and 24.3; 3.2, 4.2, 34.2 and 43.2; Benny can make 10 numbers (12 if he includes 0.2 and 0.4). These are 0.24, 0.42, 2.04, 2.40, 4.02, 4.20, 20.4, 24.0, 40.2 and 42.0.

Chapter 1 Revising and improving

Unit 1.3 Practice Book 5A, pages 7–8

Question 2

> **2** Simplify the numbers using the properties of decimals. The first one has been done for you.
> (a) 1.50 = 1.5
> (b) 0.0110 = ☐
> (c) 6.0600 = ☐
> (d) 120.000 = ☐
> (e) 80.030 = ☐
> (f) 16.200 = ☐

What learning will pupils have achieved at the conclusion of Question 2?

- Pupils will have understood that numbers that look different can have the same value.
- Pupils will be able to exploit the structure of decimal numbers to identify ways to change the look of a number without changing its value.

Activities for whole-class instruction

- Write 3.72 onto a place value chart. Ask pupils to draw a number line and mark 2, 3, 4, 5 and 3.72 on the line.
- Now add an extra column to the right of the 2 (a thousandths column) and write a 0, making 3.720. Ask pupils to mark this new number on their number line.
- Remind pupils that when zeros are added or removed at the end of the decimal part of a decimal number, the value of the number remains constant. Say: *Although the numbers might look different, they have the same value.*
- Repeat with 15.48, asking pupils to show this on a number line, and discuss where 15.480, 15.4800, 15.48000 will be on the number line. Ask: *What can you say about adding zeros to the end of a decimal number and how it changes the number?* Pupils should discuss and generate a statement. Share ideas and agree an appropriate 'All say ...' statement for the class to repeat. It might be:

All say ... Adding zeros to the end of a decimal number does not change the number because the zeros do not represent any value.

- Write a decimal number on the board in two different ways (for example 3.08 and 3.0800) and ask pupils to write a third way of writing the decimal, which looks different but has the same value. Pupils should show their whiteboards to demonstrate understanding.
- Give each pupil a sheet of A4 paper and ask them to fold it in half, in half and in half again so that the sheet is divided into eight boxes. Now ask each pupil to write different decimals in the four boxes on the left, and to write a decimal that looks different but has the same value in the opposite box, so that they end up with something like this:

3.07	3.0700
91.28	91.280
3.70	3.700
3.17	3.170000

- Pupils then cut or tear their sheets into cards and pass to their partner, who has to match the four pairs of equivalent decimal numbers. (You might like to encourage them to keep the integer part of their numbers the same to increase the challenge of matching for their partner.)
- Pupils should complete Question 2 in the Practice Book.

Same-day intervention

- Use a place value chart and place value counters. Use the counters to construct a decimal number with one decimal place, such as 4.2, and represent this in the place value chart like this:

100	10	1	.	0.1	0.01
		1		0.1	
		1		0.1	
		1		0.1	
		1			
		1			

(1) (0.1)
(1) (1) (0.1)
(1) (0.1)

- Write the decimal number on a whiteboard and ensure that pupils are able to connect the three different representations.

4.2

- Now add a zero to the number written on the whiteboard and discuss with pupils how this will affect the two other representations.

4.20

19

Chapter 1 Revising and improving Unit 1.3 Practice Book 5A, pages 7–8

- Agree with the pupils that the other representations do not change because nothing has been added, and so the value of the decimal number must still be the same.
- Add a second zero to the decimal number and repeat, again agreeing that the other representations do not change and so the value of the decimal number must still be the same.
- Now use a number line and mark on 4.2. Discuss with pupils where 4.20 and 4.200 would go on the line and agree that they all occupy the same point on the number line.
- Ensure that pupils understand that, because these numbers are all at the same place on the number line, they all have the same value.

Same-day enrichment

- Give pupils **Resource 5.1.3b** Numbers and shapes, in which they are given decimal numbers with digits replaced by symbols and are asked to identify which digit has been replaced with each shape.

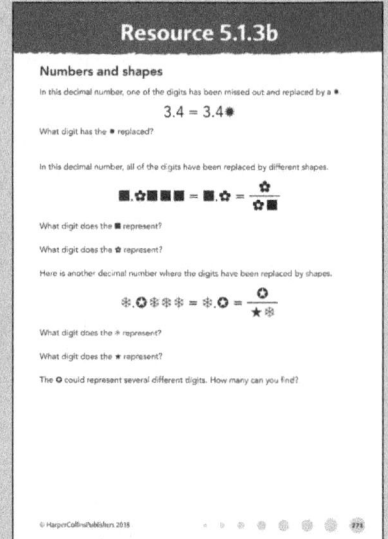

Answers: ✹ = 0; ■ = 0, ✿ = 1; ✣ = 0, ★ = 1, ✪ could represent 2, 3, 4, 5, 6, 7, 8 or 9.

Question 3

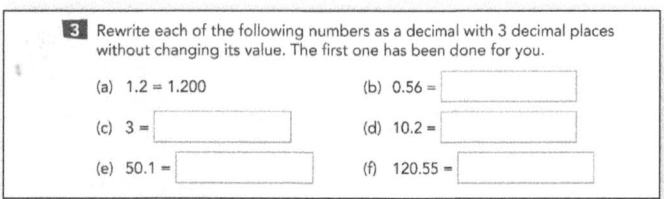

What learning will pupils have achieved at the conclusion of Question 3?
- Pupils will have understood that numbers that look different can have the same value.
- Pupils will be able to exploit the structure of decimal numbers to identify ways to change the look of a number without changing its value.

Activities for whole-class instruction

- Remind pupils that the number of decimal places is the number of digits that are written to make up the decimal part of a decimal number.
- On the board, write some decimal numbers, for example 3.14, 3.1, 3.141 592 7, 3.10, 3.140 000 0 and ask pupils to write down on mini whiteboards which of these have one decimal place, which have two decimal places and so on.
- Next, ask for a decimal number with two decimal places that has a whole number part of 38. Again, deal with mistakes when they show you their answers, and finally get them to show you a number that:
  - is written to two decimal places,
  - has a whole number part of 38
  - and has the same value as 38.4.
- Pupils should complete Question 3 in the Practice Book.

Same-day intervention

- Draw a line on the board, followed by a decimal point and three empty boxes.

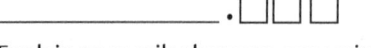

- Explain to pupils that you can write any set of digits on the line, and then fill the boxes with a digit each and you will always have a number that is written with three decimal places.
- Invite pupils to give you some numbers that are written to three decimal places either by telling you their number (pay particular attention to the correct vocabulary) or by writing on a mini whiteboard.
- Once you are confident that pupils understand what a number with three decimal places looks like, write a number on the board with two decimal places, 35.81, and ask pupils to write a number that has the same value but has three decimal places.

Chapter 1 Revising and improving

Unit 1.3 Practice Book 5A, pages 7–8

- Repeat this, writing a number with one decimal place and asking them to write a number that has the same value but with five decimal places, or with seven decimal places.
- By encouraging pupils to add more and more zeros, you are guiding them towards a generalisation that no matter how many zeros are added, the value of the number won't change.

Same-day enrichment

- Give pupils **Resource 5.1.3c** Less, same, more grid and ask them to place numbers in the grid according to the rules.

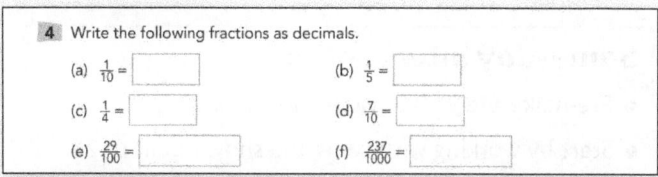

Answers: Various answers are possible, depending on the changes pupils make. For example:
3.1, 3.13, 3.014
X, 3.14, 3.140
3.4, 4.24, 13.14

Question 4

4. Write the following fractions as decimals.
(a) $\frac{1}{10} =$
(b) $\frac{1}{5} =$
(c) $\frac{1}{4} =$
(d) $\frac{7}{10} =$
(e) $\frac{29}{100} =$
(f) $\frac{237}{1000} =$

What learning will pupils have achieved at the conclusion of Question 4?

- Pupils will have understood that numbers that look different can have the same value.
- Pupils will be able to convert between fractions where the denominator is 10, 100 or 1000 and their decimal equivalents.

Activities for whole-class instruction

- Write 0.1 in the middle of the board and ask pupils for other ways to represent it. In pairs they should each write or draw as many representations as they can on their mini whiteboards, then gather their answers together.
- You will gather a broad range of solutions, some of which are suggested below; ensure that the two highlighted representations are included.

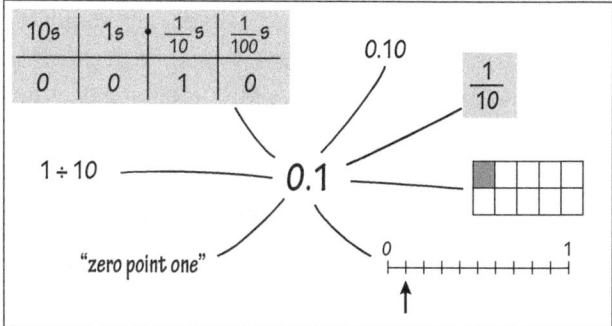

- Explore each representation, asking the pupils that came up with them to explain them to the rest of the class. Now, leaving the original on the board, start a diagram like this and ask pupils to complete it on their whiteboards.

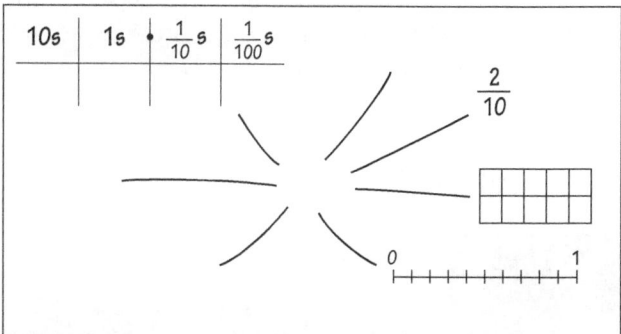

- Gather responses and discuss what is the same and what is different about the two different spider diagrams.
- Ensure that pupils make the connections between the decimal notation, the place value chart and the fraction notation.
- Pupils should complete Question 4 in the Practice Book.

Same-day intervention

- Work with pupils to fold a strip of paper into 10 equal sections.
- Discuss with pupils the fraction of the strip that each section represents and agree that this is one tenth. Write $\frac{1}{10}$ in the first section, then $\frac{2}{10}$, $\frac{3}{10}$ ... and so on until the whole strip has been completed. Count in tenths with pupils both forwards and back.

Chapter 1 Revising and improving

Unit 1.3 Practice Book 5A, pages 7–8

- Now turn the strip over and repeat, but filling in 0.1, 0.2 and so on. (Ensure that, when you turn the paper over, you do it in such a way that $\frac{1}{10}$ is written on the reverse of 0.1, $\frac{2}{10}$ on the reverse of 0.2 and so on.)
- Count in 0.1s with pupils both forwards and back.
- In pairs, pupils hold the strip of paper between them so that one can see the fractions and the other can see the decimals. Pupils take turns to ask each other to point to a value. For example, the pupil looking at the fraction side might ask their partner to point at $\frac{3}{10}$. Their partner, who can only see the decimals, should point to 0.3. Are they both touching the same segment?

Same-day enrichment

- Present pupils with the following statement:
  Rana answered Question 4 and said:
  Because $\frac{7}{10}$ = 0.7, $\frac{29}{100}$ = 0.29, and $\frac{237}{1000}$ = 0.237, the rule to change a fraction with 10, 100 or 1000 as the denominator is to write 0. and then write the numerator.
- Ask them to explain why Rana is wrong. They should provide some examples that show that Rana is wrong and to see if they can find a rule that **does** always work for these fractions.

Question 5

5. Convert these measures using a suitable decimal number.
(Note: £1 = 100p and 1 m = 100 cm.)

(a) 1p = ☐ pounds   (b) 15p = ☐ pounds

(c) 220p = ☐ pounds   (d) £5 and 5p = ☐ pounds

(e) 5 cm = ☐ m   (f) 10 cm = ☐ m

(g) 550 cm = ☐ m   (h) 3 m 18 cm = ☐ m

What learning will pupils have achieved at the conclusion of Question 5?

- Pupils will have understood that numbers that look different can have the same value.

Activities for whole-class instruction

- Show a 1p and a £1 coin and ask pupils how many 1p coins make up £1. Write on the board and say together:

 *One hundred 1p coins make one pound.*

- Show a centimetre on a metre rule and ask pupils how many centimetres make one metre. Write on the board and say together:

 *One hundred centimetres make one metre.*

- Underneath this, write 1p = £0.01 and 1 cm = 0.01 m.
- Explore with pupils how 2p and 2 cm would be written in £ and in metres, and write this on the board:
  2p = £0.02 and 2 cm = 0.02 m
- Now look at 20p and 20 cm and repeat.
- Ask pupils to work in pairs and to agree on a rule that will allow them to change pounds into pence and pence into pounds, and then one to change metres into centimetres and centimetres into metres. Gather some of the rules on the board and ask pupils what is the same and what is different about the rules.
- Use a place value slider (**Resource 5.1.3d** Place value slider) to show the conversion between pounds and pence, and metres and centimetres, and agree that all the digits slide by two spaces when converting between them.

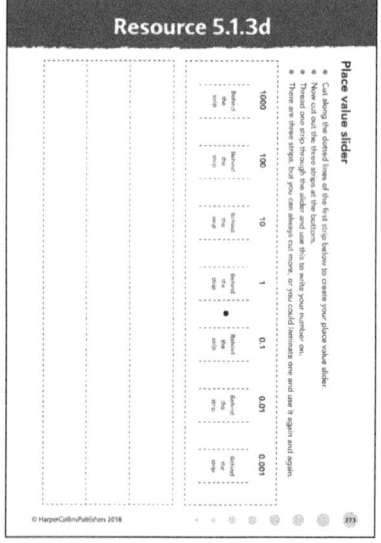

Resource 5.1.3d

- Pupils should complete Question 5 in the Practice Book.

Same-day intervention

- Pre-make a few place value sliders.
- Start by working with coins and show pupils £1.25. Write 1.25 on your place value slider and show pupils how to convert this to pence by sliding the digits.
- Now write 245 on your place value slider in pence and ask pupils what they need to do to the digits to find out what this is in pounds and pence

Chapter 1 Revising and improving Unit 1.3 Practice Book 5A, pages 7–8

> • Now write 250 on your place value slider and again tell pupils that this is a value in pence. Ask them to make the correct amount using as few coins as possible.

Same-day enrichment

- Give pupils some blank paper and ask them to fold it in half, half and half again to give eight sections.
- Pupils now use these sections to create a set of cards, writing pairs of values that are equal but written differently (such as 3 cm and 0.03 m or £4.75 and 435p).
- When enough cards have been made, pupils play 'Snap' using their cards, aiming to match equal quantities.

Question 6

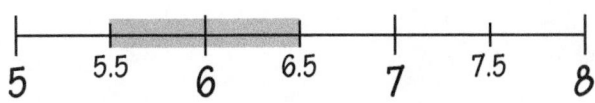

6 Round the following decimals to their nearest whole numbers.
0.09   0.9   59.3   219.5

What learning will pupils have achieved at the conclusion of Question 6?

- Pupils will be able to use their understanding of place value to identify the nearest integers to a given decimal number.

Activities for whole-class instruction

- Draw a number line on the board and mark it like this:

  5   5.5   6   6.5   7   7.5   8

- Explain that you are thinking of a number that is in the highlighted section and ask them what it might be. Ask them to write their suggestions on mini whiteboards, and gather and record some of their answers on your board.
- If you need a greater variety of numbers, tell them that the number you are thinking of has two decimal places, or three decimal places.
- Ask them what it is about their numbers that tells them that they are in the required section of the number line. Ask them what the largest and smallest numbers could be.
- Explain that all of these numbers are closer to 6 than to any other whole number, and ask them how they might know this from the decimal number.

- Agree that the numbers between 5.5 and 6.5 fit the criteria, and remind them that the rule is that, where a number is precisely half way between two whole numbers, the number 'rounds' to the next whole number.
- Challenge pupils to write on their whiteboards a number that will round to 16 to the nearest whole number. (16 has been used here as it builds on the previous example of 6. Drawing attention to the fact that the tens, hundreds … digits are irrelevant in making the choice about the nearest whole number.) Gather some responses, then ask if they can repeat this for 116.
- Pupils should complete Question 6 in the Practice Book.

(i) Avoid using the language 'round up' and 'round down'; instead, use 'rounds to…' A common misconception is to assume that, since 4.7 'rounds up' to 5 the ones value increases by 1, 4.2 must 'round down' to 3 because the ones value should decrease. Instead, say that '4.7 rounds to 5' and that '4.2 rounds to 4'.

Same-day intervention

- Work with a number line and slide your finger or a pencil along it. Ask frequently and repetitively: *Which number am I closest to? Which number am I closest to? Which number am I closest to?*
- Now ask pupils to point to a decimal that is closer to 3 than any other whole number. Ask them to say the decimal out loud. If they chose a number more than 3, ask them to point to another decimal that is closer to 3 than any other whole number, but is less than 3 (or vice versa).
- Repeat with another example, and another.
- Now ask pupils to shade a copy of a number line to capture all the decimals that will round to 3 when rounded to the nearest whole number.
- If appropriate, challenge them with a number that is just off the number line, perhaps asking them whether 10.6 would round to 10 or 11.

Chapter 1 Revising and improving

Unit 1.3 Practice Book 5A, pages 7–8

Same-day enrichment

- Give pupils **Resource 5.1.3e** Rounders, in which they are asked to write a set of decimal numbers that will all round to the same whole number.

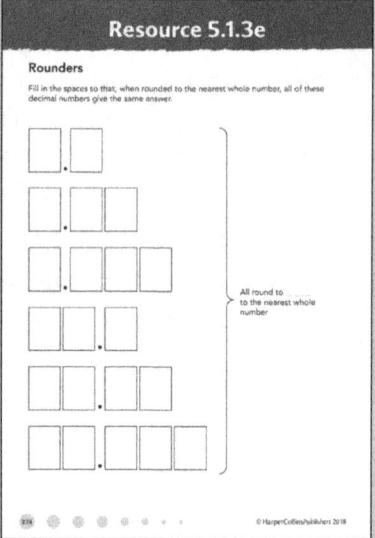

Answers: Various answers are possible. All decimals should round to 10, however. For example: 9.7, 9.86, 9.938, 10.4, 10.32, 10.109.

Challenge and extension question

Question 7

> **7** A decimal number with 2 decimal places has the following features:
> (1) The value of the whole number part is 5 greater than the greatest 1-digit number.
> (2) The sum of the digits in the tenths and hundredths places is 16.
> What could the number be?

This question challenges pupils to solve a complex problem and, in doing so, to practise their use of the vocabulary of place value. There are several different possible correct solutions (since the order of the digits making the decimal part is not determined), and this provides an opportunity for pupils to reason and to recognise that there need not necessarily be only one correct answer.

Chapter 1 Revising and improving

Unit 1.4
Decimals (2)

Conceptual context

While the previous unit focused on equality, and on different ways to represent the same value, this unit looks at inequality and strategies to compare different values.

The size of a decimal is first considered as a distance from zero, and then this size is abstracted, deepening pupils' key understanding that the further to the left a digit appears, the greater the impact that digit has on the value of the number.

Learning pupils will have achieved at the end of the unit

- Pupils will have used a number line to order decimals (Q1)
- Pupils will have understood that the same decimal number can be represented in different ways (Q2, Q4)
- Pupils will be able to write simple decimals as fractions (Q2, Q3)
- Pupils will be able to compare two decimals written up to three decimal places and use inequality symbols to express the relationship (Q3, Q5)

Resources

place value chart; place value counters; counters; mini whiteboards; **Resource 5.1.4a** Statement; **Resource 5.1.4b** Decimals maze

Vocabulary

decimal, tenths, hundredths, thousandths, greater than, less than, decimal places

Chapter 1 Revising and improving Unit 1.4 Practice Book 5A, pages 9–11

Question 1

> **1** Work on the number line.
> (a) Mark these numbers on the number line: 0.5, 10, 5.5, 19.5, 8.5, 14.5, 16.5. (Hint: Use the space both above and below the number line.)
>
> 0 1 2 3 4 5 6 7 8 9 10 11 12 13 14 15 16 17 18 19 20
>
> (b) (i) Which one of the numbers in Question (a) is the greatest? ☐
> (ii) Which one is the smallest? ☐
> (c) Write the numbers in order, starting with the smallest.

What learning will pupils have achieved at the conclusion of Question 2?

- Pupils will have used a number line to order decimals.

Activities for whole-class instruction

- Draw a number line, labelling one end as 0 and the other end as 10, but ensure that the line overruns a little, like this:

  0 1 2 3 4 5 6 7 8 9 10

- Note that a number line has an arrow pointing to the right to show that it does not end. Once negative numbers have been introduced the arrow will also be used on the left.
- Point to a marker on the number line and ask pupils to write down on their mini whiteboards the value of the number you are pointing at. Initially, start with integers, ensuring that you include zero, then point to two consecutive integers in turn, for example 7 and 8.
- Now point to 7.5, then 8.5, then 6.5. As you point to these values, say together for example:

   *7.5 is larger than 7 but not as large as 8.*

- Point to the far end of the line, past the 10, and ask pupils what value they think it might have.
- Now draw a second number line, but this time leave it blank. Ask pupils to draw a blank number line on their mini whiteboards.

- Tell pupils that you're thinking of a number and ask them to mark your number somewhere on their blank number line. Now ask a pupil to think of a number that is 'one more' than your number and ask pupils to mark this on their number line. Ask them to hold up their whiteboards and ensure that they understand that the larger number is conventionally to the right of the smaller number.
- Tell them that your number was 13.5 and ask them to write down what the other pupil's number must have been.
- Ask them to write the integer that is between your two decimal numbers and to show you on their boards.
- Ensure that pupils understand the conventions of the number line and are able to place 14 as the integer between the two decimals.
- Pupils should complete Question 1 in the Practice Book.

Same-day intervention

- Work with pupils to draw a number line and to label the integers. Choose two consecutive integers, for example 3 and 4, and tell pupils that exactly half way between them is the number 3.5.
- Ensure that they recognise that the integer part of the number relates to the lower integer in the pair of consecutive whole numbers and that 0.5 is another way to write $\frac{1}{2}$, so 3.5 means 'three and another 0.5 or one half'.
- Now ask pupils to label all of the other halfway points (0.5, 1.5, 2.5 …).
- Count together in halves from 5 to 7, naming the numbers as 5, 5.5, 6, 6.5 and so on. Then ask pupils to do the same from 10.5 to 13.
- Count backwards together between other pairs. Refer to the process interchangeably as 'counting in halves' and 'counting in 0.5s'.

Same-day enrichment

- Tell pupils that Sarah counted up in 0.5s from 0 to 100. Ask: *How many times did Sarah say 'five'?*
- This task will challenge pupils to structure their reasoning in a systematic way. It is important that they realise that every pair of integers has a 'point five' between them.

Chapter 1 Revising and improving

Unit 1.4 Practice Book 5A, pages 9–11

Question 2

2 Write the following decimals as fractions.

(a) 0.1 = ☐   (b) 0.01 = ☐   (c) 0.23 = ☐
(d) 0.2 = ☐   (e) 0.5 = ☐   (f) 0.99 = ☐

What learning will pupils have achieved at the conclusion of Question 2?
- Pupils will have understood that the same decimal number can be represented in different ways.
- Pupils will be able to write simple decimals as fractions.

Activities for whole-class instruction
- Draw a number line on the whiteboard marked in 10 equal sections, and then mark in some of the values like this:

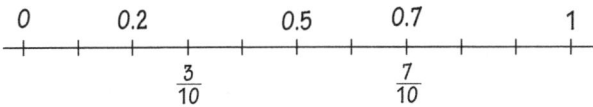

- Invite pupils to come to the board to complete the missing values, then use the number line to count with the class, tapping first above the line, then below so the count goes 'zero, zero point one, one tenth, zero point two, two tenths, zero point three, three tenths …' and so on.
- Rub off the value in the bottom row and repeat the task, counting above and below the line.
- Finally, rub off the values in the top row too and repeat the task again.
- Pupils should complete Question 2 in the Practice Book.

Same-day intervention
- Use two place value charts and some counters as shown. Explain to pupils that zero point one and one tenth are different ways of writing the same value.

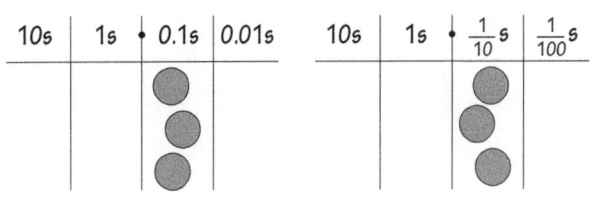

- Working in pairs, pupils take turns making a number on one of the place value charts, with their partner making the equivalent number on the other.
- When they have made a number they should say it out loud.
- Repeat this, building to numbers with two decimal places, modelling the correct way to say the decimal and the fraction as you work with pupils.
- When they are able to say decimals and fractions correctly, put the counters away and explain that you are going to imagine there are, for example, five counters in the 0.1s column. Ask them how they would say that using tenths. Record this using mathematical notation, $0.5 = \frac{5}{10}$, either on paper or on a whiteboard.
- Repeat for other 'imagined' counters.
- Next, write a decimal and ask pupils to write it as a fraction. Pupils work in pairs and take turns, challenging each other to write equivalent fractions and decimals.

Same-day enrichment
- Tell pupils that Matilda noticed that, when writing $\frac{1}{10}$ as a decimal, she wrote the denominator backwards, and put in a decimal point, which gave 0.1.
- Matilda tried this with $\frac{1}{100}$ too and found that it worked, correctly giving 0.01.
- Will Matilda's rule always work? Ask pupils to explain why.

Question 3

3 Fill in the ◯ with >, < or =.

(a) 2.05 ◯ 1.99   (b) 0.75 ◯ $\frac{3}{4}$ (c) 32.35 ◯ 31.78
(d) 0.909 ◯ 0.901   (e) $\frac{1}{10}$ ◯ 0.08   (f) 50.1 ◯ 49.9

What learning will pupils have achieved at the conclusion of Question 3?
- Pupils will be able to write simple decimals as fractions.
- Pupils will be able to compare two decimals written up to three decimal places and use inequality symbols to express the relationship.

Chapter 1 Revising and improving

Unit 1.4 Practice Book 5A, pages 9–11

Activities for whole-class instruction

- In Year 4, pupils completed the following statement:

When comparing two decimals, we first compare the _____ part; the larger the whole number part, the _____ the number. If the whole number parts are the same, then we compare the digits in the _____ place; the larger the digit in the _____ place, the greater the decimal number and so on.

- Write or project the statement onto the board, or give pupils **Resource 5.1.4a** Statement for them to write on.

Answers: whole number, larger, tenths, tenths.

- Write two decimal numbers on the board, for example 45.17 and 45.31, and ask pupils whether they can remember, or work out, what the missing words in the statement must be by thinking about how they would decide which of the two numbers is larger. Give them time to work and discuss in pairs and then gather some answers.

- Now write up another pair of decimals, 2.003 and 2.01, and have the class test whether the rules they have written work.

- If you have more than one answer from the class, spend time working with them to discuss which is the correct answer and, if you have more than one mathematically correct answer, is one 'better' than the other?

- Pupils should complete Question 3 in the Practice Book.

Same-day intervention

- Ensure that pupils have a correct copy of the statement from **Resource 5.1.4a**.

- Use two place value charts and set them up using counters so that they represent two different numbers. For example:

- Discuss with pupils which of the two numbers is the greater, using the statement from the book and working through column by column on the place value chart. Use inequality notation to compare the two decimals.

- Now tell pupils that you are going to change one column so that the other number becomes greater. Discuss with pupils which digit should be changed. Gather their responses and ensure they understand that changing the whole number part will make the greatest impact on the value of the number.

- Set up a different pair of numbers, ensuring that the whole number and the tenths part are equal, for example:

- Again, ask pupils which column could be changed to make the other number greater. Ask: *Can it be done by adding just one counter?*

- The intention is that pupils learn to work systematically through a number, starting at the furthest left digit and working to the right.

Chapter 1 Revising and improving

Unit 1.4 Practice Book 5A, pages 9–11

Same-day enrichment

- Give pupils **Resource 5.1.4b** Decimals maze, in which they complete a maze by always moving to the greatest decimal number. (Pupils should finish at 3.14159.)

Resource 5.1.4b

Decimals maze

Start at 0.06 and move through the maze, always moving to the greatest decimal number that is above, below, to the left or to the right of the square you are in. What number on the bottom row do you finish at?

0.05	0.06	0.009	0.08	0.0801	0.08011
0.0095	0.061	0.064	0.07	0.067	0.7
0.29999	0.000009	0.061	0.069	0.7051	0.705
1.5	0.812	0.80409	0.8042	0.8041	0.5
0.1000	0.91	0.9	0.83	0.38	3.1
0.92	0.93	0.80	0.823	0.83	3.8
0.1999	0.991	0.999	0.9999	2.99999	4.31
4.776	0.990	0.909	3.14159	3.099232	8.94

Answer: Final number = 3.14159.

Question 4

4 Multiple choice questions. (For each question, choose the correct answer and write the letter in the box.)

(a) There are ☐ thousandths in 0.1.
   A. 1   B. 10   C. 100   D. 1000

(b) There are ☐ decimals with 1 decimal place greater than 0 but less than 1.
   A. 2   B. 5   C. 9   D. 10

(c) The smallest decimal number with 1 decimal place is ☐.
   A. 0   B. 0.1   C. 0.01   D. 1

(d) The smallest decimal number with 2 decimal places is ☐.
   A. 0.99   B. 0.10   C. 0.01   D. 0.50

What learning will pupils have achieved at the conclusion of Question 4?

- Pupils will have understood that the same decimal number can be represented in different ways.

Activities for whole-class instruction

- Construct a place value chart and use it to explore the different ways of moving between the columns.
- Ask pupils to draw a place value chart on their mini whiteboards like the one shown below, and to mark the smallest possible number (that is greater than 0) on their chart.

100	10	1	•	0.1	0.01	0.001

- Now ask them to write the largest number that it is possible to write on their chart.
- Next, add an extra column on both sides of the chart and repeat the questions, gathering some answers and ensuring that pupils understand that the lower the digit is, and the further to the right it is, the smaller its value.
- Use place value counters and say to pupils that you have 28 of the 0.1 counters. Ask pupils to write a number with the same value as twenty-eight 0.1 counters on their place value chart, reminding them that they can only use single digits in each column of the chart.
- Gather and discuss their solutions and agree that this should be recorded as 2.8. Some pupils are likely to have written 28 in the 0.1s column. Ask pupils to explain and describe how this has the same value but is not the correct way to use a place value table.
- Ask pupils to imagine that you have 128 of the 0.1 counters. How would you record this on a place value chart using only one digit in each column? Again, discuss and explore this with pupils.
- Now write 0.35 in the place value chart and ask pupils how many 0.01 counters you would need to make that value. How many 0.001 counters?
- Pupils should complete Question 4 in the Practice Book.

Chapter 1 Revising and improving   Unit 1.4 Practice Book 5A, pages 9–11

Same-day intervention

- Use a place value chart and counters. Start counting up in 0.01s, placing counters in the hundredths column as you count. When you reach 0.09, as you place the next counter down, say: *Ten 0.01s make one 0.1* and replace the 10 counters with one in the tenths column. Keep counting, placing counters in the hundredths column until you have reached at least 0.21.
- Now tell pupils that you are going to count up in 0.1s and repeat the task, saying: *Ten 0.1s make 1* each time you reach the next integer.
- The intention of the counting is to make explicit to pupils the pattern and structure that every 10 counters in one column get swept up and moved to the next column.
- Next, say to pupils that you would like to count to 34 in 0.1s! Ask them whether you will count more than 34 numbers. Or less. Ask how they know.
- Use their discussion to ask how many 0.1s there are in 34. Start by making 34 out of place value counters using 3 tens and 4 ones.
- Now work with one of the tens counters and show that it can be replaced by 10 ones. Repeat this for the remaining tens counters.
- Now take one of the ones counters and show that it can be replaced by ten 0.1 counters. Stress again that the number still has the same value.
- Replace another ones counter with ten 0.1 counters and ask pupils how many 0.1 counters you'll need to replace all of the ones. Agree that replacing each one with ten 0.1s means that you will need 10 times as many 0.1 counters.
- Ask pupils how many ones counters you would need to make 23, then ask how many 0.1 counters you would need. Focus on multiplying by 10 as a strategy.
- When appropriate, ask pupils how many 0.01 counters you would need to make 34. Discuss strategies and remind them how many 0.1s were needed. Ask questions such as:
  - Will there be more 0.1s or more 0.01s needed to make 34?
  - How many 0.01s have the same value as 0.1? How many have the same value as 1?
- Use pupils' answers to show that conversion can be carried out by multiplication.

Same-day enrichment

- Ask pupils to work in pairs or small groups. Give them the following starting point for a question:
  There are _____ 0.01s in 3.2.
- Ask them to write four options to make a multiple choice question. Tell pupils to consider what mistakes might be made and ask them to construct their possible responses so that people will fall into their trap!
- Repeat using the following starting question:
  The largest decimal with two decimal places that is greater than 0 but less than 1 is _____.
- Ask pupils to work in their pairs or groups to write their own set of multiple choice questions, using those in the book as examples. They should consider mistakes that they think people might make and use these to create the different choices.
- If appropriate, you might like to use some of these questions when working with the whole class.

Question 5

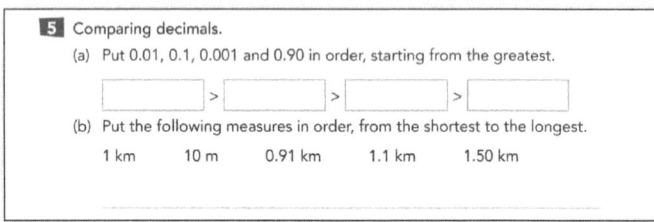

What learning will pupils have achieved at the conclusion of Question 5?

- Pupils will be able to compare two decimals written up to three decimal places and use inequality symbols to express the relationship.

Activities for whole-class instruction

- Write two integers on the board, for example 463 and 364. Ask pupils to draw a blank number line on their mini whiteboards and to mark the two numbers on it.
- Now place a decimal point in one of the numbers so that it reads, for example, 463 and 36.4. Ask pupils to add this new number to their number line.
- Ask pupils to think about where else they could place the decimal point without changing the order of the digits in the two numbers, and to mark all possible solutions

Chapter 1 Revising and improving

Unit 1.4 Practice Book 5A, pages 9–11

on their number lines. Explain that it is not possible to be entirely accurate, but they should ensure that the numbers are in the correct order on the line.

- Ask one or two pupils to work on your board so that their work can be used for the whole class to discuss. Then use their work to draw attention to the way that, when the decimal point is placed in a similar position in each number, the number derived from 463 is always larger than the value derived from 364 (so 463 > 364, 46.3 > 36.4, 4.63 > 3.64; some may have decided to include some additional zeroes to give, for example, 0.0463 > 0.0364).
- Draw pupils' attention to the way that this replicates a place value chart and that, no matter how they adjust the digits in the place value chart, as long as they adjust the digits in both numbers by the same amount, the same number will always be greater.
- Review the process for comparing decimals, shown on **Resource 5.1.4a** Statement.
- Pupils should complete Question 5 in the Practice Book.

Same-day intervention

- Give pupils a place value grid and some digit cards. Ask them to make a decimal number on the place value grid using the cards 0, 0, 1 and 2 and to say the number that they have made out loud to their partner.
- Working with one pupil at the front of the group, copy their number using cards and a place value grid of your own. Then reach out to your cards and swap the positions of two cards.
- Discuss whether this has made the value bigger or smaller, ensuring that you refer to the column heading to justify the change in value, as well as the rules that pupils wrote down in Question 2. Compare the two numbers and place a mini whiteboard between your two place value grids, writing either a < or a >, as appropriate.
- Pupil pairs should make a number, then swap the digits and use the column headings to compare. Ask them to record the two numbers they use and which is the larger number, or whether they are the same, using >, < or =.
- When pupils are confident, rather than swap the position of two digits, give them an extra digit to slide into their arrangement, and ask them to compare the resulting decimal number with the original.

- The key teaching point here is to draw pupils' attention to the column headings and the way they influence the value of the number.

Same-day enrichment

- Present pupils with the following problem:

  Fiona says that, if she has a decimal number, placing an extra zero somewhere in the decimal part will always make a smaller number. For example, starting with 3.41 and placing a 0 between the 4 and the 1 gives 3.401 and 3.401 < 3.41. Does Fiona's rule always work?

- Ask pupils to explain and justify their answer with examples.

Challenge and extension question

Question 6

6 Use 0, 1, 2, 3 and the decimal point to write the decimal numbers described below.

(a) All the decimal numbers less than 1 with 2 decimal places.

(b) All the decimal numbers greater than 2 with 3 decimal places and with a 1 in the tenths place.

(c) All the decimal numbers between 0 and 3 with a 2 in the hundredths place.

This question challenges pupils to think deeply about the impact of a digit's position in a number, and the value of that number. You might like to equip pupils with sticky notes or counters with the digits 0, 1, 2 and 3 written on them. Encourage pupils to pay attention to the way they work on this problem and to compare their strategies with those of other pupils. This task gives a good opportunity to focus on working systematically to ensure that all possible solutions have been found.

Chapter 1 Revising and improving

Unit 1.5
Mathematics plaza – Which area is larger?

Conceptual context

This is the final unit in a chapter that provides the opportunity for pupils to strengthen and extend previous knowledge. Although the chapter is varied, this particular unit's focus is pupils' understanding of the relationship between the dimensions of squares and rectangles, their perimeter and area. In particular, pupils will explore the concept that, given the same perimeter, the 'squarer' the rectangle, the larger the area.

As mentioned elsewhere in the series, the title 'Mathematics plaza' suggests the idea of an open space to investigate and wander around. In Unit 1.5, pupils have the space to investigate – exploring and applying previously learned concepts of perimeter and area to each problem.

Learning pupils will have achieved at the end of the unit

- Pupils' understanding of the concepts of area, perimeter and the dimensions of squares and rectangles will have been extended (Q1, Q2)
- Ideas about how area and/or perimeter might change will have been explored – particularly when the dimensions of a square or rectangle are altered (Q1, Q2, Q3)
- Knowledge of area will have been applied in a real-life context (Q3)
- Pupils will have applied their knowledge of number bonds and factors of given numbers to investigate perimeter and area (Q2, Q3)

Resources

large squared grid; squared paper; string; **Resource 5.1.5** One step at a time

Vocabulary

side length, perimeter, area, square centimetres (cm^2), square metres (m^2), maximum/maximise

Chapter 1 Revising and improving

Unit 1.5 Practice Book 5A, pages 12–15

Question 1

> **1** Write your answers in the spaces.
> (a) The side length of a square is 1 cm. What is the area of the square?
>
> (b) If the side length of the square is doubled, what is the area of the square?
>
> (c) If the side length of the square is tripled, what is the area of the square?
>
> (d) What is the area of the square if its side length is increased to 4 times its original length?
>
> And if it is increased to 5 times its original length?
>
> (e) What pattern can you see?

What learning will pupils have achieved at the conclusion of Question 1?

- Pupils' understanding of the concepts of area, perimeter and the dimensions of squares and rectangles will have been extended.
- Ideas about how area and/or perimeter behave will have been explored – particularly when the dimensions of a shape are altered.

Activities for whole-class instruction

- Give pupils a minute to write down as many facts as they can about the properties of squares. Draw a square on the board and encourage pupils to come up and point to its various parts, sharing their facts as they do so.
- Point to the distance around the outside of the square and ask: *What is this called? How many measurements do you need to know to work out the perimeter? What is perimeter measured in?* Point to the space inside the square and ask: *What is this called? How many measurements do you need to know to work out the area? What is area measured in?* Establish that, to find the amount of space covered by a square (its area), all pupils need to know is one side length.
- Display a line on the board and label it '2 cm' (it does not have to be to scale). Explain that this is the side of a square. Ask: *How would you find the area of the square?* Previously, pupils will have counted squares to find the area. They should now be able to identify that the area of a square or rectangle is found by multiplying its length by its width.

All say... *Area is the amount of space covered by a two-dimensional object. The area of a rectangle or square can be calculated by multiplying the length by the width.*

- Establish that the area of the square will be 4 cm². Draw a table to record the dimensions of the square:

Side length (cm)	Area (cm²)
2	4

- Extend the line so that it is now double the length. Explain that you have added 2 cm to the side length of the square. Ask: *What will the area of the new square be?* Repeat this for two further extensions so that the table of results now looks like this:

Side length (cm)	Area (cm²)
2	4
4	16
6	36
8	64

- Ask: *What patterns can you see?* Give pupils time in pairs to consider this. Share their ideas and emphasise how to describe a pattern – as 'something happens, something else happens'.
- The pattern here is fairly complex, but is accessible to pupils:

  As the side length increases by 2 cm, the area increases by 8 more than the previous increase:

  4 + 12 = 16

  16 + (12 + 8) = 36

  36 + (20 + 8) = 64

- Ask: *What will the next row be?* (side length: 10; area = 64 + (28 + 8) = 100) Ensure that pupils understand why they worked in this way. Ask: *Why do you think it is useful to write these results in a table? Why is it important to collect four or five examples of a set of numbers before looking for patterns?*
- Pupils should complete Question 1 in the Practice Book.

Same-day intervention

- Provide pupils with loops of string about 1 m long (they do not need to know how long it is). In pairs, ask them to use their fingers to make four corners so that it becomes a square.

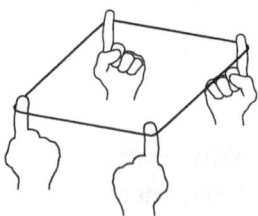

- Ask: *Where is the length? Where is the perimeter? Where is the area? What do we know about the width?*

- Explain that you have a second loop of string that will mean each side will be twice as long (it will need to be 2 m long). Ask: *What do you expect will happen to the area of the square you make? Are we keeping anything the same?*

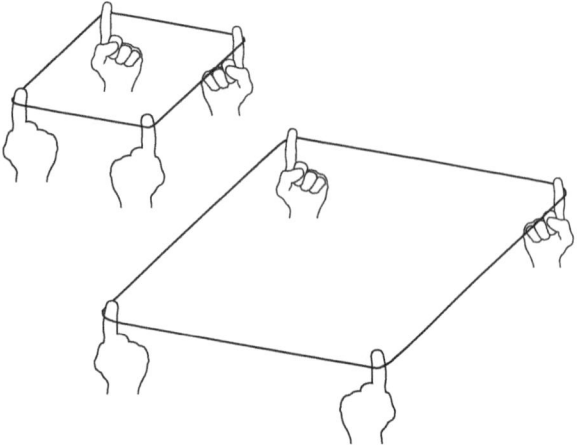

- Establish that the side lengths have increased, the perimeter has increased and the area has increased. Repeat for a side length three times the length of the original square.

- When pupils have built these concrete connections between dimensions, perimeter and area, provide them with squared paper and ask them to complete the same activity pictorially – this time counting squares to see how the area changes as the original side length doubles, then triples.

- It is important that pupils understand that doubling the side length of a square does not mean that its perimeter doubles, but leads to a more-than-doubling of its area (four times as large).

Same-day enrichment

- Set pupils challenges to investigate further patterns of changes in area when the dimensions of a rectangle (including squares) change. These may include:
  - Start with a square with side length 2 cm. Find the area.
    Double the length (but not the width). Find the area.
    Triple the original length (but not the width). Find the area.
    … and so on.
  - Start with a square with side length 10 cm. Find the area.
    Take 1 cm away from the side length. Find the area.
    Take 2 cm away from the original side length. Find the area.
    … and so on.

- Challenge pupils to work out several areas in the series and then predict what the next area will be based on the patterns they have found.

Chapter 1 Revising and improving

Unit 1.5 Practice Book 5A, pages 12–15

Question 2

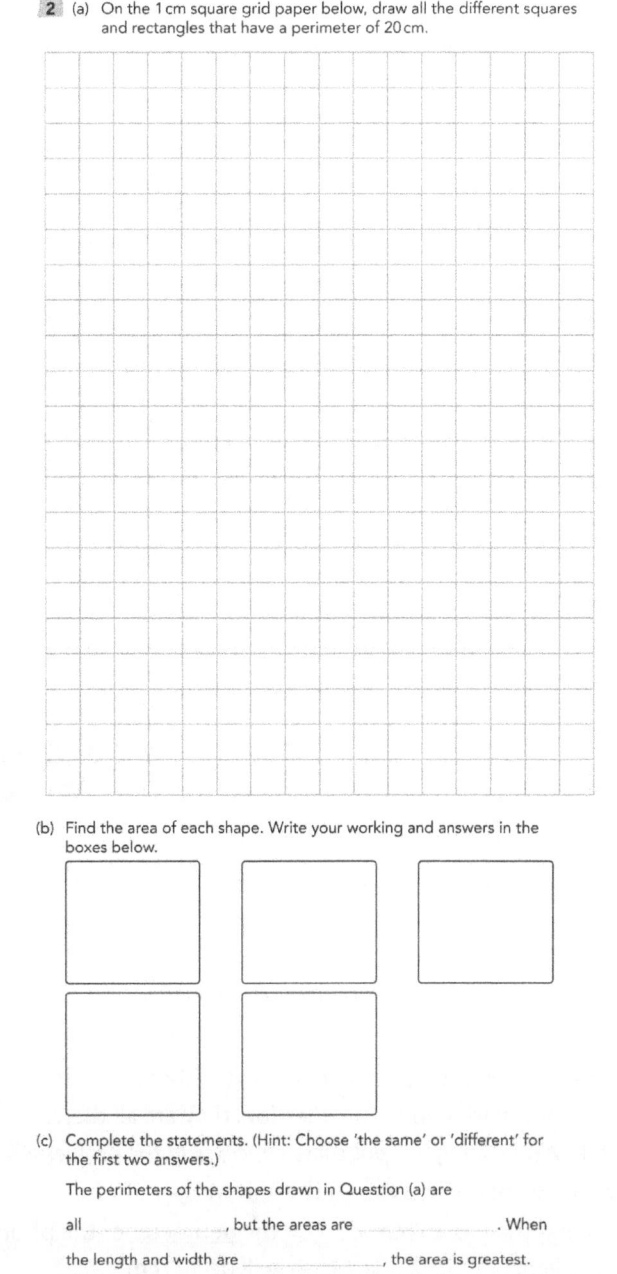

Activities for whole-class instruction

- Ask: *Do you think a shape can have the same perimeter as another shape but look different?* Check pupils understand that different shapes can have the same perimeter.

- Explain that, after considering how the areas of squares change when their dimensions change (Question 1), they will now be thinking about how the areas of rectangles and squares change when their dimensions change, but their perimeters remain the same. Ask: *Do you think a shape can have the same perimeter as another shape but have a different area?* Pupils should explain their answers.

- Display a large squared grid. Pupils should visualise a shape with a perimeter of 24 cm. Ask: *What does your shape look like? What is its area?* Ask: *If I wanted to find every possible rectangle (and square) with a perimeter of 24 cm, where should I start? Why?* For example, pupils could start with a 1 × 11 rectangle, then progress to a 2 × 10 rectangle and so on. Choose pupils to draw these systematically on squared paper and complete a table of results (showing the length, width and area). When all rectangles have been drawn ask: *What is the same about all your shapes? What is different? Which has the largest area? Which has the next largest area?*

- Pupils should complete Question 2 in the Practice Book.

Same-day intervention

- Provide pupils with loops of string about 1 m long. In pairs, ask them to use their fingers to make four corners so that it becomes a square or rectangle. Call out 'Change!', and pupils should then alter the dimensions of their shape. Do this several times and then ask pupils to analyse what has been happening. Ask: *What has stayed the same?* (the perimeter) *What has changed?* (the length, width and area)

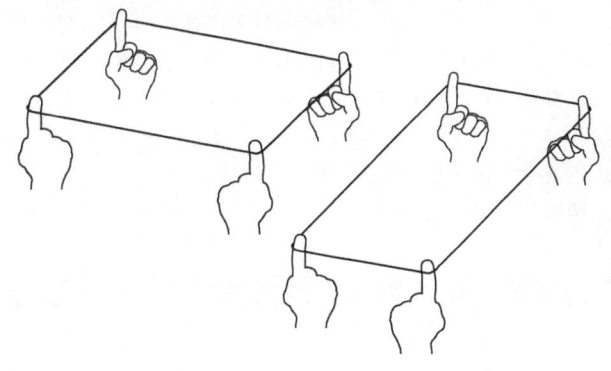

What learning will pupils have achieved at the conclusion of Question 2?

- Pupils' understanding of the concepts of area, perimeter and the dimensions of squares and rectangles will have been extended.

- Ideas about how area and/or perimeter might change will have been explored – particularly when the dimensions of a square or rectangle are altered.

- Pupils will have applied their knowledge of number bonds and factors of given numbers to investigate perimeter and area, respectively.

Chapter 1 Revising and improving

Unit 1.5 Practice Book 5A, pages 12–15

- Give pupils squared paper and give them a similar challenge. This time, give them a fixed perimeter of 18 cm and encourage them to explore the different rectangles they can draw. Ask: *What is the same? What is different? What are their areas?*

Same-day enrichment

- Provide pupils with a copy of **Resource 5.1.5** One step at a time.

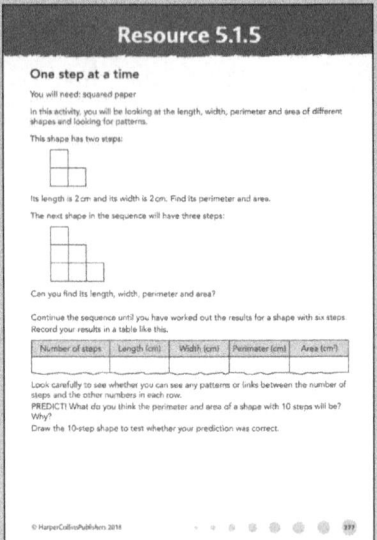

- The resource provides pupils with instructions for the following investigation into how the perimeter and area of rectilinear shapes change as a sequence is followed. Pupils should consider the following 'step' shape containing two steps and with length and width of 2 cm, recording its perimeter and area.
- They should then consider a step shape with three steps and with length and width of 3 cm, then 4 cm and so on. After six steps, pupils are challenged to predict what the perimeter and area of a shape with 10 steps will be (they can do this by multiplying by 4 to find the perimeter and finding the total of 10 + 9 + 8 + 7… and so on to find the area).
Answers: Perimeter = 8 cm, Area = 3 cm^2
Length = 3 cm, Width = 3 cm, Perimeter = 12 cm, Area = 6 cm^2

No of steps	L (cm)	W (cm)	P (cm)	A (cm^2)
4	4	4	16	10
5	5	5	20	15
6	6	6	24	21

A shape with 10 steps will have a perimeter of 40 cm (length × 4 = perimeter) and an area of 55 cm^2 (10 + 9 + 8 + 7… etc.)

Question 3

3 Evie wants to make a rectangular (not including square) window with a perimeter of 140 cm for her lizard's home. How can she design the length and width of the window in order to get the maximum possible sunlight through the window? (Note: Use whole centimetres for the length and width and make a table to investigate the possible dimensions.)

Length (cm)			
Width (cm)			
Area (cm^2)			

What learning will pupils have achieved at the conclusion of Question 3?

- Ideas about how area and/or perimeter might change will have been explored – particularly when the dimensions of a square or rectangle are altered.
- Knowledge of area will have been applied in a real-life context.
- Pupils will have applied their knowledge of number bonds and factors of given numbers to investigate perimeter and area, respectively.

Activities for whole-class instruction

- Display the following problem:
  Samantha has 100 cm of fairy lights and wants to use them to form a frame around a photo of her family. She wants the photo to cover as much space as possible on the wall. What size should she print the photo?
- Write the words 'length', 'width', 'rectangle', 'perimeter' and 'area' on the board. Explain that, although these are not mentioned in the question, they are all there. Ask: *Where can you spot these concepts in the problem?* Establish that they refer to the following:

"Samantha has 100 cm of fairy lights …"   = the <u>perimeter</u> of the photo will be 100 cm

"… form a frame around …"   = the length of lights equals the perimeter of the photo

"… print the photo …"   = the photo is a <u>rectangle</u> (or possibly a square)

"… as much space as possible"   = largest <u>area</u>

"What size …"   = what <u>length</u> and <u>width</u>

- Challenge pupils to rewrite the problem using these terms. For example:

The perimeter of a rectangle is 100 cm. What should its length and width be to ensure that the area is as large as possible?

Chapter 1 Revising and improving

Unit 1.5 Practice Book 5A, pages 12–15

- Ask: *Do you think you will find the answer straight away or will you need to try a few measurements? How will you record your results to help you compare them?* Encourage pupils to make a prediction about what they think they might find – the perimeter of the rectangle is constant. Does this mean the area will stay the same even if the length and width change?

- Ask: *What length and width will give a perimeter of 100 cm?* Remind pupils that the perimeter of a rectangle is found by using the formula 2l + 2w or 2(l + w). Choose a length to start with (for example 20 cm) and agree that a 20 cm × 30 cm photo will have a perimeter of 100 cm.

- Record the length, width and area as the first row in a table. Ask pupils how they think they should explore the possible areas. Some may suggest varying the length by 1 cm and see how that affects the area. Others may choose an easier number (for example another multiple of 10).

- The correct answer is a 25 cm × 25 cm square, which gives the maximum photo size of 625 cm².

- Repeat for similar problems. For example:

  A farmer has a coil of chicken wire that is 30 m long. He wants to make a chicken coop with the largest possible area. What dimensions should his coop have?

- Pupils should complete Question 3 in the Practice Book.

Same-day intervention

- Split the group into pairs and give each pair a loop of string. To begin with, ensure that all groups have the same length.

- Challenge pupils to make a rectangle (or square) that they think has the largest possible area. If all pupils have the same length of string then it should be interesting to compare their ideas. Encourage them to discuss whose shape looks the largest and reinforce the concept of area, if appropriate (the largest area will be the shape nearest to a square). They could draw around their shape onto squared paper and count the squares.

- Repeat the activity, this time using loops of different lengths. Observe whether pupils decide on the shape nearest to a square once more. Ask: *Why do you think the shape that is nearest to a square gives the largest area?*

- Give pupils squared paper and explain that they have a fixed perimeter of 30 cm. Ask them to find the square or rectangle that has the largest area. Encourage them to predict before they investigate. Ask: *Which shape are you going to start with? Why?*

Same-day enrichment

- Set pupils the following challenge, where they are encouraged to explore different perimeters that give a consistent area. Display this problem:

  A farmer wants to grow rhubarb and has decided to set aside 24 m² of his land to grow it on. It doesn't matter what shape it is planted in. However, he wants to fence the area off. As fencing is expensive, he wants to spend as little money as possible. What should the dimensions of the land be to plant the rhubarb?

- Pupils should realise that this problem is asking them to minimise perimeter while keeping the area 24 m².

- Encourage them to record their answers either in a table or pictorially and then present their findings to the class. Ask: *What if the area was 100 m²? Is there a general rule you can apply, whatever the area?*

Challenge and extension questions

Questions 4 and 5

> 4 Mr Wood wants to build a rectangular sheep pen. One side of the sheep pen will be an old wall, as shown in the figure. Mr Wood has enough materials to build a new wall 32 m long. Help Mr Wood to design the sheep pen. How long and wide should it be in order to have the maximum possible area? What is the maximum area? (Note: Use whole metres for the length and width and make a table to investigate the possible dimensions.)

> 5 After the length of a rectangular field is increased by 3 m and the width is increased by 5 m, it becomes a square and its area has increased by 153 m². What was the area of the original rectangular field? (Hint: First draw a diagram to investigate.)

Pupils are given two problems where they are expected to apply their knowledge of area in real-life contexts. The first gives a tweak to more standard questions of area and perimeter by giving pupils a scenario where one of the sides of a rectangle exists already (i.e. only three sides of the rectangle are needed). Pupils should compare the area of the different rectangles that can be formed using a limited length of 32 m (it is suggested that a table be used to do this). Their aim is to create a rectangle that will maximise the area.

Chapter 1 Revising and improving

Unit 1.5 Practice Book 5A, pages 12–15

The second problem is a challenging one, and pupils should draw a diagram to help visualise the mathematics. The extension to the field (153 m²) can be viewed as two rectangles (3 m × the side length of the square A and 5 m × the side length of the square A) minus the part where they overlap, which we know is 15 m² (because 3 × 5 = 15). Or, put a different way:

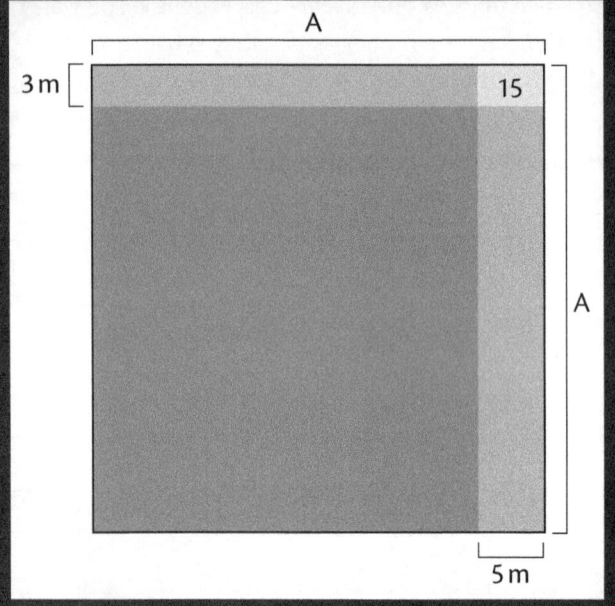

$$(3 \times A) + (5 \times A) = 153 + 15$$
So ... $$A \times (3 + 5) = 168$$
$$A \times 8 = 168$$

Side A is found by dividing 168 by 8 to get 21 metres. From this information, pupils can then derive the original rectangle's dimensions and, from these, its original area.

Chapter 1 test (Practice Book 5A, pages 16–19)

Test question number	Relevant unit	Relevant questions within unit
1	Unit 1.1	Q1
2	Unit 1.1	Q1
3	Unit 1.1	Q2
4	Unit 1.2	Q3
5	Unit 1.4	Q2
6	Unit 1.1	Q3
	Unit 1.3	Q1, Q2
	Unit 1.5	Q1
7	Unit 1.2	Q1, Q2
8	Unit 1.2	Q4
	Unit 1.5	Q3

Chapter 2
Large numbers and measures

Chapter overview

Area of mathematics	National Curriculum statutory requirements for Key Stage 2	Shanghai Maths Project reference
Number – number and place value	Year 5 Programme of study: Pupils should be taught to:	
	■ read, write, order and compare numbers to at least 1 000 000 and determine the value of each digit	Year 5, Units 2.1, 2.2, 2.3
	■ count forwards or backwards in steps of powers of 10 for any given number up to 1 000 000	Year 5, Units 2.1, 2.2, 2.3
	■ round any number up to 1 000 000 to the nearest 10, 100, 1000, 10 000 and 100 000	Year 5, Units 2.4, 2.5
	■ solve number problems and practical problems that involve all of the above.	Year 5, Units 2.4, 2.5
	Year 6 Programme of study: Pupils should be taught to:	
	■ read, write, order and compare numbers up to 10 000 000 and determine the value of each digit	Year 5, Unit 2.1, 2.2, 2.3
	■ round any whole number to a required degree of accuracy	Year 5, Units 2.4, 2.5
	■ solve number and practical problems that involve all of the above.	Year 5, Units 2.1, 2.2, 2.3, 2.4, 2.5
Measurement	Year 5 Programme of study Pupils should be taught to:	
	■ convert between different units of metric measure (for example, kilometre and metre; centimetre and metre; centimetre and millimetre; gram and kilogram; litre and millilitre)	Year 5, Units 2.6, 2.7, 2.8
	■ use all four operations to solve problems involving measure [for example, length, mass, volume, money] using decimal notation, including scaling.	Year 5, Units 2.6, 2.7, 2.8

Chapter 2 Large numbers and measures

Unit 2.1 Knowing large numbers (1)

Conceptual context

The first three units in this chapter explain the mathematical magnitudes of millions (and later billions), and how to read and write these very large numbers. Pupils are already familiar with the concept of place value where each new column on the left is 10 times bigger than the column on its right.

ⓘ A continuous string of numbers would be very difficult to read. To make reading them easier, numbers are separated into groups of three. Each group contains three subgroups: ones, tens and hundreds. This is illustrated in the place value table below.

Millions			Thousands			Ones		
Hundreds	Tens	Ones	Hundreds	Tens	Ones	Hundreds	Tens	Ones

To read numbers without a place value chart, numbers are separated into groups of three, beginning from the right. Numbers are then read from the left, beginning with the largest group. Thus 123456789 is separated from the right to become 123 456 789 and is read from the left as one hundred and twenty-three million, four hundred and fifty-six thousand, seven hundred and eighty-nine.

Learning pupils will have achieved at the end of the unit

- Pupils will have identified the place value of each digit in numbers containing up to nine digits (Q1, Q2, Q3, Q4)
- Pupils will have established that large numbers are written as groups of three digits, separated into groups from the right (Q1)
- Reading and writing numbers containing up to nine digits will have been practised (Q1, Q2, Q3, Q4)
- The use of place value tables will have been extended to include millions (Q1, Q2)
- The use of zero as a placeholder will have been extended so it is understood in numbers containing up to nine digits (Q1, Q2, Q3, Q4)
- Pupils will have explored partitioning numbers containing up to nine digits (Q2)

Resources

place value chart; place value arrow cards (to include millions); mini whiteboards; **Resource 5.2.1a** Making 9-digit numbers; **Resource 5.2.1b** Value of the 4 in 9-digit numbers; **Resource 5.2.1c** Population numbers; **Resource 5.2.1d** 9-digit numbers in numerals and words; **Resource 5.2.1e** 9-digit number puzzles

Vocabulary

ten thousands, hundred thousands, millions, ten millions, hundred millions, placeholder

Chapter 2 Large numbers and measures   Unit 2.1 Practice Book 5A, pages 20–24

Question 1

> **1** Fill in the spaces to make each statement correct.
> (a) Counting from the right, a large number can be separated into groups: ones group, thousands group, millions group, with each group containing three places for different values: ones, tens and hundreds. Complete the table below.
>
> | Group | Millions | | | Thousands | | | Ones | | |
> |---|---|---|---|---|---|---|---|---|---|
> | Place value | | Ten millions | | | | Thousands | | | Tens |
>
> (b) The value of a digit is ☐ times the value of the same digit in the place to its right.
> (c) 378 028 867 consists of ☐ millions, ☐ thousands and ☐ ones.
> (d) When reading a large number, we start from the left with the largest group. For a number whose largest group is millions, we first read the millions group, then the _____ group and finally the _____ group. 378 028 867 is read as _____
>
> (e) When writing a large number of five or more digits in numerals, we start from the left with the largest group, and leave a space between each group (counting from right to left). Twenty-one million, one thousand and thirty-six is written as ☐.

What learning will pupils have achieved at the conclusion of Question 1?

- Pupils will have identified the place value of each digit in numbers containing up to nine digits.
- Pupils will have established that large numbers are written as groups of three digits, separated into groups from the right.
- Reading and writing numbers containing up to nine digits will have been practised.
- The use of place value tables will have been extended to include millions.
- The use of zero as a placeholder will have been extended so it is understood in numbers containing up to nine digits.

Activities for whole-class instruction

- Write the following six-digit number on the board: 357 246. Ask a pupil to read the number and discuss the place value of each digit.

  3 is three hundred thousand

  5 is fifty thousand

  7 is seven thousand

  2 is two hundred

  4 is forty

  6 is six

- Agree that each column is 10 times bigger than the column on its right. Draw the following chart, showing only the six right-hand columns, leaving space to add three more columns to the left:

Millions			Thousands			Ones		
Hundreds (of millions)	Tens (of millions)	Ones (of millions)	Hundreds (of thousands)	Tens (of thousands)	Ones (of thousands)	Hundreds (of ones)	Tens (of ones)	Ones (of ones)

- Ask: *What would be the place value of a seventh column?* Agree 'millions' and add the column as shown. Then agree that the next two columns are 'ten millions' and 'hundred millions' and add those.

- Discuss how the numbers are separated into groups of three on the chart. Each group contains three subgroups: ones, tens and hundreds.

- Draw a nine-column place value chart on the board and ask pupils for digits to populate every cell. For example:

Millions			Thousands			Ones		
3	5	2	6	3	9	2	3	7
2	9	0	3	0	6	4	1	8

- Read the first number out loud: *Three hundred and fifty-two million, six hundred and thirty-nine thousand, two hundred and thirty-seven.* Pupils repeat together. Repeat for the second number

- Give pupils a blank nine-column place value chart and ask individual pupils to choose digits to fill places on the chart. Together read the number. Repeat with more numbers until pupils show confidence. Include numbers containing one or more zeros, for example:

Millions			Thousands			Ones		
2	6	0	1	4	7	5	6	9
4	1	0	0	6	9	3	0	7
5	0	0	0	5	0	0	0	5
7	0	8	0	0	0	8	0	7

   *When reading a large number, start from the left with the largest group. For a number whose largest group is millions, read millions, thousands, ones.*

- We need to be able to read large numbers without relying on a place value chart. Explain that when writing, the millions group, thousands group and ones group are separated by a small space between each group. Once the number has been written down correctly, it can be read from the left.

  ⓘ Pupils may see large numbers separated by commas, for example: 3,421,509

Chapter 2 Large numbers and measures

Unit 2.1   Practice Book 5A, pages 20–24

Explain to them that this is another way of writing large numbers by separating the groups of three digits with commas rather than spaces, like this:
3 421 509

Answers: 218 342 902; 218 902 342; 342 218 902; 342 902 218; 902 218 342; 902 342 218; individual answers

- Pupils should complete Question 1 in the Practice Book.

Same-day intervention

- Give pupils mini whiteboards and ask them to draw the following simple place value chart.

Millions	Thousands	Ones

- Prepare some cards with three-digit numbers, for example 340, 210, 902.
- Pick one of the cards, for example 902, and say this is the number of ones. Ask pupils to fill in the chart.
- Repeat with another card to give the thousands, for example 340, and the final card is the number of millions, 210.

Millions	Thousands	Ones
210	340	902

- Now ask the pupils to read the number. Agree that it is two hundred and ten million, three hundred and forty thousand, nine hundred and two. Pupils should now write this number on their whiteboards, leaving a small space between each group.
- Shuffle the cards and repeat to give a different number.

Same-day enrichment

- Give pupil pairs **Resource 5.2.1a** Making 9-digit numbers.

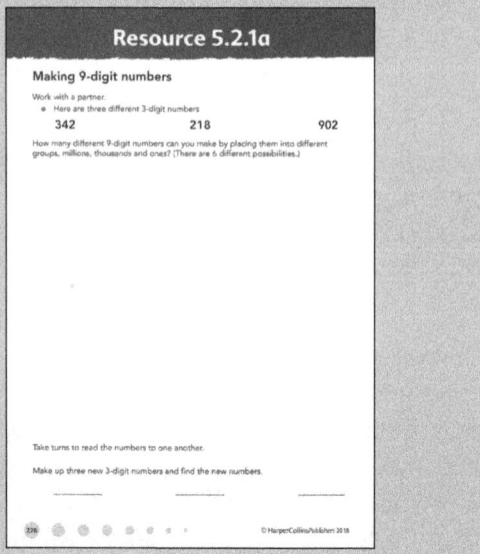

Question 2

2 Complete the place value chart for each number and fill in the blanks. The first one has been done for you.

(a) 4019

Thousands	Hundreds	Tens	Ones
4	0	1	9

Read as: <u>Four thousand and nineteen</u>

4019 = <u>4</u> × 1000 + <u>0</u> × 100 + <u>1</u> × 10 + <u>9</u> × 1

   = <u>4000 + 0 + 10 + 9</u>

(b) 25 198

Ten thousands	Thousands	Hundreds	Tens	Ones

Read as: _____

25 198 = _____ + _____ + _____ + _____ + _____

      = _____ + _____ + _____ + _____ + _____

(c) 412 708

Hundred thousands	Ten thousands	Thousands	Hundreds	Tens	Ones

Read as: _____

412 708 = _____ + _____ + _____ + _____

       + _____

       = _____ + _____ + _____ + _____

       + _____

(d) 2 395 198

Millions	Hundred thousands	Ten thousands	Thousands	Hundreds	Tens	Ones

Read as: _____

2 395 198 = _____ + _____ + _____ + _____

         + _____ + _____

         = _____ + _____ + _____ + _____

         + _____ + _____

42

Chapter 2 Large numbers and measures Unit 2.1   Practice Book 5A, pages 20–24

(e) 76 203 000

Ten millions	Millions	Hundred thousands	Ten thousands	Thousands	Hundreds	Tens	Ones

Read as: _____

76 203 000 = ____ + ____ + ____ + ____
         + ____ + ____ + ____
       = ____ + ____ + ____ + ____
         + ____ + ____

What learning will pupils have achieved at the conclusion of Question 2?

- Pupils will have identified the place value of each digit in numbers containing up to nine digits.
- Reading and writing numbers containing up to nine digits will have been practised.
- The use of place value tables will have been extended to include millions.
- The use of zero as a placeholder will have been extended so it is understood in numbers containing up to nine digits.
- Pupils will have explored partitioning numbers containing up to nine digits.

Activities for whole-class instruction

- Ask pupils to read the following number: 256 389. Establish the place value of each digit and work together to write the number in expanded form:

  256 389 = 2 × 100 000 + 5 × 10 000 + 6 × 1000 + 3 × 100 + 8 × 10 + 9

  = 200 000 + 50 000 + 6000 + 300 + 80 + 9

- Repeat with numbers containing millions, for example: 41 308 058.

  41 308 058 = 4 × 10 000 000 + 1 × 1 000 000 + 3 × 100 000 + 0 × 10 000 + 8 × 1000 + 0 × 100 + 5 × 10 + 8

  = 40 000 000 + 1 000 000 + 300 000 + 0 + 8000 + 0 + 50 + 8

- Pupils should complete Question 2 in the Practice Book.

Same-day intervention

- Give pupil pairs **Resource 5.2.1b** Value of the 4 in 9-digit numbers. Pupils may work individually or with a partner.

Resource 5.2.1b

Value of the 4 in 9-digit numbers

Here are some 9-digit numbers.
Write the value of the 4 in each of the numbers in words and numerals.
The first one has been done for you.

Number	Value of the 4 in words	Value of the 4 in numerals
232 456 198	Four hundred thousand	400 000
140 732 009		
576 321 946		
476 319 072		
563 709 954		
734 870 982		
653 247 017		
198 035 461		
762 490 083		
762 864 201		

Compare your answers with those of a partner.
Take turns to read the numbers to each other.

Answers: forty million, 40 000 000; forty, 40; four hundred million, 400 000 000; four, 4; four million, 4 000 000; forty thousand, 40 000; four hundred, 400; four hundred thousand, 400 000; four thousand, 4000.

Chapter 2 Large numbers and measures

Unit 2.1   Practice Book 5A, pages 20–24

Same-day enrichment

- Give pupil pairs **Resource 5.2.1c** Population numbers. Pupils may work individually or with a partner.

Answers: 1. United States; 2. New Zealand; 3. France; 4. Brazil, Japan, Mexico, Russia, United States; 5. and 6. individual answers.

Completed table: twenty-four million, four hundred and fifty thousand, five hundred and sixty-one; two hundred and nine million, two hundred and eighty-eight thousand two hundred and seventy-eight; 64 979 548; eighty-two million, one hundred and fourteen thousand, two hundred and twenty-four; one hundred and twenty-seven million, four hundred and eighty-four thousand, four hundred and fifty; 129 163 276; four million, seven hundred and five thousand, eight hundred and eighteen; sixty-six million, one hundred and eighty-one thousand, five hundred and eighty-five; three hundred and twenty-four million, four hundred and fifty-nine thousand, four hundred and sixty-three.

Questions 3 and 4

3 Fill in the table. The first one has been done for you.

Number in words	Number in numerals
One million, two hundred and one	1 000 201
One hundred and nineteen thousand and thirty-three	
Seventy million, seventy thousand and seven	
Nine hundred and sixty-one million, two hundred and seventy-three thousand, nine hundred and twenty-eight	
Five hundred million	

4 True or false? (Put a ✓ for true and a ✗ for false in each box.)

(a) The number consisting of two ten thousands, two one thousands, and two ones is 2 000 020 002.

(b) 50 040 600 is read as fifty thousand and forty thousand and six hundred.

(c) In a 5-digit number, the place with the highest value is the ten thousands place.

(d) Nine hundred and nine thousand and nine is written in numerals as 909 009.

What learning will pupils have achieved at the conclusion of Questions 3 and 4?

- Pupils will have identified the place value of each digit in numbers containing up to nine digits.
- Reading and writing numbers containing up to nine digits will have been practised.
- The use of zero as a placeholder will have been extended so it is understood in numbers containing up to nine digits.

Activities for whole-class instruction

- Give pupils mini whiteboards and ask them to draw a place value chart for nine-digit numbers, showing millions, thousands and ones. Check their charts.

Millions			Thousands			Ones		
Hundreds	Tens	Ones	Hundreds	Tens	Ones	Hundreds	Tens	Ones

- Ask pupils to identify particular columns by pointing to the correct column.
- Pupils should complete Questions 3 and 4 in the Practice Book.

Chapter 2 Large numbers and measures   Unit 2.1   Practice Book 5A, pages 20–24

Same-day intervention

- Give pupil pairs **Resource 5.2.1d** 9-digit numbers in numerals and words.

Answers: two hundred and ten million; two hundred and one million; two hundred million, one hundred thousand; two hundred million and ten thousand; two hundred million and one thousand; two hundred million and one hundred; two hundred million and ten; two hundred million and one; 531 642 999; 100 200 300; 777 777 777; 963 864 210; 404 303 202

Challenge and extension questions

Questions 5 and 6

5 Use four zeros and three sixes to form different 7-digit numbers as indicated.

(a) Four zeros at the end: _____

(b) Three zeros at the end: _____

(c) Two zeros at the end: _____

6 Use the six digits 3, 0, 1, 5, 7 and 9 to form the greatest and smallest possible 6-digit numbers. What is the difference between these two numbers? (Write a number sentence to show your answer.)

These questions require pupils to use reasoning to solve word problems involving place value. Preparing and answering similar problems would challenge pupils further.

Same-day enrichment

- Give pupil pairs **Resource 5.2.1e** 9-digit number puzzles. They may work individually or in pairs as appropriate. Answers will vary.

Chapter 2 Large numbers and measures

Unit 2.2
Knowing large numbers (2)

Conceptual context

The focus in this second unit is on comparing and ordering large numbers (up to nine digits). Pupils have previously ordered numbers, but in this unit they will review their understanding and extend and apply it to these large numbers.

Pupils will also learn to read and write numbers with more than nine digits, as illustrated in the table below.

Billions			Millions			Thousands			Ones		
Hundreds	Tens	Ones	Hundreds	Tens	Ones	Hundreds	Tens	Ones	Hundreds	Tens	Ones

As pupils become more familiar with handling large numbers, the abstract understanding of place value will become more embedded.

 There is one further group of numbers (trillions) that is in reasonably common use. One trillion is written 1 000 000 000 000 – it is a million million.

However, mathematicians generally use standard form to write very large numbers, so two trillion is written as 2×10^{12}. Pupils have some experience of indices/powers from square numbers ($10^2 = 100$) and units for area (cm^2). Standard form is covered in the Key Stage 3 curriculum.

Learning pupils will have achieved at the end of the unit

- Reading and writing billion numbers (10 or more digits) will have been practised (Q1, Q2)
- Pupils will have identified the place value of each digit in numbers containing up to 10 digits (Q1, Q2)
- Pupils will have explored expressing the same number in different ways (Q1, Q2)
- Pupils will have extended their understanding of ordering numbers to include numbers containing up to nine digits (Q3)
- Pupils will have extended their understanding of number lines to include very large numbers (Q4)
- Pupils will have used reasoning to solve word problems involving place value and ordering of very large numbers (Q5)
- Understanding of place value and partitioning will have been applied to addition and subtraction calculations involving large numbers (Q5, Q6)
- Pupils will have practised mental and column methods to add and subtract large numbers (Q5, Q6)

Resources

place value chart; blank number lines (class and individual); mini whiteboards; 0–9 digit cards; **Resource 5.2.2a** Matching large numbers; **Resource 5.2.2b** True or false?; **Resource 5.2.2c** Finding whole tens, hundreds and thousands; **Resource 5.2.2d** Greatest and smallest

Vocabulary

ten thousands, hundred thousands, millions, ten millions, hundred millions, billions, ten billions, hundred billions

Chapter 2 Large numbers and measures

Unit 2.2 Practice Book 5A, pages 25–28

Questions 1 and 2

1 Fill in the spaces to make each statement correct.

(a) In a 9-digit number, the place with the highest value is in the _____ place.

(b) Counting from right to left, the fifth place is the _____ place, the place to its right is the _____ place, and the place to the left of the hundred thousands place is the _____ place.

(c) 2 003 500 709 contains ☐ billions, ☐ millions, ☐ thousands and ☐ ones.

(d) In the number 10 506 000 090, the 1 is in the _____ place, standing for _____ ; the 5 is in the _____ place, standing for _____ ; the 6 is in the _____ place, standing for _____ ; and the 9 is in the _____ place, standing for _____.

(e) 913 004 consists of ☐ thousands and ☐ ones. It can also be said to consist of ☐ ones.

(f) 4000 can be seen as ☐ ones, or ☐ thousands, or ☐ hundreds.

(g) The smallest 7-digit number is ☐, the smallest 4-digit number is ☐, and the smallest 7-digit number is ☐ times the smallest 4-digit number.

2 Multiple choice questions. (For each question, choose the correct answer and write the letter in the box.)

(a) Two hundred and two thousand three hundred is written as ☐.
A. 2 002 300   B. 202 000 300   C. 202 300   D. 2 020 300

(b) In the number 6 104 510, the 4 is in the ☐ place.
A. hundreds   B. thousands
C. ten thousands   D. hundred thousands

(c) One billion is equal to ☐ millions.
A. 10   B. 100   C. 1000   D. 10 000

What learning will pupils have achieved at the conclusion of Questions 1 and 2?

- Reading and writing billion numbers (10 or more digits) will have been practised.
- Pupils will have identified the place value of each digit in numbers containing up to 10 digits.
- Pupils will have explored expressing the same number in different ways.

Activities for whole-class instruction

- Display the following place value chart.

Billions			Millions			Thousands			Ones		
Hundreds	Tens	Ones	Hundreds	Tens	Ones	Hundreds	Tens	Ones	Hundreds	Tens	Ones

- Discuss the way that the numbers are in repeating blocks of 'hundreds, tens and ones'. Ask questions such as: *What is the value of the 7th (3rd, 10th ...) digit? How many digits does one billion (million, hundred thousand ...) have?*

- Display the following number: 30 450 067 023. Ask pupils which numbers are the billions group? The millions group? The thousands group? The ones group?

- The number is made up from these groups (write on the board, set out in columns as shown):

  30 000 000 000 – thirty billion

  450 000 000 – four hundred and fifty million

  67 000 – sixty-seven thousand

  23 – twenty-three

- Tell pupils that we read the number as: *thirty billion, four hundred and fifty million, sixty-seven thousand and twenty-three.*

- Discuss how the zeros act as placeholders so that each digit can be assigned the correct value.

- Point out that, in numerals, the number can be expressed in 11 characters, while in words it requires 73 characters and two hyphens. Using the place value system is a very efficient way of recording numbers!

- Explain that the reverse process, writing numbers from words, requires pupils to identify where the digit has no value and therefore where a zero placeholder is required. This can be tricky.

- Write the number: Four billion, twenty-three million, eight thousand and two. Ask pupils to write this number in numerals on their mini whiteboards and compare it with that of a friend.

4 023 008 002

- Ask individual pupils to explain how they did it. Arranging the numbers in groups of three is the key to success. Encourage them to read the number when they have written it in numerals to check that it matches with the original.

- Repeat with more large numbers until pupils are confident.

- Pupils should complete Questions 1 and 2 in the Practice Book.

Chapter 2 Large numbers and measures

Unit 2.2 Practice Book 5A, pages 25–28

Same-day intervention

- Give pupil pairs **Resource 5.2.2a** Matching large numbers.

- An easier way of using the cards would be to lay them out face up and simply match them. Another game is to separate them into numerals and words. The numerals are spread out face up. One pupil holds the words and reads them in turn, while the other finds the matching numeral.

Same-day enrichment

- How many different 10-digit numbers can be written using only the numbers 1 and 2 and zeros as placeholders? Ask pupils to take turns to read the numbers aloud to a partner.
- Answers: 18: 2 100 000 000; 2 010 000 000; 2 001 000 000; 2 000 100 000; 2 000 010 000; 2 000 001 000; 2 000 000 100; 2 000 000 010; 2 000 000 001; 1 200 000 000; 1 020 000 000; 1 002 000 000; 1 000 200 000; 1 000 020 000; 1 000 002 000; 1 000 000 200; 1 000 000 020; 1 000 000 002.

Question 3

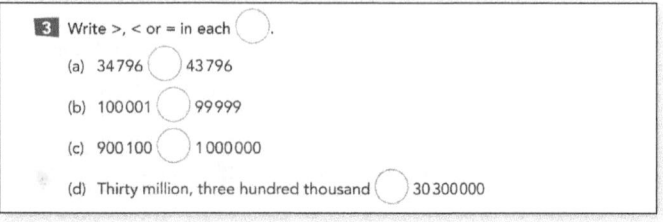

What learning will pupils have achieved at the conclusion of Question 3?

- Pupils will have extended their understanding of ordering numbers to include numbers containing up to nine digits.

Activities for whole-class instruction

- Display these large numbers and ask pupils, working in pairs, to read the numbers to their partner and to think about how to order them, starting with the greatest.

  502 089   431 796   98 821   174 968   429 762

- Discuss with pupils their strategy for ordering numbers. Ask if they spotted that one number has only five digits (98 821) and therefore must be the smallest. The other four numbers all have six digits, so they should first look for the number with the greatest number in the 'hundred thousands' column, that is 5 in 502 089. There are two numbers with 4 in the 'hundred thousands' column, so they need to compare the 'ten thousands' column; 431 796 is greater than 429 762. The remaining number, 174 968 is the smallest six-digit number. Thus, the order is 502 089 > 431 796 > 429 762 > 174 968 > 98 821.

- **Look out for** … pupils who did not spot that 98 821 was a five-digit number and reinforce the importance of the number of digits when ordering numbers.

- Show pupils another set of numbers and this time ask them to order them starting with the smallest. For example:

  319 218   319 732   31 999   318 703   319 213

- Agree that now they are looking for the number with the smallest number of digits and, where numbers have the same number of digits, for the number with the lowest value in each column, starting on the left. If the values are the same, they need to look at the next column until they find the place where the numbers differ.

- Agree that the order is:

  31 999 < 318 703 < 319 213 < 319 218 < 319 732

- Pupils should complete Question 3 in the Practice Book.

Chapter 2 Large numbers and measures Unit 2.2 Practice Book 5A, pages 25–28

Same-day intervention

- Give pupil pairs **Resource 5.2.2b** True or false? to complete.

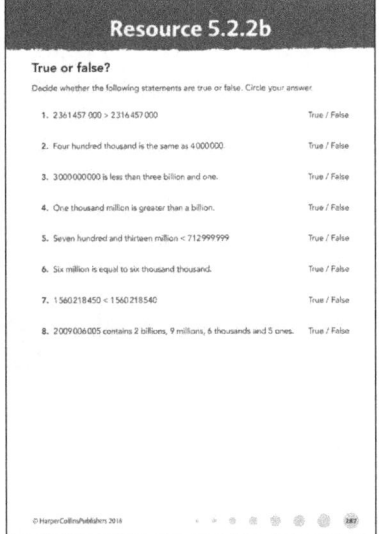

Answers: 1. True; 2. False; 3. True; 4. False; 5. False; 6. True; 7. True; 8. True

Same-day enrichment

- Pupils take turns to lay out a shuffled set of 0–9 digit cards to make a 10-digit number; encourage pupils to start from the right and to leave a small space between each group (ones, thousands, millions, billions), for example:

- Read the number together: *four billion, six hundred and twenty-three million, nine hundred and seven thousand, five hundred and eighteen.* Ask pupils to work in pairs to record each number. When each pupil has laid out a number, challenge the pairs to order the numbers and to explain their reasoning.

Question 4

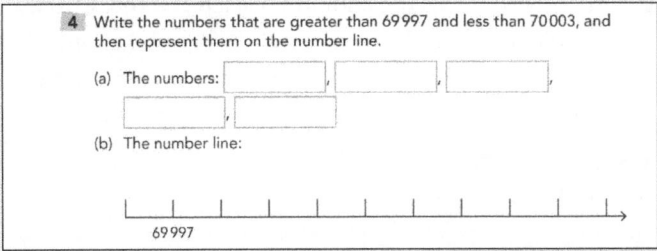

What learning will pupils have achieved at the conclusion of Question 4?

- Pupils will have extended their understanding of number lines to include very large numbers.

Activities for whole-class instruction

- Explain to pupils that number lines from zero are not practical to represent very large numbers, but using a blank number line as a visual aid to determine a range of numbers can be useful.
- Here is an example of a typical question: List the numbers greater than 799 998 and less than 800 005.
- Display part of a blank number line and explain that the intervals are ones.

|—|—|—|—|—|—|—|→
799 998   800 005

- Write 799 998 under the left-hand marker. Ask individual pupils to count on in ones to add the numbers to the line until they reach 800 005.

|—|—|—|—|—|—|—|→
799 998 799 999 800 000 800 001 800 002 800 003 800 004 800 005

- The numbers are 799 999, 800 000, 800 001, 800 002, 800 003, 800 004.
- Try another range, for example 999 995 to 1 000 002.
- Pupils should complete Question 4 in the Practice Book.

Same-day intervention

- Give pupils a blank number line. Write a five-digit number of whole thousands, for example 58 000.

|—|—|—|—|—|—|—|→
                          58 000

- Ask pupils to write the given number next to the middle marker of the line as shown. Now challenge them to complete the numbers on the number line. Pupil pairs can compare their answers. Ask individual pupils to read the numbers.
- Repeat with further numbers, including six-digit or seven-digit numbers.

Chapter 2 Large numbers and measures Unit 2.2 Practice Book 5A, pages 25–28

Same-day enrichment

- Give pupil pairs **Resource 5.2.2c** Finding whole tens, hundreds and thousands to complete

Answers 1. 67 990, 68 000, 68 010, 68 020; 2. 72 900, 73 000, 73 100, 73 200, 73 300; 3. 877 000, 878 000, 879 000, 880 000, 881 000

Questions 5 and 6

5 Subtract 23 from the smallest possible 5-digit number and add the resulting number to the largest possible 3-digit number. Show the calculations.

6 Calculate mentally or use the column method to add or subtract large numbers. Check the answers to the questions marked with *.
(a) 608 000 + 200 000
(b) 236 549 – 36 000
(c) *720 055 – 22 000
(d) 32 495 – 30 001
(e) 225 329 + 154 019
(f) *5 800 000 – 712 012

What learning will pupils have achieved at the conclusion of Questions 5 and 6?

- Pupils will have used reasoning to solve word problems involving place value and ordering of very large numbers.
- Understanding of place value and partitioning will have been applied to addition and subtraction calculations involving large numbers.
- Pupils will have practised mental and column methods to add and subtract large numbers.

Activities for whole-class instruction

- Display these numbers and use place value to answer the questions that follow together:

  2 495 301   7 283 764   34 569 547

  – Decrease each number by two million. (Answers: 495 301, 5 283 764, 32 569 547)
  – Increase each number by three hundred thousand. (Answers: 2 795 301, 7 583 764, 34 869 547)
  – Increase each number by four thousand. (Answers: 2 499 301, 7 287 764, 34 573 547)
  – Decrease each number by 10. (Answers: 2 495 291, 7 283 754, 34 569 537)

- Display the following addition calculation, which involves carrying:

  154 682

  + 238 247

- Check that pupils remember that the digits need to be correctly aligned. Ensure that they understand the value of each column, particularly the 'hundred thousands' column. Confirm that the procedures involved when using the column addition format are the same, no matter how many digits are involved.

  ```
   1 5 4 6 8 2
   2 3 8 2 4 7
   3 9 2 9 2 9
         1   1
  ```

- Discuss with pupils the addition of each column. Check they still understand that the small '1' represents one of whatever column it is in, here 'one lot of 1 hundred' and 'one lot of 10 thousand'.
- Repeat with another addition to consolidate understanding.

Chapter 2 Large numbers and measures

Unit 2.2 Practice Book 5A, pages 25–28

- Display the following four-digit subtraction, where the minuend includes a zero as a placeholder and the corresponding digit in the subtrahend is greater than zero. Look at it together. Ask a pupil to talk though the calculation, explaining the regrouping.

  $$\begin{array}{r} 6\,0\,2\,7 \\ -\;2\,6\,1\,8 \\ \hline 3\,4\,0\,9 \end{array}$$

- Agree that subtraction of very large numbers is carried out in exactly the same way – there are just more columns!

- Work through this subtraction together. Ask a pupil to talk though the calculation, explaining the regrouping.

  $$\begin{array}{r} 5\,8\,0\,7\,4\,3 \\ -\;2\,0\,8\,2\,6\,1 \\ \hline 3\,7\,2\,4\,8\,2 \end{array}$$

- Pupils should complete Questions 5 and 6 in the Practice Book.

Same-day intervention

- Give pupil pairs **Resource 5.2.2d** Greatest and smallest to complete.

  Answers

Number of digits	Smallest number	Greatest number
1	1	9
2	10	99
3	100	999
4	1000	9999
5	10 000	99 999
6	100 000	999 999
7	1 000 000	9 999 999
10	1 000 000 000	9 999 999 999

  Number of 0 digits and number of 9 digits increases by one each time; 10 – 9 = 1, 1000 – 999 = 1, 100 000 – 99 999 = 1.

  The difference will always be one.

Same-day enrichment

- Organise pupils into pairs. Give each pair six dice and ask them to take turns to roll the dice twice to create two six-digit numbers. They record the numbers as the dice are thrown from hundred thousands to ones, for example 3, 2, 6, 5, 3, 4 gives 326 534 and 2, 1, 5, 3, 2, 6 gives 215 326. They add and subtract the numbers.

  $$\begin{array}{r} 326\,534 \\ +\;215\,326 \\ \hline 541\,860 \\ {\scriptstyle 1\;\;\;1} \end{array} \qquad \begin{array}{r} 326\,534 \\ -\;215\,326 \\ \hline 111\,208 \end{array}$$

- Pupils repeat with further dice rolls.

Challenge and extension questions

Questions 7 and 8

7 Put the numbers 60 500, 50 600, 500 006, 56 000 and 65 000 in order, first from the smallest to the greatest, and then from the greatest to the smallest.

8 Find the populations of England, Scotland, Wales and Northern Ireland, and then add them up to find the total population of the United Kingdom. (State the source of your data.)

Question 8 involves researching real data. Investigating the populations of different countries is a practical and interesting way to explore very large numbers.

Chapter 2 Large numbers and measures

Unit 2.3
Knowing large numbers (3)

Conceptual context

The final unit in this series of three consolidates reading, writing, comparing and ordering large numbers.

Learning pupils will have achieved at the end of the unit

- Pupils will have used reasoning to solve word problems involving place value of large numbers (Q1, Q3)
- Pupils will have practised writing very large numbers in words from numerals (Q2)
- Real-life examples of very large numbers will have been explored (Q2)
- Pupils will have described place value in abstract terms with understanding (Q3)
- Pupils will have matched very large numbers written in words and numerals (Q4)
- Pupils will have consolidated their understanding of ordering very large numbers (Q4)

Resources

place value chart; mini whiteboards; blank A5 cards; 0–9 digit cards; 1–6 dice; **Resource 5.2.3a** Writing large numerals; **Resource 5.2.3b** How many zeros?; **Resource 5.2.3c** Digit sum equals 20; **Resource 5.2.3d** Find the match; **Resource 5.2.3e** How far to the Sun?

Vocabulary

hundred thousands, millions, ten millions, hundred millions, billions, ten billions, hundred billions

Chapter 2 Large numbers and measures

Unit 2.3 Practice Book 5A, pages 29–31

Question 1

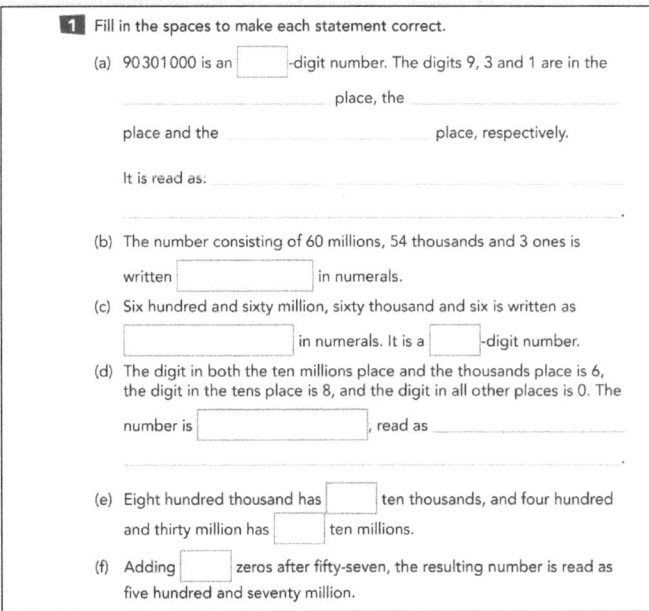

What learning will pupils have achieved at the conclusion of Question 1?

- Pupils will have used reasoning to solve word problems involving place value of large numbers.

Activities for whole-class instruction

- Display the following:

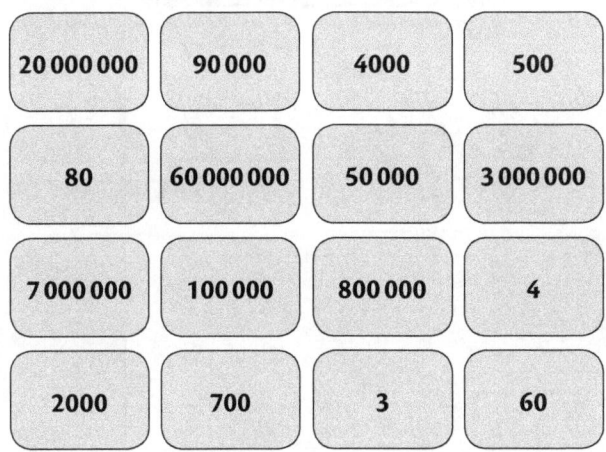

- Ask individual pupils to find and read the two six-digit numbers. Repeat with the other pairs of numbers that have the same number of digits.
- Invite a pupil to choose five cards with different numbers of digits and to arrange them in order, starting with the greatest, so that they can combine them to make a number. Zeros as placeholders should be added where necessary.

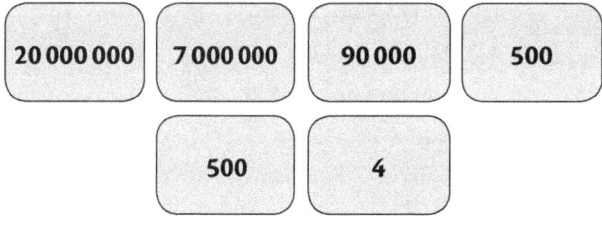

- For example, these cards make 27 090 504. Read the number together.
- Repeat with another selection of cards to make a new number. Continue with further numbers until pupils are confident handling the cards to make and read large numbers.
- Pupils should complete Question 1 in the Practice Book.

Same-day intervention

- Give pupil pairs **Resource 5.2.3a** Writing large numerals.

Answers: 1. 1 006 930; 2. 2 450 302 403; 3. 60 207; 4. 143 082; 5. 76 650 063; 6. 20 044 205 700; 7. 8 040 017; 8. 9 230 956 008; 9. 33 333; 10. 4 008 002 006

Chapter 2 Large numbers and measures

Unit 2.3 Practice Book 5A, pages 29–31

Same-day enrichment

- Give pupil pairs **Resource 5.2.3b** How many zeros?

Answers: 1. 1 000 010, 5; 2. 2 450 000 000, 7; 3. 70 007, 3; 4. 543 002, 2; 5. 6 000 363, 3; 6. 20 000 000 000, 10; 7. 8 040 002, 4; 8. 9 000 999 000, 6; 9. 33 333, 0; 10. 400 000 000 000, 11; 11. and 12. Individual answers

Question 2

2 Read the numbers underlined and write them in words below.
  (a) According to the national statistics, the number of pupils in schools in England in 2015 was 8 271 270.
  (b) According to the Guinness World Records, the largest pizza weighed 23 250 kg.
  (c) The Coral Sea is in the South Pacific Ocean, off the north-east coast of Australia. It contains the world's largest reef system and has an area of 4 791 000 square kilometres.
  (d) The distance between Pluto and the Sun is about 5 900 000 000 km.

What learning will pupils have achieved at the conclusion of Question 2?

- Pupils will have practised writing very large numbers in words from numerals.
- Real-life examples of very large numbers will have been explored.

Activities for whole-class instruction

- This question revisits writing numbers in words, using real data and measurements.
- Discuss the fact that large numbers are separated into groups of three to make reading and understanding them easier. Each group then contains three subgroups: ones, tens and hundreds. For a number that contains billions, the groups are billions, millions, thousands, ones.

 *Billions, millions, thousands, ones.*

- Pupils should complete Question 2 in the Practice Book.

Same-day intervention

- Ask pupils, working in pairs, to write 10 different 10-digit numbers where the sum of the digits is 20, for example 1 234 234 100. Then ask them to write the numbers in words (for example, one billion, two hundred and thirty-four million, two hundred and thirty-four thousand, one hundred).

Same-day enrichment

- Give pupil pairs **Resource 5.2.3c** Digit sum equals 20.

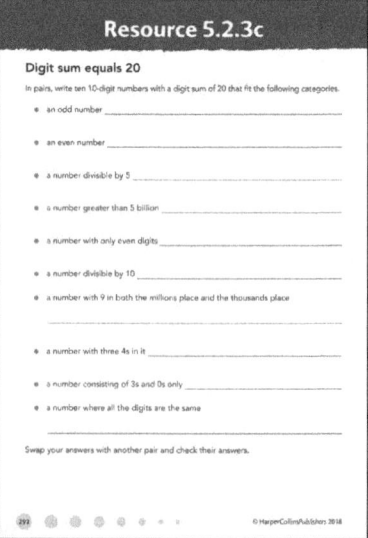

- Pairs can swap to check each other's answers.

Chapter 2 Large numbers and measures

Unit 2.3 Practice Book 5A, pages 29–31

Question 3

> 3. True or false? (Put a ✓ for true and a ✗ for false in each box.)
> (a) The greatest 7-digit number is 9 000 000.
> (b) The number consisting of 70 thousands and 500 ones is 700 500.
> (c) A large number plus a large number is also a large number.
> (d) A large number minus a large number is also a large number.

What learning will pupils have achieved at the conclusion of Question 3?

- Pupils will have described place value in abstract terms with understanding.

Activities for whole-class instruction

- Give pupils mini whiteboards and ask them to write the following number sentences:
  - the greatest five-digit number plus one
    (Answer: 99 999 + 1 = 100 000)
  - the least seven-digit number minus one
    (Answer: 1 000 000 − 1 = 999 999)
- Challenge them to write a similar number sentence. Share some of their sentences.
- Ask pupils to write one billion in numerals and to explain to their partner how the place values are arranged to facilitate reading the number. Confirm that the number is 1 000 000 000, with the zeros arranged in groups of three from the right, ones, thousands, millions and then a 1 in the tenth place making one billion.
- Show pupils 100 000 000 000 and ask a pupil to read the number. Continue with other numbers if necessary.
- Pupils should complete Question 3 in the Practice Book.

Same-day intervention

- Give pupils a nine-digit place value chart and a 1–6 dice.

Millions			Thousands			Ones		

- Explain that the aim is to make the largest possible number. Pupils take turns to roll the 1–6 dice. Each time the dice is rolled, everyone must fill in one place on the chart until the nine-digit number is complete. Once a digit has been entered it cannot be changed.
- The winner is the pupil with the highest number. (A further challenge would be for pupils to order the numbers, starting with the greatest.)
- Repeat the task but this time the aim is to make the smallest possible number (and the numbers can be ordered, starting with the smallest).

Same-day enrichment

- Present pupils with the following four numbers:
  200, 4000, 80 000, 6 000 000
- Ask: *How many different seven-digit numbers can be made using one or more of the numbers?*
  Answers: There are eight different numbers: 6 084 200, 6 084 000, 6 080 200, 6 080 000, 6 004 200, 6 004 000, 6 000 200, 6 000 000
- This could be extended to find all possible numbers with any number of digits.

Question 4

> 4. Draw a line to match each pair of the same number.
> (a) four hundred and five thousand and eight   A. 400 050 008
> (b) forty million, fifty thousand and eight   B. 40 050 008
> (c) four hundred million, fifty thousand and eight   C. 40 000 080
> (d) four billion, fifty million, eight hundred   D. 405 008
> (e) forty million and eighty   E. 4 050 000 800
> (f) Now write all the numbers in order, from the greatest to the least: _____

What learning will pupils have achieved at the conclusion of Question 4?

- Pupils will have matched very large numbers written in words and numerals.
- Pupils will have consolidated their understanding of ordering very large numbers.

Activities for whole-class instruction

- Ask pupils, working in pairs, to discuss the following questions:
  - Can a six-digit number contain millions? (No – million numbers must have at least seven digits.)
  - What is a large number? (There is no correct answer to this. It depends on the context.)
  - How many zeros follow the 1 in a billion? (nine zeros)

Chapter 2 Large numbers and measures

Unit 2.3 Practice Book 5A, pages 29–31

- Is it easier to order large numbers from the greatest to the smallest or vice versa, or does it not make any difference? (It makes no difference; just reverse the process).
- Next, ask pupils to explain the following to a partner:
  - How do you read a 10-digit number, for example 4 560 201 379?
  - How do you write a number in numerals from words, for example three billion, four hundred and twenty million, five hundred and fifty-three thousand, two hundred and six?
  - How do you order large numbers, for example 34 576 190, 34 576 321, 3 457 632?
- Listen for pupils who are able to articulate their reasoning clearly and ask them to share their explanations with the class.
- Pupils should complete Question 4 in the Practice Book.

Same-day intervention

- Give pupil pairs **Resource 5.2.3d** Find the match.

- Pairs can swap to check each other's answers.
  Answers: 1. A; 2. B; 3. B; 4. A; 5. A; 6. B; 7. A; 8. B

Same-day enrichment

- Give pupil pairs **Resource 5.2.3e** How far to the Sun?

Planet	Distance to the Sun (km)	Distance to the Sun (km) in words
Earth	149 600 000	one hundred and forty-nine million, six hundred thousand
Jupiter	778 369 000	**seven hundred and seventy-eight million, three hundred and sixty-nine thousand**
Mars	227 937 000	**two hundred and twenty-seven million, nine hundred and thirty-seven thousand**
Mercury	57 900 000	fifty-seven million, nine hundred thousand
Neptune	4 496 976 000	**four billion, four hundred and ninety-six million, nine hundred and seventy-six thousand**
Saturn	1 427 034 000	one billion, four hundred and twenty-seven million, thirty-four thousand
Uranus	2 870 658 000	**two billion, eight hundred and seventy million, six hundred and fifty-eight thousand**
Venus	108 160 000	one hundred and eight million, one hundred and sixty thousand

Neptune > Uranus > Saturn > Jupiter > Mars > Earth > Venus > Mercury

Challenge and extension questions

Questions 5, 6 and 7

5 You are given two numbers: 5976 and 1432. Subtract 4 from the first number and add 4 to the second number. Repeat. How many times do you have to do this before they become equal?

6 Joe and Alan are playing number games. Joe says, 'I am thinking of a 6-digit number, which is greater than the greatest 5-digit number. The digit in its highest value place is 1, and the digit in all the other places is 0.' Alan got the correct answer immediately. What is the number?

7 Remove four digits from the 10-digit number 5 704 590 212 so that, without changing the order, the 6-digit number made up of the remaining six digits has the greatest value. What is the 6-digit number? Repeat the activity, but this time remove four digits to leave the 6-digit number with the smallest value. What is the number?

- These questions require pupils to use reasoning to solve word problems involving place value of large numbers.

Chapter 2 Large numbers and measures

Unit 2.4
Rounding of large numbers (1)

Conceptual context

Pupils already know how to round numbers to the nearest 10, 100 and 1000. This unit extends this to rounding larger numbers to 1000 and 10 000.

ⓘ Using number lines provides pupils with a visual image that they can use mentally when rounding; pupils can see which 100/1000/10 000 is 'nearest' and, therefore, which is the correct number to round to.

Numbers that are 'halfway' are always rounded to the next 100/1000/10 000.

Learning pupils will have achieved at the end of the unit

- Number lines will have been used to determine the 'nearness' of whole hundreds in relation to intermediate numbers (Q1, Q2)
- Pupils will have identified the whole hundreds numbers immediately before and following three-digit numbers, the whole thousands numbers immediately before and following four-digit numbers and the whole ten thousands numbers immediately before and following five-digit numbers (Q1, Q2, Q3)
- Pupils will have practised rounding numbers to the nearest 1000, 10 000, 100 000 and 1 000 000 (Q4, Q5, Q6)

Resources

0–1000 number line (class and individual); 0–10 000 number line (class and individual); 10 m measuring tape; 1–6 dice; 0–9 digit cards; mini whiteboards; **Resource 5.2.4a** What's the shape? **Resource 5.2.4b** Find and make mystery shapes; **Resource 5.2.4c** Using rounding to calculate approximate answers; **Resource 5.2.4d** Rounding to 100 000

Vocabulary

round to the nearest ..., interval, halfway, midpoint

Chapter 2 Large numbers and measures

Unit 2.4 Practice Book 5A, pages 32–35

Question 1

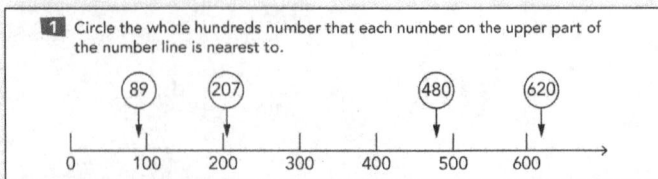

1. Circle the whole hundreds number that each number on the upper part of the number line is nearest to.

What learning will pupils have achieved at the conclusion of Question 1?

- Number lines will have been used to determine the 'nearness' of whole hundreds in relation to intermediate numbers.
- Pupils will have identified the whole hundreds numbers immediately before and following three-digit numbers, the whole thousands numbers immediately before and following four-digit numbers and the whole ten thousands numbers immediately before and following five-digit numbers.

Activities for whole-class instruction

- Display a 0–1000 number line.

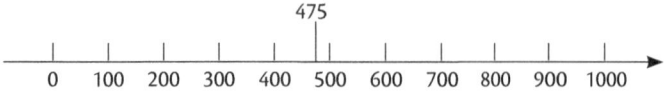

- Count the hundreds together.
- Ask a pupil to show the position of 475 on the number line. Choose a pupil to point out the whole hundreds on each side of the 475: 400 and 500. Agree that it is closer to 500.
- Choose another pupil to show the position of 920.

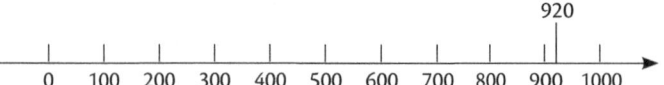

- Agree that the whole hundreds on each side of 920 are 900 and 1000 and that 920 is closer to 900.
- Pupils should complete Question 1 in the Practice Book.

Same-day intervention

- Open a 10 m measuring tape and ask a pupil to find 235 cm. Choose another pupil to identify the whole hundreds on each side: 200 cm and 300 cm. Ask which one 235 cm is nearest to and agree that it is closer to 200 cm. It is only 35 cm away as opposed to 300 cm, which is 65 cm away.
- Repeat with more measurements until pupils are confident that measurements with 5 or more in the tens position are closer to the higher number and measurements with 4 or less in the tens position are closer to the lower number.

Same-day enrichment

- Give pupil pairs a set of 0–9 digit cards. The first player shuffles the cards, turns over three cards to make a three-digit number, identifies the closest whole hundreds number and records it. The other player takes their turn.
- After 10 rounds, add up the scores, and the player with the higher total is the winner.

Questions 2 and 3

2. Write the whole ten thousands numbers that come before and after a, b, c, d and e. Put a ✓ against the ten thousands number that each number is nearest to.

3. Write the whole ten thousands numbers before and after each of the following numbers. Put a ✓ next to its nearest ten thousands number.

	32 108	
	105 213	
	971 234	
	120 087	
	6 401 239	
	396 042	

What learning will pupils have achieved at the conclusion of Questions 2 and 3?

- Number lines will have been used to determine the 'nearness' of whole hundreds in relation to intermediate numbers.
- Pupils will have identified the whole hundreds numbers immediately before and following three-digit numbers, the whole thousands numbers immediately before and following four-digit numbers and the whole ten thousands numbers immediately before and following five-digit numbers.

Chapter 2 Large numbers and measures

Unit 2.4 Practice Book 5A, pages 32–35

Activities for whole-class instruction

- Display a 0–10 000 number line.

  ```
                                    6350
  |—————————————————————————|—————————————→
  0  1000 2000 3000 4000 5000 6000 7000 8000 9000 10 000
  ```

- Choose a pupil to show the position of 6350 on the number line. Invite pupils to identify the whole thousands immediately before and following the number. Ask: *Which is the nearest whole thousand?* Agree that 6350 is closer to 6000.

  ```
                                          7820
  |————————————————————————————|———————————→
  0  1000 2000 3000 4000 5000 6000 7000 8000 9000 10 000
  ```

- Choose a pupil to show the position of 7820 on the number line. Invite pupils to identify the whole thousands immediately before and following the number. Ask: *Which is the nearest whole thousand?* Agree that 7820 is closer to 8000.

- Ask: *Is 3500 closer to 3000 or 4000?* Agree it is exactly the midpoint. Explain to pupils that, although it is halfway, by convention the number is rounded to the next whole thousand, in this instance 4000. Remind them that this is how they approached rounding to the nearest ten and nearest hundred, so 35 is rounded to 40 and 350 is rounded to 400.

- Pupils should complete Questions 2 and 3 in the Practice Book.

Same-day intervention

- Give pupils **Resource 5.2.4a** What's the shape?

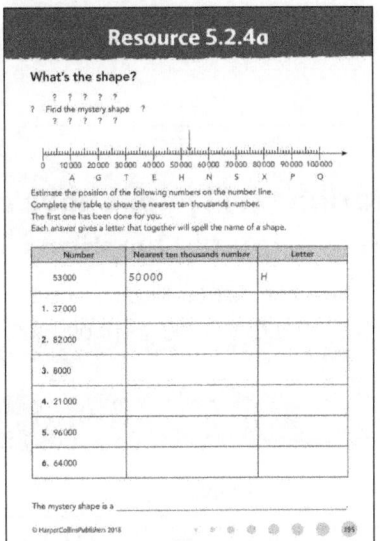

  Answer: 1. 40 000, E; 2. 80 000, X; 3. 10 000, A; 4. 20 000, G; 5. 100 000, O; 6. 60 000, N; HEXAGON

Same-day enrichment

- Give pupils **Resource 5.2.4b** Find and make mystery shapes

  Answers: 1. 40 000, E; 2. 80 000, X; 3. 10 000, A; 4. 20 000, G; 5. 100 000, O; 6. 60 000, N; HEXAGON; individual numbers

Question 4

> 4 Round each of the following numbers to the nearest ten thousand.
>
> (a) 10 999 ≈
> (b) 56 089 000 ≈
> (c) 443 219 ≈
> (d) 1 096 789 ≈
> (e) 9167 ≈
> (f) 9 950 123 ≈

What learning will pupils have achieved at the conclusion of Question 4?

- Pupils will have practised rounding numbers to the nearest 1000, 10 000, 100 000 and 1 000 000.

Activities for whole-class instruction

- In the previous question, pupils estimated the position of numbers and investigated which whole thousand the number was nearest to.

  - 6350 is closer to 6000, so the number would be rounded to 6000.
  - 7820 is closer to 8000, so the number would be rounded to 8000.

- Ask pupils to locate the positions of 500, 5500 and 8500 on the number line. Agree that the numbers are exactly midway between the whole thousands.

  ```
       500                   5500              8500
  |—————|——————————————————————|————————————————|——→
  0  1000 2000 3000 4000 5000 6000 7000 8000 9000 10 000
  ```

59

Chapter 2 Large numbers and measures Unit 2.4 Practice Book 5A, pages 32–35

- Remind them that, by convention, numbers with a 5 in the hundreds place are rounded to the next thousand. 500 is rounded to 1000, 5500 rounded to 6000 and 8500 rounded to 9000.

 *To round to the nearest 1000, look at the hundreds digit. A hundreds digit of 4 or less is rounded to the previous thousand. A hundreds digit of 5 or more is rounded to the next thousand.*

- Ask: *If you are rounding to the nearest 10 000, which digit determines whether the number is rounded up or down?* Confirm that it is the digit in the thousands column.

- Pupils should complete Question 4 in the Practice Book.

Answers: 1. 34 000 + 63 000 = 97 000; 2. 72 000 + 19 000 = 91 000; 3. 55 000 + 23 000 = 78 000; 4. 18 000 + 54 000 = 72 000; 5. 32 000 + 16 000 + 42 000 = 90 000

Questions 5 and 6

5 Approximate these measures.
  (a) £81 023 ≈ _____ thousand pounds
  (b) 119 412 m ≈ _____ thousand metres
  (c) 2 095 802 m ≈ _____ million metres
  (d) £999 999 ≈ _____ million pounds

6 A wholesale fruit market has 136 090 kg of apples, 59 400 kg of bananas, 70 020 kg of oranges and 1 064 999 kg of pears.
  (a) Read and write these numbers in words:
    136 090: _____
    59 400: _____
    70 020: _____
    1 064 999: _____
  (b) Round each number to the nearest ten thousand.
    136 090 ≈ ☐   59 400 ≈ ☐
    70 020 ≈ ☐   1 064 999 ≈ ☐
  (c) Write the numbers in order, starting from the greatest.

Same-day intervention

- Shuffle a pack of 0–9 digit cards. Turn over four cards, for example 2 9 0 5. Challenge pupils to arrange the cards in different ways so that they round to as many different thousand numbers as possible.
- For the numbers above, (0)952 rounds to 1000; 2095 rounds to 2000; 2952 rounds to 3000; 5092 rounds to 5000; 5925 rounds to 6000; 9205 rounds to 9000; 9520 rounds to 10 000.
- Repeat with new cards.

Same-day enrichment

- Give pupils **Resource 5.2.4c** Using rounding to calculate approximate answers.

  Resource 5.2.4c
  Using rounding to calculate approximate answers
  Rounding is useful for calculating approximate answers to calculations. Here are some calculations. Round the numbers to the nearest ten thousand and add them mentally to calculate approximate answers.
  1. 34 379 + 62 587
  2. 71 976 + 19 219
  3. 54 563 + 23 143
  4. 18 432 + 53 937
  5. 32 435 + 15 643 + 41 702
  Ask your teacher whether you should do the actual calculations.

- If time permits, pupils could carry out the actual calculations and compare the approximate answer with the accurate one.

What learning will pupils have achieved at the conclusion of Questions 5 and 6?

- Pupils will have practised rounding numbers to the nearest 1000, 10 000, 100 000 and 1 000 000.

Activities for whole-class instruction

- Display the following image:

 **Price** £124 499    **Price** £1 345 482    **Price** £473 264

Chapter 2 Large numbers and measures

Unit 2.4 Practice Book 5A, pages 32–35

- The image shows three houses that cost very different amounts of money. Read the prices together. Choose a pupil to put the prices in order.
- Explain that house prices are often rounded to whole hundreds, thousands or ten thousands. Work together to round the prices to see how they appear to change:

Rounded to ...	House 1 £124 499	House 2 £1 345 482	House 3 £473 264
... nearest 10			
... nearest 100			
... nearest 1000			
... nearest 10 000			
... nearest 100 000			

- Answers for reference:

Rounded to ...	House 1 £126 499	House 2 £1 345 482	House 3 £473 264
... nearest 10	£126 500	£1 345 480	£473 260
... nearest 100	£126 500	£1 345 500	£473 300
... nearest 1000	£126 000	£1 345 000	£473 000
... nearest 10 000	£130 000	£1 350 000	£470 000
... nearest 100 000	£100 000	£1 300 000	£500 000

- Ask: *How did you round to the nearest ten/hundred/thousand?*

To round to the nearest 1000, look at the hundreds digit. A hundreds digit of 4 or less is rounded to the previous thousand. A hundreds digit of 5 or more is rounded to the next thousand.

To round to the nearest 10 000, look at the thousands digit. A thousands digit of 4 or less is rounded to the previous ten thousand. A thousands digit of 5 or more is rounded to the next ten thousand.

- Pupils should complete Questions 5 and 6 in the Practice Book.

Same-day intervention

- Write these house prices on the board:
  A £256 000   **B** £144 000   **C** £348 000
- Point out that these prices are in whole thousands. Ask pupils, working in pairs, to work out the highest and lowest price in whole hundreds that will round to these whole thousand figures.
- Answers: **A** £256 400, £255 500; **B** £144 400, £143 500; **C** £348 400, £347 500
- Now ask pupils to try rounding A, B and C to the nearest ten thousand.
- Answers: **A** £260 000; **B** £140 000; **C** £350 000

Same-day enrichment

- Ask pupils to explain how to round numbers to 100 000.
- Give pupils **Resource 5.2.4d** Rounding to 100 000.

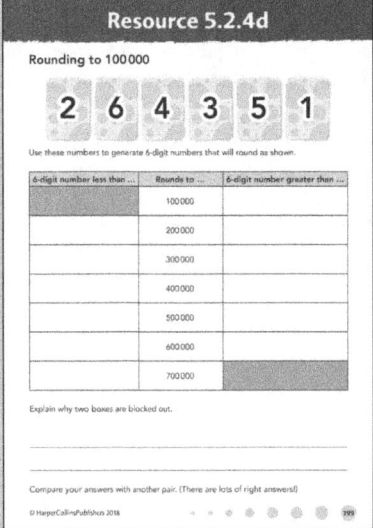

- Pupils can compare their answers with another pair.
  Answer: There is no 6-digit number less than 100 000. Also, a 6-digit number more than 700 000 that rounds to 700 000 must have a 7 digit in it.

Challenge and extension questions

Questions 7 and 8

7 Complete each statement (rounding to the nearest whole number).
  (a) Use 3 zeros and 4 sevens to make a number. The greatest number is _____, which is read as _____
  Rounding it to the nearest ten thousand, the result is _____.
  (b) To make 56 ▪13 589 ≈ 56 million true, the digit in the ▪ could be _____. The greatest possible digit in the ▪ is _____.
  (c) To make 1 09▪ 028 ≈ 1 million and 100 thousands, ▪ could be _____. The smallest possible digit in the ▪ is _____.
  (d) 10 056 217 101 ≈ _____ billion.

8 Use 2 sevens and 5 zeros to make two different 7-digit numbers with the smallest possible difference. Write both numbers.

While these questions do not involve rounding, they require a deep understanding of place value.

Chapter 2 Large numbers and measures

Unit 2.5
Rounding of large numbers (2)

Conceptual context

In this unit, pupils will extend rounding to the nearest 100 000 and 1 000 000.

Learning pupils will have achieved at the end of the unit

- Pupils will have identified the whole ten thousands number, the whole hundred thousands number and the whole millions number on each side of very large numbers (Q1, Q2)
- Pupils will have practised rounding numbers to the nearest 1000, 10 000, 100 000 and 1 000 000 (Q3, Q4, Q5)

Resources

blank 0–6 dice; mini whiteboards; **Resource 5.2.5a** Tick the nearest …; **Resource 5.2.5b** Best estimates; **Resource 5.2.5c** Newspaper reporting

Vocabulary

number line, round to the nearest …, interval, halfway, midpoint

Chapter 2 Large numbers and measures

Unit 2.5 Practice Book 5A, pages 36–37

Questions 1 and 2

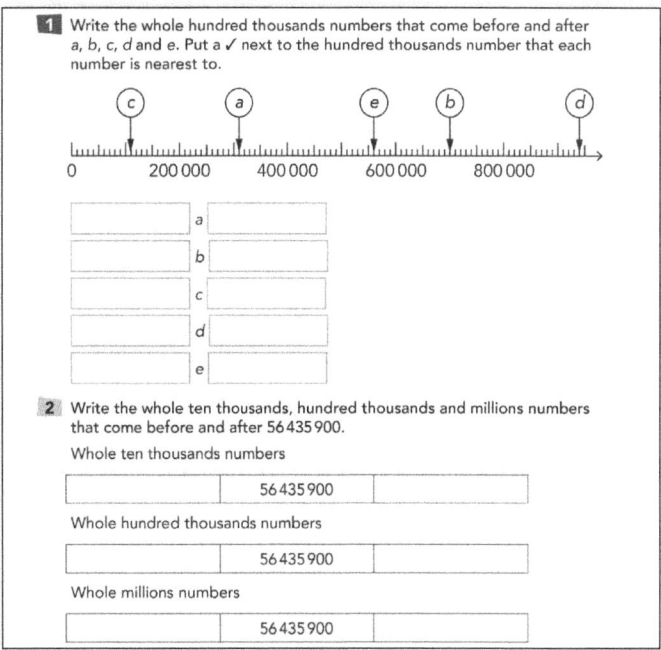

What learning will pupils have achieved at the conclusion of Questions 1 and 2?

- Pupils will have identified the whole ten thousands number, the whole hundred thousands number and the whole millions number on each side of very large numbers.

Activities for whole-class instruction

- On the board, write 530 000 and 540 000. Ask pupils to write a number that lies between these two numbers.
- Look at some of the numbers that pupils have written and discuss whether they are nearer to 530 000 or 540 000. Agree that, to decide this, the digit they need to look at is the thousands digit. A thousands digit of 5 or more means the number is nearer to 540 000, while a thousands digit below 5 means it is nearer to 530 000.
- On the board, write 12 000 000 and 13 000 000 and ask pupils to write a number that lies between these two numbers.
- Look at some of the numbers that pupils have written and discuss whether they are nearer to 12 million or 13 million. Agree that, to decide, the digit they need to look at is the hundred thousands digit. A hundred thousands digit of 5 or more means the number is nearer to 13 million, while a hundred thousands digit below 5 means it is nearer to 12 million.
- Pupils should complete Questions 1 and 2 in the Practice Book.

Same-day intervention

- Give pupils **Resource 5.2.5a** Tick the nearest …

Answers: 1. Nearest 1000 – 3 678 000; nearest 10 000 – 3 680 000; nearest 100 000 – 3 700 000; nearest 1 000 000 – 4 000 000.

2.

Millions	Thousands			Ones			
	100s	10s	1s	100s	10s	1s	Tick
6	4	7	3	8	2	0	
Tick the nearest 100							
6	4	7	3	8	0	0	✓
6	4	7	3	9	0	0	
Tick the nearest 1000							
6	4	7	3	0	0	0	
6	4	7	4	0	0	0	✓
Tick the nearest 10 000							
6	4	7	0	0	0	0	✓
6	4	8	0	0	0	0	
Tick the nearest 100 000							
6	4	0	0	0	0	0	
6	5	0	0	0	0	0	✓
Tick the nearest 1 000 000							
6	0	0	0	0	0	0	✓
7	0	0	0	0	0	0	

Chapter 2 Large numbers and measures

Unit 2.5 Practice Book 5A, pages 36–37

Same-day enrichment

- Give pupils mini whiteboards. Mark a blank dice with 2 × 10 000, 2 × 100 000 and 2 × 1 000 000.
- Choose a pupil to write a seven-digit number on the board and roll the dice. The group should write the nearest whole 10 000, whole 100 000 or whole 1 000 000, depending on the dice roll. The chosen pupil writes their answer on the board. Check answers.
- Continue until each pupil has had a turn at rolling the dice.

Questions 3, 4 and 5

3 Fill in the boxes to make each statement correct.
When we round a number, we first decide which digit is the last digit to keep. If the next digit to its right is ☐ or more, we increase it by 1 and all the digits to its right change to zero (known as rounding up). If the next digit is less than ☐, we leave it the same and all the digits to its right change to zero (known as rounding down).

4 Round the following numbers to the nearest 1000, 10 000, 100 000 and 1 000 000.

	5 375 021	9 988 522	1 240 641	1 000 234
Nearest 1000				
Nearest 10 000				
Nearest 100 000				
Nearest 1 000 000				

5 A 5-digit number, after being rounded to the nearest 10 000, is 90 000. What is the greatest possible value of this number? What is its smallest possible value?

What learning will pupils have achieved at the conclusion of Questions 3, 4 and 5?

- Pupils will have practised rounding numbers to the nearest 1000, 10 000, 100 000 and 1 000 000.

Activities for whole-class instruction

- Ask a pupil to shuffle a pack of 1–9 digit cards and lay out seven of them to make a seven-digit number, for example:

  5 7 4 3 8 1 9

- Read the number together. Agree that it is five million, seven hundred and forty-three thousand, eight hundred and nineteen.

- Mark the sides of a blank dice with 10, 100, 1000, 10 000 100 000 and 1 000 000.
- Roll the dice and ask pupils to round the number to this digit.
- For example, if the dice roll is 1000, pupils need to identify the thousands digit, 3 thousands, and then look at the digit immediately to the right, 8 hundreds. Three thousand, eight hundred is nearer to 4000 than 3000, so the number is rounded to 5 744 000.
- If the dice roll is 1 000 000, pupils need to identify the millions digit, 5 millions, and then look at the digit immediately to the right, 7 hundred thousand. Five million, seven hundred thousand is nearer to 6 000 000 than 5 000 000, so the number is rounded to 6 000 000.
- Choose another pupil to lay out another number and repeat with new dice rolls. Invite individual pupils to explain the rounding process as above.
- Display a 0–10 000 number line with intervals of 1000 marked.

  0 1000 2000 3000 4000 5000 6000 7000 8000 9000 10 000

- Ask: *What number is halfway between 0 and 1000.* Agree that it is 500. Ask pupils if it is nearer to 0 or nearer to 1000. Agree that it is the same distance to both numbers. Remind pupils that, by convention, the midpoint is rounded to the next whole number, so 500 is rounded to 1000, 1500 rounded to 2000 and so on.
- Ask: *What is the smallest number that is nearest to 1000?* Agree 500. Ask: *What is the largest number that is nearest to 1000?* Agree 1499. Continue by looking at the smallest and greatest numbers that round to 2000. Confirm that the numbers are 1500 and 2499.
- Invite pupils to discuss the pattern of numbers with a partner and choose an individual to explain. This can be expressed as:
  Smallest number = thousand number − 500
  Largest number = thousand number + 499
- Discuss these number statements with pupils.
- Choose individual pupils to tell you the smallest and largest numbers that round to other whole thousands. Ask pupils to explain to a partner how to round a number. Share ideas with examples.
- Pupils should complete Questions 3, 4 and 5 in the Practice Book.

Chapter 2 Large numbers and measures   Unit 2.5 Practice Book 5A, pages 36–37

Same-day intervention

- Give pupils **Resource 5.2.5b** Best estimates.

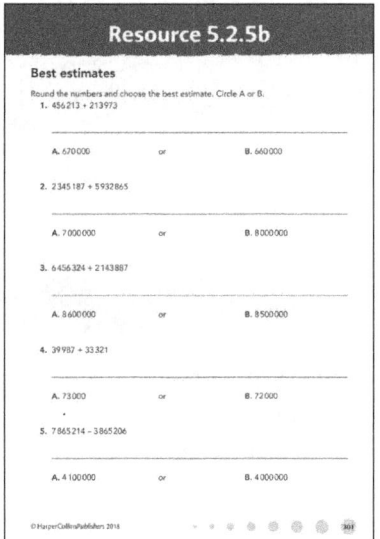

Answers: 1. A. 460 000 + 210 000 = 670 000;
2. B. 2 000 000 + 6 000 000 = 8 000 000; 3. A. 6 500 000 + 2 100 000 = 8 600 000; 4. A. 40 000 + 33 000 = 73 000; 5. B. 7 900 000 − 3 900 000 = 4 000 000

Challenge and extension question

Question 6

6 A number consists of 6 hundred thousands, 4 thousands, 5 hundreds and 3 ones. What number is it? When it is rounded to the nearest hundred thousand, what is the resulting number? What is the smallest number it can be added to so that when the sum is rounded the result is 610 thousand?

This question is a multi-stage word problem that requires pupils to have a secure understanding of rounding. Pupils could use a number line for support to visualise the problem.

Same-day enrichment

- Give pupils **Resource 5.2.5c** Newspaper reporting.

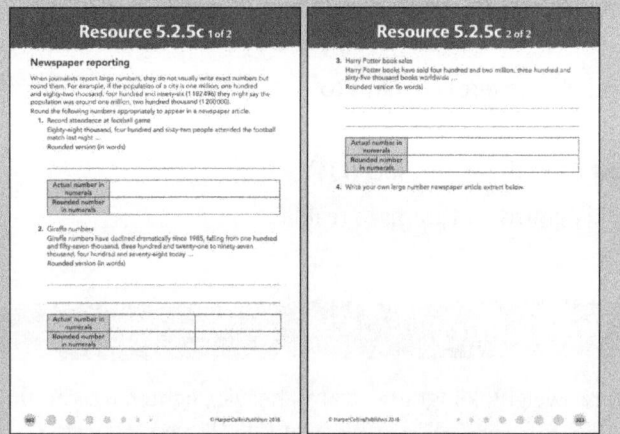

Answers: 1. Eighty-eight thousand. 88 462, 88 000;
2. one hundred and fifty-seven thousand; ninety-seven thousand; 157 321, 157 000; 97 478, 97 000 (or 97 500);
3. (over) four hundred million; 402 365 000, (over) 4 000 000.

Chapter 2 Large numbers and measures

Unit 2.6
Converting kilograms and grams

Conceptual context

This unit acts as both revision and application of the concept of conversion between kilograms and grams. Pupils will already know that 1 kg = 1000 g. Here they are provided with opportunities to convert, compare and also calculate with these units. Pupils will need to apply their knowledge of multiplying and dividing by 1000 when moving between the two units, allowing them to express answers in different ways.

Learning pupils will have achieved at the end of the unit

- Pupils will know that mass and weight are not the same thing and that scales are designed to measure weight and display mass (Q1)
- The concepts of kilograms and grams will have been revised as pupils review the relationship between the two (Q1)
- The concepts of kilograms and grams will have been revised as pupils explore suitable units to measure the mass of everyday objects (Q2)
- The concepts of kilograms and grams will have been revised as pupils convert kilograms to grams and vice versa (Q3)
- Pupils will know that, to enable comparison, measurements must be in the same units (Q4)
- Pupils will have applied their knowledge of converting between kilograms and grams in real-life contexts (Q5, Q6)

Resources

1 kg weight or equivalent; 1 g weight or equivalent; mini whiteboards; luggage tags; string; **Resource 5.2.6a** What's my unit? (1); **Resource 5.2.6b** What's my unit? (2), **Resource 5.2.6c** Mammal masses; **Resource 5.1.3d** Place value slider (from Chapter 1)

Vocabulary

mass, weight, kilograms, grams, heavier, lighter, weighs, unit (of measurement), convert, multiply, divide

Chapter 2 Large numbers and measures

Unit 2.6 Practice Book 5A, pages 38–40

Questions 1 and 2

> **1** The relationship between kilograms and grams is:
> 1 kilogram = ☐ grams
>
> **2** Write a suitable unit in each space: kilograms (kg) or grams (g).
> (a) The mass of a puppy is about 2 _____ .
> (b) The mass of a bag of crisps is about 250 _____ .
> (c) The mass of a rhinoceros is about 2000 _____ .
> (d) A pear weighs about 100 _____ .
> (e) Ben weighs about 30 _____ .
> (f) A rubber weighs about 6 _____ .

What learning will pupils have achieved at the conclusion of Questions 1 and 2?

- Pupils will know that mass and weight are not the same thing and that scales are designed to measure weight and display mass.
- The concepts of kilograms and grams will have been revised as pupils review the relationship between the two.
- The concepts of kilograms and grams will have been revised as pupils explore suitable units to measure the mass of everyday objects.

Activities for whole-class instruction

(i) It is important to know the difference between 'mass' and 'weight' – the two terms that, in everyday use, are often used interchangeably but that actually mean different things

Mass is the **amount of matter** that something contains. Grams and kilograms are units for measuring mass.

Weight is the **force** exerted by gravity pulling on the object. Newtons are the units used for measuring force, including weight.

The weight of an object will change if gravity changes, since it is related to gravity. This is why astronauts experience weightlessness in space – their mass has not changed but gravity has, so their weight has changed too.

Scales measure a pushing or pulling force – therefore they actually measure weight. However, the display on the dial or scale shows 'kg' because scales measure weight and display mass. In everyday language we all refer to this as weight, though it is not strictly correct. Scales are set up to measure force and translate that into a mass (by carrying out the calculation that is appropriate for the force of gravity here on Earth).

- Begin by writing the words 'MASS' and 'WEIGHT' on the board and asking pupils whether they know the difference between the two terms. Use the example of the astronaut (see Information point) to help pupils understand. Emphasise that weight is a force, so weight can be measured on scales, for example the weight of a person on bathroom scales.
- Explain that weighing scales actually convert the measurement of weight, carry out a calculation involving the force of gravity, and display the result as mass. So, although in everyday language we talk about something 'weighing' 5 kilograms, we should actually be saying it has a mass of 5 kilograms.

 Mass is the **amount of matter** that something contains. Weight is the force exerted by gravity pulling on the object.

- Ask pupils if they have heard of newtons. Explain that newtons are the units of measurement for measuring force. (If you have any spring balances in school, they might be marked in newtons.) Pupils do not need to work with newtons in maths; however, it is helpful if they appreciate that weight, since it is a force, is not actually measured in the same units that are used to measure mass.
- Place a kilogram bag of rice (1 kg) and a paper clip (1 g) inside a box. Choose pupils to pick up both objects from the box without looking at them and compare them using words. Obviously, the kilogram will feel a lot heavier, but challenge pupils to consider how much heavier they think it is. Explain that the two units are one kilogram and one gram. Ask pupils whether they remember how many grams are in a kilogram.

 1 kilogram equals 1000 grams.

- Explain that you have a set of scales that measure mass, but that the part that shows the unit of measurement is not working – can pupils help? Display the following measurements on the board:

A bag of potatoes = 2

A packet of crisps = 30

A book = 500

- Ask pupils to write the unit of measurement (either g or kg) on their mini whiteboards and then vote which they think each object is being measured in. Discuss pupils' reasons.
- Write the following measurement: An adult = 80 000

Chapter 2 Large numbers and measures

Unit 2.6 Practice Book 5A, pages 38–40

Look out for ... pupils might think that heavier objects are always measured in kg simply because they are heavier. This is a common misconception. Remind pupils that the length of a classroom could be measured in metres, centimetres or even millimetres, so they should not assume that the unit must be kg simply because the object is heavy.

- Pupils should complete Questions 1 and 2 in the Practice Book.

Same-day intervention

- Provide pupil pairs with a set of cards taken from **Resource 5.2.6a** What's my unit? (1). These contain a series of objects with a numerical value. Pupils should shuffle their cards and work with a partner to sort them into two groups, discussing whether they are measured in kilograms or grams.

- Afterwards, bring pairs together to discuss. For those that pupils were unsure of, ask: *Why did you find this particular one difficult?* (These will often be the values where a large object has a value in grams or a smaller object has a value in kilograms.) Use concrete experience of mass (i.e. handling plastic weights or known objects) to enable pupils to explore some comparisons.

Same-day enrichment

- Provide pupils with one set of four cards taken from **Resource 5.2.6b** What's my unit? (2). These include objects and masses (units omitted) that must be matched. Each set of four cards is designed to be compared separately, so pupils should deal with a set at a time.

- Pupils should work in pairs and then join together as a larger group, discussing why they have paired up the cards in the way that they have.

Question 3

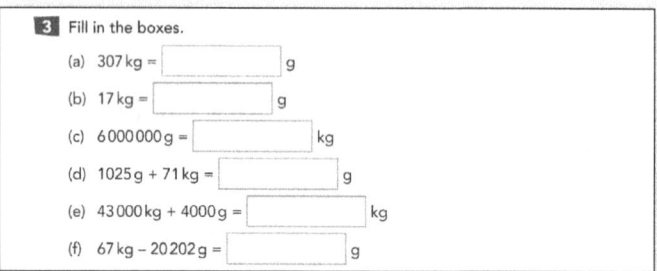

What learning will pupils have achieved at the conclusion of Question 3?

- The concepts of kilograms and grams will have been revised as pupils convert kilograms to grams and vice versa.

Activities for whole-class instruction

- Write: 1 kg = __ g and 250 kg = __ g.

Chapter 2 Large numbers and measures

Unit 2.6 Practice Book 5A, pages 38–40

- Ask: *What is 1 kg equivalent to in grams?* Show 1 g and 1 kg objects and say: *The mass of this* (point to the 1 kg object) *is 1000 times the mass of this* (point to the 1 g object).

   *The mass of the bag of rice is 1000 times the mass of the paper clip.*

- Ask: *The mass of 250 of these* (point to the 1 kg object) *is how many times the mass of this* (point to the 1 g object)? *How can we find the answer?*

- Establish that, as a single 1 kg object is equivalent to 1000 g, pupils will need to multiply the number of objects given in the question (250) by 1000 to find the answer. Give pupils time to work out the answer on their whiteboards, then choose some good examples to share with the class. Ask: *What strategy did you use to multiply 250 by 1000?*

  (i) Adding three zeros on the end of a number may have worked in this instance, but is not a good strategy for pupils to rely on (nor is crossing off three zeros when it comes to dividing by 1000). As soon as they have to multiply a decimal by 1000 or are asked to divide a number by 1000 without three zeros to cross out, this trick will fail them. Ensure that the examples discussed involve shifting digits three columns to the left or right instead.

- Write other conversions for pupils to complete. For example:

  3 000 000 g = _____ kg
  56.21 kg = _____ g
  4500 g + 37 kg = _____ g
  56 000 kg + 1000 g = _____ kg
  85 kg − 10 710 g = _____ g

- For each one, ask: *What is tricky about this question? Do you think you need to multiply or divide by 1000 to find the answer? Why? Is there anything else you need to do?*

- Pupils should complete Question 3 in the Practice Book.

Same-day intervention

- Revise the equivalence of 1 kg and 1000 g and check that pupils are confident when describing how to convert between the two (i.e. by multiplying or dividing by 1000).

- Pupils will need to use a place value slider (used previously – see **Resource 5.1.3d** Place value slider).

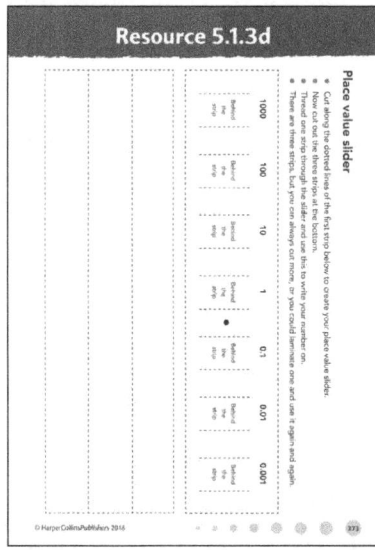

- Write 450 ml = ___ litres. Choose a pupil to write this number on one of their strips and place it in the slider. Ask: *To convert millilitres to litres, what do we need to do? In which direction will the digits move? How many places?* Agree that pupils will need to divide by 1000, which means shifting the digits three columns to the right. Choose a pupil to pull the strip so that it now shows the correct number. Ask: *How do we write this number?* (Pupils will need to show the decimal point and a placeholder zero in the ones place; they do not need to include the zero in the hundredths place.)

- Repeat for further conversions; pupils should challenge each other.

Same-day enrichment

- Challenge pupils to invent their own conversion problems for others to solve. Give pupils two luggage tags and a length of string. On the first luggage tag, pupils write a measure of mass, expressed in kilograms (46 kg), grams (25 500 g), a combination of both (7 kg 350 g) or as a calculation (13 kg − 52 g). On the second luggage tag, pupils write an equivalent mass. Each of the examples in brackets might be rewritten as follows:

  46 kg = 46 000 g
  25 500 g = 25.5 kg
  7 kg 350 g = 7350 g (or 7.35 kg)
  13 kg − 52 g = 12 948 g (or 12.948 kg)

Chapter 2 Large numbers and measures

Unit 2.6 Practice Book 5A, pages 38–40

- Pupils then tie each end of their piece of string to connect the equivalent luggage tags. They place one end of the string into a container so that one tag is inside the container and the other dangles outside.

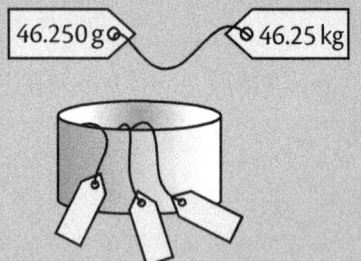

- Pupils then take turns to 'go fishing' for a pair, taking a tag and working out what will be on the corresponding tag before removing it to check. Points should be awarded for each mass that pupils can correctly convert.

- 'I can convert 820 g to kilograms by dividing by 1000 and finding that it is equal to 0.82 kg. Now both measurements are in kilograms I can compare them. 8.2 kg is more than 0.82 kg.'

Or ...

- 'I can convert 8.2 kg to grams by multiplying by 1000 and finding that it is equal to 8200 grams. Now both measurements are in grams I can compare them. 8200 grams is more than 820 grams.'

- Ask pupils to describe the comparison using the >, < or = symbols. Ensure that the equivalence is written using the original numbers on the whiteboards rather than the converted values.

- Repeat for one or two further examples using the table and then change the numbers on the grid and repeat. Include masses expressed using two units of measurement (2 kg 500 g), as well as those expressed as additions (1 kg + 5000 kg), to make sure pupils read each value very carefully before converting and comparing.

- Pupils should complete Question 4 in the Practice Book.

Question 4

4. Write >, < or = in each ◯.
   - (a) 5 kg ◯ 500 g
   - (b) 6000 g ◯ 6 kg
   - (c) 7800 kg ◯ 8 000 000 g
   - (d) 90 000 kg ◯ 9 000 000 g
   - (e) 13 000 kg ◯ 1000 kg + 200 kg
   - (f) 4000 kg ◯ 7000 g

What learning will pupils have achieved at the conclusion of Question 4?

- Pupils will know that, to enable comparison, measurements must be in the same units.

Activities for whole-class instruction

- Draw the following grid on the board. Ask pupils to choose one of the values and write it on their mini whiteboards:

8200 kg	8200 g	8.2 kg
80 000 g	8.2 kg	82 g
820 g	8 200 000 g	0.82 kg

- Choose two pupils to come to the front and show their whiteboards. Ask: *Before we compare these, do we need to convert either measurement? Why/why not? Which is larger? How do you know?* Encourage pupils to apply their knowledge of converting kilograms and grams when answering. For example, if the whiteboards show 8.2 kg and 820 g, pupils might reason as follows:

Same-day intervention

- Cut out the cards from **Resource 5.2.6c** Mammal masses. These show the masses of a number of different mammals, expressed in either kilograms or grams.

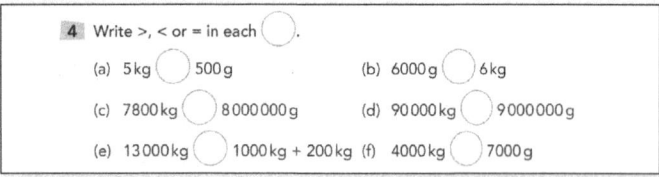

- Choose two cards to show pupils. These should be two animals whose masses are both expressed using different units of measurement. For example:
  Koala = 9300 g   Large hairy armadillo = 2 kg

Chapter 2 Large numbers and measures

Unit 2.6 Practice Book 5A, pages 38–40

- Ask: *Why might the masses of these two creatures be tricky for some students to compare? What do we need to do to find out which is heavier?* Encourage pupils to draw their own place value grids on their mini whiteboards and model how to convert one of the masses to the same unit of measurement as the other. It will be interesting if pupils choose which measurement they convert and then compare their results at the end – does it matter which one they converted? Ask pupils which symbol they would use in between the two cards to show which is larger: >, < or =. Repeat for different pairs of mammals.

Same-day enrichment

- Pupils should each have a set of cards from **Resource 5.2.6c** Mammal masses. Pupils shuffle the cards and share them equally with each other. Players take turns to compare both masses, converting one of them to the same unit as the other if they are different. They then write this as a comparison statement using >, < or = symbols. They get two points for doing so correctly and win both cards. The winner is the player with the most cards at the end.

Questions 5 and 6

> **5** Multiple choice questions. (For each question, choose the correct answer and write the letter in the box.)
>
> (a) A truck is loaded with 3 machine tools and 450 kg of accessories. Each machine tool weighs 800 kg. The truck is loaded with the total mass of ☐.
>
> A. 2050 kg   B. 2850 kg   C. 2150 kg   D. 1250 g
>
> (b) There is 482 000 kg of sand in a builders' yard. If a dumper truck can be loaded with 4000 kg of sand, how many trucks will be needed to transport all the sand in one go? ☐
>
> A. 120 trucks   B. 121 trucks   C. 122 trucks   D. 123 trucks
>
> (c) 30 kg 900 g = ☐ g
>
> A. 30 900   B. 903   C. 1200   D. 3900
>
> **6** Solve these problems.
>
> (a) Tom's mother bought 4 bottles of sunflower oil. Each bottle weighs 2500 g. Find the total mass of the 4 bottles, first in grams and then in kilograms.
>
> (b) 8 electrical machines are loaded onto a truck, which has a loading capacity of 5000 kg. The mass of each machine is 620 kg. Does the total mass of all the machines exceed the loading capacity of the truck?
>
> (c) Martha's uncle harvested 5000 kg of pears in his orchard last year into boxes. If each box can be filled with 25 kg of pears, how many boxes can be filled with all the pears?

What learning will pupils have achieved at the conclusion of Questions 5 and 6?

- Pupils will have applied their knowledge of converting between kilograms and grams in real-life contexts.

Activities for whole-class instruction

- Provide pupils with the following problem:
  - A delivery firm has been asked to deliver three large photocopiers to an office block. Each photocopier weighs 135 000 grams. The firm's lorry cannot carry more than 400 kg. Can it deliver the photocopiers in one journey?

- Ask: *What are the important pieces of information in this problem?* Challenge pupils to rephrase the problem so that it is just about the numbers (i.e. without any real-life context). For example:
  'Are three lots of 135 000 g more or less than 400 kg?'

- Ask pupils what they need to do to find the answer. Encourage them to talk through and plan these steps before carrying them out:

  1. Convert 135 000 grams to kilograms (or convert 400 kilograms to grams) to make the two measurements easier to compare.

  2. Multiply the mass of one copier by three to find the total mass.

  3. Compare the total mass with the total load that the lorry can carry and decide whether the lorry must make more than one journey.

- Pupils should then complete each step to find that the lorry cannot carry all three photocopiers at once:
  135 000 g ÷ 1000 = 135 kg
  135 kg × 3 = 405 kg
  405 kg > 400 kg

- Go through the same process (of expressing as a numerical problem, planning the steps and then calculating them) for further problems that require calculating using measurements of mass, converting between kg and g and applying to a real-life context. For example:
  - A large box of books weighs 30 kg. A lorry is carrying 510 kg of such boxes. How many boxes is it carrying?
  - Bags of potatoes weigh 1250 g. A local restaurant orders five of these bags. What mass of potatoes does it receive? Find the answer in grams and then kilograms.

Chapter 2 Large numbers and measures

Unit 2.6 Practice Book 5A, pages 38–40

- A gritter lorry can carry 3000 kg of grit for spreading on the roads. The council grit store currently holds 132 000 kg of grit. How many lorryloads is this?
- Pupils should complete Questions 5 and 6 in the Practice Book.

Same-day intervention

- Ask pupils to write these words on mini whiteboards: CONVERT, COMPARE, CALCULATE.
- Display the following problem:
  - A large Boxer dog weighs 28 000 g. The Labrador next door weighs 3 kg less. How many kilograms does the Labrador weigh?
- Ask pupils to point to the words they think they need to do to find the answer.
- Ask these questions:

  Do you need to convert any of the measurements? If so, which one and how will you convert it?

  Is the question asking you to compare any masses?

  Is it asking you to calculate using them?

  What do you need to do to find the answer?

- Establish that pupils should convert the Boxer's mass to kilograms before subtracting to find the answer. Repeat for further problems, including those where pupils are asked to compare two masses and need to convert to do so.

Same-day enrichment

- Allow pupils to use any of the Resource cards from **Resource 5.2.6a** What's my unit? (1) or **Resource 5.2.6c** Mammal masses as mass facts that will inform the following activity. (Although the cards for **Resource 5.2.6a** do not have units of measurement on, it should be straightforward for pupils to assign the appropriate units.)
- Challenge pupils to use the information to write their own multi-step problems based on mass (where one of the steps involves converting between units). Pupils should share their problems for peers to solve.

Challenge and extension questions

Questions 7 and 8

7 True or false? (Put a ✓ for true and a ✗ for false in each box.)

(a) 1000 g of cotton is lighter than 1 kg of iron.

(b) There are two lots of 10 000 grams in 20 kilograms.

(c) 1 kg is 30 g heavier than 70 g.

8 The mass of a box of apples was 46 kg inclusive of the mass of the box. After selling half the apples, the mass was 26 kg. What was the mass of the box?

In this section, pupils are given two questions to develop their understanding of the measurement of mass. Question 7 contains a set of true/false statements where pupils need to convert between units. These include two-step conversions that require slightly more thought ('There are two 10 000 grams in 20 kilograms').

Question 8 is a multi-step problem where pupils are expected to derive the mass of a basket when they are only given two facts: the combined mass of the basket and the apples within it and the combined mass when half of the apples are gone. Pupils will need to first find the mass of half of the apples, double it to find the full mass of the apples, and finally subtract this from the initial combined measurement to be left with the mass of the basket.

Chapter 2 Large numbers and measures

Unit 2.7
Litres and millilitres (1)

Conceptual context

This is the first of two units focusing on conversion between litres and millilitres. Pupils begin by reviewing their knowledge that 1 litre = 1000 ml and move on to apply it when converting, comparing and calculating.

Pupils first encountered litres and millilitres in Year 2 (Units 8.6 and 8.7). Since that time, their knowledge of numbers and calculating has developed, expanding their scope to convert between litres and millilitres with greater understanding and accuracy, involving more demanding numbers than in Year 2. By teaching this unit here (immediately following one about kilograms and grams), pupils are likely to notice and understand the similarities when converting, as both sets of units involve multiplying and dividing by 1000.

Learning pupils will have achieved at the end of the unit

- The concepts of litres and millilitres will have been revised as pupils review the relationship between the two and perform simple calculations based on this (Q1, Q2)
- The concepts of litres and millilitres will have been revised as pupils explore suitable units to measure the capacity of everyday objects (Q3)
- Greater fluency in converting between litres and millilitres will have been developed (Q4)
- Pupils will have applied their knowledge of converting between litres and millilitres when solving real-life problems (Q5)

Resources

examples of different containers to demonstrate ml and l; two measuring jugs; large washing-up bowl or tray; **Resource 5.2.7a** Blank measuring jugs; **Resource 5.2.7b** Right or wrong units?; **Resource 5.2.7c** Converting card challenge

Vocabulary

litres, millilitres, unit (of measure), convert, multiply, divide

Chapter 2 Large numbers and measures

Unit 2.7 Practice Book 5A, pages 41–43

Questions 1 and 2

> **1** Fill in the spaces to make each statement correct.
> (a) The amount of liquid is often expressed in millilitres and litres. When measuring a small amount of liquid, we usually use millilitres as the unit of measure. When measuring a _____ amount of liquid, we usually use _____ as the unit of measure.
> (b) 1 millilitre can be written as 1 ml. 1 litre can be written as 1 l or 1 L.
> 1 l = ☐ ml.
>
> **2** Which measuring cups of water can be added together to fill up a 1 litre bottle?
> Write the number sentence. _____
>
> [Beakers A, B, C, D showing measurements at 100, 300, 500, 700]

What learning will pupils have achieved at the conclusion of Questions 1 and 2?

- The concepts of litres and millilitres will have been revised as pupils review the relationship between the two and perform simple calculations based on this.

Activities for whole-class instruction

- Although pupils have learned something about litres and millilitres previously (in Year 2), they have not focused on this aspect of measurement since then, so a quick review is appropriate now.
- Ask:
  – *What liquids might we measure in everyday life? How could we measure them?*
  – *What units of measurement do we use to record an amount of liquid?*
- Putting petrol into a car or buying milk from the supermarket are suggestions pupils may put forward, with the units suggested as gallons/pints. If so, explain that these are imperial measures, which pupils will be looking at later in the year (see Unit 9.4).
- Ask pupils whether they have any idea what a millilitre looks like. Most pupils will have experience of spoons and syringes that are supplied with over-the-counter children's medicines.
- Ask: *Why is a millilitre not a useful measure for measuring large amounts of liquid? What unit can we use instead?* Remind pupils that we group together a number of millilitres and call them 1 litre. Display a 1 litre measuring jug. Ask pupils how many millilitres they think there are in 1 litre. Does this remind them of the relationship between any other measures (there are 1000 m in 1 km and 1000 g in 1 kg). Show pupils the numbers on the side of the jug and ask them what they notice. What is half a litre?
- Ask: *Given your experience of converting between measures, how will the fact that there are 1000 ml in 1 litre affect things when you have to convert between the two? What will you have to do? Is this just the same as converting between kg and g or km and m?*
- Take two containers and fill them to 200 ml and 800 ml, respectively. Ask: *What will be the total amount of water if we add these together?* Establish that 200 + 800 = 1000 and 1000 ml = 1 litre.
- Use the blank template taken from **Resource 5.2.7a** Blank measuring jugs to display further amounts of water (in ml) and ask pupils whether they will make 1 litre.

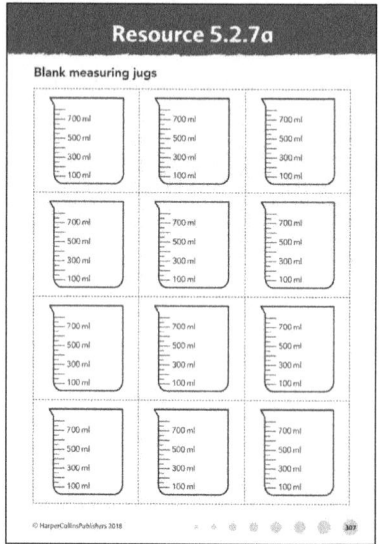

- Pupils should complete Questions 1 and 2 in the Practice Book.

Same-day intervention

- Place a large washing-up bowl or tray in the centre of a desk (to limit spillages!). Measure out 1 litre of water into a measuring jug and ask pupils how many millilitres there are. Tip away 500 ml of the water into a second measuring jug without showing pupils how much water now remains in the first. Encourage pupils to read the second measurement and express this as a subtraction:
  The original amount of water minus 500 ml equals the amount of water left:
  1000 − 500 = 500 ml
- Ensure pupils are aware that 500 ml is half a litre. They will have experience of 500 ml bottles of water and fizzy drinks – explain that two of these equal 1 litre.

Chapter 2 Large numbers and measures

Unit 2.7 Practice Book 5A, pages 41–43

- Repeat the activity, starting with 1 litre and tipping off a different multiple of 100 each time. What do pupils expect will be left and why? Use the activity to help pupils form their own number bonds to 1000, helping to embed the concept of 1 litre equalling 1000 millilitres.

Same-day enrichment

- Provide pupils with copies of **Resource 5.2.7a** Blank measuring jugs. They should colour in a water level (deciding whether to label in multiples of 100 or 50) on their jugs. Pupils should swap cards with a partner to try to make 1 litre – there may be several ways to do this.
- Once they have completed the task in pairs, pupils should join together in groups of four, shuffling all their cards and placing them upside down in the centre of the table. Pupils should take turns to take a card and then either keep or reject it. The first to make 1 litre wins, and pupils can play again. By including multiples of 50 in the activity, pupils can practise more complex ways of making 1 litre.

Question 3

3 Write a suitable unit in each space: litres or millilitres.

(a) A tank of petrol: 30 _____
(b) A bottle of cooking oil: 2 _____
(c) A tub of yogurt: 250 _____
(d) A bottle of eye drops: 5 _____
(e) A cup of water: 200 _____
(f) A bottle of cola: 600 _____
(g) A bottle of liquid medicine: 10 _____

What learning will pupils have achieved at the conclusion of Question 3?

- The concepts of litres and millilitres will have been revised as pupils explore suitable units to measure the capacity of everyday objects.

Activities for whole-class instruction

- Ask pupils to name the units of measurement they would use to measure an amount of a liquid. Ask: *How would you measure it? What is 1 litre equivalent to?*

- Explain that when liquids are sold, the law says that they must be labelled with the amount that is contained within so customers know how much they are buying. Write the following list on the board and explain that these are taken from the labels on different items.

OBJECT	AMOUNT OF LIQUID
A can of lemonade	330
A teaspoon of cough medicine	5
A carton of apple juice	1
A bottle of water	500
A watering can	5500

- Ask: *Is there a problem with these measurements?* Share ideas. Encourage pupils to use what they know of the size of 1 ml and 1 l when justifying their answers.
- Challenge pupils to think beyond the concept of simply choosing litres to measure large objects or millilitres to measure small quantities – for example a watering can is quite large but is measured in millilitres in the list provided; a bathful of water could be described as 80 000 ml.
- Pupils also need to appreciate that large numbers do not necessarily indicate that the units are millilitres – for example a swimming pool holds approximately 475 000 litres.
- Pupils should complete Question 3 in the Practice Book.

Same-day intervention

- Lead a discussion with pupils to establish a few familiar references or benchmarks. For example:
  A teaspoon of water as an example of 5 ml
  A bottle of water as an example of 500 ml (or half a litre)
  A large carton of orange juice as an example of 1 litre
  A large bottle of lemonade as an example of 2 litres
- List a series of containers that hold different amounts of liquid and give only the numerical value of that amount. For example:
  A bottle of eye drops = 5 ___
  A watering can = 5 ___
  A mug of tea = 200 ___
  A bottle of blackcurrant squash = 2.5 ___
  A saucepan of water = 700 ___
- Pupils should work in pairs to discuss each one and then write ml or l as they think appropriate. Encourage the group to then explain their answers by relating them to the concrete examples in front of them.

Chapter 2 Large numbers and measures

Unit 2.7 Practice Book 5A, pages 41–43

Same-day enrichment

- Provide pairs of pupils with a copy of the playing board on **Resource 5.2.7b** Right or wrong units?

- Both pupils will need a set of different-coloured plastic counters. They take turns to choose one of the squares for their partner to answer. Each square contains a measurement. The pupil answering should decide whether the unit of measurement shown is right or wrong. What should the unit of measurement be? They should discuss their answers each time and talk about why a different unit of measurement is needed. To add variety, the statements include a handful of concepts other than measuring liquid (area, length and so on). Pupils place one of their counters on each statement they correctly answer. The player with more counters on the board at the end wins.

Question 4

4 Convert these measures.

(a) 2 l = _____ ml   (b) 800 l = _____ ml

(c) 82 000 ml = _____ litres   (d) 50 l = _____ ml

(e) 21 600 ml = _____ l   (f) 30 003 ml = _____ l _____ ml

What learning will pupils have achieved at the conclusion of Question 4?

- Greater fluency in converting between litres and millilitres will have been developed.

Activities for whole-class instruction

- On the board, write: 7 l = ___ ml   400 ml = ___ l. Ask pupils to explain how they would find the missing values and, importantly, **why**. Ensure they are aware that the concept of multiplying or dividing by 1000 is to do with the equivalence of the units (1 litre equals 1000 millilitres). Ask: *How do you multiply or divide by 1000 quickly?*

- Draw a blank place value grid. Model the number 7 in the first equation. Ask: *If 1 litre equals 1000 millilitres, how can we convert from litres to millilitres?* Establish that pupils need to multiply by 1000. Ask: *Do you need the place value grid to work this out or can you answer it mentally?* Share answers. Model some concretely by asking a pupil to move the digit three places to the left on the board. Ask: *Why three places? How can we show that the digit has moved?* Remind pupils that zeros are used as placeholders to show the empty hundreds, tens and ones places.

M   HTh   TTh   Th   H   T   O · t   h   th

7 litres is the same as 7000 millilitres.

- Refer to the second equation (400 ml = ___ l) and model the number 400 on the place value grid. Ask: *How can we find what 400 ml is equivalent to in litres?* Some pupils may try multiplying by 1000 again, so ensure they understand that they now need to divide by 1000. Again, choose a pupil to model the shift in digits to the right this time. Ask: *Where do we need to use a zero as a placeholder? Do we need to write the digits after the 4 (i.e. as 0.400)? Why not?*

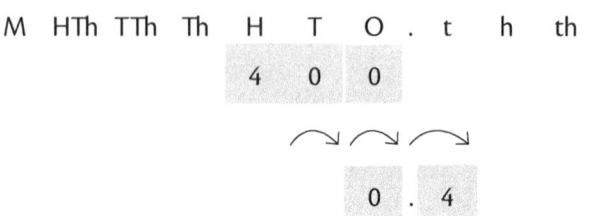

400 millilitres is the same as 0.4 litres.

- Repeat the exercise using different numbers, varying the order of the units of measurement and the unknown value, and increasing the complexity. For example: 57 000 ml = ___ l

Chapter 2 Large numbers and measures

Unit 2.7 Practice Book 5A, pages 41–43

30 l = ___ ml
31 l 450 ml = ___ ml
70 008 ml = ___ l ___ ml

- Pupils should complete Question 4 in the Practice Book.

Same-day intervention

- Ensure pupils understand that there are 1000 millilitres in a litre. Place eight trays (or similar) in a row on the table-top and label them according to the place value columns from Ten Thousands to Thousandths. Use a small circle to represent the decimal point.

- Display the following equivalence: 46 litres = ___ millilitres. Spend time discussing with pupils what this means. Show them a millilitre and the size of a litre container and ensure they understand that what they are finding out is how many millilitres are equal to 46 litres. Place digit cards onto the trays to show the number 46. Ask:
  *How many millilitres are in **one** litre?*
  *So what do we need to multiply 46 by to find the number in **forty-six** litres?*
  How do we multiply by a thousand?

- Choose pupils to model this by moving the card three places to the left. Ask: *How can we show that these digits represent Ten Thousands and Thousands? What can we use as a placeholder?*

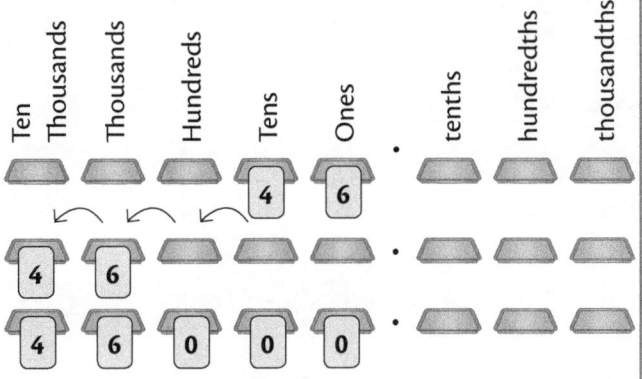

- Repeat with other examples, continuing to focus on litres to millilitres.
- Next, give examples that require converting millilitres to litres. Include values that result in simple decimals (for example 250 ml = ___ litres).

Same-day enrichment

- Give pupils **Resource 5.2.7c** Converting card challenge.

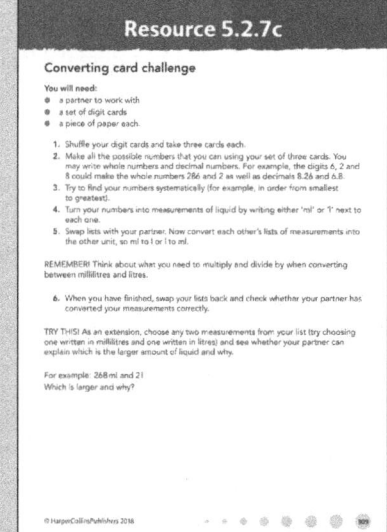

- The resource sheet asks pupils to take three digit cards each and make all the possible numbers they can (including decimals). Encourage them to do this systematically. They write the numbers on paper. Pupils should then give each number a unit of measurement (either litres or millilitres) and swap with a partner who should find equivalent measurements by converting to the alternative unit. They then swap their lists back so that each pupil can check the conversions are correct.

- As an extension, pupils can choose any two measurements from their list (ideally, one measured in litres and one measured in millilitres); their partner must explain which is the larger and why.

Question 5

> 5 Solve these problems.
> (a) Samia bought a 2 litre bottle of orange juice. After pouring 400 ml into a cup, how many millilitres of orange juice were left?
>
> (b) A 2 litre bottle of orange juice was shared equally among 8 children. How many millilitres of orange juice did each child get?

What learning will pupils have achieved at the conclusion of Question 5?

- Pupils will have applied their knowledge of converting between litres and millilitres when solving real-life problems.

Chapter 2 Large numbers and measures

Unit 2.7 Practice Book 5A, pages 41–43

Activities for whole-class instruction

- Display the following scenario:
  - Isla opens a 2 litre bottle of milk at breakfast time. She pours 200 ml onto her breakfast cereal. How many millilitres are still in the bottle?
- Ask: *What would make this problem easier to answer?* Establish that both measurements are given using different units and, in order to compare, the units need to be the same. Ask: *Should you convert the amount the bottle holds to millilitres or the amount Isla pours onto her cereal into litres. Why?* Agree that the answer needs to be in millilitres, so it is sensible to convert both to millilitres rather than litres.
- Ask pupils to complete the calculation on their whiteboards: 2000 − 200 = 1800, reminding them that, as they converted to the correct unit at the beginning, they now do not need to do anything else and the answer is 1800 ml.
- Ask: *What if the question asked: 'How much milk is still in the bottle? Is there another way to answer this question?* Establish that pupils could give the equivalent values of 1.8 l or even 1 litre 800 millilitres, both of which equal 1800 ml.
- Repeat for further simple application problems where pupils are required to convert before calculating. For example:
  - Kieran's nan fills a 4 litre watering can and uses it to water 10 plants in her garden. They each get the same amount of water. How many millilitres of water does each plant receive?
  - Grace tips 1.2 litres of water into a bowl. She can tip in a further 2300 millilitres before the bowl is full. How many millilitres in total can the bowl hold?
- Pupils should complete Question 5 in the Practice Book.

Same-day intervention

- Provide pupils with two 1 litre measuring jugs and challenge them to model Question 5a concretely. Ask: *How many millilitres do you have to begin with? How do you know? Where is the liquid level in the first jug after you pour 400 ml out? What will the level in your other jug be? How can we write this as a calculation?*
- Can pupils tell you that the answer can be expressed as either 1600 ml or 1 litre 600 ml?

- Pupils should then attempt to model Question 5b in the same way. If they find it difficult at first, remind them that they can divide by 8 by halving three times (half of 2 litres = 1 litre, half of 1 litre = 500 ml, half of 500 ml = 250 ml). Give pupils further problems to model and then express as a calculation.

Same-day enrichment

- Draw the following table on the board:

1300 ml	150 ml	190 ml	6400 ml
700 ml	1900 ml	640 ml	1500 ml
220 ml	800 ml	2200 ml	900 ml

- Pupils should make up questions about liquids that have these 12 answers. Explain that there is an additional challenge: the questions must not mention millilitres at all. Questions might have more than one step.
- Pupils should give their questions to a partner to solve.

Chapter 2 Large numbers and measures

Unit 2.7 Practice Book 5A, pages 41–43

Challenge and extension questions

Questions 6 and 7

6 Multiple choice questions. (For each question, choose the correct answer and write the letter in the box.)

(a) 3 l 30 ml = ☐ ml
   A. 3300   B. 3030   C. 3003   D. 303

(b) 7000 ml and 3 l is equal to ☐.
   A. 7003 ml   B. 1000 ml   C. 10 ml   D. 10 l

(c) 4 bottles of 600 ml of a drink is equal to ☐ bottles of 200 ml of the drink.
   A. 3   B. 6   C. 12   D. 18

(d) 1 litre of juice is shared by 16 children in a nursery. Each child gets 50 ml. There are ☐ left.
   A. 800 ml   B. 20 ml   C. 2 l   D. 200 ml

7 375 ml of concentrated grape juice was added to 11 litres of water and then equally shared by 25 workers. How many millilitres of grape juice did each worker get?

In this section, pupils are given two questions to develop their understanding of the measurement of liquids.

Question 6 contains a set of multiple choice questions where they need to convert between units. These include problems that require slightly more thought, as they are expressed using both units (for example, 7000 ml and 3 l is equal to ___), as well as those with more than one step (for example the final problem, where pupils are expected to convert 1 litre to millilitres before dividing by 16 and recording the remainder).

In Question 7, pupils are given a scenario where they must add an amount of concentrated orange juice (in ml) and an amount of water (l) – converting the litres to millilitres before adding. They should then divide this total by the number of workers to find out how many millilitres of the resulting diluted juice each worker gets.

Chapter 2 Large numbers and measures

Unit 2.8
Litres and millilitres (2)

Conceptual context

During this unit, pupils consolidate their understanding of conversion between litres and millilitres, revisiting the concepts studied in the previous unit.

Pupils' fluency with conversion of measures is developed to include ordering quantities that are represented in both litres and millilitres. To do this, pupils are required to convert so they can compare the measurements.

Learning pupils will have achieved at the end of the unit

- The concepts of litres and millilitres will have been consolidated as pupils choose appropriate quantities to describe everyday measurements (Q1)
- Pupils will be increasingly fluent when converting between litres and millilitres (Q2, Q3)
- Pupils will have applied their knowledge about converting between litres and millilitres when ordering quantities and solving real-life problems (Q3, Q4)

Resources

measuring jug (1 litre); measuring cylinder (millilitres); mini whiteboards; **Resource 5.2.8a** How much liquid?; **Resource 5.2.8b** Quantity cards

Vocabulary

litres, millilitres, unit (of measure), convert, multiply, divide

Chapter 2 Large numbers and measures

Unit 2.8 Practice Book 5A, pages 44–46

Question 1

> **1** Draw lines to match the pairs. Use a ruler.
> (a) a spoon of medicine   A. 1000 ml
> (b) a can of soft drink   B. 5 l
> (c) a bottle of cooking oil   C. 330 ml
> (d) a bottle of milk   D. 18 l
> (e) a bucket of water   E. 5 ml

What learning will pupils have achieved at the conclusion of Question 1?

- The concepts of litres and millilitres will have been consolidated as pupils choose appropriate quantities to describe everyday measurements.

Activities for whole-class instruction

- On the board, write: 1 litre, 1 millilitre. Ask pupils to suggest real-life examples of liquids that are equivalent to these. For example: '1 litre is about the same as the quantity of apple juice in a large carton' and '1 millilitre is about the same as the quantity of liquid in a single teardrop'.
- Write the amounts 5 l and 5 ml and ask the same question (this time, the amounts are approximately equal, respectively, to the quantity of water in a watering can and the quantity of medicine in a teaspoonful). Ask pupils to explain why they have chosen their particular examples. They should be able to justify their choices, relating them to known amounts. Repeat for the quantities 50 l and 50 ml.
- Write the following list on the board:

    a bucket

    a bath

    a soup tin

    a lemonade can

    a teaspoon

    an eggcup

- Ask pupil pairs: *How much water would be needed to fill each of these? Do you think the measurement is most likely to be given in litres or millilitres? Why?* Share ideas.
- Write the following:

    330 ml

    380 ml

    40 ml

    6 litres

    5 ml

    80 litres

- Pupils should match these up with the original list. Ask: *Were any of your estimates very different from these? Which ones?*
- Pupils should complete Question 1 in the Practice Book.

Same-day intervention

- Ensure pupils have access to a 1 litre measuring jug and also a measuring cylinder that shows smaller quantities (e.g. up to 100 ml). Begin by ensuring that pupils are able to visualise what 1 litre and 1 millilitre look like. Pupils should use these concepts as reference points when distinguishing between the two units of measurement.
- Fill a mug with water and ask pupils to estimate how much of the measuring jug it will fill. Ask: *Do you think we should give this measurement in millilitres or litres? Why? How many millilitres of water do you think are in the mug?* Choose pupils to check their estimates by using the measuring jug. Repeat for other containers. Relate these to previous measurements, for example, show them a bottle of water and ask: *If a mug holds __ ml, how many ml do you think this bottle will hold?*

Same-day enrichment

- Provide pupils with copies of **Resource 5.2.8a** How much liquid?

> **Resource 5.2.8a**
> How much liquid?
> CHALLENGE 1:
> Match the quantities to complete the sentences.
> Share your answers with your partner. Are they the same?
>
> A teaspoon of food colouring   200 ml
> A large carton of pure apple juice   2 litres
> A bathful of water   375 000 litres
> A mop bucket of water   500 ml
> A large bottle of cola   1.5 litres
> A drinking carton of orange squash (the ones with the straw)   15 litres
> A kettle of water   1 litre
> A drinking bottle of mineral water   75 litres
> The water in a swimming pool   5 ml
>
> CHALLENGE 2:
> Write your own facts about millilitres and litres. However, you are not allowed to use the words millilitres or litres! You will need to use the different quantities from Challenge 1 to help you.
>
> For example:
> 'There are about 100 teaspoons of water in a drinking bottle of mineral water!'
> 'About 375 000 cartons of apple juice are the same as the quantity of water in a swimming pool!'

- This challenge has two parts – first pupils must match up the different measurements and then they write statements relating the items to each other.

Chapter 2 Large numbers and measures

Unit 2.8 Practice Book 5A, pages 44–46

Question 2

> 2 Fill in the spaces.
> (a) When measuring the amount of a liquid such as water or oil,
> we can use _____ and _____ as units of measurement.
> (b) 1000 ml of water can fill up a water bottle of ☐ litre(s).
> (c) 2 l of beverage can fill up ☐ cups of 500 ml each.
> (d) 13 l = _____ ml   (e) 12 000 ml = _____ litres
> (f) 10 000 ml = _____ litres   (g) 51 500 ml = _____ ml
> (h) 2 l + 21 000 ml = _____ litres   (i) 4 l 567 ml = _____ ml
> (j) 56 010 ml = _____ l _____ ml   (k) 10 700 ml = _____ l _____ ml

What learning will pupils have achieved at the conclusion of Question 2?

- Pupils will be increasingly fluent when converting between litres and millilitres.

Activities for whole-class instruction

- Write the following quantities on the board:

500 ml	5 l	50 l	$\frac{11}{2}$ l	1.05 l
1050 ml	$\frac{1}{2}$ l	5000 ml	50 000 ml	5500 ml

- Explain that each quantity has an equivalent in the other row. Give pupils time to pair up the quantities and share their answers.

- Play a game of 'Conversion tennis'. Split pupils into two teams – Team A (the question setters) and Team B (the converters). Pupils in Team A should write a quantity of liquid on their mini whiteboards. This may take the form of a measurement written in:
  - litres [3 litres]
  - millilitres [290 ml]
  - a combination of the two [4 l 500 ml]
  - addition form [2 litres + 1500 millilitres].

- Choose a pupil from Team A to reveal the quantity written on their mini whiteboard. Team B should respond by converting the measurement to a different unit. For example, 290 ml is converted to 0.29 l and 2 litres + 1500 millilitres could be converted to either 3.5 litres or 3500 ml. Play then returns to Team A who should suggest another quantity and so on. Team B get a point for each quantity they convert correctly. After a set number of rounds of 'Conversion tennis', swap team roles and repeat so that both groups of pupils get to practise converting the quantities.

- Pupils should complete Question 2 in the Practice Book.

Same-day intervention

- Ask: *What do you need to multiply or divide by to change from millilitres into litres or from litres into millilitres? Why is this? How do we multiply or divide a number by 1000?* Ensure pupils recognise that this is not simply a case of 'adding three zeros on the end' and, in fact, entails shifting the digits three places. Provide pupils with place value sliders and a set of quantity cards (see **Resource 5.2.8b** Quantity cards).

Resource 5.2.8b

Quantity cards

7500 ml	1200 ml	6 litres	7.5 litres	13 litres
500 ml	750 ml	280 ml	1 litre	3 litres
12 000 ml	20 000 ml	10 litres	1.9 litres	0.4 litres
3400 ml	200 ml	120 ml	0.25 litres	15 litres
7500 ml	1200 ml	6 litres	7.5 litres	13 litres
500 ml	750 ml	280 ml	1 litre	3 litres
12 000 ml	20 000 ml	10 litres	1.9 litres	0.4 litres
3400 ml	200 ml	120 ml	0.25 litres	15 litres

- Pupil pairs take one card at a time and convert the quantity to a different unit of measurement, using the place value sliders to support their calculations. They should write the equivalent converted quantity on the reverse of each card. Ask: *If you are converting from a small unit of measurement to a large unit of measurement (ml into l), do you need to multiply or divide to find the answer? How do you know? Is this the same for converting other units?*

Same-day enrichment

- Pupils should work in groups of three or four and play the following 'Chinese whispers'-style game. Each pupil should begin by drawing a 3 × 3 grid on a piece of paper and, in each cell, write a quantity expressed in both millilitres and litres. For example:

45 000 ml	1.35 l	0.78 l
4000 ml	20 l	359 ml
660 ml	7200 ml	45.7 l

Chapter 2 Large numbers and measures

Unit 2.8 Practice Book 5A, pages 44–46

- This is their master copy and they should keep it during the activity. They should then make a second copy of the grid, this time on a mini whiteboard, writing their name at the top of the whiteboard. This will then be passed from person to person around the group.
- Each time pupils get passed a whiteboard, they should rub out each of the quantities and convert them so that each is expressed using a different unit of measurement. The above grid would then be written as:

45 l	1350 ml	780 ml
4 l	20 000 ml	0.359 l
0.66 l	7.2 l	45 700 ml

- The whiteboards are then passed again and the quantities converted again. Pupils keep doing this until they receive their own whiteboard back. They should then check that the quantities inside the grid are equivalent to those that they originally wrote. If there are any differences, they should consider why that particular quantity proved difficult to convert!

Question 3

> 3 Write the following quantities in order.
> (a) From the greatest to the least.
> 600 ml   5900 ml   7 l   5970 ml   70 l
>
> (b) From the least to the greatest.
> 260 ml   2060 ml   2 l   200 ml   20 l

What learning will pupils have achieved at the conclusion of Question 3?

- Pupils will be increasingly fluent when converting between litres and millilitres.
- Pupils will have applied their knowledge about converting between litres and millilitres when ordering quantities and solving real-life problems.

Activities for whole-class instruction

- Write the following quantities, one each, onto five mini whiteboards:
  800 ml   2300 ml   3 l   2170 ml   80 l
- Without revealing the numbers to the class, give five pupils a whiteboard each.

- Explain to the class that the five pupils each have a quantity of liquid written on their whiteboard and the aim is to put them in order from greatest amount to least. Ask: *As you have to compare them to order them, would you rather that these quantities were written using the same or different units of measurements? Why?* Ensure pupils recognise that measurements that are expressed using the same unit are easier to compare than those that are written using different units. The five pupils should now reveal their quantities. Agree that 3 litres and 80 litres should be converted and written as 3000 ml and 80 000 ml so that all measurements are in millilitres.
- Ask pupils to work in pairs and consider the number of moves that are necessary to put the quantities in order from greatest amount to least. For example, the above set of quantities can be reordered in three moves:

800 ml	2300 ml	3000 ml	2170 ml	80 000 ml
80 000 ml	800 ml	2300 ml	3000 ml	2170 ml
80 000 ml	3000 ml	800 ml	2300 ml	2170 ml
80 000 ml	3000 ml	2300 ml	2170 ml	800 ml

- Ask pupils to explain how they found the answer. They should understand that, in order to compare and order the quantities of liquid, they need to convert the amounts (even if they do so mentally, without actually altering the amounts on the whiteboards).
- Repeat the activity for different sets of quantities, including also ordering from least to greatest quantity.
- Pupils should complete Question 3 in the Practice Book.

Same-day intervention

- Pupils should use the quantity cards that were used in the Same-day intervention for Question 2 (**Resource 5.2.8b Quantity cards**). If the Same-day intervention activity for Question 2 has not been done beforehand, begin with this.
- Shuffle the cards and then deal any five randomly in a row onto the table. Discuss how to compare the different quantities shown and what pupils need to do to make it easier to order them from least to greatest quantity.

83

Chapter 2 Large numbers and measures

Unit 2.8 Practice Book 5A, pages 44–46

- Pupils should begin by converting as many of the cards as they need to in order for all the cards to show either millilitres or litres. As the cards have already been converted during Same-day intervention Q2 (with the equivalent quantity written on the reverse), pupils can simply flip them over to check that their conversion is correct. Once the cards are all displaying the same unit of measurement, ask pupils to order them correctly.
- Repeat for different sets of five cards.

Same-day enrichment

- Pupils should work in groups of three. Pupil A begins by writing a list of quantities of liquid in order (greatest quantity to least or vice versa). These quantities should all be written using the same unit of measurement (millilitres or litres).
- They pass this list to Pupil B whose role is then to alter some of the units of measurement and change the sequence so the list ceases to be in order.
- This new list is then passed to Pupil C who must write them in the correct order, using conversion between litres and millilitres to help compare the quantities. Pupil A can use their original list to check whether their answer is correct.

Question 4

> 4 Solve these problems.
> (a) 16 crates of coconut milk were delivered to a supermarket. Each crate had ten 350 ml cartons of coconut milk. How many litres of coconut milk were delivered?
>
> (b) There are 625 ml of soya milk in 5 packs of the same size. How many millilitres of soya milk are there in 8 packs? How many litres are there?

What learning will pupils have achieved at the conclusion of Question 4?

- Pupils will have applied their knowledge about converting between litres and millilitres when ordering quantities and solving real-life problems.

Activities for whole-class instruction

- Display the following problem:

   – Cans of orangeade are sold in packs of six. Each can contains 330 ml of orangeade and there are 11 packs on the shelf. How many litres of orangeade are on the shelf?

- Ask: *Which pieces of information are important to understand and solve the problem?*

  Look out for … pupils who do not recognise that, as well as the various numbers, the phrase 'How many litres' in the final sentence is important. It is this phrase that introduces the element of conversion to the problem. Without it, the problem is simply a multiplication problem. By asking 'How many litres', the problem involves division to convert the final total of millilitres to litres.

- Ask pupils to draw a quick sketch to summarise the scenario. Check that these refer to 11 groups of 6 with one of each 6 labelled with 330 ml. Explain that pupils are not expected to work out the answer yet, but give them time to discuss with a partner what their strategy would be. Ask: *How many steps are needed? What are they?* Share ideas and agree there are different ways of getting to the same answer. Ask pupils to write these as a number sentence containing several steps.

- Possible strategies include:

Strategy	STEP 1	STEP 2	STEP 3
A	Work out 330 × 6 to find out the number of ml in a pack.	Multiply the answer by 11 to find out the number of ml on a shelf.	Divide by 1000 to convert the number of ml to litres.
Number sentence	330 × 6 × 11 ÷ 1000		
B	Work out 6 × 11 to find out the number of cans on the entire shelf.	Multiply the answer by 330 to find out the number of ml on the shelf.	Divide by 1000 to convert the number of ml to litres.
Number sentence	6 × 11 × 330 ÷ 1000		
C	Divide 330 by 1000 to convert the number of ml in one can to litres.	Multiply the answer by 6 to find out the number of litres in a pack.	Multiply the answer by 11 to find out the number of litres on a shelf.
Number sentence	330 ÷ 1000 × 6 × 11		

Chapter 2 Large numbers and measures

Unit 2.8 Practice Book 5A, pages 44–46

- Ask pupils to circle the part in the number sentence that shows the conversion. Pupils should then work through their number sentence to find the answer.
- Repeat the process for further multi-step problems involving converting between litres and millilitres. For example:
  - There are 12 litres of orange juice in two multipacks (the same size). How many millilitres will there be in five similar multipacks?
  - A gardener has three watering cans that all can hold 4500 ml of water when full. She fills all three watering cans twice when watering the garden. How many litres of water has she used in total?
- Pupils should complete Question 4 in the Practice Book.

Same-day intervention

- Display the following problem:
  - A bottle of mineral water contains 600 ml. How many millilitres of water do 10 bottles contain?
- Ask: *How would you draw this as a bar diagram?* Establish that the problem might be represented like this:

- Ask: *What does each smaller bar represent? What are they worth? What does the long bar represent? How will you find out what it is worth?* Establish that the answer is found by multiplying 600 ml (water in one bottle) by 10 (the number of bottles). Ask pupils to make one small change to the question so that it adds an element of conversion into the problem. For example:
  - A bottle of mineral water contains ~~600 ml~~ 0.6 litres. How many millilitres of water do 10 bottles contain?
  - A bottle of mineral water contains 600 ml. How many ~~millilitres~~ litres of water do 10 bottles contain?
- Ask: *How do these changes affect what you need to do to find the answer?* Compare the problem with the original question and ask pupils what is the same and what is different. Give pupils time to solve the new conversion problem.
- Give pupils further simple problems to discuss, represent using bar models, alter to add the element of conversion, and then solve.

Same-day enrichment

- Draw the following table on the board:

Flavour	Quantity
pineapple juice	200 ml
orangeade	500 ml
cranberry juice	300 ml
coconut milk	30 ml
lemon juice	100 ml
a squirt of lime juice	10 ml
apple juice	750 ml
pomegranate juice	20 ml

- Challenge pupils to devise their own cocktail recipe. They should give it a name and work out the total quantity and tell these to a partner, for example: 'Fab Fruity Fizz' = 1.375 litres. Partners should work out what the recipe might be by finding ingredients that add together to make the total quantity.

Challenge and extension question

Question 5

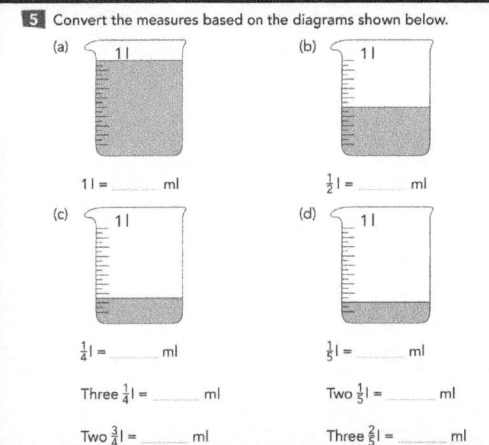

Pupils are challenged to consider various fractions of a litre (1 whole, $\frac{1}{2}$, $\frac{1}{4}$ and $\frac{1}{5}$) in terms of millilitres, using visual representations to aid their understanding. This concept is then extended as pupils are asked to use their knowledge to express multiple fractions of a litre (for example two lots of $\frac{3}{4}$).

Chapter 2 Large numbers and measures

Chapter 2 test (Practice Book 5A, pages 47–52)

Test question number	Relevant unit	Relevant questions within unit
1	No specific unit	
2	No specific unit	
3	No specific unit	
4	Unit 2.1	Q1, Q2, Q3, Q4
	Unit 2.2	Q1, Q2, Q3, Q4, Q5
	Unit 2.3	Q1, Q2, Q3, Q4
	Unit 2.4	Q1, Q2, Q3, Q4, Q5, Q6
	Unit 2.5	Q4, Q5, Q6
	Unit 2.6	Q3
	Unit 2.7	Q4
	Unit 2.8	Q2, Q3
5	Unit 2.4	Q2, Q3, Q4, Q5, Q6
	Unit 2.5	Q1, Q2, Q3, Q4, Q5
	Unit 2.6	Q5
6	No specific unit	
7	Unit 2.6	Q6
	Unit 2.7	Q5
	Unit 2.8	Q4

Chapter 3
Dividing by 2-digit numbers

Chapter overview

Area of mathematics	National Curriculum statutory requirements for Key Stage 2	Shanghai Maths Project reference
Number – multiplication and division	Year 5 Programme of study: Pupils should be taught to: ■ multiply numbers up to 4 digits by a one- or two-digit number using a formal written method, including long multiplication for two-digit numbers	Year 5, Unit 3.3
	■ multiply and divide numbers mentally drawing upon known facts	Year 5, Unit 3.1
	■ multiply and divide whole numbers and those involving decimals by 10, 100 and 1000	Year 5, Units 3.4, 3.5, 3.6, 3.8
	■ solve problems involving multiplication and division including using their knowledge of factors and multiples, squares and cubes	Year 5, Units 3.1, 3.2, 3.3, 3.4, 3.5, 3.6, 3.7, 3.8
	■ solve problems involving addition, subtraction, multiplication and division and a combination of these, including understanding the meaning of the equals sign	Year 5, Units 3.5, 3.6
	■ solve problems involving multiplication and division, including scaling by simple fractions and problems involving simple rates.	Year 5, Units 3.1, 3.2, 3.4
Number – addition, subtraction, multiplication and division	Year 6 Programme of study: Pupils should be taught to: ■ multiply multi-digit numbers up to 4 digits by a two-digit whole number using the formal written method of long multiplication	Year 5, Units 3.6, 3.7, 3.8
	■ divide numbers up to 4 digits by a two-digit whole number using the formal written method of long division, and interpret remainders as whole number remainders, fractions, or by rounding, as appropriate for the context	Year 5, Units 3.3, 3.4, 3.5, 3.6, 3.7, 3.8
	■ perform mental calculations, including with mixed operations and large numbers	Year 5, Units 3.1, 3.2, 3.3, 3.4, 3.5, 3.6, 3.7, 3.8

■ use their knowledge of the order of operations to carry out calculations involving the four operations	Year 5, Units 3.7, 3.8
■ solve problems involving addition, subtraction, multiplication and division	Year 5, Units 3.1, 3.2, 3.3, 3.4, 3.5, 3.6, 3.7, 3.8
■ use estimation to check answers to calculations and determine, in the context of a problem, an appropriate degree of accuracy.	Year 5, Units 3.3, 3.4, 3.5, 3.6, 3.7, 3.8

Chapter 3 Dividing by 2-digit numbers

Unit 3.1
Speed, time and distance (1)

Conceptual context

In Year 4, pupils learned to multiply by two-digit and three-digit numbers. They developed mental and written methods for multiplication and used what they know about multiples and factors to help determine quotients when working with division, for example, knowing that 4 × 60 = 240 and 5 × 60 = 300, then 275 ÷ 60 will give a quotient of 4 and a remainder because it is between 240 and 300.

Pupils have related division involving a number of ones, for example 48 ÷ 6, to division involving the same number of tens, 480 ÷ 60, recognising that both give rise to the same quotient.

They have worked with a real-life application for multiplication and division as they explored 'work rates', using practical activities to help develop conceptual understanding.

In this unit, pupils continue to secure and apply connections between multiplication and division as they discover the relationship between speed, distance and time, recognising that speed can be calculated by dividing the distance covered by the time taken.

Learning pupils will have achieved at the end of the unit

- Conceptual understanding of the relationship between speed, time and distance will have been developed through the use of practical activities (Q1, Q2)
- Pupils will have applied knowledge of multiplication and division – and the relationship between them – to work with problems related to speed, time and distance (Q1, Q2, Q4)
- Pupils will have practised calculating and comparing speeds shown in different units of measurement (Q2, Q4)
- Pupils will have recognised and explained why speeds may be shown using different units of measurement (Q3)
- An understanding of the relationship between speed, distance and time will have been applied to a range of problems (Q4, Q5)

Resources

stopwatches; metre sticks or trundle wheels; chalk or tape; calculators; arrays and place value counters as required; **Resource 5.3.1a** Fastest first! (1); **Resource 5.3.1b** Fastest first! (2); **Resource 5.3.1c** Recording speeds; **Resource 5.3.1d** Car journeys; **Resource 5.3.1e** Solving problems about speed

Vocabulary

speed, distance, time, dividend, divisor, quotient

Chapter 3 Dividing by 2-digit numbers   Unit 3.1 Practice Book 5A, pages 53–55

Question 1

> **1** True or false? (Put a ✓ for true and a ✗ for false in each box.)
> (a) Speed tells how fast a moving object travels. ☐
> (b) Distance tells how much time a moving object has spent in motion. ☐
> (c) If Mr Lee walks 2 km in two hours, then his speed is 1 km per hour. ☐
> (d) If a bird flies at a speed of 2 m per second, then it can fly 120 m per minute. ☐
> (e) In a running race, the winner runs at the fastest speed and is the first person to cross the finish line. ☐

What learning will pupils have achieved at the conclusion of Question 1?

- Conceptual understanding of the relationship between speed, time and distance will have been developed through the use of practical activities.
- Pupils will have applied knowledge of multiplication and division – and the relationship between them – to work with problems related to speed, time and distance.

Activities for whole-class instruction

- In the hall or playground, divide pupils into groups of four. Give each group a stopwatch. Ask each group to measure out a distance between 5 m and 10 m. (This range can be greater or smaller depending on the space available.) Pupils should use chalk or tape to mark out their starting and finishing points for their distance. Can they record the distance in centimetres?
- Pupils should take it in turns to time and record how long it takes in seconds to:
  - walk the total distance
  - run or jog the total distance
  - hop the total distance.
- Return to the classroom and share some of the results, comparing, for example:
  - how long it took to walk a longer distance compared to a shorter distance
  - how long it took to run or jog a distance compared to hopping the same distance
  - how much further a pupil who was running was able to travel in a similar time to another pupil who hopped.
- Ask: *What generalisations can we make about the time it took compared to the distance we travelled and how fast or slow we travelled?* Establish that we can use the term 'speed' to describe how fast we travelled, but this depends on the distance and the time taken.

ⓘ Speed is about the relationship between the two measures, distance and time, rather than just about how quickly an object moves. Speed is the rate at which an object moves and can be found by dividing the measurement of distance by the time taken.

- Display the following scenarios on the board:
  - *A tortoise travelled a distance of 25 metres and a hare travelled a distance of 20 metres. Which was faster?*
  - *Two animals both travelled 25 metres – one walked and one ran. Which was travelling at the greater speed?*
  - *A lion and a hyena both walked for 4 hours. Which travelled further?*
- Discuss how, in each scenario, there is not enough information to answer the question, for example say:
  - *We know the tortoise travelled further but we don't know how long it took to travel 25 m. It might have taken a whole day, so its speed might have been very slow – we don't know what the speed was without knowing the time taken.*
  - *The animal that ran didn't necessarily travel faster – we also need to know how long it took.*
  - *Knowing how long the lion and hyena walked for does not tell us how far they travelled – we would need to know how fast (what speed) they were walking.*
- Focus on the terms 'speed', 'distance' and 'time'. Can pupils use each term to describe the activity they did and what they recorded? Establish that 'speed' is how fast an object travels over a distance, 'time' is how long it takes to travel the distance and 'distance' is how far an object travels.
- Share some examples about speed, distance and time, for example:
  - *A car travels at a speed of 50 kilometres per hour. In 2 hours, it travels a distance of 100 km.*
  - *A ball travels 40 metres through the air. It takes 5 seconds in total. It travelled at a speed of 8 metres per second.*
  - *A tortoise walks at a speed of 7 centimetres per second. In 10 seconds, it travelled a distance of 70 cm.*
- Can pupils work out the connection between the values? Look together at the use of multiplication and division.
- (NOTE: Keep all the distances and times from the Whole-class activities to use in the next session.)
- Pupils should complete Question 1 in the Practice Book.

Chapter 3 Dividing by 2-digit numbers

Unit 3.1 Practice Book 5A, pages 53–55

Same-day intervention

- Discuss other examples in everyday life or science where the notion of speed, time and distance are also used, for example in sport, transport and fact files about animals.
- Ask pupils to make a list of faster 'objects' and one of 'slower' objects. Can they explain that a faster 'object' will cover more distance than a slower object in the same time or that a faster 'object' will take less time to cover the same distance?
- Look together at some of the statements in Question 1, drawing out the use of multiplication and division as appropriate.

Same-day enrichment

- Give pupils **Resource 5.3.1a** Fastest first! (1). Can they arrange the cards in order, fastest first? They should use the clues to help them make decisions.

Answers: Cards should be arranged in order from fastest to slowest.

Question 2

	Speed	Time	Distance
🚶		3 hours (h)	42 km
🚌		5 minutes (min)	4500 m
🏍		20 seconds (s)	400 m

What learning will pupils have achieved at the conclusion of Question 2?

- Conceptual understanding of the relationship between speed, time and distance will have been developed through the use of practical activities.
- Pupils will have applied knowledge of multiplication and division – and the relationship between them – to work with problems related to speed, time and distance.
- Pupils will have practised calculating and comparing speeds shown in different units of measurement.

Activities for whole-class instruction

- Tell pupils that they are going to calculate their own speed when walking, hopping and running and make accurate comparisons. Ensure that pupils recognise that 'speed' is used to represent how fast an object travels over a distance.
- Can pupils explain how the speed in the following example can be calculated?
  - *A car travels a distance of 90 kilometres in 3 hours.*
- Agree that the speed is 30 km per hour, and can be found by dividing the distance travelled by the time taken. Record the speed as 30 km/h

  (All say...) *Speed is equal to the distance travelled divided by the time taken.*

- Record this as:

  SPEED = DISTANCE ÷ TIME TAKEN

- Show pupils the following table showing the time taken for an adult to complete the activities. Explain that the speeds will be calculated as centimetres per second (cm/s).

	Distance 1200 cm		
Activity	Walking	Running	Hopping
Time taken	6 seconds	3 seconds	8 seconds
Speed (cm/s)			

- Look together at mental and written strategies to divide 1200, including the use of known facts and place value. Ask: *How can you show each speed as metres per second?* Record these as 0.5 m/s, 4 m/s and 0.75 m/s.
- Pupils should work with a partner to calculate and compare their speed for each activity using a division

Chapter 3 Dividing by 2-digit numbers

Unit 3.1 Practice Book 5A, pages 53–55

method of their choice. They should ignore any remainders for this activity. Can pupils write each speed as metres per second?

- Share some of the results, focusing on how it is now much easier to compare activities over different distances. Explain that when a pupil runs, say 750 cm in 10 seconds, and another runs 600 cm in 8 seconds, it is much harder to say who was faster without calculating the speed, whereas comparing two pupils who ran the same distance is much easier as we only need to compare the time taken.

- Pupils should complete Question 2 in the Practice Book.

Same-day intervention

- Give pupils **Resource 5.3.1b** Fastest first! (2). Pupils should work in pairs to discuss and arrange the cards in order, fastest first.

Answers: Cards should be arranged in order from fastest to slowest.

Same-day enrichment

- Work together as a group to solve the following problem using the clues provided. Who is the fastest?

  Alvin takes 60 seconds longer to run the same distance as Beth.

  Sally runs 0.3 km further than Beth.

  Anita runs at a speed of 2.5 m/s.

  Alvin takes four minutes to run a distance of 540 m.

  It takes Sally 180 seconds longer to run her distance than Alvin.

  [Solution: Beth 3 m/s, Anita 2.5 m/s, Alvin 2.25 m/s, Sally 2 m/s]

- Discuss a useful starting point for the problem. Why is the first clue not a useful starting place? Look together at conversions to ensure that all speeds are recorded in the same way.

Questions 3 and 4

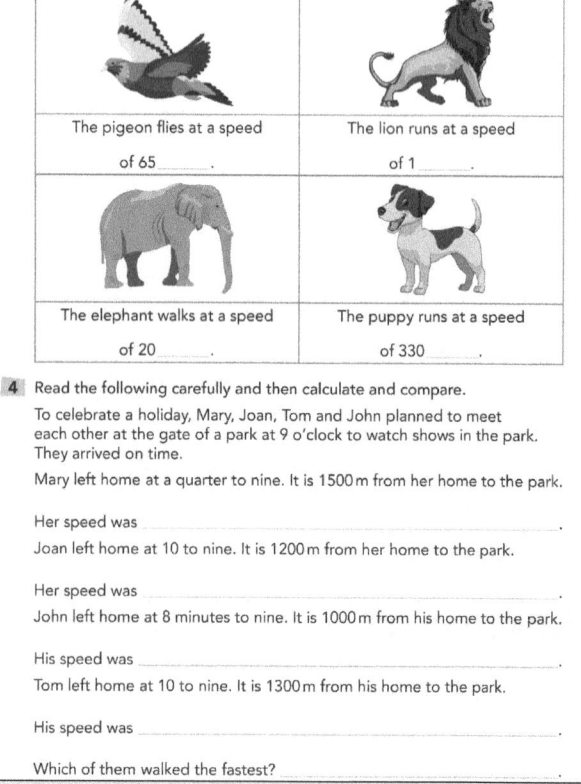

Chapter 3 Dividing by 2-digit numbers

Unit 3.1 Practice Book 5A, pages 53–55

What learning will pupils have achieved at the conclusion of Questions 3 and 4?

- Pupils will have recognised and explained why speeds may be shown using different units of measurement.
- Pupils will have applied knowledge of multiplication and division – and the relationship between them – to work with problems related to speed, time and distance.
- Pupils will have practised calculating and comparing speeds shown in different units of measurement.
- An understanding of the relationship between speed, distance and time will have been applied to a range of problems.

Activities for whole-class instruction

- Discuss the different units of measurements that the pupils have used so far to work with speed. Record these on the board as:

  cm/s   **m/s**   **m/min**   **km/h**.

- Can pupils give an example of different 'things' that travel at speeds that would be recorded in this way? Can they explain why each unit of measurement may be used? For example, ask: *Why would the speed of a car be recorded as km/h rather than cm/s? What unit of measurement would you use to measure the speed of a snail?*
- Revisit the speeds in cm/s and m/s recorded during the practical activities. Ask: *Which things (natural or human-made) move faster or slower than your walking speed?*
- Suggest that metres per hour (m/h) and kilometres per minute (km/m) can also be used to record speed. Ask: *What is the speed 3 km/h given as metres per hour?* (3000 m/h) *What is 600 km/h given as kilometres per minute?* (10 km/m)
- Give an example of an object moving at such speed, for example the typical cruising speed of a commercial jet aircraft is between 740 and 930 km/h. Can pupils calculate these speeds as kilometres/minute? Display the image below for support, and quickly look at strategies to divide 740 and 930 by 60, relating this to 74 ÷ 6 and 93 ÷ 6.

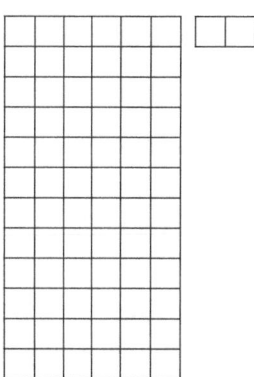

This shows 74 divided into groups of 6.

There are 12 groups of 6 and 2 single ones left over.

So, 74 ÷ 6 = 12 r 2.

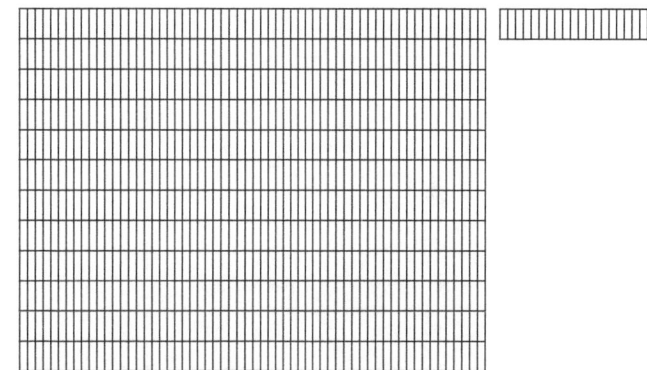

This shows 740 divided into groups of 60.

There are 12 groups of 60 and 20 left over.

So, 740 ÷ 60 = 12 r 20.

- Show pupils the following information about the arrival and departure times of two different aeroplanes.

	Departure	Arrival	Distance
Aeroplane A	10:00	13:00	2100 km
Aeroplane B	11:30	15:30	3200 km

- Ask pupils to discuss how they can find out which aeroplane travelled at a greater speed. Do they recognise that they must first calculate the time taken?
- Pupils should now calculate the speed of each aeroplane and record this as kilometres per hour. Revisit the calculation required to calculate speed.

 *All say...* *Speed is equal to the distance travelled divided by the time taken.*

- Agree that Aeroplane B (800 km/h) travels at a faster speed than Aeroplane A (700 km/h). Establish that it would have been easier to compare two aeroplanes that departed at the same time and travelled the same distance, but when this is not the case we must calculate the speed to help us make an accurate comparison.

Chapter 3 Dividing by 2-digit numbers

Unit 3.1 Practice Book 5A, pages 53–55

- Pupils should complete Questions 3 and 4 in the Practice Book.

Same-day intervention

- Give pupils **Resource 5.3.1c** Recording speeds. They should take it in turns to shuffle each set of cards and pick one from each pile.
- Can they calculate the speed each time and record it using an appropriate unit of measurement? For example, they pick the '120 metres' card and the '6 hours' card and record the speed as 20 m/h.

Resource 5.3.1c

Recording speeds

10 minutes	3 minutes
3 hours	6 hours
12 minutes	12 hours
4 minutes	2 hours
10 hours	120 metres
60 metres	2400 metres
360 metres	72 metres
240 kilometres	48 kilometres
36 kilometres	12 kilometres

Same-day enrichment

- Give pupils **Resource 5.3.1d** Car journeys. Can they use the information given to complete the table and find out which car travelled at the greatest speed?

Resource 5.3.1d

Car journeys

a) Fill in the missing information about the car journeys.

	Departure	Arrival	Distance (km)	Speed (km/h)
Car A	08:00	13:00	310	
Car B	09:00	16:00	413	
Car C	11:30		114	57
Car D	13:00	16:00	237	
Car E	14:30	18:30	272	
Car F	16:00	20:00	332	
Car G		21:00	240	80

b) Which car was travelling at the greatest speed?

Answers: a) 62, 59, 13:30, 79, 68, 83, 18:00; b) Car F.

Question 5

5 Solve these problems.
(a) Andrew walked to Jim's house for a party. The distance between their houses is 800 m. Andrew left home at 10 past 10 and arrived at 18 minutes past 10.

Find Andrew's walking speed. _____

(b) The distance between place A and place B is 800 km. A train leaves place A at 5 o'clock and arrives at place B at 10 o'clock.

Find the speed of the train. _____

What learning will pupils have achieved at the conclusion of Question 5?

- An understanding of the relationship between speed, distance and time will have been applied to a range of problems.

Activities for whole-class instruction

- Explain to pupils that they are going to use what they know about the relationship between speed, distance and time to help solve different problems. Give pupils the following scenario about Mrs Allan and Mr Tai's journey to work:

Mrs Allan walks a distance of 600 m to work every day.

She leaves at 7:40 a.m. and arrives at 8:00 a.m.

Mr Tai walks a distance of 0.72 km to work every day.

He leaves 10 minutes earlier than Mrs Allan but arrives at the same time.

Who is walking at the faster speed?

- Pupils should work in pairs to solve the problem. Do they recognise that the distances are given in different units of measurement?

Look out for … pupils who find it difficult to divide by a multiple of 10 and do not relate, say 600 ÷ 20 to 60 ÷ 2, recognising that the quotient is the same. It would be useful to use squared paper to sketch an array to show each division or use 60 ones and 60 tens place value counters.

- Agree that Mrs Allan walks at 30 m/min and Mr Tai at 24 m/min, so she is faster.

Chapter 3 Dividing by 2-digit numbers

- Look at similar examples together where the time (making these a multiple of 10 minutes each time) has to be found each time before calculating the speed. Be sure to ask for speeds using different units of measurement so pupils have to convert first. For example:

A bus departs at 10 past 1 and arrives at the train station at 10 to 2.

The total distance is 3000 m.

What speed was it travelling?

- Can pupils give the speed in both m/min and km/min?
- Pupils should complete Question 5 in the Practice Book.

Same-day intervention

- Look together at the problems in Question 5, addressing any issues as required.
- Provide pupils with some start and finish times for different journeys, again making the intervals a multiple of 10 minutes. Can they work together to calculate the speed each time? Focus on strategies to divide by a number of tens, using arrays or place value counters as required.

Same-day enrichment

- Give pupils **Resource 5.3.1e** Solving problems about speed. Ask them to explore the problems. Can they find the speed that each bus travelled and give a possible departure and arrival time for the three buses?

Answers: Departure and arrival times will vary.
Bus A: 50 min, 192 m/min
Bus B: 40 min, 240 m/min
Bus C: 30 min, 320 m/min

Challenge and extension question

Question 6

6. The distance of the London marathon is 42 km and 195 m. Famous British marathon runner Paula Radcliffe is the women's world record holder in the marathon with her time of 2 hours, 15 minutes and 25 seconds.

Her running speed is about _____ m/s.

This problem requires pupils to work with approximations and convert between different units of measurement. The distance given is 42 km and 195 m and the time given is 2 hours, 15 minutes and 25 seconds, but the approximate speed is asked for as metres per second. Using 42 000 m as an approximate distance and 140 minutes as an approximate time will be useful.

Chapter 3 Dividing by 2-digit numbers

Unit 3.2
Speed, time and distance (2)

Conceptual context

In the previous unit, pupils learned that speed is about the relationship between the two measures, distance and time – it is a rate at which an object moves.

Pupils are developing their understanding that comparison is difficult when a number of variables are involved and that calculating speed enables comparisons to be made. This understanding will be developed further in this unit.

Pupils will explore methods for calculating in order to solve problems using the relationship between time, distance and speed.

Learning pupils will have achieved at the end of the unit

- Pupils will have applied knowledge of multiplication and division – and the relationship between them – to work with problems related to speed, time and distance (Q1, Q2, Q3)
- An understanding of conversion will have been applied as pupils solve problems involving different units of measurement (Q2, Q4)
- Pupils will be able to recognise when they can simply compare information about the time taken or distance travelled by objects to say which is fastest or when they have to carry out a calculation (Q2, Q4)
- An understanding of conversion will have been applied as pupils solve problems involving different units of measurement (Q4)

Resources

counters; paper clips; **Resource 5.3.2a** Speedy dominoes (1); **Resource 5.3.2b** In a spin; **Resource 5.3.2c** Speedy dominoes (2); **Resource 5.3.2d** Speed problems

Vocabulary

speed, distance, time, dividend, divisor, quotient

Chapter 3 Dividing by 2-digit numbers

Unit 3.2 Practice Book 5A, pages 56–58

Questions 1 and 2

> **1** Fill in the blanks. The first one has been done for you.
>
> Distance = Speed (×) Time
>
> Time = _____ ◯ _____
>
> Speed = _____ ◯ _____
>
> **2** Compare and then write the answers.
> (a) The distance between the school and the museum is 1 km. Both Bill and Jim walked to the museum from their school. Bill left at 16:00 and arrived at 16:15. Jim left at 16:05 and arrived at 16:18.
>
> Who walked faster? _____
>
> When the distance is the same, we can compare the time.
>
> The less the time, the _____ the speed.
>
> (b) Emmy and Joanne left school and walked home at 15:30. By 15:50 both of them reached their homes. The distance between Emmy's home and the school is 1500 m while the distance between Joanne's home and the school is 1650 m.
>
> Who walked faster? _____
>
> When the time taken is the same, we can compare the distance.
>
> The greater the distance travelled, the _____ the speed.

What learning will pupils have achieved at the conclusion of Questions 1 and 2?

- Pupils will have applied knowledge of multiplication and division – and the relationship between them – to work with problems related to speed, time and distance.
- An understanding of conversion will have been applied as pupils solve problems involving different units of measurement.
- Pupils will be able to recognise when they can simply compare information about the time taken or distance travelled by objects to say which is fastest or when they have to carry out a calculation.

Activities for whole-class instruction

- Remind pupils about the scenarios they discussed as part of the previous unit.
  - *A tortoise travelled a distance of 25 metres and a hare travelled a distance of 20 metres. Which was faster?*
  - *Two animals both travelled 25 metres – one walked and one ran. Which was travelling at the greater speed?*
  - *A lion and a hyena both walked for 4 hours. Which travelled further?*
- Ask: *What information must we also know each time to answer the questions? Is the missing information related to time, distance or speed?* Pupils should discuss the scenarios in turn and prepare to explain their decisions.

- Agree that we need to know the following information about each scenario:
  - how long it took the hare and the tortoise to each travel the given distances (time is missing)
  - the time taken by the two animals (time is missing)
  - the speed at which the lion and the hyena travelled (speed is missing).
- Display the information shown below to now include the missing information for each scenario.
  - *A tortoise travelled a distance of 25 metres and a hare travelled a distance of 20 metres. The tortoise took 25 minutes and the hare took 2 minutes. Which was faster?*
  - *Two animals both travelled 25 metres – one walked and one ran. The second animal took 30 seconds longer than the first animal. Which was travelling at the greater speed?*
  - *A lion and a hyena both walked for 4 hours. The lion walked at a speed of 5 km/h. The hyena walked at a speed of 4 km/h. Which travelled further?*
- Remind pupils that speed can be calculated as:

  SPEED = DISTANCE ÷ TIME TAKEN

- Can they answer the first two questions? Suggest that they may not need to calculate the speed in both questions.
- Agree that the hare is faster with a speed of 10 m/min, whereas the tortoise's speed is only 1 m/min. Explain that as the distances travelled and the time taken are different each time, the speed needs to be calculated. Ask: *If we had been told that the hare took 2 minutes to travel 20 metres and the tortoise took 2 minutes to travel 2 metres, would we need to calculate the speed to see which animal was faster?*

When the time taken is the same, we can compare the distance. The greater the distance travelled, the faster the speed.

- Look in more detail at the second question, asking pupils to explain why it was not necessary to calculate the actual speed. Establish that as the animals travelled the same distance, we only need to compare the time taken, so animal 1 was faster as it took less time. Refer back to the activities the pupils did in the hall or playground, agreeing that it was easier to compare how much faster or slower an activity was completed when the distance travelled was the same.

When the distance is the same, we can compare the time. The less time, the faster the speed.

97

Chapter 3 Dividing by 2-digit numbers

Unit 3.2 Practice Book 5A, pages 56–58

- Finally, look together at the third question, agreeing that we now know about the time taken and the speed at which each animal travelled. Ensure that pupils recognise that both animals walked for the same length of time but at different speeds, so they did not walk the same distance.

- Explain that we need to know how to use this information to answer the question. Ask pupils initially to use all the information we know about the hare from the first question to explore other relationships between speed, distance and time. For example:

  SPEED = DISTANCE ÷ TIME

  $10 = 20 ÷ 2$

- Ask them to imagine that we do not know the distance travelled by the hare, but only the speed and time taken. Can pupils explain how we could use the other two values to find the distance? What do they notice?

- Agree that the values for time and speed can be multiplied to give the distance, 20. Record this as:

  $20 = 10 × 2$

  DISTANCE = SPEED × TIME

   *To find the distance, we multiply the speed by the time taken.*

- Display the following to demonstrate why multiplying the values for speed and time give the distance travelled.

  | 1 hour | 10 km | | 10 km travelled in 1 hour |
  | 2 hours | 10 km | 10 km | 20 km travelled in 2 hours |

- Work through the representation for 1 hour and then for 2 hours, referring to the speed as 10 km 'per' hour, so 10 km in one hour and 2 lots of 10 km in two hours. Can pupils explain how far the hare will have travelled in 3 hours? Agree this as $10 × 3 = 30$ km, drawing an extra row of 10 km bars below the image to show this.

- Return together to the question about the lion and the hyena. Can pupils sketch bars to represent the distance each animal travelled? Can they show this as a calculation using DISTANCE = SPEED × TIME? Agree that the lion travels 20 km ($5 × 4$) and the hyena only 16 km ($4 × 4$).

- Remind pupils that we can calculate speed when we know the measurement for time and distance. We can also calculate distance when we know about speed and time. Ask: *How could we calculate time when we know about speed and distance?* Can pupils work together to decide how to use the values for the lion's speed and distance travelled to find the time taken?

- Agree that the value for distance can be divided by the value for speed to give the time taken. Record this as:

  $4 = 20 ÷ 5$

  TIME = DISTANCE ÷ SPEED

   *To find the time taken, we divide the distance travelled by the speed.*

- Pupils should complete Questions 1 and 2 in the Practice Book.

Same-day intervention

- Look together at the problems in Question 2, including strategies to calculate a time interval, for example using a number line to count up from 16:05 to 16:18 if needed. Briefly remind pupils of 24-hour clock notation, agreeing these as 4:05 p.m. and 4:18 p.m., although this conversion is not needed for pupils to calculate.

- Ensure that pupils recognise that in part (a) the distance is the same and in part (b) the time taken is the same.

- Return to some of the data collected from the activities in Unit 3.1 and compare the speeds of activities over the same distance or those that took approximately the same speed over different distances. Can pupils explain who/which activity was faster each time?

Same-day enrichment

- Give pupils **Resource 5.3.2a** Speedy dominoes (1). Can pupils work together to arrange all the dominoes (loop cards) so that each question is answered?

Answers: Animals should be in the following order (starting at any point): Dog, Rabbit, Pony, Lion, Cat, Horse, Squirrel, Fox, Mouse, Bird (and then back to Dog).

Chapter 3 Dividing by 2-digit numbers

Unit 3.2 Practice Book 5A, pages 56–58

Question 3

3 Fill in the table.

Speed	Time	Distance
	6 min	504 m
7 km/h		119 km
118 m/min	8 min	

What learning will pupils have achieved at the conclusion of Question 3?

- Pupils will have applied knowledge of multiplication and division – and the relationship between them – to work with problems related to speed, time and distance.

Activities for whole-class instruction

- Show pupils the following multiplication and division calculations:

  132 × 5   156 ÷ 6   288 ÷ 9   112 × 7

- Ask: *What strategies can we use to solve these calculations?* Look together at possible strategies, to include:
  - Using knowledge of multiplying by 10 to support multiplying by 5, for example:
    132 × 5 = 132 × 10 ÷ 2 or 132 ÷ 2 × 10.
  - Partitioning to find part products, for example:
    112 × 7 = (100 × 7) + (12 × 7).
  - Partitioning into groups of the divisor, for example:
    288 ÷ 9 = (270 ÷ 9) + (18 ÷ 9).
  - Column methods for multiplication and division.

- Discuss the use of brackets to organise parts of the calculation and to show what to do first.

- Display the following table. Ask pupils to discuss the information that it shows and the information that is missing. Can they explain how the missing information can be found? Do they notice that the calculations needed include those practised earlier?

Speed	Time	Distance
112 km/h	7 hr	
	6 min	156 m
9 m/s		288 m
5 m/min	132 min	
	10 hr	750 km

- Revisit the formulae found in the previous session.

  SPEED = DISTANCE ÷ TIME
  DISTANCE = SPEED × TIME
  TIME = DISTANCE ÷ SPEED

- Look at the first three rows of the table together, deciding what information is already known and what needs to be found. Look carefully at the units of measurement given and how these should be used to express the missing information, for example 112 km/h and 7 h in the first row, so the distance should be given in kilometres (km).

- Ask pupils to practise writing the calculations alongside the formula, for example:

  DISTANCE = SPEED × TIME   784 km = 112 km/h × 7 h

- Pupils should complete the final two rows of the table, identifying and explaining which calculation they will need to use and why.

- Pupils should complete Question 3 in the Practice Book.

Same-day intervention

- Present the different formula used to work with speed, time and distance on different cards.

  | SPEED = DISTANCE ÷ TIME |

  | DISTANCE = SPEED × TIME |

  | TIME = DISTANCE ÷ SPEED |

- Look in turn at each row of the table from the Practice Book. Can pupils choose the formula that is needed each time and explain why? For example, explaining what information they know already and what they need to find out.

- Check strategies for multiplication and division, modelling as required.

- Take one formula card at a time. Can pupils make up their own pair of values for the known values each time, for example make up 200 m for distance and 12 minutes for the time taken, and explain what they will need to do to find the unknown value (distance)? They do not need to calculate, but explain how they would use the information, for example 'To find the speed I need to divide 200 by 12. The speed will be written as metres per minute.'

99

Chapter 3 Dividing by 2-digit numbers

Unit 3.2 Practice Book 5A, pages 56–58

Same-day enrichment

- Give pupils **Resource 5.3.2b** In a spin, a paper clip and pencil for the spinner and two different-coloured sets of counters. Pupils should work in pairs.

- They take it in turns to spin the spinner and choose a value from the corresponding section of the grid, for example spin 'speed' and choose a value from the 'speed' section of the grid. They use the value, for example 6 km/h for speed, and then make up two other values, for example one for time and one for distance, that would result in the value chosen from the grid. Pupils should record each of their goes on the table.

Question 4

4 Solve these problems.
  (a) It took Emily 5 minutes to walk 400 m while it took Samantha 4 minutes to walk 360 m. Who walked faster?

  (b) Alvin and his mother left home at 7 o'clock in the morning. His mother drove to her office at a speed of 700 m/min and Alvin cycled to school at a speed of 16 km/h. Both of them reached their destinations at half past seven. Find out the distance between Alvin's mother's office and their home. How about the distance between Alvin's home and his school?

  (c) A bicycle travels at 18 km/h and a motorcycle travels 27 km/h faster than the bicycle. How many kilometres can a motorcycle travel in 8 hours?

  (d) Tim left home at 7 o'clock in the morning for school. After walking for 2 minutes he realised he had left his maths homework at home. So he went back to get his homework and arrived at the school at 28 minutes past 7. Given Tim walked at 100 m/min, and it took him 4 minutes to get home and find the homework, what is the distance between his home and the school?

What learning will pupils have achieved at the conclusion of Question 4?

- An understanding of conversion will have been applied as pupils solve problems involving different units of measurement.
- Pupils will be able to recognise when they can simply compare information about the time taken or distance travelled by objects to say which is fastest or when they have to carry out a calculation.

Activities for whole-class instruction

- Share the three sets of problems shown below. Pupils should discuss each scenario with a partner, deciding what information they already know and what needs to be found out.

Faster?	Shorter time?	Longer distance?
Ben runs at 4 km/h. Sam runs at 50 m/min.	Asha's journey takes 45 minutes. Nina's journey starts at 8:03 a.m. and ends at 8:53 a.m.	Luka cycles for 10 km. Alice cycles from her house to the beach and back. The distance from her house to the beach is 4000 m.

Chapter 3 Dividing by 2-digit numbers

Unit 3.2 Practice Book 5A, pages 56–58

Look out for ... pupils who do not notice that an immediate comparison of speed, time or distance cannot be made because units of measurement are not the same or must be calculated first, for example thinking that Sam must be running faster than Ben because 50 is larger than 4.

- Ask: *What makes the first problem trickier to solve? Would it be easier if Sam's speed was also given in km/h? Why?* Pupils should discuss how Sam's speed could be given in km/h. Can they explain that there are 60 minutes in an hour, so the number of metres should be multiplied by 60?
- Revisit strategies to multiply 60 by 50 by breaking down the multiples of 10 to show the calculation as 6 × 10 × 5 × 10 and rearranged as 6 × 5 × 100 so that known facts and place value can be simply applied. Agree that 4 m/min is equivalent to 3000 m/h or 3 km/h, so Ben is faster.
- Now consider the second scenario. Agree that we are not given Nina's journey time, but we can calculate it by comparing the start and finish times. Look at strategies to calculate time intervals, for example using a number line, if needed.

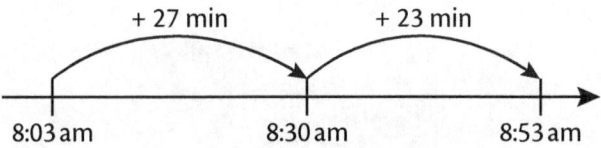

- Pupils should explain that Nina's journey is 5 minutes longer than 45 minutes.
- Finally, consider the third scenario. Do pupils recognise that the distances are given in different units? Can they convert 4000 m to km? Agree that there are 1000 metres in a kilometre, so 4000 m is equivalent to 4 lots of 1 km.

 *Four thousand metres is equal to four lots of 1 km, 4 km.*

- Ask: *What do we know about the distance that Alice cycles? What do we need to do?* Establish that we only know the distance to the beach, so we need to double that value to find the total distance cycled. Can pupils explain that Luka cycled the longer distance, 10 km, which is 2 km further than 8 km (2 × 4 km).

- Display the following problems.

Distance?	Faster?	Shorter time?
Ben runs at 4 km/h. Sam runs at 50 m/min. It takes both Ben and Sam half an hour to run from their homes to the park. How far do they each live from the park?	Asha's journey of 90 km takes 45 minutes. Nina's journey starts at 8:03 a.m. and ends at 8:53 a.m. Her journey is a distance of 150 km. Who travelled at the faster speed?	Luka cycles for 10 km at a speed of 20 km/h. Alice cycles from her house to the beach and back at a speed of 8 km/h. The distance from her house to the park is 4000 m. Whose journey took the shorter time?

- Assign a problem each to different groups of pupils. Can they work together to explain what each problem is asking and how it can be solved? Work with groups as required to make sense of the new problems, bringing the class back together to clarify any points or to revisit the formulae for calculating speed, time or distance. Pupils should prepare to feed back to the rest of the class, explaining any decisions they have made.
- Confirm the following solutions, writing the calculations that were used each time:
  - Ben lives 2 km from the park because 4 × 0.5 = 2 or half of 4 is 2.
  - Sam lives 1.5 km from the park because 3 × 0.5 = 1.5 or half of 3 is 1.5.
  - Nina's journey is faster with a speed of 3 km/min because 150 ÷ 50 = 3.
  - Asha's journey is slower with a speed of 2 km/min because 95 ÷ 45 = 2.
  - Luka and Alice took the same time of half an hour (30 min) to complete their cycle rides because 10 ÷ 20 = 0.5 or $\frac{1}{2}$ and 4 ÷ 8 = 0.5 or $\frac{1}{2}$.
- Pupils should complete Question 4 in the Practice Book.

Chapter 3 Dividing by 2-digit numbers

Unit 3.2 Practice Book 5A, pages 56–58

Same-day intervention

- Give pupils **Resource 5.3.2c** Speedy dominoes (2). Can pupils work together to arrange all the dominoes (loop cards) so that each question is answered?

Answers: Animals should be in the following order (starting at any point): Dog, Rabbit, Pony, Lion, Cat, Horse, Squirrel, Fox, Mouse, Bird (and then back to Dog).

Same-day enrichment

- Show pupils **Resource 5.3.2d** Speed problems. Work together as a group, discussing starting points and what is known and unknown. Can pupils use the information to complete the table and give possible departure and arrival times for each coach? Can they explain how they can use the given information to help them? Look at strategies for dividing 420 by 80. Can pupils explain why the quotient will be the same as for 42 by 8?

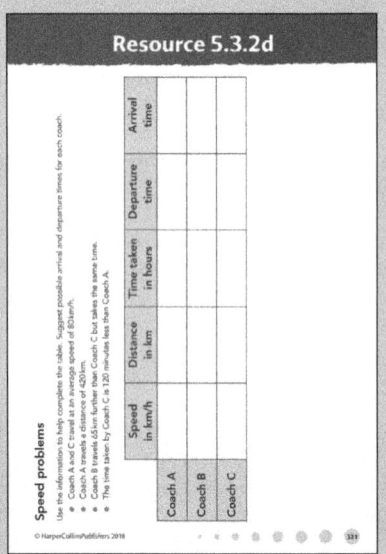

Challenge and extension question

Question 5

5. Four pupils were having a 100 m running race. Lily ran at 8 m/s, Anna took 13 seconds, Linda took 12 seconds and Mary ran at 7 m/s.

Who ran the fastest among the four pupils? _____

This problem requires pupils to compare the information about four runners to find the fastest over the same distance.

Pupils should recognise that the given speeds of both Lily and Mary can be easily compared, with Lily being the faster of the two. Additionally, the times taken by Linda and Anna can be easily compared, with Linda taking the least amount of time.

Pupils should be able to explain that they now need only to consider Linda and Lily. However, as the information about them is different, they must either use a formula to calculate Linda's speed or Lily's time to help them compare.

They should be encouraged to use estimations and what they know to determine that Linda's speed is a bit faster than 8 m/s or explain the strategies they will use to calculate 100 ÷ 8 to find Lily's time is 12.5 seconds.

Chapter 3 Dividing by 2-digit numbers

Unit 3.3
Dividing 2-digit or 3-digit numbers by a 2-digit number (1)

Conceptual context

In Year 4, pupils strengthened connections between multiplication and division, focusing on dividing by a number of tens and multiplying by a number of tens. Pupils made a link between dividing by a number of tens or hundreds (for example 630 ÷ 90 or 630 ÷ 9) and dividing by a number of ones (for example 63 ÷ 9), explaining how the dividend and quotient are related each time.

In this unit, pupils' understanding of division is extended to dividing by a two-digit number using what they know about dividing by a number of tens to help make decisions about the approximate size of the quotient. Pupils apply this understanding to the column method of division.

They continue to make decisions about problems relating to speed, time and distance, recognising that the object travelling at a greater speed is faster.

Learning pupils will have achieved at the end of the unit

- A flexible approach to using known division facts and place value to help solve related calculations will have been developed (Q1)
- Pupils will be able to identify an equivalent simple division fact because they understand that the quotient is the same if the dividend and divisor are both multiplied by the same factor (Q1, Q3)
- Pupils will have related division to multiplication, recognising that they can multiply the divisor to determine how many groups of the divisor are in the dividend (Q2, Q3)
- Mental methods to multiply a two-digit number by a one-digit number will have been applied as pupils find multiples that are close to a given dividend (Q2, Q3)
- Procedural skills of dividing by a two-digit number using a column method (and conceptual understanding of why the procedure is effective) will have been developed (Q3)
- Pupils will be able to explain that when comparing speeds, the object with the greater speed is faster and that this means the same distance will be covered in less time (Q4)

Resources

place value counters; squared paper; 1–6 dice; **Resource 5.3.3a** More than, less than or equal; **Resource 5.3.3b** Dividing by 24; **Resource 5.3.3c** What division am I solving?; **Resource 5.3.3d** Fastest and slowest; **Resource 5.3.3e** Fastest first

Vocabulary

division, divide, dividend, divisor, quotient, remainder, equivalent, multiple, speed

Chapter 3 Dividing by 2-digit numbers

Unit 3.3 Practice Book 5A, pages 59–62

Question 1

1 Work these out mentally and then write the answers.
(a) 6 ÷ 2 =
(b) 8 ÷ 4 =
(c) 9 ÷ 3 =
(d) 21 ÷ 7 =
(e) 60 ÷ 2 =
(f) 80 ÷ 4 =
(g) 90 ÷ 3 =
(h) 210 ÷ 7 =
(i) 600 ÷ 20 =
(j) 80 ÷ 40 =
(k) 90 ÷ 30 =
(l) 210 ÷ 70 =
(m) 600 ÷ 200 =
(n) 800 ÷ 400 =
(o) 900 ÷ 300 =
(p) 2100 ÷ 700 =

What learning will pupils have achieved at the conclusion of Question 1?

- A flexible approach to using known division facts and place value to help solve related calculations will have been developed.
- Pupils will be able to identify an equivalent simple division fact because they understand that the quotient is the same if the dividend and divisor are both multiplied by the same factor.

Activities for whole-class instruction

- Give pupils sets of place value counters. Ask them to arrange:
  - 8 ones counters into rows of 4 ones
  - 8 tens counters into rows of 4 tens
  - 8 hundreds counters into rows of 4 hundreds.
- Can pupils explain what is the same and what is different about each array?
- Using the image below, ensure that pupils recognise the following:
  - all the arrays have the same number of counters in total
  - the numbers of rows and columns are the same
  - the value of each row, column or total becomes 10 times larger each time
  - the value of each row, column and total in the array of hundreds counters is 100 times larger than the array of ones counters.

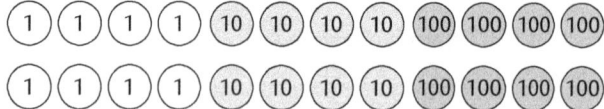

- Pupils should now use the rows and columns of each array to help write the related multiplication and division statements.
- Record these as:

  2 × 4 = 8   2 × 40 = 80   2 × 400 = 800
  4 × 2 = 8   4 × 20 = 80   4 × 200 = 800
  8 ÷ 4 = 2   80 ÷ 40 = 2   800 ÷ 400 = 2
  8 ÷ 2 = 4   80 ÷ 20 = 4   800 ÷ 200 = 4

- Agree that we can also use the commutativity of multiplication to record other facts, for example 40 × 2 and 400 × 2.
- Focus on the division statements. Ask: *What do you notice about the dividend, the divisor and the quotient each time?* Establish that these are equivalent divisions as the quotient is the same for each row of calculations. Look together at the dividend and divisor each time, agreeing that both are scaled by the same amount, for example 80 is 10 times larger than 8 and 40 is 10 times larger than 4.

  All say ... *Eighty divided by forty is the same as eight divided by four.*

- Ask pupils to create their own sentence to explain what division(s) 800 ÷ 400 is equivalent to.
- Show pupils the following set of divisions:

  12 ÷ 3   120 ÷ 3   120 ÷ 30
  1200 ÷ 30   1200 ÷ 300

- Read each division together using the language of ones, tens and hundreds to describe them, for example 12 ones divided by 3 ones, 12 tens divided by 3 ones and so on.
- Pupils should work in pairs to reason about which divisions are equivalent and will result in the same quotient. Can they explain why the division that shows a number of ones (12) divided by a number of ones (3) and the division showing 12 tens divided by 3 tens will result in the same quotient?

(i) When the dividend and the divisor are scaled by the same amount, the quotient will remain the same. Pupils will later relate this to other scale factors and not just multiples of 10 or 100. For example 12 ÷ 4 is an equivalent division to 24 ÷ 8 because both the dividend and the divisor are twice the size.

- Return to the divisions 120 ÷ 3 and 1200 ÷ 30, agreeing that these do not have the same number of tens (3 tens) or hundreds (3 hundreds) as the divisor, for example the dividend 12 ones has been scaled by 10 to give 12 tens but the divisor has not. Use the image below to model this.

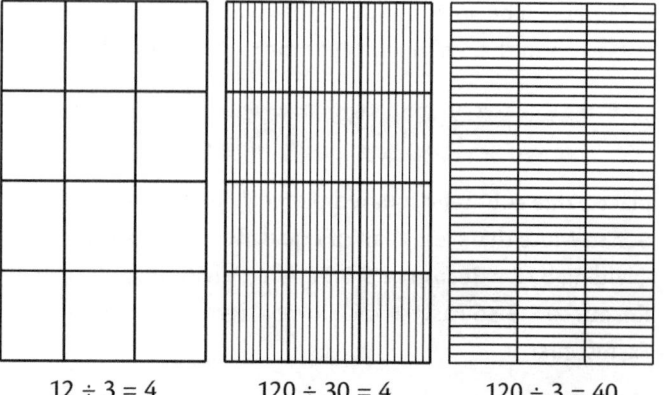

12 ÷ 3 = 4   120 ÷ 30 = 4   120 ÷ 3 = 40

104

Chapter 3 Dividing by 2-digit numbers

Unit 3.3 Practice Book 5A, pages

- Agree that 120 ÷ 3 gives a quotient that is 10 times larger than 12 ÷ 3 because 120 is 10 times larger than 12 but the divisor is the same. Ask: *How many times larger is the quotient for 1200 ÷ 30 than 120 ÷ 30? Why?*

1200 ÷ 30 is 10 times larger than 120 ÷ 30 because the dividend 1200 is 10 times larger.

- Give pupils the opportunity to reason about another set of divisions in the same way, explaining which are equivalent and which are not. For example:

  15 ÷ 5   150 ÷ 5   150 ÷ 50
  1500 ÷ 500   1500 ÷ 50

- Pupils should complete Question 1 in the Practice Book.

Same-day intervention

- Look together at the examples from Question 1 using counters or sketching arrays to show which divisions are equivalent. Can pupils explain why some divisions are not equivalent? They should be able to explain that 60 ÷ 2 is not equivalent to 6 ÷ 2 because 6 tens is being divided by 2 rather than 6 ones. The dividend 60 is 10 times larger than 6, but the divisor is still the same.

Same-day enrichment

- Give pupils **Resource 5.3.3a** More than, less than or equal. Pupils should use each of the division calculations once, writing them in the empty spaces to make all statements correct.
- Pupils can then make up their own puzzle for others to solve in the same way.

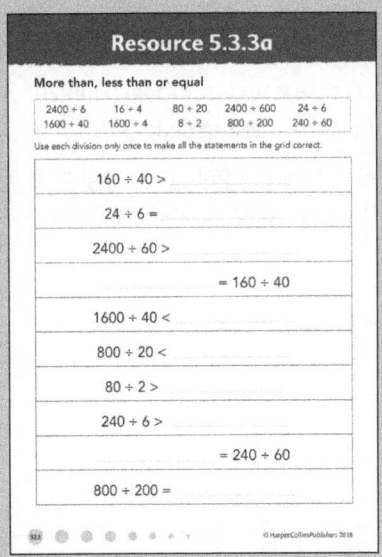

Question 2

2 Answer the questions about each calculation and then calculate the answer.

(a) In 99 ÷ 23 =

How many twenty-threes are there in 99?

Think: How many _____ are there in 99?

There are _____ in 99. The quotient is _____ .

_____ × 23 = _____ .

The remainder _____ is _____ than the divisor.

The quotient is _____ .

(b) In 517 ÷ 63 =

How many sixty-threes are there in 517?

Think: How many _____ are there in 517?

There are _____ in 517. The quotient is _____ .

_____ × 63 = _____ .

The remainder _____ is _____ than the divisor.

The quotient is _____ .

What learning will pupils have achieved at the conclusion of Question 2?

- Pupils will have related division to multiplication, recognising that they can multiply the divisor to determine how many groups of the divisor are in the dividend.
- Mental methods to multiply a two-digit number by a one-digit number will have been applied as pupils find multiples that are close to a given dividend.

Activities for whole-class instruction

- Show pupils the following multiplication calculations:

  6 × 39   6 × 63   5 × 68   3 × 73
  4 × 86   7 × 42

- Draw two circles on the board to show sets, one labelled 'products greater than 300' and the other labelled 'products less than 300'.

- Ask: *What does approximate mean?* Agree that it means 'close to'. Discuss how rounding can help to find answers that will be close to the accurate answers; rounding can give approximate answers, or approximations.

- Ask pupil pairs to round each of the calculations on the board so that you could easily find approximate answers and then work out those approximations mentally. Can pupils tell you the following? (Write each original calculation in the correct set.)

  – 6 × 40 = 6 × 4 × 10, *so the product of 6 × 39 is approximately 240*

Chapter 3 Dividing by 2-digit numbers Unit 3.3 Practice Book 5A, pages 59–62

- $6 \times 60 = 6 \times 6 \times 10$, so the product of 6×63 is approximately 360
- $5 \times 70 = 5 \times 7 \times 10$, so the product of 5×68 is approximately 350
- $3 \times 70 = 3 \times 7 \times 10$, so the product of 3×73 is approximately 210
- $4 \times 90 = 4 \times 9 \times 10$, so the product of 4×86 is approximately 360
- $7 \times 40 = 7 \times 4 \times 10$, so the product of 7×42 is approximately 280

- Focus on the first example. Ask: *Will 6 × 40 be more or less than 6 × 39? Why?* Repeat for others on the list.
- Explain that pupils are going to use their knowledge about multiplication and approximating to help make decisions about division calculations. Show the division 89 ÷ 22, reading this together as '89 divided by 22'.

- Ask: *How many twenty-twos are there in 89? Who is right, Alfie or Nisha? How do you know?* Can pupils use approximation to explain that 5 × 22 is more than 5 × 20, so the product is more than 100? Agree that the quotient must be less than five.
- **Look out for** … pupils who do not recognise that the product must be less than 89, perhaps sketching rows of 22 to make up an array to show that four rows of 22 is one less than 89, but another row of 22 is more than 89.
- Establish that there are 4 twenty-twos in 89 because 4 × 22 = 88, so the quotient must be 4. It cannot be more because if another 22 (the divisor) is added, the dividend (89) is exceeded.
- Sketch a quick array (see below) to show that there are 4 twenty-twos in 89 and to establish the remainder. Model mental methods of multiplication, for example finding the part products 4 × 20 and 4 × 2 to establish that 4 × 22 = 88.

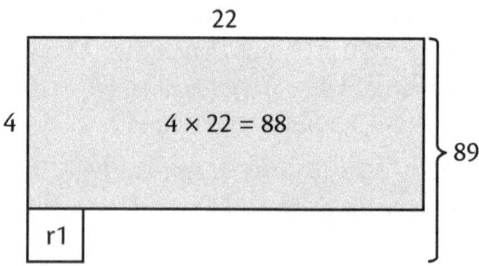

- Record this as:

  89 ÷ 22   There are 4 twenty-twos in 89.

  The quotient is 4.

  4 × 22 = 88

  The remainder is 1.

- Show pupils another calculation: $39\overline{)245}$. Ask: *How many thirty-nines are there in 245? How can we use approximation to help?* Pupils should work together, recognising that 6 × 39 is a bit less than 6 × 40 = 240. Remind them to use mental methods of multiplication.
- Ask pupils to quickly sketch an array to represent the division. Share the arrays and use them to complete the sentences as before:

  $39\overline{)245}$ There are 6 thirty-nines in 245.

  The quotient is 6.

  6 × 39 = 234

  The remainder is 11.

  The remainder is less than the divisor.

- Pupils should complete Question 2 in the Practice Book.

Same-day intervention

- Give pupils **Resource 5.3.3b** Dividing by 24. They should first complete the multiplication facts about 24 and then use them to help solve a set of divisions with divisor, 24. There is an additional problem that requires pupils to find the missing dividend.
- Discuss the different problems as required, moving between the intervention group and enrichment group.

Chapter 3 Dividing by 2-digit numbers

Unit 3.3 Practice Book 5A, pages 59–62

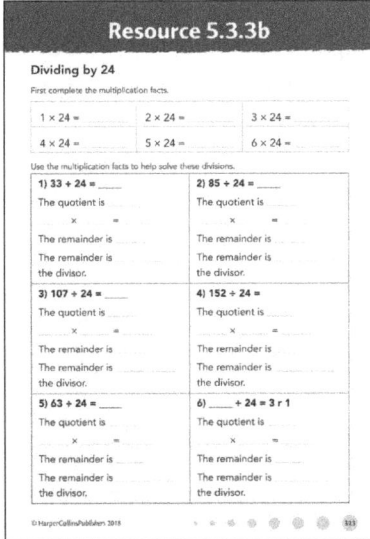

Answers: 24, 48, 72, 96, 120, 144
1) 1 r 9, 1, 1 x 24 = 24, 9, less than
2) 3 r 13, 3, 3 x 24 = 72, 13, less than
3) 4 r 11, 4, 4 x 24 = 96, 11, less than
4) 6 r 8, 6, 6 x 24 = 144, 8, less than
5) 2 r 15, 2, 2 x 24 = 48, 15, less than
6) 73, 3, 3 x 24 = 72, 1, less than

Same-day enrichment

- Give pupils **Resource 5.3.3c** What division am I solving? Three children are talking about the multiplications they used to help solve divisions. Pupils should use the information to reason about the possible divisions the children have been solving.

- During the activity, discuss examples of divisions that the children could not be solving, for example Ben cannot be solving 279 ÷ 42 because 7 × 42 = 280 and this is larger than the dividend 279. This division would result in a smaller quotient.

Question 3

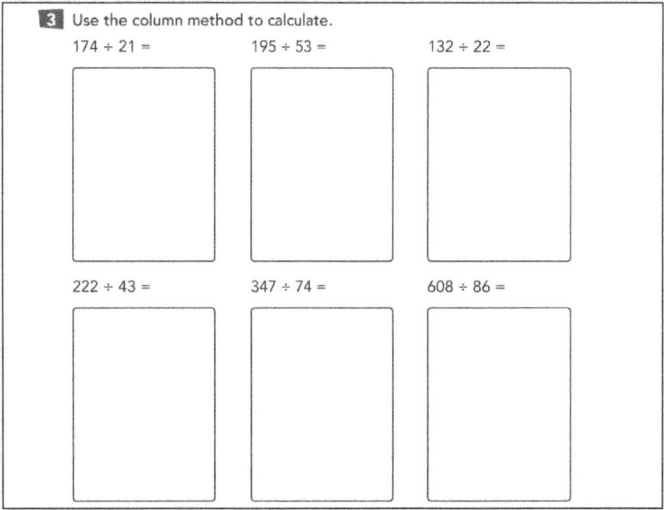

What learning will pupils have achieved at the conclusion of Question 3?

- Pupils will be able to identify an equivalent simple division fact because they understand that the quotient is the same if the dividend and divisor are both multiplied by the same factor.

- Pupils will have related division to multiplication, recognising that they can multiply the divisor to determine how many groups of the divisor are in the dividend.

- Mental methods to multiply a two-digit number by a one-digit number will have been applied as pupils find multiples that are close to a given dividend.

- Procedural skills of dividing by a two-digit number using a column method (and conceptual understanding of why the procedure is effective) will have been developed.

Activities for whole-class instruction

- Give pairs of pupils a 1–6 dice and display the calculations shown below.

84 ÷ 20	274 ÷ 91	454 ÷ 92	190 ÷ 90
476 ÷ 77	68 ÷ 42	540 ÷ 88	157 ÷ 38
285 ÷ 69	151 ÷ 33	143 ÷ 68	45 ÷ 34
124 ÷ 61	204 ÷ 50	243 ÷ 82	175 ÷ 29

- Explain that pupils should take it in turns to roll the dice to generate an approximate quotient. They should work together to find a division on the grid that matches this approximate quotient. For example, having rolled 2, select 124 ÷ 61.

- Share ideas and reasoning. Discuss whether the actual quotients will be more or less than the approximations.

Chapter 3 Dividing by 2-digit numbers

Unit 3.3 Practice Book 5A, pages 59–62

- Focus on 157 ÷ 38, agreeing that a good estimate is 4 because 160 ÷ 40 = 4 and 4 × 40 = 160. Explain that the calculation can be completed using the column method, setting this out as:

  38)‾157‾

- Ask: *How many 38s are in 157?* Agree that 4 × 40 = 160, so the answer will be close to 4. Ask: *Will the answer be 4? Are there more than 4 thirty-eights in 157?*

- Can pupils multiply 38 by 4 mentally, by finding part products and combining? So, 4 × 38 = 4 × 30 + 4 × 8 = 120 + 32 = 152. They might round and adjust: 4 × 38 = (4 × 40) − (4 × 2) = 160 − 8 = 152.

- Agree that 152 is less than the dividend 157, so 4 is indeed the quotient – as long as another 38 (the divisor) cannot be added without exceeding 157 (the dividend). Since the remainder is only 5 – less than 38 – the quotient is 4.

- Record this step in the column method, asking pupils to identify the parts of the calculation, for example dividend, divisor and so on.

```
       4
  38)157
     152     (4 × 38)
     ___
       5
```

All say... *157 ÷ 38 is 4 remainder 5 because 157 is 5 more than 4 × 38.*

 ... pupils who find it difficult to identify the dividend, the divisor, the quotient and the remainder. Rewrite the calculation as 157 ÷ 38 = 4 r5 and ask pupils to sketch a matching array, identifying the parts of the calculation each time.

- Practise a few more examples from the grid together, for example 151 ÷ 33 and 285 ÷ 69, recording each in the column method. Use pupils estimated quotients from the start of the lesson to inform choices and focus on the use of mental methods of multiplication. Ask pupils to identify the dividend, divisor, quotient and remainder each time.

- Pupils should complete Question 3 in the Practice Book.

Same-day intervention

- Work through the examples in Question 3 together, using rounding to help approximate quotients. Identify equivalent divisions that can be used. Practise each step of the column method, relating this to a matching array each time.

- You may find it useful to build up the arrays on squared paper using repeated addition and then multiplication to identify the quotient. For example, for 174 ÷ 21:

21	1 × 21 = 21
21	2 × 21 = 42
21	3 × 21 = 63
21	4 × 21 = 84
21	5 × 21 = 105
21	6 × 21 = 126
21	7 × 21 = 147
21	8 × 21 = 168

r6

- Choose another division from the grid used in the whole-class instruction for pupils to practise independently.

Same-day enrichment

- Pupils should use the divisions from the grid where approximate quotients were 6 in the whole-class session. They should find the actual quotient and determine a remainder using the column method.

- Can they make up some more divisions of their own that result in the quotient 6? They should prove their ideas to a partner using approximation and then the column method. How many different divisions can they make with the quotient 6?

Chapter 3 Dividing by 2-digit numbers

Unit 3.3 Practice Book 5A, pages 59–62

Question 4

> **4** These animals are having a 1 km running race. Look at their speeds and answer the questions.
>
> 12 m/s   10 m/s   13 m/s
>
> In 1st place is _____
>
> Reason: _____
>
> In 2nd place is _____
>
> Reason: _____
>
> In 3rd place is _____
>
> Reason: _____

What learning will pupils have achieved at the conclusion of Question 4?

- Pupils will be able to explain that when comparing speeds, the object with the greater speed is faster and that this means the same distance will be covered in less time.

Activities for whole-class instruction

- Remind pupils about the work they have been doing related to speed, time and distance. Display the following scenarios:
  - Beth and Kit run a 100 metre race. Beth finishes the race in 14.2 seconds and Kit in 13.9 seconds.
  - Two buses each travel for 2 hours. One bus travels a distance of 48 km and the other travels 36 km.
  - Jade and Sam both cycle the same distance around the park. Jade cycles at 12 km/h and Sam at 13 km/h.
- Ask: *Who or what is faster each time? What can you compare? What does it tell you?*
- Display each scenario in turn, together with a writing frame for discussion.
  - Beth and Kit run the same distance and the time for each is given in seconds.
    - by comparing _____
      we can see _____
      (must have been _____).
  - The two buses travel for the same length of time and the distances are both given in kilometres.
    - by comparing _____
      we can see _____
      (must have been _____).
  - Jade and Sam cycle the same distance and the speeds are given using the same measurement.
    - by comparing _____
      we can see _____
      (must have _____).
- Fill in the missing sections as follows:
  - Beth and Kit run the same distance and the time for each is given in seconds.
    - by comparing <u>the number of seconds it took to run the distance</u> we can see <u>who did it in fewer seconds</u> (must have been <u>running faster</u>).
  - The two buses travel for the same length of time and the distances are both given in kilometres.
    - by comparing <u>the distance travelled in the time</u> we can see <u>which bus travelled further</u> (must have been <u>moving faster</u>).
  - Jade and Sam cycle the same distance and the speeds are given using the same measurement.
    - by comparing <u>the speed at which each was travelling</u> we can see <u>who was cycling faster</u> and (must have <u>finished first</u>).
- Pupils should complete Question 4 in the Practice Book.

Same-day intervention

- Give pupils **Resource 5.3.3d** Fastest and slowest. Can they find the fastest and slowest thing each time?

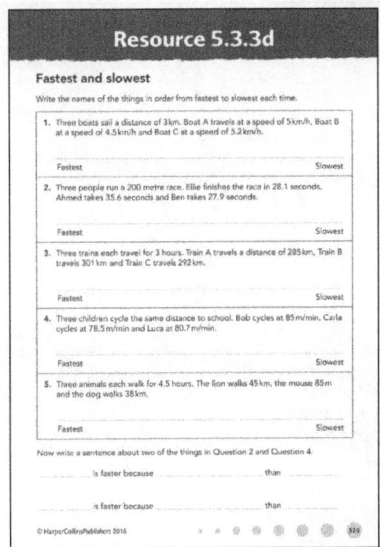

Answers: 1. Boat C, Boat A, Boat B; 2. Ben, Ellie, Ahmed; 3. Train B, Train C, Train A; 4. Bob, Luca, Carla; 5. Lion, Dog, Mouse; Various sentences possible.

109

Chapter 3 Dividing by 2-digit numbers

Unit 3.3 Practice Book 5A, pages 59–62

Same-day enrichment

- Introduce the problem set out on **Resource 5.3.3e** Fastest first. Ensure that pupils understand that they must find the child who runs at the greatest speed each time using the given clues.
- Each set of clues gives the same information, either time and distance or just speed. However, the information is not given in the same units of measurement each time, so pupils are required to convert. Discuss conversions and the decisions pupils must make each time to find the fastest runners.
- Finally, pupils should compare the three fastest runners from the races and apply formulae as required to find who ran at the greatest speed, second greatest speed and third greatest speed.

Answer: Jane, Anesha, Jemma

Challenge and extension question

Question 5

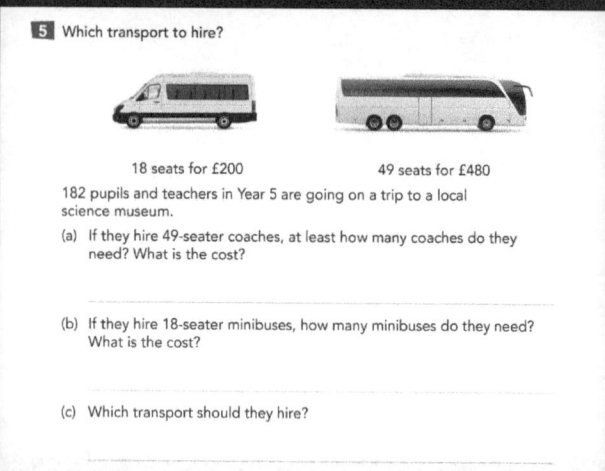

In this problem, pupils are required to find the lowest number of 18-seater coaches and the lowest number of 49-seater coaches that can be hired to take a group of 182 pupils and teachers on a trip. They must also calculate the cost each time and then use this information to decide which is the better deal.

They should apply strategies to divide 182 by 18 and then by 49, recognising that 180 is 10 × 18 but that an extra coach is required as they interpret the remainder in the context of the problem.

Column or mental methods of division can be applied as pupils reason about the number of 49s in 182, perhaps relating this to the number of 50s in 182. Pupils should be able to explain that the actual remainder for the division 182 ÷ 49 does not need to be found as another group of 49 cannot be made but an extra coach is still required for the pupils and teachers who are left over.

Chapter 3 Dividing by 2-digit numbers

Unit 3.4
Dividing 2-digit or 3-digit numbers by a 2-digit number (2)

Conceptual context

In the previous unit, pupils' understanding of division was extended to dividing by a two-digit number using what they know about dividing by a number of tens to help make decisions about the size of the quotient. They used strategies of rounding and mental multiplication to find approximate products that could be used to inform decisions about possible quotients, for example for the division 245 ÷ 39 they used the multiplication 6 × 40 = 240 to estimate the quotient as 6. Pupils also connected their understanding of equivalent division to begin to think about approximations, for example for 245 ÷ 39, relating 240 ÷ 40 to the division 24 ÷ 4, recognising that the quotient for each will be the same.

Pupils began to apply this understanding to the column method of division, which will be further developed in this unit.

Learning pupils will have achieved at the end of the unit

- Pupils will be able to identify an equivalent division fact because they understand that the quotient is the same if the dividend and divisor are both multiplied by the same factor (Q1, Q2, Q3, Q4)
- Pupils will have related division to multiplication, recognising that they can multiply the divisor to determine how many groups of the divisor are in the dividend (Q1, Q2, Q3)
- Mental methods to multiply a two-digit number by a one-digit number will have been applied as pupils find multiples that are close to a given dividend (Q1, Q3)
- Understanding of the relationship between the size of the divisor and the possible size of a remainder will have been strengthened (Q1, Q2)
- Conceptual understanding of dividing by a two-digit number using a column method will have been developed (Q2, Q4)
- Pupils' application of the inverse will have been consolidated as they reason about missing number problems (Q3)
- The relationship between division and multiplication will have been strengthened as pupils solve word problems (Q5)

Resources

counting stick; highlighter pens; pencil and paper; **Resource 5.3.4a** Guess the group; **Resource 5.3.4b** The divisor is 32; **Resource 5.3.4c** Division errors; **Resource 5.3.3c** What division am I solving? (from Unit 3.3); **Resource 5.3.4d** Domino divisors; **Resource 5.3.4e** Writing division problems

Vocabulary

division, divide, dividend, divisor, quotient, remainder, equivalent, multiple

Chapter 3 Dividing by 2-digit numbers

Unit 3.4 Practice Book 5A, pages 63–66

Question 1

1 For each calculation, complete the statements then work out the answer. The first one has been done for you.

(a) 51)̄160

Think: When 16 ÷ 5, the quotient is ☐3☐.

We get: ☐3☐ × 51 = ☐153☐.

The quotient is __just right__. (Choose: just right, too big or too small.)

(b) 63)̄480

Think: When 48 ÷ 6, the quotient is ☐.

We get: ☐ × 63 = ☐.

The quotient is _____. (Choose: just right, too big or too small.)

Change the quotient to ☐.

☐ × 63 = ☐.

The remainder is ☐; it is _____ than the divisor.

Therefore, the quotient ☐ is the right choice.

(c) 93)̄360

Think: When 36 ÷ 9, the quotient is ☐.

We get: ☐ × 93 = ☐.

The quotient is _____. (Choose: just right, too big or too small.)

Change the quotient to ☐.

☐ × 93 = ☐.

The remainder is ☐; it is _____ than the divisor.

Therefore, the quotient ☐ is the right choice.

(d) 43)̄334

Think: When 33 ÷ 4, the quotient is ☐.

We get: ☐ × 43 = ☐.

The quotient is _____. (Choose: just right, too big or too small.)

Change the quotient to ☐.

☐ × 43 = ☐.

The remainder is ☐; it is _____ than the divisor.

Therefore, the quotient ☐ is the right choice.

What learning will pupils have achieved at the conclusion of Question 1?

- Pupils will be able to identify an equivalent simple division fact because they understand that the quotient is the same if the dividend and divisor are both multiplied by the same factor.
- Pupils will have related division to multiplication, recognising that they can multiply the divisor to determine how many groups of the divisor are in the dividend.
- Mental methods to multiply a two-digit number by a one-digit number will have been applied as pupils find multiples that are close to a given dividend.
- An understanding of the relationship between the size of the divisor and the possible size of a remainder will have been strengthened.

Activities for whole-class instruction

- Using a counting stick or a number line with 10 divisions, count together in steps of 70 from zero. Stop after four steps (280). Ask: *How many 70s are in 280? How do you know?*
- Pupils should record a matching multiplication and division statement. Record these as 4 × 70 = 280 and 280 ÷ 70 = 4.

 *4 × 7 tens equals 28 tens, so 28 tens divided by 7 tens is 4.*

- Ask pupils for an equivalent division that gives the same quotient. (28 ÷ 7 = 4) Agree that if we counted in steps of 7, it would also take 4 steps of 7 to reach 28.
- Return to the counting stick and continue to count in steps of 70, this time stopping after 7 steps (490). Ask: *How many 70s are in 490? So how many 7s are in 49?* Again, pupils should write matching multiplication and division statements, agreeing that 49 ÷ 7 is an equivalent division.
- Show the following image of the counting stick with the number marked.

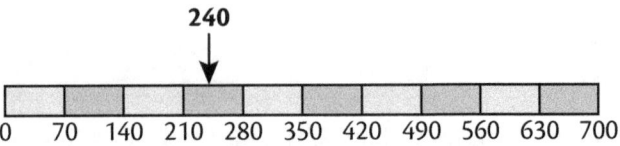

- Ask: *What is 240 divided by 70? What is the quotient? Are there as many as four 70s in 240? How do you know?*

112

Chapter 3 Dividing by 2-digit numbers

Unit 3.4 Practice Book 5A, pages 63–66

Are there more than two 70s in 240? How do you know? Invite pupils to discuss the questions and to explain their answers.

- Share ideas, establishing that:
  - there are more than two 70s in 240 because another group of 70 can be made from the remaining 100
  - the quotient 2 is too small
  - there are less than four 70s in 240 as another 40 is needed to make a fourth group
  - the quotient 4 is too big
  - there are three 70s in 210, which is less than 240, but the reminder is not big enough to make another group of 70
  - the quotient 3 is correct.
- Record this together as:

  $$70\overline{)240}^{\ 3\ r\ 30}$$

  $210 \div 70 = 3$
  $3 \times 70 = 210$
  The remainder is 30.

- Now show pupils the following division, establishing that it is different because the divisor is not a multiple of 10:

  $370 \div 72$

- Explain that we can still use division facts that we know to help us estimate quotients. Ask: *How many 7s are in 37?* (5) Can pupils explain why you have asked this question rather than how many 70s are in 370?
- Agree that $37 \div 7$ and $370 \div 70$ are equivalent divisions as they share the same quotient. It is often easier to work with smaller numbers. Discuss how, in this case, it is easy to use the number of tens in the dividend and the divisor to keep the calculation simple.
- Return to the division $370 \div 72$. Write: 'When $37 \div 7$, the quotient is 5'. Ask pupils to suggest how they could find out whether the quotient, 5, will be too big, too small or just right for the division $370 \div 72$. Agree that the size of the remainder is important.
- Look together at strategies for 72×5, for example finding part products or multiplying by 10 and then halving. Agree that $72 \times 5 = 360$, which is 10 less than 370, so the remainder is 10. Ask: *How do we know that the quotient is not too small? How do we know that the quotient is not too big?*

(i) To help check whether the quotient that has been calculated is correct, pupils should recognise that if another group of the divisor can be made with the remainder, the quotient is too small. If the quotient multiplied by the divisor results in a number larger than the dividend, the quotient is incorrect; it is too big.

- Complete the recording for the division so it reads as:

  $370 \div 72$ When $37 \div 7$, the quotient is 5.
  $5 \times 72 = 360$
  The quotient is just right.
  The remainder is 10.

- Discuss the following divisions in the same way:

  $370 \div 78$ $415 \div 71$

- Can pupils explain which equivalent divisions they can use to help estimate the quotient each time? Which tens numbers will they use for the dividend and the divisor? Establish that $37 \div 7$ and $370 \div 70$ are equivalent divisions and that $41 \div 7$ and $410 \div 70$ are also equivalent.
- Agree that the quotient for both $37 \div 7$ and $41 \div 7$ is 5. (There will be a remainder in both cases.) Split the class into two groups, asking one half to reason about the estimated quotient for $370 \div 78$ and the other, $415 \div 71$. Can they explain whether the quotient will be too small, too big or just right?

Look out for ... pupils who struggle to make the connection between multiplication and division, not recognising that they can multiply 78 by 5 or 71 by 5 to help make decisions. Return to the counting stick and the matching statements made earlier, looking at the relationship between the operations.

- Share ideas, establishing that:
  - $5 \times 78 = 390$ is larger than the dividend 370, so the quotient 5 is too big. The quotient 4 should be tried.
  - $5 \times 71 = 355$ is smaller than the dividend 415. The remainder is 60, so another group of 71 cannot be made.
- Finally, agree and record the calculations, for example:

  $370 \div 78$ When $37 \div 7$, the quotient is 5.
  $5 \times 78 = 390$
  The quotient is too big.
  Change the quotient to 4.
  $4 \times 78 = 312$
  The remainder is 58. The quotient of 4 is correct.

- Pupils should complete Question 1 in the Practice Book.

Chapter 3 Dividing by 2-digit numbers

Unit 3.4 Practice Book 5A, pages 63–66

Same-day intervention

- Look together at the examples from Question 1, drawing out equivalent divisions to help make decisions. Focus particularly on the divisions where the estimated quotients were too big, discussing why this is the case. Revise strategies for mental multiplication as required.
- Work together on another division, 230 ÷ 45, using 23 ÷ 4 to estimate the quotient. Can pupils explain why you have chosen 23 ÷ 4? Use the counting stick or number lines to record jumps of 45 to help find the product of 5 × 45.

Same-day enrichment

- Give pupils **Resource 5.3.4a** Guess the group. They should match the questions to the correct group of children, using the information about divisions to help them. They should record the remainder each time.

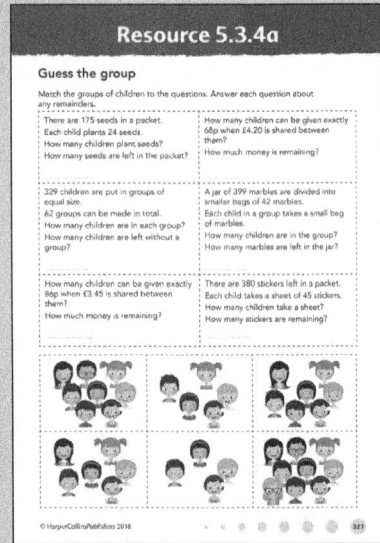

Answers: 7 children, 7 seeds remaining; 6 children, 12p remaining; 5 children in each group, 4 children remaining; 9 children in the group, 21 marbles remaining; 4 children, 1p remaining; 8 children, 20 stickers remaining.

Question 2

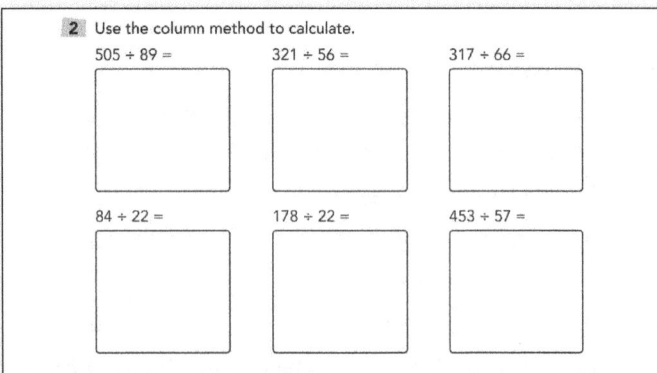

What learning will pupils have achieved at the conclusion of Question 2?

- Pupils will be able to identify an equivalent simple division fact because they understand that the quotient is the same if the dividend and divisor are both multiplied by the same factor.
- Pupils will have related division to multiplication, recognising that they can multiply the divisor to determine how many groups of the divisor are in the dividend.
- An understanding of the relationship between the size of the divisor and the possible size of a remainder will have been strengthened.
- Conceptual understanding of dividing by a two-digit number using a column method will have been developed.

Activities for whole-class instruction

Activities for whole-class instruction

- Show pupils the image of the 'Quotient spinner'.

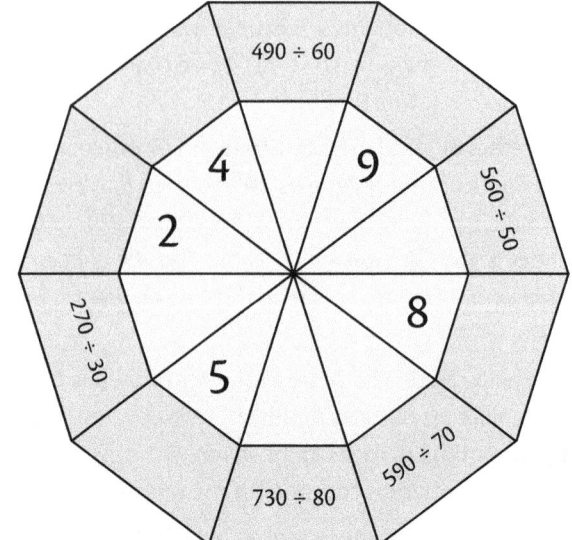

Chapter 3 Dividing by 2-digit numbers

Unit 3.4 Practice Book 5A, pages 63–66

- Explain that some of the information on the quotient spinner is missing. Assign the missing quotients to half the class and the missing divisions to the other, establishing that the missing divisions involve multiples of 10. Can pupils use equivalent divisions to help finding missing quotients? Can they use division facts and place value to find missing divisions?

- Share pupils' ideas, exploring the missing quotients and relating these to equivalent divisions. Discuss the remainders each time, agreeing that these are less than the divisor, so an additional group cannot be made.

- Say that you have also been thinking about some possible division statements for the quotient 4. Share the division 310 ÷ 80. Ask: *What equivalent division should I use to check?* (31 ÷ 8) Establish that the quotient 4 is too large, so the division is not possible for this quotient. Can pupils explain how the dividend can be changed so that the quotient is 4?

- Look together at pupils' ideas for other quotients, using equivalents to check each time.

- Suggest that 743 ÷ 95 will also give the quotient 8. Ask: *Is the quotient too big, too small or just right?* Agree that when 74 is divided by 9, the quotient is 8 and that 8 × 95 = 760. However, 760 is larger than the dividend 743, so the quotient is too big. The quotient is 7.

- Sketch an array:

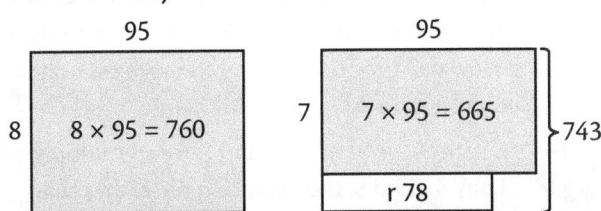

- Use the column method to model the division as:

$$\begin{array}{r} 7 \text{ r } 78 \\ 95 \overline{)743} \\ 665 \quad (7 \times 95 = 665) \\ \hline 78 \end{array}$$

- Give pupils the opportunity to practise the column method with the following divisions:

  595 ÷ 73   492 ÷ 68   276 ÷ 35

- Work together as required to estimate quotients, apply mental strategies of multiplication and calculate remainders.

- Pupils should complete Question 2 in the Practice Book.

Same-day intervention

- Give pupils **Resource 5.3.4b** The divisor is 32. Pupils will solve a set of divisions with divisor 32, using the column method. Ask pupils to choose one of the calculations and to sketch a matching array in their books.

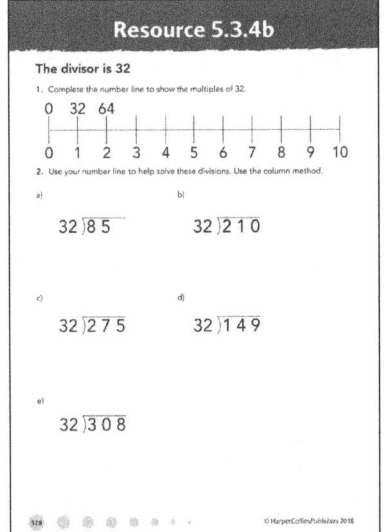

Answers: 1. 96, 128, 160, 192, 224, 256, 288, 320; 2. a) 2 r 21 b) 6 r 18 c) 8 r 19 d) 4 r 21 e) 9 r 20

Same-day enrichment

- Give pupils **Resource 5.3.4c** Division errors and highlighter pens. They should check each division carefully, highlighting and correcting errors.

Chapter 3 Dividing by 2-digit numbers

Unit 3.4 Practice Book 5A, pages 63–66

Question 3

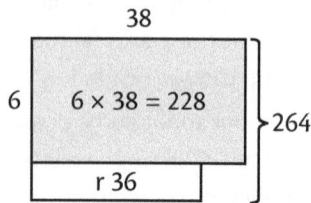

What learning will pupils have achieved at the conclusion of Question 3?

- Pupils will be able to identify an equivalent simple division fact because they understand that the quotient is the same if the dividend and divisor are both multiplied by the same factor.
- Pupils will have related division to multiplication, recognising that they can multiply the divisor to determine how many groups of the divisor are in the dividend.
- Mental methods to multiply a two-digit number by a one-digit number will have been applied as pupils find multiples that are close to a given dividend.
- Pupils' application of the inverse will have been consolidated as they reason about missing number problems.

Activities for whole-class instruction

- Share the following problem with the pupils.

Mr Golding, I would like the hall set out in rows of 38 chairs for the school concert, please.

That's fine, Mrs McNeal. We have 264 chairs we can use!

- Ask: *How do we know that Mr Golding will not be able to set out 10 rows of 38 chairs? How can we estimate the numbers of rows of chairs he can have?*
- Discuss using estimates for 264 ÷ 38, for example 260 ÷ 30 and 260 ÷ 40. (Pupils should use equivalent divisions 26 ÷ 3 and 26 ÷ 4 to help them.) Can pupils explain that 26 ÷ 4 is the most helpful calculation because 38 is closer to 40? Agree that 260 ÷ 40 and 26 ÷ 4 both give the quotient 6.

- Confirm that the quotient 6 is correct as 6 × 38 = 228, which is less than 264. Also agree that another row of 38 chairs cannot be made as the remainder is less than 38.

 *There are six 38s in 265. The remainder is less than the divisor.*

- Write '6 × 38 < 264 and 38 × 6 < 264'. Pupils could sketch an array to show this.

```
          38
      ┌─────────┐
   6  │ 6 × 38  │ ┐
      │  = 228  │ │ 264
      ├─────────┤ │
      │  r 36   │ ┘
      └─────────┘
```

- Conclude that Mr Golding can set out 6 rows of 38 chairs.
- Now explain that Mrs McNeal is unhappy that there are only 6 rows and asks Mr Golding to find another arrangement using fewer chairs in each row. Mr Golding records the following multiplication statements to help him decide the greatest number of rows he can make each time.

  32 × ☐ < 264   30 × ☐ < 264   27 × ☐ < 264

- Pupils should discuss Mr Golding's multiplication statements and explain what each one represents, for example 'He is planning to make rows of 32 and wants to find out how many 32s are in 264.' Pupils should discuss with a partner how they will work out the missing numbers. How will they use division to make estimates and use equivalent divisions to help them?
- **Look out for** … pupils who use trial and error to multiply, say 32 by 4, then 5, then 6 and so on, rather than using the inverse, division, to help make decisions. Refer back to the statements made previously, 6 × 38 < 264, and discuss how we got to this using division, rewriting this as 264 ÷ 38 to remind them.
- Agree that the missing numbers in the statements are as follows, and these are the largest possible numbers:

  32 × 8 < 264   30 × 8 < 264   27 × 9 < 264

- Pupils should complete Question 3 in the Practice Book.

Chapter 3 Dividing by 2-digit numbers

Unit 3.4 Practice Book 5A, pages 63–66

Same-day intervention

- Give pupils **Resource 5.3.3c** What division am I solving? (from Unit 3.3) and work on the problem together.

Same-day enrichment

- Give pupils **Resource 5.3.4d** Domino divisors. They should work in pairs, taking turns to lay a domino that shows the largest possible missing number each time.
- Alternatively, pupils can play the game together or individually, seeing how quickly they can lay all dominoes.

Question 4

4. Write the number sentences and then calculate.
  (a) 192 is divided by 32. What is the quotient?

  (b) What times 43 is 344?

  (c) What is the quotient of 100 000 divided by 10?

  (d) What is the quotient of 100 000 divided by 100?

What learning will pupils have achieved at the conclusion of Question 4?

- Pupils will be able to identify an equivalent simple division fact because they understand that the quotient is the same if the dividend and divisor are both multiplied by the same factor.
- Conceptual understanding of dividing by a two-digit number using a column method will have been developed.

Activities for whole-class instruction

- Split the class into three groups, labelling them 'dividend', 'divisor' and 'quotient'. Each pupil requires a pencil and paper.
- Display the following grid of numbers. Pupils should choose a number from the section for their group.

Dividends	Divisors	Quotients
276	28	5
350	33	6
387	45	7
186	52	8
465	63	9

- Explain that they will collect different division calculations by meeting a pupil from a different group. They should work together to solve the calculation using mental or column methods before moving on to another partner.
- Model the activity using the following examples:
  - *When a 'dividend', for example 276, meets a 'divisor', for example 33, they solve 276 ÷ 33 = ☐.*
  - *When a 'divisor', for example 45, meets a 'quotient', for example 8, they solve ☐ ÷ 48 = 8 by multiplying 48 × 8.*
  - *When a 'dividend', for example 276, meets a 'quotient', for example 5, they solve 276 ÷ ☐ = 5, reasoning about the largest divisor that can be used to give the quotient.*

Chapter 3 Dividing by 2-digit numbers

Unit 3.4 Practice Book 5A, pages 63–66

- Remind pupils that they may also need to think about remainders.
- Give pupils 10–15 minutes to collect and solve division calculations before sharing them together. Revisit the column method of division as required. (Keep a copy of the shared divisions for the next session.) Ask questions such as:
  - *When ... is divided by ... what is the quotient?*
  - *What is ... times ...?*
  - *What division gave you the largest quotient?*
  - *What division gave you the smallest quotient?*
  - *What was the largest remainder you found? Why?*
  - *What strategies did you use to multiply?*
  - *What equivalent divisions did you use?*
- Pose the following question: *What times 52 is 416?*
- Ask: *What is the question asking? What will we need to do?* Agree that the question is asking us to find how many times 52 goes into 416 (or how many 52s are in 56) or what can we multiply 52 by to get the product 416. Discuss how division can be used to solve this using $416 ÷ 52 = \square$.
- Explain that a similar activity was carried out using the following dividends, divisors and quotients.

Dividends	Divisors	Quotients
1000	1	20
2000	10	40
10 000	100	50

- Can pupils work together to create different division calculations in the same way, imagining, for example, that a pupil with dividend 1000 met another with divisor 100 or a pupil with divisor 10 met a pupil with the quotient 20?
- Collect ideas as a class, focusing on place value to multiply or divide by a number of tens or hundreds.
- Pupils should complete Question 4 in the Practice Book.

Same-day intervention
- Give pupils **Resource 5.3.4c** Division errors and highlighter pens. They should highlight errors and correct any wrong calculations.

Same-day enrichment
- Work with pupils to revisit the use of the column method to multiply three-digit by two-digit numbers. Challenge them to find the smallest and the largest possible product. Give pupils the following division calculations. Can they write word problems to match each calculation?

  576 ÷ 8   401 ÷ 6   389 ÷ 7   818 ÷ 9

- They should share them with a partner who must explain why the problem does or does not match.

Question 5

> 5 A team of road maintenance workers are repairing an 855 metre-long road. The workers have completed 162 m of the road. For the remaining part, if they repair 63 m of the road each day, how many more days do they need to complete their work?

What learning will pupils have achieved at the conclusion of Question 5?

- The relationship between division and multiplication will have been strengthened as pupils solve word problems.

Chapter 3 Dividing by 2-digit numbers

Unit 3.4 Practice Book 5A, pages 63–66

Activities for whole-class instruction

- Remind pupils about some of the division calculations they collected during the previous session, for example:
  - 210 ÷ 24
  - 186 ÷ 28
  - 350 ÷ 45
- Convert them into word problems, for example:

  Sami has 210 stickers in his collection.

  He uses 24 of them on the front of his sticker book.

  He arranges the rest in groups of 28 on the pages in his book.

  How many pages does he fill?

  How many stickers are left over?
- Pupils should discuss the problem, deciding what it is asking.
- Remind pupils that bar models are helpful to represent the problem. Ask: *What does each part represent? How do you know? Is there a remainder?*

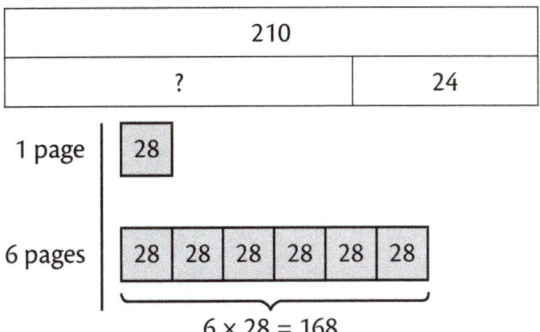

- Pupils should discuss the representations, explaining how each relates to the problem. Do they recognise the division 186 ÷ 28 that may have been completed during the first activity? Agree that there is a remainder because 168 is less than the dividend 186.

 *There are six 28s in 168. The remainder, 18, is less than the divisor.*

- Give pupils another problem using the same context. For example:

  Nisha has 400 stickers in her collection.

  She uses 50 of them on the front of her sticker book.

  She arranges the rest in groups of 45 on the pages in her book.

  How many pages does she fill?

  How many stickers are left over?
- Can they draw a bar model to represent the problem?
- Pupils should complete Question 5 in the Practice Book.

Same-day intervention

- Work together to represent the following problem using bar models.

  Benji has a 400 cm ball of string.

  He cuts off 13 cm and then divides the rest into 33 cm lengths.

  How many 33 cm lengths can he make?

  What length piece is remaining?
- Can pupils make up some problems of their own with a subtraction step followed by one of these divisions?

  256 ÷ 7   324 ÷ 6

Same-day enrichment

- Give pupils **Resource 5.3.4e** Writing division problems. Pupils will write their own problems. Encourage pupils to think about different contexts for their problems, for example money and other units of measurement such as time, capacity or mass.

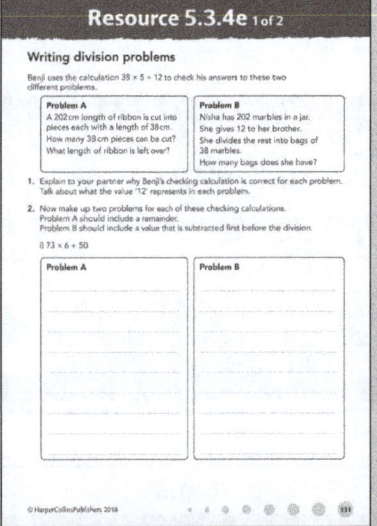

Answers: 1. Problem A: 5 pieces, remainder 12 cm; 2. Problem B: 5 bags (the 12 represents the number of marbles she gives to her brother); 3. Various answers possible.

Chapter 3 Dividing by 2-digit numbers Unit 3.4 Practice Book 5A, pages 63–66

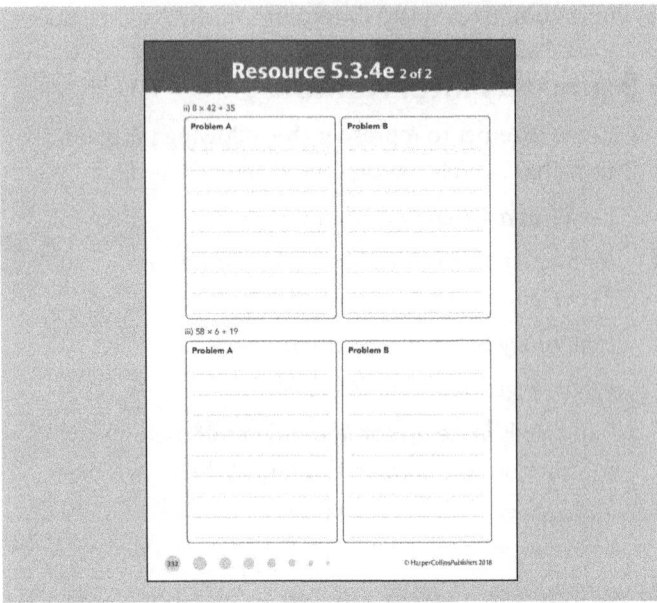

Challenge and extension question

Question 6

6 A tunnel is 760 m long. A 240 m-long train is travelling at 25 m per second. How long will it take to pass through the tunnel?

Pupils are required to draw on their experiences of solving speed, distance and time problems, recognising that to calculate time they must divide the distance by the speed. However, this problem is more complex as pupils have to allow for the length of the train and the final part of it exiting the tunnel.

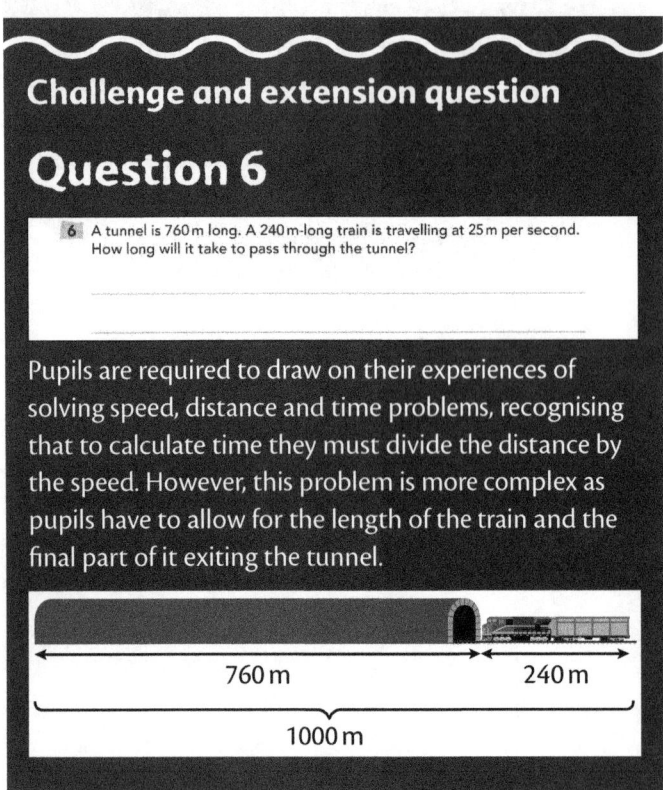

Chapter 3 Dividing by 2-digit numbers

Unit 3.5
Dividing 2-digit or 3-digit numbers by a 2-digit number (3)

Conceptual context

In the previous unit, pupils developed their understanding of equivalent divisions to help estimate a quotient. They recognised that the estimated quotient could be just right or too big depending on the size of the actual divisor. They used multiplication to check the size of the quotient and adjusted it when the product was larger than the dividend. Pupils further applied this understanding to the column method of division, recognising that they could simply look at the number of tens in the divisor and dividend to help find an equivalent division to make an approximation, for example 265 ÷ 32 can be estimated as 260 ÷ 30, which has the same quotient as the division 26 ÷ 3.

Learning is further developed in this unit as pupils consolidate their use of the column method and apply their understanding of the relationship between multiplication and division to solve a range of problems.

Learning pupils will have achieved at the end of the unit

- Pupils will have related division to multiplication, recognising that they can multiply the divisor to determine how many groups of the divisor are in the dividend (Q1, Q2, Q3)
- Pupils will be able to recognise and explain why divisions are equivalent (Q1, Q2)
- Conceptual understanding of dividing by a two-digit number using the column method will have been strengthened (Q1, Q2)
- Pupils will have fluently applied their understanding of remainders to help reason about the quotient for related divisions, for example comparing the quotient for 174 ÷ 48 and 274 ÷ 48 (Q2)
- The language of division and multiplication will have been used flexibly to describe calculations (Q3, Q4)
- The relationship between division and multiplication will have been strengthened as pupils solve a range of problems (Q4)

Resources

counting stick; place value counters; base 10 blocks; **Resource 5.3.5a** Sorting quotients; **Resource 5.3.5b** Quotient spinner; **Resource 5.3.5c** What number am I?; **Resource 5.3.5d** Bar models

Vocabulary

division, divide, dividend, divisor, quotient, remainder, equivalent, multiple

Chapter 3 Dividing by 2-digit numbers

Unit 3.5 Practice Book 5A, pages 67–70

Question 1

1 For each calculation, complete the statements then work out the answer.

(a) 28)89

Think: When 80 ÷ 20, the quotient is ☐.

☐ × 28 = ☐.

The quotient is _____ (Choose: just right, too big or too small); change the quotient to ☐.

☐ × 28 = ☐.

The remainder is ☐; it is _____ than the divisor.

Therefore, the quotient ☐ is the right choice.

(b) 28)80

Think: When 80 ÷ 20, the quotient is ☐.

☐ × 28 = ☐.

The quotient is _____ (Choose: just right, too big or too small); subtract 1, it is ☐.

☐ × 28 = ☐.

Again subtract 1, it is ☐.

☐ × 28 = ☐.

The remainder is ☐; it is _____ than the divisor.

Therefore, the quotient ☐ is the right choice.

(c) 38)278

Think: When 270 ÷ 30, the quotient is ☐.

When 270 ÷ 40, the quotient is ☐.

The quotient ☐ is the right choice.

(d) 57)421

Think: When 420 ÷ 50, the quotient is ☐.

When 420 ÷ 60, the quotient is ☐.

The quotient ☐ is the right choice.

(e) 19)134

Think: Both have the same first digit and 13 < 19.

Try the number ☐ as an initial quotient.

130 ÷ 20, the quotient is ☐.

The quotient ☐ is the right choice.

(f) 78)732

Think: Both have the same first number and 73 < 78.

Try ☐ as an initial quotient.

730 ÷ 80, the quotient is ☐.

The quotient ☐ is the right choice.

What learning will pupils have achieved at the conclusion of Question 1?

- Pupils will have related division to multiplication, recognising that they can multiply the divisor to determine how many groups of the divisor are in the dividend.
- Pupils will be able to recognise and explain why divisions are equivalent.
- Conceptual understanding of dividing by a two-digit number using the column method will have been strengthened.

Activities for whole-class instruction

- Write '523 ÷ 68 = ☐'. Agree that we can use division fact 52 ÷ 6 to help approximate the quotient as 8.
- Write 'When 520 ÷ 60, the quotient is 8'. Tell pupils that you think the actual quotient will be less than 8. Ask: *Why do you think I am saying this? What do think I have noticed?* Discuss pupils' ideas, establishing that the divisor 68 is closer to 70 than it is to 60; so it might not be possible to make as many groups as the initial estimate suggests.
- Ask: *How could you find out whether the quotient, 8, will be too big for 523 ÷ 68?*
- Multiply 8 × 68 together and agree that the product, 544, is bigger than the dividend, so the quotient is not 8.
- Multiply 7 × 68 together (or subtract 68 from 544) to find 7 × 68 = 476.
- Agree that, with a quotient of 7, the remainder (47) is less than the divisor, so 7 is the quotient.
- Pupil pairs should work through the following calculations in the same way.

  394 ÷ 48   740 ÷ 59   94 ÷ 27   263 ÷ 32

- Discuss answers and establish that when the divisor is close to the next multiple of 10, the quotient is likely to be smaller than for the estimated division that used the previous multiple of 10.

(i) Pupils will discover that when they make approximations using the tens digit in a divisor that is close to the next multiple of 10, for example when 520 ÷ 60 is used to estimate 523 ÷ 68, it is likely that the quotient will need to be revised downwards. They will not learn this as a rule but will have experience that means they are open to the possibilities and will not assume it is always about the tens value in the divisor, for example not assuming that dividing by 60 (when dividing by 68) will best inform the size of the quotient but that dividing by 70 may well do.

Chapter 3 Dividing by 2-digit numbers

Unit 3.5 Practice Book 5A, pages 67–70

- Show the following four calculations:

  345 ÷ 36 = ☐
  639 ÷ 65 = ☐
  512 ÷ 54 = ☐
  451 ÷ 47 = ☐

- Ask: *Without calculating the answers, what is similar about all of these?* Agree that both the dividend and the divisor start with the same digit. So, focusing on the first digit only does not help to estimate a quotient. Therefore, we must consider the first two digits of the dividend.

- Write:

  34 < 36
  63 < 65
  51 < 54
  45 < 47

- Ask: *Why does comparing the pairs of numbers in this way help to show that the quotient must be less than 10?* Set out the first example in the column format:

  ```
          0   0
    3 6 | 3   4   5
  ```

  Discuss how nothing can be entered in the hundreds or tens column of the answer because 340 is less than 10 times 36. Start working through the second example on the board using the column format:

  ```
          0   0
    6 5 | 6   3   9
  ```

  Agree that the same thing happens – the first two digits of the dividend need to be at least as big as the divisor if the quotient is going to have 1 in the tens column. Repeat with the other two examples.

- Ask: *What could I change the divisor or dividend to that would give a quotient of 10 or more?* Pupils should discuss with a partner. Share ideas. They should suggest divisors of 63 or less – or dividends of 650 or more.

- Pupils should complete Question 1 in the Practice Book.

Same-day intervention

- Look together at Question 1, drawing out equivalent divisions to help make decisions. Use place value counters to work through the calculations. Focus particularly on the divisions where the estimated quotients were too big, discussing why this is the case.
- Revise strategies for mental multiplication as required.

Same-day enrichment

- Give pupils **Resource 5.3.5a** Sorting quotients. Pupils should sort the divisions by the size of the quotients as given.

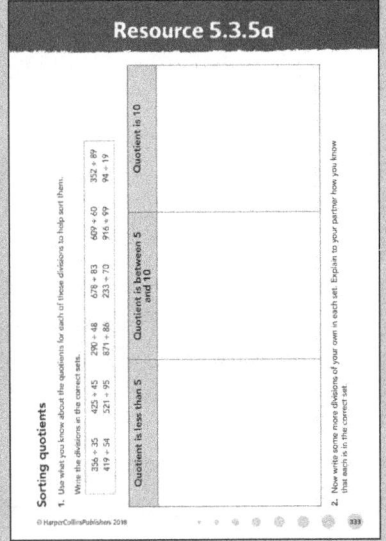

Answers: Quotient is less than 5: 233 ÷ 70; Quotient is between 5 and 10: 419 ÷ 54, 425 ÷ 45, 521 ÷ 95, 290 ÷ 48, 678 ÷ 83, 916 ÷ 99; Quotient is 10: 356 ÷ 35, 871 ÷ 86, 609 ÷ 60; 2. Various answers possible.

Question 2

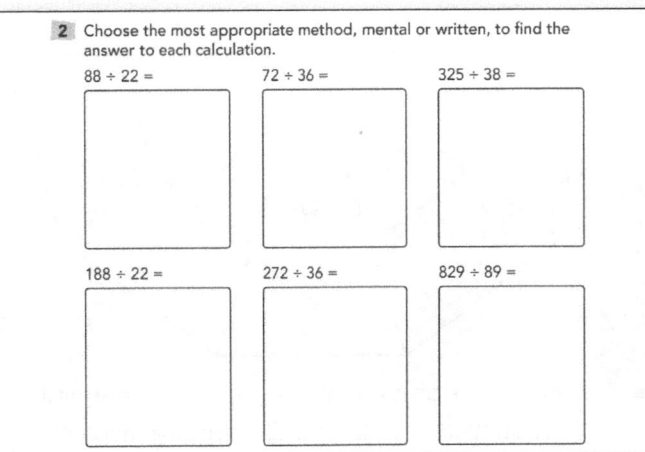

Chapter 3 Dividing by 2-digit numbers

Unit 3.5 Practice Book 5A, pages 67–70

What learning will pupils have achieved at the conclusion of Question 2?

- Pupils will have related division to multiplication, recognising that they can multiply the divisor to determine how many groups of the divisor are in the dividend.
- Pupils will be able to recognise and explain why divisions are equivalent.
- Conceptual understanding of dividing by a two-digit number using the column method will have been strengthened.
- Pupils will have fluently applied their understanding of remainders to help reason about the quotient for related divisions, for example comparing the quotient for 174 ÷ 48 and 274 ÷ 48.

Activities for whole-class instruction

- Show pupils the image of the 'Quotient spinner'.

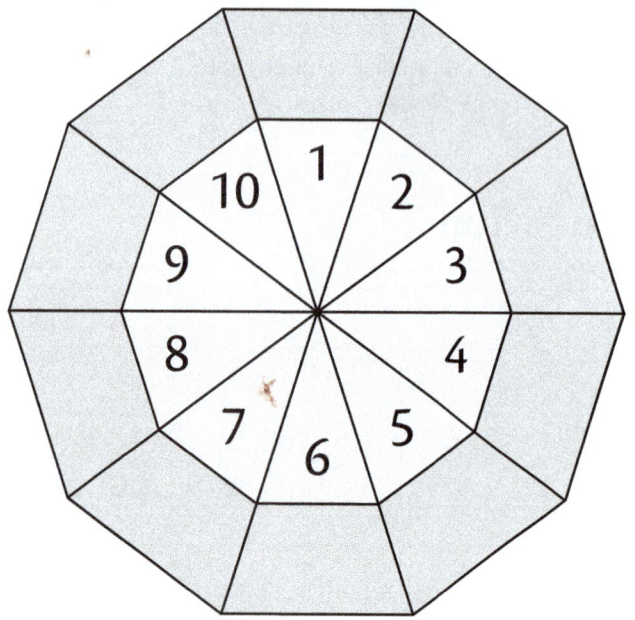

- Explain that the divisions on the spinner are missing and only the quotients can be seen. The missing divisions all have two-digit divisors. Pupils should work in pairs to agree and record one possible division calculation for each segment around the outside of the spinner.

  Look out for … pupils who are randomly trying divisions. Encourage them to use equivalent divisions and known facts for a given quotient to help make decisions.

- Share ideas, exploring possible divisions. Discuss any remainders that might occur, for example for the quotient 5, a possible division is 215 ÷ 40 = 5 r 15, agreeing that the remainder is less than the divisor.

- Suggest that 300 ÷ 47 is another possible division that gives the quotient 7. Ask: *What equivalent division should I use to check?* (30 ÷ 4 or 30 ÷ 5) *Why?* Discuss responses.
- Return to the spinner and suggest that a good starting point to find a possible division is to simply multiply the quotient by a two-digit number, for example 7 × 23. Can pupils explain why you have made this suggestion? Can they explain what they would need to do so the division has a remainder?
- Pupils should complete Question 2 in the Practice Book.

Same-day intervention

- Give pupils **Resource 5.3.5b** Quotient spinner. They will use the column method to complete each of the divisions.

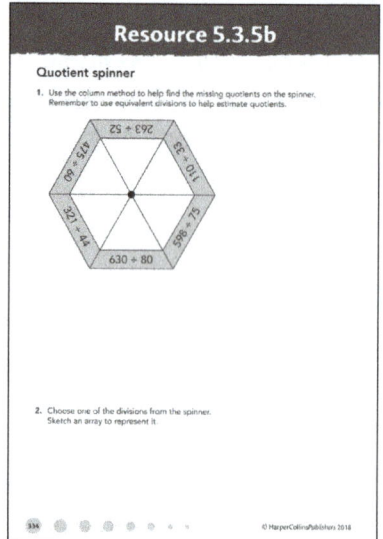

Answers: 1. Quotients as follows: 263 ÷ 52 = 5, 110 ÷ 33 = 3, 598 ÷ 75 = 7, 630 ÷ 80 = 7, 321 ÷ 44, 475 ÷ 60 = 7; 2. Array should reflect one of the divisions.

Same-day enrichment

- Work with the pupils to reason about related divisions (see below). Can pupils reason about the quotient for the first division each time to predict the quotients for the related divisions?

146 ÷ 32	246 ÷ 32	346 ÷ 32
285 ÷ 67	385 ÷ 67	485 ÷ 67
374 ÷ 84	574 ÷ 84	774 ÷ 84

Chapter 3 Dividing by 2-digit numbers

Unit 3.5 Practice Book 5A, pages 67–70

Question 3

> **3** Write the number sentences and then calculate the answer.
> (a) How many times 48 is 384?
>
> (b) 59 times a number is 413. What is the number?
>
> (c) At least how much needs to be taken away from 960 so there is no remainder when it is divided by 42?

What learning will pupils have achieved at the conclusion of Question 3?

- Pupils will have related division to multiplication, recognising that they can multiply the divisor to determine how many groups of the divisor are in the dividend.
- The language of division and multiplication will have been used flexibly to describe calculations.

Activities for whole-class instruction

- Pupils work in small groups with tens and ones place value counters (or base 10 blocks). Ask: *How can you arrange the counters to show how many times 30 goes into 240?* For example:

  (10) (10) (10)
  (10) (10) (10)
  (10) (10) (10)
  (10) (10) (10)
  (10) (10) (10)
  (10) (10) (10)
  (10) (10) (10)
  (10) (10) (10)

- Can pupils write a division statement to match their representation? (240 ÷ 30 = 8) Agree that 30 goes into 240 eight times.
- Now ask pupils to arrange the counters to show how many times 40 goes into 240. Can they write the matching division sentence? (240 ÷ 40 = 6) Agree that 40 goes into 240 six times.
- Suggest that there will be a remainder when 240 is divided by 50. Ask: *What number can be subtracted from the dividend 240 so there is no remainder when it is divided by 50?*

 ... pupils who do not recognise that by subtracting the remainder 40, the number that is left (200) must be exactly divisible by 50 and will leave no remainder. Use an array to show this, removing the remainder of 40 and agreeing that 200 can be divided by 50 leaving no remainder, counting the 20 tens to show this.

- Challenge pupils to now arrange counters to show how many times 50 goes into 185. Can they use their arrangement to:
  - describe the matching division?
  - show how much needs to be subtracted from 185 so that there is no remainder when it is divided by 50?
  - explain how many times 50 is 150?
- Show the following array to agree answers to each of the questions above:

[array of tens blocks and ones]

- Discuss the questions together agreeing that:
  - the calculation is 185 ÷ 50 = 3 r 35, so 50 goes into 185 three times.
  - 35 must be subtracted from 185 so that there is no remainder when it is divided by 50.
  - 150 is three times 50.
- Explain that you now want to find out how many 32s there are in 185. Ask: *What can we do to solve this?* Agree that we can count in 32s up to 185 or divide 185 by 32. Can pupils estimate the quotient? For example, using 180 ÷ 30 (18 ÷ 3). Can they explain why the estimated quotient 6 is too big?
- Agree that 185 ÷ 32 = 5 r 25 because 5 × 32 = 160.

  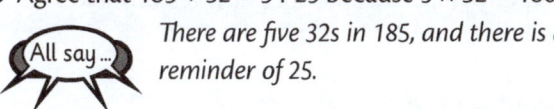 *There are five 32s in 185, and there is a reminder of 25.*

- Can pupils sketch an array to show this?
- Say that 32 times a number is 192. Can pupils explain how to solve this? Do they notice that this is one group of 32 more than 160? Agree that 192 ÷ 32 = 6, so 32 times 6 is 192.
- Pupils should complete Question 3 in the Practice Book.

Chapter 3 Dividing by 2-digit numbers

Unit 3.5 Practice Book 5A, pages 67–70

Same-day intervention

- Give pupils base 10 blocks. Ask them to use the blocks to show how many 40s are in 212. Can they write a matching division? Can they explain what should be subtracted from 212 so there is no remainder when it is divided by 40?
- Explore other divisions using the dividend 212 in the same way, for example how many 30s are in 212. Discuss the amount to be subtracted each time so there is no remainder, focusing on why the amount changes.

Same-day enrichment

- Give pupils **Resource 5.3.5c** What number am I? They should work with a partner and decide how they will prove their solutions. (Note: the first mystery number is 419 and the second is 16.)

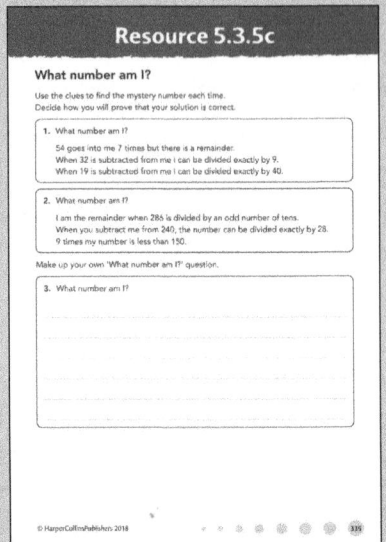

Answers: 1. 419; 2. 16; 3. Various answers possible.

Question 4

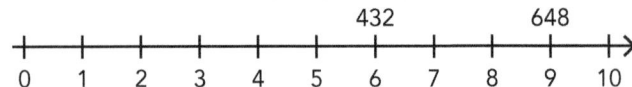

4 In a spring week, there were 1000 birds visiting an island in their migration from south to north. Among them, 130 were cuckoos. How many were other species of birds? Excluding the remainder, how many times as many as cuckoos were the other species of birds? What is the remainder?

What learning will pupils have achieved at the conclusion of Question 4?

- The language of division and multiplication will have been used flexibly to describe calculations.
- The relationship between division and multiplication will have been strengthened as pupils solve a range of problems.

Activities for whole-class instruction

- Show pupils a partially completed double-sided number line. Ask: *What does it show? How do you know?* Agree that it is the 72 times table.

```
                        432             648
|---|---|---|---|---|---|---|---|---|---|-->
0   1   2   3   4   5   6   7   8   9   10
```

- Pupils should find the other missing numbers using strategies of multiplication to help them. Complete the number line together.
- Share the following problems:
  – *A ticket for a coach tour costs £72. How many tickets can be bought for £450?*
  – *A ticket for a coach tour costs £72. The Jackson family has saved £300 for a trip. How much money will they have left after buying four tickets?*
- Can pupils use the number line to help solve the problems? Can they explain what division statement each problem represents?
- Invite pupils to make up division problems that use other values on the number line. Share the problems, agreeing quotients and remainders each time.
- Share another problem. Can they explain why it is different?
  – *A birthday party costs £432 in total. £72 was spent on party games. The rest was spent on food and drink. How many times more money was spent on food and drink than on games?*
- Ask: *What is the question asking? What should we do first?* Agree that we need to calculate the amount spent on food and drink so we can compare it with the amount spent on party games. Establish that £360 must have been spent on food and drink because £432 – £72 = £360.
- Sketch the following bar model.

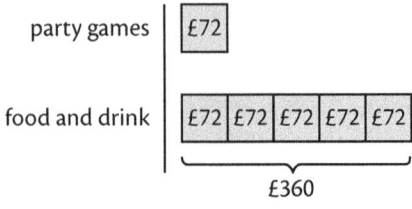

- Ask: *How do you know that the bar model represents the problem?* Agree that 5 times 72 is £360, so the amount spent on food and drink is five times more than that spent on party games.
- Finally, share the following problem. Pupils should work together to find what calculations are required to solve it.

There are 800 spectators at a sports event.

Chapter 3 Dividing by 2-digit numbers

Unit 3.5 Practice Book 5A, pages 67–70

120 of the spectators are children.

How many adults are there?

Excluding any remainders, how many times more adults are there than children?

- Establish these as:
  - the subtraction 800 − 120 = 680 to find the number of adults
  - the division 680 ÷ 120 to find out how many times more adults than children there are.
- Focus on the division 680 ÷ 120. Pupils should use multiplication facts to show that the quotient is 5 because 5 × 12 = 60. Conclude that there are 5 times as many adults than children at the event.
- Pupils should complete Question 4 in the Practice Book.

Same-day intervention

- Work together to represent the problem in Question 4 using bar models. Can pupils identify the two calculations required? Can they explain why 87 ÷ 13 can be used to solve the division 870 ÷ 13?
- Return to the problem about the sporting event from the whole-class instruction. Work together to represent the problem using the bar model.

Same-day enrichment

- Give pupils **Resource 5.3.5d** Bar models. Pupils should find the calculations required each time. They should show 'how many times more' each time using bar models.

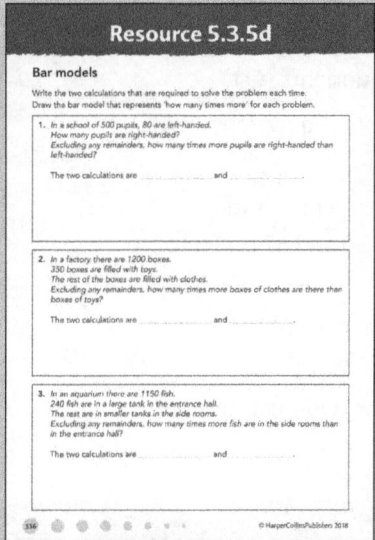

Answers: Bar models should reflect 'how many times more'. Calculations (excluding remainders) should be:
1. 500 − 80 = 420, 420 ÷ 80 = 5; 2. 1200 − 350 = 850, 850 ÷ 350 = 2; 3. 1150 − 240 = 910, 910 ÷ 240 = 3.

Challenge and extension question

Question 5

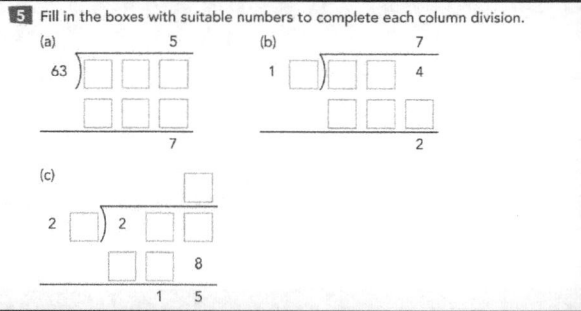

Pupils are required to reason about missing digits in column divisions, applying understanding of the relationship between the dividend, divisor, quotient and remainder.

In the first example, they should notice that they can find the dividend by multiplying the quotient by the divisor before adding the remainder.

In the other examples, only the tens value is given in the divisor. Ignoring the remainder 2, pupils should reason about a ones digit that when multiplied by 7 gives a product with 2 in the ones position, for example 7 × 6 = 42.

Knowing this, they can find the missing values as 7 × 16 + 2 = 114.

Chapter 3 Dividing by 2-digit numbers

Unit 3.6
Dividing multi-digit numbers by a 2-digit number (1)

Conceptual context

In the previous unit, pupils reasoned about the size of a quotient using equivalent divisions to help make decisions. They began to recognise when an estimated quotient needs to be adjusted, explaining whether it is too big, too small or just right. Pupils learned that they need to look at more than just the first digit of each number when judging appropriate equivalent divisions; they learned that it often makes sense to use 'next 10' divisors, recognising, for example, that for 645 ÷ 39, an approximation using 640 ÷ 40 is better than 640 ÷ 30.

In this unit, pupils will develop flexibility in their approach as they also use other mental strategies for division and further consolidate the use of the column method. They will strengthen their understanding of why a division will result in a one- or two-digit quotient, making generalisations and explaining decisions.

Learning pupils will have achieved at the end of the unit

- Pupils will have continued to strengthen their understanding of the relationship between division and multiplication, recognising that they can multiply the divisor to determine how many groups of the divisor are in the dividend (Q1)
- Pupils will have drawn on their understanding of partitioning to find part quotients (Q1)
- A flexible approach to using known division facts and place value to help solve equivalent and related calculations will have been applied (Q1, Q2)
- Strategies to approximate quotients will have been developed as pupils use the next and previous multiples of 10 for the divisor, for example for 371 ÷ 53, use 371 ÷ 50 and 371 ÷ 60 to estimate (Q1, Q2)
- Fluency in dividing by a two-digit number using the column method will have been strengthened (Q3)
- Pupils will be able to recognise and explain when a quotient will be a one- or two-digit number (when dividing a three-digit number by a two-digit number) (Q4, Q5)

Resources

calculators; squared paper; highlighter pens; 0–9 dice; sets of different-coloured counters; **Resource sheet 5.3.6a** Squared paper; **Resource 5.3.6b** Division errors; **Resource 5.3.6c** Quotient sort; **Resource 5.3.6d** Rolling digits

Vocabulary

division, divide, dividend, divisor, quotient, remainder, equivalent, multiple

Chapter 3 Dividing by 2-digit numbers

Unit 3.6 Practice Book 5A, pages 71–74

Question 1

> **1** Use the steps shown to help find the answer to each calculation.
> (a) 204 ÷ 12
> 12 × 10 = ☐
> 12 × 20 = ☐
> First: ☐ ÷ 12 = ☐
> Then: 84 ÷ 12 = ☐
> Therefore: 204 ÷ 12 = ☐
>
> (b) 2128 ÷ 38
> 38 × 50 = ☐
> 38 × 60 = ☐
> First: ☐ ÷ 38 = ☐
> Then: ☐ ÷ 38 = ☐
> Therefore: 2128 ÷ 38 = ☐

What learning will pupils have achieved at the conclusion of Question 1?

- Pupils will have continued to strengthen their understanding of the relationship between division and multiplication, recognising that they can multiply the divisor to determine how many groups of the divisor are in the dividend.
- Pupils will have drawn on their understanding of partitioning to find part quotients.
- A flexible approach to using known division facts and place value to help solve equivalent and related calculations will have been applied.
- Strategies to approximate quotients will have been developed as pupils use the next and previous multiples of 10 for the divisor, for example for 371 ÷ 53, use 371 ÷ 50 and 371 ÷ 60 to estimate.

Activities for whole-class instruction

- Show pupils the following multiplication calculations:
  67 × 34   58 × 45   82 × 63   45 × 29
- Suggest that the product for 67 × 35 will be more than the product for 67 × 30 but less than the product for 67 × 40. Pupils should use calculators to check this. Ask pupils to make statements about the products of the other multiplications in the same way, again using the calculator to check each time.
- Now show the following division calculations:
  272 ÷ 34   2610 ÷ 45   378 ÷ 63   1218 ÷ 29
- Ask: *Can we make similar statements about quotients for these? Is the quotient for 272 ÷ 34 likely to be more or less or the same as the quotient for 272 ÷ 30? And for 272 ÷ 40?* Agree that the estimated quotient for 272 ÷ 30 is 9 and for 272 ÷ 40 is 6. Ask: *How can we now use multiplication to find the actual quotient?*
- Pupils should work together to find the products of 34 × 9 and 34 × 6, discussing whether the quotients are just right, too big or too small for 272 ÷ 34.

- Share ideas and record that:
  272 ÷ 34
  34 × 9 = 306 (quotient is too big)
  34 × 6 = 204 (quotient is too small because more groups of 34 can be made)
  First 204 ÷ 34 = 6 (so we know the quotient is at least 6).
- Ask: *How many more 34s are there?* Agree that the difference between the dividend and 6 × 34 must be found. (272 − 204 = 68)
  Then 68 ÷ 34 = 2.
  Therefore, 272 ÷ 34 = 6 + 2.
- Ask: *What strategy have I used here? Why?* Agree that 272 has been partitioned into 204 and 68 and the quotients for each part have been found and then recombined to find the quotient for the starting dividend.
- Discuss the second example together. First, sketch an array 'A', representing what is already known.

Array A

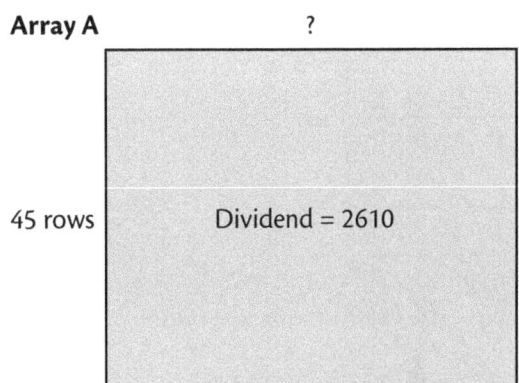

- Write '2610 ÷ 45 = ___' under the array. Circle the 26 in the dividend and the 4 in the divisor. Agree that the quotient might be 60 because 26 ÷ 4 = 6, so 260 ÷ 4 = 60.
- If a visual representation is required, use the following arrays to revisit and show that the quotient (and remainder) for 260 ÷ 4 is 10 times larger than for 26 ÷ 4.

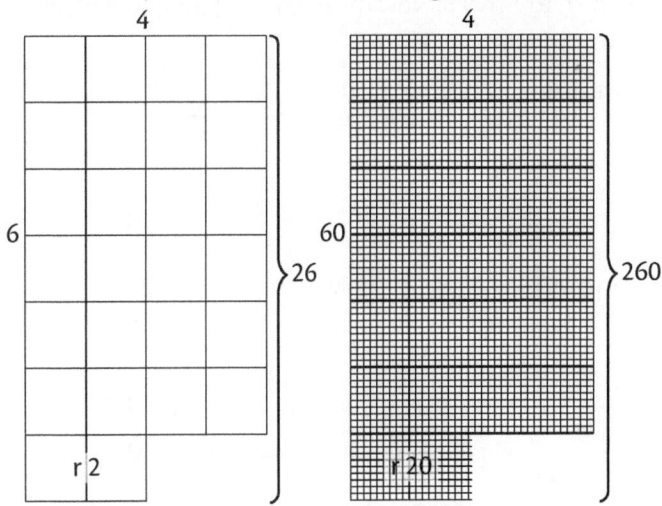

129

Chapter 3 Dividing by 2-digit numbers

Unit 3.6 Practice Book 5A, pages 71–74

- Return to Array A. Check 45 × 60 = 2700. Agree that this is more than 2610, so the quotient 60 is too big.
- Check the smaller quotient of 50. 45 × 50 = 2250. Agree that this is less than 2610, so the quotient is at least 50 but less than 60.
- Sketch Array B:

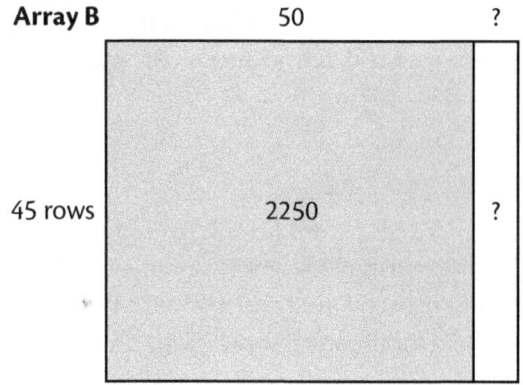

- Agree that the tens digit of the quotient is now known. Begin to complete the column representation of the calculation:

```
           5
   4 5 | 2 6 1 0
         2 2 5 0   (subtract 50 × 45)
           3 6 0
```

- Ask: *How many more 45s are in 360?* Agree 8 × 45 = 360. Now complete the column representation.

```
           5 8
   4 5 | 2 6 1 0
         2 2 5 0   (subtract 50 × 45)
           3 6 0
           3 6 0   (subtract 8 × 45)
           0 0 0
```

- Return to Array B. Now the unknown part quotient and part dividends are known.

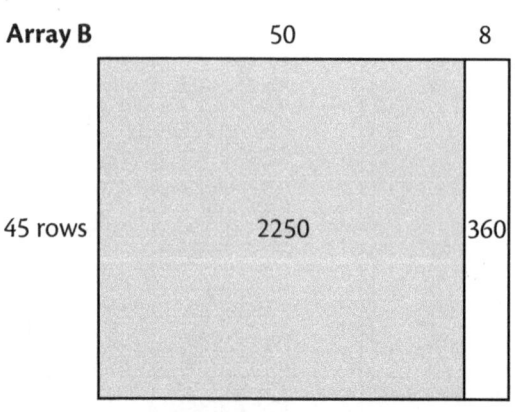

- Write:

  dividend = 2250 + 360 = 2610

  quotient = 50 + 8 = 58

- Pupils should practise the method to find the quotients for 378 ÷ 63 and 1218 ÷ 29. Share solutions, addressing any errors as required. Focus on the fact that the divisor 29 is close to 30, so the quotient will be closer to the estimate 1200 ÷ 30 than it is to 1200 ÷ 20.
- Pupils should complete Question 1 in the Practice Book.

Same-day intervention

- Look together at 204 ÷ 12 in Question 1. Ask pupils to discuss why the first step shows 12 × 10 and 12 × 20. Establish that the divisions 200 ÷ 10 = 20 and 200 ÷ 20 = 10 have been used to approximate the quotient for 204 ÷ 12.
- Pupils should sketch a 12 × 10 array and a 12 × 20 array on squared paper. (**Resource 5.3.6a** Squared paper)

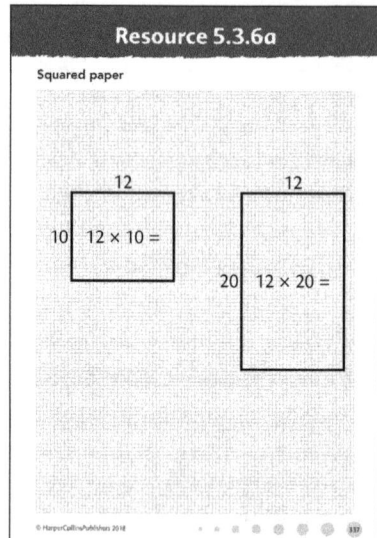

- Can pupils calculate the product for each? Can they explain why the quotient 10 is too small and that the quotient 20 is too big?
- Point to the array for 12 × 10, say: *First 12 × 10 = 120.* Explain that this will be one part of the actual array we need to find.
- Ask: *How many small squares should the second part of the array show so that there are 204 in total when both parts are put together?* Agree that this can be found by subtracting 120 from 204. (84)
- Explain that we now need to find how many more groups of 12 there are in 84 so we know how many rows to add to the array. Pupils should use multiplication facts to identify this as 7.

Chapter 3 Dividing by 2-digit numbers

Unit 3.6 Practice Book 5A, pages 71–74

- Ask pupils to show the second part of the array by adding another 8 rows. Label the array:

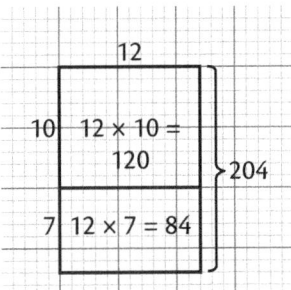

 *First 12 × 10 = 20. Then 84 ÷ 12 = 7. Therefore, 204 ÷ 12 = 10 + 7.*

- Pupils should practise sketching their own arrays to help calculate 345 ÷ 15.

Same-day enrichment

- Give pupils **Resource 5.3.6b** Division errors and highlighter pens. They should check and correct the calculations shown.

Answers: 1. 8; 2. 9; 3. 47; 4. 11; 5. 63; 6. 43.

Questions 2 and 3

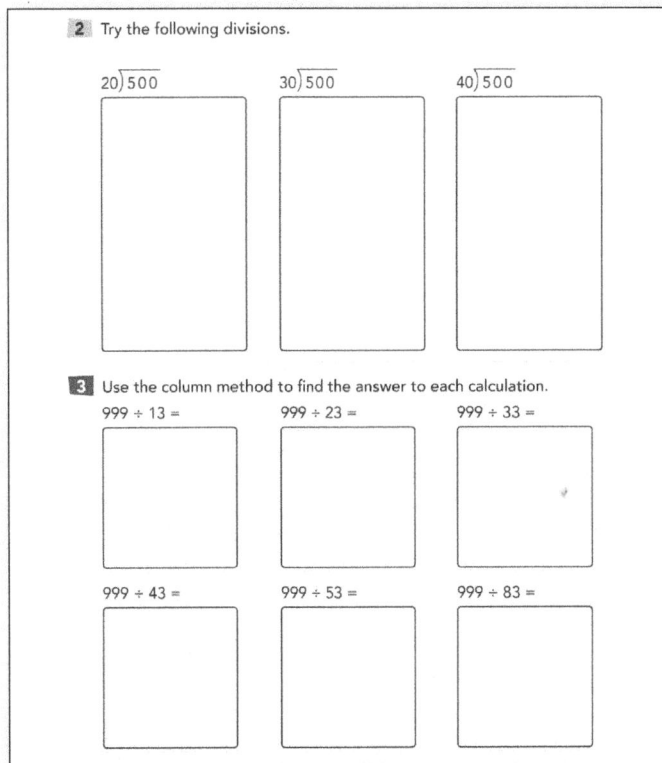

What learning will pupils have achieved at the conclusion of Questions 2 and 3?

- A flexible approach to using known division facts and place value to help solve equivalent and related calculations will have been applied.
- Strategies to approximate quotients will have been developed as pupils use the next and previous multiples of 10 for the divisor, for example for 371 ÷ 53, use 371 ÷ 50 and 371 ÷ 60 to estimate.
- Fluency in dividing by a two-digit number using the column method will have been strengthened.

Activities for whole-class instruction

- Show pupils the following images. Ask: *What division calculations do they represent? What is the same and what is different about them?*

Chapter 3 Dividing by 2-digit numbers

Unit 3.6 Practice Book 5A, pages 71–74

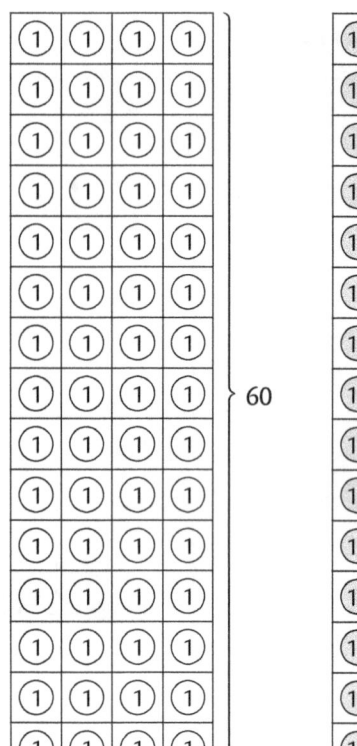

- Establish that the two calculations are 60 ÷ 4 and 600 ÷ 40. Both images have the same number of counters set out in the same number of rows and columns. This shows that the relationship between the numbers that are represented is the same for both calculations. The total value of the arrays is different, as is the value of each row, but the quotient is the same for both.

- Ask: *How do these equivalent divisions help solve the following calculations?*

  604 ÷ 42   604 ÷ 43   604 ÷ 45

- Agree that the equivalent division 60 ÷ 4 can be used to quickly find the quotient. Ask pupils to use the column method to complete each of the calculations. Can they explain why the estimated quotient 15 is too big?

- Record each of the calculations on the board, reasoning about the size of the quotient and remainder each time.

```
        1  4   remainder 16
   4 2| 6  0  4
        4  2  0   (10 × 42)
        1  8  4
        1  6  8   (4 × 42)
              1  6
```

```
        1  4   remainder 2
   4 3| 6  0  4
        4  3  0   (10 × 43)
        1  7  4
        1  7  2   (4 × 43)
              2
```

```
        1  3   remainder 19
   4 5| 6  0  4
        4  5  0   (10 × 45)
        1  5  4
        1  3  5   (3 × 45)
              1  9
```

- Now show the following arrays. Can pupils explain what divisions they represent and why the quotient is smaller each time? Suggest that they imagine the number of columns (representing the divisor) increasing and visualise what happens to the number of rows. Of course, using rows to represent the divisor would also be appropriate.

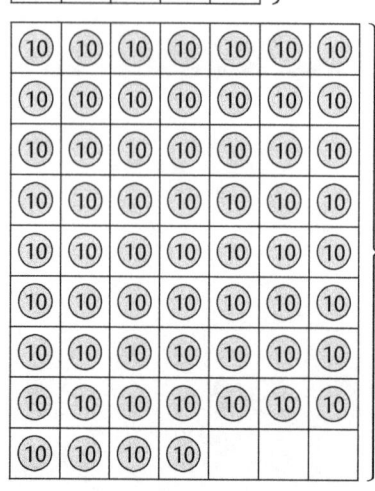

Chapter 3 Dividing by 2-digit numbers

Unit 3.6 Practice Book 5A, pages 71–74

- Ask pupils to explain how they can use what they know to solve the following divisions. Can they use the column method to show their working?

  608 ÷ 54   608 ÷ 74

- Can pupils tell you:
  - why the actual quotient for the first division is smaller than the estimate?
  - why the quotient from the estimate for the second example is just right?
  - how the array can be visualised each time as the dividend remains the same but the number of columns and, therefore, rows will change?

- Finally, show the following:

  600 ÷ 80   600 ÷ 90   599 ÷ 83   599 ÷ 93

- Pupils should first estimate the quotient for 600 ÷ 80 and 600 ÷ 90 before finding the actual answers using the column method. Ask: *Why might the division 600 ÷ 80 be a more useful approximation for 599 ÷ 83 than 500 ÷ 80?* Agree that 599 is closer to 600 than to 500.

- Establish that when the dividend is close to the next multiple of 100, the quotient is likely to be larger than for the estimated division that uses the previous multiple of 100.

- Share the answers to each division, discussing why the actual quotients are just right or too big for each division.

- Pupils should complete Questions 2 and 3 in the Practice Book.

Same-day intervention

- Give pupils **Resource 5.3.6c** Quotient sort. They should use the column method to solve each division calculation.

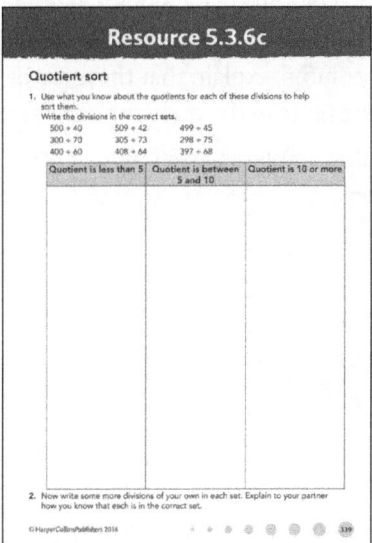

Answers: 1. Quotient is less than 5: 300 ÷ 70, 305 ÷ 73, 298 ÷ 75; Quotient is between 5 and 10: 400 ÷ 60, 408 ÷ 64, 396 ÷ 68; Quotient is 10 or more: 500 ÷ 40, 509 ÷ 42, 499 ÷ 45; 2. Various answers possible.

Same-day enrichment

- Give pupils the following problem to solve. Work with the group as needed to help pupils reason about possible solutions.

  > Nisha uses the same digit four times and one other digit to make all of these calculations correct.
  > Which digits did she use?
  >
  > ☐ 0 0 ÷ ☐ 0 = 8 r 20
  >
  > ☐ 0 1 ÷ ☐ 8 = 7 r 85
  >
  > ☐ 9 6 ÷ ☐ 9 = 6 r 62

- Can pupils make up their own missing digit problem for their partner to solve?

Questions 4 and 5

4 Fill in the hundreds place in each dividend below with a number starting from 1 to 9 in order and then find the quotient and remainder. Identify patterns from these divisions.

(a)

35)☐ 3 5   35)☐ 3 5   35)☐ 3 5

35)☐ 3 5   35)☐ 3 5   35)☐ 3 5

35)☐ 3 5   35)☐ 3 5   35)☐ 3 5

(b) Pattern identified:

When the hundreds place is filled with any of the digits _____, the quotient is a 1-digit number.

When the hundreds place is filled in with either _____, the quotient is a 2-digit number.

5 Fill in the missing numbers to make each statement correct.

(a) The quotient of 268 ÷ 26 is a ☐-digit number.

The highest value place of the quotient is in the _____ place.

The quotient is ☐.

(b) The quotient of 268 ÷ 38 is a ☐-digit number.

The digit of the quotient in the highest-value place is ☐.

(c) When the quotient of 5■6 ÷ 53 is a 2-digit number, the least possible number in the ■ is ☐.

(d) The highest-value place of the quotient of 336 ÷ 3■ is in the tens place; the greatest possible number in the ■ is ☐.

Chapter 3 Dividing by 2-digit numbers

Unit 3.6 Practice Book 5A, pages 71–74

What learning will pupils have achieved at the conclusion of Questions 4 and 5?

- Pupils will be able to recognise and explain when a quotient will be a one- or two digit number (when dividing a three-digit number by a two-digit number).

Activities for whole-class instruction

- Show pupils the following quotient sorting table:

Quotient is less than 10 (a one-digit number)	Quotient is 10 or more (a two-digit number)

- Give pupils a few minutes to work together to suggest possible divisions to go in each part of the table. Take feedback, quickly estimating and checking the calculations using mental or column methods used in the unit so far.

- Suggest that the division 432 ÷ 53 has a quotient that is less than 10. Ask: *How do I know that the quotient is a one-digit number without calculating? How can I change the divisor so that the quotient is 10 or more?*

- Establish that 432 ÷ 43 gives a quotient of 10 (because 430 ÷ 43 = 10) and therefore any divisor greater than this will result in a quotient that is a one-digit number.

 *The first two digits in the dividend must be equal to or greater than the divisor to give a two-digit quotient.*

- Record the division as:

```
         8   r 8
5 3 ) 4 3 2
```

- Discuss how nothing can be entered in the hundreds or tens column of the answer because 430 is less than 10 times 53.

- Write the calculations 432 ÷ 43 and 432 ÷ 53 in the correct place in the sorting table. Ask: *Where should 432 ÷ 33 and 432 ÷ 63 go in the table? Why?*

- Show the calculations 641 ÷ 64 and 541 ÷ 64. Ask: *What do you notice about this pair of calculations? What do you know about the dividend for 641 ÷ 64? Do pupils know that the quotient is 10?*

- Agree that the value of the dividend in the second calculation is 100 less, but the divisor is the same. Ask pupils to describe the two arrays that they need to visualise and describe the difference to a partner. Share ideas.

- Establish that the quotient for 541 ÷ 64 must be less than 10 because the dividend is smaller than 640 – the quotient is a one-digit number. Can pupils reason about the quotients for 441 ÷ 64 and 341 ÷ 64? Will they also be one-digit numbers?

- Write all the calculations in the correct place in the table, listing those with one-digit divisors as follows so patterns become clear. For example:

541 ÷ 64

441 ÷ 64

341 ÷ 64

- Ask pupils to continue the pattern, reducing the dividend by 100 each time and keeping the divisor the same. What do they notice? (All quotients are one-digit numbers when the hundreds digit in the dividend is 5, 4, 3, 2 or 1)

- Pupils should reason about the quotients for the following, explaining whether the quotient will be a one-digit or a two-digit number:

758 ÷ 53   358 ÷ 53   538 ÷ 53
258 ÷ 53   858 ÷ 53

- Can they explain, for example, that the dividend in 758 ÷ 53 is greater than in 530 ÷ 53, so the quotient must be a two-digit number, but the dividend in 358 ÷ 53 is less than in 530 ÷ 53, so the quotient is a one-digit number?

- They should check each calculation using a division method of their choice, for example partitioning to find part-quotients or using the column method.

- Return to the table, explaining that all the examples in the left-hand column are divisions where the highest value place in the quotient is the ones. Moving on to the right-hand column, explain that these are divisions where highest-value place in the quotient is the tens.

- Pupils should complete Questions 4 and 5 in the Practice Book.

Chapter 3 Dividing by 2-digit numbers

Unit 3.6 Practice Book 5A, pages 71–74

Same-day intervention

- Sketch the following two arrays on squared paper. Use **Resource 5.3.6a** Squared paper.

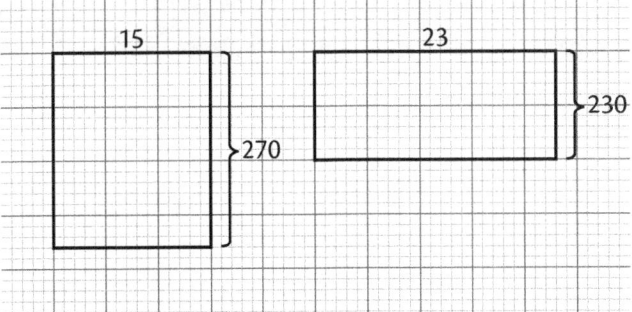

- Ask: *How do you know that both divisions give a two-digit quotient?* Establish that 10 or more groups have been made, and this is shown by the number of rows in the array.

- Can pupils identify the two divisions the arrays represent? Record these as 270 ÷ 15 = 18 and 230 ÷ 23 = 10.

- Ask pupils to explain what they notice about the number of tens in the dividend 270 (27 tens) compared to the divisor (15). They should notice that there are more tens, so more than 10 groups of 15 can be made as 10 × 15 = 150.

 *The first two digits in the dividend must be equal to or greater than the divisor to give a two-digit quotient.*

- Ask pupils to now sketch an array to show that 135 ÷ 15 = 9. Can they explain why the quotient is a one-digit number by comparing 13 tens in the divisor and the divisor 15? Can they explain that 10 × 15 is more than 135?

- Pupils should sketch two arrays of their own to show divisions with a two-digit division – one with a one-digit quotient and the other with a two-digit quotient. Can they identify the divisions they have represented? Can they explain the size of the quotients by comparing the number of tens in the dividend and the divisor?

Same-day enrichment

- Give pairs of pupils **Resource 5.3.6d** Rolling digits, two sets of different-coloured counters (one set for each player) and a 0–9 dice. They roll the dice and reason about whether the quotient will be a one-digit or a two-digit number.

Chapter 3 Dividing by 2-digit numbers · Unit 3.6 Practice Book 5A, pages 71–74

Challenge and extension question

Question 6

6. Fill in the boxes with suitable numbers to complete the column division.

Pupils are required to reason about missing digits in column division calculations.

The first thing they should do is list what they can see or infer from what they see, for example for the first calculation:

- The quotient has two digits.
- The first multiple of 26 to be subtracted from the dividend has 2 in the hundreds column, therefore must be 260. This also shows that the missing digit in the quotient is 1.
- The remainder is 22.

There is sufficient information here to deduce the dividend since the quotient, divisor and remainder are known. So, dividend = 19 × 26 + 22 = 516.

The second calculation is particularly challenging since there are unknown values in the quotient, divisor and dividend. Pupils should notice and reason that:

- The quotient is between 20 and 29. That is, the dividend is at least 20 times the divisor. So the missing digit in the divisor is not 1.
- The dividend is a multiple of 10 between 900 and 990.
  - Dividing the largest possible dividend (990) by the smallest possible quotient (20) gives the largest possible divisor (49).
  - Dividing the smallest possible dividend (900) by the largest possible quotient (29) give the smallest possible divisor (31).
- The ones digit in the divisor is 8, so there are only two possible divisors, 38 and 48.
- There is a remainder 2, so the dividend is 2 more than a multiple of the divisor. Therefore, the divisor cannot be 48 because 48 × 20 = 960 with no remainder.

- A divisor of 38 seems the only possible divisor, so, for the quotient to be at least 20, the dividend must be at least 960. Trial and elimination reveal that the dividend can only be 990 and the quotient 26.

Chapter 3 Dividing by 2-digit numbers

Unit 3.7
Dividing multi-digit numbers by a 2-digit number (2)

Conceptual context

In this unit, pupils continue to reason about a range of division problems. They revisit the order of operations and use this knowledge to reorder calculations to make them simpler and calculate smartly. Pupils further explore the language that can be used to describe a multiplication or division, using this understanding fluently to help identify the calculations required to solve it. Teaching will focus on mental as well as written methods.

Learning pupils will have achieved at the end of the unit

- Pupils will be able to explain why the quotient for a division is double or half that of a related division, for example 360 ÷ 60 has a quotient that is half of 360 ÷ 30 (Q1)
- Pupils will be able to explain why a quotient will be smaller or larger when comparing divisions using the same dividend (Q2)
- Fluency in dividing by a two-digit number using the column method will have been strengthened (Q2)
- Pupils will have flexibly used a range of mental strategies to carry out calculations using all four operations (Q3)
- Pupils will be able to explain when a calculation can be reordered to make it simpler (Q3, Q4)
- The language of division and multiplication will have been used flexibly to describe calculations (Q4)
- Pupils will be able to reason how many digits there will be in a quotient after a division (Q5)

Resources

place value counters or cubes; calculators; **Resource 5.3.7a** Comparing quotients; **Resource 5.3.7b** Quotient families; **Resource 5.3.7c** Larger or smaller?; **Resource 5.3.7d** Quotient puzzle (1); **Resource 5.3.7e** Picture problems; **Resource 5.3.7f** Calculation problems (1); **Resource 5.3.7g** Calculation problems (2); **Resource 5.3.7h** Missing numbers

Vocabulary

division, divide, dividend, divisor, quotient, remainder, equivalent, multiple, double, half

Chapter 3 Dividing by 2-digit numbers

Unit 3.7 Practice Book 5A, pages 75–77

Question 1

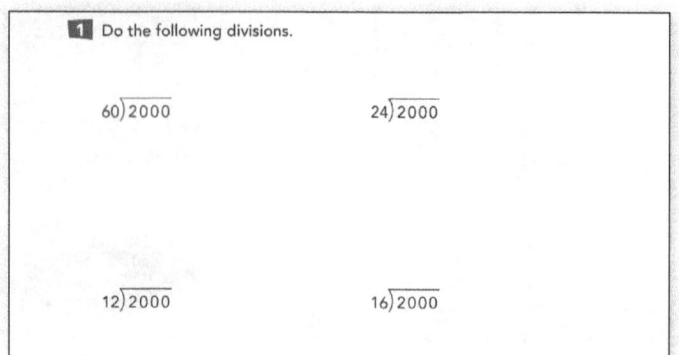

What learning will pupils have achieved at the conclusion of Question 1?

- Pupils will be able to explain why the quotient for a division is double or half that of a related division, for example 360 ÷ 60 has a quotient that is half of 360 ÷ 30.

Activities for whole-class instruction

- Discuss the relationships between the quotients for each of the following pairs of divisions:
  - 32 ÷ 8 and 320 ÷ 8
  - 40 ÷ 5 and 400 ÷ 50
  - 60 ÷ 12 and 600 ÷ 12
- Agree that:
  - The quotient for 320 ÷ 8 is 10 times larger than for 32 ÷ 8 because the dividend is 10 times larger.
  - The quotients for 40 ÷ 5 and 400 ÷ 50 are the same because both the dividend and the divisor in 400 ÷ 50 have been made 10 times larger. They are equivalent divisions.
  - The quotient for 600 ÷ 12 is 10 times larger than for 60 ÷ 12 because the dividend is 10 times larger.

 *When the dividend is 10 times larger and the divisor is the same, the quotient is 10 times larger.*

- Now show the following divisions:

  3200 ÷ 8   4000 ÷ 50   6000 ÷ 12

- Ask: *How do the quotients compare this time? Why?* Agree that the quotients are now all 10 times larger than for 320 ÷ 8, 400 ÷ 50 and 600 ÷ 12 because only the dividends are all 10 times larger.
- Give small groups of pupils a set of cards from **Resource 5.3.7a** Comparing quotients. They should shuffle the cards and pick a pair of divisions at a time. As a group, pupils should compare the calculations and explain the relationship between the quotients. The cards should be returned to the pile and re-shuffled between turns. (Note that some cards have the same calculations.)

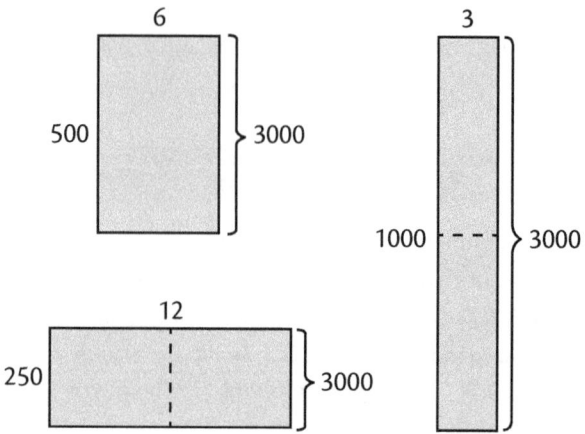

- Show pupils some cards that you have been comparing.

  | 3000 ÷ 6 | 3000 ÷ 12 | 3000 ÷ 3 |

- Suggest that you only need to find the quotient for 3000 ÷ 6 to know what the quotients will be for the others. Pupils should discuss your suggestion and prepare to feedback.
- Sketch arrays to confirm that the quotient for 3000 ÷ 12 will be half the size because the size of each group has doubled (or double the number of groups are made); the quotient for 3000 ÷ 3 will be double the size because the size of each group has halved (or half the number of groups are made).

- Finally, look together at the following divisions:

  15)4000   20)4000   30)4000   16)4000

- Ask: *How can we solve each of these divisions?* Pupils should discuss their strategies and solve. Do they recognise that the answer to the division 3000 ÷ 40 must be half the size as the answer for 3000 ÷ 20?

Chapter 3 Dividing by 2-digit numbers

Unit 3.7 Practice Book 5A, pages 75–77

- Share ideas, using the column method as required, drawing on the following:
  - that 4000 ÷ 15 gives a quotient that is 10 times larger than for 400 ÷ 15
  - the equivalent division 40 ÷ 2 can be used for 400 ÷ 20, so 4000 ÷ 20 is 10 times larger still
  - 4000 ÷ 30 can be solved using what we know about 4000 ÷ 15. The divisor is doubled, so the quotient will be halved
  - The first step in the calculation 4000 ÷ 16 is to look at 400 ÷ 16, which will be smaller than the quotient for 400 ÷ 10 but larger than the quotient for 400 ÷ 20. We can also use the very useful fact that 25 × 4 = 100, so 25 × 16 = 400, so 250 × 16 = 4000 to help us.
- Pupils should complete Question 1 in the Practice Book.

Same-day intervention

- Work together through the examples in Question 1, looking for related divisions and those that might use the very important fact that 4 × 25 = 100, discussed in the lesson.
- Can pupils explain how they would solve the following pairs of divisions?

  360 ÷ 12 and 3600 ÷ 12

  4000 ÷ 50 and 4000 ÷ 25

Same-day enrichment

- Give pupils **Resource 5.3.7b** Quotient families. Can they find families of divisions that share quotients or where quotients are double/half of another?

Question 2

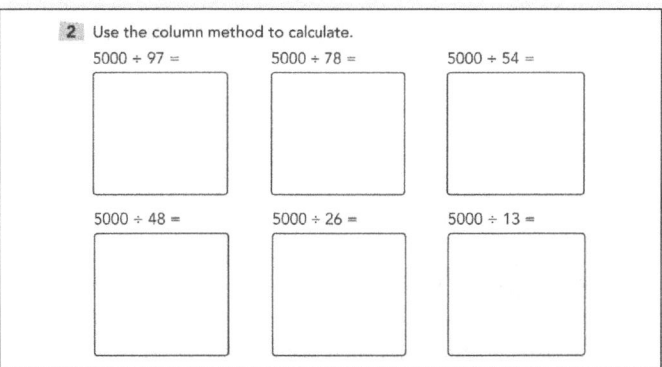

What learning will pupils have achieved at the conclusion of Question 2?

- Pupils will be able to explain why a quotient will be smaller or larger when comparing divisions using the same dividend.
- Fluency in dividing by a two-digit number using the column method will have been strengthened.

Activities for whole-class instruction

- Give pupils set of hundreds place value counters or cubes, where each represents 100. Ask: *Can you show me 200 divided by 40 as an array?* Can pupils explain how the quotient will change for the division 200 ÷ 20 without making the array? Agree that the quotient will be double the size because the size of each group (40) is halved (20).
- Ask pupils to explain whether the quotient will be smaller or larger than the quotient for 200 ÷ 40 for the following divisions:

  200 ÷ 50   200 ÷ 30   200 ÷ 60   200 ÷ 10

- They should quickly rearrange their counters or cubes to prove their thinking, finding the answer to each division.

   *When the dividend is the same, if the divisor gets smaller, the quotient gets larger.*

- Can pupils complete the sentence stem, 'When the dividend is the same ...' to explain what happens when the divisor gets larger?
- Explain that the dividend, 200, is now made 10 times larger for each of the divisions above. Can pupils record the new calculations and explain to a partner what will happen to the size of the quotient each time?

Chapter 3 Dividing by 2-digit numbers

Unit 3.7 Practice Book 5A, pages 75–77

- Record the calculations as 2000 ÷ 50, 2000 ÷ 30, 2000 ÷ 60, 200 ÷ 10 and agree that the quotients will be 10 times larger. Can pupils explain why the remainders will also be 10 times larger?
- Show the following calculations on the board. Can pupils explain whether the quotient will be smaller or larger than for 2000 ÷ 40 each time?

  41)2000   36)2000   18)2000   65)2000

- Pupils should complete each calculation using the column method, using estimates to help decide how many groups of the divisor there will be. Take feedback, recording each calculation on the board. For example:

  ```
              4  8    remainder 16
      4 1 ) 2  0  0  0
            1  6  4  0   (4 × 41)
               3  6  0
               3  2  8   (8 × 41)
                  3  2
  ```

- Pupils should complete Question 2 in the Practice Book.

Same-day intervention

- Give pupils **Resource 5.3.7c** Larger or smaller? They should compare the pairs of division calculations and insert the correct symbols. The last example is a little different as the dividends are not the same, so must be calculated.

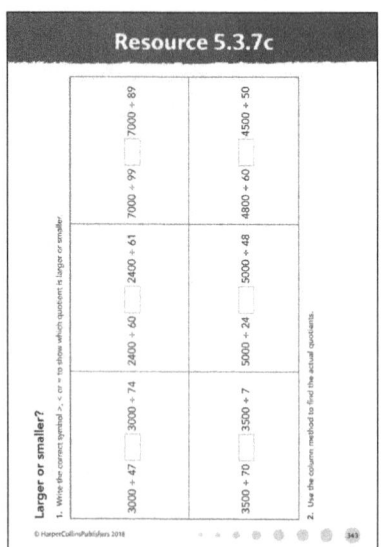

Answers: 1. >, >, <; <, >, <; 2. Column method used correctly.

Same-day enrichment

- Give pupils **Resource 5.3.7d** Quotient puzzle (1). Pupils should calculate quotients and complete the puzzle. They should use the column method to check any calculations as required.

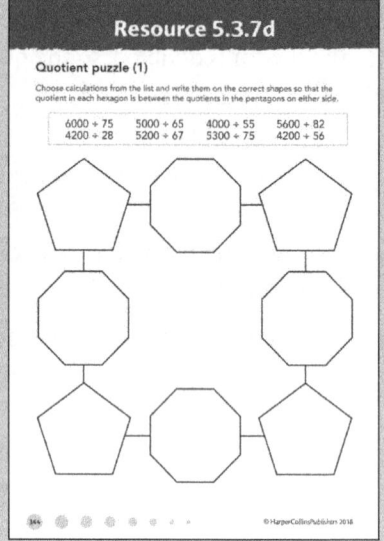

Question 3

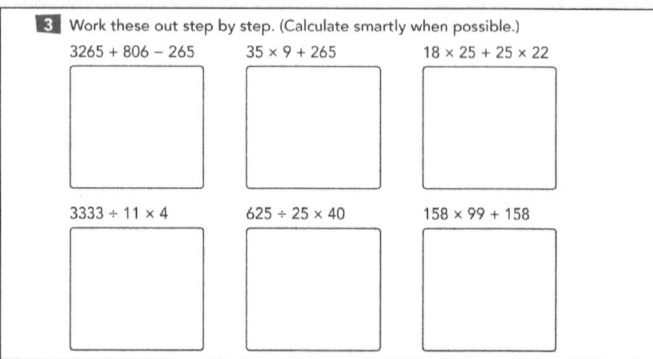

What learning will pupils have achieved at the conclusion of Question 3?

- Pupils will have flexibly used a range of mental strategies to carry out calculations using all four operations.
- Pupils will be able to explain when a calculation can be reordered to make it simpler.

Activities for whole-class instruction

- Show pupils the following pictures. Ask: *What calculations can we use to find the total number of marbles each time?*

Chapter 3 Dividing by 2-digit numbers

Unit 3.7 Practice Book 5A, pages 75–77

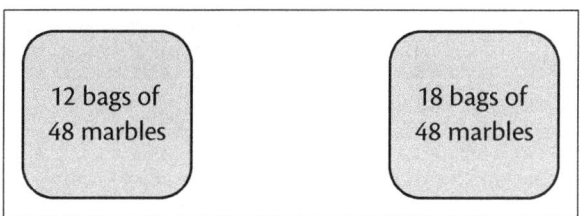

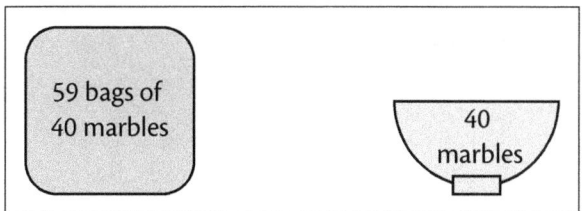

- Take feedback, agreeing that the calculations are:
  - 12 × 48 + 18 × 48
  - 200 + 16 × 25
  - 59 × 40 + 40
- Discuss strategies for solving each, focusing on the following:
  - Calculation 1:
    - There are 12 + 18 lots of 48 here. This (30 × 48) could be solved as 3 × 48 × 10.
  - Calculation 2:
    - This is solved as a multiplication (16 × 25) and an addition. However, both parts can be considered as multiples of 25, which would give 8 × 25 + 16 × 25, which is 24 × 25.
    - Knowledge of the number of 25s in 100 helps here, to change to 6 × 100.
  - Calculation 3:
    - The extra 40 marbles can be seen as another group of 40, so the calculation is simply 60 × 40.
    - 60 × 40 can be solved using factors as 6 × 4 × 100.
- Pupils should now solve the following calculations, discussing strategies with a partner:

  800 − 35 × 20   50 + 200 ÷ 4
  15 × 60 + 60 × 15   75 + 75 × 19

- Address any issues, reinforcing that multiplication and division are carried out before addition and subtraction.

- Now discuss another picture and the story it shows, establishing that there are 480 marbles in the container and then 195 are added but 95 are subtracted.

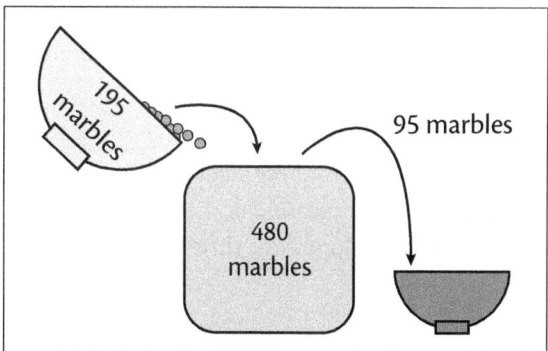

- Ask: *How many marbles are in the container now? What calculation should we write?*
- Record the calculation as 480 + 195 − 95 and as 195 + 480 − 95, agreeing that the order does not matter.

 *We can reorder calculations that only involve addition and subtraction.*

- Pupils should discuss the most efficient way to solve this. Do they notice that they can calculate smartly by first subtracting 95 from 195 so only the addition 480 + 100 is necessary?
- Quickly practise strategies to calculate smartly using a few more examples:

  3499 + 5750 − 499   4563 − 299 + 399
  5000 − 2750 − 250

- Revisit the fact that we can reorder a calculation involving only addition and subtraction. Ask: *Can we also reorder calculations involving only multiplication and division? Why/why not?* Agree that multiplication and division are the inverse of each other and both have the same importance. Therefore, we can choose whether to multiply first or divide.
- Show this using the following examples:

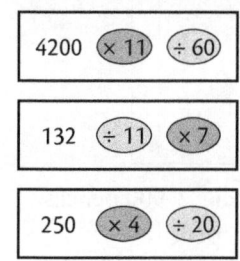

- Explain that in the first calculation, you have noticed an easy division calculation using 42 ÷ 6, so you will do this one first. Reorder the calculation to show this, agreeing that the answer is 70 × 11 (770).

  4200 ÷ 60 × 11

Chapter 3 Dividing by 2-digit numbers

Unit 3.7 Practice Book 5A, pages 75–77

- Ask: *What about the other calculations? Should I change the order of those?* Agree that 132 ÷ 11 is an easy calculation and that 250 × 4 is simply 1000, making the second part of each calculation straightforward. So, the second and third parts do not need to be reordered.
- Pupils should quickly copy the calculations below and test these ideas, explaining why reordering may be a useful strategy for some of these calculations. Encourage them to circle the multiplication part to be done and the division part to be done each time before making a decision.

  7000 × 45 ÷ 7   375 × 48 ÷ 100
  4500 × 11 ÷ 90   500 ÷ 50 × 32

- Take feedback, agreeing that reordering the first and third calculations as 7000 ÷ 7 × 45 and 4500 ÷ 90 × 11 make the calculations simpler as 1000 × 45 and 50 × 11.

 *We can decide what to do first when a calculation involves only multiplication and division.*

- Pupils should complete Question 3 in the Practice Book.

Same-day intervention

- Give pupils **Resource 5.3.7e** Picture problems. Can they write and solve the calculations each image represents? Allow pupils time to work on the activity and then ask them to explain their answers.

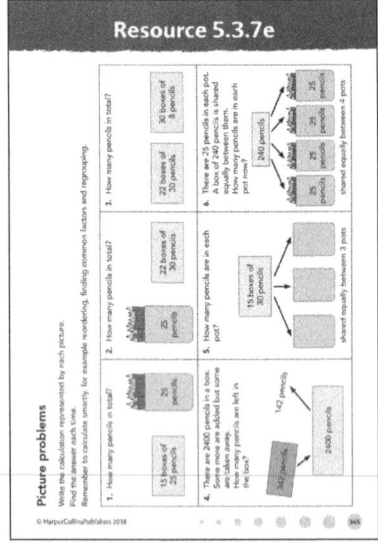

Answers: 1. 400 pencils; 2. 685 pencils; 3. 900 pencils; 4. 2600 pencils; 5. 150 pencils; 6. 85 pencils.

Same-day enrichment

- Explain that you would like pupils to first write a word problem or sketch a picture problem (as for the marbles in the whole-class activity above) to match three of the calculations in Question 3.
- They should then make a list of their own calculations that they would reorder or regroup using common factors to help solve them and another list of those they would not reorder. They should explain their decisions to a partner.

Questions 4 and 5

4 Write the number sentences and then calculate the answer.
  (a) When the product of 84 and 14 is divided by 49, what is the quotient?

  (b) How many times 18 is the sum of the greatest 3-digit number and the greatest 2-digit number?

  (c) When the product of two fifteens is divided by 225, what is the quotient?

5 Multiple choice questions. (For each question, choose the correct answer and write the letter in the box.)
  (a) In the division sentences below, the quotient that is a 2-digit number is ☐.
      A. 2188 ÷ 22   B. 324 ÷ 55   C. 843 ÷ 8   D. 3838 ÷ 28
  (b) A 4-digit number is divided by a 2-digit number. The quotient is ☐.
      A. 2-digit number
      B. 3-digit number
      C. 1-digit number
      D. 2-digit number or 3-digit number

What learning will pupils have achieved at the conclusion of Questions 4 and 5?

- Pupils will be able to explain when a calculation can be reordered to make it simpler.
- The language of division and multiplication will have been used flexibly to describe calculations.
- Pupils will be able to reason how many digits there will be in a quotient after a division.

Chapter 3 Dividing by 2-digit numbers

Unit 3.7 Practice Book 5A, pages 75–77

Activities for whole-class instruction

- Give pupils **Resource 5.3.7f** Calculation problems (1).

- Ask: *How do you know that the children are all talking about calculations that can be solved using division?* Pupils should discuss the question and justify their thinking.

- Conclude that division can be used to solve each calculation. Together, record the calculations that the problems represent and the divisions that can be used to solve them.
  - 45 × ☐ = 945   So 945 ÷ 45 = ☐
  - 6300 = ☐ × 90 (or ☐ × 90 = 6300)   So 6300 ÷ 90 = ☐
  - 400 = 25 × ☐ (or 25 × ☐ = 400)   So 400 ÷ 25 = ☐
  - ☐ × 60 = 7200 (or 60 × ☐ = 7200)   So 7200 ÷ 60 = ☐

- Focus on the divisions 945 ÷ 45, 6300 ÷ 90 and 7200 ÷ 60. Ask: *How many digits will each of the quotients have? How do you know?*

- Discuss how we know that:
  - For a two-digit quotient, the first two digits of the dividend need to be at least as big as the divisor. In 945 ÷ 45 we can see that 94 > 45 and 45 times 10 is 450. The quotient will be a two-digit number.
  - 6300 ÷ 90 will also have a two-digit quotient because the smallest three-digit quotient is 100 and 90 × 100 is 9000, which is much bigger than the dividend 6300.
  - 7200 ÷ 60 will have a three-digit quotient because the smallest three-digit quotient is 100 and 60 × 100 is 6000, which is smaller than the dividend 7200 – more than 100 groups of the divisor can be made.

- Pupils should quickly solve the divisions to find the answers to the problems, using what they know about the number of digits in the quotients to help make decisions. Discuss when known facts and place value could be used or when a column method was useful.

- Write:
  1470 ÷ 32 = ☐   1210 ÷ 11 = ☐

- Can pupils make up two problems like those discussed by the children that would be represented by these division sentences?

- Share different examples, confirming whether they do or do not work for the divisions involved. Discuss strategies to find the actual answers, asking a pupil to model the column method for 1470 ÷ 32.

- Finally, share the following problems:
  - *The product of 30 and 20 is divided by 15. What is the quotient?*
  - *The product of two 20s is divided by 50. What is the quotient?*

- Can pupils write the calculations they need to use to solve them? Can they explain why there are two steps to each problem?

- Give pupils **Resource 5.3.7g** Calculation problems (2). It shows two children talking about some calculations. Ask: *Why has each child said that? What have they noticed?* Agree that Nisha has spotted that 30 ÷ 15 is 2, so the calculation is simply 2 × 20. Benji has seen that 20 × 20 = 400, and this can easily be divided by 50.

- Point out that sometimes there is no way to make the calculation simpler, so it should just be carried out in the order it is written in, for example 365 × 45 ÷ 17.

- Pupils should complete Questions 4 and 5 in the Practice Book.

Chapter 3 Dividing by 2-digit numbers

Unit 3.7 Practice Book 5A, pages 75–77

Same-day intervention

- Look at the problems in Question 4 together, discussing the calculations that each represent and the divisions that are necessary.
- Can pupils write similar problems for the calculations $24 \times 21 \div 7$ and $60 \times 60 \div 12$? Can they explain how they will solve each one and whether the calculations can be reordered to make them simpler?
- Can they explain how many digits will be in each quotient?

Same-day enrichment

- Give pupils **Resource 5.3.7h** Missing numbers. They should find the missing numbers to complete each of the problems.

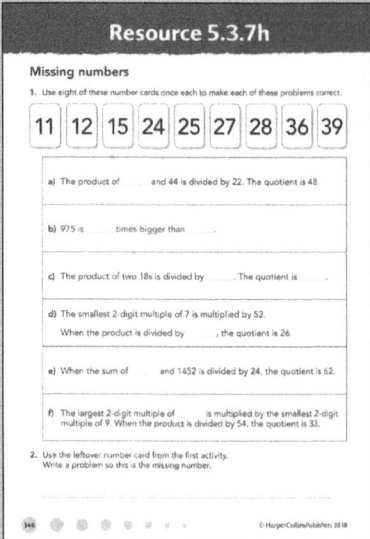

Answers: 1. a) 24; b) 25, 39; c) 27, 12; d) 28; e) 36; f) 11; 2. Pupils' own answers.

Challenge and extension question

Question 6

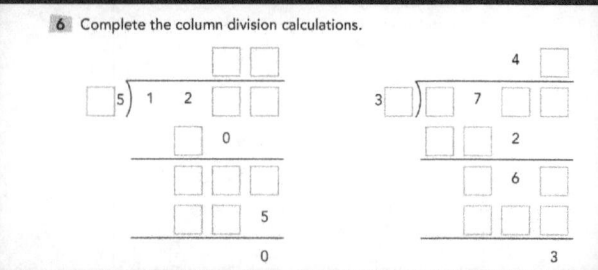

Pupils are required to reason about missing digits in column division calculations. The first thing they should do is list what they can see or infer from what they see. For example, for the first calculation:

- They should recognise that the initial step in the first example is a three-digit number divided by a two digit number and the largest multiple that can be made is a two-digit number.
- The divisor must be 45 because more groups of 15, 25 and 35 could be made. A divisor of 55 would result in a three-digit multiple as $2 \times 55 = 110$ and $1 \times 55 = 55$; another group can still be made.
- There is also no remainder, so the final division involves a dividend that is exactly divisible by 45.

In the second example, pupils should recognise that:

- The largest possible number for the dividend is less than $50 \times 40 = 2000$ (estimation for 49×39), so the first digit in the dividend must be 1.
- The first digit in the quotient is 4, so 4×3 is less than 17 tens but also ends in the digit 2 ($38 \times 4 = 152$).
- When 152 is subtracted the remainder is 26, so the first three digits of the dividend are 178.
- The final stage is to find a multiple of 38 that is 3 less than 26.
- When 38 is multiplied by 7 the product is 266, so the final digit in the dividend is 9.

Chapter 3 Dividing by 2-digit numbers

Unit 3.8
Practice and exercise

Conceptual context

In this chapter, pupils have extended their understanding of division to work with two-digit divisors.

They have developed a range of mental methods, allowing them to make informed decisions about the most efficient way to calculate. Pupils understand how to predict the approximate size of a quotient.

The relationship between multiplication and division has been further strengthened as pupils work flexibly with both operations, interchanging as necessary to solve a range of problems.

Conceptual understanding of dividing by a two-digit number using the column method has been developed throughout the chapter so that pupils can calculate confidently and fluently.

In this unit, pupils will practise and apply their learning in a range of contexts.

Learning pupils will have achieved at the end of the unit

- Pupils will have applied their knowledge of division flexibly in different contexts (Q1)
- Pupils will have drawn on a range of mental strategies to carry out calculations using all four operations (Q1)
- Understanding of the order of operations will have been strengthened as pupils solve a range of problems (Q1, Q3)
- Pupils will be able to explain when a calculation can be reordered to make it simpler and so calculate more efficiently (Q1, Q3)
- Pupils' fluency when dividing by a two-digit number using the column method will have continued to develop (Q2)
- The language of division and multiplication will have been used flexibly to describe calculations (Q4)
- Pupils will be able to recognise and explain how many digits there will be in a quotient after a division (Q5)

Resources

Resource 5.3.8a Using known facts; **Resource 5.3.8b** The answer is the same; **Resource 5.3.8c** Quotient puzzle (2); **Resource 5.3.8d** Making calculations; **Resource 5.3.8e** Using bar models; **Resource 5.3.8f** Division calculations; **Resource 5.3.8g** Quotient cruncher

Vocabulary

division, divide, dividend, divisor, quotient, remainder, equivalent, multiple, double, half

Chapter 3 Dividing by 2-digit numbers

Unit 3.8 Practice Book 5A, pages 78–80

Question 1

1 Work these out mentally and then write the answers.
(a) 35 × 20 = ☐
(b) 36 × 5 ÷ 18 = ☐
(c) 79 × 0 × 12 = ☐
(d) 6800 ÷ 34 = ☐
(e) 86 × 5 − 30 = ☐
(f) 100 − 100 ÷ 25 = ☐
(g) 9300 ÷ 31 = ☐
(h) 3000 ÷ 25 = ☐
(i) 2000 ÷ 500 = ☐
(j) 1000 ÷ 250 = ☐
(k) 9000 ÷ 3000 = ☐
(l) 10 000 ÷ 100 = ☐

What learning will pupils have achieved at the conclusion of Question 1?

- Pupils will have applied their knowledge of division flexibly in different contexts.
- Pupils will have drawn on a range of mental strategies to carry out calculations using all four operations.
- Understanding of the order of operations will have been strengthened as pupils solve a range of problems.
- Pupils will be able to explain when a calculation can be reordered to make it simpler and so calculate more efficiently.

Activities for whole-class instruction

- Show or give pupils **Resource 5.3.8a** Using known facts. Can they quickly complete the answers before checking with a partner?

Resource 5.3.8a

100 ÷ 25	24 × 5	5 × 50
24 × 10	half of 48	16 × 20
4 × 25	double 16	48 ÷ 24
10 × 100	50 × 0	100 ÷ 4

- Revisit any strategies or connections as required, ensuring that pupils have recognised that:
  - 24 × 5 is half of 24 × 10
  - 16 × 20 can be seen as 16 × 2 × 10 using factors so that double 16 can be carried out first
  - half of 48 is the same as 48 ÷ 2 = 24, so 48 ÷ 24 = 2

  - the product is always zero when a factor in a multiplication is zero.

- Show pupils the following three sets of calculations:

45 + 0 × 50	32 × 45 ÷ 16	4800 ÷ 24
48 × 5 ÷ 24	20 ÷ 40 × 16	78 − 200 ÷ 25
1000 ÷ 25	2000 ÷ 40	10 × 24 × 2

- Suggest that the 'known facts' you have been discussing may come in useful here. Split the class into three groups, assigning each a set of calculations to discuss. Can they explain which of the facts they can use each time and how?

- Take feedback from each group, referring to the use of the known facts and/or place value each time, for example 1000 ÷ 25 is 10 times larger than 100 ÷ 25. Focus particularly on the following calculations:
  - multiplication should be carried out first in 45 + 0 × 50
  - division should be carried out first in 78 − 200 ÷ 25
  - 48 × 5 ÷ 24, 32 × 45 ÷ 16 and 20 ÷ 40 × 16 involve only multiplication and division and can be reordered to simplify the calculations:

  48 (×5) (÷24)   48 (÷24) (×5)
  32 (×45) (÷16)   32 (÷16) (×45)
  20 (÷80) (×16)   20 (×16) (÷80)

- Pupils should complete Question 1 in the Practice Book.

Same-day intervention

- Discuss each of the calculations in Question 1, drawing out the following points:
  - when multiplication or division has to be carried out first and why
  - when a calculation can be reordered and why this decision might be made
  - the use of known facts, such as 4 × 25 = 100 and doubles/halves
  - the use of place value and known facts, for example relating 3000 ÷ 25 to 1000 ÷ 25, which is 10 times larger than 100 ÷ 25 = 4
  - equivalent divisions, for example 9000 ÷ 3000 and 9 ÷ 3.
- Can pupils use some more of the facts from the session in different ways to make up their own calculations for their partner to solve?

Chapter 3 Dividing by 2-digit numbers

Unit 3.8 Practice Book 5A, pages 78–80

Same-day enrichment

- Give pupils **Resource 5.3.8b** The answer is the same. Can they arrange the number cards so the answer to each calculation is the same two-digit *even* number? Do they recognise that the calculation 99 × 0 + ☐ helps to initially identify the two-digit number as one of the actual number cards 12, 44 or 60?

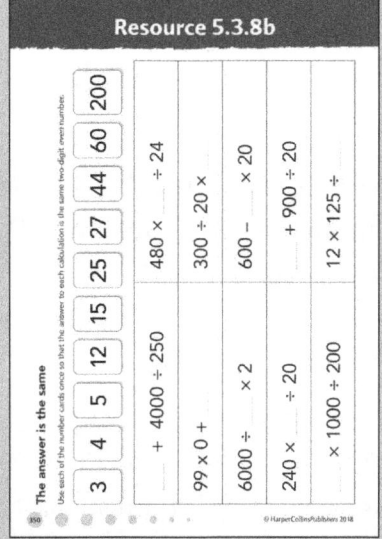

Answers: 44, 3; 60, 4; 200, 27; 5, 15; 12, 25.

Question 2

2. Use the column method to calculate. Check the answers to the questions marked with *.
   (a) 3025 × 88 =   (b) *3296 ÷ 32 =   (c) *2551 ÷ 42 =

What learning will pupils have achieved at the conclusion of Question 2?

- Pupils' fluency when dividing by a two-digit number using the column method will have continued to develop.

Activities for whole-class instruction

- Show pupils the following digits and divisions:

  2   4   5   6   7   8

  ☐☐☐☐ ÷ ☐☐
  ☐☐☐ ÷ ☐☐

- Ask: *When the digits are used only once in a calculation, what is the largest quotient we can make for each calculation?* Give pupils times to discuss this, reasoning about the positions of the digits.

- Agree that the largest quotient each time will arise from the largest possible dividends and the smallest possible divisors. Focus on 8765 ÷ 24 and 876 ÷ 24.

- Pupils should now find the actual quotient for 8765 ÷ 24, making an approximation first. Can they explain whether the quotient will have two or three digits?

- Write the full method on the board for pupils to check against their own. Look at what is known about 8000 ÷ 25 and 9000 ÷ 25 to help make decisions.

```
          3  6  5    remainder 5
     2 4 | 8  7  6  5
           8  6  4  0    36 × 24
           ─────────
                 1  2  5
                 1  2  0    5 × 24
                 ─────
                       5
```

- Ask: *Do we need to calculate to find the quotient for 876 ÷ 24? Why?* Agree that we already know it is 36 because the first stage in the column method shows us. Also 876 is approximately 10 times smaller than 8765, so the quotient will also be approximately 10 times smaller.

- Challenge pupils to find the calculations that result in the smallest quotient. Discuss the position of the digits, agreeing that we are now looking for the smallest three- or four-digit dividend and the largest divisor. (2456 ÷ 87 and 245 ÷ 87)

- Can pupils:
  - explain how many digits the quotient will have?
  - estimate the quotient for 2456 ÷ 87 and use the column method to check?
  - explain why they do not need to calculate 245 ÷ 87?

- Explain that you would like to check their answer to the calculation 2456 ÷ 87 without doing the actual division. Ask pupils what you should do. Agree that multiplication can be used to check.

- Can pupils explain that you need to first multiply 87 by 28 before adding the remainder 20? Record the method on the board as a reminder.

Chapter 3 Dividing by 2-digit numbers

Unit 3.8 Practice Book 5A, pages 78–80

```
       8 7
×      2 8
-----------
     6 9 6    87 × 8 ones
   1 7 4 0    87 × 2 tens
   -------
   2 4 3 6
     1 1
```

2436 + 20 = 2456

- Pupils should complete Question 2 in the Practice Book.

Same-day intervention

- Give pupils **Resource 5.3.8c** Quotient puzzle (2). Pupils should calculate quotients and complete the puzzle. They should use the column method to check any calculations as required.

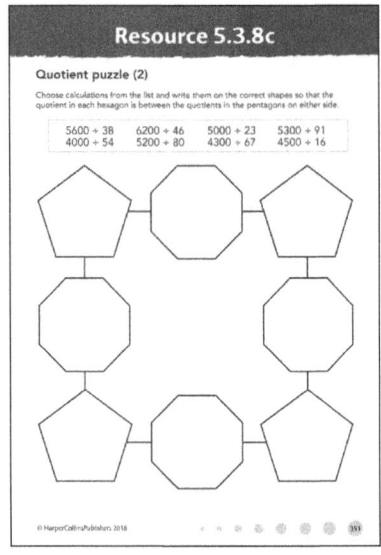

Same-day enrichment

- Pupils further explore quotients by developing the activity from the main session, but this time creating divisions that give rise to the following quotients:
  - a one-digit quotient
  - a three-digit quotient
  - a quotient of 10 (for example 724 ÷ 68)
  - a quotient between 20 and 30
  - a quotient between 200 and 300.
- Can they explain when a quotient of a certain size is not possible and why?

Question 3

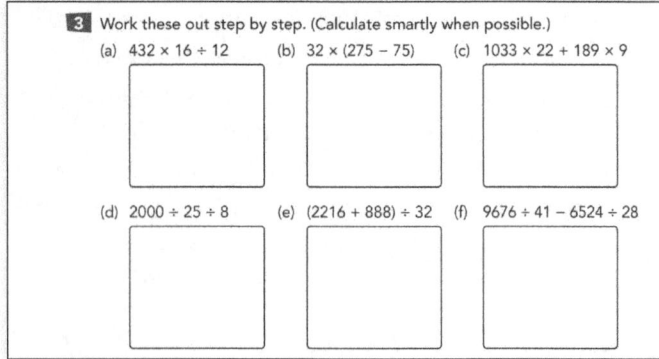

What learning will pupils have achieved at the conclusion of Question 3?

- Pupils will be able to explain when a calculation can be reordered to make it simpler and so calculate more efficiently.

Activities for whole-class instruction

- Show pupils the following calculations that have already been solved. Explain that some of the answers are incorrect.

56 + 34 × 20 = 1800	99 × 100 + 75 × 4 = 10 200
720 × 19 ÷ 90 = 152	45 × (40 + 60) = 1860
8800 × 50 ÷ 11 = 4000	1000 ÷ 25 − 900 ÷ 30 = 10

(1250 + 725) ÷ 25 = 79
25 × 8 × 12 = 2000
53 × 2 + 8 × 53 = 530

- Give pupils time to discuss each calculation, explaining any errors that have been made.
- Look at the incorrect solutions in turn, focusing on errors that have arisen from:
  - not carrying out a multiplication or division before a subtraction or addition
  - not carrying out a calculation inside a bracket first
  - mistakes in place value
  - mistakes when using multiplication or division facts.
- Agree correct solutions for each of the calculations discussed.
- Discuss why the calculations 720 × 19 ÷ 90 and 8800 × 50 ÷ 11 could be more easily solved by reordering them as 720 ÷ 90 × 19 and 8800 ÷ 11 × 50. Review strategies to multiply by 19 using rounding and adjusting, and multiplying by 50 using × 100 and then ÷ 2.

Chapter 3 Dividing by 2-digit numbers

Unit 3.8 Practice Book 5A, pages 78–80

- Pupils should complete Question 3 in the Practice Book.

Same-day intervention

- Work together with the pupils **Resource 5.3.8d** Making calculations. Cut out the operation cards and lay them in a pile face down. Pupils should position cards in the spaces to make calculations and explain to a partner how they would complete the calculation in a way that makes it simpler where possible.
- Can pupils explain which part of the calculation they should do first and why?
- Put the operation cards back in the pile, shuffle and repeat. Pupils should continue to pick cards to make different calculations in the same way.

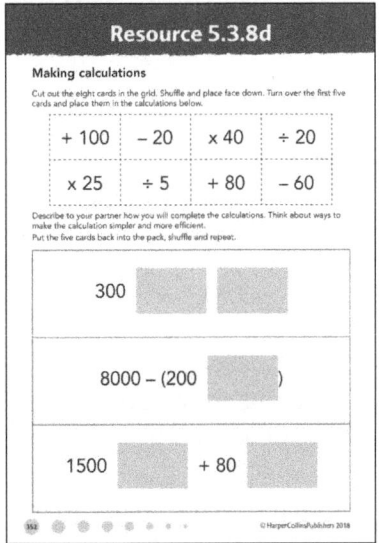

Same-day enrichment

- Pupils should first discuss any strategies they used to 'calculate smartly' in Question 3.
- In pairs, they should write a word problem to match each of the calculations. Can they include aspects of measurement, for example money or length?

Question 4

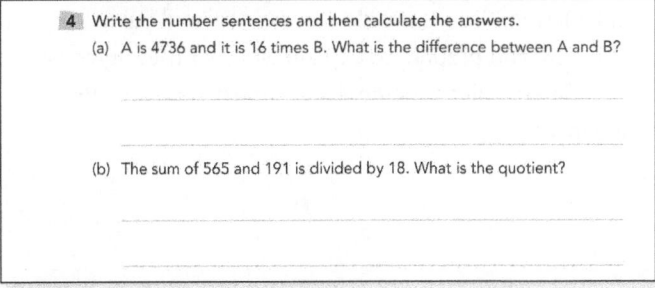

What learning will pupils have achieved at the conclusion of Question 4?

- The language of division and multiplication will have been used flexibly to describe calculations.

Activities for whole-class instruction

- Show pupils the following images, explaining that they each represent the same problem.

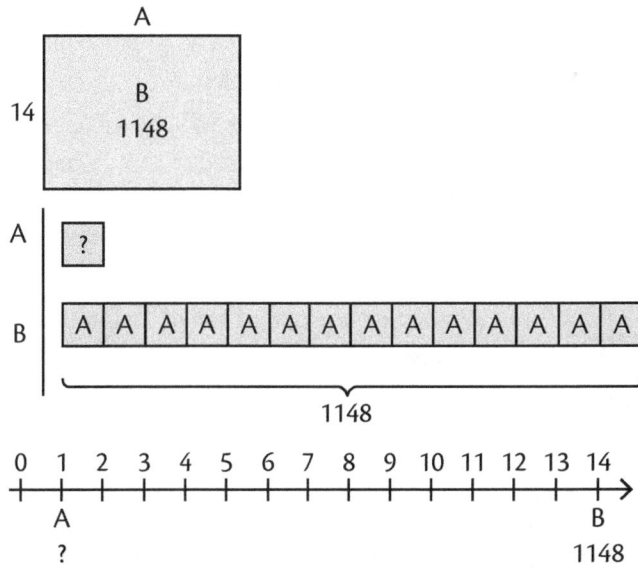

- Split the class into three groups, assigning them each an image to discuss. Can they reason about the problem their image represents and how they know?
- Take feedback, agreeing that the value of B is 14 times larger than the value of A. We can find the value of A by dividing 1148 by 14. Look at how the image shows this each time.
- Suggest that the following problems match the images:
  - A value (A) is multiplied by 14. The product (B) is 1148. What is the value of A?
  - A × 14 = B. When B is 1148, what is the value of A?
  - B is 1148 and it is 14 times A. What is the value of A?
  - B is 14 times larger than A. When B is 1148, what is A?
- Pupils should discuss your suggestions, comparing them with their own ideas. Can they explain why each problem does match?
- Ask pupils to find the value of A using a division method of their choice. Agree that this is 82 and can be checked using 82 × 14 = 1148.
- Return to the bar model diagram. Ask: *How can we use the image to help find the difference between the values of A and B?* Agree that the difference between the values is the same as 13 groups of A. Show this on the bar model as:

Chapter 3 Dividing by 2-digit numbers

Unit 3.8 Practice Book 5A, pages 78–80

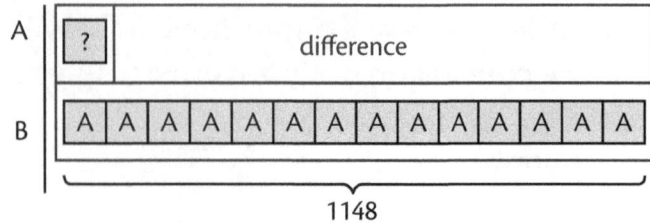

- Establish that 13 groups of A is 1066, which is one group of 82 less than 1148. Conclude that the difference between the values A and B is 1066.
- Finally, explain that the next part of the problem is that the sum of A and B is divided by 30. Can pupils explain what calculation needs to be completed?
- Record this as (1148 + 82) ÷ 30. Ask: *Why have I used brackets?* Agree that brackets are used to show what needs to be done first, and if we did not use them the division would need to be carried out first, and we do not want to do this.
- Pupils should complete the calculation in their own way. Agree that the answer to the problem is 41.
- Pupils should complete Question 4 in the Practice Book.

Same-day intervention

- Give pupils **Resource 5.3.8e** Using bar models. They should first discuss what each problem is asking and the calculations they will need to use. Pupils may find it useful to work with a partner when starting to represent and solve the problems.
- Allow them some time to work on the problems before joining the group. Discuss how the problems are similar to those in Question 3, looking together at the use of bar models each time.

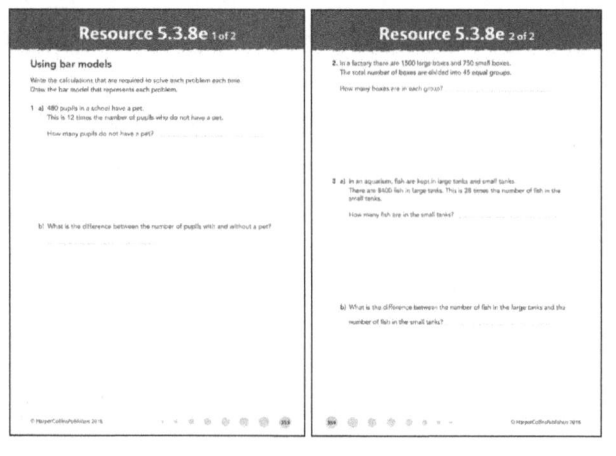

Answers: 1. a) 40; b) 440; 2. (1500 + 750) ÷ 45 = 50 boxes; 3. a) 8400 ÷ 28 = 300 fish; b) 8400 − 300 = 8100 fish.

Same-day enrichment

- Show pupils the different calculations that have been used to solve five different problems.

  576 ÷ 18   (2670 + 4930) ÷ 19   1587 ÷ 23
  (750 − 294) ÷ 57   1248 ÷ 26

- Can pupils make up their own problems to go with each calculation using the context of values A and B? Discuss the first example, 576 ÷ 18, agreeing a possible solution to the problem before they continue on their own. For example *B is 18 times larger than A. When B is 576, what is the value of A?* Can they explain that the difference between values A and B in this example is 576 − 32 or 17 × 32?
- Pupils should select three of the problems and represent them using the bar model.

Question 5

> 5 Fill in the missing numbers to make each statement correct.
> (a) Find the quotients of the following division calculations.
> 125 ÷ 25 = ☐   1250 ÷ 25 = ☐   1275 ÷ 25 = ☐
> (b) When the quotient of 440 ÷ ■3 is a 2-digit number, the greatest possible number in the ■ is ☐.
> (c) When the quotient of 9■95 + 95 is a 3-digit number, the least possible number in the ■ is ☐; in this case, the quotient is ☐ and the remainder is ☐. When the quotient is a 2-digit number, the greatest possible number in the ■ is ☐; in this case, the quotient is ☐ and the remainder is ☐.

What learning will pupils have achieved at the conclusion of Question 5?

- Pupils will be able to recognise and explain how many digits there will be in a quotient after a division.

Activities for whole-class instruction

- Give pupils **Resource 5.3.8f** Division calculations. This shows two children talking about two division calculations. Pupils should discuss Ami and Luka's thinking and prepare to explain whether they agree or not. Discuss ideas and agree that both Ami and Luka are incorrect.

Chapter 3 Dividing by 2-digit numbers

Unit 3.8 Practice Book 5A, pages 78–80

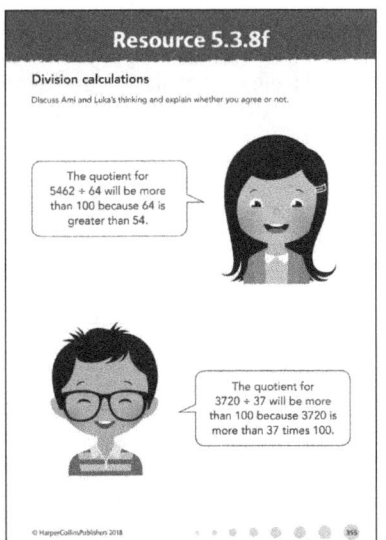

 *The first two digits in a four-digit dividend must be equal to or greater than the divisor to give a three-digit quotient.*

- Pupils should use this generalisation to quickly sort these divisions into those with a one-digit and those with a two-digit divisor.

  7832 ÷ 87   4091 ÷ 49   5480 ÷ 54
  2653 ÷ 25   8375 ÷ 84   4442 ÷ 43

- Look at each division in turn, being sure to include the following, for example:

  - 7832 ÷ 87   The quotient is a two-digit number because 87 × 100 is 8700. The first two digits in the dividend are 78, and this is less than the divisor 87. The highest-value place in the quotient is the tens.

  - 5480 ÷ 54   The quotient is a three-digit number because 54 × 100 is 5400. The highest-value place in the quotient is the hundreds.

  - 4442 ÷ 43   The quotient is a three-digit number because 43 × 100 is 4300 and 44 is more than 43. The highest-value place in the quotient is the hundreds.

- Return to each calculation in turn to find the quotients and any remainders.

- Finally, show pupils the following divisions with missing digits:

  6320 ÷ ☐4   5☐63 ÷ 57   4625 ÷ 4☐

- Split the class into two groups, labelling one group as 'three-digit quotients' and the other as 'two-digit quotients'. They should reason about the possible missing digits that result in a quotient to match their group. For example, for the 'two-digit quotient' group, choose 7 as the missing digit in the first division numbers because 6320 ÷ 74 will result in a two-digit quotient. Encourage pupils to find more than one solution for each division.

- Share ideas, focusing on the largest and smallest missing digit each time. Can pupils find the quotient and any remainders for their calculations?

- Pupils should complete Question 5 in the Practice Book.

Same-day intervention

- Give pupils **Resource 5.3.8g** Quotient cruncher. They should work in pairs to reason about the size of the quotient each time. Pupils should use the sentence from the session, 'The first two digits in a four-digit dividend must be equal to or greater than the divisor to give a three-digit quotient' to help make decisions.

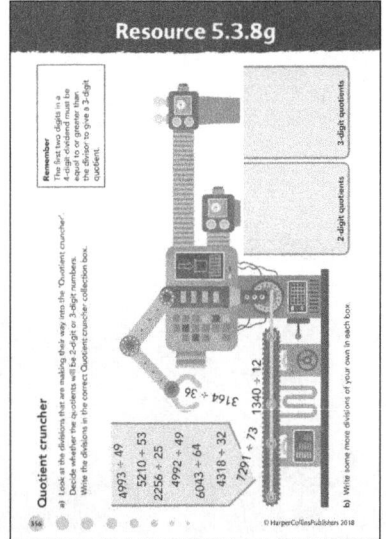

Answers: a) 2-digit quotients: 5210 ÷ 53, 2256 ÷ 25, 6043 ÷ 64, 7291 ÷ 73, 3164 ÷ 36; 3-digit quotients: 4993 ÷ 49, 4992 ÷ 49, 4318 ÷ 32, 1340 ÷ 12; b) Various answers possible.

Same-day enrichment

- Share the following word problems with the group.

  - £2460 is shared equally between a *number of people*. They each receive less than £100.
    How many people could there be?
    How many people could there not be?

  - 3350 kg of sand is divided into 32 kg sacks.
    How many 32 kg sacks will there be?
    Another 4450 kg of sand is divided into 45 kg crates.
    Will there be enough sand for 10 of these crates?

- Give pupils time to solve the problems and then share ideas about possible solutions. Focus particularly on problem 1 as there is more than one solution to the problem.

- Can pupils make up a problem of their own for others to solve that draws on two-digit or three-digit quotients?

Chapter 3 Dividing by 2-digit numbers

Unit 3.8 Practice Book 5A, pages 78–80

Challenge and extension question

Question 6

> 6 The distance between City A and City B is 220 km. How long will it take you to get there if you have the following means of transportation?
>
> | Means of transportation | Speed | Time |
> |---|---|---|
> | On foot | 5 km/h | |
> | By scooter | 20 km/h | |
> | By motorcycle | 40 km/h | |
> | By bus | 80 km/h | |
> | By train | 110 km/h | |
> | By high-speed train | 275 km/h | |

Pupils are required to draw on their understanding of working with speed, distance and time to calculate the time taken at the given speeds to travel a distance of 220 km using different means of transport.

Pupils should reason about division strategies they can apply to solve each calculation and when they can use what has already been calculated to help them, for example already knowing about a speed of 20 km/h they can recognise that the time will be halved for 40 km/h and halved again for 80 km/h.

Chapter 3 test (Practice Book 5A, pages 81–84)

Test question number	Relevant unit	Relevant questions within unit
1	Unit 3.3	Q1
	Unit 3.7	Q3
	Unit 3.8	Q1, Q3
2	Unit 3.6	Q3
	Unit 3.7	Q2
	Unit 3.8	Q2
3	Unit 3.7	Q3
	Unit 3.8	Q3
4	Unit 3.6	Q5
	Unit 3.7	Q5
	Unit 3.8	Q5
5	Unit 3.1	Q5
	Unit 3.2	Q2
	Unit 3.6	Q5
	Unit 3.7	Q3, Q5
	Unit 3.8	Q5
6	Unit 3.2	Q4
	Unit 3.4	Q5
	Unit 3.5	Q5
7	Unit 3.1	Q2
	Unit 3.2	Q3

Chapter 4
Comparing fractions, improper fractions and mixed numbers

Chapter overview

Area of mathematics	National Curriculum statutory requirements for Key Stage 2	Shanghai Maths Project reference
Number – fractions (including decimals and percentages)	Year 5 Programme of study: Pupils should be taught to:	
	• compare and order fractions whose denominators are all multiples of the same number	Year 5, Unit 4.2, 4.3, 4.4
	• identify, name and write equivalent fractions of a given fraction, represented visually, including tenths and hundredths	Year 5, Unit 4.4
	• recognise mixed numbers and improper fractions and convert from one form to the other and write mathematical statements > 1 as a mixed number [for example $\frac{2}{5} + \frac{4}{5} = 1\frac{1}{5}$]	Year 5, Unit 4.5
	• add and subtract fractions with the same denominator and denominators that are multiples of the same number	Year 5, Unit 4.6, 4.7
	• multiply proper fractions and mixed numbers by whole numbers, supported by materials and diagrams	Year 5, Unit 4.8

Chapter 4 Comparing fractions, improper fractions and mixed numbers

Unit 4.1
Comparing fractions (1)

Conceptual context

This is the first of four units that develop pupils' understanding of comparing fractions. Pupils have already had some experience of comparing and ordering fractions with the same denominator in Year 3; this unit will build on these early experiences and will provide a range of visual representations to support pupils' conceptual understanding of comparing fractions. Within this unit there will be a focus on precise language to ensure pupils fully understand the role of the numerator and denominator when comparing fractions. It is also important that pupils understand inequality symbols; symbolic notation will be used frequently within this and subsequent units to compare two or more fractions.

Learning pupils will have achieved at the end of the unit

- Pupils will have expanded their repertoire of visual representations that support their thinking about fractions (Q1)
- Pupils will be able to compare fractions of shapes and quantities less than 1 with the same denominator (Q2)
- Symbolic notation will have been used to compare fractions less than 1 with the same denominator (Q2)
- Pupils will be able to order fractions with the same denominator using pictorial representations to support their understanding (Q3)
- Pupils will understand how to compare fractions with the same denominator that are presented symbolically (Q4)

Resources

paper strips divided into equal parts; interlocking cubes in two different colours; dice with three sides labelled greater and three sides labelled smaller; mini whiteboards; spinner labelled $\frac{1}{6}, \frac{2}{6}, \frac{3}{6}, \frac{4}{6}, \frac{5}{6}, \frac{6}{6}$; inequality symbol on paper; equals symbol on paper; three large dice each labelled $\frac{1}{12}, \frac{3}{12}, \frac{4}{12}, \frac{6}{12}, \frac{9}{12}, \frac{11}{12}$; scissors; **Resource 5.4.1a** Comparing tenths

Vocabulary

numerator, denominator, inequality

Chapter 4 Comparing fractions, improper fractions and mixed numbers Unit 4.1 Practice Book 5A, pages 85–87

Question 1

> **1** Use the diagram to complete the statements.
>
> (a) | $\frac{1}{7}$ | $\frac{1}{7}$ | $\frac{1}{7}$ | $\frac{1}{7}$ | $\frac{1}{7}$ | $\frac{1}{7}$ | $\frac{1}{7}$ |
>
> | $\frac{1}{7}$ | $\frac{1}{7}$ | $\frac{1}{7}$ | $\frac{1}{7}$ | $\frac{1}{7}$ | $\frac{1}{7}$ | $\frac{1}{7}$ |
>
> $\frac{3}{7}$ means ☐ lots of $\frac{1}{7}$. $\frac{6}{7}$ means ☐ lots of $\frac{1}{7}$.
>
> Therefore $\frac{3}{7}$ is _____ than $\frac{6}{7}$. (Choose 'greater' or 'less'.)
>
> (b) For fractions that have the same denominator, the greater the numerator is, the _____ the fraction is, and the smaller the _____ is, the smaller the fraction is.

What learning will pupils have achieved at the conclusion of Question 1?

- Pupils will have expanded their repertoire of visual representations that support their thinking about fractions.

Activities for whole-class instruction

- Show pupils a paper strip divided into nine equal parts.

- Ask: *What fraction of the whole does each part represent?* Establish that each part represents $\frac{1}{9}$ because the whole has been divided into nine equal parts. Select a pupil to label each part $\frac{1}{9}$. Ask a different pupil to shade the bar, $\frac{1}{9}$ at a time, while the rest of the class count in ninths: $\frac{1}{9}, \frac{2}{9}, \frac{3}{9}$ …

- Holding the fraction bar, fold it so that the pupils can see a certain number of shaded parts, for example:

| $\frac{1}{9}$ | $\frac{1}{9}$ | $\frac{1}{9}$ | $\frac{1}{9}$ | $\frac{1}{9}$ | $\frac{1}{9}$ |

- Ask: *What fraction of the whole can you see?* Together, count in ninths up to $\frac{7}{9}$. Ask: *What fraction of the whole is hidden?* If necessary, show the hidden parts to establish $\frac{2}{9}$ of the whole are hidden. Repeat by folding to show a different number of shaded parts.

- Show pupils a new paper strip divided into nine equal parts. Select a pupil to label each part $\frac{1}{9}$. Ask a different pupil to shade the bar, $\frac{1}{9}$ at a time, while the rest of the class count, but tell the pupils that you would like them to count in a different way this time. Emphasise that each segment of the bar is called a 'one-ninth'. So, one segment should be referred to as 'one (PAUSE) one-ninth' and two segments of the bar should be referred to as 'two (PAUSE) one-ninths' and so on. Count together along the whole bar for one-ninths.

- Holding the fraction bar, fold it so that the pupils can see a certain number of shaded parts: for example:

| $\frac{1}{9}$ | $\frac{1}{9}$ | $\frac{1}{9}$ | $\frac{1}{9}$ | $\frac{1}{9}$ | $\frac{1}{9}$ | $\frac{1}{9}$ |

- Ask: *How many lots of $\frac{1}{9}$ can you see?* If necessary, count in one-ninths to establish pupils can see 'seven one-ninths'. Ask: *How many one-ninths are hidden?* If necessary, show the hidden parts to establish 'two one-ninths' are hidden. Repeat by folding to show a different number of shaded parts if appropriate.

> (i) It is important that pupils know $\frac{7}{9}$ means 'seven one-ninths'; they will need this understanding when comparing fractions with the same denominator.

- Display two paper strips divided into nine equal parts. Ask pupils to label each part $\frac{1}{9}$ and ask a different pupil to shade any number of parts on each strip, for example:

| $\frac{1}{9}$ | $\frac{1}{9}$ | $\frac{1}{9}$ | $\frac{1}{9}$ | $\frac{1}{9}$ | $\frac{1}{9}$ | $\frac{1}{9}$ | $\frac{1}{9}$ | $\frac{1}{9}$ |

| $\frac{1}{9}$ | $\frac{1}{9}$ | $\frac{1}{9}$ | $\frac{1}{9}$ | $\frac{1}{9}$ | $\frac{1}{9}$ | $\frac{1}{9}$ | $\frac{1}{9}$ | $\frac{1}{9}$ |

- Ask: *How many lots of $\frac{1}{9}$ are shaded on each strip?* Establish correct responses by counting in 'one-ninths' if necessary. Ask: *What fraction of the whole is shaded on each strip?* Establish correct responses by confirming, 'Three lots of $\frac{1}{9}$ means "three, (PAUSE) one-ninths" or $\frac{3}{9}$' and 'seven lots of $\frac{1}{9}$ means "seven (PAUSE) one-ninths" or $\frac{7}{9}$.'

- Ask: *Which fraction is greater, $\frac{3}{9}$ or $\frac{7}{9}$? How do you know?* Give pupils time to discuss responses before taking feedback. Ensure pupils identify that $\frac{7}{9}$ is greater than $\frac{3}{9}$ because seven lots of $\frac{1}{9}$ have been shaded, and this is greater than three lots of $\frac{1}{9}$.

For fractions that have the same denominator, a larger numerator means the fraction is larger.

- Show pupils a paper strip divided into 12 equal parts. Ask: *What fraction of the whole does each part represent?* Establish that each part represents $\frac{1}{12}$ because the whole has been divided into 12 equal parts. Label each part $\frac{1}{12}$. Shade seven lots of $\frac{1}{12}$:

| $\frac{1}{12}$ | $\frac{1}{12}$ | $\frac{1}{12}$ | $\frac{1}{12}$ | $\frac{1}{12}$ | $\frac{1}{12}$ | $\frac{1}{12}$ | $\frac{1}{12}$ | $\frac{1}{12}$ | $\frac{1}{12}$ | $\frac{1}{12}$ | $\frac{1}{12}$ |

- Ask: *How many lots of $\frac{1}{12}$ have been shaded?* Confirm seven lots of $\frac{1}{12}$ or 'seven one-twelfths' have been shaded. Ask: *What fraction of the whole has been shaded?* Confirm $\frac{7}{12}$ of the whole shape have been shaded.

- Provide pairs of pupils with a fraction strip divided into 12 equal parts. Tell pupils to label the fraction strip in $\frac{1}{12}$ and to shade a number of twelfths so that less than $\frac{7}{12}$ is shaded. Stick shaded strips to the board and examine

Chapter 4 Comparing fractions, improper fractions and mixed numbers   Unit 4.1 Practice Book 5A, pages 85–87

different responses. Ask: *Are they all correct? How do you know?* Ensure pupils identify that less than $\frac{7}{12}$ is shaded if fewer than seven lots of $\frac{1}{12}$ are shaded. Ask pupils to identify all possible fractions less than $\frac{7}{12}$ that can be represented on the fraction strip.

All say… *For fractions that have the same denominator, the smaller the numerator is, the smaller the fraction is.*

- Pupils should complete Question 1 in the Practice Book.

Same-day intervention

- Show pupils a stack of 11 interlocking cubes in 2 different colours, for example red and blue:

- Ask: *What fraction of the whole does each cube represent?* Establish that each cube represents $\frac{1}{11}$ (one-eleventh) because the whole has been made up of 11 cubes. Ask: *What fraction of the bar is red?* Count in 'lots of $\frac{1}{11}$' to establish six lots of $\frac{1}{11}$ are red, so $\frac{6}{11}$ is red. Repeat with blue.
- Provide pupils with a pile of interlocking cubes in the same two colours if possible. Tell pupils to create a stack the same length as the original with greater than $\frac{6}{11}$ red. Give pupils time to explore this before sharing responses. Establish which fractions could have been created.
- Using the different stacks created by the pupils, select two stacks to compare. Ask pupils to compare the two stacks using full sentences, for example '$\frac{8}{11}$ of Stack 1 is red because eight lots of $\frac{1}{11}$ are red. $\frac{2}{11}$ of Stack 2 is red because two lots of $\frac{1}{11}$ are red. Therefore, Stack 1 has a greater amount of red because $\frac{8}{11}$ is greater than $\frac{2}{11}$.'

Stack 1

Stack 2

- Repeat with two different stacks.

Same-day enrichment

- Provide pairs of pupils with strips of paper, divided into 11 equal parts, and a dice, with three sides labelled 'greater' and three sides labelled 'smaller'. Pupils compete against their partner.
- Individually, pupils shade any number of parts on their strip of paper and establish what fraction of the whole is shaded. Once both pupils have identified what fraction of the whole is shaded, roll the dice. If the dice lands on 'greater' the person who has shaded the greater fraction of the whole is the winner, if the dice lands on 'smaller' the person who has shaded the smaller fraction of the whole is the winner. Play five rounds.
- Ask pupils to consider: *Is this just a game of chance or can you select certain fractions that will increase your chance of winning this game? Which fractions are 'best' to go for? Why?*

Question 2

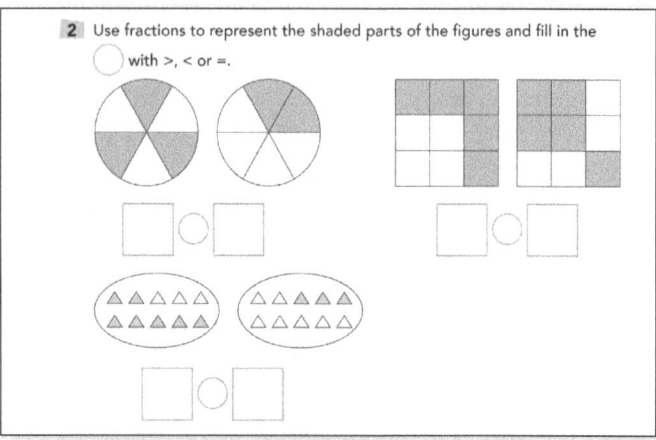

2 Use fractions to represent the shaded parts of the figures and fill in the ◯ with >, < or =.

What learning will pupils have achieved at the conclusion of Question 2?

- Pupils will be able to compare fractions of shapes and quantities less than 1 with the same denominator.
- Symbolic notation will have been used to compare fractions less than 1 with the same denominator.

Chapter 4 Comparing fractions, improper fractions and mixed numbers   Unit 4.1 Practice Book 5A, pages 85–87

Activities for whole-class instruction

- Show pupils the following sets of images:

Set 1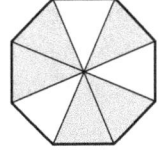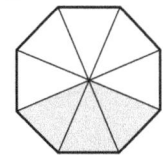

Set 2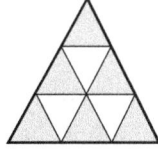

Set 3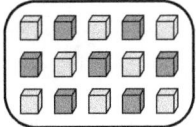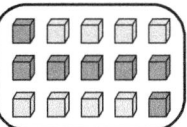

- Examine the shapes in Set 1. Ask pupils to identify what fraction of each shape is shaded. Establish that $\frac{5}{8}$ and $\frac{3}{8}$ are shaded, respectively, count the total number of parts and then count the number of shaded parts if necessary. Ask: *Which shape has the greater fraction shaded?* Ensure pupils identify and can explain that the shape on the left has the greater fraction shaded because five lots of $\frac{1}{8}$ are shaded, and this is greater than three lots of $\frac{1}{8}$.

 *Five lots of $\frac{1}{8}$ are greater than three lots of $\frac{1}{8}$.*

- Examine the shapes in Set 2. Ask pupils to identify what fraction of each shape is shaded. Establish that $\frac{5}{9}$ and $\frac{6}{9}$ are shaded, respectively. Ask: *Which shape has the smaller fraction shaded?* Ensure pupils identify and can explain that the shape on the left has the smaller fraction shaded because five lots of $\frac{1}{9}$ are shaded, and this is smaller than six lots of $\frac{1}{9}$.

 *Five lots of $\frac{1}{9}$ are smaller than six lots of $\frac{1}{9}$.*

- Examine the shapes in Set 3. Ask pupils to identify what fraction of each group is shaded. Establish that $\frac{7}{15}$ are shaded in both sets. Ensure pupils identify that both sets have the same fraction shaded because seven lots of $\frac{1}{15}$ are shaded in both sets.

Look out for … pupils who interpret fractions as a ratio of 'shaded parts : unshaded parts' rather than a proportion of the total number of parts. If this happens, encourage pupils to count the number of parts and record the denominator. Then count the number of shaded parts and record the numerator to reinforce the role of the numerator and denominator.

- Provide mini whiteboards and ask pupils to work in pairs to record the three comparisons using fraction notation and >, < and = symbols.

ⓘ Pupils were first introduced to inequality symbols in Year 1, and they were encouraged to remember the 'small' end always points to the smaller number.

Small < **Big**   **Big** > Small

Pupils will need to understand that this applies to fractions as well as integers.

- Pupils should complete Question 2 in the Practice Book.

Same-day intervention
- Provide pairs of pupils with a copy of **Resource 5.4.1a** Comparing tenths (if possible printed on card). Pupils to play the game using their understanding of <, > and = to compare tenths.

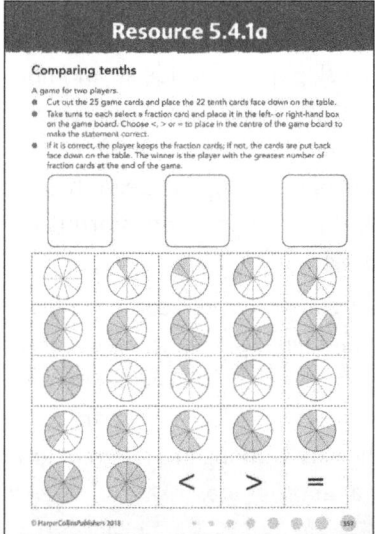

Same-day enrichment
- Ask: *Is it always, sometimes or never true that $\frac{2}{8}$ is smaller than $\frac{3}{8}$?* Pupils should provide examples to support their decision. Encourage pupils to consider different-sized wholes to deepen their thinking. Ask: *Can you draw two shapes that show $\frac{2}{8}$ is bigger than $\frac{3}{8}$?*

Chapter 4 Comparing fractions, improper fractions and mixed numbers   Unit 4.1 Practice Book 5A, pages 85–87

Question 3

> **3** Colour $\frac{3}{8}$, $\frac{7}{8}$ and $\frac{1}{8}$ in the following diagram. Write them in order below, starting from the smallest.

What learning will pupils have achieved at the conclusion of Question 3?

- Pupils will be able to order fractions with the same denominator using pictorial representations to support their understanding.

Activities for whole-class instruction

- Provide pupils with a strip of paper divided into seven equal parts. Ask pupils to shade any number of parts. Group pupils into threes (ensuring each pupil has shaded a different number of parts); ask them to identify what fraction of each strip has been shaded. Ask pupils to order the three fraction strips starting from the smallest fraction.

- On mini whiteboards, pupils complete the following statement for their three fraction strips: ____ < ____ < ____. They share with another group of three who confirm if they are correct. Swap pupils so they are working in a different group of three and repeat as appropriate.

- **Look out for** … pupils who forget which way round the inequality statements go. Encouraging them to remember the 'small' end always points to the smaller number may help with this.

- Present the class with three shaded bars, for example:

- Ask: *What fraction of each bar is shaded?* Establish $\frac{1}{9}$, $\frac{7}{9}$ and $\frac{4}{9}$ are shaded, by counting if necessary. Ask pupils to put these diagrams in order starting with the greatest. Ensure pupils order them: $\frac{7}{9}$, $\frac{4}{6}$, $\frac{1}{9}$.

- Ask: *Can you tell me what fraction of each bar is unshaded, without counting them? How did you know?*

- (i) Ensure pupils are asked to order from largest to smallest as well as from smallest to largest. Their natural instinct is to order starting with the smallest, so they need to appreciate that numbers can be ordered both ways.

- Ask: *If I shaded one more part on each diagram would it change the order?* Confirm that the order would not change because each strip has increased by the same amount.

- Ask pupils where the following bars would be positioned within this set of fractions:

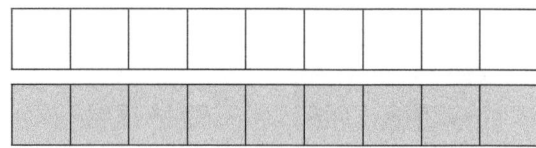

- Ensure pupils position these bars correctly within the set of fractions.

- Pupils should complete Question 3 in the Practice Book.

Same-day intervention

Provide pairs of pupils with strips of paper divided into six equal parts, a spinner labelled $\frac{1}{6}$, $\frac{2}{6}$, $\frac{3}{6}$, $\frac{4}{6}$, $\frac{5}{6}$, $\frac{6}{6}$ and an inequality symbol and equals symbol on paper. Ask Pupil A to spin the spinner and shade the fraction generated on a strip of paper. Pupil A decides whether they think the next fraction spun will be greater or less than the first fraction and shows their prediction using the fraction strip and the inequality/equals symbols, for example:

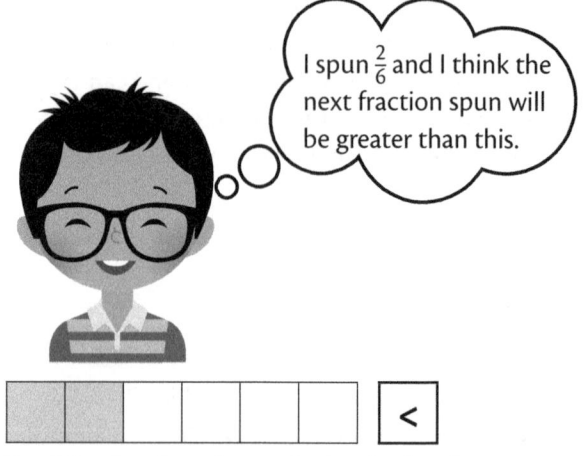

I spun $\frac{2}{6}$ and I think the next fraction spun will be greater than this.

- Pupil B spins the spinner, shades the fraction spun on a strip of paper and adds it to the inequality statement. If the statement is correct, Pupil A gets a point. If the statement is incorrect, Pupil B gets a point. Swap roles.

Chapter 4 Comparing fractions, improper fractions and mixed numbers   Unit 4.1 Practice Book 5A, pages 85–87

Same-day enrichment

- Display four shaded bars:

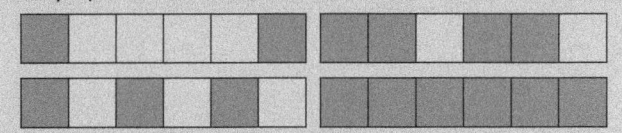

- Choose any three to make this statement correct.

- Ask: *How many different ways can you make the statement correct?* Add a further shaded bar. Ask: *How many different ways can you now make the statement correct?*

Question 4

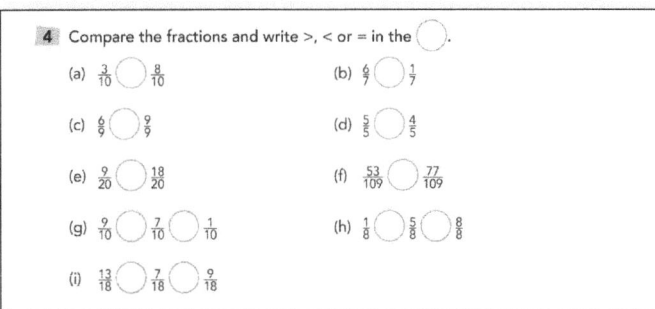

4 Compare the fractions and write >, < or = in the ◯.

(a) $\frac{3}{10}$ ◯ $\frac{8}{10}$ (b) $\frac{6}{7}$ ◯ $\frac{1}{7}$

(c) $\frac{6}{9}$ ◯ $\frac{9}{9}$ (d) $\frac{5}{5}$ ◯ $\frac{4}{5}$

(e) $\frac{9}{20}$ ◯ $\frac{18}{20}$ (f) $\frac{53}{109}$ ◯ $\frac{77}{109}$

(g) $\frac{9}{10}$ ◯ $\frac{7}{10}$ ◯ $\frac{1}{10}$ (h) $\frac{1}{8}$ ◯ $\frac{5}{8}$ ◯ $\frac{8}{8}$

(i) $\frac{13}{18}$ ◯ $\frac{7}{18}$ ◯ $\frac{9}{18}$

What learning will pupils have achieved at the conclusion of Question 4?

- Pupils will understand how to compare fractions with the same denominator that are presented symbolically.

Activities for whole-class instruction

- Present the class with two large dice both labelled $\frac{1}{12}$, $\frac{3}{12}$, $\frac{4}{12}$, $\frac{6}{12}$, $\frac{9}{12}$, $\frac{11}{12}$. Select two pupils to roll the dice and present the fractions rolled to the class. Pupils then use their hands to create an inequality or equals symbol to compare the fractions, for example:

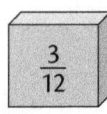 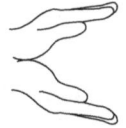 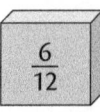

- Ask pupils to explain their choice using precise terminology. Swap pupils and repeat as appropriate.

 *The smaller end of the inequality symbol always points to the smaller number.*

- Present pupils with a third large dice labelled $\frac{1}{12}$, $\frac{3}{12}$, $\frac{4}{12}$, $\frac{6}{12}$, $\frac{9}{12}$, $\frac{11}{12}$. Ask three different pupils to roll the three dice and present the fractions rolled to the class, for example:

 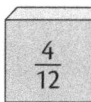 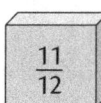

- Ask pupils to use their hands to create an inequality or equals symbol to compare the first two fractions. Ask pupils to explain their choice using precise language. Select a pupil to stand between the two fractions, using their hands to represent the correct symbol. Ask pupils to use their hands to create an inequality or equals symbol to compare the second and third fractions. Ask pupils to explain their choice using precise terminology. Select a pupil to stand between these fractions, using their hands represent the correct symbol.

- Pupils work in pairs to record this fraction comparison on mini whiteboards using symbolic notations, for example:

$$\frac{9}{12} > \frac{4}{12} < \frac{11}{12}$$

- Repeat as appropriate.

Look out for … pupils who find it tricky to compare fractions that are not organised from smallest to largest or largest to smallest. Encouraging them to select two fractions to compare and identify the correct inequality or equals symbol before moving on to another two may help with this.

- Pupils should complete Question 4 in the Practice Book.

Same-day intervention

- Ask: *How many different ways can you make this statement true?*

$$\frac{7}{15} > \frac{\square}{15}$$

Do you think there will be more or fewer ways of making this statement true for fractions less than or equal to 1?

$$\frac{7}{15} < \frac{\square}{15}$$

Can you think of another statement that will have the same number of ways you can make it true?

Same-day enrichment

- Say to pupils: *Predict how many different ways there are of making this statement true:*

$$\frac{\square}{15} < \frac{7}{15} < \frac{\square}{15}$$

Justify your prediction.

Chapter 4 Comparing fractions, improper fractions and mixed numbers   Unit 4.1 Practice Book 5A, pages 85–87

Challenge and extension questions

Questions 5 and 6

5 Put the fractions $\frac{7}{8}$, $\frac{2}{8}$, $\frac{1}{8}$, $\frac{5}{8}$ and $\frac{3}{8}$ in order, from the smallest to the greatest.

☐ ☐ ☐ ☐ ☐

6 Put the fractions $\frac{30}{80}$, $\frac{1}{80}$, $\frac{18}{80}$, $\frac{79}{80}$ and $\frac{50}{80}$ in order, from the greatest to the smallest.

☐ ☐ ☐ ☐ ☐

These questions require pupils to draw on their understanding of ordering fractions with the same denominator. This involves ordering fractions from least to greatest or greatest to least.

Question 7

7 Four groups of children in a Year 5 class borrowed 39 skipping ropes from the school sports shed. The first group received 8, the second group received 10, the third group got 11, and the fourth group received all of the remaining ones.

What fraction of the ropes did the fourth group borrow? _____

This question presents a contextualised problem that will require pupils to add or subtract fractions to or from 1 whole and calculate fractions of quantities.

Chapter 4 Comparing fractions, improper fractions and mixed numbers

Unit 4.2
Comparing fractions (2)

Conceptual context

In the previous unit, pupils compared and ordered fractions with the same denominator; in this unit they will compare fractions with different denominators and a numerator or 1. Pupils will need to understand that when comparing unit fractions, the bigger the denominator the smaller the fraction. This thinking is different to the way fractions were compared in the previous chapter when pupils needed to understand that a bigger numerator resulted in a bigger fraction.

Learning pupils will have achieved at the end of the unit

- Pupils will have reinforced their use of visual representations that support their thinking about fractions (Q1)
- Pupils will understand that when comparing unit fractions for the same-sized whole, smaller fractions have greater denominators (Q1, Q2, Q3)
- Pupils will be able to compare fractions of shapes with a numerator of 1 (Q2)
- Symbolic notation will have been used to order fractions with a numerator of 1 (Q2)
- Pupils will understand how to compare fractions with a numerator of 1 that are presented symbolically (Q3)

Resources

a jug of squash; transparent cups; mini whiteboards; paper rectangles; 1–10 dice; sticky notes; **Resource 5.4.2a** Fraction wall template; **Resource 5.4.2b** Ordering shaded fractions

Vocabulary

numerator, denominator, unit fraction, inequality

Chapter 4 Comparing fractions, improper fractions and mixed numbers   Unit 4.2 Practice Book 5A, pages 88–90

Question 1

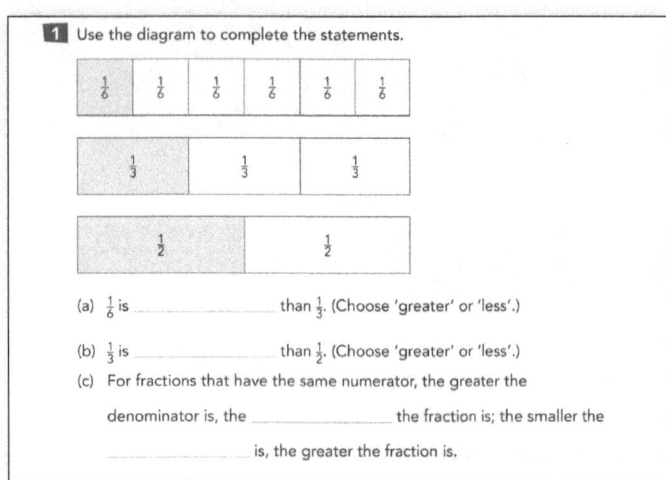

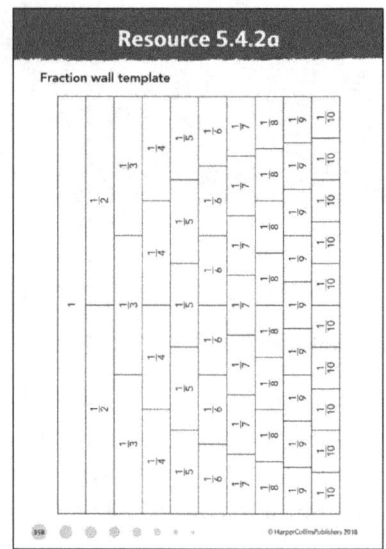

What learning will pupils have achieved at the conclusion of Question 1?

- Pupils will have reinforced their use of visual representations that support their thinking about fractions.
- Pupils will understand that when comparing unit fractions for the same-sized whole, smaller fractions have greater denominators.

Activities for whole-class instruction

- Show pupils a jug of squash and say that it is to be shared equally between four people. Pour the liquid so it is distributed equally between four cups. Ask: *What fraction of the whole jug of squash does each cup hold?* Agree $\frac{1}{4}$.
- Ask: *If we are to share the same liquid equally between five people, will each cup contain more or less liquid?* Draw a line to show the level of squash on each cup. Pour all the squash back into the jug before sharing it equally between five cups. Ask: *What fraction of the whole jug of squash does each cup hold?* Agree $\frac{1}{5}$ and that each cup now contains less squash.
- Ask: *If we are to share the same squash equally between six people, will each cup contain more or less squash?* Pour all the squash back in the jug before sharing it equally between six cups. Predict and check that each cups holds $\frac{1}{6}$ and that each cup now contains even less liquid.

 *The greater the number of parts the whole is divided into, the smaller each part will be.*

- Provide pupils with a copy of **Resource 5.4.2a** Fraction wall template

- Tell pupils to shade $\frac{1}{2}, \frac{1}{3}, \frac{1}{4}, \frac{1}{5}, \frac{1}{6}, \frac{1}{7}, \frac{1}{8}, \frac{1}{9}$ and $\frac{1}{10}$. Ask: *What do you notice about the size of the shaded part as the denominator gets larger?* Establish that the larger the denominator the smaller each part will be.
- Ask pupils to identify two unit fractions on the fraction wall that will make this statement correct and write their number sentence on their mini whiteboards in the form:
$\frac{1}{\square} > \frac{1}{\square}$
- Share responses and agree there are many correct answers. Ask: *What generalisations can we make about all of these inequality statements?* Give pupils time to examine the inequality statements before taking responses. Agree that the larger unit fractions always have the smaller denominators.

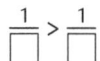 ... pupils who think $\frac{1}{5}$ is larger than $\frac{1}{3}$ because 5 is larger than 3. Further sharing of objects into a different number of equal parts and comparing the size of the parts will help to develop pupils' understanding of this.

- Working in pairs, give pupils two sticky notes each. On one sticky note ask them to write the largest unit fraction they can think of and on the other sticky note ask them to write the smallest unit fraction they can think of. Display responses on the board. Identify that the largest unit fraction is $\frac{1}{1}$, but there is no specific smallest unit fraction because we will always be able to find a smaller unit fraction that the one that is given. Illustrate this with some of the examples displayed.

 *When comparing unit fractions, smaller fractions have greater denominators.*

- Pupils should complete Question 1 in the Practice Book.

Chapter 4 Comparing fractions, improper fractions and mixed numbers   Unit 4.2 Practice Book 5A, pages 88–90

Same-day intervention

- Ask pupils to cut their shaded copies of **Resource 5.4.2a** Fraction wall template into rows. Select two rows and say two comparison sentences that identify which unit fraction is 'greater' and which is 'less', for example:

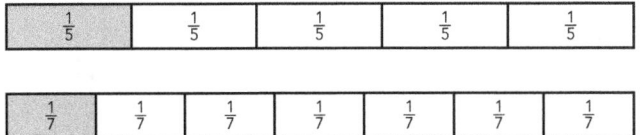

$\frac{1}{5}$ is greater than $\frac{1}{7}$.
$\frac{1}{7}$ is less than $\frac{1}{5}$.

- Record the two comparison sentences symbolically.
- Select two different fraction bars to compare. Repeat with three more pairs.

Same-day enrichment

- In pairs, pupils take turns to write down and then say the name of a unit fraction. Each unit fraction must be smaller than the previous one. What is the smallest unit fraction pupils can think of? How would this be written? How would this be named in words? Discuss which fractions are easier and which are harder to name in words.

Question 2

2 Fill in the spaces.
(a) Use a fraction to represent the shaded part in each figure below.

(b) Put the fractions from part (a) in order, starting from the greatest.

(c) From the above, we found that if the whole is the same, the more parts the whole is equally divided into, the _____ each part gets. Therefore, for a fraction with a numerator of 1, the greater the denominator is, the _____ the fraction is.

What learning will pupils have achieved at the conclusion of Question 2?

- Pupils will understand that when comparing unit fractions for the same-sized whole, smaller fractions have greater denominators.
- Pupils will be able to compare fractions of shapes with a numerator of 1.
- Symbolic notation will have been used to order fractions with a numerator of 1.

Activities for whole-class instruction

- Set up three tables with one 'chocolate bar' on each table:

- Explain that 10 pupils will come out one at a time and will stand behind a table. Once all 10 pupils have chosen where to stand, the chocolate will be shared equally between the number of pupils behind the table. Ask pupils, one at a time, to select which table they wish to stand behind. After four pupils have positioned themselves, pause and ask what fraction of the whole bar each pupil will currently get. Establish that if there is one pupil standing behind the table they will get all of the chocolate bar. If there are two pupils standing behind the table, the chocolate bar will be divided into two equal parts and each pupil will get $\frac{1}{2}$ of the chocolate bar.

Chapter 4 Comparing fractions, improper fractions and mixed numbers   Unit 4.2   Practice Book 5A, pages 88–90

- Choose more pupils to stand behind a table. After seven pupils have positioned themselves, pause and ask what fraction of the whole bar each pupil will get. Pupils will probably have divided themselves equally between the tables so there are two pupils at two of the tables and three pupils at one of the tables. Ask the class to draw images on mini whiteboards that represent how the three chocolate bars will be divided into equal parts. Pupils should notice that the more pupils the chocolate bar is shared between, the smaller the amount of chocolate each person will receive. Ask: *What fraction of a bar of chocolate will each child get? Who will get the most/ least chocolate?*

- Continue until all 10 pupils are positioned and ask what fraction of the whole bar each pupil will now get. Ask the class to draw images on mini whiteboards that represent how the three chocolate bars will be divided into equal parts. Agree which pupils will get the most chocolate and which will get the least. Ask: *What fraction of a bar of chocolate will each child get? Would you prefer to stand in a group with lots of people or a few people? Why?* Record the fractions symbolically and order them from smallest to largest.

For the same-sized whole, the more parts the whole is equally divided into, the smaller each part gets.

- Present the class with four fractions written on the board:

I've ordered these fractions from smallest to largest.

$$\frac{1}{2} \quad \frac{1}{3} \quad \frac{1}{4} \quad \frac{1}{5}$$

- Suggest that Boris has incorrectly ordered these fractions from smallest to largest. Ask: *What could you draw or show to help him understand that they are incorrectly ordered?* Give pupils time to work in pairs before presenting their feedback to another pair. Evaluate. Who has provided the clearest justification as to why this is incorrect? Ask: *How should the fractions be ordered from smallest to largest?*

For a fraction with a numerator of 1, smaller fractions have greater denominators.

(i) Ensure pupils are asked to order from largest to smallest as well as from smallest to largest. Their natural instinct is to order starting with the smallest, so they need to appreciate that numbers can be ordered both ways.

- Pupils should complete Question 2 in the Practice Book.

Same-day intervention

- Provide pairs of pupils with five paper rectangles. Tell them to divide each rectangle into a different number of equal parts and for one part to be shaded. Label the fraction of the whole that each shaded part represents. Pupils should order fractions from largest to smallest. Next, ask pupils to order the same rectangles from smallest to largest. Ask: *What did you have to do?*

- Give pupils another rectangle and ask them to divide it into a different number of equal parts and shade one part. Ask: *What fraction of the whole does the shaded part represent? Where would this rectangle be positioned?*

Same-day enrichment

- Provide pairs of pupils with a copy of **Resource 5.4.2b** Ordering shaded fractions. Pupils should cut out the circles and order the fractions from largest to smallest. Ask: *What fraction is shaded on each circle? How can you justify that this is the correct order?* Identifying that the unshaded part of each circle is a unit fraction will enable pupils to apply their understanding of ordering unit fractions within a different context.

- Ask pupils to divide the remaining two circles into equal parts and shade some parts so that one circle will be at either end of the sort.

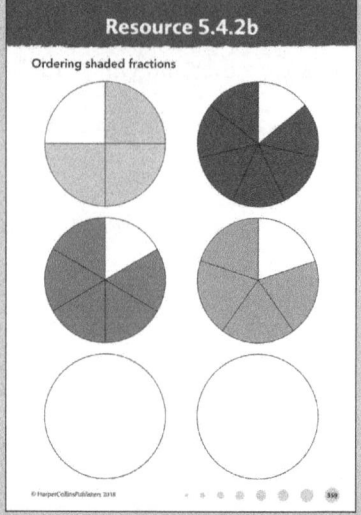

Answers: Fractions should be arranged $\frac{6}{7}, \frac{5}{6}, \frac{4}{5}$ and $\frac{3}{4}$. Remaining fractions should be greater than $\frac{6}{7}$ (for example, $\frac{7}{8}$) and less than $\frac{3}{4}$ (for example $\frac{2}{3}$) respectively.

Chapter 4 Comparing fractions, improper fractions and mixed numbers   Unit 4.2 Practice Book 5A, pages 88–90

Question 3

> **3** Compare the fractions and write >, < or = in the ◯.
> (a) $\frac{1}{10}$ ◯ $\frac{1}{8}$ (b) $\frac{1}{6}$ ◯ $\frac{1}{7}$
> (c) $\frac{1}{9}$ ◯ $\frac{1}{15}$ (d) $\frac{1}{4}$ ◯ $\frac{1}{40}$
> (e) $\frac{1}{21}$ ◯ $\frac{1}{20}$ (f) $\frac{1}{109}$ ◯ $\frac{1}{77}$
> (g) $\frac{1}{9}$ ◯ $\frac{1}{7}$ ◯ $\frac{1}{5}$ (h) $\frac{1}{8}$ ◯ $\frac{1}{18}$ ◯ $\frac{1}{108}$

What learning will pupils have achieved at the conclusion of Question 3?

- Pupils will understand how to compare fractions with a numerator of 1 that are presented symbolically.
- Pupils will understand that when comparing unit fractions for the same-sized whole, smaller fractions have greater denominators.

Activities for whole-class instruction

- Present pupils with the following inequality statement:

  $\frac{1}{\Box} < \frac{1}{\Box}$

- Use a 10-sided dice to roll two numbers. Pupils should use the numbers rolled to represent the denominators in the two fractions in the number statement so that the statement is true and write it on their mini whiteboards. Share answers.

- Now roll the 10-sided dice three times and present the numbers rolled to the class. Ask pupils to select two of the three numbers to make the statement correct. Agree all possible responses. Repeat with four numbers, ensuring pupils find all possible answers.

  > *All say ...* For a fraction with a numerator of 1, smaller fractions have greater denominators.

- Repeat with the following inequality statement:

  $\frac{1}{\Box} < \frac{1}{\Box} < \frac{1}{\Box}$

- Roll the 10-sided dice three times and present the numbers rolled to the class.

- Next, roll four times. Ask pupils to select three of the four numbers to make the statement correct. Agree all possible responses.

   ... pupils who find it hard to order fractions that are not consecutive unit fractions, for example $\frac{1}{4}$, $\frac{1}{5}$, $\frac{1}{6}$. Pupils need to appreciate that they are not continuing a sequence, that each fraction is a value in its own right.

Positioning and ordering fractions on a number line may help to reinforce this.

- Repeat the dice activity using:

  $\frac{1}{\Box} < \frac{1}{\Box} > \frac{1}{\Box}$

- Roll the 10-sided dice three times. Ask: *Is there only one possible answer?* Agree that there is more than one possible way this statement can be completed with three numbers. Now roll the dice four times. Ask pupils to select three of the four numbers to make the statement correct. Agree all possible responses.

- Pupils should complete Question 3 in the Practice Book.

Same-day intervention

- Tell pupils that some of the following inequality statements below include an error. Ask pupils to identify the errors and correct them. Provide pupils with a copy of **Resource 5.4.2a** Fraction wall template for support with the first two statements. Encourage pupils to draw a number line to help answer the last two statements, if required.
  - $\frac{1}{3} > \frac{1}{7}$
  - $\frac{1}{6} < \frac{1}{12}$
  - $\frac{1}{300} > \frac{1}{200}$
  - $\frac{1}{5} > \frac{1}{50}$

- Pupils write their own set of inequality statements like the ones above including some errors. They ask their partner to identify the errors and correct them.

Same-day enrichment

- Tell pupils that the following inequality statements below include a number of errors. Ask pupils to identify the errors and correct them.
  - $\frac{1}{3} > \frac{1}{7} > \frac{1}{12} > \frac{1}{10}$
  - $\frac{1}{36} < \frac{1}{6} < \frac{1}{12} < \frac{1}{24}$
  - $\frac{1}{300} > \frac{1}{200} > \frac{1}{500} < \frac{1}{100}$
  - $\frac{1}{5} > \frac{1}{50} < \frac{1}{55} > \frac{1}{15}$

- Pupils write their own inequality statements like the ones above including an error or errors. They ask their partner to identify the errors and correct them.

165

Chapter 4 Comparing fractions, improper fractions and mixed numbers   Unit 4.2   Practice Book 5A, pages 88–90

Challenge and extension questions

Questions 4, 5 and 6

4 Put the fractions $\frac{1}{9}$, $\frac{1}{36}$, $\frac{1}{27}$, $\frac{1}{18}$ and $\frac{1}{81}$ in order, from the smallest to the greatest.

☐ ☐ ☐ ☐ ☐

5 Put the fractions $\frac{1}{10}$, $\frac{1}{20}$, $\frac{1}{70}$, $\frac{1}{100}$ and $\frac{1}{40}$ in order, from the greatest to the smallest.

☐ ☐ ☐ ☐ ☐

6 There are two boxes of chocolates. The first box has 30 chocolates and the second has 20 chocolates. Alex takes $\frac{1}{5}$ of the chocolates from the first box and his brother takes $\frac{1}{4}$ of the chocolates from the second box.

Who takes more? _____

Questions 4 and 5 require pupils to draw on their understanding of ordering fractions with a numerator of 1. This involves ordering fractions from least to greatest or greatest to least.

Question 6 presents a contextualised problem that will require pupils to calculate fractions of quantities in order to compare amounts from different-sized wholes.

Chapter 4 Comparing fractions, improper fractions and mixed numbers

Unit 4.3
Comparing fractions (3)

Conceptual context

In the previous unit, pupils compared and ordered unit fractions with different denominators, in this unit they will compare and order fractions with the same numerator and different denominators, but the numerator is often greater than 1. In the previous unit, pupils developed their understanding that when comparing fractions with the same numerator, smaller fractions have greater denominators. This knowledge will be applied here as pupils compare and order (non-unit) fractions with the same numerators and increasingly large denominators.

Learning pupils will have achieved at the end of the unit

- Pupils will be able to identify fractions of shaded shapes divided into equal parts (Q1)
- Understanding of equivalent fractions will have been reinforced (Q1)
- Pupils will understand that when comparing fractions with the same numerator, smaller fractions have greater denominators (Q1, Q2, Q3)
- Symbolic notation will have been used to compare and order fractions with the same numerators and different denominators (Q2)
- Pupils will be able to find the difference between two fractions with the same denominator (Q3)
- Pupils will be able to compare fractions with the same denominator to solve word problems (Q3)

Resources

three identical cakes (or use modelling clay); plastic knife; mini whiteboards; scissors; spinners labelled $\frac{3}{3}, \frac{3}{4}, \frac{3}{5}, \frac{3}{6}, \frac{3}{7}, \frac{3}{8}, \frac{3}{9}, \frac{3}{10}, \frac{3}{11}, \frac{3}{12}$; small pieces of card; two different-coloured pieces of ribbon; **Resource 5.4.3a** Shaded rectangles; **Resource 5.4.3b** Sorting circles; **Resource 5.4.3c** Comparing parts of a rectangle; **Resource 5.4.2a** Fraction wall template (from the previous unit); **Resource 5.4.3d** Fraction number lines; **Resource 5.4.3e** Fractions to position on number lines

Vocabulary

numerator, denominator, unit fraction, non-unit fraction, inequality

Chapter 4 Comparing fractions, improper fractions and mixed numbers   Unit 4.3 Practice Book 5A, pages 91–93

Question 1

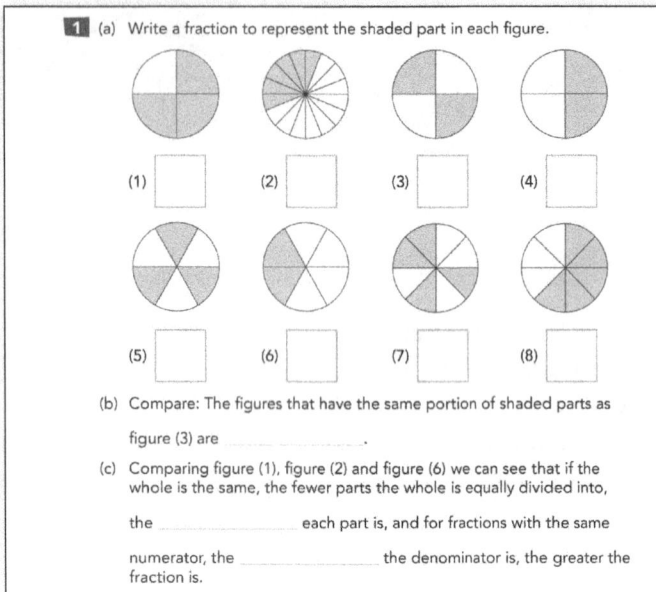

1 (a) Write a fraction to represent the shaded part in each figure.

(1) ☐ (2) ☐ (3) ☐ (4) ☐
(5) ☐ (6) ☐ (7) ☐ (8) ☐

(b) Compare: The figures that have the same portion of shaded parts as figure (3) are _____.

(c) Comparing figure (1), figure (2) and figure (6) we can see that if the whole is the same, the fewer parts the whole is equally divided into, the _____ each part is, and for fractions with the same numerator, the _____ the denominator is, the greater the fraction is.

What learning will pupils have achieved at the conclusion of Question 1?

- Pupils will be able to identify fractions of shaded shapes divided into equal parts.
- Understanding of equivalent fractions will have been reinforced.
- Pupils will understand that when comparing fractions with the same numerator, smaller fractions have greater denominators.

Activities for whole-class instruction

- Show two identical cakes and tell pupils that one is to be shared equally between four people and one is to be shared equally between five people.

A   B

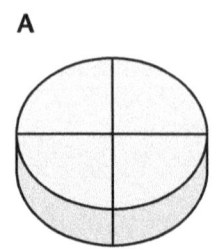   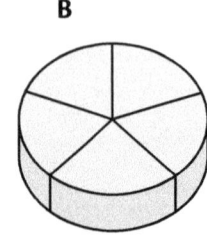

- Ask: *What fraction of cake A will each person get if it is cut into four equal parts?* Agree $\frac{1}{4}$ of the cake. Ask: *Will the people who are sharing cake B get more or less cake than the people who are sharing cake A?* Establish that each person who is sharing cake B will get one $\frac{1}{5}$ of the cake if it is cut into five equal parts and that this is less than one $\frac{1}{4}$.

Cut the cakes into the correct number of equal parts and compare the sizes of one part from cake A and one part from cake B.

- Record '$\frac{1}{4} > \frac{1}{5}$' on the board.
- Introduce a third identical cake. State that this cake will be shared equally between six people.

C

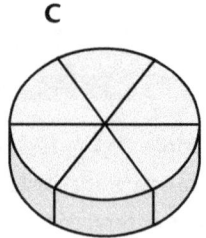

- Ask: *Will the people sharing this cake get more or less than the people sharing cake A? Cake B?* Establish that each person who is sharing cake C will get one $\frac{1}{6}$ of the cake if it is cut into six equal parts and that this is less than one $\frac{1}{4}$ and one $\frac{1}{5}$. Cut the cake into six equal parts and compare the sizes of one part with those of a part from cake A and a part from cake B.
- Record '$\frac{1}{4} > \frac{1}{5} > \frac{1}{6}$' on the board.

(All say...) *The fewer parts the whole is equally divided into, the larger each part is.*

- Show this image:

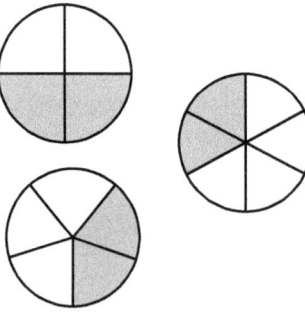

- Ask: *What fraction of each circle is shaded? Which circle has the most shading? Which circle has the least shading?* Ask pupils to record an inequality statement on mini whiteboards that compares two of the circles. Share ideas.

- Now ask pupils to record an inequality statement that compares all three circles. Ask: *Can you think of another inequality statement?* Pupils should identify several possible inequality statements involving all three fractions, for example:

$\frac{2}{4} > \frac{2}{5} > \frac{2}{6}$ $\frac{2}{6} < \frac{2}{5} < \frac{2}{4}$

$\frac{2}{6} < \frac{2}{4} > \frac{2}{5}$ $\frac{2}{4} > \frac{2}{6} < \frac{2}{5}$

Write: $\frac{2}{\Box} < \frac{2}{6} < \frac{2}{5} < \frac{2}{4} < \frac{2}{\Box}$

Chapter 4 Comparing fractions, improper fractions and mixed numbers Unit 4.3 Practice Book 5A, pages 91–93

- Ask: *Can you think of two fractions that would make this statement correct?* Pupils should discuss with a partner. Ask: *Can you think of any alternatives? What do you notice about the fractions that are smaller than $\frac{2}{6}$?* Agree that the denominator needs to be greater than 6.

> All say... *When comparing fractions with the same numerator, smaller fractions have larger denominators.*

- Ask: *What do you notice about the fractions that are greater than $\frac{2}{4}$?* Agree that the denominator needs to be smaller than 4.
- Give pupil pairs **Resource 5.4.3a** Shaded rectangles. Ask pupils to work out what fraction of each rectangle is shaded.
- Pupils should cut out the rectangles and sort them into groups based on a mathematical property. Ask pairs to share the way they sorted the rectangles with another pair. Ask: *Has anyone sorted the rectangles based on the size of the denominator?* Tell the rest of the class to sort them in this way if they haven't already done so. Ask: *Has anyone sorted the rectangles based on the size of the numerator? Has anyone sorted them into equivalent fractions?* Tell the rest of the class to sort them in these ways if they haven't already done so. Ask: *How else could we sort the rectangles?*

- Pupils should complete Question 1 in the Practice Book.

Same-day intervention

- Give pupil pairs **Resource 5.4.3b** Sorting circles. Ask pupils to shade $\frac{2}{4}, \frac{2}{6}, \frac{2}{8}$ and $\frac{2}{12}$ of a circle on the sheet. Ask: *What do you notice about the size of each part in these four circles?* Ensure pupils notice that the greater the number of parts each circle is divided into, the smaller each part is.
- Ask pupils which circle has the most shaded parts? Which has the least shaded parts? Tell pupils to select two of these circles and record an inequality statement. Select two further circles and record another inequality statement. Repeat two more times.
- Shade $\frac{3}{4}, \frac{3}{6}, \frac{3}{8}$ and $\frac{3}{12}$ of a circle on the sheet. Repeat the questions above for these four circles.
- Shade $\frac{4}{4}, \frac{4}{6}, \frac{4}{8}$ and $\frac{4}{12}$ of a circle on the sheet. Repeat the questions above for these four circles.
- Tell pupils to cut the 12 circles out and sort them into equivalent fractions.

Chapter 4 Comparing fractions, improper fractions and mixed numbers   Unit 4.3 Practice Book 5A, pages 91–93

Same-day enrichment

- Provide pupil pairs with **Resource 5.4.3c** Comparing parts of a rectangle. Ask pupils to work out what fraction of the whole each part represents. Pupils may wish to use cutting or folding to help with this.
- Tell pupils to select two parts and record an inequality or 'equal to' statement. Then, select two more parts and record another inequality or 'equal to' statement. Repeat two more times.
- Tell pupils to select three parts and record an inequality or 'equal to' statement. Select three further parts and record another inequality or 'equal to' statement. Repeat two more times.

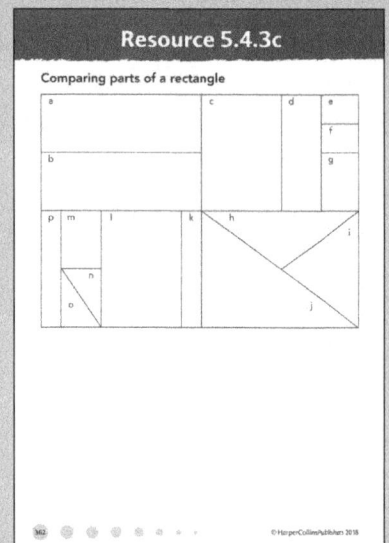

Answers: a. $\frac{1}{8}$, b. $\frac{1}{8}$, c. $\frac{1}{8}$, d. $\frac{1}{16}$, e. $\frac{1}{64}$, f. $\frac{1}{64}$, g. $\frac{1}{32}$, h. $\frac{1}{16}$, i. $\frac{1}{16}$, j. $\frac{1}{8}$, k. $\frac{1}{32}$, l. $\frac{1}{8}$, m. $\frac{1}{32}$, n. $\frac{1}{64}$, o. $\frac{1}{64}$, p. $\frac{1}{32}$

Question 2

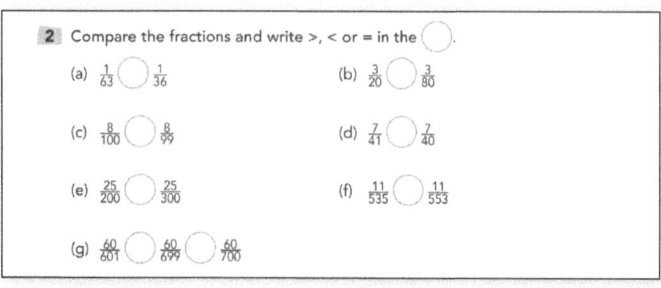

What learning will pupils have achieved at the conclusion of Question 2?

- Pupils will understand that when comparing fractions with the same numerator, smaller fractions have greater denominators.
- Symbolic notation will have been used to compare and order fractions with the same numerators and different denominators.

Activities for whole-class instruction

- Provide pupils with a copy of **Resource 5.4.2a** Fraction wall template (from the previous unit).

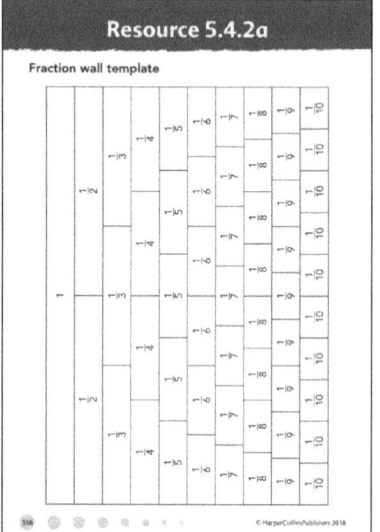

- Tell pupils to shade $\frac{2}{2}, \frac{2}{3}, \frac{2}{4}, \frac{2}{5}, \frac{2}{6}, \frac{2}{7}, \frac{2}{8}, \frac{2}{9}$ and $\frac{2}{10}$. Ask: *What do you notice about the size of the shaded part as the denominator gets larger?* Establish that as the denominator gets larger, the fraction shaded gets smaller.
- Ask: *What are two fractions with a numerator of 2 that will make this statement correct?*

$$\frac{2}{\square} > \frac{2}{\square}$$

- Share responses on mini whiteboards and agree there are many correct answers. Ask: *What generalisations can we make about all of these inequality statements?* Give pupils time to examine the inequality statements before taking responses. Agree that, when the numerators are the same, the larger fractions always have smaller denominators.

 *For fractions with the same numerator, the fraction gets larger as the denominator gets smaller.*

Chapter 4 Comparing fractions, improper fractions and mixed numbers Unit 4.3 Practice Book 5A, pages 91–93

- **Look out for** ... pupils who think $\frac{2}{7}$ is larger than $\frac{2}{5}$ because 7 is larger than 5. Further sharing of objects into a different number of equal parts, comparing the size of the parts and selecting two parts will help to develop pupils' understanding of this.
- Show a spinner labelled $\frac{3}{3}, \frac{3}{4}, \frac{3}{5}, \frac{3}{6}, \frac{3}{7}, \frac{3}{8}, \frac{3}{9}, \frac{3}{10}, \frac{3}{11}, \frac{3}{12}$.

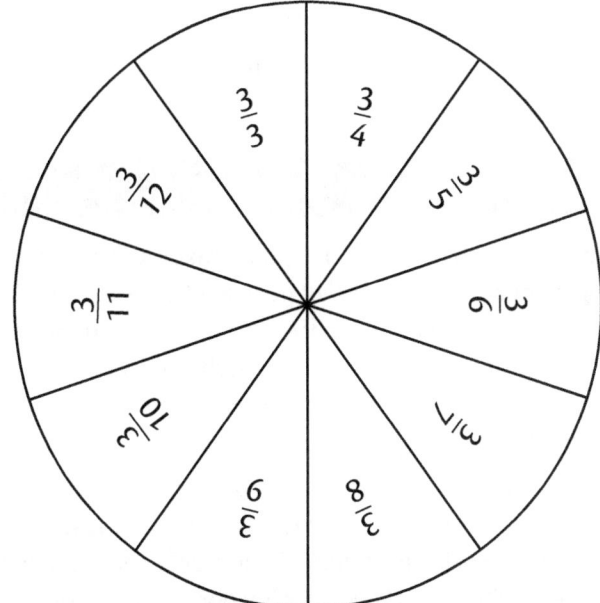

- Tell pupils that you are going to spin the spinner three times and record the fractions generated, for example:
  $\frac{3}{7}$ $\frac{3}{11}$ $\frac{3}{10}$
- Pupils should record the three fractions on mini whiteboards and insert inequality symbols between each of the fractions to make the statement correct. Encourage pupils to use the fraction wall image for support if appropriate. Spin the spinner again to generate three further fractions and complete an inequality statement for these fractions. Repeat as appropriate.
- Pupil pairs should record four inequality statements for fractions with a numerator of 3. Tell them to write three statements that are correct and one statement that is incorrect. Swap with another pair and ask them to identify the incorrect statement and explain why it is incorrect using the fraction wall for support if necessary. Ask pupils to make the incorrect statements correct.
- Pupils should complete Question 2 in the Practice Book.

Same-day intervention

- Give pupil pairs **Resource 5.4.3d** Fraction number lines. Pupils should look at the number of equal parts that each number line is divided into and label each number line using fractions.

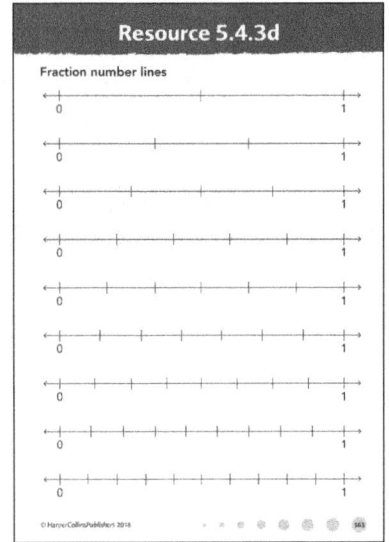

- Ask pupils to record $\frac{4}{4}, \frac{4}{5}, \frac{4}{6}, \frac{4}{7}, \frac{4}{8}, \frac{4}{9}, \frac{4}{10}$ on seven small pieces of card and lay them face down on the table. They should select two cards, turn them over and locate the fraction on the corresponding fraction number line. Ask pupils to compare the two fractions and record an inequality statement using < or > symbols. Return the cards to the table and repeat five more times.

Chapter 4 Comparing fractions, improper fractions and mixed numbers   Unit 4.3 Practice Book 5A, pages 91–93

Same-day enrichment

- Give pupil pairs **Resource 5.4.3e** Fractions to position on number lines. Pupils should cut out the 16 cards and lay them face down on the table. Ask pupils to draw a blank number line labelled 0 at one end and 1 at the other. Pupils take turns to select a card and label the position of this fraction on the number line. The first pupil to correctly position three fractions on the number line, without any of their opponent's fractions between them, is the winner. Repeat as appropriate.

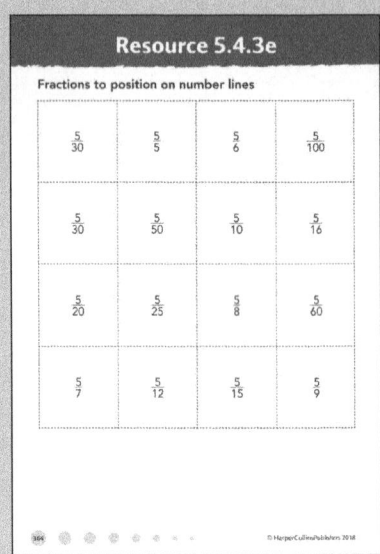

Question 3

3 Fill in the missing numbers to make each statement correct.

(a) There are ☐ lots of $\frac{1}{15}$ in $\frac{7}{15}$. After taking away 3 lots of $\frac{1}{15}$, it is ☐.

(b) Five lots of $\frac{1}{13}$ make ☐. Four lots of $\frac{1}{13}$ make ☐.
The difference between them is ☐.

(c) A 2 metre-long piece of string is cut into 5 equal pieces. Each piece is ☐ of the string and it is ☐ m long.
Four pieces are ☐ of the string, and the length of each piece is ☐ m.

(d) There are 19 boys in a maths class, which is $\frac{19}{37}$ of the class.
The number of girls in the class is ☐.

What learning will pupils have achieved at the conclusion of Question 3?

- Pupils will understand that when comparing fractions with the same numerator, smaller fractions have greater denominators.
- Pupils will be able to find the difference between two fractions with the same denominator.
- Pupils will be able to compare fractions with the same denominator to solve word problems.

Activities for whole-class instruction

- Show a length of ribbon. Tell pupils that it will be cut into eight equal parts. Ask: *What fraction of the whole will each part be?* Agree that each part will be $\frac{1}{8}$. Cut the ribbon into eight equal parts and count each part in eighths. Ask: *How many lots of $\frac{1}{8}$ make up the whole ribbon?* Agree that eight lots of $\frac{1}{8}$ make up the whole ribbon.

- Hold up two of the pieces of ribbon. Ask: *What fraction of the whole is this?* Agree that this is $\frac{2}{8}$ or $\frac{1}{4}$ because two lots of $\frac{1}{8}$ are being held up. Hold up a different number of pieces of ribbon and ask what fraction of the whole this is. Repeat as appropriate.

- Hold up all eight pieces of ribbon. Ask: *After taking away three lots of $\frac{1}{8}$, how many lots of $\frac{1}{8}$ will be left?* Model taking away three lots of $\frac{1}{8}$ and agree that five lots of $\frac{1}{8}$ will remain. Repeat the activity taking away a different fraction each time.

- Hold up two pieces of ribbon in your left hand and five pieces of ribbon in your right hand; tell pupils how many pieces you are holding in each hand. Ask: *How many more pieces of ribbon am I holding in my right hand than in my left hand?* Continue to hold the ribbon in your two hands and tell the pupils that you are holding $\frac{2}{8}$ of the ribbon in your left and $\frac{5}{8}$ of the ribbon in your right hand. Ask: *What is the difference between $\frac{2}{8}$ and $\frac{5}{8}$?* Ensure pupils work out that the difference is $\frac{3}{8}$. Repeat the questioning with a second piece of ribbon divided into 12 equal parts.

- Tell pupils that Alice has written 20 party invitations. She is going to invite 35 people to her party. Ask: *What fraction of the total number of invitations has she written?* Pupils should discuss. Share ideas and agree $\frac{20}{35}$. Ask: *What fraction of the total number of invitations does Alice still have to write?* Agree $\frac{15}{35}$.

- Tell pupils that Alice writes five more invitations. Ask: *What fraction of the total number has she now written? What fraction of the total number does she still have to write?* Repeat with Alice having written eight more invites.

Chapter 4 Comparing fractions, improper fractions and mixed numbers   Unit 4.3 Practice Book 5A, pages 91–93

- Pupils should complete Question 3 in the Practice Book.

Same-day intervention

- Display the following table:

Time taken (in hours)	Total distance run (in miles)
1	5
2	10
3	14
4	19
5	23
6	26

- Explain that these data show information about one person who ran a marathon. Ask: *What was the total distance?* Agree 26 miles.

- Ask: *How many miles had the person run after one hour? Two hours?* Repeat for each hour. Ask: *What fraction of the total distance had the person run after one hour?* Repeat for each hour. Ask: *What fraction of the total distance is left after one hour?* Repeat for each hour.

Same-day enrichment

- Display the following table:

Time taken (in hours)	Runner A Total distance run (in miles)	Runner B Total distance run (in miles)
1	5	6
2	10	13
3	14	19
4	19	24
5	23	26
6	26	

- Explain that these data show information about two people who ran a marathon. Ask: *What was the total distance?* Agree 26 miles.

- Ask: *What fraction of the total distance had each person run after one hour?* Repeat for each hour. Ask: *After four hours, what fraction of the total distance is left for each runner? What was the greatest distance covered by either runner in one hour? What was the shortest distance covered by either runner in one hour?*

- Pupils write their own fraction questions relating to these data for their partner to solve.

Challenge and extension questions

Questions 4 and 5

4 Put the fractions $\frac{5}{123}, \frac{5}{999}, \frac{5}{656}, \frac{5}{50}$ and $\frac{5}{11}$ in order, from the smallest to the greatest.

5 Put the fractions $\frac{4}{7}, \frac{2}{11}$ and $\frac{2}{5}$ in order, from the greatest to the smallest.

These questions require pupils to draw on their understanding of ordering fractions with the same numerator; they involve ordering fractions from least to greatest or greatest to least.

Questions 6 and 7

6 A snail and an ant had a race to climb a wall. The snail climbed $\frac{9}{15}$ m and the ant climbed $\frac{9}{20}$ m. Who climbed higher?

7 Tom and Mary had two cups of drinks with the same amount in each. Tom drank $\frac{3}{4}$ of his and Mary drank $\frac{2}{5}$ of hers.

Who drank more?

These questions present contextualised problems that will require pupils to compare fractions of quantities linked to measures.

Chapter 4 Comparing fractions, improper fractions and mixed numbers

Unit 4.4
Comparing fractions (4)

Conceptual context

Pupils were introduced to equivalent fractions in Year 3 where they identified equivalent fractions with small denominators in diagrams and pictures. They will build on this understanding, together with their knowledge of division as equal sharing in order to compare fractions. Pupils will compare fractions with increasingly large denominators; this will lead to them being able to generalise about the characteristics of equivalent fractions when represented symbolically.

Learning pupils will have achieved at the end of the unit

- The concept of equal sharing will have been used to develop pupils' understanding of equivalent fractions (Q1)
- Pupils will understand how to compare fractions of quantities (Q1)
- Pupils will understand that the multiplicative relationship between the numerator and the denominator stays the same for equivalent fractions (Q2, Q3)
- Symbolic notation will have been used to identify equivalent fractions (Q2)
- Pupils will be able to recognise common equivalent fractions (Q3)
- Pupils will be able to add and subtract fractions less than 1 with the same denominator (Q4)

Resources

bags of sweets (or non-edible alternatives); mini whiteboards; equal-length strips of paper; a variety of coins; rectangles of paper; sticky notes; **Resource 5.4.4a** Fractions of quantities; **Resource 5.4.4b** Equivalent fraction puzzle

Vocabulary

equivalent, numerator, denominator

Chapter 4 Comparing fractions, improper fractions and mixed numbers Unit 4.4 Practice Book 5A, pages 94–97

Question 1

1 Read the story and then answer the questions.

> Once upon a time, an old monkey gave some young monkeys some peaches to share. The old monkey gave one of the young monkeys a basket of peaches and said, 'These are for six of you to share.'
>
> The young monkey thought it was too few and asked for more. The old monkey said, 'OK, you can have one more basket, but to share with 12 monkeys.' The young monkey was very happy with this.

(a) Given that each basket contains the same number of peaches, what do you think about the story?

_____

_____

Lee thinks:
> Six monkeys share a basket of peaches. Each monkey can have $\frac{1}{6}$ of the peaches. Two baskets of peaches are shared by 12 monkeys. Each monkey has $\frac{2}{12}$ of the peaches.

Ming thinks:
> As learned earlier, we know different fractions can represent the same part of an object, and $\frac{1}{6}$ and $\frac{2}{12}$ are equal. Therefore, the number of peaches that each monkey has is the same either way.

(b) Do you think Lee or Ming is right? Why?

_____

_____

What learning will pupils have achieved at the conclusion of Question 1?
- The concept of equal sharing will have been used to develop pupils' understanding of equivalent fractions.
- Pupils will understand how to compare fractions of quantities.

Activities for whole-class instruction

- Show pupils a bag of sweets and tell pupils that it is to be shared equally between three people. Ask: *What fraction of the whole bag will each person get?* Agree $\frac{1}{3}$.
- Show two further bags of sweets and tell the class that all the bags have exactly the same number of sweets in them. Explain that these two bags are to be shared equally between six people. Ask: *Would you rather be in the group that is sharing one bag of sweets between three or the group that is sharing two bags of sweets between six?* Pupils should discuss with a partner and prepare a justification for their decision before sharing ideas.

- Draw a bar model on the board; tell pupils that it represents one bag of sweets. Divide it into three equal parts. Ask a pupil to label the fractional value of each part and shade one part to represent how much of the whole one person will get.

$\frac{1}{3}$	$\frac{1}{3}$	$\frac{1}{3}$

- Agree that each person would get $\frac{1}{3}$ of the whole bag of sweets.
- Draw two bars, each identical in size to the previous one, and divide both into six parts. Ask a pupil to label the fractional value of each part on both bars.

$\frac{1}{6}$	$\frac{1}{6}$	$\frac{1}{6}$	$\frac{1}{6}$	$\frac{1}{6}$	$\frac{1}{6}$
$\frac{1}{6}$	$\frac{1}{6}$	$\frac{1}{6}$	$\frac{1}{6}$	$\frac{1}{6}$	$\frac{1}{6}$

- Agree that each person would get $\frac{1}{6}$ of each bag of sweets. Record $\frac{1}{6} + \frac{1}{6} = \frac{2}{6}$ symbolically on the board.
- Compare $\frac{1}{3}$ with $\frac{1}{6} + \frac{1}{6} = \frac{2}{6}$.

- Agree that when sharing one bag between three, each person would get $\frac{1}{3}$ of a bag and when sharing two bags between six, each person would get $\frac{2}{6}$ of a bag; both groups would get the same amount of sweets.

> *All say...* When the amount to be shared is doubled and the number of people sharing it is doubled, everyone still receives the same amount.

- Encourage pupils to talk in full sentences when comparing two fractions to ensure they understand the people in the second group will receive $\frac{2}{6}$ of a bag of sweets rather than $\frac{2}{6}$ of the whole (two bags of sweets). Visual representations are important for pupils to form this concept and will support their explanations.

- Show pupils three further bags of sweets and tell them that all the bags have exactly the same number of sweets in them. Explain that these three bags are to be shared equally between nine people. Tell pupils that the people in this group will get the same as the people in the previous groups. Ask pupils to draw an image to explain why this is true.

> *Look out for* ... pupils who find it hard to understand that two or more fractions can represent the same amount, for example $\frac{1}{3} = \frac{2}{6} = \frac{3}{9}$. Continuing to represent the problem visually will help them to comprehend the concept of equivalence within fractions.

Chapter 4 Comparing fractions, improper fractions and mixed numbers Unit 4.4 Practice Book 5A, pages 94–97

- Show pupils the following image:

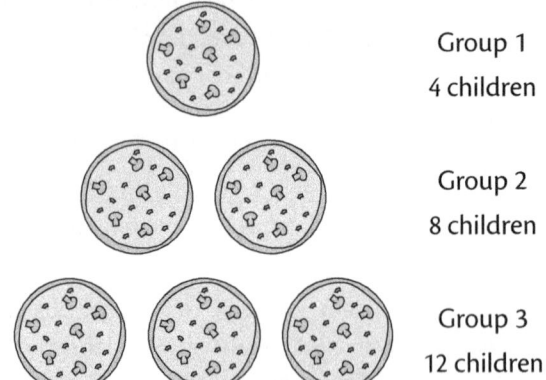

Group 1
4 children

Group 2
8 children

Group 3
12 children

- Ask: *Which group of children will get the most pizza?* Ensure pupils notice each group will receive the same amount of pizza by working out that each child will get the equivalent of $\frac{1}{4}$ of a pizza.
- Ask pupils to consider how many pizzas would be needed for a fourth group of 16 children to ensure they also received the same amount of pizza. What about seven pizzas? How many children could share these equally to ensure they also received the same amount of pizza? Tell pupils to choose their own number of pizzas and work out how many children could share them equally and still receive the same amount.
- Pupils should complete Question 1 in the Practice Book.

Same-day intervention

- Provide pairs of pupils with a selection of coins and a copy of **Resource 5.4.4a** Fractions of quantities. Pupils should cut out the cards and organise them into equivalent groups. Ask: *What value does each card represent? How can you justify that the equivalents are equal?*

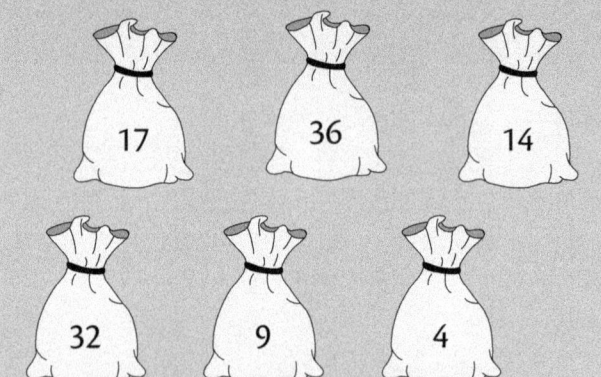

- Ask pupils to record four fraction statements involving quantities (similar in style to the ones on the other cards) on the blank cards. Ensure the four fractions are equivalent. If further practice is required, pupils could play a matching pairs game using these cards.
Answers: Equal to 2: $\frac{1}{3}$ of 6, $\frac{1}{10}$ of 20, $\frac{1}{6}$ of 12, $\frac{1}{5}$ of 10; Equal to 5: $\frac{1}{12}$ of 60, $\frac{1}{8}$ of 40, $\frac{1}{2}$ of 10, $\frac{1}{5}$ of 25; Equal to 10: $\frac{1}{2}$ of 20, $\frac{1}{8}$ of 80, $\frac{1}{4}$ of 40, $\frac{1}{10}$ of 100; Equal to 25: $\frac{1}{4}$ of 100, $\frac{1}{2}$ of 50, $\frac{1}{8}$ of 200, $\frac{1}{10}$ of 250.

Same-day enrichment

- Show pupils the following image:

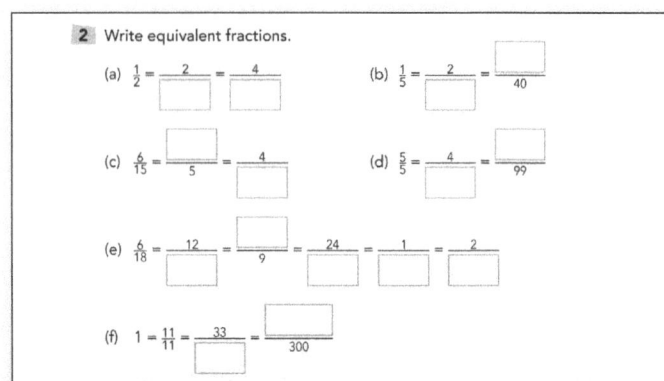

- Explain that six bags of sweets are to be distributed between a group of five girls and a group of nine boys. No sweets can be taken out of the bags until all the bags have been distributed among the two groups to ensure everyone in both groups will receive the same amount. Which bags should the girls receive and which bags should the boys receive to ensure each child will get the same amount of sweets? Is there more than one way this can be done?

Question 2

2 Write equivalent fractions.

(a) $\frac{1}{2} = \frac{2}{\boxed{}} = \frac{4}{\boxed{}}$ (b) $\frac{1}{5} = \frac{2}{\boxed{}} = \frac{\boxed{}}{40}$

(c) $\frac{6}{15} = \frac{\boxed{}}{5} = \frac{4}{\boxed{}}$ (d) $\frac{5}{5} = \frac{4}{\boxed{}} = \frac{\boxed{}}{99}$

(e) $\frac{6}{18} = \frac{12}{\boxed{}} = \frac{\boxed{}}{9} = \frac{24}{\boxed{}} = \frac{1}{\boxed{}} = \frac{2}{\boxed{}}$

(f) $1 = \frac{11}{11} = \frac{33}{\boxed{}} = \frac{\boxed{}}{300}$

Chapter 4 Comparing fractions, improper fractions and mixed numbers   Unit 4.4 Practice Book 5A, pages 94–97

What learning will pupils have achieved at the conclusion of Question 2?
- Pupils will understand that the multiplicative relationship between the numerator and the denominator stays the same for equivalent fractions.
- Symbolic notation will have been used to identify equivalent fractions.

Activities for whole-class instruction

- Present pupils with the following images:

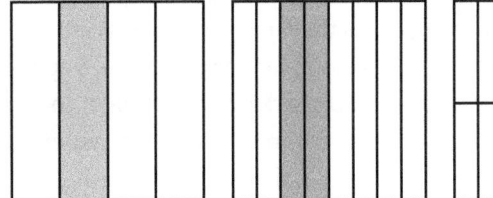

- Ask: *What is the same and what is different about the three rectangles?* Pupils should tell you that:
  - the rectangles are the same shape and size
  - they are all divided into a different number of equal parts
  - the same amount of space is shaded on each of the three rectangles.
- Ask: *What fraction of each rectangle is shaded?* Agree $\frac{1}{4} = \frac{2}{8} = \frac{4}{16}$.

 *When two or more fractions represent the same amount they are equivalent.*

- Provide pairs of pupils with a rectangle of paper and ask them to show another fraction that is equivalent to $\frac{1}{4}$. Stick responses to the board and ask pupils to work out what fraction each image represents. Establish that they are all equivalent.
- Display the following images:

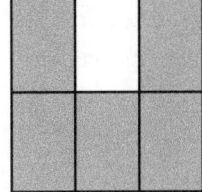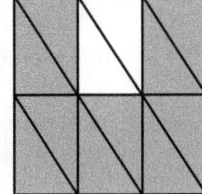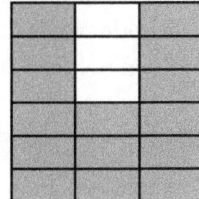

- Ask: *What is the same and what is different about these three rectangles?* Pupils should tell you that:
  - the rectangles are the same shape and size
  - they are all divided into a different number of equal parts
  - the same amount of space is shaded on each of the three rectangles.
- Ask: *What fraction of each rectangle is shaded?* Agree $\frac{5}{6} = \frac{10}{12} = \frac{15}{18}$.
- Provide pairs of pupils with a rectangle of paper and ask them to show another fraction that is equivalent to $\frac{5}{6}$. Stick responses to the board and ask pupils to work out what fraction each image represents. Establish that they are all equivalent.
- Write:

  $\frac{1}{3}$ $\frac{2}{6}$ $\frac{3}{9}$ $\frac{4}{12}$

- Ask: *What is the same and what is different about these four fractions?* Pupils should tell you that the fractions are equivalent in value but have different-sized numerators and denominators.
- Ask: *What is the relationship between the numerator and the denominator in each fraction?* Agree that the denominator is three times larger than the numerator in each fraction.
- Ask: *What fraction, with a numerator of 5, is equivalent to $\frac{1}{3}$? How do you know?* Can pupils tell you that the denominator will need to be three times as large as the numerator for the fraction to be equivalent to $\frac{1}{3}$. So, if the new numerator is 5, the denominator will be 15. So, the fraction will be $\frac{5}{15}$.
- Ask: *What fraction, with a numerator of 10, is equivalent to $\frac{1}{3}$?* Agree $\frac{10}{30}$. Can pupils justify this? Repeat with different numerators.

 *When the denominator is three times the numerator, the fraction is equivalent to $\frac{1}{3}$.*

- Ask: *What fraction, with a denominator 18, is equivalent to $\frac{1}{3}$? How do you know?* Can pupils explain that dividing the denominator by three will determine the value of the numerator. Repeat with different denominators.
- Write:

  $\frac{2}{5}$ $\frac{4}{10}$ $\frac{6}{15}$ $\frac{8}{20}$

- Tell pupils that these four fractions are equivalent. Ask: *What do you notice about the numerators in these four fractions?* Agree that they increase by two each time. Ask: *What do you notice about the denominator in these four fractions?* Agree that they increase by five each time. Ask: *What are the next three fractions in this sequence?*
- Write $\frac{9}{15}$ on the board. Provide pupils with sticky notes and ask them to identify as many equivalent fractions

Chapter 4 Comparing fractions, improper fractions and mixed numbers Unit 4.4 Practice Book 5A, pages 94–97

as they can for $\frac{9}{15}$. Stick responses on the board. Who can come up with the most complicated fraction? Share strategies for identifying equivalent fractions.

Look out for … pupils who find it hard to 'scale back' when identifying equivalent fractions and can only 'scale up'. Ensure pupils are not always presented with fractions in their simplest form to ensure that they have opportunities to 'convert in both directions'.

- Pupils should complete Question 2 in the Practice Book.

Same-day intervention

- Find five ways to make each of these statements true:

  $\frac{1}{\square} = \frac{2}{\square}$ $\frac{1}{\square} = \frac{3}{\square}$ $\frac{2}{\square} = \frac{3}{\square}$ $\frac{\square}{20} = \frac{\square}{30}$

- Pupils may find a fraction wall useful to support working with this activity.

Same-day enrichment

- Present pupils with the following set of fractions:

  $\frac{6}{10}$ $\frac{3}{5}$ $\frac{18}{20}$ $\frac{9}{15}$

- Ask: *Which one is the odd one out and why? What about this list?*

  $\frac{30}{100}$ $\frac{3}{10}$ $\frac{6}{20}$ $\frac{3}{9}$

- Ask pupils to come up with their own sets of four fractions, each with one odd one out for a partner to identify.

Question 3

> **3** Complete each statement.
>
> (a) Mary was given half of half a cake; she was given ☐ of the cake.
>
> (b) Write any three fractions that are equal to $\frac{1}{3}$: ☐, ☐ and ☐.
>
> (c) 3 lots of $\frac{1}{6}$ equal ☐ lots of $\frac{1}{12}$
>
> (d) After folding a square piece of paper in half twice, each part is ☐ of the square.

What learning will pupils have achieved at the conclusion of Question 3?

- Pupils will understand that the multiplicative relationship between the numerator and the denominator stays the same for equivalent fractions.
- Pupils will be able to recognise common equivalent fractions.

Activities for whole-class instruction

- Provide pupils with a strip of paper, one per pair. Ask them to fold the paper so it is divided into any number of equal parts and then open the paper out. Ask: *Who has divided the whole into two equal parts? Who has divided the whole into four equal parts? Who has divided the whole into a different number of equal parts?* Ask pupils to tell their partner what fraction of the whole each part represents on their strip of paper.

- Tell pupils to refold their paper strip and to fold it once more so they are halving each of the parts. Ask pupils to predict how many parts they now have. Ask: *What fraction of the whole does each part represent?* Ask pupils to open their paper out and check what fraction of the whole each part now represents on their strip of paper. Record responses on a table on the board, for example:

Fraction each part initially represented	Fraction each part represents after halving each part
$\frac{1}{2}$	$\frac{1}{4}$
$\frac{1}{3}$	$\frac{1}{6}$
$\frac{1}{4}$	$\frac{1}{8}$
$\frac{1}{5}$	$\frac{1}{10}$
$\frac{1}{6}$	$\frac{1}{12}$

- Ask pupils to generalise about the relationship after halving each part. Ensure pupils notice the denominator doubles because the number of parts doubles but that each part is half the size. Ask: *What is half of $\frac{1}{10}$? What is half of $\frac{1}{46}$?* Repeat with other fractions.

- Draw pupils' attention back to their fraction strips and shade four parts. They should complete the following sentence: 'We have shaded four lots of ____; this is equivalent to ____ lots of ____'. Ask pupils to identify an equivalent fraction for the amount shaded. You may wish to guide pupils to considering how the paper was initially folded to help with the identification of an equivalence, for example:

Chapter 4 Comparing fractions, improper fractions and mixed numbers   Unit 4.4 Practice Book 5A, pages 94–97

We shaded four lots of $\frac{1}{10}$; this is equivalent to two lots of $\frac{1}{5}$.

- Pupils share equivalence statements with another pair. Do they agree? Identify other equivalence statements using the fractions strips for support.
- Display the images below:

We shaded four lots of $\frac{1}{12}$ and two lots of $\frac{1}{6}$, but it doesn't look like they are equivalent.

- Ask pupils to consider how they can prove the shaded parts on the two bars are equal. Demonstrate the equivalence by cutting and rearranging the parts if necessary.
- Provide pupils with another strip of paper, identical in size to the previous strip. Using folding and shading, ask pupils to show a fraction that is equivalent to their previous fractions but where the shaded parts are not positioned consecutively on the left side of the image.
- Pupils should complete Question 3 in the Practice Book.

Same-day intervention

- Present pupils with the following set of fractions:

$\frac{3}{4}$	$\frac{3}{5}$	$\frac{6}{15}$	$\frac{8}{20}$
$\frac{6}{10}$	$\frac{10}{15}$	$\frac{9}{15}$	$\frac{1}{5}$
$\frac{2}{3}$	$\frac{4}{6}$	$\frac{1}{3}$	$\frac{2}{5}$

- Ask pupils to sort the fractions into three groups of equivalent fractions. There should be three fractions left over. Can pupils write two equivalent fractions to go with each of the three leftover fractions.

Same-day enrichment

- Provide pupils with a copy of **Resource 5.4.4b** Equivalent fraction puzzle. Ask pupils to place fractions in the three-by-three grid so that no fractions in the same column or row are equivalent.

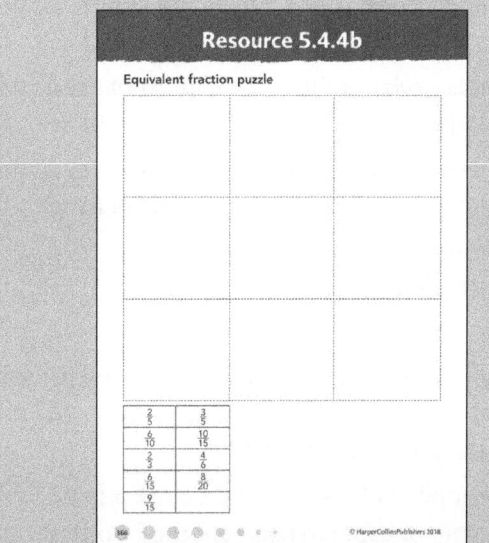

Question 4

4 An ant was crawling from Place A to Place B.
The ant crawled $\frac{4}{12}$ m on the first day and $\frac{6}{12}$ m on the second day.

(a) How many metres did the ant crawl on these two days?

(b) How many metres away is it to Place B after two days' crawling?

Chapter 4 Comparing fractions, improper fractions and mixed numbers   Unit 4.4 Practice Book 5A, pages 94–97

What learning will pupils have achieved at the conclusion of Question 4?

- Pupils will be able to add and subtract fractions less than 1 with the same denominator.

Activities for whole-class instruction

- Present pupils with the following image:

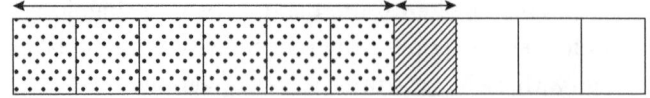

- Ask pupils to consider what this image could represent. Share ideas; aim for different contexts. For each one ask:
  - *What does the whole represent?* (a real-life situation, for example number of packets of biscuits in the cupboard)
  - *What does each part represent?* ($\frac{1}{10}$ of the whole – what is this in the context of a real-life situation?)
  - *What is represented by the spotted section?* ($\frac{6}{10}$ of the whole – what is this in the context of a real-life situation?)
  - *What is represented by the striped section?* ($\frac{4}{10}$ of the whole – what is this in the context of a real-life situation?)
  - *What remains unshaded?*
- Repeat as appropriate.
- Pupils should complete Question 4 in the Practice Book.

Same-day intervention

- Provide pupils with a strip of paper. Ask pupils to use the strip of paper to represent the following information about a journey.

Journey time	Fraction of total distance travelled
1st hour	$\frac{3}{8}$
2nd hour	$\frac{2}{8}$

- Ask: *How many equal parts does the strip of paper need to be divided into? What does each part represent? What will represent the first hour of the journey? What will represent the second hour of the journey?*
- Ask pupils questions relating to this scenario. Encourage pupils to use their fraction strips for support.

Same-day enrichment

- Draw the image below.

- Ask pupils to decide a context that this image could represent. Write three word problems relating to this context that involve fractions. Give the questions to a partner to solve.

Challenge and extension questions

Question 5

5 Walking from Place A to Place B took Tim $\frac{3}{7}$ hours and Sam $\frac{4}{14}$ hours.
   Who walked faster? _____

This question presents a word problem that requires pupils to compare fractions with related denominators to identify which is smaller.

Question 6

6 Three pizzas of the same size are shared equally by four children.
   How many pizzas can each child have? Show your working. _____

To answer this question, pupils will need to draw on their understanding of division to identify a fraction of a quantity within a real-life context.

Chapter 4 Comparing fractions, improper fractions and mixed numbers

Unit 4.5
Improper fractions and mixed numbers

Conceptual context

Pupils were introduced to mixed numbers in Year 2 where they identified fractional numbers greater than 1 and positioned them on a number line. They will build on this understanding in order to identify improper fractions using pictorial representations and number lines to support their thinking. Pupils will learn the terminology: proper fractions, improper fractions and mixed numbers and will generalise about the characteristics of these three groups of numbers. Pupils will compare and order mixed numbers and improper fractions and will draw on their knowledge of multiplication and division facts to convert from improper fractions to mixed numbers and vice versa. The understanding that is developed within this unit will be required within the remainder of Chapter 4 as pupils solve fraction calculations involving numbers beyond 1.

Learning pupils will have achieved at the end of the unit

- Pupils will be able to interpret and represent improper fractions and mixed numbers pictorially (Q1)
- Pupils will understand the terms: proper fraction, improper fraction and mixed number (Q2, Q4)
- Pupils will recognise: proper fractions, improper fractions and mixed numbers (Q2)
- Pupils will be able to locate mixed numbers, improper fractions and proper fractions on a number line (Q3)
- Pupils will be able to reason about proper fractions, improper fractions and mixed numbers using their understanding about the characteristics of these numbers (Q4)
- Pupils will be able to convert mixed numbers to improper fractions (Q5)
- Pupils will be able to convert improper fractions to whole numbers or mixed numbers (Q6)

Resources

bars of chocolate divided into equal pieces (or a non-edible equivalent); mini whiteboards; whole straws and straws cut into eighths; selection of cards with proper fractions, improper fractions and mixed numbers on them; small sticky notes; counting stick; strips of paper; number line from 0–5; sugar paper; transparent cups labelled in quarters; squash; interlocking cubes; dienes equipment; **Resource 5.4.5a** Fraction sort; **Resource 5.4.5b** Improper fractions and mixed number pairs

Vocabulary

numerator, denominator, mixed number, proper fraction, improper fraction, convert

Chapter 4 Comparing fractions, improper fractions and mixed numbers   Unit 4.5 Practice Book 5A, pages 98–100

Question 1

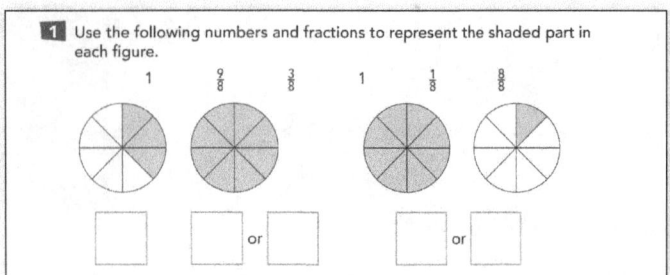

What learning will pupils have achieved at the conclusion of Question 1?

- Pupils will be able to interpret and represent improper fractions and mixed numbers pictorially.

Activities for whole-class instruction

- Show pupils a whole bar of chocolate divided into equal parts and a single piece from the same-sized bar. Ask: *How much chocolate is there?* Share ideas, ensuring pupils speak in full phrases, for example 'Seven pieces of chocolate; one bar of chocolate and one piece of chocolate; one whole bar and one-sixth of a bar.'

- Write:
  $1\frac{1}{6} = \frac{7}{6}$
- Ask: *Both of these fractions represent the quantity of chocolate. Why do they look different? Why are they the same?* Establish that one bar of chocolate is the whole and each part is $\frac{1}{6}$ of a bar. Count in sixths to demonstrate there are $\frac{7}{6}$ and that this can be recorded as 1 whole bar and $\frac{1}{6}$ of a bar.
- Add another piece of chocolate. Ask: *How could this be expressed as a fraction?* Count in sixths to demonstrate that there are $\frac{8}{6}$ and that this can be recorded as 1 whole bar and $\frac{2}{6}$ of a bar. Ask pupils to record these fractions on mini whiteboards. Add additional pieces of chocolate and repeat if appropriate.

ⓘ Pupils often have difficulty thinking of fractions being greater than 1, probably because their experience so far has been with fractions that are smaller than 1. Counting in fractions, perhaps on a number line, will help pupils to understand that fractions can go beyond 1.

- Show pupils the following images:

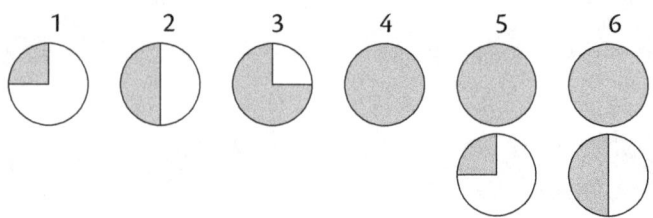

- Tell pupils that they are going to count in quarters. Count forwards starting with $\frac{1}{4}$. Pause on $\frac{2}{4}$ and agree that it is equivalent to $\frac{1}{2}$. Continue the count until $\frac{4}{4}$ is reached. Establish that this is equivalent to 1 whole. Identify that Image 5 represents both $\frac{5}{4}$ and $1\frac{1}{4}$ and that Image 6 represents $\frac{6}{4}$ and $1\frac{2}{4}$ or $1\frac{1}{2}$.
- Select pupils to label each image before repeating the count both forwards and backwards. Discuss how you are counting either in quarters ($\frac{1}{4}, \frac{2}{4}, \frac{3}{4}, \frac{4}{4}, \frac{5}{4}$ ...) or wholes and quarters ($\frac{1}{4}, \frac{2}{4}, \frac{3}{4}, 1, 1\frac{1}{4}$ ...) but do not introduce the language of mixed numbers or improper fractions yet; this will be introduced in Question 2.
- Ask pupils to draw the next image in this sequence and label it. Agree that it will be $1\frac{3}{4}$ or $\frac{7}{4}$. Repeat with subsequent images if appropriate.

Look out for ... pupils who swap the numerator and the denominator because they think the smaller number is always the numerator. Reminding pupils of the roles of both the numerator and the denominator will help with this.

- Pupils should complete Question 1 in the Practice Book.

Same-day intervention

- Provide pupils with a pile of whole straws and straws cut into eighths. Establish that the smaller straws represent eighths by lining up eight small straws and comparing them with a single whole straw. Record: $\frac{8}{8} = 1$.
- Tell pupils to select one straw and one small part of a straw. Ask: *What does this represent as a fraction?* Agree 1 whole and $\frac{1}{8}$, which should be written as $1\frac{1}{8}$. Remind pupils that $\frac{8}{8} = 1$, therefore it could also be seen as $\frac{8}{8}$ and $\frac{1}{8}$, which is $\frac{9}{8}$.
- Select one straw and three small straws and repeat. Repeat with other amounts if appropriate.

Chapter 4 Comparing fractions, improper fractions and mixed numbers   Unit 4.5 Practice Book 5A, pages 98–100

Same-day enrichment

- Show pupils the following images:

  Image 1   Image 2

- Discuss the fractions represented. Can pupils see:
  - $1\frac{1}{2}$ or $\frac{3}{2}$ in Image 1?
  - $\frac{2}{4}$ or $\frac{6}{4}$ in Image 2?
- Ask pupils to draw another similar bar image showing a number of thirds. Ask: *Can you make any generalisations – something that happens every time?*

Question 2

> **2** Sort these fractions into proper fractions, improper fractions and mixed numbers.
>
> $\frac{7}{12}$ $\frac{5}{3}$ $7\frac{1}{18}$ $\frac{3}{2}$ $1\frac{4}{5}$ $\frac{79}{100}$ $30\frac{1}{2}$ $\frac{181}{365}$ $\frac{13}{12}$ $\frac{19}{6}$ $5\frac{1}{4}$
>
> Proper fractions:
>
> Improper fractions:
>
> Mixed numbers:

What learning will pupils have achieved at the conclusion of Question 2?
- Pupils will understand the terms: proper fraction, improper fraction and mixed number.
- Pupils will recognise: proper fractions, improper fractions and mixed numbers.

Activities for whole-class instruction

- From a selection of cards that show a proper fraction, improper fraction or mixed number, position the cards on the board in three groups. At this stage, do not have headings for the groups but sort them according to whether they are a proper fraction, improper fraction or a mixed number.
- Ask: *What do you notice? What is the same about the numbers within each group?* Encourage pupils to generalise about the properties of the numbers within each group and use this to generate headings for the group based on the characteristics identified.

- Introduce pupils to the terms 'proper fraction', 'improper fraction' and 'mixed number' and identify what each one means.

A proper fraction is a fraction where the numerator is less than the denominator. An improper fraction is a fraction where the numerator is greater than or equal to the denominator. A mixed number is a whole number and a fraction combined.

- Ask pupils to consider which name describes the fraction cards in each group.
- In pairs, ask pupils to write a number on a sticky note that could be added to each group. Stick the numbers in the correct positions on the board and check for accuracy.

Look out for … pupils who misunderstand mixed numbers and ignore either the fractional part or the whole number. Reminding pupils of the role of both the whole number and the fractional part may help with this.

- Pupils should complete Question 2 in the Practice Book.

Same-day intervention

- Provide pupils with a copy of **Resource 5.4.5a** Fraction sort. Ask pupils to sort the numbers under the headings: 'Proper fraction', 'Improper fraction' and 'Mixed number'. If necessary, encourage pupils to draw a pictorial representation, similar to those in Question 1, to support their thinking.
- Tell pupils to add two more numbers to each group.

Resource 5.4.5a

Fraction sort

$\frac{9}{16}$	$1\frac{5}{6}$	$\frac{5}{4}$
$3\frac{2}{3}$	$\frac{16}{9}$	$\frac{17}{20}$
$\frac{1}{100}$	$5\frac{1}{10}$	$\frac{10}{5}$
$\frac{13}{6}$	$\frac{2}{3}$	$4\frac{3}{5}$

Answers: Proper fraction: $\frac{9}{16}, \frac{17}{20}, \frac{1}{100}, \frac{2}{3}$; Improper fraction: $\frac{5}{4}, \frac{16}{9}, \frac{10}{5}, \frac{13}{6}$; Mixed number: $1\frac{5}{6}, 3\frac{2}{3}, 5\frac{1}{10}, 4\frac{3}{5}$.

Chapter 4 Comparing fractions, improper fractions and mixed numbers Unit 4.5 Practice Book 5A, pages 98–100

Same-day enrichment

- Ask pupils to write numbers under each of the headings 'Proper fraction', 'Improper fraction' and 'Mixed number' according to the following criteria:
  - a number with a numerator of 3
  - a number with a denominator of 7
  - a number where the numerator and the denominator are even
  - a number where the numerator and the denominator are odd
  - a number with a numerator greater than 100
  - a number with a denominator greater than 100.
- Discuss ideas.

Question 3

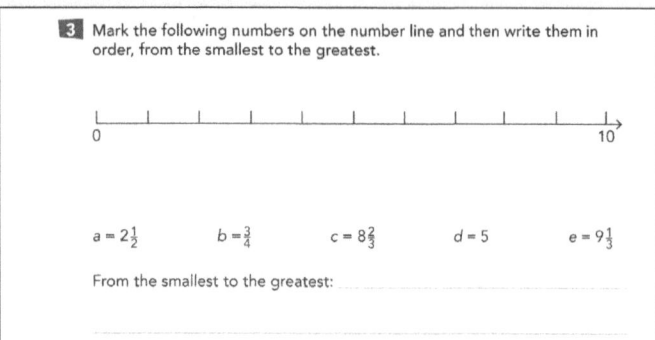

3 Mark the following numbers on the number line and then write them in order, from the smallest to the greatest.

$a = 2\frac{1}{2}$ $b = \frac{3}{4}$ $c = 8\frac{2}{3}$ $d = 5$ $e = 9\frac{1}{3}$

From the smallest to the greatest:

What learning will pupils have achieved at the conclusion of Question 3?

- Pupils will be able to locate mixed numbers, improper fractions and proper fractions on a number line.

Activities for whole-class instruction

- Show a counting stick with 0 labelled at one end and 5 at the other.

  0   5

- Together, locate 1, 2, 3 and 4. Add these numbers to the counting stick using sticky notes.
- Ask: *What would go between 0 and 1? 1 and 2? 2 and 3?* Pupils should label each interval with either a proper fraction or a mixed number. Count up and back in proper fractions and mixed numbers.

- Ask: *What else could 1 be labelled as?* Agree $\frac{2}{2}$. Ask pupils to label all intervals as improper fractions. Count up and back in improper fractions.
- Change the counting stick so it is labelled 0 at one end and $2\frac{1}{2}$ at the other. Repeat the line of questioning above. Change the counting stick so it is labelled 0 at one end and $3\frac{1}{3}$ at the other. Repeat the questions.
- (i) Pupils need to understand that fractions can represent a point on a number line because they are numbers in their own right.
- Provide pairs of pupils with a strip of paper. Ask them to label 0 at one end and 4 at the other. Ask pupils to label where 1, 2 and 3 would be. Ask pupils to label $2\frac{1}{2}$. Share ideas by holding up strips.
- Pupils should label where $\frac{5}{4}$ would be. Repeat with other mixed numbers and improper fractions.
- Ask pupils to choose other numbers to position and label along the number line. Tell pupils to ensure they include proper fractions, improper fractions and mixed numbers. Swap number lines with another pair and check. Are there any you disagree with? Ask: *Which were easier/harder to position? Why?*
- Look out for ... pupils who position $\frac{3}{4}$ where 3 should be because they are thinking the number line is 0–1 rather than 0–4. Reading a range of measuring scales, for example rulers, weighing scales or thermometers, may help pupils to understand intermediate points for numbers beyond 1.
- Looking at the number line from the previous activity, ask pupils to identify a number between:
  - 1 and 2
  - 2 and 3
  - $3\frac{1}{2}$ and 4
  - $\frac{6}{4}$ and $\frac{8}{4}$
  - $\frac{9}{4}$ and $\frac{12}{4}$.
- Ask pupils to record their responses on mini whiteboards. Using the number line for support, ask pupils to order these fractions from least to greatest. Swap with a partner and check for accuracy.
- Pupils should complete Question 3 in the Practice Book.

Chapter 4 Comparing fractions, improper fractions and mixed numbers Unit 4.5 Practice Book 5A, pages 98–100

Same-day intervention

- Show a 0–5 number line and a list of mixed numbers and proper fractions smaller than 5. Ask pupils to pick four numbers and position them on the number line. Encourage pupils to label where the whole numbers will be to support their thinking. Next, ask them to order them from least to greatest. Repeat as appropriate.

Same-day enrichment

- Give pupils the following list:
  $\frac{7}{4}$ $3\frac{5}{8}$ $5\frac{1}{3}$ $\frac{4}{7}$ $\frac{16}{4}$ $\frac{4}{16}$ $7\frac{2}{3}$ $\frac{3}{5}$ $\frac{15}{3}$
- Pupils should:
  - order them from least to greatest
  - add one more proper fraction, improper fraction and mixed number and correctly position these within the list.

Question 4

> 4 Read these statements and write 'true' or 'false'.
>
> (a) $2\frac{3}{5}$ is read as two and three fifths.
>
> (b) All proper fractions are less than 1.
>
> (c) All improper fractions are greater than 1.
>
> (d) The numerator of a proper fraction is always less than its denominator.
>
> (e) The numerator of an improper fraction is always greater than its denominator.
>
> (f) A proper fraction can be converted to a mixed number.
>
> (g) An improper fraction can be converted to a mixed number.
>
> (h) A mixed number can be converted to an improper fraction.

What learning will pupils have achieved at the conclusion of Question 4?

- Pupils will understand the terms: proper fraction, improper fraction and mixed number.
- Pupils will be able to reason about proper fractions, improper fractions and mixed numbers using their understanding about the characteristics of these numbers.

Activities for whole-class instruction

- Split the class into three groups. Ask pupils to brainstorm everything they know about either proper fractions, improper fractions or mixed numbers and record ideas as a group on a large sheet of paper. Share ideas. What else would the class like to add to each group's ideas?
- Write 'The numerator of an improper fraction is greater than the denominator.' Ask: *Is this always, sometimes or never true?* Pupil pairs should identify examples where it is true and examples where it is not true, which can lead to a generalisation.
- Agree that it is sometimes true because an improper fraction can have a numerator that is equal to the denominator. Ask pupils to record five improper fractions where the numerator is equal to the denominator.

An improper fraction is a fraction where the numerator is greater than or equal to the denominator.

- Write 'Improper fractions are greater than 1.' Ask: *Is this always, sometimes or never true?* Pupil pairs should identify examples where it is true and examples where it is not true, which can lead to a generalisation.
- Agree that it is sometimes true because an improper fraction can be equal to 1. Ask pupils to record five improper fractions that are equal to 1. Identify that these are all fractions where the numerator and the denominator are equal.

Fractions that are equal to 1 are improper fractions.

- Pupils should complete Question 4 in the Practice Book.

Same-day intervention

- Ask pupils to provide a justification for the following statements:
  - $\frac{3}{7}$ is a proper fraction
  - $\frac{9}{5}$ is an improper fraction
  - $3\frac{1}{2}$ is a mixed number
  - $\frac{9}{5}$ isn't a proper fraction
  - $5\frac{1}{3}$ isn't an improper fraction
  - $\frac{10}{10}$ isn't a proper fraction.

Same-day enrichment

- Ask pupils to write five true or false statements relating to proper fractions, improper fractions and mixed numbers. They give them to their partner to answer.

Chapter 4 Comparing fractions, improper fractions and mixed numbers   Unit 4.5 Practice Book 5A, pages 98–100

Question 5

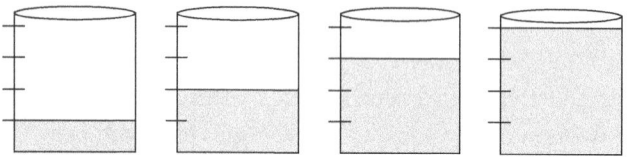

5 Convert the mixed numbers to improper fractions.
(a) $2\frac{1}{3}=$ ☐   (b) $1\frac{5}{8}=$ ☐   (c) $6\frac{7}{9}=$ ☐   (d) $60\frac{37}{39}=$ ☐

What learning will pupils have achieved at the conclusion of Question 5?

- Pupils will be able to convert mixed numbers to improper fractions.

Activities for whole-class instruction

- Show pupils four transparent cups containing squash, one $\frac{1}{4}$ full, one $\frac{2}{4}$ full, one $\frac{3}{4}$ full and one full. Ensure each cup is marked in $\frac{1}{4}$ intervals. Ask: *Which cup has the most squash? Which cup has the least squash?*

- Focus pupils' attention on the cup that is full and agree that the amount of squash in 1 full cup is equivalent to $\frac{4}{4}$. If necessary, pour four lots of $\frac{1}{4}$ into an identical cup to convince pupils of the equivalence. Ask: *How many quarters in two cups? How many quarters in three cups?* If necessary, fill cups with quarter measures to convince pupils of the equivalencies.

- Record:
  - 1 cup = $1 \times \frac{4}{4} = \frac{4}{4}$
  - 2 cups = $2 \times \frac{4}{4} = \frac{8}{4}$
  - 3 cups = $3 \times \frac{4}{4} = \frac{12}{4}$

- Ask pupils what they notice about this sequence. Establish that because there are four quarters in a whole the number of cups needs to be multiplied by 4 to calculate the total number of quarters.

- Tell pupils to complete the sequence for four cups, five cups and six cups.

All say... *To calculate the number of quarters, we multiply the number of wholes by 4 because there are 4 quarters in 1 whole.*

- Ask pupils to examine 1 full cup and a cup that is $\frac{1}{4}$ full.

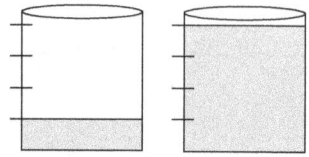

- Ask: *How much squash is there?* Ensure pupils identify there is 1 full cup and a cup that is $\frac{1}{4}$ full. Ask: *How could this be recorded as a mixed number?* Agree $1\frac{1}{4}$. Ask: *What would this be if it were converted to an improper fraction?* Agree $\frac{5}{4}$ because $\frac{4}{4} + \frac{1}{4} = \frac{5}{4}$. Record this information in a table:

Quantity of liquid expressed as a mixed number	Quantity of liquid expressed as an improper fraction
$1\frac{1}{4}$	$\frac{5}{4}$
$1\frac{2}{4}$	
$1\frac{3}{4}$	
2	
$2\frac{1}{4}$	
$2\frac{2}{4}$	
$2\frac{3}{4}$	
3	

- Using the marked cups and squash, ask pupils to explore other mixed numbers and complete the table.

- Ask: *If I had five and a quarter cups of squash, what would this be converted to as an improper fraction?* Represent this scenario using the cups and squash.

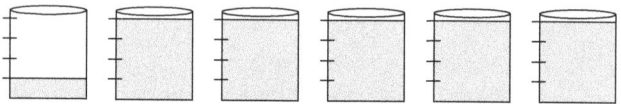

- Counting in lots of $\frac{4}{4}$, ask pupils to count the amount of liquid in the full cups: $\frac{4}{4}, \frac{8}{4}, \frac{12}{4}, \frac{16}{4}, \frac{20}{4}$. Establish it is $\frac{20}{4}$ in the full cups. Ask pupils to add on the $\frac{1}{4}$ full cup of squash to identify that the total is $\frac{21}{4}$.

- Record the above calculations symbolically:

$$1 + 1 + 1 + 1 + 1 + \frac{1}{4} = 5\frac{1}{4}$$
$$\frac{4}{4} + \frac{4}{4} + \frac{4}{4} + \frac{4}{4} + \frac{4}{4} + \frac{1}{4} = \frac{21}{4}$$

- Establish that this shows the total amount of liquid by repeated addition. How could it be solved more efficiently using multiplication? Encourage pupils to notice that finding five lots of $\frac{4}{4}$ results in $5 \times \frac{4}{4} = \frac{20}{4}$.

- Ask: *Imagine the cups were divided into fifths and we had 5 and $\frac{1}{5}$ cups of squash. What would we multiply by to calculate the number of fifths in 5 cups?* Agree we would multiply by 5 because there are 5 fifths in 1 whole, so we need to multiply the number of wholes by 5.

- Ask: *What if the cups were divided into sixths and we had 5 and $\frac{1}{6}$ cups of squash?* Agree we would multiply the number of wholes by 6 because there are 6 sixths in a whole.

Chapter 4 Comparing fractions, improper fractions and mixed numbers   Unit 4.5 Practice Book 5A, pages 98–100

- Ask: *What generalisations can you make about the number we multiply by to calculate the total number of parts within the wholes?* Agree we multiply by the number of parts 1 whole has been equally divided into.

 *To calculate the total number of parts in the wholes we multiply the number of wholes by the number of parts each whole is equally divided into.*

 … pupils who add or multiply the denominator when working out the amount of whole parts. Reminding pupils of the number of parts the whole has been equally divided into may help with this.

- Pupils should complete Question 5 in the Practice Book.

Same-day intervention

- Provide pupils with interlocking cubes. Ask them to build a tower of 5 cubes. Tell pupils this represents 1 tower. Ask: *What does 1 cube represent?* Agree, $\frac{1}{5}$ of a tower. Ask: *What do 2 cubes represent? 3 cubes? 4 cubes?*
- Ask: *How many fifths in 1 tower? How many fifths in 2 towers? 3 towers?* Show pupils four complete towers of 5 cubes and one tower of 3 cubes.
- Change to towers of 3 and 7 and ask similar questions.
- Ask: *How could you express $5\frac{2}{5}$ as an improper fraction?* They first need to realise that the answer must be in fifths because a number of fifths is included in the number given. Then, they should consider how many fifths in 1 whole and then multiply by the number of wholes (5).

Same-day enrichment

- Provide pupils with a number line from 0 to 5. Ask pupils to position and label eight mixed numbers on the line. Convert the mixed numbers to improper fractions.

Question 6

6 Convert the improper fractions to whole numbers or mixed numbers.
(a) $\frac{31}{7}$ = _____   (b) $\frac{53}{8}$ = _____
(c) $\frac{81}{9}$ = _____   (d) $\frac{97}{30}$ = _____

What learning will pupils have achieved at the conclusion of Question 6?

- Pupils will be able to convert improper fractions to whole numbers or mixed numbers.

Activities for whole-class instruction

- Show pupils the following image:

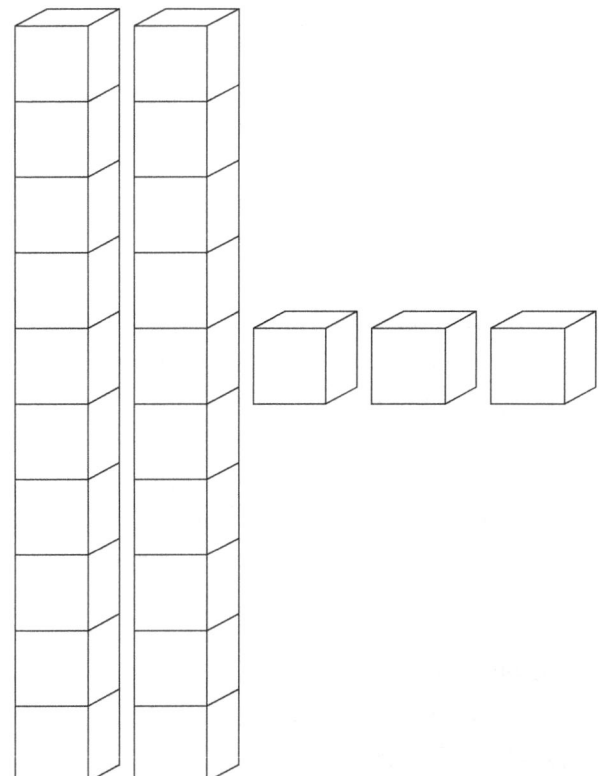

- Tell pupils that each tower represents $\frac{10}{10}$ and is equivalent to 1. Ask: *What does 1 of the cubes represent?* Agree, $\frac{1}{10}$. Ask: *How many lots of $\frac{10}{10}$ are there?* Agree that there are 2 lots of $\frac{10}{10}$ and that this equals $\frac{20}{10}$. Ask: *How many lots of $\frac{1}{10}$ are there?* Agree that there are 3 lots of $\frac{1}{10}$. Ask: *How many tenths are there altogether?* If necessary, pupils can count the individual cubes to identify there are $\frac{23}{10}$. Tell pupils to convert this to a mixed number. Establish that this will be $2\frac{3}{10}$ because there are 2 towers and $\frac{3}{10}$ of a tower. Repeat with other images if appropriate.

- Pupils should construct $\frac{56}{10}$ using base 10 blocks. Repeat the questioning above. Repeat with other improper fractions.

- Record $\frac{46}{8}$ on the board. Ask: *What would this be converted to as a mixed number?* Pupils should identify how many complete lots of $\frac{8}{8}$ can be made from $\frac{46}{8}$. Write: $\frac{8}{8} + \frac{8}{8} + \frac{8}{8} + \frac{8}{8} + \frac{8}{8} = \frac{40}{8}$. Ask: *How many eighths are left?* Establish that $\frac{6}{8}$ remain. This means $\frac{46}{8} = 5\frac{6}{8}$. Repeat with other mixed number fractions.

 *When converting improper fractions to mixed numbers we need to find out how many times the denominator goes into the numerator to calculate the number of wholes.*

- Pupils should complete Question 6 in the Practice Book.

Chapter 4 Comparing fractions, improper fractions and mixed numbers Unit 4.5 Practice Book 5A, pages 98–100

Same-day intervention

- Provide pupils with a number line from 0 to 5 with divisions for quarters marked on it. Ask pupils to position and label the following fractions:

  $\frac{54}{4}$ $\frac{20}{4}$

  $\frac{8}{4}$ $\frac{18}{4}$

  $\frac{15}{4}$ $\frac{10}{4}$

  $\frac{12}{4}$ $\frac{16}{4}$

- Convert the improper fractions to mixed numbers using towers of four interlocking cubes for support if necessary. Repeat, using a different denominator.

Same-day enrichment

- Provide pairs of pupils with a copy of **Resource 5.4.5b** Improper fractions and mixed number pairs. They match the improper fractions to the whole numbers or mixed numbers.
- Pupils should make three more matching pairs on the blank cards. They swap these with another pair who should match them.

Resource 5.4.5b

Improper fractions and mixed number pairs

$4\frac{8}{9}$	$\frac{47}{9}$	$\frac{29}{7}$
$\frac{32}{7}$	$\frac{44}{9}$	$5\frac{1}{7}$
$\frac{54}{9}$	$4\frac{1}{7}$	$5\frac{2}{9}$
$\frac{36}{7}$	6	$4\frac{4}{7}$

Answers: $4\frac{8}{9}$ and $\frac{44}{9}$, $5\frac{1}{7}$ and $\frac{36}{7}$, $4\frac{1}{7}$ and $\frac{29}{7}$, $5\frac{2}{9}$ and $\frac{47}{9}$, 6 and $\frac{54}{9}$, $4\frac{4}{7}$ and $\frac{32}{7}$.

Challenge and extension questions

Question 7

7 Complete the following table. One has been done for you.

Quantity	As a decimal	As a mixed number	As an improper fraction
2 m 10 cm	2.1 m	$2\frac{1}{10}$ m	$\frac{21}{10}$ m
90 minutes	___ h	___ h	___ h
5 kg 200 g	___ kg	___ kg	___ kg
1650 ml	___ l	___ l	___ l
30 km 200 m	___ km	___ km	___ km

8 (a) If $\frac{5}{\triangle + 2}$ is an improper fraction and $\triangle$ is a whole number (including 0), then $\triangle$ can be _____.

(b) If a is a whole number, $\frac{8}{a}$ is a proper fraction, and $\frac{a}{5}$ is an improper fraction, then the value of a can be _____.

This question requires pupils to use their knowledge of decimals, mixed numbers and improper fractions to convert units of measure.

Question 8

This question requires pupils to apply their understanding of both proper and improper fractions to identify unknowns within an abstract problem.

Chapter 4 Comparing fractions, improper fractions and mixed numbers

Unit 4.6
Adding and subtracting fractions with related denominators (1)

Conceptual context

This is the first of two units that develop pupils' skills in adding and subtracting fractions with related denominators. This unit will build on the concept of adding and subtracting fractions with the same denominator that has been developed in Year 3 and Year 4. Pupils will be required to use their understanding of equivalent fractions as they convert fractions so they have the same denominator; they will draw on their knowledge of multiples and factors.

In Unit 4.5, pupils developed their understanding of mixed numbers and improper fractions; this new learning will be required within this unit because some answers will be greater than 1. In the next unit, pupils will be adding and subtracting improper fractions and mixed numbers with related denominators.

Learning pupils will have achieved at the end of the unit

- Pupils will understand that the multiplicative relationship between the numerator and the denominator stays the same for equivalent fractions (Q1, Q2)
- Pupils will be able to fluently identify equivalent fractions when represented only symbolically (Q1, Q2)
- Pupils will be able to mentally add and subtract fractions with the same denominator, which results in an answer less than or equal to 1 (Q3)
- Pupils will understand how to add fractions with related denominators (Q4)
- Pupils will understand how to subtract fractions with related denominators (Q5)
- Pupils will be able to add and subtract fractions with related denominators to solve contextualised problems (Q6)

Resources

paper triangles; strip of paper divided into 12 equal parts; paper circles; fraction strips divided into equal parts; **Resource 5.4.6a** Equivalent fractions – extending beyond 1; **Resource 5.4.6b** Equivalent fractions – beyond 1; **Resource 5.4.6c** Adding and subtracting fractions mentally

Vocabulary

equivalent, numerator, denominator, related denominators, multiple, mixed number, proper fraction, improper fraction

Chapter 4 Comparing fractions, improper fractions and mixed numbers Unit 4.6 Practice Book 5A, pages 101–104

Question 1

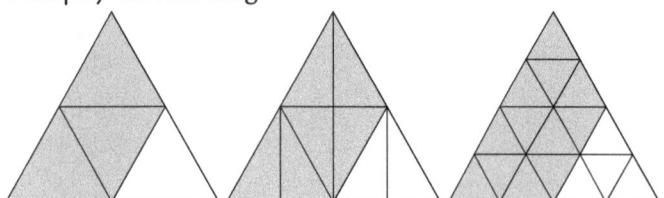

What learning will pupils have achieved at the conclusion of Question 1?

- Pupils will understand that the multiplicative relationship between the numerator and the denominator stays the same for equivalent fractions.
- Pupils will be able to fluently identify equivalent fractions when represented only symbolically.

Activities for whole-class instruction

- Display the following:

- Ask: *What is the same and what is different about the three triangles?* Pupils should tell you that:
  - the triangles are the same shape and size
  - they are all divided into a different number of equal parts
  - the same amount of space is shaded on each of the three triangles.
- Ask: *What fraction of each triangle is shaded?* Agree $\frac{3}{4} = \frac{6}{8} = \frac{12}{16}$.

   *When two or more fractions represent the same amount they are equivalent.*

- Give pairs of pupils a paper triangle and ask them to show another fraction that is equivalent to $\frac{3}{4}$. Stick responses to the board and identify the fraction that each image represents. Establish that they are all equivalent because the numerator is $\frac{3}{4}$ the size of the denominator.

   *When the numerator is $\frac{3}{4}$ the size of the denominator, the fraction is equivalent to $\frac{3}{4}$.*

- Display the following:

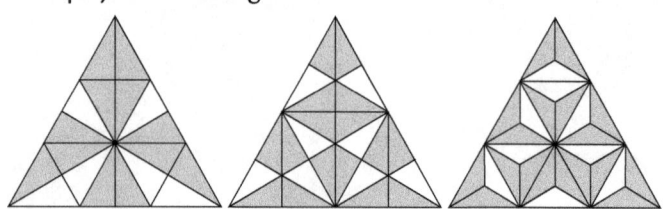

- Ask: *What is the same and what is different about these three triangles?* Pupils should tell you that:
  - the triangles are the same shape and size
  - they are all divided into a different number of equal parts
  - the same amount of space is shaded on each of the three triangles.
- Ask: *What fraction of each triangle is shaded?* Agree $\frac{12}{18} = \frac{16}{24} = \frac{18}{27}$.
- Give pairs of pupils a paper triangle and ask them to show another fraction that is equivalent to these fractions. Stick responses to the board and identify what fraction each image represents. Establish that they are all equivalent because the numerator is $\frac{2}{3}$ the size of the denominator.

   *When the numerator is $\frac{2}{3}$ the size of the denominator, the fraction is equivalent to $\frac{2}{3}$.*

- (i) Equivalence is an important mathematical idea; therefore, pupils should experience a variety of representations to support their understanding of this.

- Display the following:

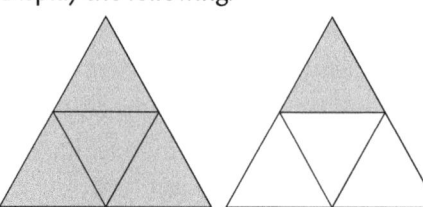

- Tell pupils that this represents $1\frac{1}{4}$. Ask: *What does this represent as an improper fraction?* Agree $\frac{5}{4}$. Provide pairs of pupils with two paper triangles and ask them to represent another fraction that is equivalent to $\frac{5}{4}$. Stick responses to the board and identify what fraction each image represents. Do pupils know that, as long as the numerator and denominator are multiplied by the same factor, the fractions are equivalent? Therefore, a triangle divided into 15, with 12 parts shaded, might be a solution, but there are many others.
- Write:

  $\frac{5}{4}$ $\frac{10}{8}$ $\frac{15}{12}$ $\frac{20}{16}$

Chapter 4 Comparing fractions, improper fractions and mixed numbers   Unit 4.6   Practice Book 5A, pages 101–104

- Ask: *What is the same and what is different about these four fractions?* Pupils should tell you that the fractions are equivalent in value but have different-sized numerators and denominators.
- Ask: *What is the relationship between the numerator and the denominator in each fraction?* Agree that the numerator is $1\frac{1}{4}$ times the denominator.
- Ask: *What fraction, with a denominator of 20, is equivalent to $\frac{5}{4}$? How do you know?* Can pupils tell you that the numerator will need to be $1\frac{1}{4}$ times the size of the denominator for the fraction to be equivalent to $\frac{5}{4}$? If the denominator is 20, the numerator will be $1\frac{1}{4} \times 20 = 25$. Therefore, the fraction will be $\frac{25}{20}$.
- Ask: *What fraction, with a denominator of 24, is equivalent to $\frac{5}{4}$?* Agree $\frac{30}{24}$. Can pupils justify this? Repeat with different denominators.

 When the numerator is $1\frac{1}{4}$ times the denominator, the fraction is equivalent to $\frac{5}{4}$.

- Pupils should complete Question 1 in the Practice Book.

Same-day intervention

- Provide pairs of pupils with a copy of **Resource 5.4.6a** Equivalent fractions – extending beyond 1. Pupils should cut up the cards and organise them into equivalent groups. They might draw pictorial representations to support their thinking. Ask them to justify their decisions.
- Ask them to add one more fraction to each group.

Answers:
$\frac{2}{5} = \frac{4}{10} = \frac{6}{15}, \frac{8}{20}$ $\frac{6}{5} = \frac{12}{10} = \frac{18}{15} = \frac{24}{20}$

$\frac{4}{5} = \frac{8}{10} = \frac{12}{15}, \frac{16}{20}$ $\frac{3}{5} = \frac{6}{10} = \frac{12}{20}$

Same-day enrichment

- Provide pairs of pupils with a copy of **Resource 5.4.6b** Equivalent fractions – beyond 1. Pupils should write three improper fractions that are equivalent to the fractions given. Ask them to justify their decisions.
- Cut up the cards and play pairs.

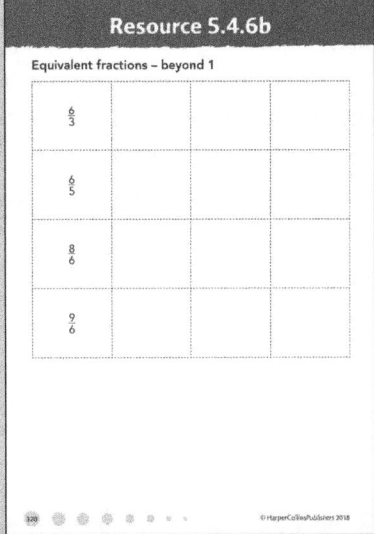

Answers: Various answers possible. Fractions should be equivalent.

Question 2

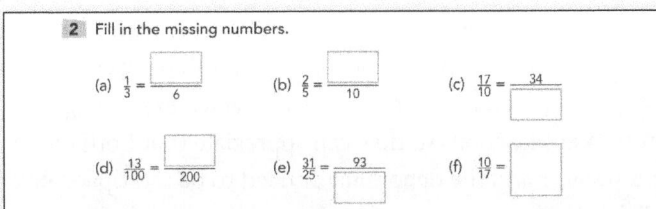

What learning will pupils have achieved at the conclusion of Question 2?

- Pupils will understand that the multiplicative relationship between the numerator and the denominator stays the same for equivalent fractions.
- Pupils will be able to fluently identify equivalent fractions when represented only symbolically.

Activities for whole-class instruction

- Write:

$\frac{1}{\square} = \frac{2}{\square}$

Chapter 4 Comparing fractions, improper fractions and mixed numbers Unit 4.6 Practice Book 5A, pages 101–104

- Ask pupil pairs to record five equivalences that will make this statement correct. Share ideas. Ask: *What is the same and what is different about these statements?* Pupils should tell you that the numerators are always 1 and 2 but the denominators change.
- Ask: *What is the relationship between the numerators?* Agree that one numerator is twice the other. Ask: *What is the relationship between the denominators?* Agree that one denominator is twice the other.
- Ask: *If the smaller denominator is 7, what would the other denominator be? How do you know?* Repeat with different denominators.
- Write the following incomplete equivalency statement on the board:

  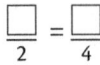

- Ask pupil pairs to record five equivalences that will make this statement correct. Share ideas. Ask: *What is the same and what is different about these equivalency statements?* Pupils should tell you that the denominators are always 2 and 4 but the numerators change.
- Ask: *What is the relationship between the denominators in each statement?* Agree that one denominator is twice the other. Ask: *What is the relationship between the numerators in each equivalency?* Agree that one numerator is twice the other.
- Ask: *If the first numerator is 5, what would the second numerator be? How do you know?* Repeat with different numerators.

(i) Pupils need to notice the relationship between the numerators or denominators when examining equivalent fractions so they can appreciate that both the numerator and the denominator need to be multiplied or divided by the same amount to remain equivalent.

- Write the following sequence on the board:
  - $\frac{3}{5} \times \frac{2}{2} = \frac{6}{10}$
  - $\frac{3}{5} \times \frac{3}{3} = \frac{9}{15}$
  - $\frac{3}{5} \times \frac{4}{4} = \frac{12}{20}$
  - $\frac{3}{5} \times \frac{5}{5} = \frac{15}{25}$
  - $\frac{3}{5} \times \frac{6}{6} = \frac{18}{30}$
- Ask: *What do you notice?* Ensure pupils notice that multiplying the numerator and denominator by the same number results in an equivalent fraction. Ask pupils to record the next three calculations in this sequence. Agree equivalencies.

 *To find an equivalent fraction, both the numerator and the denominator need to be multiplied or divided by the same amount.*

- Present the following statements:
  - For any fraction, if we double the numerator and the denominator, the new number will be:
    1) half the size of the original fraction
    2) equal in size to the original fraction
    3) double the size of the original fraction.
- Ask pupils to select which statement they believe to be correct and to justify their answers. Agree that the new number will be equal to the original fraction.
- Pupils should complete Question 2 in the Practice Book.

Same-day intervention
- Find two possible answers for each of the following statements:
  - a fraction that is equivalent to $\frac{1}{2}$ that has either a numerator or a denominator of 6
  - a fraction that is equivalent to $\frac{1}{3}$ that has either a numerator or a denominator of 6
  - a fraction that is equivalent to $\frac{2}{3}$ that has either a numerator or a denominator of 6.
- Pupils make up their own statements for a partner to solve.

Same-day enrichment
- Ask: *Using the numbers 1, 2, 3, 4, 6, 8 or 12, how many different ways can you make this equivalency statement correct?*

  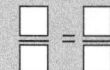

- Tell pupils to consider both proper and improper fractions.

Question 3

3 Work these out mentally. Write the answers.

(a) $\frac{1}{5} + \frac{1}{5} =$ (b) $\frac{4}{7} - \frac{2}{7} =$ (c) $\frac{3}{10} + \frac{7}{10} =$

(d) $\frac{9}{13} - \frac{5}{13} =$ (e) $\frac{8}{9} - \frac{4}{9} =$ (f) $\frac{13}{23} + \frac{5}{23} =$

Chapter 4 Comparing fractions, improper fractions and mixed numbers Unit 4.6 Practice Book 5A, pages 101–104

What learning will pupils have achieved at the conclusion of Question 3?

- Pupils will be able to mentally add and subtract fractions with the same denominator, which results in an answer less than or equal to 1.

Activities for whole-class instruction

- Ask pairs of pupils to draw a number line from 0 to 1 labelled in jumps of $\frac{1}{20}$:

- Explain that this is a competitive game for two players that will require mental addition and subtraction of fractions. (Pupils learned to add and subtract fractions with the same denominator in Year 4).

  – Player 1 chooses a number on the line and crosses it out. They then choose a second number and cross that out. Player 1 mentally calculates the sum or difference of the two numbers and circles the answer.

  – Player 2 starts by crossing off the number Player 1 has just circled and then chooses a second number to cross out.

  – Both players then find the sum or difference of the two numbers and circle the answer. Play continues in this way with each player starting with the number that has just been circled by their opponent. The loser of the game is the player who cannot find the number they need. Repeat the game considering winning strategies.

- Ask: *Which calculations were easy to work out mentally?* Share strategies. Ask: *Which calculations were harder? Why?*

- Working mentally, ask pairs of pupils to sort the following calculations into those that are correct and those that are incorrect:

  $\frac{2}{5} + \frac{3}{5} = \frac{5}{10}$ $\frac{9}{11} - \frac{4}{11} = \frac{5}{11}$

  $\frac{7}{10} - \frac{7}{10} = 0$ $\frac{7}{18} + \frac{5}{18} = \frac{12}{18}$

  $\frac{15}{19} - \frac{11}{19} = \frac{5}{19}$ $\frac{8}{11} - \frac{3}{11} = \frac{5}{0}$

  $\frac{4}{20} + \frac{3}{20} + \frac{2}{20} = \frac{9}{20}$ $\frac{7}{13} + \frac{5}{13} = \frac{11}{13}$

- Pupil pairs should explain to another pair why the incorrect calculations are wrong. Ask: *What should the answers be?* Agree answers.

 *When adding or subtracting fractions with the same denominator, the denominator does not change.*

- Pupils should complete Question 3 in the Practice Book.

Same-day intervention

- Using a number line from 0 to 1 labelled in jumps of $\frac{1}{20}$, ask pupils to complete the following calculations:

  $\frac{6}{20} + \frac{5}{20} =$ $\frac{14}{20} - \frac{5}{20} =$

  $\frac{8}{20} + \frac{7}{20} =$ $\frac{6}{20} - \frac{5}{20} =$

  $\frac{5}{20} + \frac{9}{20} =$ $\frac{15}{20} - \frac{9}{20} =$

  $\frac{4}{20} + \frac{5}{20} + \frac{6}{20} =$ $\frac{17}{20} - \frac{1}{20} - \frac{9}{20} =$

  $\frac{11}{20} + \frac{1}{20} + \frac{3}{20} + \frac{7}{20} =$ $\frac{16}{20} - \frac{2}{20} - \frac{8}{20} - \frac{5}{20} - \frac{1}{20} =$

- Ask: *Consider which strategy you used for each calculation. What affected your choice of strategy?*

Chapter 4 Comparing fractions, improper fractions and mixed numbers Unit 4.6 Practice Book 5A, pages 101–104

Same-day enrichment

- Provide pairs of pupils with a copy of **Resource 5.4.6c** Adding and subtracting fractions mentally. Pupils play a game against their partner focusing on speed and accuracy. Ask them to consider: *When did you decide to add? When did you decide to find the difference? Why?*

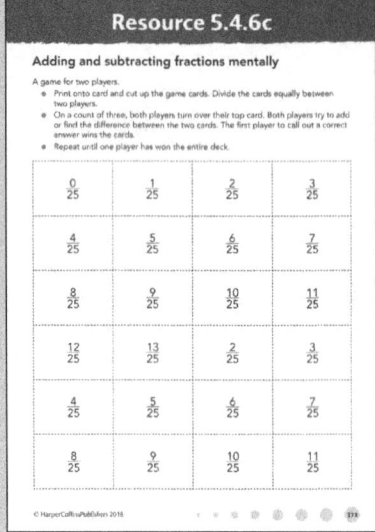

Question 4

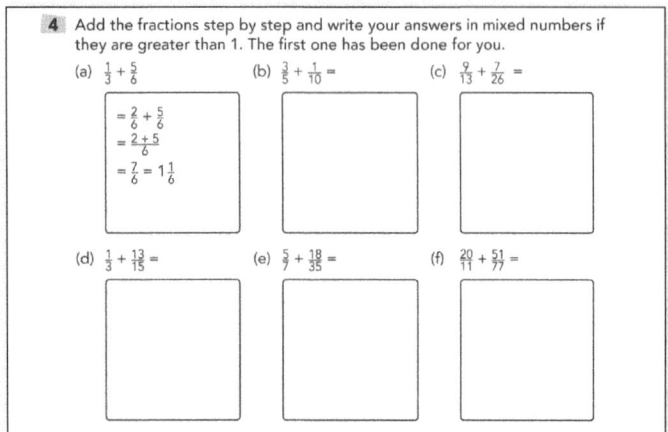

What learning will pupils have achieved at the conclusion of Question 4?

- Pupils will understand how to add fractions with related denominators.

Activities for whole-class instruction

- Introduce the following context:
  - Poppy ate $\frac{3}{8}$ of a pizza. Flo ate $\frac{1}{4}$ of a pizza. How much pizza have they eaten altogether?

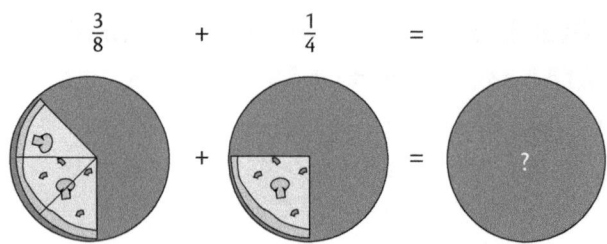

- Give pupils paper circles and ask them to investigate. If necessary, suggest cutting or folding to help. Agree the correct answer is $\frac{5}{8}$ because adding $\frac{1}{4}$ is equivalent to adding $\frac{2}{8}$. Share a variety of approaches to solving this problem.

- Ask: *What about if Poppy ate $\frac{5}{8}$ and Flo ate $\frac{1}{4}$?* Agree the correct answer is $\frac{7}{8}$ because adding $\frac{1}{4}$ is equivalent to adding $\frac{2}{8}$. Share strategies.

- Ask: *What if Poppy ate $\frac{3}{10}$ and Flo ate $\frac{2}{5}$?* Give pupils time to discuss. Ask: *What is the relationship between the two denominators?* Agree that one denominator is a multiple of the other. Explain that these are called fractions with related denominators.

 *When one denominator is a multiple of another denominator, the denominators are related.*

- Discuss how, when adding fractions with related denominators, one denominator can be converted to the other so that both fractions have the same denominator, making the adding or subtracting easy.

- Write:

$$\frac{3}{10} + \frac{2}{5}$$
$$= \frac{3}{10} + \frac{4}{10}$$
$$= \frac{3+4}{10}$$
$$= \frac{7}{10}$$

- Ask pupils to talk a partner through the strategy. Afterwards, ask: *Why did I convert the $\frac{2}{5}$ to $\frac{4}{10}$?* Model a second calculation if appropriate.

- Present pupils with the following fractions:

$$\frac{1}{2} \quad \frac{3}{4} \quad \frac{5}{8} \quad \frac{7}{16} \quad \frac{13}{32}$$

- Pupil pairs should select two fractions. Convert one fraction so that both fractions have the same denominator, for example $\frac{5}{8}$ and $\frac{13}{32}$ require pupils to convert $\frac{5}{8}$ to $\frac{20}{32}$. Repeat with different fractions.

Look out for … Pupils who convert the denominator but forget to make the corresponding change to the numerator; asking if the fraction is still equivalent should help to identify this error.

- Write:

Chapter 4 Comparing fractions, improper fractions and mixed numbers Unit 4.6 Practice Book 5A, pages 101–104

$\frac{5}{7} + \frac{15}{28}$

- Pupil pairs should solve this using the strategy outlined above. Ask: *Which fraction will you convert? What will you convert it to? What do you notice about the answer?*
- Agree that the answer is greater than 1. Together, record as both improper fraction and mixed number. Agree the answer is $\frac{35}{28}$ or $1\frac{7}{28}$. Repeat with further calculations if required.
- Pupils should complete Question 4 in the Practice Book.

Same-day intervention

- Provide pupils with a fraction strip labelled in sixths and another labelled in twelfths.

$\frac{1}{6}$	$\frac{1}{6}$	$\frac{1}{6}$	$\frac{1}{6}$	$\frac{1}{6}$	$\frac{1}{6}$

$\frac{1}{12}$	$\frac{1}{12}$	$\frac{1}{12}$	$\frac{1}{12}$	$\frac{1}{12}$	$\frac{1}{12}$	$\frac{1}{12}$	$\frac{1}{12}$	$\frac{1}{12}$	$\frac{1}{12}$	$\frac{1}{12}$	$\frac{1}{12}$

- Write:
  $\frac{2}{6} + \frac{5}{12} =$
- Ask pupils to identify an equivalent fraction for $\frac{2}{6}$ so it has the same denominator as $\frac{5}{12}$. Using the fraction strips, prove $\frac{2}{6} = \frac{4}{12}$. Ask pupils to complete the calculation $\frac{4}{12} + \frac{5}{12}$. Agree the answer is $\frac{9}{12}$.
- Repeat with other calculations involving sixths and twelfths.

Same-day enrichment

- Write:
  $\frac{\square}{\square} + \frac{\square}{\square} = 1\frac{1}{4}$
- Choosing two fractions with related denominators, find five ways to make this statement correct.
- Select a different mixed number fraction as the total. Repeat the activity above.

Question 5

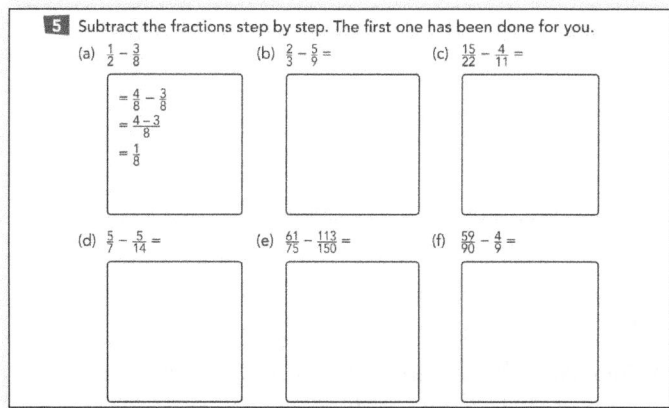

What learning will pupils have achieved at the conclusion of Question 5?

- Pupils will understand how to subtract fractions with related denominators.

Activities for whole-class instruction

- Introduce the following context:
  - *After a party, there was some pizza left over. There was $\frac{1}{2}$ a Margarita left and $\frac{1}{6}$ of a Hawaiian. How much more Margarita was left than Hawaiian?*

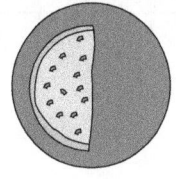 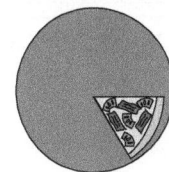

- Give pupils paper circles and ask them to investigate. If necessary, suggest pupils use cutting or folding to help with their investigating. Agree the correct answer is $\frac{2}{6}$ or $\frac{1}{3}$ because $\frac{1}{2}$ is equivalent to $\frac{3}{6}$ and $\frac{3}{6} - \frac{1}{6} = \frac{1}{6}$. Share a variety of approaches to solving this problem.

 … pupils who try to subtract $\frac{1}{6}$ of a $\frac{1}{2}$ rather than $\frac{1}{6}$ of a whole pizza.

- Ask: *What about if $\frac{2}{6}$ of the Hawaiian was left? How much more Margarita would there now be?* Agree $\frac{1}{6}$. Share strategies.
- Ask: *What if there was $\frac{7}{12}$ of a Margarita left and $\frac{1}{3}$ of a Hawaiian?* Allow pupils time to discuss. Ask: *What is the relationship between the two denominators?* Agree that one denominator is a multiple of the other, remind pupils that these are called fractions with related denominators.

 *When one denominator is a multiple of another denominator, the denominators are related.*

Chapter 4 Comparing fractions, improper fractions and mixed numbers Unit 4.6 Practice Book 5A, pages 101–104

- Discuss how, when adding fractions with related denominators, one denominator can be converted to the other so that both fractions have the same denominator, making the adding or subtracting easy.
- Write:

$$\frac{7}{12} - \frac{1}{3}$$
$$= \frac{7}{12} - \frac{4}{12}$$
$$= \frac{7 - 4}{12}$$
$$= \frac{3}{12}$$

- Pupil pairs should talk a partner through the strategy. Afterwards, ask: *Why did I convert the $\frac{1}{3}$ to $\frac{4}{12}$?* Model a second calculation if appropriate.

Look out for … pupils who convert the denominator but forget to make the corresponding change to the numerator, asking if the fraction is still equivalent should help to identify this error.

- Pupils should complete Question 5 in the Practice Book.

Same-day intervention

- Provide pupils with a fraction strip labelled in eighths and a fraction strip labelled in sixteenths.

$\frac{1}{16}$	$\frac{1}{16}$	$\frac{1}{16}$	$\frac{1}{16}$	$\frac{1}{16}$	$\frac{1}{16}$	$\frac{1}{16}$	$\frac{1}{16}$	$\frac{1}{16}$	$\frac{1}{16}$	$\frac{1}{16}$	$\frac{1}{16}$	$\frac{1}{16}$	$\frac{1}{16}$	$\frac{1}{16}$	$\frac{1}{16}$
$\frac{1}{8}$		$\frac{1}{8}$		$\frac{1}{8}$		$\frac{1}{8}$		$\frac{1}{8}$		$\frac{1}{8}$		$\frac{1}{8}$		$\frac{1}{8}$	

- Write:

$$\frac{7}{8} - \frac{5}{16} =$$

- Ask pupils to identify an equivalent fraction for $\frac{7}{8}$ so it has the same denominator as $\frac{5}{16}$. Using the fraction strips, prove $\frac{7}{8} = \frac{14}{16}$. Ask pupils to complete the calculation $\frac{14}{16} - \frac{5}{16}$. Agree the answer is $\frac{9}{16}$.
- Repeat with other calculations involving eighths and sixteenths.

Same-day enrichment

- Present pupils with the following lengths:

$\frac{1}{4}$ of a metre	$\frac{27}{32}$ of a metre
$\frac{17}{64}$ of a metre	$\frac{5}{8}$ of a metre
$\frac{9}{16}$ of a metre	$\frac{1}{2}$ a metre

- Ask pupils to select two lengths and find the difference. Ask: *What is the greatest difference? What is the smallest difference?*

Question 6

6. When Andrew said how many books he had, Jason said that he had two thirds as many as Andrew, and his younger sister Amy said she had one ninth as many as Andrew. Answer the following questions. Show your working.

   (a) Comparing the numbers of books Jason and Amy have, who has more books? _____

   (b) Express the number of books Jason and Amy have in total as a fraction of what Andrew has. ☐

   (c) Express the difference between the numbers of books Jason and Amy have as a fraction of what Andrew has. ☐

   (d) If Andrew has 18 books, how many books do Jason and Amy have altogether? (Use two different ways to find the answer.)
   Method 1:   Method 2:

What learning will pupils have achieved at the conclusion of Question 6?

- Pupils will be able to add and subtract fractions with related denominators to solve contextualised problems.

Activities for whole-class instruction

- Present the following information:

Year group	Fraction of total amount raised for new library books
3	$\frac{3}{12}$
4	$\frac{1}{6}$
5	$\frac{1}{3}$
6	$\frac{6}{24}$

- Ask pupil pairs to answer:
  - Which class raised the greatest amount?
  - Which class raised the least?
  - Which classes raised the same amount?
- Ask pupils to choose two classes and work out what fraction of the total amount they raised.
- Ask pupils to choose two classes and work out the difference between the amounts raised.

Chapter 4 Comparing fractions, improper fractions and mixed numbers Unit 4.6 Practice Book 5A, pages 101–104

- Share strategies and check for accuracy. Ask: *Can you think of a different strategy for the same calculation?*
- Pupils should complete Question 6 in the Practice Book.

Same-day intervention

- Present the following information about a class reading book:

Day of the week	Fraction of total amount read
Monday	$\frac{1}{4}$
Tuesday	$\frac{5}{32}$
Wednesday	$\frac{1}{8}$
Thursday	$\frac{7}{32}$
Friday	$\frac{3}{16}$

- Ask pupil pairs to answer:
  - On which day did the class read the most?
  - On which day did the class read the least?
  - How much of the book is left to read?
- Encourage pupils to convert all fractions so they have the same denominator.
- Ask pupils to pick two days and work out the total/difference.
- Share strategies and check for accuracy. Ask: *Can you think of a different strategy for the same calculation?*

Same-day enrichment

- Ask pupils to create their own table that summarises the fraction of a book read across a whole week. Agree that fractions should not add up to more than 1. Can pupils select fractions that have different denominators for each day of the week?

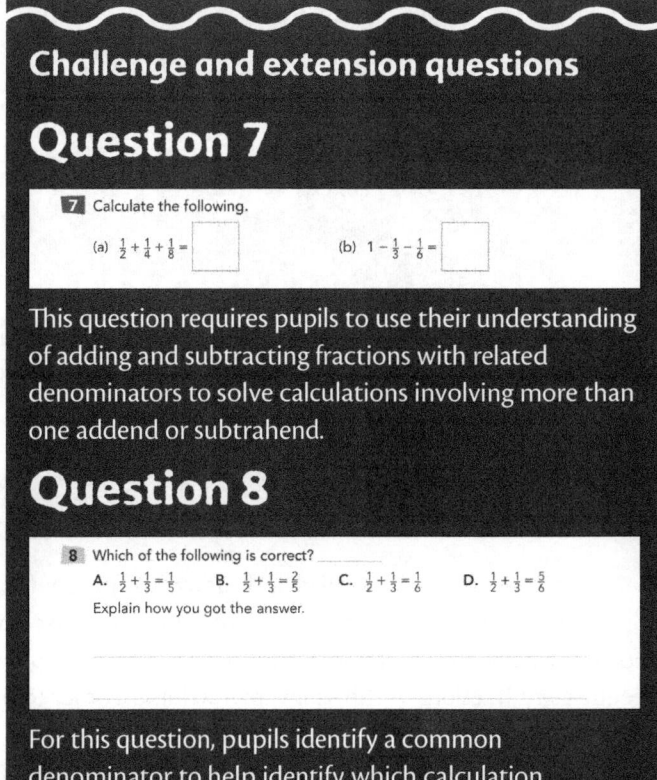

Challenge and extension questions

Question 7

7 Calculate the following.

(a) $\frac{1}{2} + \frac{1}{4} + \frac{1}{8} =$ ☐ (b) $1 - \frac{1}{3} - \frac{1}{6} =$ ☐

This question requires pupils to use their understanding of adding and subtracting fractions with related denominators to solve calculations involving more than one addend or subtrahend.

Question 8

8 Which of the following is correct? _____

A. $\frac{1}{2} + \frac{1}{3} = \frac{1}{5}$ B. $\frac{1}{2} + \frac{1}{3} = \frac{2}{5}$ C. $\frac{1}{2} + \frac{1}{3} = \frac{1}{6}$ D. $\frac{1}{2} + \frac{1}{3} = \frac{5}{6}$

Explain how you got the answer.

For this question, pupils identify a common denominator to help identify which calculation is correct.

Chapter 4 Comparing fractions, improper fractions and mixed numbers

Unit 4.7
Adding and subtracting fractions with related denominators (2)

Conceptual context

In the previous unit, pupils added and subtracted proper fractions with related denominators. In this unit, they will add and subtract improper and mixed numbers with related denominators and will give the answers as whole or mixed numbers. Pupils will use their understanding of equivalent fractions as they convert fractions in order to operate with them and convert improper fractions to mixed numbers; this will require them to draw on their knowledge of multiples and factors. In Year 6, pupils will add and subtract improper fractions and mixed numbers with different denominators that are not related.

Learning pupils will have achieved at the end of the unit

- Pupils will be able to mentally add and subtract proper and improper fractions with related denominators (Q1)
- Pupils will be able to add whole numbers and proper fractions (Q2)
- Pupils will be able to subtract proper fractions from whole numbers (Q3)
- Pupils will be able to add and subtract improper fractions with related denominators and can give the answer as a whole or mixed number (Q4)
- Pupils will be able to add and subtract mixed numbers with related denominators and can give the answer as a whole or mixed number (Q5)
- Pupils will be able to add and subtract improper fractions and mixed numbers with related denominators to solve decontextualised problems (Q6)
- Pupils will be able to add and subtract improper fractions and mixed numbers with related denominators to solve contextualised problems (Q7)

Resources
strips of paper divided into an equal number of parts; a 10-sided dice; sheets of paper

Vocabulary
proper fraction, improper fraction, mixed number, multiple, factor, related denominator, minuend, subtrahend

Chapter 4 Comparing fractions, improper fractions and mixed numbers Unit 4.7 Practice Book 5A, pages 105–107

Question 1

> **1** Work these out mentally. Write the answers.
>
> (a) $\frac{1}{7} + \frac{4}{7} =$ ☐   (b) $\frac{1}{5} - \frac{1}{5} =$ ☐   (c) $\frac{3}{2} + \frac{1}{8} =$ ☐
>
> (d) $\frac{8}{9} - \frac{1}{3} =$ ☐   (e) $\frac{5}{7} + \frac{7}{56} =$ ☐   (f) $1 - \frac{9}{10} =$ ☐

What learning will pupils have achieved at the conclusion of Question 1?

- Pupils will be able to mentally add and subtract proper and improper fractions with related denominators.

Activities for whole-class instruction

- Write:
  $\frac{1}{3} + \frac{4}{9} =$
- Provide pupil pairs with a strip of paper divided into nine equal parts. Ask: *How will you use the strip to explain how to solve this calculation?* Share ideas.
- Can pupils show that $\frac{1}{3} = \frac{3}{9}$ and $\frac{3}{9} + \frac{4}{9} = \frac{7}{9}$? Ask: *What did you multiply the numerator and denominator by to find an equivalent fraction for $\frac{1}{3}$ that has a denominator of 9? Why?* Discuss what happens when thirds are converted to ninths – how there will be three times as many because each third becomes 3 ninths.

When thirds are converted to ninths there will be three times as many because each third becomes 3 ninths.

- Agree that, for the fractions shown as thirds, both the numerator and the denominator must be multiplied by 3 to show how many ninths are equivalent. Repeat with other examples if appropriate.
- Write:
  $\frac{13}{15} - \frac{2}{3} =$
- Provide pupil pairs with a strip of paper divided into 15 equal parts. Ask: *How will you use the strip to explain how to solve this calculation?* Share ideas.
- Can pupils show that $\frac{2}{3} = \frac{10}{15}$ and $\frac{13}{15} - \frac{10}{15} = \frac{3}{15}$? Ask: *What did you multiply the numerator and denominator by to find an equivalent fraction for $\frac{2}{3}$ that has a denominator of 15? Why?* Discuss what happens when thirds are converted to fifteenths – how there will be five times as many because each third becomes 5 fifteenths.

When thirds are converted to fifteenths there will be five times as many because each third becomes 5 fifteenths.

- Agree that, for the fractions shown as thirds, therefore both the numerator and the denominator need to be multiplied by 5. Repeat with other fractions if appropriate.

> (i) Pupils will need a good understanding of equivalence to be able to add and subtract fractions with related denominators. Therefore, choosing images (such as the paper strip) where pupils can clearly identify both denominators can help them to see the equivalence.

- Show the following calculations:
  $\frac{35}{56} + \frac{2}{8} = \frac{37}{58}$
  $\frac{35}{56} + \frac{2}{8} = \frac{50}{56}$
  $\frac{35}{56} + \frac{2}{8} = \frac{49}{56}$
  $\frac{35}{56} + \frac{2}{8} = \frac{37}{56}$
- Ask: *Which calculation is correct? What error has been made in the other three calculations?* Agree that $\frac{35}{56} + \frac{2}{8} = \frac{49}{56}$ because $\frac{2}{8}$ is equivalent to $\frac{14}{56}$ and $\frac{35}{56} + \frac{14}{56} = \frac{49}{56}$.
- Show the following calculations:
  $\frac{11}{8} - \frac{3}{4} = \frac{8}{4}$
  $\frac{11}{8} - \frac{3}{4} = \frac{8}{8}$
  $\frac{11}{8} - \frac{3}{4} = \frac{5}{4}$
  $\frac{11}{8} - \frac{3}{4} = \frac{5}{8}$
- Ask: *Which calculation is correct? What error has been made in the other three calculations?* Agree that $\frac{11}{8} - \frac{3}{4} = \frac{5}{8}$ because $\frac{3}{4}$ is equivalent to $\frac{6}{8}$ and $\frac{11}{8} - \frac{6}{8} = \frac{5}{8}$.
- **Look out for** … pupils who subtract both the numerator and the denominator. These pupils are treating the numerator and the denominator as separate whole numbers and need to be reminded of the role of both numbers within a fraction.
- Pupils should complete Question 1 in the Practice Book.

Chapter 4 Comparing fractions, improper fractions and mixed numbers Unit 4.7 Practice Book 5A, pages 105–107

Same-day intervention

- Show the following calculations:

$\frac{4}{8} + \frac{1}{4} =$	$\frac{5}{6} - \frac{1}{3} =$
$\frac{2}{6} + \frac{1}{12} =$	$\frac{9}{10} - \frac{1}{2} =$
$\frac{3}{10} + \frac{2}{5} =$	$\frac{9}{12} - \frac{1}{6} =$
$\frac{5}{8} + \frac{1}{16} =$	$\frac{9}{20} - \frac{1}{4} =$
$\frac{3}{18} + \frac{4}{6} =$	$\frac{7}{8} - \frac{3}{4} =$

- Ask: *Which fraction will you convert in each calculation? What will you convert it to? Why?* Provide pupils with strips of paper to help identify equivalent fractions if necessary.
- Ask pupils to solve the calculations and position the answers on a number line from 0 to 1.

Same-day enrichment

- Ask pupils to select three fractions from the following list to make the calculation correct:

$\frac{1}{4}$ $\frac{1}{5}$ $\frac{1}{10}$ $\frac{1}{20}$ $\frac{1}{40}$

____ + ____ + ____ = $\frac{1}{2}$

- They should explain to a partner how they know they are correct.
- Next, they make their own problem like this for a partner to solve.
- Ask: *Can you set a similar problem involving subtraction?*

Questions 2 and 3

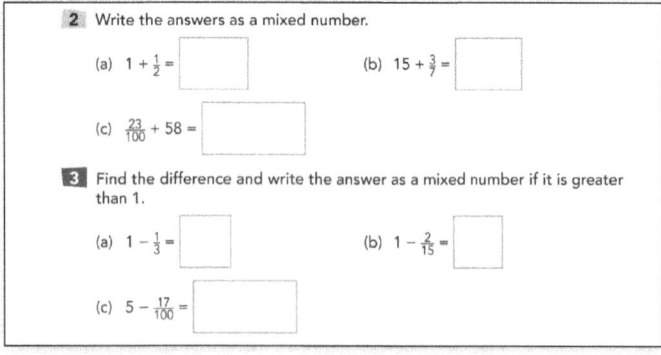

What learning will pupils have achieved at the conclusion of Questions 2 and 3?

- Pupils will be able to add whole numbers and proper fractions.
- Pupils will be able to subtract proper fractions from whole numbers.

Activities for whole-class instruction

- Introduce the following scenario:
  - *I spend two hours watching a football match. I spend $\frac{3}{4}$ of an hour in total travelling to and from the game. How much time is this altogether?*
- Ask pupils to record a number sentence for this calculation. Agree 2 hours $+ \frac{3}{4}$ of an hour is $2 + \frac{3}{4} = 2\frac{3}{4}$ hours.
- Ask: *What if the match lasted for three hours?* Record the number sentence now. Agree 3 hours $+ \frac{3}{4}$ of an hour is $3 + \frac{3}{4} = 3\frac{3}{4}$ hours. Ask: *What changes and what stays the same?* Agree that the fraction part of the mixed number stays the same but the whole number increases by 1 because the number of hours has increased by 1.
- Ask: *What if the match lasted for three hours and I spent 5/6 of an hour in total travelling to and from the game?* Record the number sentence now. Agree 3 hours $+ \frac{5}{6}$ of an hour is $3 + \frac{5}{6} = 3\frac{5}{6}$ hours. Ask: *What changes and what stays the same?* Agree that the whole number part stays the same but the fraction part has changed because the amount of time travelling has increased to $\frac{5}{6}$ of an hour.
- Repeat this activity changing the whole numbers and fractions as appropriate.

 *When adding a whole number and a proper fraction you combine the two numbers to get the total.*

- Show the following:

  $3 - \frac{6}{13} = 2\frac{7}{13}$

  $3 - \frac{7}{13} = 2\frac{6}{13}$

  $3 - \frac{8}{13} = 2\frac{5}{13}$

  $3 - \frac{9}{13} = 2\frac{4}{13}$

- Ask: *What changes and what stays the same?* Give pupils time to discuss responses with partners. Agree:
  - the minuend stays the same
  - the subtrahend increases by $\frac{1}{13}$ each time
  - the whole number in the answer stays the same
  - the answer decreases by $\frac{1}{13}$ each time.

Chapter 4 Comparing fractions, improper fractions and mixed numbers Unit 4.7 Practice Book 5A, pages 105–107

- Ask pupils to write the next three calculations in this sequence. Check the answers are correct. Repeat with a different sequence of subtraction calculations if required.

  (i) Pupils will need to use their knowledge of number bonds when subtracting proper fractions from whole numbers.

- Write:

  ____, 3, $3\frac{2}{3}$, $4\frac{1}{3}$, 5, ____

- Ask: *What are the missing numbers?* Pupils should discuss with a partner. Ask: *What is happening in this sequence?* Agree that each number increases by $\frac{2}{3}$ to get the next number and that the missing numbers are $2\frac{1}{3}$ and $5\frac{2}{3}$.

- Repeat with:

  ____, 7, $7\frac{3}{4}$, $8\frac{1}{2}$, $9\frac{1}{4}$, 10, ____

- Pupils should complete Questions 2 and 3 in the Practice Book.

Same-day intervention

- Show the following:

Whole numbers	Proper fractions
1	$\frac{1}{4}$
9	$\frac{5}{6}$
5	$\frac{11}{12}$
7	$\frac{1}{2}$
3	$\frac{1}{8}$
4	$\frac{3}{4}$

- Throw a 10-sided dice. Pupil pairs should select one whole number and one proper fraction from the table that can be added/subtracted to make an answer that is as close as possible to the number thrown. Ask: *How do you know this is the closest possible answer?* Repeat with a different target number.

Same-day enrichment

- Show the following:
  - $5 + \frac{5}{6}$
  - $6 - \frac{11}{12}$
  - $7 - \frac{4}{9}$
  - $\frac{1}{3} + 6$
  - $\frac{1}{2} + 5 + \frac{1}{4}$
  - $\frac{4}{6} + 6 - \frac{1}{3}$
  - $7 - \frac{2}{3} + \frac{1}{6}$
  - $\frac{4}{16} + 6 + \frac{1}{4}$

- Ask pupils to solve the calculations and order the answers from smallest to largest.

Question 4

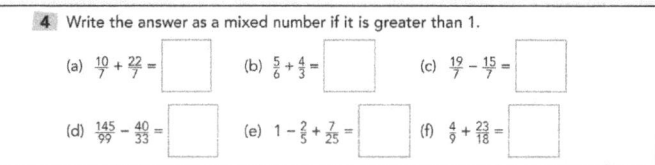

4 Write the answer as a mixed number if it is greater than 1.

(a) $\frac{10}{7} + \frac{22}{7} =$ ☐   (b) $\frac{5}{6} + \frac{4}{3} =$ ☐   (c) $\frac{19}{7} - \frac{15}{7} =$ ☐

(d) $\frac{145}{99} - \frac{40}{33} =$ ☐   (e) $1 - \frac{2}{5} + \frac{7}{25} =$ ☐   (f) $\frac{4}{9} + \frac{23}{18} =$ ☐

What learning will pupils have achieved at the conclusion of Question 4?

- Pupils will be able to add and subtract improper fractions with related denominators and can give the answer as a whole or mixed number.

Activities for whole-class instruction

- Provide pupils with strips of paper divided into seven equal parts.

- Write:

  $\frac{15}{7} + \frac{11}{7} =$

- Ask: *How can we use the strips to represent $\frac{15}{7}$?* Give pupils time to consider this in pairs before taking feedback. Agree that 1 full strip is $\frac{7}{7}$, therefore $\frac{15}{7}$ is represented by 2 full strips and 1 strip with $\frac{1}{7}$ shaded:

Chapter 4 Comparing fractions, improper fractions and mixed numbers   Unit 4.7   Practice Book 5A, pages 105–107

- Ask: *How can we use the strips to represent $\frac{11}{7}$?* Establish $\frac{11}{7}$ can be represented by 1 full strip, which represents $\frac{7}{7}$, and 1 strip with $\frac{4}{7}$ shaded:

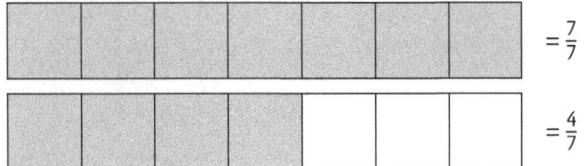

$= \frac{7}{7}$

$= \frac{4}{7}$

- Write:
$\frac{15}{7} + \frac{11}{7} = \frac{15+11}{7} = \frac{26}{7}$

- Ask: *What do you notice about this calculation?* Draw pupils' attention to the fact that the numerators are added together but the denominator remains unchanged. Also emphasise that because the denominator is the same for both addends, it only needs to be written once. Ask: *What is $\frac{26}{7}$ equivalent to as a mixed number?* Show this is represented by 3 full strips of $\frac{7}{7}$ and 1 strip with $\frac{5}{7}$, therefore the answer is $3\frac{5}{7}$. Repeat with other calculations if appropriate.

 *When adding two fractions with the same denominator, the denominator does not change.*

- Write:
$\frac{24}{11} - \frac{15}{11} =$

- Model this strategy on the board:
$\frac{24}{11} - \frac{15}{11} = \frac{24-15}{11} = \frac{9}{11}$

- Ask: *What do you notice about this calculation?* Draw pupils' attention to the fact that the numerators are subtracted but the denominator remains unchanged. If necessary, represent this on strips of paper divided into 11 equal parts. Repeat with other calculations if appropriate.

 *When subtracting fractions with the same denominator, the denominator does not change.*

- Show the following:
$\frac{15}{7} + \frac{3}{14} =$

- Remind pupils that when adding fractions with related denominators we need to convert one of the fractions to an equivalent fraction so they both have the same denominator. Share the following strategy and ask pupils to observe what is happening:

$\frac{15}{7} + \frac{3}{14}$

$= \frac{30}{14} + \frac{3}{14}$

$= \frac{30+3}{14}$

$= \frac{33}{14}$

$= 2\frac{5}{14}$

- Tell pupils to talk a partner through the strategy. Ask: *Why did I convert the $\frac{15}{7}$ to $\frac{30}{14}$? How do we know $\frac{33}{14}$ is equivalent to $2\frac{5}{14}$?* Model a second calculation if appropriate.

- Show the following:
$\frac{5}{3}$ $\frac{5}{6}$ $\frac{15}{12}$ $\frac{13}{24}$ $\frac{21}{48}$

- Ask pupil pairs to select two fractions. Convert one fraction so that both have the same denominator; for example, to make $\frac{5}{3}$ and $\frac{15}{12}$ equivalent, $\frac{5}{3}$ can be converted to twelfths ($\frac{20}{12}$). Check that pupils know that $\frac{15}{12}$ cannot be converted to thirds because both numerator and denominator would need to be divided by 4, and 15 cannot be divided by 4 and give a whole number.

- Using the strategy outlined above, ask pupils to add their two fractions and present the answer as a mixed number if the answer is greater than 1. Repeat with different fractions.

Look out for … pupils who convert the denominator but forget to make the corresponding change to the numerator. Asking if the fraction is still equivalent will help to identify this error.

- Remind pupils that when subtracting fractions with related denominators we need to convert one of the fractions to an equivalent fraction so they both have the same denominator. Share the following strategy and ask pupils to observe what is happening:

$\frac{95}{50} - \frac{11}{10}$

$= \frac{95}{50} - \frac{55}{50}$

$= \frac{95-55}{50}$

$= \frac{40}{50}$

- Tell pupils to talk a partner through the strategy. Ask: *Why did I convert the $\frac{11}{10}$ to $\frac{55}{50}$?* Model a second calculation if appropriate.

- Pupils should complete Question 4 in the Practice Book.

Chapter 4 Comparing fractions, improper fractions and mixed numbers Unit 4.7 Practice Book 5A, pages 105–107

Same-day intervention

- Provide pupils with fraction strips labelled in sixths and a fraction strip labelled in twelfths.

| $\frac{1}{6}$ | $\frac{1}{6}$ | $\frac{1}{6}$ | $\frac{1}{6}$ | $\frac{1}{6}$ | $\frac{1}{6}$ |

| $\frac{1}{12}$ | $\frac{1}{12}$ | $\frac{1}{12}$ | $\frac{1}{12}$ | $\frac{1}{12}$ | $\frac{1}{12}$ | $\frac{1}{12}$ | $\frac{1}{12}$ | $\frac{1}{12}$ | $\frac{1}{12}$ | $\frac{1}{12}$ | $\frac{1}{12}$ |

- Write:
$\frac{7}{6} + \frac{15}{12} =$
- Ask pupils to identify an equivalent fraction for $\frac{7}{6}$ so it has the same denominator as $\frac{15}{12}$. Using the fraction strips, prove $\frac{7}{6} = \frac{14}{12}$. Pupils should solve $\frac{15}{12} + \frac{14}{12} =$ ____. Agree the answer is $\frac{29}{12}$ or $2\frac{5}{12}$.
- Repeat with other calculations containing improper fractions involving sixths and twelfths.

Same-day enrichment

Show the following:

$= 2\frac{5}{6}$

Ask pupils to choose three fractions with related denominators and find four ways to make this statement correct. Then, repeat with a different mixed number fraction as the total.

Question 5

5 Complete the following addition and subtraction of fractions. Write the answer as a mixed number if it is greater than 1. One has been done for you.

(a) $2\frac{3}{7} + 1\frac{5}{7}$
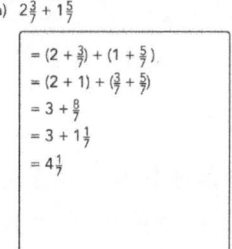

(b) $10\frac{10}{13} - 5\frac{3}{13}$
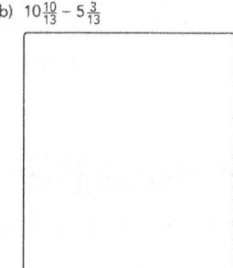

(c) $3\frac{4}{9} - 3\frac{5}{18}$
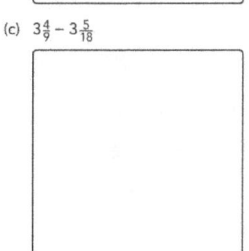

(d) $12\frac{2}{3} - 10\frac{7}{12}$
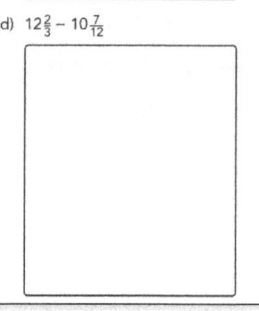

What learning will pupils have achieved at the conclusion of Question 5?

- Pupils will be able to add and subtract mixed numbers with related denominators and be able to give the answer as a whole or mixed number.

Activities for whole-class instruction

- Tell pupils:
  - *Oscar was running a race. He ran $3\frac{5}{8}$ of a kilometre in the first 15 minutes. He ran $2\frac{1}{4}$ of a kilometre in the second 15 minutes. How far had he run in total after 30 minutes?*
- Share the following image:

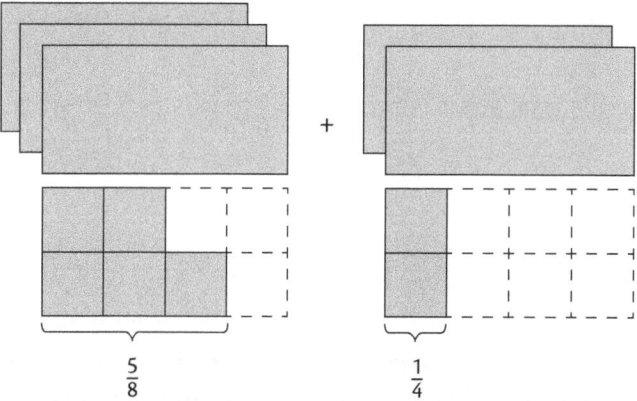

- Ask: *What does one sheet of paper represent?* Agree 1 km. Ask: *How many compete kilometres has Oscar run after 30 minutes?* Agree that he has run five full kilometres because there are five full sheets. Ask: *Oscar ran further than 5 km. How much further?* Agree that Oscar has also ran $\frac{5}{8}$ of a km and $\frac{1}{4}$ of a km. Establish that these are related fractions because one denominator is a multiple of the other. Agree that $\frac{1}{4} = \frac{2}{8}$ and $\frac{5}{8} + \frac{2}{8} = \frac{7}{8}$.
- Share the following strategy and ask pupils to observe what is happening:

$3\frac{5}{8} + 2\frac{1}{4} = 3\frac{5}{8} + 2\frac{2}{8}$

$= (3 + \frac{5}{8}) + (2 + \frac{2}{8})$

$= (3 + 2) + (\frac{5}{8} + \frac{2}{8})$

$= 5 + \frac{7}{8}$

$= 5\frac{7}{8}$

- Tell pupils to talk a partner through the strategy. Ask: *Why did I convert the $\frac{1}{4}$ to $\frac{2}{8}$?* Model a second calculation if appropriate.

Chapter 4 Comparing fractions, improper fractions and mixed numbers Unit 4.7 Practice Book 5A, pages 105–107

Look out for … pupils who add the whole number part to the numerator of the fractional part, for example $3\frac{5}{8} + 2\frac{1}{4} = \frac{8}{8} + \frac{3}{4}$. This error shows a lack of understanding about what mixed numbers are and that they are made up of a whole number part and a fractional part. Asking pupils how many wholes there are will support their understanding of this.

- Tell pupils:

  I had $3\frac{1}{4}$ litres of milk in the fridge. I used $1\frac{7}{8}$ litres of milk. How much milk was left?

- Share the following image:

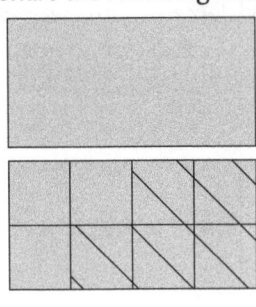

- Ask: *How does this image represent $3\frac{1}{4} - 1\frac{7}{8}$?* Give pupils time to examine the image before sharing responses.

- Ask: *What does one sheet of paper represent?* Agree that one sheet of paper represents 1 litre. Ask: *How many full litres did I start with?* Agree 3 full litres to start with. Ask: *How much more milk did I have?* Agree I also had $\frac{1}{4}$ of a litre of milk and that this is equivalent to $\frac{2}{8}$. Ask: *How many full litres were used?* Agree 1 full litre; this is represented by the full sheet of paper that has been crossed out. Ask: *How much more milk was used?* Agree $\frac{7}{8}$ of a litre was also used, and this is represented by the crossed out $\frac{7}{8}$. Agree $1\frac{3}{8}$ is left.

- Share the following strategy and ask pupils to observe what is happening:

  $3\frac{1}{4} - 1\frac{7}{8} = 3\frac{2}{8} - 1\frac{7}{8}$
  $= 3\frac{2}{8} - 1 - \frac{7}{8}$
  $= 2\frac{2}{8} - \frac{7}{8}$
  $= 1\frac{3}{8}$

- Tell pupils to talk a partner through the strategy. Ask: *Why did I convert $\frac{1}{4}$ to $\frac{2}{8}$? How could you prove $2\frac{2}{8} - \frac{7}{8} = 1\frac{3}{8}$ using the sheets of paper?* Model a second calculation if appropriate.

- Pupils should complete Question 5 in the Practice Book.

Same-day intervention

- Present pupils with the following fractions:

  $3\frac{2}{3}$ $1\frac{5}{6}$ $2\frac{7}{12}$ $4\frac{15}{24}$

- Pupils should find two fractions that:
  - have a total of:
    - $6\frac{1}{4}$
    - $6\frac{11}{24}$
  - have a difference of:
    - $2\frac{1}{24}$
    - $1\frac{5}{6}$

- Pupils should represent the fractions with sheets of paper (as above) to support their thinking.

Same-day enrichment

- Ask pupils to find two fractions with:
  - a sum of $5\frac{9}{14}$ and a difference of $\frac{13}{14}$
  - a sum of $8\frac{3}{4}$ and a difference of $1\frac{11}{12}$
  - a sum of $7\frac{1}{3}$ and a difference of $3\frac{5}{6}$.

Questions 6 and 7

> **6** A number has $\frac{5}{6}$ subtracted from it and then has $\frac{1}{3}$ added to it; the answer is $\frac{2}{3}$. What is the start number? _____
>
> **7** An electrician used some electrical wire to wire a new building. On the first day he planned to use $1\frac{2}{3}$ m of the wire, on the second day he planned to use $\frac{3}{5}$ m more than on the first day, and on the third day he planned to use 2 m more than on the second day. If the wire was 10 m long, would it have been long enough? Why or why not?

What learning will pupils have achieved at the conclusion of Questions 6 and 7?

- Pupils will be able to add and subtract improper fractions and mixed numbers with related denominators to solve decontextualised problems.
- Pupils will be able to add and subtract improper fractions and mixed numbers with related denominators to solve contextualised problems.

Chapter 4 Comparing fractions, improper fractions and mixed numbers Unit 4.7 Practice Book 5A, pages 105–107

Activities for whole-class instruction

- Show the following:

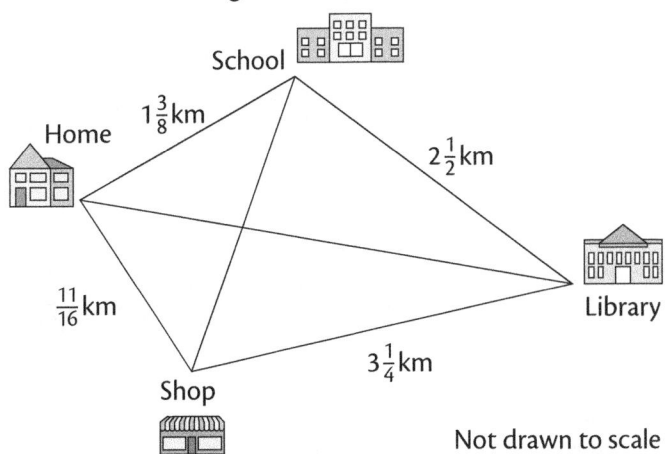

Not drawn to scale

- Ask: *If I were at home, how far would I need to cycle to go to the library via the school?* Agree the calculation is $1\frac{3}{8}$ km $+ 2\frac{1}{2}$ km $= 3\frac{7}{8}$ km. Repeat with other journeys.
- Ask: *How much further is it from the library to the shop than from the library to the school?* Agree $\frac{3}{4}$ km further. Repeat with other comparisons.
- Ask: *If I travelled $5\frac{3}{4}$ km, what journey could I have taken?* Agree I could have travelled from the school to the shop via the library or vice versa. Repeat with other distances.
- Ask: *I travelled from home to the library and then to school. My total journey distance was $7\frac{1}{8}$ km. How far is it from home to the library?* Give pupils time to work in pairs to consider what the unknown is within this calculation. Agree that the unknown is ____ $+ 2\frac{1}{2}$ km $= 7\frac{1}{8}$ km. Ask: *Who will solve this by counting up? Who will solve this by subtracting?* Compare strategies and agree the answer is $4\frac{5}{8}$.
- Ask: *I travelled from home to school and then to the shop. My total journey distance was $3\frac{9}{16}$ km. How far is it from school to the shop?* Compare strategies and agree the answer is $2\frac{3}{16}$.
- Pupils should complete Questions 6 and 7 in the Practice Book.

Same-day intervention

- Provide pupils with the above plan. Ask them to identify three new questions for a partner to solve. Swap questions and solve using visual representations or written calculations to support their thinking.

Same-day enrichment

- Pupils should design their own plan of a town (similar to the one above). They consider fractions with related denominators for the distances and write three questions for a partner to solve. They swap questions and solve.

Challenge and extension question

Question 8

8. While working on addition and subtraction involving mixed numbers, Dan found another method to find the answer, that is, first convert all the mixed numbers to improper fractions and then add or subtract them. Can you use Dan's method to find the answers to the following questions? Show your working.

(a) $9\frac{6}{19} + \frac{11}{19} =$

(b) $3\frac{2}{3} - 2\frac{7}{9} =$

This question requires pupils to examine an alternative way to add and subtract mixed numbers by converting them to improper fractions before solving the calculation.

Chapter 4 Comparing fractions, improper fractions and mixed numbers

Unit 4.8
Multiplying fractions by whole numbers

Conceptual context

This unit will introduce pupils to the multiplication of fractions by whole numbers. It will draw on their understanding of multiplication as repeated addition, which has already been explored with whole numbers, and will apply this to multiplying proper fractions and mixed numbers by whole numbers. Visual images will be used to help pupils see this relationship between multiplication and addition and will enable them to develop a range of strategies when solving multiplication questions involving fractions. Pupils will be required to use their knowledge of multiplication facts when multiplying the numerator by a whole number and will use their understanding of equivalence to convert improper fractions to mixed numbers. In Year 6, pupils will multiply one fraction by another fraction.

Learning pupils will have achieved at the end of the unit

- Through revisiting the link between multiplication and repeated addition, pupils will have found that when a proper fraction is added repeatedly to itself, the numerators are added but the denominator stays the same (Q1)
- Pupils will have applied the concept of multiplication as repeated addition in order to multiply a fraction by a whole number (Q2)
- Pupils will have understood how the multiplication of a fraction by a whole number can be represented symbolically and can manipulate the numbers appropriately within a calculation (Q3)
- Pupils will be able to solve multistep calculations that involve the multiplication of fractions by whole numbers (Q4)
- Pupils will be able to multiply fractions by whole numbers to solve contextualised problems (Q5, Q6)

Resources

strips of paper divided into an equal number of parts; 2 × 4 grids; sticky labels; number lines from 0 to 40; coloured pencils; **Resource 5.4.8a** Calculation match

Vocabulary

numerator, denominator, proper fraction, improper fraction, mixed number, addend, function machine

Chapter 4 Comparing fractions, improper fractions and mixed numbers   Unit 4.8 Practice Book 5A, pages 108–111

Question 1

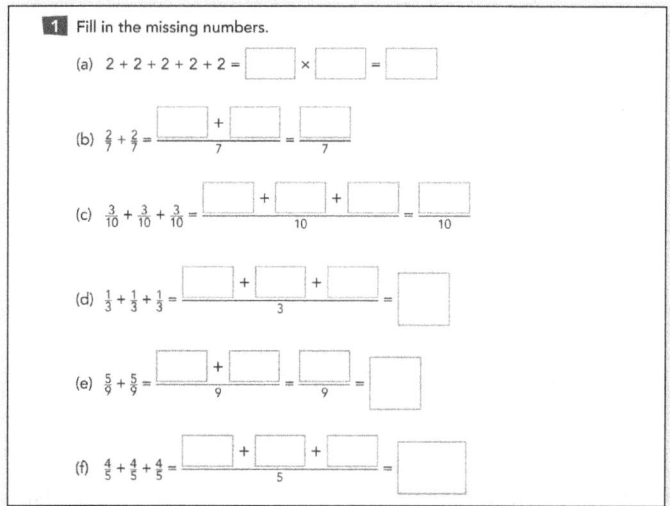

What learning will pupils have achieved at the conclusion of Question 1?

- Through revisiting the link between multiplication and repeated addition, pupils will have found that when a proper fraction is added repeatedly to itself, the numerators are added but the denominator stays the same.

Activities for whole-class instruction

- Show pupils a small chocolate bar and tell them that it contains $\frac{2}{7}$ of the recommended daily allowance (RDA) of sugar for a child. Ask: *What fraction of a child's RDA would 2 bars contain?* Agree that this would be $\frac{2}{7} + \frac{2}{7} = \frac{4}{7}$. Record this on the board. Ask: *What about 3 bars?* Agree $\frac{2}{7} + \frac{2}{7} + \frac{2}{7} = \frac{6}{7}$. Ask: *What about 4 bars?* Agree $\frac{2}{7} + \frac{2}{7} + \frac{2}{7} + \frac{2}{7} = \frac{8}{7} = 1\frac{1}{7}$ and that this would be greater than the recommended daily allowance because the total is greater than 1.

- Write the following:
$\frac{2}{7} + \frac{2}{7} + \frac{2}{7} + \frac{2}{7} = \frac{2 + 2 + 2 + 2}{7} = \frac{8}{7} = 1\frac{1}{7}$

- Ask: *What do you notice about this calculation?* Draw pupils' attention to the fact that the numerators are added together but the denominator remains unchanged. Also explain that because the denominator is the same for all addends, it only needs to be written once.

 *All say…* When adding two fractions with the same denominator, the denominator does not change.

- Together, count up in jumps of $\frac{4}{7}$, starting at 0. Stop at $\frac{28}{7}$. Record the sequence so far, showing each value as a fraction and as a mixed number:

0	$\frac{4}{7}$	$\frac{8}{7}$	$\frac{12}{7}$	$\frac{16}{7}$	$\frac{20}{7}$	$\frac{24}{7}$	$\frac{28}{7}$
0	$\frac{4}{7}$	$1\frac{1}{7}$	$1\frac{5}{7}$	$2\frac{2}{7}$	$2\frac{6}{7}$	$3\frac{3}{7}$	4

- Ask: *What is the first whole number that appears in the sequence?* Agree that the first time a whole number appears in the sequence is at $\frac{28}{7}$, which is 4. Together, write a number sentence to represent this:
$\frac{4}{7} + \frac{4}{7} + \frac{4}{7} + \frac{4}{7} + \frac{4}{7} + \frac{4}{7} + \frac{4}{7} = \frac{28}{7}$

- Tell pupils that this can be written as:
$\frac{4 + 4 + 4 + 4 + 4 + 4 + 4}{7} = \frac{28}{7}$

- Pupil pairs should construct another sequence, counting in jumps of $\frac{5}{9}$ to $\frac{45}{9}$. Agree that:
$\frac{5}{9} + \frac{5}{9} + \frac{5}{9} + \frac{5}{9} + \frac{5}{9} + \frac{5}{9} + \frac{5}{9} + \frac{5}{9} + \frac{5}{9} = \frac{45}{9}$
and
$\frac{5 + 5 + 5 + 5 + 5 + 5 + 5 + 5 + 5}{9} = \frac{45}{9}$

- Pupils should complete Question 1 in the Practice Book.

Same-day intervention

- Provide pupils with a strip of paper divided into three equal parts and a selection of different-coloured pencils. Tell pupils to shade $\frac{3}{11}$, then shade another $\frac{3}{11}$ in a different colour. Ask: *What is $\frac{3}{11} + \frac{3}{11}$?* Agree $\frac{6}{11}$. Tell pupils to shade another $\frac{3}{11}$ in a different colour. Ask: *What is $\frac{3}{11} + \frac{3}{11} + \frac{3}{11}$?* Agree $\frac{9}{11}$. Tell pupils to shade another $\frac{3}{11}$ in a different colour. Establish that a second strip of paper is required because the total will be greater than 1. Ask: *What is $\frac{3}{11} + \frac{3}{11} + \frac{3}{11} + \frac{3}{11}$?* Agree $\frac{12}{11}$ or $1\frac{1}{11}$.

- Record number sentences describing how the sequence developed:
$\frac{3}{11} + \frac{3}{11} + \frac{3}{11} + \frac{3}{11} = \frac{12}{11}$
and
$\frac{3 + 3 + 3 + 3}{11} = \frac{12}{11}$

- Repeat with different fractions.

Same-day enrichment

- Explain that a jug holds $\frac{2}{7}$ of a litre. Ask:
  - *How much liquid is in 4 full jugs?*
  - *What number sentence describes this?*
  - *Is there another way to write this?*
  - *How many jugs are needed to hold 2 litres? What number sentence describes this?*
  - *How many jugs are needed to hold 3 litres? What number sentence describes this?*

Question 2

Chapter 4 Comparing fractions, improper fractions and mixed numbers Unit 4.8 Practice Book 5A, pages 108–111

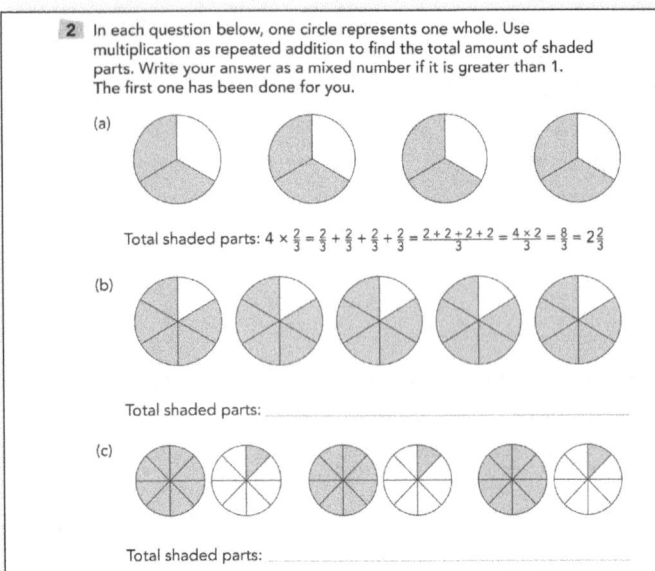

What learning will pupils have achieved at the conclusion of Question 2?

- Pupils will have applied the concept of multiplication as repeated addition in order to multiply a fraction by a whole number.

Activities for whole-class instruction

- Introduce the following context:
  - George's stride length is $\frac{2}{3}$ of a metre.
- Ask: *If George takes two strides, how far will he have travelled?* Agree $\frac{2}{3}$ of a metre + $\frac{2}{3}$ of a metre = $\frac{4}{3}$ of a metre, and this is equivalent to $1\frac{1}{3}$ metres.
- Show pupils the following image:

- Ask: *How does the image represent this scenario?* Can pupils explain that each bar represents 1 whole metre and $\frac{2}{3}$ of each bar is shaded, which represents George's stride length? Give pupils strips of paper divided into three equal parts and ask them create a representation for George having taken three strides. Ask: *How far would he have travelled?* Ensure pupils shade three lots of $\frac{2}{3}$ and identify $\frac{2}{3}$ of a metre + $\frac{2}{3}$ of a metre + $\frac{2}{3}$ of a metre = $\frac{6}{3}$ of a metre = 2 metres.
- Show the following calculation on the board:
  $3 \times \frac{2}{3} = \frac{2}{3} + \frac{2}{3} + \frac{2}{3} = \frac{2+2+2}{3} = \frac{3 \times 2}{3} = \frac{6}{3} = 2$

- Ask: *What do you notice?* Pupils should tell you that the numerator is multiplied by the whole number but the denominator remains unchanged; also, that because the denominator is the same for all addends, it only needs to be written once.

All say ... *When multiplying a fraction by a whole number, you multiply the numerator but the denominator does not change.*

(i) Pupils will have experienced multiplication as repeated addition with whole numbers but may not appreciate that this also applies to fractions. Presenting this visually and symbolically may help pupils to see the relationship.

- Using strips of paper divided into three equal parts (or drawings of these), ask pupils to work in pairs to calculate $5 \times \frac{2}{3}$ of a metre. Agree the answer is $\frac{10}{3}$ of a metre, which is equivalent to $3\frac{1}{3}$ metres. Ask pupils to record their working as a number sentence. Share ideas.
- Tell pupils:
  - Oscar's stride length is $1\frac{1}{6}$ of a metre.
- Ask: *If Oscar takes two strides, how far will he have travelled?* Pupil pairs should calculate $2 \times 1\frac{1}{6}$ metres. Agree, $\frac{14}{6}$ of a metre, which is equivalent to $2\frac{2}{6}$ metres. Pupils should record this as a number sentence. Share ideas. Repeat with a different number of strides for more practice if appropriate.
- Pupils should complete Question 2 in the Practice Book.

Same-day intervention

- Provide pupils with 2 × 4 grids and establish that 1 grid represents 1 whole.

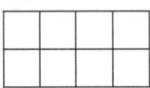

- Tell pupils to shade $\frac{3}{8}$ on four grids. Ask: *What multiplication calculation does this represent?* Agree $4 \times \frac{3}{8}$. Ask: *What addition calculation does this represent?* Agree this represents $\frac{3}{8} + \frac{3}{8} + \frac{3}{8} + \frac{3}{8}$. Ask: *How many eighths are shaded?* Count four lots of $\frac{3}{8}$ and agree $\frac{12}{8}$ are shaded. To reinforce the relationship between multiplication and repeated addition, model recording this calculation as:

  $\frac{3}{8} + \frac{3}{8} + \frac{3}{8} + \frac{3}{8} = \frac{12}{8}$

  and

  $\frac{3+3+3+3}{8} = \frac{12}{8}$

- Repeat this activity, multiplying $\frac{3}{8}$ by different whole numbers.
- Repeat but change the $\frac{3}{8}$ to $\frac{5}{8}$.

Chapter 4 Comparing fractions, improper fractions and mixed numbers Unit 4.8 Practice Book 5A, pages 108–111

Same-day enrichment

- Ask pupils to use their understanding of multiplication as repeated addition to identify the unknowns in the following calculations:
  - $2\frac{1}{3} = b + b + b$ $2\frac{1}{3} = b \times c$
- Ask: *What is the value of c? What is the value of b?*
  - $7\frac{3}{7} = d + d + d + d$ $7\frac{3}{7} = d \times e$
- Ask: *What is the value of e? What is the value of d?*

Question 3

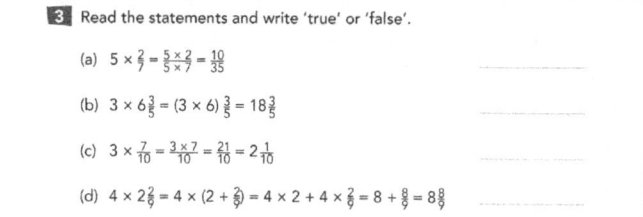

What learning will pupils have achieved at the conclusion of Question 3?

- Pupils will have understood how the multiplication of a fraction by a whole number can be represented symbolically and can manipulate the numbers appropriately within a calculation.

Activities for whole-class instruction

- Give pupils **Resource 5.4.8a** Calculation match. Tell pupils that each calculation in the top row matches an equivalent calculation in the bottom row. Pupil pairs should work together to match the calculations and provide a clear justification for their decision. Share ideas, discussing reasoning about why calculations are equivalent. Pupils may find it helpful to use number lines to support their justifications.

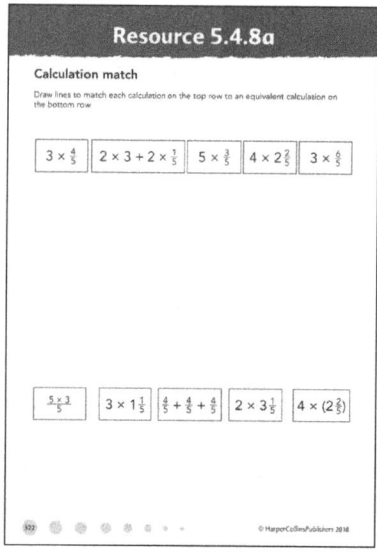

Answers:

$3 \times \frac{4}{5} = \frac{4}{5} + \frac{4}{5} + \frac{4}{5}$

$2 \times 3 + 2 \times \frac{1}{5} = 2 \times 3\frac{1}{5}$

$5 \times \frac{3}{5} = \frac{5 \times 3}{5}$

$4 \times 2\frac{2}{5} = 4 \times (2\frac{2}{5})$

$3 \times \frac{6}{5} = 3 \times 1\frac{1}{5}$

- Write the following:

  $3 \times 2\frac{5}{7}$

- Pupil pairs should record different ways this calculation could be represented as number sentences. Share ideas. If necessary, represent the calculation using shaded bars to support pupils' understanding.

- Write the following:

  $(3 \times 2) + \frac{5}{7}$

- Ask: *Is this fraction equivalent to the original calculation?* Agree that this is not equivalent because the $\frac{5}{7}$ has not been multiplied by the whole number.

- Write the following:

  $(3 \times 2) + \frac{3 \times 5}{3 \times 7}$

- Ask: *Is this fraction equivalent to the original calculation?* Agree that this is not equivalent because both the numerator and the denominator have been multiplied by the whole number.

 *When multiplying a fraction by a whole number, you multiply the numerator but the denominator does not change.*

- Pupils should complete Question 3 in the Practice Book.

Chapter 4 Comparing fractions, improper fractions and mixed numbers Unit 4.8 Practice Book 5A, pages 108–111

Same-day intervention

- Show the following:
$4 \times \frac{5}{9} = \frac{4 \times 5}{4 \times 9}$
$3 \times 1\frac{2}{9} = (3 \times 1) + \frac{2}{9}$
$5 \times 4\frac{1}{9} = 4\frac{1}{9} + 4\frac{1}{9} + 4\frac{1}{9} + 4\frac{1}{9}$
- Provide pupils with strips of paper divided into nine equal parts and ask them to use these to justify why the calculations are incorrect. Ask pupils to provide a correct number sentence for each of the calculations.

Same-day enrichment

- Show the following:
$4 \times \frac{5}{9}$ $3 \times 1\frac{2}{9}$ $5 \times 4\frac{1}{9}$
- Ask pupils to write three statements that are equivalent to each of the calculations above and one incorrect statement. Pupils should swap incorrect statements for their partner to consider what error has been made.

Question 4

4 Multiplying fractions by whole numbers.

(a) $5 \times \frac{1}{2} =$

(b) $\frac{3}{10} \times 3 =$

(c) $8 \times 5\frac{2}{15} + \frac{8}{15} =$

(d) $12 \times 12\frac{1}{5} =$

(e) $3\frac{5}{12} \times 5 - 4 \times 2\frac{1}{12} =$

(f) $0 \times 6\frac{11}{100} + 1 \times 4\frac{19}{100} - 2 \times 2\frac{3}{100} =$

What learning will pupils have achieved at the conclusion of Question 4?

- Pupils will be able to solve multistep calculations that involve the multiplication of fractions by whole numbers.

Activities for whole-class instruction

- Using sticky labels, label half the class with a whole number less than 20 and the other half with a proper fraction. Ask pupils to pair up so each pair consists of a whole number and a proper fraction. Ask pupils to work together to multiply the two numbers together.

Encourage pupils to record their working if necessary. Share answers with another pair and check for accuracy. Swap pairings and repeat the activity.

- Change the proper fraction labels for mixed number labels and repeat the activity.
- Present pupils with the following image:

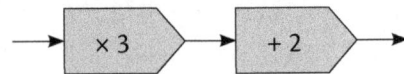

- Ask: *If I input 5 into the function machine, what would the output be?* Agree 17 because $5 \times 3 = 15$ and $15 + 2$ is 17. Record $5 \times 3 + 2 = 17$ on the board. Repeat with other whole numbers.
- Ask: *If I input $\frac{4}{5}$ into the function machine, what would the output be?* Agree $4\frac{2}{5}$ because $\frac{4}{5} \times 3 = \frac{12}{5} = 2\frac{2}{5}$ and $2\frac{2}{5} + 2$ is $4\frac{2}{5}$. Record $\frac{4}{5} \times 3 + 2 = 4\frac{2}{5}$ on the board. Repeat with other proper fractions.
- Ask: *If I input $4\frac{3}{7}$ into the function machine, what would the output be?* Agree $15\frac{2}{7}$ because $4\frac{3}{7} \times 3 = 13\frac{2}{7}$ and $13\frac{2}{7} + 2 = 15\frac{2}{7}$. Repeat with other mixed numbers.
- Present pupils with the following image:

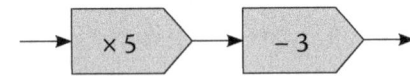

- Input whole numbers, proper fractions and mixed numbers into this function machine. Repeat the line of questioning above.
- Present pupils with the following calculation:
$4\frac{2}{10} \times 3 - 2 \times 3\frac{4}{10} =$
- Ask: *In what order should we carry out this calculation? Which part of the calculation needs to be calculated first? Why?* Agree that multiplication and division take priority over addition and subtraction, therefore the two multiplication elements need to be calculated first.
- Ask: *What is $4\frac{2}{10} \times 3$?* Agree $12\frac{6}{10}$. Ask: *What is $2 \times 3\frac{4}{10}$?* Agree $6\frac{8}{10}$.
- Record $12\frac{6}{10} - 6\frac{8}{10}$ on the board for pupils to calculate. Agree that the final answer is $5\frac{8}{10}$.
- Repeat with other multistep calculations involving multiplication of fractions if appropriate.

(i) Pupils will have knowledge of general rules of the order of operations and will have explored these with whole numbers; they will be required to apply this understanding to multistep calculations involving fractions.

- Pupils should complete Question 4 in the Practice Book.

Chapter 4 Comparing fractions, improper fractions and mixed numbers Unit 4.8 Practice Book 5A, pages 108–111

Same-day intervention

- Show the following:

Whole numbers		
2	3	4
5	6	7
8	9	10

Fractions and mixed numbers		
$\frac{1}{2}$	$\frac{1}{3}$	$\frac{1}{4}$
$\frac{3}{5}$	$\frac{4}{5}$	$\frac{9}{10}$
$1\frac{2}{5}$	$2\frac{1}{3}$	$3\frac{1}{6}$

- Pupils play against a partner. The pair will need a number line from 0 to 40 and each pupil will need a different-coloured pencil. Decide who goes first. Take turns to choose a whole number and a fraction or mixed number. Multiply the two numbers together and mark the answer on the number line. Keep taking turns until someone has marked three numbers next to each other on the number line.

Same-day enrichment

- Write the following:

| 2 | 3 | 4 | $\frac{3}{4}$ | $1\frac{1}{2}$ | $2\frac{1}{4}$ |

- Ask pupils to use three of the numbers to make each of the calculations correct.

  ____ × ____ + ____ = $14\frac{1}{4}$

  ____ ÷ ____ × ____ = $1\frac{1}{2}$

  ____ × ____ − ____ = $2\frac{1}{2}$

  (____ + ____) × ____ = $10\frac{1}{2}$

- Pupils make their own multistep missing number calculation for a partner to solve. Make sure it involves multiplying a fraction by a whole number.

Questions 5 and 6

5 A rectangular pool is 9 metres long and $5\frac{1}{2}$ metres wide. Find its perimeter and area.

6 On a trip, Joshua drove from Cardiff to London and then to Edinburgh. It took him two and three-quarter hours to drive from Cardiff to London on the first day. On the second day, he drove from London to Edinburgh. The journey took him three times longer than the journey from Cardiff to London.

(a) How long did it take Joshua to drive from London to Edinburgh?

(b) How much longer did it take Joshua to drive from London to Edinburgh than from Cardiff to London?

(c) How much time did it take Joshua to drive from Cardiff to London and then from London to Edinburgh?

What learning will pupils have achieved at the conclusion of Questions 5 and 6?

- Pupils will be able to multiply fractions by whole numbers to solve contextualised problems.

Activities for whole-class instruction

- Show the following image:

4 m

- Explain that this image represents a plan of a bedroom. Ask: *What is the area of the bedroom?* Take responses. Ask pupils to share their strategies on the board. Can pupils tell you that they need to multiply 4 m by $2\frac{1}{2}$ m

Chapter 4 Comparing fractions, improper fractions and mixed numbers   Unit 4.8   Practice Book 5A, pages 108–111

to calculate the total area: $4\,m \times 2\tfrac{1}{2}\,m = 10\,m^2$. This can also be illustrated visually by dividing the plan up into square metres:

- Ask: *What is the perimeter of the bedroom?* Take responses. Ask pupils to share their strategies on the board. Ensure pupils identify that they need to add the total of all the side lengths to calculate the perimeter: $4\,m + 4\,m + 2\tfrac{1}{2}\,m + 2\tfrac{1}{2}\,m = 13\,m$.
- Ask: *What if the width were increased from $2\tfrac{1}{2}\,m$ to $3\tfrac{1}{3}\,m$; what would the area and the perimeter be now?* Take responses. Agree that the area would now be 4 metres × $3\tfrac{1}{3}\,m = 13\tfrac{1}{3}\,m^2$ and that the perimeter would now be $4\,m + 4\,m + 3\tfrac{1}{3}\,m + 3\tfrac{1}{3}\,m = 14\tfrac{2}{3}\,m$.
- Ask: *How much larger is the area?* Agree that the difference in the area is $13\tfrac{1}{3}\,m^2 - 10\,m^2 = 3\tfrac{1}{3}\,m^2$. Ask: *How much larger is the perimeter?* Agree that the difference in the perimeter is $14\tfrac{2}{3}\,m - 13\,m = 1\tfrac{2}{3}\,m$.
- Pupils should complete Questions 5 and 6 in the Practice Book.

Same-day intervention

- Show the following image:

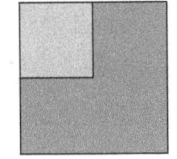

- Tell pupils that each side of the smaller square is half the length of a side of the larger square. Ask: *What is the area of the smaller square? What is the perimeter of the smaller square?*
- Ask: *What if each side of the smaller square is $\tfrac{1}{3}$ the length of a side of the larger square? What is the area of the smaller square now? What is the perimeter of the smaller square now?*

Same-day enrichment

- Show the following image:

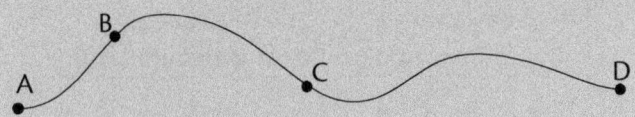

- Tell pupils this image represents a cycle ride. It took $1\tfrac{2}{3}$ hours to cycle from A to B. It took twice as long to cycle from B to C. It took the same length of time to cycle from C to D as it took to cycle from A to C. Ask:
  - *How long did it take to cycle from B to C?*
  - *How long did it take to cycle from C to D?*
  - *How long did the entire cycle last for?*
  - *How much longer did it take to cycle from B to C than from A to B?*
  - *How much longer did it take to cycle from C to D than from B to C?*

Challenge and extension question

Question 7

7 Calculate the following and write the answer as a mixed number if it is greater than 1.

(a) $7 \times 5\tfrac{1}{2} + \tfrac{5}{6} =$

(b) $10 \times 3\tfrac{11}{12} - 12 \times 2\tfrac{3}{60} =$

Pupils are required to use their understanding of adding and subtracting fractions with related denominators and their knowledge of multiplying fractions by whole numbers to solve multistep calculations.

Chapter 4 Comparing fractions, improper fractions and mixed numbers   Unit 4.8   Practice Book 5A, pages 112–115

Chapter 4 Test (Practice Book 5A, pages 112–115)

Test question number	Relevant unit	Relevant questions within unit
1	Unit 4.6	Q3, Q4
	Unit 4.7	Q1, Q2
	Unit 4.8	Q2, Q3, Q4
2	Unit 4.6	Q4, Q5
	Unit 4.7	Q1, Q2
	Unit 4.8	Q2, Q3, Q4
3	Unit 4.1	Q2, Q3
	Unit 4.3	Q1
	Unit 4.4	Q2
4	Unit 4.1	Q4
	Unit 4.2	Q1, Q3
	Unit 4.3	Q1, Q2
	Unit 4.4	Q2
	Unit 4.5	Q3
5	Unit 4.1	Q4
	Unit 4.5	Q3
6	Unit 4.4	Q1, Q3
	Unit 4.5	Q4
	Unit 4.6	Q6
7	Unit 4.5	Q6
	Unit 4.7	Q7
	Unit 4.8	Q5, Q6

Chapter 5
Consolidation and enhancement

Chapter overview

Area of mathematics	National Curriculum statutory requirements for Key Stage 2	Shanghai Maths Project reference
Number – number and place value	Year 5 Programme of study: Pupils should be taught to:	
	■ read, write, order and compare numbers to at least 1 000 000 and determine the value of each digit	Year 5, Units 5.1, 5.2
	■ count forwards or backwards in steps of powers of 10 for any given number up to 1 000 000	Year 5, Units 5.1, 5.2
	■ round any number up to 1 000 000 to the nearest 10, 100, 1000, 10 000 and 100 000	Year 5, Units 5.1, 5.2
	■ solve number problems and practical problems that involve all of the above	Year 5, Units 5.1, 5.2
	■ read Roman numerals to 1000 (M) and recognise years written in Roman numerals.	Year 5, Units 5.7
Number – number and place value	Year 6 Programme of study: Pupils should be taught to:	
	■ read, write, order and compare numbers up to 10 000 000 and determine the value of each digit	Year 5, Units 5.1, 5.2
	■ round any whole number to a required degree of accuracy.	Year 5, Units 5.1, 5.2
Number – addition and subtraction	Year 5 Programme of study: Pupils should be taught to:	
	■ solve addition and subtraction multi-step problems in contexts, deciding which operations and methods to use and why.	Year 5, Units 5.3, 5.4

Number – multiplication and division	Year 5 Programme of study: Pupils should be taught to: ■ solve problems involving addition, subtraction, multiplication and division and a combination of these, including understanding the meaning of the equals sign ■ solve problems involving multiplication and division, including scaling by simple fractions and problems involving simple rates.	Year 5, Units 5.5, 5.6 Year 5, Units 5.5, 5.6
Number – addition, subtraction, multiplication and division	Year 6 Programme of study: Pupils should be taught to: ■ use their knowledge of the order of operations to carry out calculations involving the four operations.	Year 5, Units 5.3, 5.4, 5.5, 5.6
Statistics	Year 4 Programme of study: Pupils should be taught to: ■ interpret and present discrete and continuous data using appropriate graphical methods, including bar charts and time graphs ■ solve comparison, sum and difference problems using information presented in bar charts, pictograms, tables and other graphs.	Year 5, Unit 5.8 Year 5, Unit 5.8
Statistics	Year 5 Programme of study: Pupils should be taught to: ■ solve comparison, sum and difference problems using information presented in a line graph ■ complete, read and interpret information in tables, including timetables.	Year 5, Unit 5.8 Year 5, Unit 5.8

Chapter 5 Consolidation and enhancement

Unit 5.1
Large numbers and rounding (1)

Conceptual context

The first two units in this chapter revisit reading, writing and rounding large numbers. The concept of place value, where each new column on the left is 10 times bigger than the column on its right, is now embedded. Pupils are able to identify each digit and know when and how to use zero as a placeholder.

To read large numbers, digits are separated into groups of three, beginning from the right. Each group comprises hundreds, tens and ones. Numbers are read from the left, beginning with the largest group. 987654321 is separated from the right to become 987 654 321 and is read from the left as nine hundred and eighty-seven million, six hundred and fifty-four thousand, three hundred and twenty-one.

Pupils have experience of rounding numbers to the nearest specified multiple of 10. By convention, the digit 5, although midway is rounded to the next multiple.

4 587 321 rounded to the nearest million becomes 5 000 000

4 487 321 rounded to the nearest million becomes 4 000 000.

Learning pupils will have achieved at the end of the unit

- Pupils will have practised counting forwards and backwards in steps of powers of 10 for any given number (Q1)
- Expressing the same number in different ways will have been consolidated (Q1)
- Pupils will have identified the place value of each digit in numbers containing up to 10 digits (Q1, Q4)
- Pupils will be able to talk about place value with understanding (Q1, Q4)
- Reading and writing very large numbers will have been practised (Q1, Q2, Q3, Q4)
- Pupils will have used reasoning to solve word problems involving place value (Q1, Q4)
- Pupils will have extended their understanding of comparing and ordering very large numbers (Q5)
- Pupils will have practised rounding numbers to the nearest 1000, 10 000, 100 000, 1 000 000 and 10 000 000 (Q6)

Resources

A5 cards labelled Thousand, Ten Thousand, Hundred Thousand, Million; mini whiteboards; glue sticks; ordinal A5 cards (labelled 1st to 9th); **Resource 5.5.1a** Counting in steps; **Resource 5.5.1b** Find the number; **Resource 5.5.1c** 1, 2, 3 and zeros; **Resource 5.5.1d** Change the order

Chapter 5 Consolidation and enhancement

Unit 5.1 Practice Book 5A, pages 116–119

Question 1

1. Fill in the spaces to make each statement correct.
   (a) Counting in 100 000s.
   Forwards: 11 000, 111 000, 211 000, 311 000, ☐,
   ☐, 611 000
   Backwards: 1 000 000, ☐, 800 000, ☐,
   ☐, 500 000

   (b) When counting large numbers, ☐ ten thousands is one hundred thousand; ☐ ten millions is one hundred million.

   (c) Ones, tens, hundreds, thousands, ten thousands, hundred thousands, millions, ten millions, hundred millions, billions, ten billions, are all units of _____. The multiplication from one unit to the next unit is by 10.

   (d) The two nearest whole million numbers to 1 567 000 are ☐ and ☐.

   (e) 43 007 070 is read in words as _____
   It consists of ☐ thousands and ☐ ones.

   (f) In a 3-digit number, the digit in the tens place is 1 greater than the digit in the ones place and 3 greater than the digit in the hundreds place. The digit in the hundreds place is half of 10.
   The number is ☐.

What learning will pupils have achieved at the conclusion of Question 1?

- Pupils will have practised counting forwards and backwards in steps of powers of 10 for any given number.
- Expressing the same number in different ways will have been consolidated.
- Pupils will have identified the place value of each digit in numbers containing up to 10 digits.
- Pupils will be able to talk about place value with understanding.
- Reading and writing very large numbers will have been practised.
- Pupils will have used reasoning to solve word problems involving place value.

Activities for whole-class instruction

- Display the number 7 777 777 and read the number together. Shuffle four A5 cards marked as follows:

| Thousand | Ten Thousand | Hundred Thousand | Million |

- Choose a card at random, and ask pupils to count in steps of that number. Discuss and record the sequence.

For example, counting in steps of ten thousand gives 7 777 777, 7 787 777, 7 797 777, 7 807 777, 7 817 777 … Repeat with another card.

- Try more numbers, perhaps a six-digit number (for example 567 567) and an eight-digit number (78 787 878). Choosing numbers with six digits or greater means that the sequence will quickly cross a number boundary.

- Display the following number, 2 499 999. Ask pupils to write the nearest million on mini whiteboards. Agree that it is 2 000 000 because the hundred thousands number is 4. Repeat with the following numbers, 3 613 613, 1 900 523, 7 388 291, choosing individual pupils to explain their reasoning.

- Pupils should complete Question 1 in the Practice Book.

Same-day intervention

- Give pupil pairs **Resource 5.5.1a** Counting in steps, and paper and a glue stick to make the sequences.

Resource 5.5.1a

Counting in steps

The numbers in the grid can be sorted into three sequences, counting in steps of:
1. 1000
2. 10000
3. 100000

Cut out the numbers and arrange the sequences in increasing order.

70 000	200 000	34 000	700 000	110 000
500 000	80 000	170 000	40 000	120 000
35 000	1 000 000	32 000	110 000	39 000
800 000	140 000	300 000	31 000	600 000
37 000	30 000	90 000	38 000	15 000
100 000	400 000	36 000	160 000	900 000

Answers: 1. 30 000, 31 000, 32 000, 34 000, 35 000, 36 000, 37 000, 38 000, 39 000, 40 000; 2. 70 000, 80 000, 90 000, 100 000, 110 000, 120 000; 3. 100 000, 200 000, 300 000, 400 000, 500 000, 600 000, 700 000, 800 000, 900 000, 1 000 000.

Same-day enrichment

- Read Question 1(f) together. Challenge pupil pairs to write similar questions for a five-digit and a six-digit number. Invite pupils to try each other's number puzzles.

Chapter 5 Consolidation and enhancement

Unit 5.1 Practice Book 5A, pages 116–119

Questions 2 and 3

2 Read out and write the following numbers in words.
(a) 4 204 322
(b) 10 025 090
(c) 20 000 200
(d) 1 010 101 010

3 Write the following numbers in numerals.
(a) Fifty-nine million, five hundred and eight thousand, eight hundred and eighty.
(b) Four hundred million, eight hundred and fifty-four thousand, five hundred.
(c) Two million, six hundred and sixteen thousand, three hundred and twenty-nine.
(d) One hundred and ten million, four hundred and nine thousand and eleven.

What learning will pupils have achieved at the conclusion of Questions 2 and 3?
- Reading and writing very large numbers will have been practised.

Activities for whole-class instruction

- Work together to add column headings to this place value chart:

- Here is the finished chart:

Billions			Millions			Thousands			Ones		
Hundreds	Tens	Ones	Hundreds	Tens	Ones	Hundreds	Tens	Ones	Hundreds	Tens	Ones

- Display the grid below. Ask pupils to read each number in turn to a partner and check they agree. Choose individual pupils to read the numbers aloud.

A	B	C	D
14 325 201	32 327 089	2 360 320 158	929 430
E	F	G	H
602 424 321	42 567 026 749	1 427 007	190 721 802

- Give pupils mini whiteboards. Say: *Two million, forty thousand.* Ask pupils to write the number in words and then in numerals on their boards. Repeat with the following numbers:
  - six million, five hundred
  - four billion and seventy
  - ten billion and three.

- Support any pupils who find this challenging by showing them how to write sets of three dashes, placing the numbers and then adding zeros as required.

- Pupils should complete Questions 2 and 3 in the Practice Book.

Same-day intervention

- Give pupils **Resource 5.5.1b** Find the number. They should circle the matching numerals and words.

Answers: 1. 54 600; 2. 6 300 000; 3. 750 020;
4. 42 000 000 000; 5. 81 000 081; 6. 35 053 000 000;
7. 9 009 909; 8. 2 060 600.

Chapter 5 Consolidation and enhancement

Unit 5.1 Practice Book 5A, pages 116–119

Same-day enrichment

- Give pupils **Resource 5.5.1c** 1, 2, 3 and zeros. Peer marking the answers will give pupils additional practice.

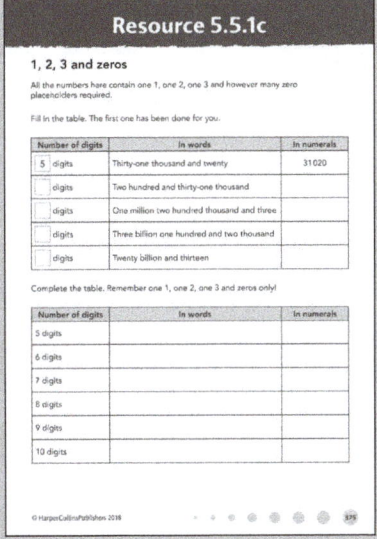

Answers: Table 1: 6, 231 000; 7, 1 200 003; 10, 3 000 102 000; 11, 20 000 000 013; Table 2: Various answers possible.

Question 4

4. Multiple choice questions. (For each question, choose the correct answer and write the letter in the box.)
   (a) The number consisting of 3 ten-millions, 6 millions and 9 thousands is ☐.

   A. 369 000 B. 3 609 000 C. 36 009 000 D. 30 609 000

   (b) In a large number, from the ones place to the left, the fourth place is ☐; the place to the right of the hundred millions place is ☐.

   A. the thousands place B. the ten thousands place
   C. the hundred thousands place D. the ten millions place

   (c) ☐ different 4-digit numbers can be formed using the digits 0, 1, 5 and 9.

   A. 16 B. 18 C. 20 D. 24

What learning will pupils have achieved at the conclusion of Question 4?

- Pupils will be able to talk about place value with understanding.
- Pupils will have identified the place value of each digit in numbers containing up to 10 digits.
- Reading and writing very large numbers will have been practised.
- Pupils will have used reasoning to solve word problems involving place value.

Activities for whole-class instruction

- Display the number grid again:

A	B	C	D
14 325 201	32 327 089	2 360 320 158	929 430
E	F	G	H
602 424 321	42 567 026 749	1 427 007	190 721 802

- Ask questions to check understanding of place value, such as:
  - *Which is the smallest number? Explain how you know.*
  - *Which is the largest number? Explain how you know.*
  - *Which numbers are less than a billion? Explain how you know.*
  - *Find the number with a zero placeholder in the 100 000s place (1 000 000s place, …).*
  - *The value of one place is the same in every number. Which place is it?*

- Pupils should complete Question 4 in the Practice Book.

Same-day intervention

- Choose a pupil to write a nine-digit number on the board. Shuffle a pack of ordinal A5 cards, 1st to 9th and select one. Agree the value of the chosen digit. Choose two more cards and work out the value of those digits. For example, 356 408 129, card selected 6th. Say: *The value of the sixth digit is four hundred thousand.* Repeat with new numbers.

Same-day enrichment

- Say that in a six-digit odd number, the odd digits appear in decreasing order. The only other digit is zero. Ask pupils to find all the possibilities.
- Investigate the possibilities for a seven-digit odd number, where the odd digits are in increasing order, for example 1 003 579.

Question 5

5. Compare each pair of numbers below. Write > or < in the ◯.
   (a) 9676 ◯ 9767   (b) 800 100 ◯ 810 000
   (c) 4 406 000 ◯ 446 000   (d) 559 999 ◯ 590 000
   (e) 900 009 ◯ 900 090   (f) 100 001 ◯ 10 001

Chapter 5 Consolidation and enhancement   Unit 5.1 Practice Book 5A, pages 116–119

What learning will pupils have achieved at the conclusion of Question 5?

- Pupils will have extended their understanding of comparing and ordering very large numbers.

Activities for whole-class instruction

- Show pupils the following numbers:

  3 347 456   **2 347 456**

- Ask pupils to explain to a partner which is larger and how they know. Agree that the first number is larger because there are 3 millions in that number and only 2 millions in the right-hand-number. Check that pupils understand they don't need to consider the other digits.

- Look at this pair of numbers:

  2 347 456   **2 547 456**

- Ask pupil pairs which is larger and how they know. Establish that the second number is larger because both numbers have 2 millions, so the next column to the right must be considered. There are 5 hundred thousands in that number and only 3 hundred thousands in the other one.

- Ask: *Which is the larger of this pair of numbers?*

  2 347 456   **2 367 456**

- Establish that the second number is larger because there are six lots of ten thousand in that number and only four lots of ten thousand in the other one.

 *To order numbers, compare digits from the left.*

- Pupils should complete Question 5 in the Practice Book.

Same-day intervention

- Ask pupils to collect six mobile phone numbers. Rewrite them as large numbers and order them from the largest.

Same-day enrichment

- Give pupil pairs **Resource 5.5.1d** Change the order. Peer marking the answers will give pupils further experience of handling and ordering large numbers.

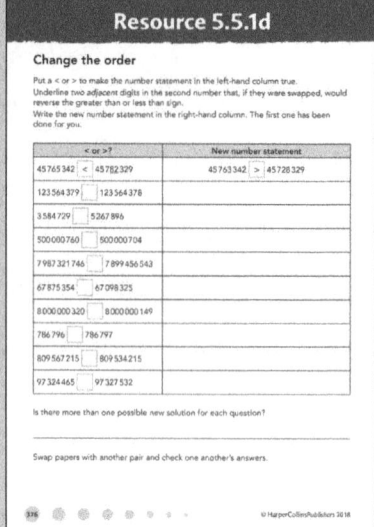

Answers: >, <, >, >, >, >, <, >, <; There is more than one possible new solution for each question.

Question 6

	To the nearest ten thousand	To the nearest hundred thousand	To the nearest ten million
36 890 700			
98 970 076			
109 827 000			

6 Round the numbers and complete the table.

What learning will pupils have achieved at the conclusion of Question 6?

- Pupils will have practised rounding numbers to the nearest 1000, 10 000, 100 000, 1 000 000 and 10 000 000.

Activities for whole-class instruction

- Ask pupils to explain rounding to the nearest …
- Tell pupils that rounding is sometimes called 'rounding off'; they both mean the same.
- Display the number:

  65 362 749

Chapter 5 Consolidation and enhancement

Unit 5.1 Practice Book 5A, pages 116–119

- Ask: *What is this number rounded to the nearest ten million? ... to the nearest million? ... hundred thousand? ... ten thousand? ... thousand?* Give pupils mini whiteboards to record their answers. Invite individual pupils to explain the process for each rounding. Repeat with another number if necessary.

 ... pupils who are uncertain how to round the digit 5.

 The digit 5 is the exact midpoint but by convention is rounded to the next specified power of 10.

- Pupils should complete Question 6 in the Practice Book.

Same-day intervention

- Ask pupils to collect six mobile phone numbers. Rewrite them as large numbers and round them to the nearest 10 000, 100 000 and 1 000 000. For example: 07577 543764 is 7 577 543 764; rounded to 10 000 is 7 577 500 000; rounded to 100 000 is 7 577 600 000; rounded to 1 000 000 is 7 578 000 000.

Same-day enrichment

- Display the number:

  3 547 382 916

- Round this number to the nearest:
  - billion
  - hundred million
  - ten million
  - million
  - hundred thousand
  - ten thousand
  - thousand
  - hundred
  - ten.

Challenge and extension questions

Questions 7 and 8

7 Use 8, 3, 5 and three 0s to form 6-digit numbers according to the conditions given.

(a) The greatest number is _____ ; rounding it to the nearest ten thousand, it is _____ .

(b) The least number is _____ ; rounding it to the nearest hundred thousand, it is _____ .

(c) The numbers with three zeros at the end are _____

(d) The numbers without zeros next to each other are _____

8 If a number is rounded to the nearest million, it is 5 000 000. The greatest possible value of this number is _____ and the least possible value is _____ .

The challenge and extension questions are problem-solving tasks that require a deep understanding of place value and rounding. Preparing and answering similar problems would challenge pupils further.

Chapter 5 Consolidation and enhancement

Unit 5.2
Large numbers and rounding (2)

Conceptual context

This second unit gives further practice reading, writing, comparing and ordering large numbers.

Pupils have experience of rounding numbers to the *nearest* specified multiple of 10. This is sometimes called 'rounding off'.

In this unit, pupils will also learn to round up and round down.

Learning pupils will have achieved at the end of the unit

- Pupils will have identified the place value of each digit in numbers containing up to 10 digits (Q1, Q2, Q3)
- Pupils will have described place value with understanding (Q1, Q2, Q3)
- Reading and writing very large numbers will have been practised (Q1, Q2)
- Pupils will have practised rounding numbers to the nearest 1000, 10 000, 100 000, 1 000 000 and 10 000 000 (Q1, Q2, Q3)
- Pupils will have used reasoning to solve word problems involving place value (Q1, Q2)

Resources

0–9 A5 digit cards; mini whiteboards; **Resource 5.5.2a** Five numbers; **Resource 5.5.2b** Number questions; **Resource 5.5.2c** Rounding 'to the nearest …' or 'up to the next …'; **Resource 5.5.2d** Rounding statements

Vocabulary

round to the nearest, round up to the next, rounding off

Chapter 5 Consolidation and enhancement

Unit 5.2 Practice Book 5A, pages 120–123

Questions 1 and 2

1 Complete each statement.

(a) Starting from the ones place to the left, the sixth place is the _____ place and the ten billions place is the _____ place.

(b) The least 7-digit number with 3 zeros and 4 fours is _____.

(c) If the hundred millions place of a number is its highest value place, it is a ____-digit number.

(d) A number consists of 3 hundred-millions, 5 millions, 2 thousands and 1 one. The number is _____.

(e) Two hundred and six million and sixty is written in numerals as _____.

(f) One billion, eight thousand and three is written in numerals as _____.

(g) 25 700 890 is an ____-digit number. The digit 5 is in the _____ place and it represents five _____.

(h) Starting from the left, the first 7 in the number 7 807 321 is in the _____ place, the second 7 is in the _____ place, and the difference between the values they stand for is _____.

(i) If a number is rounded to the nearest million, the result is 258 million.

The greatest possible value of this number is _____

and the least possible value is _____.

2 Multiple choice questions. (For each question, choose the correct answer and write the letter in the box.)

(a) In the following numbers, the number with 2 in the millions place is ____.

A. 202 205 808 B. 220 208 505 C. 20 208 505 D. 2 220 208 505

(b) One hundred and one thousand, three hundred is written as ____.

A. 1 001 300 B. 101 000 300 C. 101 300 D. 1 010 300

(c) Seven billion, five hundred thousand and sixty is written as ____.

A. 700 050 060   B. 700 500 060
C. 7 000 500 060   D. 40 070 050 060

(d) If a multi-digit number has only non-zero digits in its ten thousands place and ones place, then it is a ____ at least.

A. 4-digit number   B. 5-digit number
C. 6-digit number   D. 7-digit number

(e) Rounding the number 19▩324 to the nearest ten thousand, the result is 190 000. The least number that can be filled in the space is ____.

A. 0   B. 4   C. 5   D. 6

What learning will pupils have achieved at the conclusion of Questions 1 and 2?

- Pupils will have identified the place value of each digit in numbers containing up to 10 digits.
- Pupils will have described place value with understanding.
- Reading and writing very large numbers will have been practised.
- Pupils will have practised rounding numbers to the nearest 1000, 10 000, 100 000, 1 000 000 and 10 000 000.
- Pupils will have used reasoning to solve word problems involving place value.

Activities for whole-class instruction

- Ask 10 pupils to stand in a line. Shuffle a pack of 0–9 A5 digit cards and give each pupil a card. (If the pupil on the extreme left is holding the zero, then ask that pupil to move to the other end of the line). Invite a pupil to arrange the line to make it resemble a very large number, moving the line into groups of three from the right so that there is a small space between each set. For example:

  7 154 390 268

- Ask pupils to write the value of the 1, 2, 3, 4, 5, 6, 7, 8 and 9 in turn on mini whiteboards in numerals and words. Thus 1 is 100 000 000 / one hundred million; 2 is 200 / two hundred, and so on.

- Display the number:

  9 151 675 796

- Ask: *How many digits does the number have?* Confirm that it is a 10-digit number. Invite a pupil to read the number. Agree that it is nine billion, one hundred and fifty-one million, six hundred and seventy-five thousand, seven hundred and ninety-six.

- Invite a pupil to say the value of the two 6s. (6 ones and 6 hundred thousand) Ask: *What is the difference between the values they stand for?* Confirm that it is 100 000.

- Repeat with the two 5s in the number. Agree they are 5 thousand and 50 million, 50 million is 1000 times greater. Continue by establishing the difference between the values of the two 1s, the two 7s and the two 9s.

- Pupils should complete Questions 1 and 2 in the Practice Book.

Chapter 5 Consolidation and enhancement Unit 5.2 Practice Book 5A, pages 120–123

Same-day intervention

- Give pupils **Resource 5.5.2a** Five numbers. Ask them to look at the numbers and answer the questions.

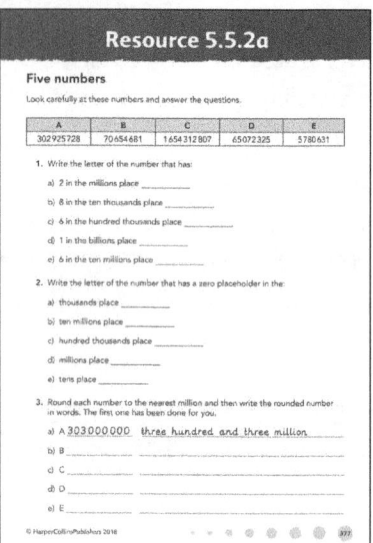

Answers: 1. a) A, b) E, c) B, d) C, e) D; 2. a) E, b) A, c) D, d) B, e) C; 3. b) 71 000 000, seventy-one million, c) 1 654 000 000, one billion, six hundred and fifty four million; d) 65 000 000, sixty-five million; e) 6 000 000, six million.

Same-day enrichment

- Give pupils **Resource 5.5.2b** Number questions. Ask them to look at the numbers and answer the questions.

Answers: 1. to 5 various answers possible; 6. a) E, b) A, c) D, d) B, e) C; 7. a) 303 000 000, three hundred and three million; b) 71 000 000, seventy-one million; c) 1 654 000 000, one billion, six hundred and fifty-four million; d) 65 000 000, sixty-five million; e) 6 000 000, six million; 8. 6 000 000, 65 000 000, 71 000 000, 303 000 000, 1 654 000 000.

Question 3

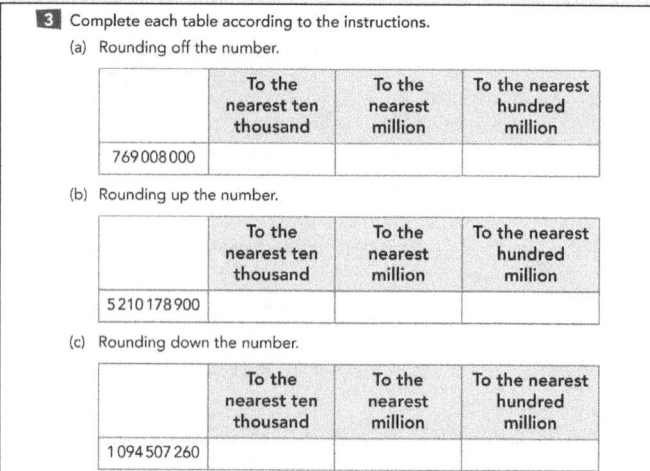

What learning will pupils have achieved at the conclusion of Question 3?

- Pupils will have identified the place value of each digit in numbers containing up to 10 digits.
- Pupils will have described place value with understanding.
- Pupils will have practised rounding numbers to the nearest 1000, 10 000, 100 000, 1 000 000 and 10 000 000.
- Pupils will have learned to round up and round down.

Activities for whole-class instruction

- Explain to pupils that until now they have been rounding numbers to the *nearest* specified multiple of 10. This is the most common way to round numbers and gives the best estimate for calculations, but sometimes they may be asked to round in a different way.
- To 'round up to the next …', means that numbers are rounded up to the next specified multiple of 10 even if the starting number is not half way or more to the next multiple. For example, 5 243 871 rounded up to the nearest million is 6 000 000, even though the number is closer to 5 000 000.
- Try some examples together, for example:
  - 34 541 rounded off to the nearest thousand is 35 000
  - 34 541 rounded up to the nearest thousand is 35 000.
- Continue with further examples until pupils can confidently follow the 'round to the nearest …' and 'round up to the nearest …'

Chapter 5 Consolidation and enhancement

Unit 5.2 Practice Book 5A, pages 120–123

- Emphasise to pupils the importance of reading the instructions for rounding carefully. It is important to be clear about whether they should 'round (or round off) to the nearest …' or 'round up to the nearest …'; also, they need to be clear about the degree of accuracy required, that is, whether rounding is to the nearest/next 10, 100, 1000, …
- Pupils should complete Question 3 in the Practice Book.

Same-day intervention

- Give pupil pairs **Resource 5.5.2c** Rounding 'to the nearest …' or 'up to the next …' They should decide if the statements are true or false.

  Answers: 1. T; 2. F; 3. T; 4. T; 5. F; 6. T; 7. F; 8. T; 9. F; 10. F.

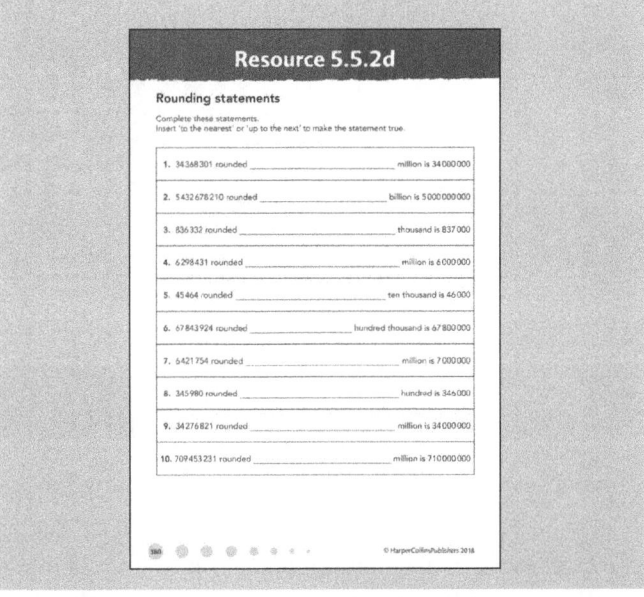

Same-day enrichment

- Give pupil pairs **Resource 5.5.2d** Rounding statements. They should complete the statements to make them true.

  Answers: 1. to the nearest; 2. to the nearest; 3. up to the next; 4. to the nearest; 5. up to the next; 6. to the nearest; 7. up to the next; 8. to the nearest or up to the next; 9. to the nearest; 10. up to the next.

Challenge and extension questions

Question 4

4 Think carefully and fill in the spaces with suitable numbers.

(a) For rounding off 14☐995 to get 150 000, the digit in the space can be either _____.

(b) For rounding off 64☐995 to get 640 000, the greatest possible digit in the space is _____.

(c) For rounding off 3674☐017 to get 36 750 000, the least possible digit in the space is _____.

(d) For rounding up 99☐345 to get 1 000 000, the digit in the space can be _____.

(e) For rounding down 3874☐017 to get 38 740 000, the greatest possible digit in the space is _____.

This question extends pupils understanding of rounding large numbers, and rounding them up or down.

Question 5

5 Let's play a number game: I am thinking of a 6-digit number. The first three digits starting from the left are all the same. The last three digits are consecutive whole numbers, counting down to 1. The sum of the six digits equals the 2-digit number at the end of the number. What number am I thinking of?

For this question, pupils are required to use logic to solve a problem involving place value. Remind pupils to consider each step sequentially and to record the stages. When they have found the six-digit number, they should check that it correctly answers each part of the question.

225

Unit 5.3
Four operations of numbers

Chapter 5 Consolidation and enhancement

Conceptual context

This unit revises the idea of the order of operations that was first introduced in Year 4.

Pupils will be encouraged to consider the difference that brackets can make in a calculation when they are placed in different positions. They will also approach mixed number problems from the position of identifying correct/incorrect ways to solve them.

> The 'order of operations' refers to the priority that each symbol takes in a calculation containing several operations. The rules are as follows:

1) × and/or ÷ take priority over + and/or − (so for 467 − 30 × 10, the multiplication should be completed first and then the subtraction).

2) Where two or more symbols have equal importance, they should be completed from left to right (so for 300 ÷ 2 × 6, the division should be completed first and then the multiplication).

3) Whatever is inside brackets overrules the order of operations and should be completed first (so for (280 + 20) × 4, the addition is given precedence over the multiplication).

Learning pupils will have achieved at the end of the unit

- Reasoning skills will have been enhanced (when deriving the correct order of operations, identifying errors in working methods and predicting the relative sizes of answers) (Q1, Q3, Q4)
- Further opportunities will have been provided to explore and consolidate knowledge of the order of operations (Q1, Q2, Q3, Q4)

Resources

mini whiteboards; plastic counters; sticky notes; operation symbol cards; sticky labels; **Resource 5.5.3a** Order of operations; **Resource 5.5.3b** Order of operations cards

Vocabulary

brackets, number sentence, mixed operations, order of operations

Chapter 5 Consolidation and enhancement

Unit 5.3 Practice Book 5A, pages 124–126

Question 1

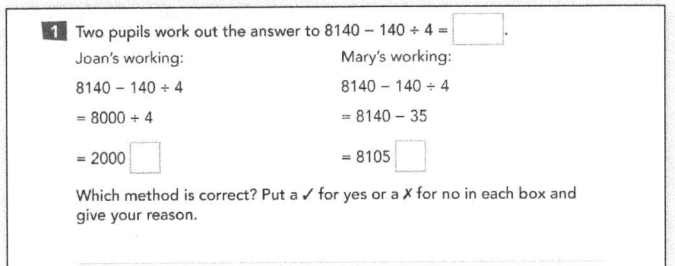

What learning will pupils have achieved at the conclusion of Question 1?

- Reasoning skills will have been enhanced (when deriving the correct order of operations, identifying errors in working methods and predicting the relative sizes of answers).
- Further opportunities will have been provided to explore and consolidate knowledge of the order of operations.

Activities for whole-class instruction

- Model the calculation of 3651 + 300 ÷ 3 by deliberately working it out wrongly (addition first, then division):

  3651 + 300 ÷ 3

  = 3951 ÷ 3

  = 1317

- Note any pupils who identify that the order of operations is wrong before being asked. Encourage pupils to recall the order of operations they used in Year 4. Ask: *Has this calculation been worked out in the correct order?*
- Display the following image to revise the order of operations.

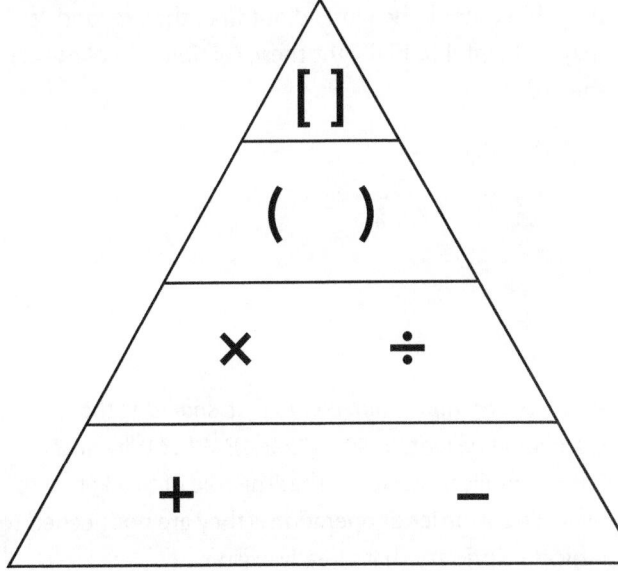

- Refer to the original calculation and ask: *How should I have worked this out?* Model this:

  3651 + 300 ÷ 3

  = 3651 + 100

  = 3751

- Model a further calculation, 5450 ÷ 5 × 2, in the following two ways:

  5450 ÷ 5 × 2   5450 ÷ 5 × 2

  = 1090 × 2   = 5450 ÷ 10

  = 2180   = 545

- Ask: *What is the difference between the two methods? Which gives the correct answer? Why?* Ensure that pupils refer to the order of operations when reasoning.
- Provide further number sentences, including those that contain brackets. For example:

  2450 ÷ 5 × 10

  (1421 + 389) × 10 − 800.

  (232 + 188) ÷ (569 − 559)

- Split pupils into pairs and ask them to work out each number sentence twice, once using the correct order of operations and once incorrectly. Choose pairs to come to the front and share their methods. Ask: *Which is correct? Why?*
- Pupils should complete Question 1 in the Practice Book.

Same-day intervention

- Provide pairs with **Resource 5.5.3a** Order of operations. Ask: *How does this pyramid help us remember the order of operations?*

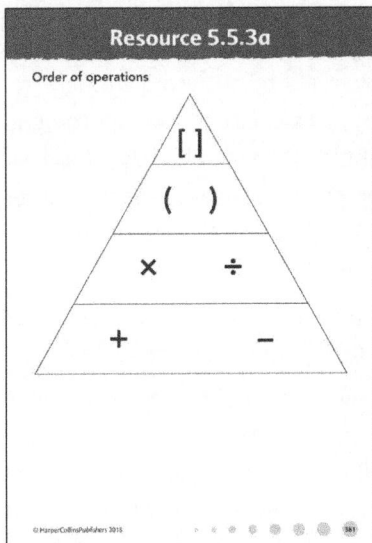

Chapter 5 Consolidation and enhancement

Unit 5.3 Practice Book 5A, pages 124–126

- Write the following on the board:
  729 − 18 ÷ 9
- Ask pupils to place two plastic counters on their pyramid to represent the two operations that need to be worked out. Ask: *Which operation is higher on the pyramid – the subtraction or the division?* Use this to discuss with pupils how this helps them identify the order – first working out 18 ÷ 9 and then 729 − 2.
- Repeat for further number sentences. For example, (476 + 14) ÷ 7. Discuss the fact that the use of brackets overrules the usual order of operations. Demonstrate this by moving the counter up the pyramid.
- Ask: *Which operation should we work out first? Why?* Pupils should find the answer by calculating 476 + 14 and then 490 ÷ 7.
- It is also important that pupils consider examples that contain operations on the same level of the pyramid. For example, 578 − 53 + 19. Revise the fact that, as − and + have equal priority, they need to be calculated in the order in which they appear.

Same-day enrichment

- Explain that in the following activity, pupils should take on the role of teachers, identifying errors and providing advice to those who need reminding of the order of operations.
- Write a variety of number sentences on the board. Pupils should answer each calculation either correctly or incorrectly (by deliberately choosing the wrong order of operations). When 'making mistakes', encourage pupils to think carefully about how a calculation might be answered wrongly (for example, working out a calculation from left to right, regardless of its symbols). They should only record each calculation and its answer (correct or otherwise). For example, 3200 + 100 ÷ 4 = 825, 4500 ÷ 10 × 2 = 900, and so on.
- Pupils should then swap responses so that they have another pupil's answers in front of them.
- Pupils then become the teacher, marking each answer and, if it is incorrect, identifying the error. They should write feedback for each incorrect answer, explaining to their 'pupil' how to rectify the error and/or how to avoid making the same mistake with the order of operations.
- Pupils should return their feedback to their author to check and see whether the error analysis and corrected calculation are appropriate.

Question 2

> 2 Write the order of operations in each calculation and then work it out step by step. The first one has been done for you.
> (a) 75 + 25 × 6
> First multiply and then add:
> 75 + 25 × 6
> = 75 + 150
> = 225
> (b) (75 + 25) × 6
> (c) 50 × 3 + 45 ÷ 3
> (d) 50 × (3 + 45) ÷ 3

What learning will pupils have achieved at the conclusion of Question 2?

- Further opportunities will have been provided to explore and consolidate knowledge of the order of operations.

Activities for whole-class instruction

- Write the following two calculations on the board:
  80 − 12 × 4   (80 − 12) × 4
- Ask: *What do you notice about these calculations? Will they give the same or different answers? Why? In what order should you work through the first calculation and why?*
- Provide pupils with sticky notes labelled 1 and 2. They should place the notes next to the parts of the calculation they think should be worked out first, then second. It may be helpful to highlight these sections to colour-code the order.

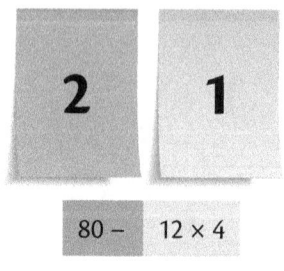

- Ask: *If the multiplication comes first, shouldn't the calculation be written 80 − (12 × 4)? Why? Why not?* Ensure pupils understand that the role of brackets is to overrule the order of operations (they are not needed to indicate a priority that already exists).

Chapter 5 Consolidation and enhancement

Unit 5.3 Practice Book 5A, pages 124–126

- Ask: *How many steps are needed to find the answer? How could you show these as a tree diagram?* Ask pupils to find the answer and explain why their working looks like this:

  80 – 12 × 4

  = 80 – 48

  = 32

- Repeat for (80 – 12) × 4, in particular focusing on how the presence of brackets has an effect on the order of operations and the answer.

- Repeat for different pairs of number sentences, where both contain the same string of numbers and operations, but only one contains brackets. For example:

  24 ÷ 2 + 2 × 10   24 ÷ (2 + 2) × 10

  Ensure pupils are also given examples (as above) where division comes before multiplication or where subtraction comes before addition. This will enable them to recognise that both operations have equivalent priority and (if there are no brackets) it is the operation that comes first when working from left to right that takes priority.

- Pupils should complete Question 2 in the Practice Book.

Same-day intervention

- Take two operation symbol cards (out of +, –, × and ÷), placing them in the order they were taken. Ask: *If this is the order in which these symbols appear in a number sentence, in what order should they be worked out?* Note any pupils who answer that it depends on whether there are any brackets. Agree that there are no brackets in this example and discuss the order. Ask: *What strategy do you use to help you remember which operations come first?*

- Write a calculation based on the symbol cards. If the cards are + and ×, the calculation could be 54 + 10 × 2. Pupils should write 1 and 2 above each symbol to show the order in which they should be calculated. Share ideas and discuss how pupils decided which should come first. Provide pupils with structured answers:

  54 + 10 × 2

  = 54 + ☐

  = ☐

- Go through each step, completing the missing values. Show (54 + 10) × 2. Ask: *How will the brackets affect the order in which you work through the calculation?*

- Repeat for different calculations, progressing to those made with three symbol cards.

Same-day enrichment

- Each pupil should devise a pair of similar three-step number sentences (one with brackets, one without). They should take it in turns to share both number sentences, giving four possibilities of the order of operations as multiple choice options. These should include the orders for both calculations as well as two incorrect answers.

- For example: 48 + 32 × 9 – 1 and 48 + 32 × (9 – 1)

  A: add   multiply   subtract
  B: multiply   add   subtract
  C: subtract   multiply   add
  D: subtract   add   multiply

- Others in the group should decide on the correct orders for both number sentences and find the answer. For example:

  48 + 32 × 9 – 1 is solved using Order B

  = 48 + 288 – 1

  = 336 – 1

  = 335

  48 + 32 × (9 – 1) is solved using Order C

  = 48 + 32 × 8

  = 48 + 256

  = 304

- Pupils score points for identifying the correct order and calculating correctly. They should repeat the activity for each of their number sentences.

Question 3

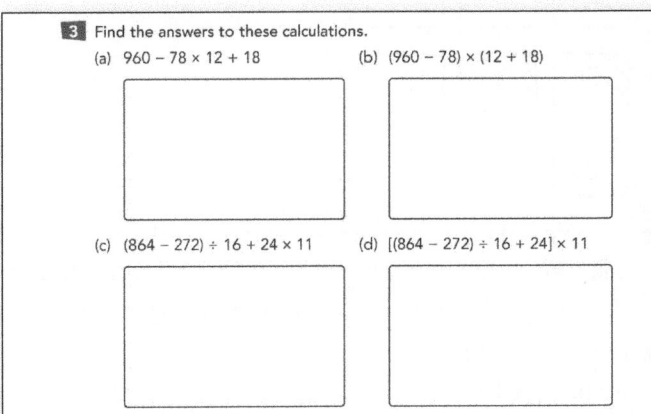

3 Find the answers to these calculations.
(a) 960 – 78 × 12 + 18
(b) (960 – 78) × (12 + 18)
(c) (864 – 272) ÷ 16 + 24 × 11
(d) [(864 – 272) ÷ 16 + 24] × 11

Chapter 5 Consolidation and enhancement

Unit 5.3 Practice Book 5A, pages 124–126

What learning will pupils have achieved at the conclusion of Question 3?

- Further opportunities will have been provided to explore and consolidate knowledge of the order of operations.
- Reasoning skills will have been enhanced (when deriving the correct order of operations, identifying errors in working methods and predicting the relative sizes of answers).

Activities for whole-class instruction

- Display the following two calculations:

  740 − 23 × 14 + 17   (740 − 23) × (14 + 17)

- Give pupils the following scenario: *Kian says that both calculations contain the same numbers, in the same order with the same operations, so they must give the same answer. Is he right? Why? Why not?*

- Discuss the differences in the order of operations for both sentences. Ask pupils to predict which of the two calculations they think will give the greatest total. Why do they think this? Although not necessary, this is a useful question to start pupils reasoning with greater depth about the effect of different orders of operations on the same number sentence.

- Use mini whiteboards to write each part of the calculation. Ask: *What do we need to do first? How do you know?* Go through the calculation, step by step, moving each operation to the fore and replacing it with its answer before continuing:

435

- Complete the second number sentence in the same way, choosing pupils to explain the order of operations. Revise the role of brackets as overruling the 'normal' order.

- Provide further examples to practise, including those with nested brackets:

  (644 + 210) ÷ 14 + 19 × 11

  [(644 + 210) ÷ 14 + 24] × 11

- Pupils should complete Question 3 in the Practice Book.

Same-day intervention

- Revise the rules for the order of operations. Provide pupils with quick instances of pairs of number sentences with and without brackets. For example:

  94 + 52 ÷ 2

  (94 + 52) ÷ 2

  36 + 14 × 30 ÷ 10

  (36 + 14) × (30 ÷ 10)

- For each example, challenge pupils to quickly write the symbols of the order of operations (without asking them to calculate anything).

- Display the following on strips of paper. Go through each number sentence in the correct order, replacing calculations with sticky labels as they are worked out.

320 + 320 ÷ 2 × 2	(320 + 320) ÷ (2 × 2)
320 + 160 × 2	(320 + 320) ÷ (4)
320 + 320	(640) ÷ (4)
640	(160)

- Provide pupils with their own sets of sticky labels or similar, replacing each expression in further examples with their equivalent values.

Same-day enrichment

- Provide pupils with a copy of **Resource 5.5.3b** Order of operations cards. Use this to set pupils a series of challenges where they are asked to write pairs of number sentences to match given clues.
- Having chosen a challenge, pupils should then share their number sentence pairs for peers to split into steps and answer. Encourage them to use reasoning to make a prediction about which answer will be largest if they are able.

Chapter 5 Consolidation and enhancement   Unit 5.3 Practice Book 5A, pages 124–126

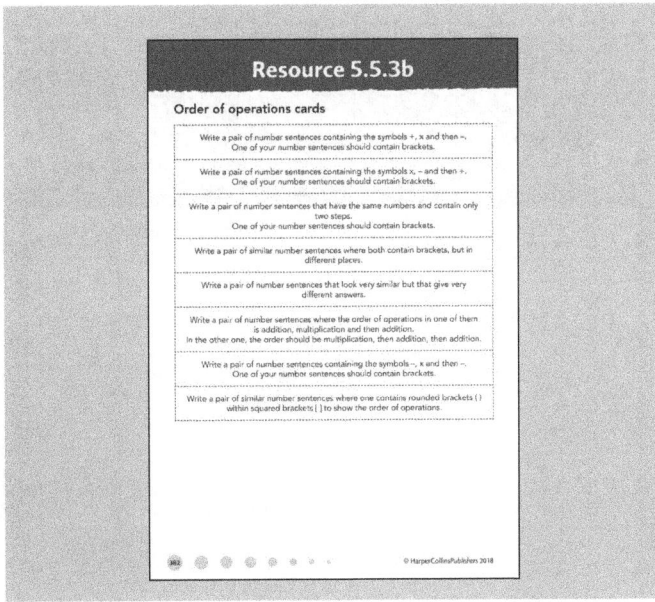

Question 4

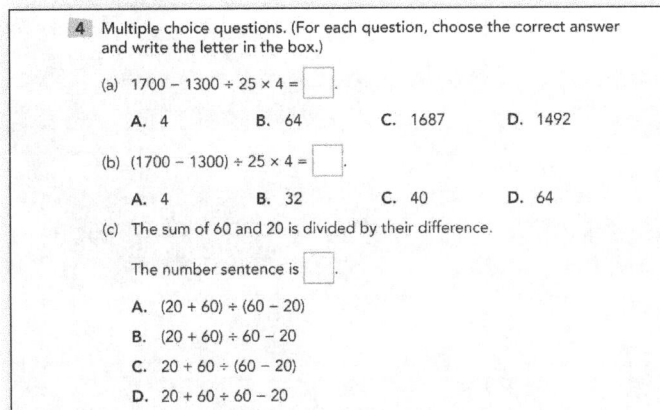

What learning will pupils have achieved at the conclusion of Question 4?

- Further opportunities will have been provided to explore and consolidate knowledge of the order of operations.
- Reasoning skills will have been enhanced (when deriving the correct order of operations, identifying errors in working methods and predicting the relative sizes of answers).

Activities for whole-class instruction

- Describe a scenario where a group of pupils have been shown a number sentence. Their addition, subtraction, multiplication and division skills are perfect, but only one of them holds up the correct answer. What mistake have the others made?

   *Only the correct order gives the correct answer.*

- Write the following multiple choice question on the board:

  1650 − 1200 ÷ 50 × 2 = ?

  A) 18   B) 1602   C) 1638   D) 4.5

- Give pupils time to consider the order of operations in the number sentence to work out the answer and then they hold up their mini whiteboard with the letter they think is correct. Revise the correct order of operations (÷, × then −) and the answer. Ask: *Where do some of the other answers come from?*

- Draw brackets around part of the number sentence: 1650 − 1200 ÷ (50 × 2). Ask pupils to show the correct letter now.

- Repeat for further number sentences where pupils vote on the correct answer each time. Include word calculation problems, for example:

  The difference between the product of 80 and 30 and the sum of 80 and 30 is …

  A) 80 × 30 − 80 + 30   B) (80 × 30) − (80 + 30)
  C) 80 × 30 − (80 + 30)   D) (80 × 30) − 80 + 30

- For further extension, introduce a 'Prove It!' element to the activity where pupils are required to justify their answers.
- Pupils should complete Question 4 in the Practice Book.

Chapter 5 Consolidation and enhancement

Unit 5.3 Practice Book 5A, pages 124–126

Same-day intervention

- Place four boxes at the front of the class, labelled A, B, C and D. Write: 600 + 100 × 2 ÷ 50 as well as four different possibilities for the order of operations and label these A, B, C and D. For example:

  A: addition → multiplication → division

  B: multiplication → division → addition

  C: multiplication → addition → division

  D: division → multiplication → addition

- Ensure that a cube is secretly placed into the box representing the correct answer (in this example, Box B).

- Encourage pupils to consider the rules they have learned, discussing in pairs which of the three orders of operations is correct. Choose pairs to check the corresponding box to see whether they are correct.

- Model the answer as a group, following the steps in option B. Repeat for different number sentences. As pupils become more confident, ask extension questions that allude to the use of brackets. For example: *How could we tweak the number sentence so that option A becomes true?*

Same-day enrichment

- Challenge pupils to devise their own three-step number sentences with a multiple choice of three or four possible answers, one of which is correct, the others of which should be plausible attempts (answers that are found by working out the operations in the wrong order). This is a harder task than it sounds as the numbers involved will have to be chosen carefully in order to still make a whole number when completed in the wrong order. Pupils should share their questions with peers, who get a point for each correctly identified answer.

Challenge and extension questions

Questions 5 and 6

5 Fill in the boxes first. Then write number sentences with mixed operations and work out the answers.

(a) 2000 →÷4→ ☐ →−323→ ☐ →×5→ ☐

Number sentence: _____

(b) ☐ →÷23→ ☐ →−76→ ☐ →×50→ 600

Number sentence: _____

6 Write the same number in the ☐ in each sentence to make the equation true.

(a) (☐ − ☐) × 5 + ☐ ÷ ☐ = 1

(b) (☐ + ☐ − ☐) ÷ (☐ + ☐) = 2

(c) ☐ ÷ ☐ + (☐ + ☐) ÷ ☐ = 3

(d) ☐ × ☐ × 2 ÷ (☐ + ☐) = 4

Pupils are given two sets of questions to further extend application of the order of operations. Question 5 involves a chain of operations (rather like a number machine) from a given input to an output (and *vice versa*). Pupils need to complete each operation, deriving the number sentence that reflects the chain as a whole. Where they are given the output first, pupils should use their knowledge of inverse operations to work backwards to establish the input.

For Question 6, pupils are required to complete a set of blank numbers in number sentences, repeating the same number throughout each sentence. Pupils should realise that each answer holds the clue to the missing numbers, but should be encouraged to use reasoning to explain why this is the case.

Chapter 5 Consolidation and enhancement

Unit 5.4
Properties of whole number operations (1)

Conceptual context

In this unit, pupils add to these strategies with the property of subtraction. This refers to the property in a subtraction with two or more subtrahends; these can be added first so as to leave one overall subtraction, for example a − b − c can be calculated as a − (b + c). This concept is applied as a further tool to enable pupils to simplify and calculate multistep number sentences (alongside prior knowledge of the order of operations and the commutative, associative and distributive laws).

Learning pupils will have achieved at the end of the unit

- A property of subtraction whereby two subtrahends can be combined to leave a one-step subtraction will have been introduced (Q1)
- Understanding of the relationship between subtraction and addition will have been deepened as pupils explore the properties of subtraction further (Q2, Q3)
- Pupils will have used the property of subtraction to simplify and calculate number sentences (Q3)
- Problem-solving skills will have been consolidated as pupils identify opportunities to use the property of subtraction in real-life contexts (Q4)

Resources

base ten blocks; 1–6 dice; a shopping receipt

Vocabulary

property of subtraction, addition, total, combine, minuend, subtrahend

Chapter 5 Consolidation and enhancement

Unit 5.4 Practice Book 5A, pages 127–129

Question 1

> **1** Work these out mentally and then write the answers.
>
> (a) $79 + 3 + 6 =$ ☐
> (b) $430 - 90 - 10 =$ ☐
> (c) $17 + 20 - 3 \times 1 =$ ☐
> (d) $96 - 16 - 4 =$ ☐
> (e) $80 - 2 \times 0 =$ ☐
> (f) $151 - (51 + 11) =$ ☐
>
> In solving the above questions, did you use any property of the subtraction operation? If so, in which questions?

What learning will pupils have achieved at the conclusion of Question 1?

- A property of subtraction whereby two subtrahends can be combined to form a one-step subtraction will have been introduced.

Activities for whole-class instruction

- Choose pupils to act out the following simple role play (referring to pupils by their letters will help later on):
  – Pupil A represents a cash machine containing £520 (modelled concretely by base ten blocks).
  – Pupil B withdraws £130.
  – Pupil C withdraws £70.
- Without counting the base ten blocks, can pupils say how much money the cash machine now has in it? How? Can they write it as a number sentence?
- Repeat the role play. This time, encourage Pupils B and C to combine the money they want to withdraw and only make one withdrawal of £200. Ask: *What do you notice? Can you write this as a number sentence?*
- Display the two number sentences as being equivalent:
  $520 - 130 - 70 = 520 - (130 + 70)$
- Ask pupils to describe these in words to provoke thought about what has happened. For example, 'When you subtract two numbers from a larger number, this is the same as combining them and subtracting their total.'
- Repeat, subtracting two amounts from another starting total.
- **Look out for** ... pupils who see the addition symbol and think that in some way they are adding to the total. The best way to combat this is to consider the brackets as a whole – these surround the amount that is going to be subtracted. The addition inside the brackets is simply a way of saying 'we are still going to take these numbers away; we are just going to combine the numbers before we do so'.

- Tell pupils that they have discovered one of the properties of subtraction – the properties are the rules that are always true for subtraction problems. Use the pupil letters from the role play to write the property using letters: $a - b - c = a - (b + c)$. Illustrate the property pictorially by showing $64 - 24 - 10$ and $64 - (24 + 10)$ as bar diagrams. Shade the parts that show what is being subtracted from 64 and show that this is the same (34) in both cases.
- Practise several further examples of the property. For example, ask: *How could we work out these subtractions in the same way?*

  $310 - 50 - 50$ $23 - 6 - 4$
  $65 - 23 - 7$ $78 - 21 - 28$

- Point out that some calculations combine more easily than others, for example 6 and 4 make 10, so $23 - 6 - 4$ instantly becomes easier when it is written as $23 - (6 + 4)$ or $23 - 10$.
- Display further calculations to answer mentally. Try 'hiding' these within a broad range of different calculations (including other subtractions as well as addition, multiplication and division calculations) so that pupils get into the habit of spotting those calculations where this property can be used. Ask pupils to only answer the calculations with which they can use this strategy to help.
- Pupils should complete Question 1 in the Practice Book.

Same-day intervention

- Split pupils into two groups. Give them the same two-digit starting number. Roll a 1–6 dice twice to generate two numbers. Group A should subtract the first number, then subtract the second. Group B should wait until they see both numbers and combine them before subtracting the total. For example:

Starting number: 57

Group A: $57 - 6 = 51$
           $51 - 1 = 50$
Group B: $6 + 1 = 7$
           $57 - 7 = 50$

- Ask: *What do you notice?* Show how both methods can be expressed as equivalent:

  $57 - 6 - 1 = 57 - (6 + 1)$

Chapter 5 Consolidation and enhancement

Unit 5.4 Practice Book 5A, pages 127–129

- Repeat for different examples. Ask further questions to encourage pupils to consider the usefulness of the strategy, for example: *Why might it be useful for Group B if the numbers on the dice are 6 and 4? If the starting number is 95, why might it be useful for Group A if the numbers are 5 and something else?*
- Encourage pupils to work out both methods themselves. Give examples that are not limited by numbers on a 1–6 dice.

Same-day enrichment

- Remind pupils of when it makes sense to use this property of subtraction and when it may be quicker not to combine the numbers. For example:

  89 – 51 – 9   51 and 9 make 60, so it is quicker to work out 89 – (51 + 9) or 89 – 60.

  178 – 78 – 15   78 can be quickly subtracted from 178 to leave 100, so it is quicker to just calculate 100 – 15.

- Challenge pupils to write three examples of each type of calculation – those that benefit from being combined before subtracting and those that do not. They should share their calculations for peers to answer (and identify the strategy that is most useful).

Question 2

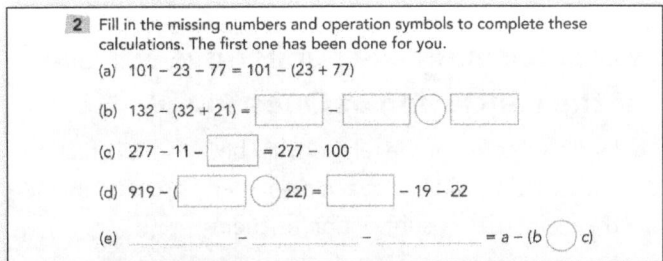

What learning will pupils have achieved at the conclusion of Question 2?

- Understanding of the relationship between subtraction and addition will have been deepened as pupils explore the properties of subtraction further.

Activities for whole-class instruction

- Remind pupils of the property of subtraction that they have been using. Write the following on the board:

  460 – 182 – 18

- Ask: *How could you use a different method to find the same answer? How would you rewrite the number sentence?* Agree that 182 and 18 could be combined to make 200 and then subtracted from 460:

  460 – 182 – 18
  = 460 – (182 + 18)

- Give two responses from imaginary pupils, discussing each as a class to provoke deeper reasoning:
  - Ellie says, 'It's a subtraction calculation, but by adding 182 and 18, aren't you making the answer bigger?'
- (Remind pupils that the bracketed addition shows what is *to be subtracted*. Adding the numbers simply combines them *ready to be subtracted*. Ensure pupils really grasp this point.)
  - Aled says, 'I can spot straight away that 182 and 18 make 200. Can't I just skip a step and write 460 – 200?'
- (The objective is to show pupils efficient subtraction strategies. So, although a question might ask pupils to write out each step, if they are working out an answer mentally this is a perfectly acceptable, and very efficient, method).
- Display blank number lines and model the two strategies that pupils have just discussed:

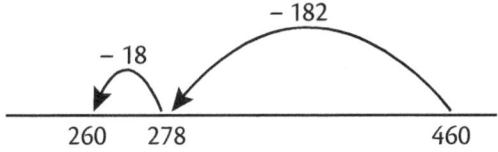

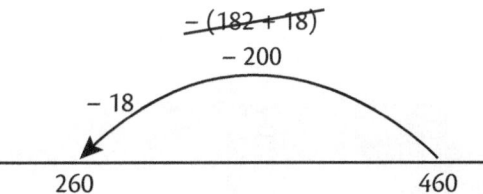

- Give pupils time to discuss in pairs why the strategy of adding the subtrahends before subtracting them works.
- Ask: *What is the same about these number lines? What is different? Can you explain why the answer is still the same, even though the second number line contains a + symbol?*
- Write:

  326 – 42 – 15 = 326 – (☐ ◯ ☐)

- Explain that each box contains a number and the circle contains an operation symbol. Ask: *What do we know about the order of operations in the second number sentence?* Ask pupils to use the property of subtraction to complete the gaps.
- Challenge pupils by querying the symbol they choose. For example, ask: *Shouldn't it be a – as both numbers are being*

235

Chapter 5 Consolidation and enhancement

Unit 5.4 Practice Book 5A, pages 127–129

taken away, not added? Draw a ring around the brackets to reinforce the fact that the amount being subtracted is contained within them.

- For each calculation, encourage pupils to model the subtraction using a blank number line to demonstrate that both strategies end with the same answer.
- Repeat for further examples with gaps in different places. Include examples where the addition has already been completed, for example:

  634 − 25 − ☐ = 634 − 200

  ... where the order is altered ...

  782 − (☐ ◯ 32) = ☐ ◯ 45 − 32

  ... and where letters replace numbers ...

  a − b − c = a ◯ (☐ ◯ ☐)

- Pupils should complete Question 2 in the Practice Book.

Same-day intervention

- Model examples where the minuend is shown concretely (using base ten blocks) and the subtrahends are shown using digit and symbol cards. For example, represent 120 − 14 − 5 as follows:

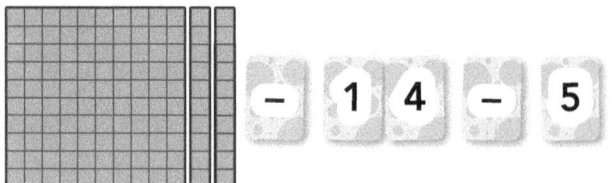

- Choose pupils to subtract 14 and then 5, describing what they are doing and how the base ten blocks change each time. Ask: *How much have you subtracted altogether?*

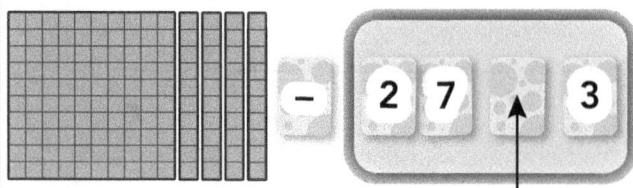

How do you know this is not a − symbol?

- Use a tray to represent brackets by placing the cards 14 + 5 in the tray. Ask: *If we add these numbers together, how many do we now need to subtract from 120?* Choose a pupil to model this.
- Ask: *Would you prefer to work out 120 − 14 − 5 or to combine 14 and 5 and work out 120 − 19? Why?*
- Repeat for further calculations, including examples where pupils have to question the symbols they are using.

Same-day enrichment

- In pairs, pupils should write a pair of equivalent number sentences demonstrating the property of subtraction they have been using. Before revealing their equation, they should use sticky notes to cover just enough numbers and symbols to allow the answer to be derived. They should share their puzzles with their partner who should use the property of subtraction to identify the missing parts and then find the answer.

Question 3

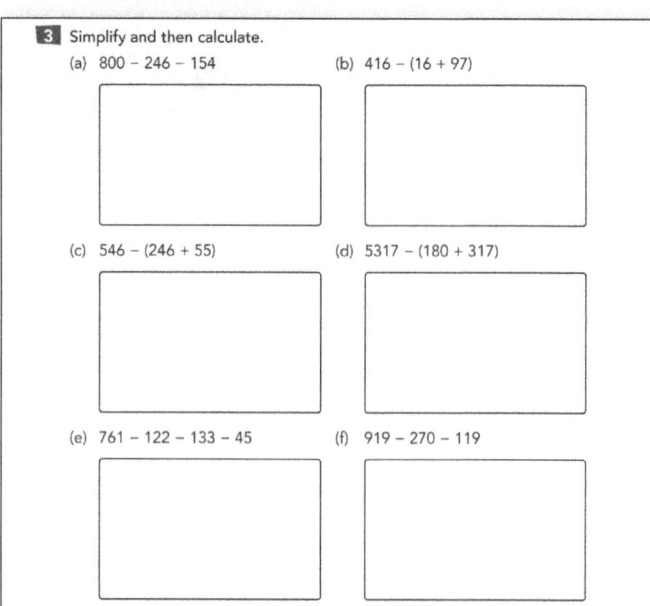

What learning will pupils have achieved at the conclusion of Question 3?

- Understanding of the relationship between subtraction and addition will have been deepened as pupils explore the properties of subtraction further.
- Pupils will have used the property of subtraction to simplify and calculate number sentences.

Activities for whole-class instruction

- Ensure pupils are able to describe the property of subtraction. Ask probing questions to ensure that they explore their reasoning more deeply, for example:
  - *How can a subtraction calculation have one of the subtraction symbols replaced with an addition symbol and still end up with the same answer? Give me an example of when this property might be useful.*

Chapter 5 Consolidation and enhancement

Unit 5.4 Practice Book 5A, pages 127–129

- *Give me an example of when you might choose **not** to add first. (For example, in the calculation 356 – 65 – 56, the 56 can be subtracted quickly, leaving the subtraction 300 – 65.) Explain this property without using any numbers at all.*
- Display a series of number sentences. Pupils should think individually about how to simplify each calculation, then discuss with a partner, and finally share answers as a class.
- Examples might include:

Example	Possible strategy	Simplified calculation
472 – (272 + 19)	Notice that 272 is easy to subtract from 472. Write as 472 – 272 – 19 and work out 472 – 272 first. Then subtract 19.	200 – 19 = 181
500 – 125 – 175	Notice that 125 and 175 can be combined to make 300. Write as 500 – (125 + 175) and work out the brackets.	500 – 300 = 200
414 – 201 – 114	Notice that 114 is easy to subtract from 414. Work out 414 – 114. Then subtract 201.	300 – 201 = 99

- Ensure that pupils can relate their strategies to the property of subtraction where they have used it. If not, they may be able to explain why they chose not to. Remind pupils that there are many ways to approach a calculation, and encourage pupils to consider which one seems the most efficient strategy to use.
- Pupils should complete Question 3 in the Practice Book.

Same-day intervention

- Write the calculation 513 – 75 – 25, where the subtrahends have been covered with sticky notes (but the subtraction symbols are still visible):

  513 – ▨ – ▨

- Explain that you are going to ask pupils to simplify the calculation before solving it. Ask: *What pairs of numbers might you be looking for if you want to simplify the calculation? Why?* Ensure that pupils understand that they are looking to find combinations that make multiples of 10 or 100 as these are easier numbers to calculate with. Possible answers might be '340 and 60', '50 and 50' and so on. Reveal the first subtrahend in the calculation by removing the sticky note.

  513 – 75 – ▨

- Ask: *What would you like the second subtrahend to be in order to help you answer the question more quickly?* Agree that 75 + 25 = 100, and so 25 would be a good number to see (encourage pupils to see that 125, 225, 335, … would be just as useful). Reveal the second subtrahend. Ask: *How can we work out the answer using the property of subtraction to help?*

  513 – (75 + 25)
  = 513 – 100
  = 413

- Ensure pupils can see the speed at which the calculation can be answered is a direct result of simplifying it (513 – 75 – 25 would take much longer).
- Repeat for further examples where part of the calculation is revealed and pupils are asked to predict what might be a helpful final number in order to simplify and then solve it.

Same-day enrichment

- Set pupils the challenge of exploring subtracting more than two numbers. Does the property work when three numbers are subtracted? Will it work for any number of subtrahends? Pupils should investigate and write each property using letters.
- Once they have found the answer, they should write their own subtractions – either in the format a – b – c – d or a – (b + c + d) for their peers to simplify and solve. Encourage them to consider the numbers that will make a calculation easier to simplify.

Question 4

4 A bicycle factory plans to make 1600 bikes in the first quarter. It made 520 bikes in January and 480 bikes in February. How many bikes does it need to make in March? (Use two methods to find the answer.)

Chapter 5 Consolidation and enhancement
Unit 5.4 Practice Book 5A, pages 127–129

What learning will pupils have achieved at the conclusion of Question 4?

- Problem-solving skills will have been consolidated as pupils identify opportunities to use the property of subtraction in real-life contexts.

Activities for whole-class instruction

- Show pupils a shopping receipt. Give them a moment to consider what it shows and then ask them to describe how a receipt works. Establish that this is a real-life example of the property of subtraction. Rather than paying for each item separately, the cashier adds them all together and then the customer pays one amount ('subtracting' one large figure). Ask: *Why is our strategy useful? What would life be like it we didn't use it?*

- Display the following problem:

  A lorry has to travel 578 miles to reach its destination. Yesterday it travelled 234 miles. Today it has travelled 66 miles. How many miles does it still have to travel?

- Ask: *What are the two methods you could use to find out the answer to the problem? Which would you choose and why?*

- Repeat for further problems so that pupils can apply the strategy in context. For example:

  Sam has £285 in his bank account. He buys a pair of trainers for £28 and a baseball cap for £13. How much does he have left?

- Pupils should complete Question 4 in the Practice Book.

Same-day intervention

- Display the following problem:

  There are 89 chickens in a field. One morning, 14 of them escape through a hole in the hedge. In the afternoon, another 16 of them leave too. How many chickens are now left?

- Ask two pupils to sit on chairs. Explain that they represent the two operations in a number sentence. Ask: *Who should complete their operation first?* Ensure pupils understand that Pupil A should work out 89 − 14 to work out how many chickens were left after the first lot escaped and then Pupil B should subtract 16 from the answer to work out how many were left at the end.

- Ask: *How else could we solve the problem?* Ensure pupils can see that this time Pupil B could find the total number of escaped chickens first (by working out 14 + 16) before Pupil A subtracts the answer from the original number of chickens to find out how many are left. Ask pupils to write these as two equivalent number sentences: 89 − 14 − 16 = 89 − (14 + 16)

- Give pupils time to devise their own word problems (and solutions) based on similar scenarios. They should share these for peers to model, then solve.

Same-day enrichment

- Pupils should invent role plays that show the two methods as real-life problems. For example, they might act out going to a shop and laboriously paying for a group of items separately (showing each individual subtraction) or the cashier totalling everything up and the customer making one payment (addition, then one subtraction).

- Pupils should show their scenes to others in the class (this might work well with the *Same-day intervention* group as it provides a visual representation of the strategies). Peers should use the strategy of their choice to solve each acted problem.

Challenge and extension questions

Question 5

5 Fill in the missing numbers and operation symbols to complete these calculations.

(a) 190 − 165 + 65 = ☐ − (☐ ○ 65)

(b) 142 − (☐ ○ 27) = 142 − 42 + ☐

Pupils are challenged to further consider the relationship between addition and subtraction, specifically whether a − b + c can be rewritten using brackets, similar to the subtraction property.

Chapter 5 Consolidation and enhancement

Unit 5.4 Practice Book 5A, pages 127–129

To answer this, pupils will again need to consider the operation inside the brackets separately, in this case considering it as the difference between b and c. Therefore, a − b + c is the same as a minus the difference between b and c or a − (b − c). The concept can be usefully demonstrated by encouraging pupils to model both calculation types on a number line:

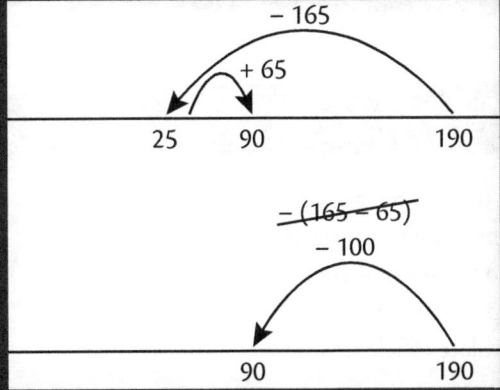

Show visually where the difference between 165 and 65 can be seen on the first number line (from 190 directly to 90) and that the second number line merely models this jump.

Question 6

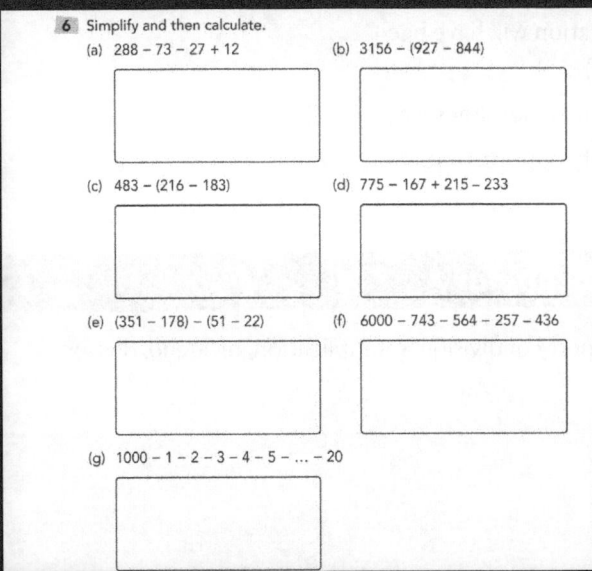

6 Simplify and then calculate.
(a) 288 − 73 − 27 + 12
(b) 3156 − (927 − 844)
(c) 483 − (216 − 183)
(d) 775 − 167 + 215 − 233
(e) (351 − 178) − (51 − 22)
(f) 6000 − 743 − 564 − 257 − 436
(g) 1000 − 1 − 2 − 3 − 4 − 5 − … − 20

Pupils are required to apply their understanding of the property of subtraction when simplifying more complex calculations. They should be encouraged to break each calculation down into parts and consider whether they can see examples of the property of subtraction that can be simplified. In some cases they should look for combinations of numbers that equal more manageable totals before finding the answers.

Chapter 5 Consolidation and enhancement

Unit 5.5
Properties of whole number operations (2)

Conceptual context

Continuing from the previous unit where pupils learned a property of subtraction, pupils are now introduced to a similar property for division. This means that where an amount is divided by two or more numbers (greater than zero), those numbers can be multiplied first to leave a one-step division. So, $a \div b \div c$ can be calculated as $a \div (b \times c)$. This concept enhances pupils' knowledge of whole number operations and gives them another strategy with which to calculate efficiently.

In the following unit, another property of division will be explored.

Learning pupils will have achieved at the end of the unit

- A property of division whereby two divisors can be multiplied to form the single divisor in a one-step division will have been introduced (Q1)
- Understanding of the relationship between division and multiplication will have been deepened as pupils explore properties of division further (Q2, Q3)
- Pupils will have used the property of division to simplify and calculate number sentences (Q2)
- Problem-solving skills will have been consolidated as pupils identify opportunities to use the property of division in real-life contexts (Q4)

Resources

mini whiteboards; beads or small countable objects; sticky notes; **Resource 5.5.5a** Blank 100 squares

Vocabulary

property of division, multiplication, dividend, divisor

Chapter 5 Consolidation and enhancement

Unit 5.5 Practice Book 5A, pages 130–132

Question 1

> **1** Fill in the missing numbers and operation symbols to complete these calculations.
>
> (a) 5100 ÷ (17 × 25) = 5100 ÷ ☐ ○ ☐
>
> (b) 1000 ÷ 25 ÷ 4 = 1000 ÷ (☐ ○ ☐)
>
> (c) 128 ÷ 8 ÷ 2 = ☐ ÷ (8 ○ 2)
>
> (d) 34 ÷ (☐ × 2) = 34 ÷ 17 ○ 2
>
> These answers are based on a property of division. As long as the numbers are greater than 0, we can write this as a ÷ b ÷ c = a ÷ (b ○ c)

What learning will pupils have achieved at the conclusion of Question 1?

- A property of division whereby two divisors can be multiplied to form the single divisor in a one-step division will have been introduced.

Activities for whole-class instruction

- Present the following scenario:
  - *200 people are leaving a concert by coach. They are split equally between two bus stops, one at the front of the building and one at the back.*
  - *Four coaches arrive at each bus stop. The same number of people get on each coach.*
- Ask: *How many people get on each coach? Can you write the calculation as a number sentence?*
- Repeat the scenario, this time expressing it slightly differently:
  - *200 people are waiting to leave a concert by coach. There are four bus stops and coaches arrive, two at a time, parking at each stop. The same number of people get on each coach.*
- Ask pupils whether they noticed the difference in the description. Can they express it as a number sentence?
- Display the two number sentences as being equivalent:
  200 ÷ 2 ÷ 4 = 200 ÷ (2 × 4)
- Ask pupils to describe the equation. For example, 'If we divide 200 by 2 and then divide the answer by 4, it is the same as dividing 200 by 8 (the product of 2 and 4)'. Challenge them to sketch the scenario:

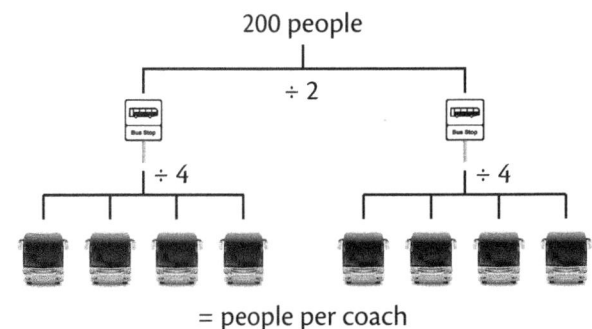

= people per coach

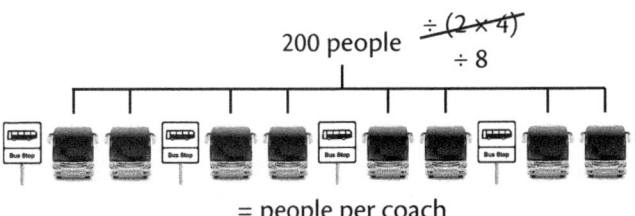

= people per coach

Look out for … pupils who see the multiplication symbol and think that in some way they are increasing the answer. This is extremely common. As with the subtraction property in Unit 5.4, the best way to combat this is to consider the brackets in their entirety – they surround the divisor. The multiplication inside the brackets is simply a way of combining the two parts of the divisor. Ask: *What have you learned before about how the size of the divisor affects the quotient?* Can pupils tell you that (if the dividend stays the same) the larger the divisor, the smaller the quotient? Can they illustrate this with examples?

- Write this property of division using letters as: a ÷ b ÷ c = a ÷ (b × c). Illustrate the property pictorially by showing 60 ÷ 2 ÷ 5 and 60 ÷ (2 × 5) as bar diagrams. Demonstrate that in both cases 60 is being divided into 10.

60	
30	30

60 ÷ 2

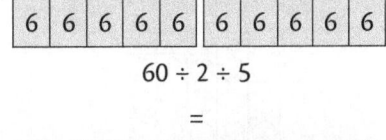

60 ÷ 2 ÷ 5

=

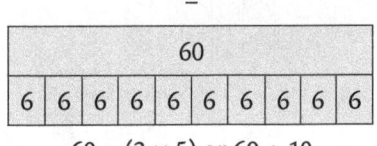

60 ÷ (2 × 5) or 60 ÷ 10

Chapter 5 Consolidation and enhancement　　　　　　　　　Unit 5.5 Practice Book 5A, pages 130–132

- As a further example to show pupils, the same model can be used to represent the calculation 140 ÷ 5 ÷ 4:

140				
28	28	28	28	28

140 ÷ 5

28	28	28	28	28
7 7 7 7	7 7 7 7	7 7 7 7	7 7 7 7	7 7 7 7

140 ÷ 5 ÷ 4

=

140
7 7 7 7 7 7 7 7 7 7 7 7 7 7 7 7 7 7 7 7

140 ÷ (5 × 4) or 140 ÷ 20

- Pupils should draw similar bar models to represent both ways of approaching the following:

　450 ÷ 25 ÷ 2　　120 ÷ 2 ÷ 2　　45 ÷ 3 ÷ 3　　312 ÷ 6 ÷ 4

- Move on to examples where some numbers and operation symbols are covered by two different-coloured sticky notes. Ask pupils to use reasoning to explain what the missing numbers and symbols are:

　420 ÷ 10 ÷ 2 = 420 ▓ (▓ ▓)

- Pupils should complete Question 1 in the Practice Book.

Same-day intervention

- Split pupils into two groups. Explain that their starting number will be 48. Write the numbers 6 and 4 on the board. Explain that pupils in Group A should physically divide 48 beads into 6 equal groups and then divide each of those into 4 equal groups. Group B should multiply 6 by 4 and then divide 48 by 24 by seeing how many groups of 24 will go into 48. For example:

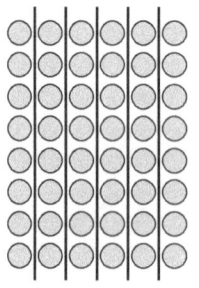

48 ÷ 6　　　48 ÷ 6 ÷ 4　=　48 ÷ (6 × 4)
　　　　　　　　　　　　　　　or 48 ÷ 24

- Ask: *What do you notice?*

- Repeat for further examples. For example: 30 ÷ 5 ÷ 2 (where the group of 30 is shown as a 5 × 6 array) and 36 ÷ 3 ÷ 2 (where the group of 36 is shown as a 6 × 6 array).
- Encourage pupils to work out both methods themselves and, where possible, become less reliant on concrete methods and more on mental strategies.

Same-day enrichment

- In pairs, pupils should write a pair of equivalent number sentences demonstrating this property of division. Before revealing their equation, they should use sticky notes to cover just enough numbers and symbols to allow the missing ones to be inferred. They should share their puzzles with their partner who should use the property of division to identify the covered parts and then find the answer.
- Encourage them to explain what they need to take into account when choosing the numbers in their equation. Does any pair of divisors work?

Question 2

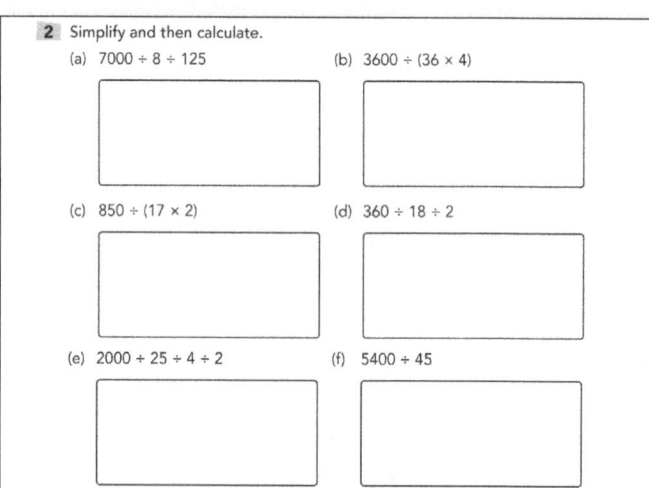

What learning will pupils have achieved at the conclusion of Question 2?

- Understanding of the relationship between division and multiplication is deepened as pupils explore the properties of division a ÷ b ÷ c = a ÷ (b × c) further.
- Pupils will have used this property of division to simplify and calculate number sentences.

Chapter 5 Consolidation and enhancement

Unit 5.5 Practice Book 5A, pages 130–132

Activities for whole-class instruction

- Ensure pupils are able to describe the property of division they have just learned. Ask questions to consolidate pupils' understanding, for example:
  - *Doesn't multiplication make numbers get larger? So, how can you replace a division symbol with a multiplication symbol and still end up with the same answer?*
  - *How could you use this property of division to help with dividing by difficult numbers?* (For example, 16 is the same as 8 × 2, so 192 ÷ 16 could be written as 192 ÷ (8 × 2), which is easier to calculate if it is considered as 192 ÷ 8 ÷ 2.)
  - *How important are the brackets in your number sentence and why?*
- Display a series of number sentences. First pupils should think individually about how to simplify each sentence, then discuss with a partner, and finally share answers as a class.
- Examples might include:

Example	Possible strategy	Simplified calculation
3000 ÷ 4 ÷ 125	Notice that 4 × 125 makes a multiple of 100. Write as 3000 ÷ (4 × 125) and work out the brackets.	3000 ÷ 500 = 6
5400 ÷ (54 × 25)	Notice that 5400 can be easily divided by 54. Write as 5400 ÷ 54 ÷ 25 and work out 5400 ÷ 54 first.	100 ÷ 25 = 4
5000 ÷ 50 ÷ 2 ÷ 5	Notice that 50 × 2 × 5 makes a multiple of 100. Write as 5000 ÷ (50 × 2 × 5)	5000 ÷ 500 = 10

- Ensure pupils link strategies to the property of division each time.
- Pupils should complete Question 2 in the Practice Book.

Same-day intervention

- Write the following calculation:

  100 ÷ 2 ÷ 10

- Provide pupils with **Resource 5.5.5a** Blank 100 squares.

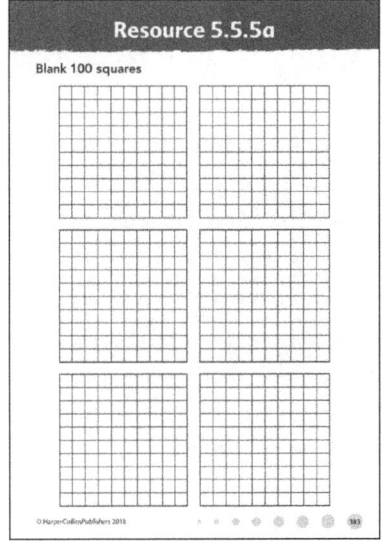

- Ask them to model the number sentence by drawing lines on their 100 square as follows:

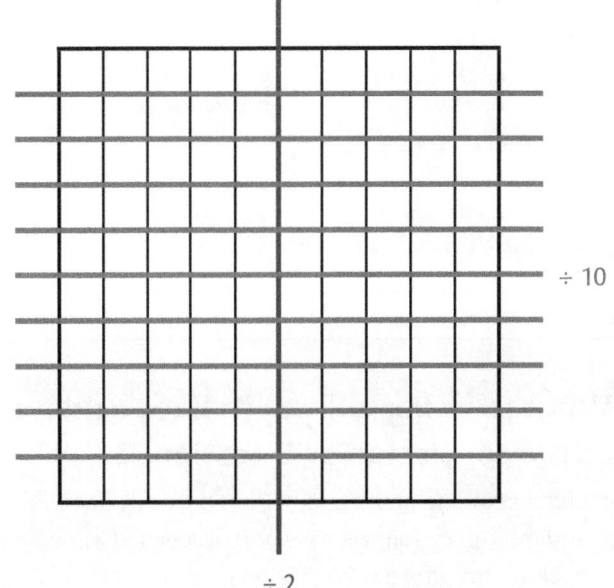

- Ask: *How many equal groups have you made?* Write:

  100 ÷ 2 ÷ 10 is the same as dividing the 100 square into 20 equal groups.

- Ask pupils what they notice. Establish that they could multiply 2 by 10 to get 20 and then split the whole amount into 20 directly. They could also divide the grid into blocks of 20 and show that there are 5 of them. Write:

  100 ÷ (2 × 10)

Chapter 5 Consolidation and enhancement

Unit 5.5 Practice Book 5A, pages 130–132

- Repeat for further division number sentences to allow pupils to identify the way the division property works. These could include:

  100 ÷ 5 ÷ 2   100 ÷ 10 ÷ 5   100 ÷ 5 ÷ 4   100 ÷ 10 ÷ 2

Same-day enrichment

- Set pupils the challenge of exploring division calculations containing more than two divisors. Does the property work for any number of divisors? Pupils should investigate and write each property using letters.
- Once they have found the answer, they should write their own divisions, either in the format a ÷ b ÷ c ÷ d or a ÷ (b × c × d) for their peers to simplify and solve. Encourage them to consider the numbers that will make a calculation easier to simplify.

Question 3

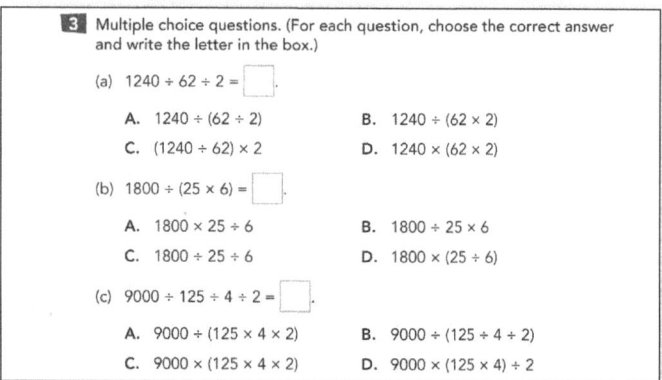

What learning will pupils have achieved at the conclusion of Question 3?

- Understanding of the relationship between division and multiplication will have been deepened as pupils explore this property of division further.

Activities for whole-class instruction

- Write the numbers 600, 6 and 2 on the board and ask pupils to write a large number sentence on their mini whiteboard that features those numbers in that order. They do not need to work out the answer – just invent the question. Explain that they are only allowed to use ÷ and/or × symbols and a pair of brackets if they wish. Encourage them to look at what their partner has written and try to write different number sentences if they can (so there is a variety).

- Choose four different pupils to stand at the front, holding up their mini whiteboards so that they show four multiple-choice answers (A, B, C or D). Ensure that one of the pupils chosen has written the sentence: 600 ÷ (6 × 2).

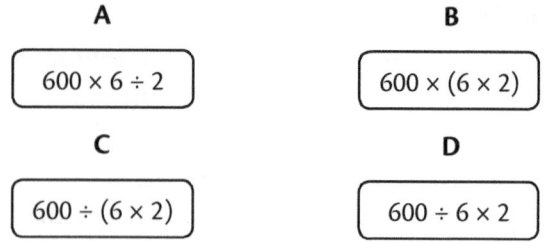

- Write 600 ÷ 6 ÷ 2. Encourage pupils to consider how they could write this another way so that it still gives the same answer. Confirm that one of the pupils at the front is showing the correct answer. Ask them to vote according to which answer they think is correct. Spend time ensuring pupils are able to explain why.
- Repeat for further self-generated multiple-choice questions. Alter the rules so that pupils work in the opposite direction too (starting with an a ÷ (b × c) calculation and linking it to an a ÷ b ÷ c calculation).
- Pupils should complete Question 3 in the Practice Book.

Same-day intervention

- Encourage pupils to model different possibilities when using the property of division. Write 20 ÷ 2 ÷ 2 = ? on the board and explain that they will be shown some possible answers. Write 20 × (2 × 2). Ask: *Is this equivalent? Why not?*
- Write three further number sentences and encourage pupils to use reasoning to explain which are equivalent, working out the answers where they are able:

  20 × (2 ÷ 2)   20 ÷ (2 × 2)   (20 ÷ 2) × 2

- Set pupils the challenge of sketching an array to show why 20 halved and halved again is the same as dividing it by 4. Repeat the activity for further number sentences, using numbers that are small enough to model using sketches or base ten blocks.

Same-day enrichment

- Pupils should complete the following activity in small groups. They should all write down a division calculation of the form a ÷ b ÷ c or a ÷ (b × c). Pupils should ensure that they have worked out the answer to their division and that it makes sense.

Chapter 5 Consolidation and enhancement

Unit 5.5 Practice Book 5A, pages 130–132

- Underneath, they should write the same three numbers four times, along with ÷ and × signs (and brackets), so that at least one of their calculations is equivalent.
- The mini whiteboards should be passed around the circle, with each pupil deciding the correct answer on the whiteboard in front of them each time. They should write these down on a piece of paper. When pupils have answered each question and the mini whiteboards have returned back to their original authors, pupils should go through their own questions, explaining to the group what the correct answer was and, crucially, why.

Question 4

4 (a) 240 pupils took part in the dance performance in a school's game day. They were grouped equally into 12 teams and each team was further grouped into two sub-teams. How many pupils were there in each sub-team on average? (Use two methods to find the answer.)

(b) Lily's class plans to plant trees. The whole class is equally grouped into four teams. £240 is used to purchase saplings. Each team plants six saplings on average. How much does each sapling cost?

What learning will pupils have achieved at the conclusion of Question 4?

- Problem-solving skills will have been consolidated as pupils identify opportunities to use the property of division in real-life contexts.

Activities for whole-class instruction

- Present the following scenario:
  - *A cinema has enough seats for 260 people. The seating is split into two equal sections with an aisle down the middle. Each section has 10 rows in it. How many seats are there in a row?*
- Ask pupils to sketch the problem for themselves. What operation(s) do they need to do to find the answer? Establish that there are two ways to find the answer:

METHOD 1:

Find the number of seats in a section by dividing 260 by 2

Find the number of seats in a row by dividing the answer by 10

Number sentence: 260 ÷ 2 ÷ 10

METHOD 2:

Find the number of rows in the whole cinema by multiplying 2 by 10

Find the number of seats in a row by dividing 260 by the answer

Number sentence: 260 ÷ (2 × 10)

- Give pupils time to check that both answers are the same. Ensure that they completely understand why Method 2 works – in effect, pupils are trying to create one division that reflects the whole problem, rather than completing two divisions in two steps (Method 1).
- Display further problems for pupils to work through. For each problem, ask: *What are the two methods you could use to find out the answer to the problem? Which would you choose and why?* Ask pupils to describe what they are doing with Method 2, in particular, so that they understand why this property of division works.
- Present the following scenario:
  - *A phone shop sells 546 mobile phone covers every week. It is open for seven days and each day it is open for six hours. The shop sells the same number of covers every hour. How many covers does it sell per hour?*
- Here, Method 2 is used to find the total number of hours the shop is open in a week before dividing the total sales by the total number of hours: 546 ÷ (6 × 7).
- Present the following scenario:
  - *A Year 5 teacher has 180 minutes before they need to go to bed. They have three piles of books left to mark. In each pile there are 20 books. To get it finished, how many minutes should they spend marking each book?*
- Here, Method 2 is used to find the total number of books before dividing the total number of minutes left by the total number of books: 180 ÷ (3 × 20).
- Pupils should complete Question 4 in the Practice Book.

Same-day intervention

- Present the following problem:
  - *There are 72 people waiting to leave a railway station in taxis. There are two rows of taxis ready to leave. Each row contains nine taxis. If the same number of people get in, how many people will be in each taxi?*

Chapter 5 Consolidation and enhancement

Unit 5.5 Practice Book 5A, pages 130–132

- Give pupils time to model the problem using whichever method they find most helpful. Ask: *How could we calculate the answer?* Establish that there are two possible methods:
- Go through Method 1 as a class before asking pupils to model it: First divide 72 by 2 to find the number of people that will go to each row of taxis. Then divide the answer by 9 to find out how many people will be in each taxi.
- Do the same for Method 2: First multiply 2 by 9 to find out the number of taxis there are altogether. Then divide 72 by the answer to find out how many people will be in each taxi.
- Ask: *How can we write these methods as number sentences?*
- With this example, it may be that finding the overall number of taxis first (Method 2) is pupils' first thought rather than Method 1. This is why they should experience a variety of problems. Different methods often seem more appropriate to different situations.
- Give pupils time to devise their own word problems (and solutions) based on similar scenarios. They should share these for peers to model, then solve.

Same-day enrichment

- Challenge pupils to write their own word problems that can be answered using either of the two methods they have learned. Explain that the easiest way to do this is to consider a large number of something that is split into a number of groups that are then themselves split into a number of groups. For example, they might write about 600 cans of soup that are packed into 10 boxes, with each box containing five trays. Or 50 children who are split between two classrooms with each classroom containing five groups. Pupils should share their problems with peers (this might work well with the *Same-day intervention* group, particularly if manipulatives are available to model the problem concretely).

Challenge and extension question

Question 5

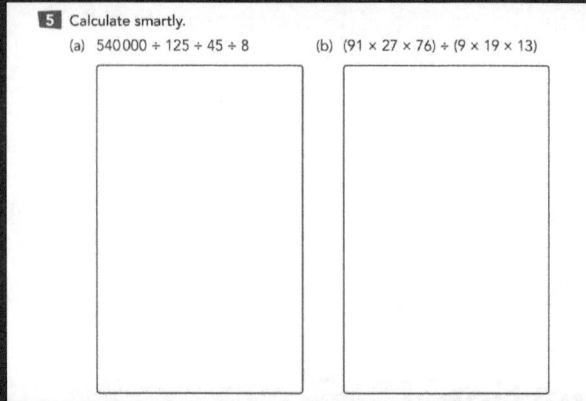

5 Calculate smartly.
(a) 540 000 ÷ 125 ÷ 45 ÷ 8
(b) (91 × 27 × 76) ÷ (9 × 19 × 13)

Pupils are given two calculations to calculate efficiently, using their knowledge of the property of division to help. The first requires them to identify that the divisors in a calculation can be combined through multiplication to leave one divisor. They should consider how to multiply these three divisors, looking for ways to combine them quickly.

In the second question, pupils are expected to reason that, where the same factors appear on both sides of a division symbol, they effectively 'cancel each other out' because the same value must be divided by itself. Therefore, by simplifying values into smaller factors, duplicate factors can often be revealed on both sides of the division symbol (on the top and bottom of a fraction) and these can then be eliminated, leaving a reduced/smaller/less complex calculation to be solved. Part b, (91 × 27 × 76) ÷ (9 × 19 × 13) is solved by factorising to:

(7 × 13 × 3 × 9 × 4 × 19) ÷ (9 × 19 × 13) =

After eliminating duplicates that appear on both sides, what is left is 7 × 3 × 4 = 84.

Chapter 5 Consolidation and enhancement

Unit 5.6
Properties of whole number operations (3)

Conceptual context

This is the last of three units where pupils are introduced to useful properties of operations, including the previous unit which featured a property of division. Here pupils are introduced to another property of division, this time relating to the fact that when both the dividend and the divisor in a calculation are either multiplied or divided by the same number, the quotient will remain the same. So, the answer to a ÷ b will be the same as (a ÷ c) ÷ (b ÷ c) and the same as (a × c) ÷ (b × c). Knowledge of this property enables pupils to identify efficient 'smart' ways to calculate.

Learning pupils will have achieved at the end of the unit

- A property of division – whereby the dividend and divisor can be multiplied by the same number (or divided by the same number) with no effect on the quotient – will have been introduced (Q1)
- Understanding of the relationship between division and multiplication will have been deepened as pupils explore the properties of division further (Q2, Q3)
- Pupils' reasoning skills will have been developed as they recognise, explain and apply this property of division (Q1, Q2, Q3)
- Pupils will have applied the property of division to simplify and calculate number sentences (Q4, Q5)

Resources

counters; several paper 100 squares; scissors; **Resource 5.5.6a** Derive the division!

Vocabulary

division, dividend, divisor, quotient, multiplication, property of division, column method

Chapter 5 Consolidation and enhancement Unit 5.6 Practice Book 5A, pages 133–137

Question 1

> **1** Complete each calculation and then fill in the spaces to make each statement correct.
>
> 24 ÷ 8 = ☐
>
> (24 × 10) ÷ (8 × 10) = ☐
>
> (24 × 3) ÷ (8 × 3) = ☐
>
> (24 ÷ 4) ÷ (8 ÷ 4) = ☐
>
> (24 ÷ 8) ÷ (8 ÷ 8) = ☐
>
> (24 × 100) ÷ (8 × 100) = ☐
>
> Observing the calculations above, we can find that when both the dividend and the divisor are _____ or _____
>
> by the same number (except zero), their _____ remains unchanged. These answers are based on a property of
>
> _____. As long as the numbers are greater than 0, we can write this as:
>
> $a \div b = (a \times c) \div (b \bigcirc c)$
>
> $a \div b = (a \div c) \div (b \bigcirc c)$

What learning will pupils have achieved at the conclusion of Question 1?

- A property of division – whereby the dividend and divisor can be multiplied by the same number (or divided by the same number) with no effect on the quotient – will have been introduced.

Activities for whole-class instruction

- Present this scenario:

  The council wants to build a car park holding 100 cars, split equally over two levels.

- Ask: *How many cars will be on each level of the car park?* Agree the problem can be represented as 100 ÷ 2 = 50 and the answer is the quotient, 50.

- Choose a pupil to cut a 100 square to represent the division and also ask: *How can we model this as a bar diagram?* Show the different representations next to each other to build connections between the concrete, pictorial and the abstract.

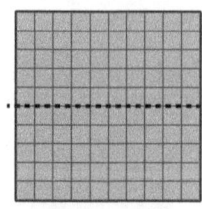

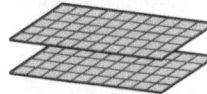

100 ÷ 2 = 50

- Explain that division calculations have an interesting property that means the numbers in the division can be altered in different ways *so that the quotient stays the same*. Alter the scenario to the following:

  The council chooses to double the total amount the car park holds to 200. But they really like the idea of keeping 50 cars per level constant. How many levels should they now build?

- Alter the calculation to 200 ÷ ? = 50 and choose pupils to demonstrate how to split two 100 squares stuck together (double 100) in order to keep the quotient (the number of cars on each level) constant. Ask: *What should we divide 'double 100' by to still have an answer of 50?* Establish that the answer is equal to double the original divisor (double 2 = 4). Again, ask pupils to represent this as a bar diagram:

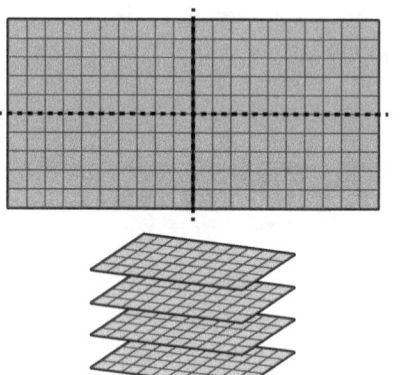

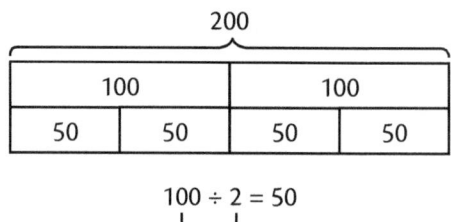

$100 \div 2 = 50$

×2 ↓   ↓ ×2

$200 \div 4 = 50$

- Consider the two calculations and how they can be written as 100 ÷ 2 = (100 × 2) ÷ (2 × 2). Ask: *Can you describe this using your own words?*

   *The quotient of 100 ÷ 2 is the same as the quotient of double 100 ÷ double 2. If we multiply both the dividend and the divisor by the same number, the quotient will stay the same.*

- Ask: *Do you think this might be true if we divided both numbers by the same number?* Alter the car park scenario as follows:

  The council decides that 100 cars is too many, so they halve the number allowed into the car park. How many levels will they need to keep 50 cars per level?

Chapter 5 Consolidation and enhancement

Unit 5.6 Practice Book 5A, pages 133–137

- Write 50 ÷ ? = 50 to clarify that this is now the calculation.
- Encourage pupils to use the various models they have used already to show that (100 ÷ 2) ÷ (2 ÷ 2) (or 50 ÷ 1) is the same as the original calculation of 100 ÷ 2.

 *The quotient of 100 ÷ 2 is the same as the quotient of half of 100 ÷ half of 2. If we divide both the dividend and the divisor by the same number, the quotient will stay the same.*

- Talk about the algebraic representation and that this property works because:

  1) The operations inside both brackets are the same, that is, the signs are either both × or both ÷.

  2) Both numbers are being altered by the same value (c), so they are being changed in *exactly the same way*.

- Pupils should complete Question 1 in the Practice Book.

Same-day intervention

When intervening with pupils who may need further support before reaching mastery, it is not a recommended tactic to merely make the numbers easier to deal with. However, in this particular case, simplifying the numbers may be a useful starting point to allow pupils to grasp the property being introduced. It allows them to focus less on the numbers and more on the process. Once they understand *why* it works, they can then apply it to more complicated calculations.

- Write the calculation 12 ÷ 2. Give the problem a context and discuss a class of 12 children being asked to split into two equal groups. Pupils should demonstrate this using counters:

  12 ÷ 2 = 6

  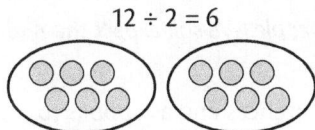

- Explain that the class size then doubles. Write the new calculation:

  12 ÷ 2 = 6
  × 2 ↓   ↓
  24 ÷ 2 = ?

- Ask: *How many pupils would you expect to be in each group now?* Establish that, because the dividend has been doubled, we'd expect the quotient to double too – the number of children in the class is twice as large, so twice as many children will be in both groups (12). Check pupils understand this and can explain it in their own words.

- Explain that the teacher in the problem thought that the children worked really well in groups of six and wants to keep them this size. Ask: *What should we divide by if we want the answer to stay the same?*

  12 ÷ 2 = 6
  × 2 ↓   ↓
  24 ÷ ? = 6

- Pupils should use counters to demonstrate this, sharing 24 into groups of six and showing that there are four groups.

  12 ÷ 2 = 6
  × 2 ↓   ↓ × 2
  24 ÷ 4 = 6

  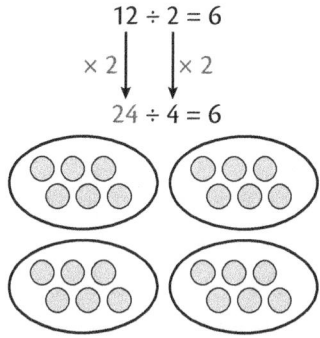

- Ask: *What do you notice?* Establish that the dividend (12) and divisor (2) have both been doubled, yet the answer stays the same. Although the class has become twice as large, the number of groups has also doubled, so the number in each group will remain the same. Discuss the property: 12 ÷ 2 = (12 × 2) ÷ (2 × 2).

 *The quotient of 12 ÷ 2 is the same as the quotient of double 12 ÷ double 2. If we multiply both the dividend and the divisor by the same number, the quotient will stay the same.*

- Repeat the activity for further examples, maintaining the simple numbers and giving each example a context that is referred to throughout.

Same-day enrichment

- Pupils should work in pairs and both write two equivalent number sentences demonstrating this property of division, for example 45 ÷ 9 = (45 × 3) ÷ (9 × 3). Before passing their mini whiteboard to their partner, they should erase two of the numbers, chosen so that they can still be inferred. For example: 45 ÷ 9 = (☐ × 3) ÷ (☐ × 3). They should then share their puzzles with their partner who should use this property of division to complete the calculation and then find the answer.

249

Chapter 5 Consolidation and enhancement

Unit 5.6 Practice Book 5A, pages 133–137

- Encourage pupils to alter their dividend and divisors in different ways. Can they give an example where the dividend and divisor are divided? How much of their puzzle can they erase and still keep it solvable?

Question 2

> 2 Find the number sentences that have the same answer as (a). Put a ✓ or a ✗ in the box.
> (a) 375 ÷ 125 = 3
> (b) (375 ÷ 3) ÷ (125 ÷ 3)
> (c) (375 ÷ 5) ÷ (125 ÷ 25)
> (d) (375 × 3) ÷ (125 ÷ 3)
> (e) (375 × 10) ÷ (125 × 10)

What learning will pupils have achieved at the conclusion of Question 2?

- Understanding of the relationship between division and multiplication will have been deepened as pupils explore properties of division further.
- Pupils' reasoning skills will be developed as they recognise, explain and apply this property of division.

Activities for whole-class instruction

- Display the following:
  $a ÷ b = (a × c) ÷ (b × c)$
  $a ÷ b = (a ÷ c) ÷ (b ÷ c)$
- Ask pupils to describe this property in their own words. For example, 'If I change the two numbers in a division calculation by multiplying or dividing them both in the same way, the answer will stay the same.'

If I change the two numbers in a division calculation by multiplying or dividing them both in the same way, the answer will stay the same.

- Present this scenario:

  A breakfast cereal company has 350 mini boxes of cereal to split between the first 50 people who enter their competition. How many boxes of cereal will each person receive?

- Remind pupils once more that the property of division is all about trying to keep the answer constant, even when the numbers in the division change. Tweak the scenario so that it now becomes:

The company really likes the idea of everyone getting seven boxes because it means they can advertise the competition as 'WIN BREAKFAST FOR A WEEK!' But they only want to offer half as many boxes (half of 350). How many people can they pick as winners?

- Rewrite the number sentence as:

  (350 ÷ 2) ÷ ? = 7

- Ask: *How should we alter the dividend so that the quotient stays as 7?*

If I change the two numbers in a division calculation by multiplying or dividing them both in the same way, the answer will stay the same.

- Agree that the two numbers must be altered in the same way. As 350 has been halved, 50 must also be halved. Write this as (350 ÷ 2) ÷ (50 ÷ 2) and ask pupils to find the answer by working out the brackets to get 175 ÷ 25 = 7.

- Write (350 × 10) ÷ (50 ÷ 10) on the board. Ask: *Is this true? How do you know?* Pupils may answer correctly that it is false because the dividend and the divisor are both being altered in different ways. However, encourage them to also consider what the calculation has become and the reason *why* it no longer works.

  (350 × 10) ÷ (50 ÷ 10) is the same as writing 3500 ÷ 10, which equals 350 boxes each, not 7.

- Return to the analogy of the competition to show that this makes no sense:

  'Let's go crazy and give away 10 times as many boxes of breakfast cereal! But we'll just split them between a tenth of the original number of people. We still expect them all to only get seven boxes!'

- Display further number sentences and ask pupils to say whether they have the same answer as 350 ÷ 50. For example:

  (350 × 10) ÷ (50 × 10)
  (350 × 10) ÷ (50 ÷ 10)
  (350 ÷ 10) ÷ (50 ÷ 2)
  (350 ÷ 5) ÷ (50 ÷ 5)

- Pupils should complete Question 2 in the Practice Book.

Chapter 5 Consolidation and enhancement

Unit 5.6 Practice Book 5A, pages 133–137

Same-day intervention

- Write on the board:

    24 ÷ 6 = ?

- Ask: *Which part of the calculation is the dividend? Which is the quotient? Which is the divisor?* Remind pupils of the property of division they have been considering – that they can alter the dividend and the divisor so that the quotient remains the same.

 *If I change the two numbers in a division calculation by multiplying or dividing them both in the same way, the answer will stay the same.*

- Split pupils into two groups and explain that one will be responsible for the dividend and the other for the divisor. Write the calculation (24 × 2) ÷ (6 × 2). Only show the first bracket to the 'dividend' group and the second bracket to the 'divisor' group. Ask each group to reveal the operation that has been applied to their number.

- Ask: *Have they changed in the same way? Will the quotient stay the same?* Establish that the calculation has now become 48 ÷ 12, which still equals 4 because both numbers were multiplied by the same amount. Repeat for further calculations related to 24 ÷ 6. For example:

    (24 ÷ 2) ÷ (6 ÷ 3)

    (24 ÷ 2) ÷ (6 × 2)

    (24 ÷ 2) ÷ (6 ÷ 2)

- Emphasise the 'meeting of minds' between the two groups and that the only way the quotient will stay the same is if both dividend and divisor are altered *in exactly the same way*. Show pupils a series of full calculations. Encourage them to circle the operations so that they can compare them immediately and recognise whether the property applies.

Same-day enrichment

- Split pupils into groups of four. Each pupil should take a piece of paper and write a division calculation at the top of it, complete with answer. They should then pass the paper to their left.

- Each pupil will now have a piece of paper with a division at the top. They should look at the calculation and, underneath it, write a division where the dividend and divisor are altered in some way (deciding whether or not they wish to keep the quotient the same or not). For example, if the original calculation is 176 ÷ 16 = 11, the second pupil's calculation might be (176 ÷ 2) ÷ (16 × 2) = 11 (which would be an example of an incorrect alteration).

- Pupils should pass their pieces of paper two more times until they then end up with their original calculation and three possible variants. Their task is to decide which of the altered divisions is the same as their original calculation. Pupils should share these problems and challenge each other with them.

Question 3

> **3** Using the above property of division calculation, fill in the spaces. Complete the statements for each division calculation by filling in the missing numbers.
>
> (a) The quotient of two numbers is 24. If the dividend is divided by 8 and the quotient remains unchanged, the divisor should be _____.
>
> (b) One number is divided by another. If the dividend is divided by 10 and the divisor is also divided by 10, the quotient remains _____.
>
> (c) One number is divided by another and the quotient is 71. If both the dividend and the divisor are multiplied by 11, the quotient is ☐.
>
> (d) ☐ ÷ 50 = 115 ÷ 5 = 230 ÷ ☐ = 460 ÷ ☐.

What learning will pupils have achieved at the conclusion of Question 3?

- Understanding of the relationship between division and multiplication will have been deepened as pupils explore properties of division further.

- Pupils' reasoning skills will have been developed as they recognise, explain and apply this property of division.

Activities for whole-class instruction

- Write a division calculation, with boxes where the unknown numbers are:

    ☐ ÷ ☐ = ☐

- Call out the terms 'dividend', 'divisor' and 'quotient' in different orders and get pupils to point to the corresponding part in the division that each term describes.

- Display the following sentence:

Chapter 5 Consolidation and enhancement

Unit 5.6 Practice Book 5A, pages 133–137

The quotient of two numbers is 30. If the dividend is divided by 8 and the quotient remains unchanged, the divisor should be ...

- Ask pupils to relate this to the blank calculation, altering it so that it looks like this:

  $$\square \div \square = 30$$
  $$\div 8 \downarrow \quad \downarrow \quad \downarrow$$
  $$\square \div \square = 30$$

- Ask: *How could we write this using letters?* For example: $a \div b = 30$ and then $(a \div 8) \div (b \square \square) = 30$. Remind pupils of the property of division and establish that the way to keep the quotient constant is to change the dividend and divisor in the same way. So the number sentence should become $(a \div 8) \div (b \div 8)$ and the original sentence should be completed with the words 'the divisor should be divided by 8'.

- Work in the same way with similar example sentences. For example:

  A number is divided by another. If the dividend is multiplied by 3 and the divisor is also multiplied by 3, the quotient will be ...

  A number is divided by another and the quotient is 26. If both the dividend and the divisor are halved, the quotient will be ...

  The quotient of a division is 82. If the divisor is doubled and the quotient stays the same, the dividend should be ...

- Pupils should complete Question 3 in the Practice Book.

Same-day intervention

- Ask pupils to all write out the division $54 \div 2$ and to work out the quotient. Display the following statement:

  The quotient of two numbers is 27. If the dividend is doubled and the quotient remains the same, the divisor must also be doubled.

- Read it aloud three times, once so that pupils can just listen to it (the key words can sometimes seem confusing), a second time where they point to the specific parts of the calculation that are being referred to, and a third time where they alter the numbers in their division (which will now read either $(54 \times 2) \div (2 \times 2)$ or $108 \div 4$ (both of which show understanding of the property of division).

- Pupils should explain why the answer has not changed. Repeat for further divisions and statements, then gradually alter the statements so that they become questions:

  The quotient of two numbers is X. If the dividend is divided by 3 and the quotient remains the same, <u>what must have happened to the divisor?</u>

Same-day enrichment

- Provide pupil pairs with **Resource 5.5.6a** Derive the division!

- The activity encourages one pupil to start with a secret division calculation and then alter it according to the property of division (so that the quotient remains the same). They then provide their partner with specific facts about the new calculation. Their partner should work backwards, using inverse operations and the facts they have been told, to derive the original 'secret' calculation. The aim of the activity is to help pupils make connections between simple division calculations and related calculations that have been altered using this property.

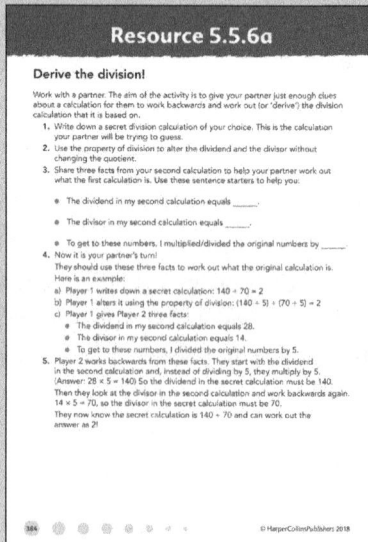

Chapter 5 Consolidation and enhancement

Unit 5.6 Practice Book 5A, pages 133–137

Questions 4 and 5

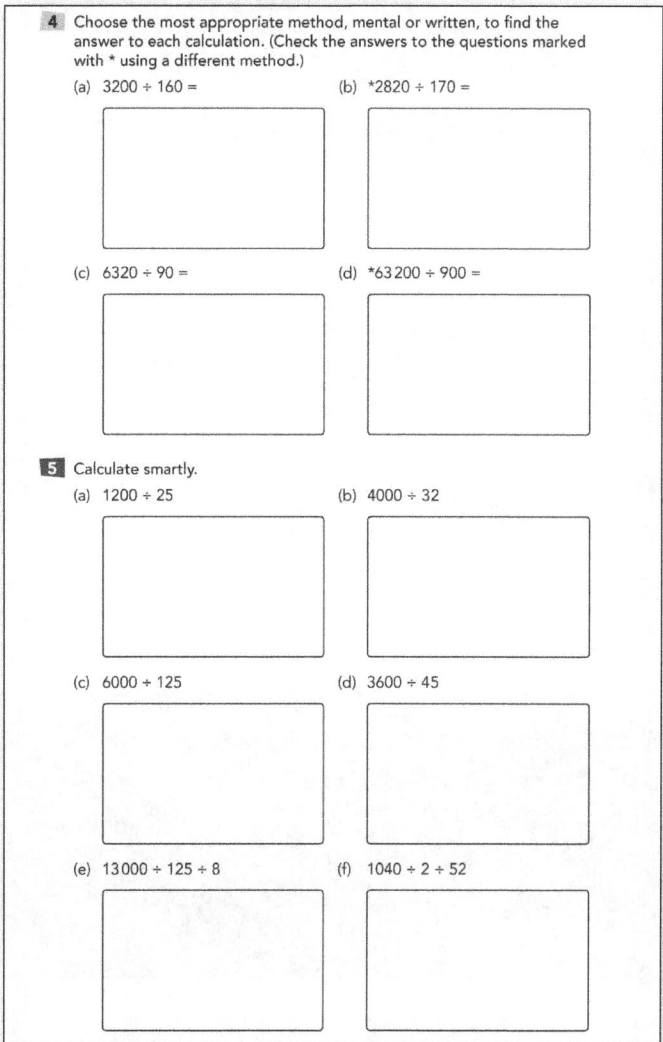

What learning will pupils have achieved at the conclusion of Questions 4 and 5?

- Pupils will have applied the property of division to simplify and calculate number sentences.

Activities for whole-class instruction

- Check that pupils can confidently describe the property of division they have learned in this unit. Ask probing questions to assess pupils' understanding, for example:
  - By multiplying the divisor in a calculation, aren't you making the number a lot bigger? So how does the answer stay the same when you are starting with a much larger number?
  - How could you use this property of division to help with dividing by difficult numbers?

  – Division and multiplication have the same priority in the order of operations. So why do we need to use brackets in number sentences that demonstrate this property of division, such as (100 × 5) ÷ (20 × 5)?

- Display a series of number sentences. Pupils should work in pairs to come up with possible simplification strategies. Examples might include:

Example	Possible strategy	Simplified calculation
2700 ÷ 54	Divide both numbers by 9 to get 300 ÷ 6 without affecting the answer. Simplify further by dividing both numbers by 3 to get 100 ÷ 2.	100 ÷ 2 = 50
1400 ÷ 25	Multiply both numbers by 4 to get 5600 ÷ 100 without affecting the answer.	5600 ÷ 100 = 56
19 000 ÷ 8 ÷ 125	Use the previous property of division to alter this to 19 000 ÷ (8 × 125).	19 000 ÷ 1000 = 19

- Ensure pupils apply the property of division each time. Note that some of these calculations benefit from dividing the dividend and divisor to make them smaller, others benefit from using multiplication to make them larger. In every instance, pupils' decisions should be based on 'what will make this calculation simpler to work out?'

- Pupils should complete Questions 4 and 5 in the Practice Book.

Same-day intervention

- Briefly revise how to divide numbers by 10 and 100. Ask pupils to write the calculation 300 ÷ 5 on their mini whiteboard. Ask them how they could alter it so that they are now dividing by 10. Remind them that, if they double the divisor, they also need to double the dividend to ensure that the answer stays the same. Pupils should cross out each number, replacing it with its double so that the calculation now reads 600 ÷ 10, and they can then work out the answer. Write the entire original calculation to show that the answer is the same for this (300 ÷ 5 = 60).

Chapter 5 Consolidation and enhancement Unit 5.6 Practice Book 5A, pages 133–137

- Give pupils further calculations where the divisor can easily be changed into either 10 or 100. For example:

  250 ÷ 5

  150 ÷ 25

  120 ÷ 20

- To practise the skill of identifying opportunities to apply this property, challenge pupils by giving them sets of three calculations to consider, where only one of the three divisors can be simplified into a ÷ 10 or ÷ 100 calculation. They should only answer the one that they can easily simplify.

Same-day enrichment

- Questions 5(e) and (f) involved two-step divisions. Set pupils the challenge of exploring similar calculations containing two divisors and applying the property of division they have studied. Does this property work for a ÷ b ÷ c? Write several examples on the board for pupils to begin with:

  Is 45 ÷ 3 ÷ 3 the same as (45 × 2) ÷ (3 × 2) ÷ (3 × 2) and (45 × 3) ÷ (3 × 3) ÷ (3 × 3)?

  Is 160 ÷ 5 ÷ 4 the same as (160 × 2) ÷ (5 × 2) ÷ (4 × 2)?

  Is 96 ÷ 8 ÷ 2 the same as (96 ÷ 2) ÷ (8 ÷ 2) ÷ (2 ÷ 2)?

  (i) Pupils should be able to explain *why* calculations with two divisors do not behave in this way. Consider whether 45 ÷ 3 ÷ 3 is the same as if each number were doubled. The first part of the calculation (the 45 ÷ 3 part) equals 15 and the property of division states that this will remain the same when both numbers are doubled (90 ÷ 6 = 15). However, instead of dividing 15 by 3 (as in the final step of the original calculation), in the doubled calculation 15 is divided by double 3, leading to a completely different answer (half as large as it should be). So the property only works for one-step divisions.

Challenge and extension questions

Question 6

6 Multiple choice questions. (For each question, choose the correct answer and write the letter in the box.)

(a) The result of 4100 ÷ 700 is ☐.

  A. quotient 5 with remainder 6
  B. quotient 5 with remainder 600
  C. quotient 500 with remainder 6
  D. quotient 500 with remainder 600

(b) One number is divided by another number. If the dividend is multiplied by 2 and the divisor is divided by 2, the quotient is ☐.

  A. unchanged
  B. multiplied by 2
  C. divided by 2
  D. multiplied by 4

(c) In 120 ÷ 40, if the dividend increases by 120, then in order to keep the quotient unchanged, the divisor should ☐.

  A. increase by 120
  B. increase by 100
  C. increase by 80
  D. increase by 40

This question focuses specifically on the property of division featured. Pupils are required to apply the property to new scenarios (for example, a calculation with a remainder). They are given a group of multiple choice answers and so are guided in their thinking.

Question 7

7 Think carefully and work out the answers.

(a) Two numbers are added together. If one addend is increased by 20 and the other addend is also increased by 20, what is the change to the sum?

(b) One number is subtracted from another number. If the subtrahend is decreased by 10 and the difference remains unchanged, what is the change to the minuend?

(c) The quotient of two numbers is 48. If the dividend is multiplied by 10 and the divisor is divided by 10, what is the quotient now?

(d) Two numbers are multiplied together. If one factor is multiplied by 10 and the other is divided by 10, does the product remain the same?

Pupils are encouraged to consider the effect that altering different parts of other calculations can have on the final answer (for example, if both addends in an addition increase by 20). These examples challenge and extend pupils' reasoning.

Chapter 5 Consolidation and enhancement

Unit 5.7
Roman numerals including thousands

Conceptual context

Pupils have previously learned about Roman numerals to 100. This unit extends the number system up to 1000.

1	5	10	50	100	500	1000
I	V	X	L	C	D	M

The symbols are generally written in order, from the largest on the left to the smallest on the right and then added together to give the number. For example:

2 is II

6 is VI

13 is XIII

25 is XXV

There is a rule when writing Roman numerals that more than three identical symbols in a row are not permitted, so 4 is not written as IIII. For numbers containing 4 or 9, I is shown preceding the next multiple (of 5, 10, 50, …).

4	6	9	10	40	60	90	110	400	600	900
IV	VI	IX	XI	XL	LX	XC	CX	CD	DC	CM

By using a combination of multiple symbols, every number can be written, for example:

112	340	400	504	600	799	949
CXII	CCCXL	CD	DIV	DC	DCCXCIX	CMXLIX

This number system differs greatly from the base ten place value system that pupils are familiar with.

Roman numerals are still used today, for example:

- names of kings, queens and popes, for example King Henry VIII, Pope John Paul II
- on clock faces
- on buildings to mark the year of construction
- in film and TV programme credits, to show the year of production.

Learning pupils will have achieved at the end of the unit

- The symbols for Roman numerals will have been revised and extended (Q1)
- Pupils will have interpreted numbers written in Roman numerals (Q1, Q2, Q3)

Chapter 5 Consolidation and enhancement Unit 5.7 Practice Book 5A, pages 138–139

- Pupils will have practised adding symbols to find the value of numbers in Roman numerals, recognising that symbols are generally written in order, from the largest on the left to the smallest on the right (Q1, Q2, Q3)
- Pupils will have explored the rule that, in Roman numerals, when a symbol for a smaller number appears to the left of any symbol, that number should be subtracted (Q2, Q3)
- Pupils will have discussed how, over time, the numeral system changed to include the concept of zero and place value (Q3)

Resources

A5 cards with 1, 5, 10, 50, 100, 500 and 1000, I, V, X, L, C, D and M; mini whiteboards; 0–9 dice; blank dice; **Resource 5.5.7a** Roman numerals; **Resource 5.5.7b** Roman numeral sequences; **Resource 5.5.7c** Famous dates; **Resource 5.5.7d** Before and after

Vocabulary

Roman numerals I, V, X, L, C, D, M

Chapter 5 Consolidation and enhancement　　　　　Unit 5.7 Practice Book 5A, pages 138–139

Question 1

> **1** Complete the table to show the value of each Roman numeric symbol in digits. One has been done for you.
>
> | Roman symbol | Value in digits |
> |---|---|
> | I | |
> | V | |
> | X | |
> | L | 50 |
> | C | |
> | D | |
> | M | |

What learning will pupils have achieved at the conclusion of Question 1?

- The symbols for Roman numerals will have been revised and extended.
- Pupils will have interpreted numbers written in Roman numerals.
- Pupils will have practised adding symbols to find the value of numbers in Roman numerals, recognising that symbols are generally written in order, from the largest on the left to the smallest on the right.

Activities for whole-class instruction

- Show a shot of the closing credits of a TV programme or film with the date in Roman numerals and ask pupils if they know what these letters represent. Agree that they are Roman numerals.
- Remind pupils that the number system the Romans used is completely different from the base ten place value system that we use today. Our system allows calculations to be carried out more easily because we can add and subtract in columns.
- Ask: *Why do we learn the Roman system?* Listen to their ideas. Explain that the Roman number system is still used today, as in TV programmes, film dates, for kings and queens. Show pupils the table of symbols.

Roman symbol	Value in numerals
I	1
V	5
X	10
L	50
C	100
D	500
M	1000

- Explain that you can easily remember the letters C for 100 and M for 1000 from words we use in English. The Latin word for 100, 'centum', has given us, for example the words **c**entury, **c**entimetre, and the word for a thousand, 'mille', has given us, for example **m**illimetre, **m**illilitre, **m**illennium.
- Give pupils mini whiteboards. Use a set of cards I, V, X, L, D, C, M. Shuffle the cards and show the top card and ask pupils to write the number for a particular symbol, for example 50. Repeat with more cards.
- Repeat using a set of numbered cards, 1, 5, 10, 50, 100, 500, 1000, this time asking the pupils to write the Roman numeral symbol on their mini whiteboard.
- When pupils are confident with the symbols, explain that to make the numbers in between, the symbols are generally written in order, from the largest on the left to the smallest on the right, and then added. Work together on some examples.

  XI = 10 + 1 = 11

  CXII = 100 + 10 + 1 + 1 = 112

  MDV = 1000 + 500 + 5 = 1505

- Give pupils further examples and ask them to write the answers on their mini whiteboards. At this stage, avoid examples where subtraction is involved (numbers involving the digits 4 and 9).

 *To work out a number from Roman numerals, arrange the symbols in decreasing order from the left and add the values.*

- Pupils should complete Question 1 in the Practice Book.

Chapter 5 Consolidation and enhancement

Unit 5.7 Practice Book 5A, pages 138–139

Same-day intervention

- Give pupil pairs **Resource 5.5.7a** Roman numerals. They play a matching game. The number of cards pupils use to play can be reduced if necessary to make the game simpler.

Same-day enrichment

- Give pupil pairs two blank 1–6 dice and ask them to label the dice as follows:

  Dice 1: I, I, V, X, L, C

  Dice 2: I, X, C, C, D, M

- Roll the two dice and make the number, by placing the larger symbol on the left. Work out the number formed by adding the symbols. For example: X and C give the number CX, which is 110.
- This can be turned into a game. Pupils take turns to roll the dice and the one with the higher number scores a point. The first pupil to reach five points is the winner.

Question 2

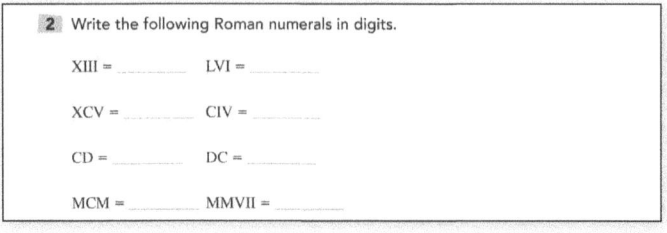

What learning will pupils have achieved at the conclusion of Question 2?

- Pupils will have interpreted numbers written in Roman numerals.
- Pupils will have practised adding symbols to find the value of numbers in Roman numerals, recognising that symbols are generally written in order, from the largest on the left to the smallest on the right.
- Pupils will have explored the rule that in Roman numerals, when a symbol for a smaller number appears to the left of any symbol that number should be subtracted.

Activities for whole-class instruction

- Put together Roman numerals in decreasing order of size and work out the numbers together by adding the symbols, for example:

  MD (1000 + 500 = 1500)

  MDC (1000 + 500 + 100 = 1600)

  MDCL (1000 + 500 + 100 + 50 = 1650)

  MDCLX (1000 + 500 + 100 + 50 + 10 = 1660)

  MDCLXV (1000 + 500 + 100 + 50 + 10 + 5 = 1665)

  MDCLXVI (1000 + 500 + 100 + 50 + 10 + 5 + 1 = 1666)

- Tell pupils there is a rule when writing Roman numerals that more than three identical symbols in a row are not permitted, so 4 is not written as IIII. A system of subtraction is employed to write numbers containing 4 or 9. In these cases the smaller number is written in front of the larger one and subtracted. This happens in six instances, 4, 9, 40, 90, 400 and 900. Display and discuss each case:

  IV is one less than 5, 4   IX is one less than 10, 9

  XL is 10 less than 50, 40   XC is 10 less than 100, 90

  CD is 100 less than 500, 400   CM is 100 less than 1000, 900

4	9	40	90	400	900
IV	IX	XL	XC	CD	CM

- By using a combination of multiple symbols and these six subtractions, every number can be written in Roman numerals.
- Practise reading Roman numerals where one of these subtractions occurs. Look for any smaller symbol in front of a larger one, and that is where subtraction takes place. For example:

258

Chapter 5 Consolidation and enhancement

Unit 5.7 Practice Book 5A, pages 138–139

In CLIX, the I is smaller than the X, so IX is 9.

Therefore CLIX = 100 + 50 + 9 = 159.

In CCXLVI, the X before L is smaller, so XL is 40.

Thus CCXLVI = 200 + 40 + 5 + 1 = 246.

- Continue with similar examples, MXCIV, CDLXII, MCMLIII, CCIX. (1094, 462, 1953, 209)
- Pupils should complete Question 2 in the Practice Book.

Same-day intervention

- Give pupil pairs two blank 1–6 dice and ask them to label the dice as follows:

  Dice 1: I, I, V, X, L, C

  Dice 2: I, X, C, C, D, M

- Roll the two dice to see what numbers can be made. For example, X and C can give the numbers XC, which is 90, and CX, which is 110. Two identical symbols will only give one number, for example II gives 2, XX, 20 and CC, 200.
- Some combinations cannot work both ways. For example, I and C can only give CI, 101. IC is not a permitted subtraction; 99 is written as 90 + 9, XCIX.
- Remind pupils of the numbers where subtraction is used.

4	9	40	90	400	900
IV	IX	XL	XC	CD	CM

- This table could be displayed.
- This can be turned into a game. Pupils take turns to roll the dice, add up the numbers they can make, and the one with the higher sum scores a point. The first pupil to reach five points is the winner.

Same-day enrichment

- Give pupil pairs **Resource 5.5.7b** Roman numeral sequences. They complete the number sequences.

  Answers: 1. I, II, III, IV, V, VI, VII, VIII, IX, X; 2. X, XX, XXX, XL, L, LX, LXX, LXXX, XC, C; 3. C, CC, CCC, CD, D, DC, DCC, DCCC, CM, M; 4. L, C, CL, CC, CCLC, CCC, CCCL, LD, LDL, D; 5. 9, 19, 29, 39, 49, 59, increasing in 10s; 6. 3, 5, 7, 9, 11, 13, 15, increasing in 2s; 7. 24, 44, 64, 84, 104, 124, increasing in 20s; 8. 99, 94, 89, 84, 79, 74, 69, decreasing in 5s.

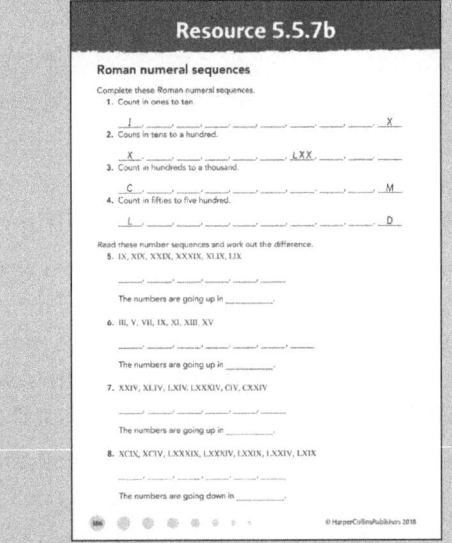

Question 3

3 Can you recognise years written in Roman numerals? Complete the table below. The first one has been done for you.

Roman numeral	MM	MD	MDLII	MCM	MCMXCV	MMXVI
Year	2000					

What learning will pupils have achieved at the conclusion of Question 3?

- Pupils will have interpreted numbers written in Roman numerals.

Chapter 5 Consolidation and enhancement

Unit 5.7 Practice Book 5A, pages 138–139

- Pupils will have practised adding symbols to find the value of numbers in Roman numerals, recognising that symbols are generally written in order, from the largest on the left to the smallest on the right.
- Pupils will have explored the rule that, in Roman numerals, when a symbol for a smaller number appears to the left of any symbol, that number should be subtracted.
- Pupils will have discussed how, over time, the numeral system changed to include the concept of zero and place value.

Activities for whole-class instruction

- Explain that sometimes pupils make mistakes when they write Roman numerals. Here is an example of when something has gone wrong: 9 is written as VIIII.
- Ask pupils to say why this is incorrect and what the correct symbols for this Roman numeral are. This is incorrect because you are not allowed to have more than three identical symbols next to one another. The correct version for 9 is IX, one less than 10. What about these?

40 is XXXX	Same error, four consecutive identical symbols; correct version, XL.
190 is CLXL	The correct way to write 90 is XC, so the number should be CXC.
1500 is DM	The largest symbol is written first, so the number should be MD.

- Display the following numbers:

  CMXCIX   M   MI

- Ask pupils to identify the numbers. Confirm that they are 999, 1000, 1001.

  CMXCIX   M   MI
  999   1000   1001

- Ask pupils to discuss with a partner the differences that they notice in the two number systems. Share some of their observations. Establish that the smallest Roman numeral has the largest number of symbols, six symbols, while the middle number has only a single symbol. The modern numbers are one three-digit and two four-digit numbers. Our number system uses position or place to determine the magnitude of a number and uses zero(s) as placeholders to ensure that the digit is in the correct place. Roman numerals have no symbol for zero; which makes column addition and subtraction impossible!

- Ask pupils to tell you the Roman number symbols from the largest to the smallest. Confirm the order of the seven symbols is M, D, C, L, X, V, I.
- Display the following number: MCMLXXXIX. Work together to deduce that the number is 1989 (1000 + 900 + 50 + 30 + 9). Try some more examples until pupils demonstrate confidence in converting Roman numerals, for example:

  MMC (2100)   MMXVIII (2018)
  MDCCXCII (1792)   MCDXLIV (1444)

(i) Fibonacci brought the Hindu-Arabic number system that we use today to Europe in the thirteenth century. The new system used 1, 2, 3, 4, 5, 6, 7, 8, 9 and 0, and with these digits any number could be written. The new system is base ten. Ten 1s make one 10, ten 10s make 100, ten 100s make 1000 and so on. Thus, the concept of place value was established. The first digit shows how many 1s are in the number, the second digit how many 10s, the third how many 100s and so on. If there are none of a particular value then we use zero as a placeholder. For example, 205 means 5 ones, 0 tens and 2 hundreds.

- Pupils should complete Question 3 in the Practice Book.

Same-day intervention

- Give pupil pairs **Resource 5.5.7c** Famous dates. They should match the famous date to the correct event.

  Answers: MM 2000; MLXVI 1066; MCCXV 1215; MCDXCII 1492; MDCLXVI 1666; MCMLII 1952; MDLXXXVIII 1588; MCMXIV 1914.

Chapter 5 Consolidation and enhancement

Unit 5.7 Practice Book 5A, pages 138–139

Same-day enrichment

- Give pupil pairs **Resource 5.5.7d** Before and after. They should work out the dates before and after each given date.

Answers:

Before	Date	After
MMVII 2007	**MMVIII** 2008	MMIX 2009
MDCCXLIX 1749	**MDCCL** 1750	MDCCLI 1751
MCMXCVIII 1998	**MCMXCIX** 1999	MM 2000
MCDXCVIII 1498	**MCDXCIX** 1499	MD 1500
MXLVII 1047	**MXLVIII** 1048	MXLIX 1049
MDCLXXXIX 1689	**MDCXC** 1690	MDCXCI 1691

Challenge and extension question

Question 4

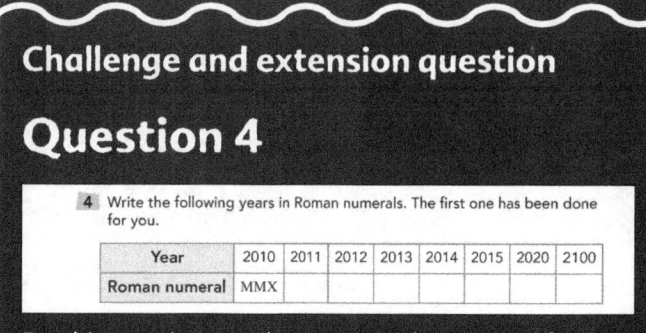

For this question, pupils are required to convert four-digit numbers into Roman numerals. This is more challenging than the reverse process covered in the unit questions.

Chapter 5 Consolidation and enhancement

Unit 5.8
Solving problems in statistics

Conceptual context

This unit revisits tables, bar charts and line/time graphs. Pupils will need to solve problems about the data, as well as interpret and construct statistical tables and graphs.

Learning pupils will have achieved at the end of the unit

- Construction and interpretation of pictograms will have been revisited (Q1)
- Pupils will have further practised interrogating data in tables to answer questions (Q2)
- Interpretation of information presented in bar charts with different scale intervals will have been explored (Q3)
- Pupils will have interrogated the data in bar charts to answer questions, including finding the total number represented (Q3)
- With support, pupils will have constructed line graphs (Q3)
- Pupils will have solved trend, sum and difference problems using data in line graphs/time graphs (Q3)

Resources

squared paper; graph paper; **Resource 5.5.8a** Favourite superheroes in Class 5A; **Resource 5.5.8b** Year 5 favourite superheroes; **Resource 5.5.8c** Javelin records; **Resource 5.5.8d** High jump results; **Resource 5.5.8e** Electric car sales; **Resource 5.5.8f** Electric bike sales

Vocabulary

data, pictogram, bar, bar chart, table, cell, vertical axis, horizontal axis, scale, interval, unit, line graph, trend, upward/downward tendency

Chapter 5 Consolidation and enhancement

Unit 5.8 Practice Book 5A, pages 140–143

Question 1

> **1** The pictogram below shows the numbers of Year 5 pupils participating in different school clubs. Use this information to find the answers to the questions.
>
> | Choir | Science | Dancing | ICT |
> |---|---|---|---|
> | △△△△△ | △△△△ | △△△ | △△△△ |
>
> Each △ stands for 5 pupils.
> Which school club has the greatest number of participating pupils?
>
> _____
>
> Which school clubs have the same number of participating pupils?
>
> _____
>
> How many more pupils are there joining choir than dancing? _____
> From the pictogram, can you tell the total number of pupils participating in different school clubs? Why or why not?
>
> _____
> _____

What learning will pupils have achieved at the conclusion of Question 1?

- Construction and interpretation of pictograms will have been revisited.

Activities for whole-class instruction

- Show pupils the following pictogram. Say: *A supermarket looked at how the 100 most popular items in the shop were packaged. Each X stands for 4 items.*

Packaging of the 100 most popular items in a supermarket

Plastic	Glass	Cardboard	Steel can	Aluminium can
X		X		
X		X		
X	X	X		
X	X	X		
X	X	X	X	
X	X	X	X	X
X	X	X	X	X

- Ask: *What is this type of chart called?* Agree that it is a pictogram. A pictogram is a chart that uses columns of pictures (or symbols) to show the numbers of items. In this pictogram, each X represents 4 items.

- Ask pupil pairs to make up questions about the pictogram. Share ideas. Possible questions might include:

  – *Which packaging material is the most/least popular?*
  – *How many items are packaged in plastic/glass/cardboard/steel can/aluminium can?*
  – *How many more items are packaged in plastic than in glass?*

- Ask: *If X represents 4 items, how could 2 items be represented?* Agree it could be either ⟩ or ⌃.

- Pupils should complete Question 1 in the Practice Book.

Same-day intervention

- Give pupils **Resource 5.5.8a** Favourite superheroes in Class 5A. They look at the pictogram and answer the questions.

  Answers: 1. Spiderman, 10; 2. Catwoman, 2; 3. 4; 4. 30; 5. Individual answers.

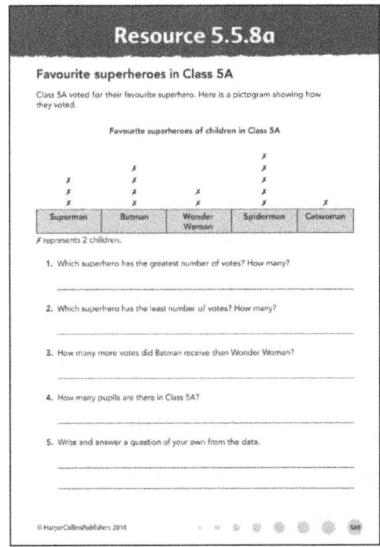

Same-day enrichment

- Give pupils **Resource 5.5.8b** Year 5 favourite superheroes. They look at the pictograms and answer the questions.

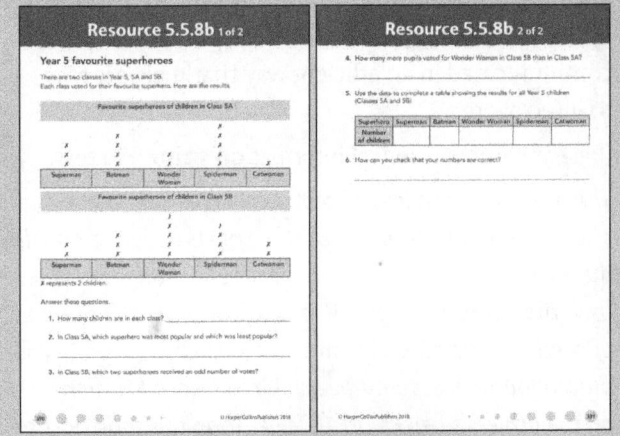

Chapter 5 Consolidation and enhancement

Unit 5.8 Practice Book 5A, pages 140–143

Answers: 1. 30 in each class; 2. Spiderman, Catwoman; 3. Spiderman, Wonder Woman; 4. 5 (9 – 4);

5.

Superhero	Number of children
Superman	10
Batman	14
Wonder Woman	13
Spiderman	17
Catwoman	6

6. Check that the total is 60; 10 + 14 + 13 + 17 + 6 = 60.

Question 2

2. Read the following table carefully and then work out the answers.

Results of standing long jump test (Year 5)

	Linda	Alvin	Bob	Peter	May
Result (cm)	242	256	261	228	219
Place					

(a) What is the difference between the longest jump and the shortest jump?

(b) According to the results, write each participating pupil's place in the table.

What learning will pupils have achieved at the conclusion of Question 2?

- Pupils will have further practised interrogating data in tables to answer questions.

Activities for whole-class instruction

- Ask: *What is a table?* Agree that a table shows numbers or quantities arranged in rows and columns. Ask: *Why are tables useful?* Elicit that tables allow data to be presented in an organised way. This allows the information to be communicated in an efficient way that makes it easy to interrogate.

- Present some numerical information written in text.

The managers of a leisure centre collected some information about the numbers taking part in sports activities one day during the summer. Over the course of the day, 160 children used the swimming pool. This was four times the number of children who played tennis and twice the number who played football. Seventy-five children enjoyed running on the athletics track and 10 fewer than this took part in gymnastics.

- Together, extract the information and present it in a table.

Number of children using leisure centre facilities				
Swimming	Tennis	Football	Running	Gymnastics
160	40	80	75	65

- Agree that the table shows the data in a more straightforward way. Questions can be asked and answered more easily.

- Challenge pupils to write their own questions from the data, involving differences and totals. Invite individual pupils to share their questions for the class to answer.

- Ask: *Can you tell how many children were at the leisure centre during the day?* Agree that you cannot because children may have taken part in more than one activity.

- Pupils should complete Question 2 in the Practice Book.

Same-day intervention

- Give pupils **Resource 5.5.8c** Javelin records. They read the information and answer the questions.

  Answers: 1. 17.5 m; 2. $8\frac{1}{2}$; 3. 8.4 m; 4. 1.9 m; 5. 24.5 m.

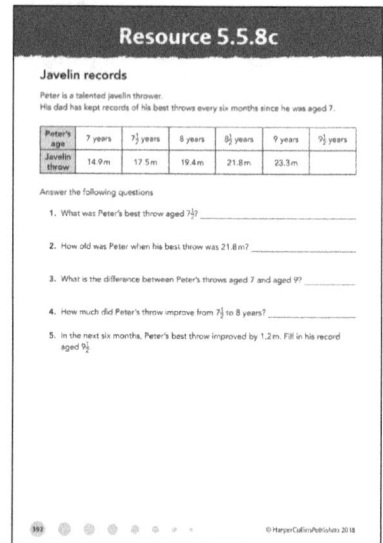

Chapter 5 Consolidation and enhancement   Unit 5.8 Practice Book 5A, pages 140–143

Same-day enrichment

- Give pupils **Resource 5.5.8d** High jump results.
  They read the information and answer the questions.
  Answers:

	Linda	Alvin	Bob	Peter	May
Height jumped	114 cm	122 cm	121 cm	112 cm	119 cm
Place	4th	1st	2nd	5th	3rd

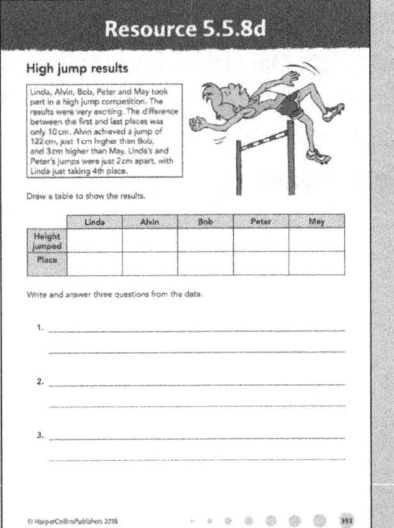

Question 3

3. The bar chart shows the production of cars each quarter for a year. Use this information to find the answers to the questions.

(Bar chart: 1st quarter 1000, 2nd quarter 1500, 3rd quarter 1300, 4th quarter 1600)

(a) The total output of the manufacturer is ☐ cars in the year.

(b) Construct a line graph using the data represented in the bar chart.

(c) According to the line graph, which of the following is true? Put a ✓ for true or a ✗ for false in each box.

   (i) The production was stable over the four quarters. ☐
   (ii) The production was steadily improving over the four quarters. ☐
   (iii) The production was steadily declining over the four quarters. ☐
   (iv) The production fluctuated over the four quarters. ☐

What learning will pupils have achieved at the conclusion of Question 3?

- Interpretation of information presented in bar charts with different scale intervals will have been explored.
- Pupils will have interrogated the data in bar charts to answer questions, including finding the total number represented.
- With support, pupils will have constructed line graphs.
- Pupils will have solved trend, sum and difference problems using data in line graphs/time graphs.

265

Chapter 5 Consolidation and enhancement

Unit 5.8 Practice Book 5A, pages 140–143

Activities for whole-class instruction

- Display the following graphs:

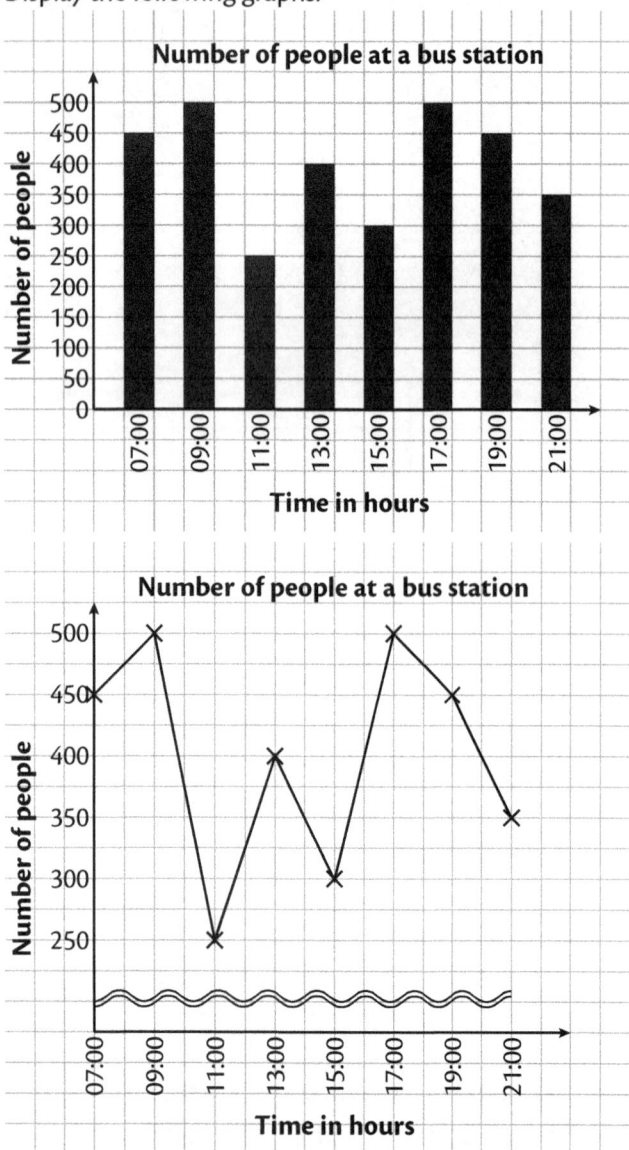

- Ask pupil pairs to look at both graphs and discuss them. Share their findings.

- Agree that they both show the same data. The first graph is a 'bar chart' and the scale interval is 100.

- The second graph is a 'line graph' and the scale interval is 50. Line graphs are used to display connected numerical information that changes over time. Time is always recorded on the horizontal axis – here it is time during the day every two hours. The data is plotted as a series of points, joined with straight lines, which allows the intermediate values to be estimated.

- Ask: *Where is the line going up/coming down and what does this mean?* Establish that where the line is in an upward direction, the value is increasing and vice versa.

Confirm that the high values show the busy times at the bus station. Agree that they correspond to 'going to work/school', 'lunchtime' and 'going home from work/school'.

- Ask: *What do the wiggly lines in the second graph show?* They show a missing part of the vertical scale so that a bigger scale can be used that will still fit on the page.

- Pupils should complete Question 3 in the Practice Book.

Same-day intervention

- Give pupils **Resource 5.5.8e** Electric car sales, as well as squared paper to draw a bar chart.

  Answers: 1. 5; 2. Main labels every 100, small intervals represent 20; 3. 210; 4. 30; 5. Years 4 & 5; 6. Sales show an upward trend, with a rapid rise between Years 4 & 5.

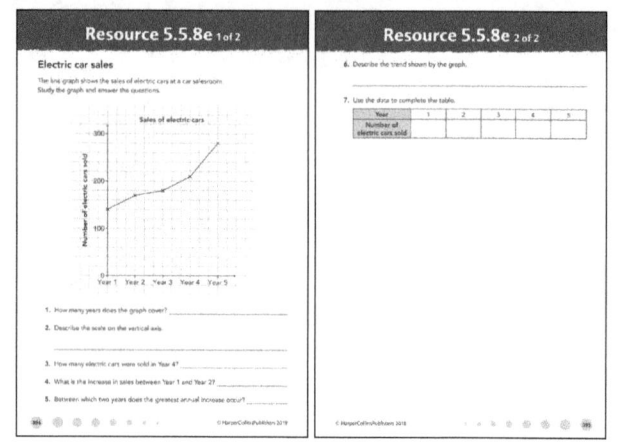

Chapter 5 Consolidation and enhancement

Unit 5.8 Practice Book 5A, pages 140–143

Same-day enrichment

- Give pupil **Resource 5.5.8f** Electric bike sales.

  Answers: 1. Sales show an upward trend, with a rapid rise between Years 4 & 5; 2a, b & c. Individual answers; 3. 390 is approximately double the sales of Year 1, so she is more or less correct: sales of 400 bikes would be exactly double.

Chapter 5 test (Practice Book 5A, pages 144–151)

Test question number	Relevant unit	Relevant questions within unit
1	Unit 5.4	Q1
2	Unit 5.6	Q4
3	Unit 5.3	Q3
	Unit 5.4	Q3
	Unit 5.5	Q2
4	Unit 5.1	Q1, Q4, Q6
	Unit 5.2	Q1, Q2, Q3
	Unit 5.4	Q2
	Unit 5.5	Q1
	Unit 5.6	Q1, Q3
5	Unit 5.6	Q2
6	Unit 5.3	Q4
	Unit 5.5	Q3
	Unit 5.7	Q1, Q2, Q3, Q4
7	Unit 5.6	Q3
8	Unit 5.4	Q4
	Unit 5.5	Q4
	Unit 5.8	Q2, Q3

Challenge and extension question

Question 4

This is a practical problem examining data from a water utility bill. Pupils are asked to examine and compare their own water bill. As they will not have access to this at school, a generic bill could be made available to them.

Resource 5.1.1

Spot the mistake

Circle the mistake and then recalculate.

1. 126 × 7 = _____

```
      1   2   6
  ×           7
  ─────────────
      8   4   2
          1   4
```

2. 25 × 32 = _____

5 × 5 × 32 = 600

5 × 32 = 160

160 × 5 = 600

3. 638 ÷ 6 = _____

```
         1   0   5   r8
     ┌─────────────
  6  )  6   3   8
        6   0   0
        ─────────
            3   8
            3   0
            ─────
                8
```

Resource 5.1.2

Shading fractions of shapes

A game for 2 players

Rules:
- Take turns to roll two 1–10 dice. Use the numbers to generate a fraction with the larger number rolled representing the denominator and the smaller number representing the numerator.
- Select a circle below and shade a number of parts to represent the fraction rolled.
- The first player to shade 8 circles correctly wins the game.
- Players may shade equivalent fractions for the numbers rolled.

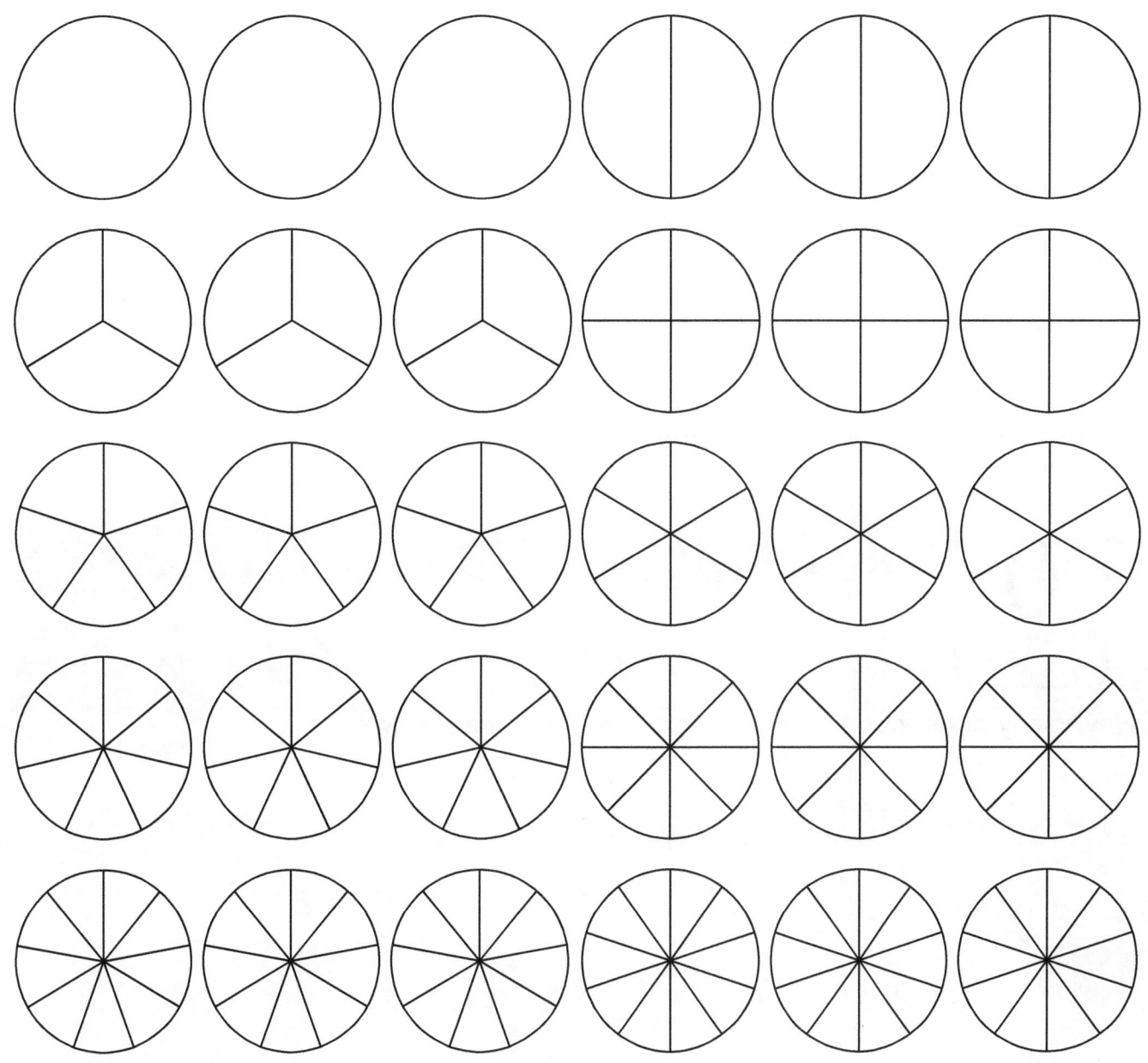

Resource 5.1.3a

Benny's cards

Benny has three digit cards, and a card with a decimal point.

| 2 | 3 | 4 | . |

The 2 card must represent 20.
List all the numbers that Benny can make using all of the cards.

Next, the 2 card must represent 0.2.
List all the numbers that Benny can make using all of the cards.

Remove the 3 card and replace it with a 0 card.

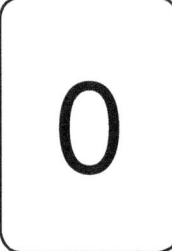

How many different decimal numbers can Benny make now?

Resource 5.1.3b

Numbers and shapes

In this decimal number, one of the digits has been missed out and replaced by a ✸.

$$3.4 = 3.4✸$$

What digit has the ✸ replaced?

In this decimal number, all of the digits have been replaced by different shapes.

$$■.✿■■■ = ■.✿ = \frac{✿}{✿■}$$

What digit does the ■ represent?

What digit does the ✿ represent?

Here is another decimal number where the digits have been replaced by shapes.

$$❄.✪✺✺ = ❄.✪ = \frac{✪}{★✺}$$

What digit does the ❄ represent?

What digit does the ★ represent?

The ✪ could represent several different digits. How many can you find?

© HarperCollins*Publishers* 2018

Resource 5.1.3c

Less, same, more grid

Make as few changes as possible to the centre number to complete the grid.

Number of digits

	Fewer	Same	More
Lower			
Same		3.14	
Higher			

Value of number

Resource 5.1.3d

Place value slider

- Cut along the dotted lines of the first strip below to create your place value slider.
- Now cut out the three strips at the bottom.
- Thread one strip through the slider and use this to write your number on.
- There are three strips, but you can always cut more, or you could laminate one and use it again and again.

1000	100	10	1	0.1	0.01	0.001
Behind the strip	Behind the strip	Behind the strip	Behind the strip	Behind the strip	Behind the strip	Behind the strip

© HarperCollins*Publishers* 2018

Resource 5.1.3e

Rounders

Fill in the spaces so that, when rounded to the nearest whole number, all of these decimal numbers give the same answer.

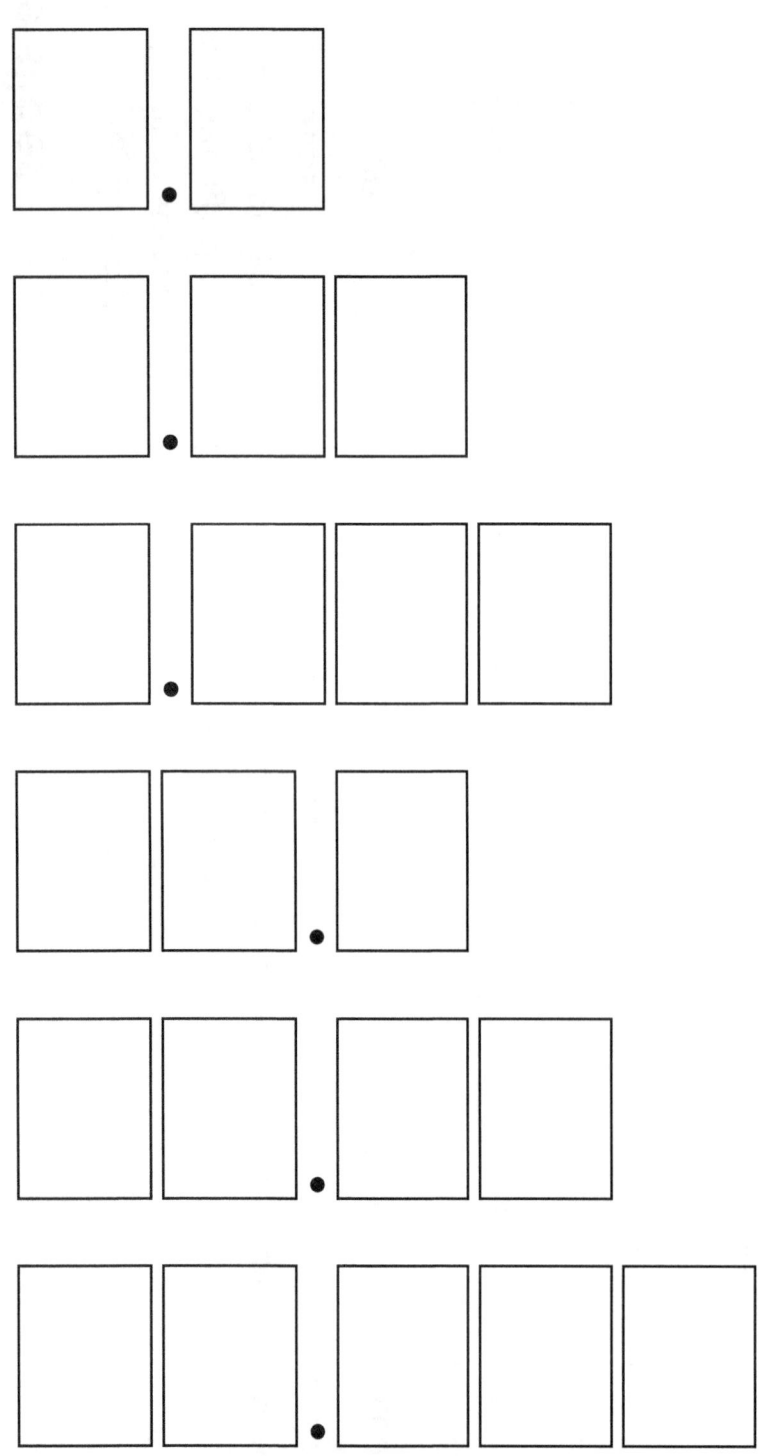

All round to _____ to the nearest whole number

Resource 5.1.4a

Statement

When comparing two decimals, we first compare the _____ part;

the larger the whole number part, the _____ the number.

If the whole number parts are the same, then we compare the digits in

the _____ place; the larger the digit in

the _____ place, the greater the decimal number and so on.

Resource 5.1.4b

Decimals maze

Start at 0.06 and move through the maze, always moving to the greatest decimal number that is above, below, to the left or to the right of the square you are in. What number on the bottom row do you finish at?

0.05	0.06	0.009	0.08	0.0801	0.08011
0.0095	0.061	0.064	0.07	0.067	0.7
0.29999	0.000009	0.061	0.069	0.7051	0.705
1.5	0.812	0.80409	0.8042	0.8041	0.5
0.1000	0.91	0.9	0.83	0.38	3.1
0.92	0.93	0.80	0.823	0.83	3.8
0.1999	0.991	0.999	0.9999	2.99999	4.31
4.776	0.990	0.909	3.14159	3.099232	8.94

Resource 5.1.5

One step at a time

You will need: squared paper

In this activity, you will be looking at the length, width, perimeter and area of different shapes and looking for patterns.

This shape has two steps:

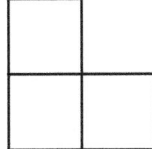

Its length is 2 cm and its width is 2 cm. Find its perimeter and area.

The next shape in the sequence will have three steps:

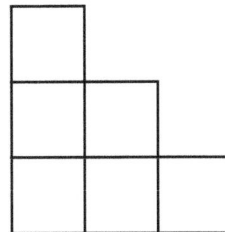

Can you find its length, width, perimeter and area?

Continue the sequence until you have worked out the results for a shape with six steps. Record your results in a table like this.

Number of steps	Length (cm)	Width (cm)	Perimeter (cm)	Area (cm^2)

Look carefully to see whether you can see any patterns or links between the number of steps and the other numbers in each row.

PREDICT! What do you think the perimeter and area of a shape with 10 steps will be? Why?

Draw the 10-step shape to test whether your prediction was correct.

Resource 5.2.1a

Making 9-digit numbers

Work with a partner.

- Here are three different 3-digit numbers

342 **218** **902**

How many different 9-digit numbers can you make by placing them into different groups, millions, thousands and ones? (There are 6 different possibilities.)

Take turns to read the numbers to one another.

Make up three new 3-digit numbers and find the new numbers.

_____   _____   _____

Resource 5.2.1b

Value of the 4 in 9-digit numbers

Here are some 9-digit numbers.
Write the value of the 4 in each of the numbers in words and numerals.
The first one has been done for you.

Number	Value of the 4 in words	Value of the 4 in numerals
232 456 198	Four hundred thousand	400 000
140 732 009		
576 321 946		
476 319 072		
563 709 954		
734 870 982		
653 247 017		
198 035 461		
762 490 083		
762 864 201		

Compare your answers with those of a partner.
Take turns to read the numbers to each other.

Population numbers

Here are the populations of 10 countries in July 2017.
Complete the table.

Country	Population (July 2017)	In words
Australia	24 450 561	
Brazil	209 288 278	
France		Sixty-four million, nine hundred and seventy-nine thousand, five hundred and forty-eight
Germany	82 114 224	
Japan	127 484 450	
Mexico		One hundred and twenty-nine million, one hundred and sixty-three thousand, two hundred and seventy-six
New Zealand	4 705 818	
Russia	143 989 754	One hundred and forty-three million, nine hundred and eighty-nine thousand, seven hundred and fifty-four
United Kingdom	66 181 585	
United States	324 459 463	

Answer these questions.
1. Which country has the largest population?

2. Which country has the smallest population?

   _____

3. Which country's population is close to the population of the United Kingdom?

   _____

4. Which countries have more than a hundred million people?

   _____

5. Here is the population of New Zealand in expanded form.
   4 705 818
   = 4 × 1 000 000 + 7 × 100 000 + 0 × 10 000 + 5 × 1000 + 8 × 100 + 1 × 10 + 8
   = 4 000 000 + 700 000 + 0 + 5000 + 800 + 10 + 8

   Choose two more countries and write their populations in expanded form.

   _____

   _____

   = _____

   = _____

   _____

   _____

   = _____

   = _____

   If time allows, use the internet to investigate the populations of more countries.

Resource 5.2.1d 1 of 2

9-digit numbers in numerals and words

Write these numbers in words.

- 210 000 000

  _____

  _____

- 201 000 000

  _____

  _____

- 200 100 000

  _____

  _____

- 200 010 000

  _____

  _____

- 200 001 000

  _____

  _____

- 200 000 100

  _____

  _____

- 200 000 010

  _____

  _____

- 200 000 001

  _____

  _____

Write these numbers in numerals.

Five hundred and thirty-one million, six hundred and forty-two thousand, nine hundred and ninety-nine

_____

One hundred million, two hundred thousand, three hundred

_____

Seven hundred and seventy-seven million, seven hundred and seventy-seven thousand, seven hundred and seventy-seven

_____

Nine hundred and sixty-three million, eight hundred and sixty-four thousand, two hundred and ten

_____

Four hundred and four million, three hundred and three thousand, two hundred and two

_____

9-digit number puzzles

Write a 9-digit number in numerals that fits the criteria. Then write the number in words.

1. All the digits are odd.

   In numerals: _____

   In words: _____

2. All the digits are even.

   In numerals: _____

   In words: _____

3. The number contains 4 zeros.

   In numerals: _____

   In words: _____

4. All the digits are less than or equal to 3.

   In numerals: _____

   In words: _____

5. Alternate digits are zero.

   In numerals: _____

   In words: _____

6. All the digits are greater than or equal to 7.

   In numerals: _____

   In words: _____

7. The sum of the digits is 20.

   In numerals: _____

   In words: _____

8. The number of millions is the same as the number of thousands and the number of ones.

   In numerals: _____

   In words: _____

Check your answers with a partner.
(It is very unlikely that any of your answers will be the same! There are so many possibilities.)

Resource 5.2.2a

Matching large numbers

Play this game with a partner.

Cut out the cards. Shuffle them and lay them face down. The first player turns over two cards. If they match, the player wins the pair and has another turn. If they are not the same, they turn them back over in the same place. The other player takes their turn. The winner is the pupil with the greater number of pairs.

one million	1 000 000	one thousand	1000
one billion	1 000 000 000	one hundred thousand	100 000
one hundred million	100 000 000	one hundred and one million	101 000 000
one billion and one	1 000 000 001	one million, one hundred and one	1 000 101
one million, one hundred and eleven thousand, one hundred and eleven	1 111 111	one billion, one million, one thousand and one	1 001 001 001

Resource 5.2.2b

True or false?

Decide whether the following statements are true or false. Circle your answer.

1. 2 361 457 000 > 2 316 457 000   True / False

2. Four hundred thousand is the same as 4 000 000.   True / False

3. 3 000 000 000 is less than three billion and one.   True / False

4. One thousand million is greater than a billion.   True / False

5. Seven hundred and thirteen million < 712 999 999   True / False

6. Six million is equal to six thousand thousand.   True / False

7. 1 560 218 450 < 1 560 218 540   True / False

8. 2 009 006 005 contains 2 billions, 9 millions, 6 thousands and 5 ones.   True / False

© HarperCollins*Publishers* 2018

Resource 5.2.2c

Finding whole tens, hundreds and thousands

1. Complete the number line, which is marked in intervals of 10.

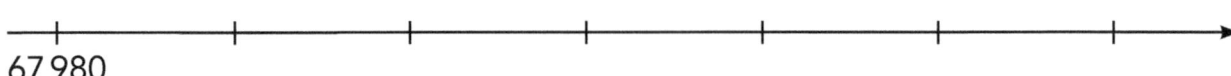
67 980

List the whole tens that are greater than 67 980 and less than 68 030.

_____

2. Complete the number line, which is marked in intervals of 100.

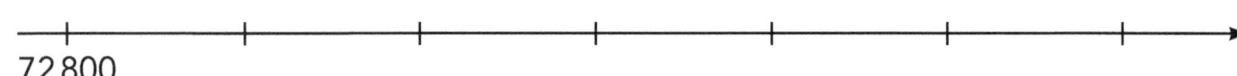
72 800

List the whole hundreds that are greater than 72 800 and less than 73 400.

_____

3. Complete the number line, which is marked in intervals of 1000.

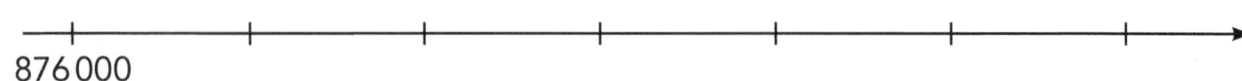
876 000

List the whole thousands that are greater than 876 000 and less than 882 000.

_____

Resource 5.2.2d

Greatest and smallest

Number of digits	Smallest number	Greatest number
1		
2		
3		
4		
5		
6		
7		
10		

Describe the patterns in the columns.

_____

_____

Write the number sentences for these calculations.
Subtract the largest single-digit number from the smallest 2-digit number.

_____

Subtract the largest 3-digit number from the smallest 4-digit number.

_____

Subtract the largest 5-digit number from the smallest 6-digit number.

_____

What do you notice? Will this always happen?

_____

© HarperCollins*Publishers* 2018

Resource 5.2.3a

Writing large numerals

Billions			Millions			Thousands			Ones		
Hundreds	Tens	Ones	Hundreds	Tens	Ones	Hundreds	Tens	Ones	Hundreds	Tens	Ones
___	___	___	___	___	___	___	___	___	___	___	___

Write each number in numerals.

Hint: Read the number carefully and complete each group – billions, millions, thousands and ones – in turn, and then add any zero placeholders.

Number in words   **Number in numerals**

1. One million, six thousand, nine hundred and thirty   _ ___ ___

2. Two billion, four hundred and fifty million, three hundred and two thousand, four hundred and three   _ ___ ___ ___

3. Sixty thousand, two hundred and seven   __ ___

4. One hundred and forty-three thousand and eighty-two   ___ ___

5. Seventy million, six hundred and fifty thousand and sixty-three   __ ___ ___

The following questions do not show the number of digits. Start by drawing those, then add the numbers and fill in with the zero placeholders.

6. Twenty billion, forty-four million, two hundred and five thousand, seven hundred

7. Eight million, forty thousand and seventeen

8. Nine billion, two hundred and thirty million, nine hundred and fifty-six thousand and eight

9. Thirty-three thousand, three hundred and thirty-three

10. Four billion, eight million, two thousand and six

© HarperCollinsPublishers 2018

Resource 5.2.3b

How many zeros?

Complete the table.
Write each number in numerals and then count the number of zero placeholders that are required.

Number in words	Number in numerals	Number of zeros
1. One million and ten		
2. Two billion, four hundred and fifty million		
3. Seventy thousand and seven		
4. Five hundred and forty-three thousand and two		
5. Sixty million, three hundred and sixty-three		
6. Twenty billion		
7. Eight million, forty thousand and two		
8. Nine billion, nine hundred and ninety-nine thousand		
9. Thirty-three thousand, three hundred and thirty-three		
10. Four hundred billion		

Make up your own numbers with the correct number of zeros.

Number in words	Number in numerals	Number of zeros
11.		1
12.		8

Resource 5.2.3c

Digit sum equals 20

In pairs, write ten 10-digit numbers with a digit sum of 20 that fit the following categories.

- an odd number _____

- an even number _____

- a number divisible by 5 _____

- a number greater than 5 billion _____

- a number with only even digits _____

- a number divisible by 10 _____

- a number with 9 in both the millions place and the thousands place

  _____

- a number with three 4s in it _____

- a number consisting of 3s and 0s only _____

- a number where all the digits are the same

  _____

Swap your answers with another pair and check their answers.

Resource 5.2.3d

Find the match

Circle the number in words that matches the numeral in the centre.

A	Numeral	B
1. thirty-four million	34 000 000	thirty-four thousand
2. two billion, three hundred and forty-five thousand	2 345 000 000	two billion, three hundred and forty-five million
3. four million, six hundred and twenty-four thousand	4 642 000	four million, six hundred and forty-two thousand
4. five hundred and six million, three hundred and four thousand, one hundred and two	506 304 102	five hundred and sixty million, three hundred and four thousand, one hundred and two
5. forty-eight million, three thousand, two hundred and fifty-eight	48 003 258	forty-eight million, thirty thousand, two hundred and fifty-eight
6. forty-three thousand and fifty-two hundred	43 520	forty-three thousand, five hundred and twenty
7. seven billion	7 000 000 000	seven million
8. nine hundred and six million, six hundred thousand, six hundred and sixty	960 600 660	nine hundred and sixty million, six hundred thousand, six hundred and sixty

© HarperCollins*Publishers* 2018

Resource 5.2.3e

How far to the Sun?

Planet	Distance to the Sun (km)	Distance to the Sun (km) in words
Earth		one hundred and forty-nine million, six hundred thousand
Jupiter	778 369 000	
Mars	227 937 000	
Mercury		fifty-seven million, nine hundred thousand
Neptune	4 496 976 000	
Saturn		one billion, four hundred and twenty-seven million, thirty-four thousand
Uranus	2 870 658 000	
Venus	108 160 000	

- Complete the table.
- Put the planets in order of distance from the Sun, starting with the greatest distance.

_____

_____

Resource 5.2.4a

What's the shape?

? ? ? ? ?
? Find the mystery shape ?
? ? ? ? ?

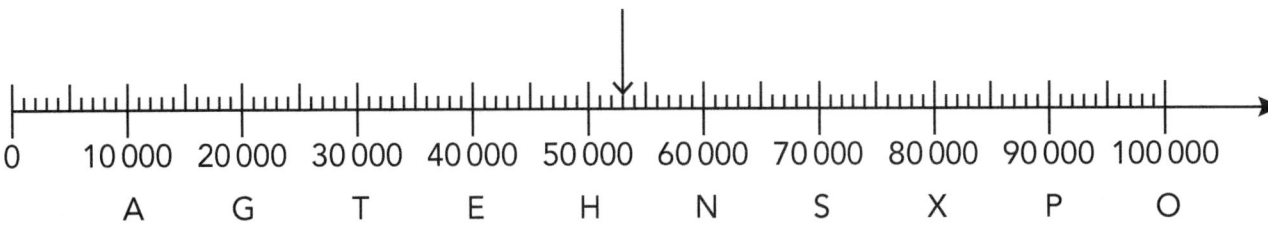

0	10 000	20 000	30 000	40 000	50 000	60 000	70 000	80 000	90 000	100 000
	A	G	T	E	H	N	S	X	P	O

Estimate the position of the following numbers on the number line.
Complete the table to show the nearest ten thousands number.
The first one has been done for you.
Each answer gives a letter that together will spell the name of a shape.

Number	Nearest ten thousands number	Letter
53 000	50 000	H
1. 37 000		
2. 82 000		
3. 8000		
4. 21 000		
5. 96 000		
6. 64 000		

The mystery shape is a _____.

Find and make mystery shapes

? ? ? ? ?
? Find the mystery shape ?
? ? ? ? ?

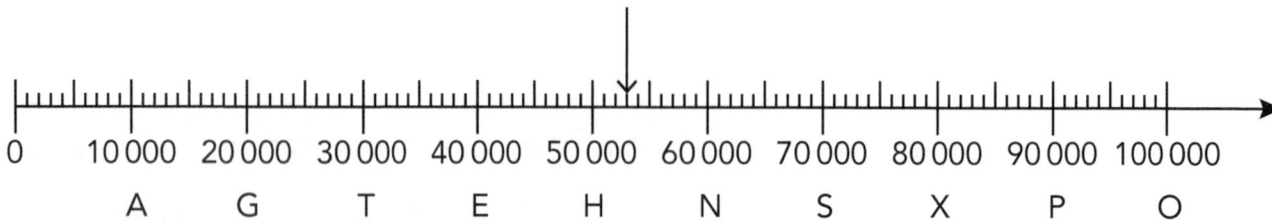

Estimate the position of the following numbers on the number line.
Complete the table to show the nearest ten thousands number.
The first one has been done for you.
Each answer gives a letter that together will spell the name of a shape.

Number	Nearest ten thousands number	Letter
53 000	50 000	H
1. 37 000		
2. 82 000		
3. 8000		
4. 21 000		
5. 96 000		
6. 64 000		

The mystery shape is a _____.

Use the table below to choose your own numbers so that the mystery shape is an octagon.

Letter	Nearest ten thousands number	Number chosen
O		
C		
T		
A		
G		
O		
N		

© HarperCollins*Publishers* 2018

Resource 5.2.4c

Using rounding to calculate approximate answers

Rounding is useful for calculating approximate answers to calculations.
Here are some calculations.
Round the numbers to the nearest ten thousand and add them mentally to calculate approximate answers.

1. 34 379 + 62 587

   _____

2. 71 976 + 19 219

   _____

3. 54 563 + 23 143

   _____

4. 18 432 + 53 937

   _____

5. 32 435 + 15 643 + 41 702

   _____

Ask your teacher whether you should do the actual calculations.

Resource 5.2.4d

Rounding to 100 000

Use these numbers to generate 6-digit numbers that will round as shown.

6-digit number less than …	Rounds to …	6-digit number greater than …
	100 000	
	200 000	
	300 000	
	400 000	
	500 000	
	600 000	
	700 000	

Explain why two boxes are blocked out.

_____

_____

Compare your answers with another pair. (There are lots of right answers!)

Resource 5.2.5a

Tick the nearest …

1. The whole hundreds, thousands, …, on each side of the number 3 678 290 have been shaded. Complete the table by ticking the nearest thousand, ten thousand, …

	Millions	Thousands			Ones			
		100s	10s	1s	100s	10s	1s	Tick
	3	6	7	8	2	9	0	
Tick the nearest 100	3	6	7	8	2	0	0	
	3	6	7	8	3	0	0	✓
Tick the nearest 1000	3	6	7	8	0	0	0	
	3	6	7	9	0	0	0	
Tick the nearest 10 000	3	6	7	0	0	0	0	
	3	6	8	0	0	0	0	
Tick the nearest 100 000	3	6	0	0	0	0	0	
	3	7	0	0	0	0	0	
Tick the nearest 1 000 000	3	0	0	0	0	0	0	
	4	0	0	0	0	0	0	

2. Complete the table in the same way for the new number: six million, four hundred and seventy-three thousand, eight hundred and twenty.

	Millions	Thousands			Ones			
		100s	10s	1s	100s	10s	1s	Tick
Tick the nearest 100								
Tick the nearest 1000								
Tick the nearest 10 000								
Tick the nearest 100 000								
Tick the nearest 1 000 000								

Resource 5.2.5b

Best estimates

Round the numbers and choose the best estimate. Circle A or B.

1. 456 213 + 213 973

    A. 670 000   or   B. 660 000

2. 2 345 187 + 5 932 865

    A. 7 000 000   or   B. 8 000 000

3. 6 456 324 + 2 143 887

    A. 8 600 000   or   B. 8 500 000

4. 39 987 + 33 321

    A. 73 000   or   B. 72 000

5. 7 865 214 − 3 865 206

    A. 4 100 000   or   B. 4 000 000

Resource 5.2.5c 1 of 2

Newspaper reporting

When journalists report large numbers, they do not usually write exact numbers but round them. For example, if the population of a city is one million, one hundred and eighty-two thousand, four hundred and ninety-six (1 182 496) they might say the population was around one million, two hundred thousand (1 200 000).

Round the following numbers appropriately to appear in a newspaper article.

1. Record attendance at football game

   Eighty-eight thousand, four hundred and sixty-two people attended the football match last night …

   Rounded version (in words)

   _____

Actual number in numerals	
Rounded number in numerals	

2. Giraffe numbers

   Giraffe numbers have declined dramatically since 1985, falling from one hundred and fifty-seven thousand, three hundred and twenty-one to ninety-seven thousand, four hundred and seventy-eight today …

   Rounded version (in words)

   _____

Actual number in numerals		
Rounded number in numerals		

3. Harry Potter book sales

   Harry Potter books have sold four hundred and two million, three hundred and sixty-five thousand books worldwide …

   Rounded version (in words)

   _____

   _____

Actual number in numerals	
Rounded number in numerals	

4. Write your own large number newspaper article extract below.

Resource 5.2.6a

What's my unit? (1)

A pineapple	A bowling ball	A grand piano	A toilet	A car
900	7	450	43	240 000
A basketball	A tennis ball	A light bulb	A football	A jelly bean
0.6	57	33	0.43	0.9
A dice	A playing card	The anchor of a cruise liner	An AA battery	A loaf of bread
4	2	11 300	24	700
An adult	A CD	A car tyre	An average baby	A wooden chair
70	15	9000	3400	9

Resource 5.2.6b

What's my unit? (2)

A house brick	A cat	A pack of cards	A human brain
3	9000	100	1.35

A sheet of paper	A blue whale's heart	An octopus	A gold bar
5	650	55 000	12.3

Resource 5.2.6c

Mammal masses

Blue whale 136 000 kg	Honey badger 10 kg	North American porcupine 8.6 kg	Fruit bat 306 g	Mongoose 2.2 kg
African elephant 4 800 000 g	Giraffe 800 kg	Large hairy armadillo 2 kg	Black-footed ferret 1021 g	Coyote 13 250 g
Hippopotamus 3 750 000 g	Grey kangaroo 28 250 g	Water buffalo 725 000 g	Giant otter 24 kg	African pygmy mouse 0.007 kg
Howler monkey 7000 g	Koala 9300 g	Cheetah 53 500 g	Moose 386 kg	Red squirrel 0.6 kg
Woodchuck 4000 g	Arctic lemming 0.085 kg	Orangutan 64 kg	Sloth bear 100 000 g	Giant panda 117.5 kg
Chimpanzee 45 000 g	Common warthog 100 kg	Lion 175 kg	Mongolian five-toed jerboa 118 g	Grey seal 268 000 g

Resource 5.2.7a

Blank measuring jugs

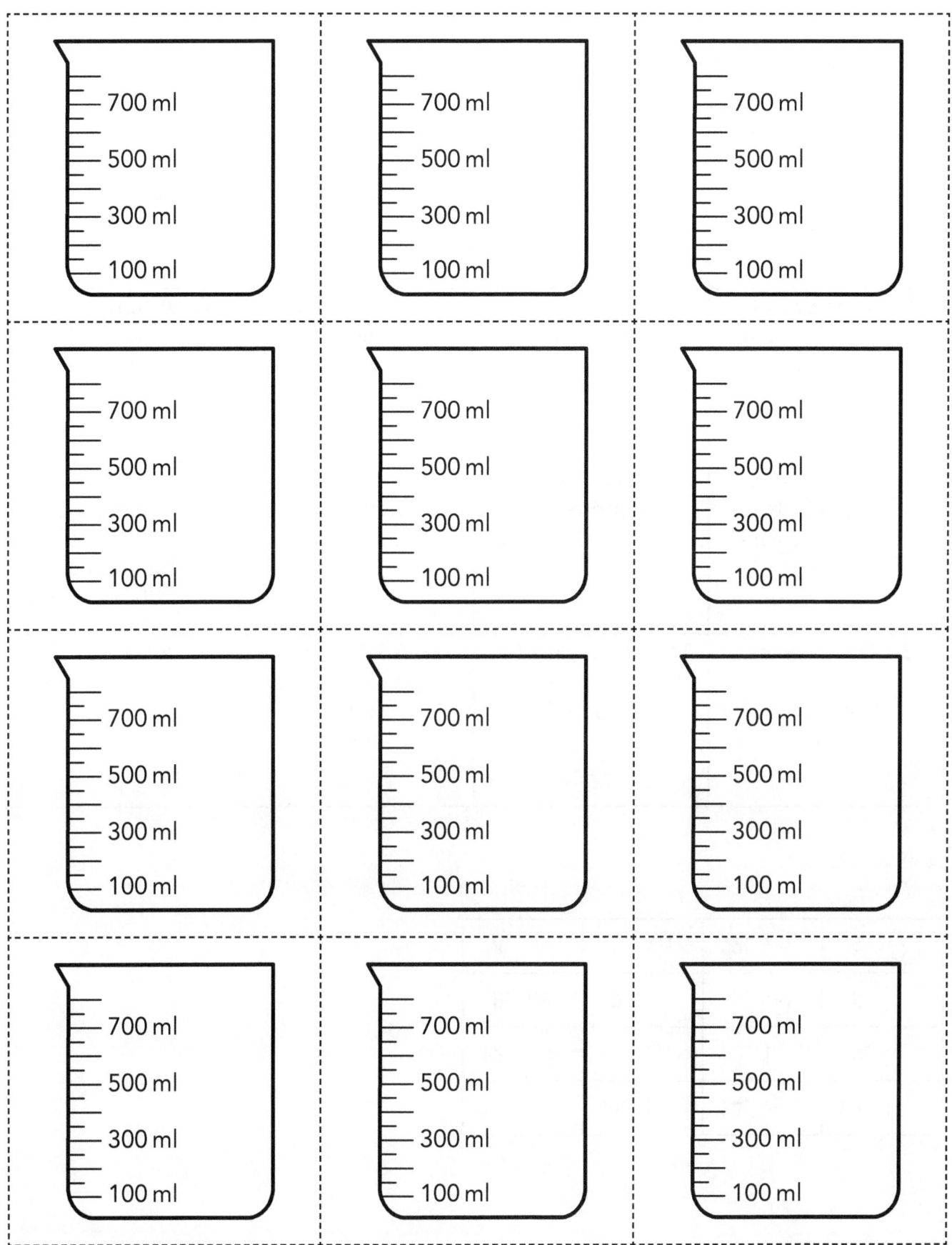

Resource 5.2.7b

Right or wrong units?

Read each measurement carefully. The numbers are all correct, but are the units of measurement right? If not, what should the units of measurement be?

1. The length of a car-park is 50 m²	2. A bottle of ear drops holds 10 l	3. The mass of a large dog is 30 g	4. A carton of milk contains 1000 l of milk
5. A car petrol tank can hold 60 ml of fuel	6. A cup of coffee contains 250 ml	7. A can of cola holds 330 l	8. A teaspoon holds 5 ml of liquid
9. A washing-up liquid bottle contains ½ ml	10. A bottle of lemonade contains 1.5 ml	11. The area of a piece of paper is 300 cm²	12. Normal water intake for an adult should be around 2000 l per day
13. The human body contains between 4 and 6 ml of blood	14. The mass of a chocolate bar is about 50 kg	15. A 70 kg man is made up of about 42 l of water	16. A bathful of water is about 80 ml

ANSWERS

1. m	2. ml	3. kg	4. ml
5. l	6. ml	7. ml	8. ml
9. l	10. l	11. cm²	12. ml
13. l	14. g	15. l	16. l

Resource 5.2.7c

Converting card challenge

You will need:
- a partner to work with
- a set of digit cards
- a piece of paper each.

1. Shuffle your digit cards and take three cards each.
2. Make all the possible numbers that you can using your set of three cards. You may write whole numbers and decimal numbers. For example, the digits 6, 2 and 8 could make the whole numbers 286 and 2 as well as decimals 8.26 and 6.8.
3. Try to find your numbers systematically (for example, in order from smallest to greatest).
4. Turn your numbers into measurements of liquid by writing either 'ml' or 'l' next to each one.
5. Swap lists with your partner. Now convert each other's lists of measurements into the other unit, so ml to l or l to ml.

REMEMBER! Think about what you need to multiply and divide by when converting between millilitres and litres.

6. When you have finished, swap your lists back and check whether your partner has converted your measurements correctly.

TRY THIS! As an extension, choose any two measurements from your list (try choosing one written in millilitres and one written in litres) and see whether your partner can explain which is the larger amount of liquid and why.

For example: 268 ml and 2 l
Which is larger and why?

Resource 5.2.8a

How much liquid?

CHALLENGE 1:
Match the quantities to complete the sentences.
Share your answers with your partner. Are they the same?

A teaspoon of food colouring	200 ml
A large carton of pure apple juice	2 litres
A bathful of water	375 000 litres
A mop bucket of water	500 ml
A large bottle of cola	1.5 litres
A drinking carton of orange squash (the ones with the straws!)	15 litres
A kettle of water	1 litre
A drinking bottle of mineral water	75 litres
The water in a swimming pool	5 ml

CHALLENGE 2:
Write your own facts about millilitres and litres. However, you are not allowed to use the words millilitres or litres! You will need to use the different quantities from Challenge 1 to help you.

For example:
'There are about 100 teaspoons of water in a drinking bottle of mineral water!'

'About 375 000 cartons of apple juice are the same as the quantity of water in a swimming pool!'

Resource 5.2.8b

Quantity cards

7500 ml	1200 ml	6 litres	7.5 litres	13 litres
500 ml	750 ml	280 ml	1 litre	3 litres
12 000 ml	20 000 ml	10 litres	1.9 litres	0.4 litres
3400 ml	200 ml	120 ml	0.25 litres	15 litres
7500 ml	1200 ml	6 litres	7.5 litres	13 litres
500 ml	750 ml	280 ml	1 litre	3 litres
12 000 ml	20 000 ml	10 litres	1.9 litres	0.4 litres
3400 ml	200 ml	120 ml	0.25 litres	15 litres

Resource 5.3.1a

Fastest first! (1)

Cut out the cards and arrange the information in order, fastest speed first.

A train journey is a distance of 200 km. The journey takes 4 hours.	A motorbike travels a distance of 180 km. The journey takes 3 hours.	Sami skates around the local park. The distance is 2 km. It takes half an hour.
Pete runs a distance of 10 000 metres in one hour.	A boat trip takes a total of 3 hours. The trip is a distance of 9 km.	A taxi travels a distance of 20 km. The journey time is 20 minutes.
A helicopter flight takes 2 hours. The flight is a distance of 70 km.	A truck travels a distance of 360 km. The journey takes 4 hours.	Alice cycles at a speed of 40 km per hour.
A car travels at a speed of 80 m per hour.	Ben walks 20 km for charity. He completes the walk in 5 hours.	A hot-air balloon travels a distance of 45 km. The journey takes 2 hours.

Resource 5.3.1b

Fastest first! (2)

Cut out the cards and arrange the information in order, fastest speed first.

Pete runs a distance of 20 km in two hours.

A motorbike travels a distance of 180 km. The journey takes 3 hours.

Sami skates around the local park. The distance is 2 km. It takes half an hour.

A train journey is a distance of 240 km. The journey takes 4 hours.

A boat trip takes a total of 3 hours. The trip is a distance of 9 km.

A taxi travels a distance of 25 km. The journey time is half an hour.

A helicopter flight takes 2 hours. The flight is a distance of 70 km.

A truck travels a distance of 420 km. The journey takes 6 hours.

Alice cycles at a speed of 40 km per hour.

A car travels at a speed of 80 km per hour.

Ben walks 20 km for charity. He completes the walk in 5 hours.

A hot-air balloon travels a distance of 45 km. The journey takes 2 hours.

© HarperCollins*Publishers* 2018

Resource 5.3.1c

Recording speeds

Shuffle each set of cards and place them face down in two piles on the table.
Pick one from each pile. What speed do you calculate from the information you have? Look carefully at the units of measurement.

10 minutes	3 minutes
3 hours	6 hours
12 minutes	12 hours
4 minutes	2 hours
10 hours	120 metres
60 metres	2400 metres
360 metres	72 metres
240 kilometres	48 kilometres
36 kilometres	12 kilometres

Car journeys

a) Fill in the missing information about the car journeys.

	Departure	Arrival	Distance (km)	Speed (km/h)
Car A	08:00	13:00	310	
Car B	09:00	16:00	413	
Car C	11:30		114	57
Car D	13:00	16:00	237	
Car E	14:30	18:30	272	
Car F	16:00	20:00	332	
Car G		21:00	240	80

b) Which car was travelling at the greatest speed? _____

Solving problems about speed

Find the speed each bus travelled in metres per minute and give a possible departure and arrival time for each bus.
- Bus A, B and C all travelled a distance of 9.6 kilometres.
- Bus A took 20 minutes longer than Bus C.
- Bus B took 10 minutes longer than Bus C.
- Bus C took half an hour to travel the total distance.

	Departure time	Arrival time	Time taken (minutes)	Speed in (m/min)
Bus A				
Bus B				
Bus C				

Resource 5.3.2a

Speedy dominoes (1)

Bird	Cat and Dog walk for the same length of time. Dog walks 10 metres further than Cat. Who is the faster?	**Lion**	Cat and Mouse each walk 20 m. Mouse takes 2 minutes longer than Cat. Who is the faster?
Pony	Dog and Lion walk at the same speed. Dog walks for 10 minutes less than Lion. Who walked further?	**Cat**	Horse starts running at 14:30. Pony starts running at 14:40. Both arrive at the lake at 14:45. They run at the same speed. Who had further to run?
Dog	Mouse runs 20 m in 5 minutes. Rabbit hops 30 m in 6 minutes. Who is the faster?	**Fox**	Bird hops for 10 minutes. Mouse runs for half that time. They travel the same distance. Who was the faster?
Mouse	Bird and Fox travel for 3 hours. Fox runs at a speed of 40 km/h. Bird flies at double the speed of Fox. Who travels further?	**Squirrel**	Fox runs at a speed of 12 m/s. Dog runs at a speed of 8 m/s. Who can run 60 m in 5 seconds?
Horse	Squirrel runs 150 m at a speed of 30 m/min. Rabbit runs 100 m at a speed of 25 m/min. Who runs for the longer time?	**Rabbit**	Horse runs 90 m in 2 minutes. Pony runs 120 m in 3 minutes. Who had a speed of 40 m/min?

Resource 5.3.2b

In a spin

1. Spin the spinner to find the value you need to use, for example 'speed'.
2. Choose a value from the matching section of the grid, for example 6 km/h.
3. Write this value in the correct column on your player table. (Write 6 km/h in the 'speed' column.)
4. Make up some values of your own to complete the row on your player table, for example distance 54 km and time 9 minutes.
5. Cover the square on the grid you have used. (6 km/h)
6. Aim to get three counters in a line on the board.

Speed		Time		Distance	
8 km/h	6 km/h	3 h	12 min	90 km	25 m
40 km/h	9 km/h	6 sec	30 min	148 m	250 cm
25 m/min	50 m/min	5 h	11 sec	189 km	132 m
10 cm/min	12 m/s	9 sec	8 hr	75 cm	240 km
20 m/min	7 km/h	50 sec	20 min	144 m	168 km

Speed	Time	Distance
6 km/h	9 h	54 km

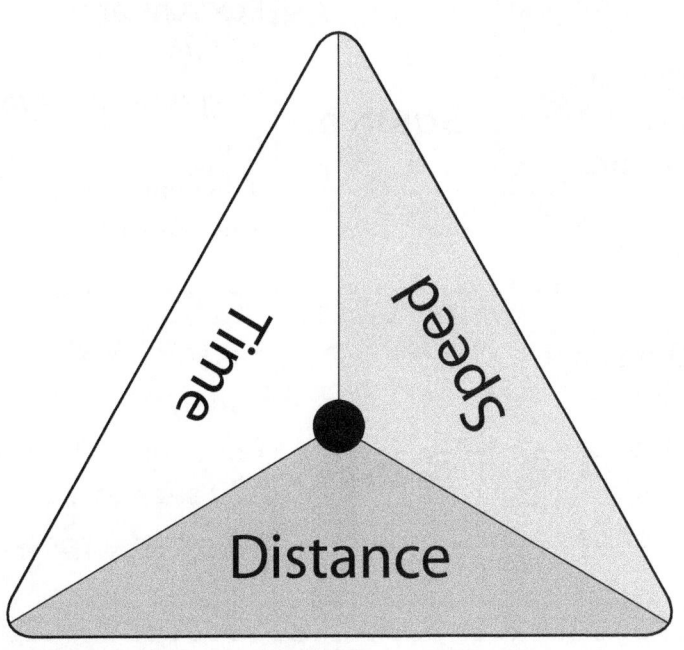

Resource 5.3.2c

Speedy dominoes (2)

Bird	Cat and Dog walk for the same length of time. Dog walks 10 metres further than Cat. Who is the faster?	**Lion**	Cat and Mouse each walk 20 m. Mouse takes 2 minutes longer than Cat. Who is the faster?
Pony	Dog and Lion walk at the same speed. Dog walks for 10 minutes less than Lion. Who walked further?	**Cat**	Horse starts running at 14:30. Pony starts running at 14:35. Both arrive at the lake at 14:45. They each run at a speed of 30 km/h. Who had further to run?
Dog	Mouse runs 20 m in 300 seconds. Rabbit hops 30 m in 6 minutes. Who is the faster?	**Fox**	Bird hops for 10 minutes. Mouse runs for half that time. They travel the same distance. Who was the faster?
Mouse	Bird and Fox travel for 3 hours. Fox runs at a speed of 40 km/h. Bird flies at double the speed of Fox. Who travels further?	**Squirrel**	Fox runs at a speed of 12 m/s. Dog runs at a speed of 8 m/s. Who can run 6000 cm in 5 seconds?
Horse	Squirrel runs 150 m at a speed of 30 m/min. Rabbit runs 100 m at a speed of 25 m/min. Who runs for the longer time?	**Rabbit**	Horse runs 90 m in 2 minutes. Pony runs 120 m in 180 seconds. Who had a speed of 40 m/min?

© HarperCollins*Publishers* 2018

Speed problems

Use the information to help complete the table. Suggest possible arrival and departure times for each coach.

- Coach A and C travel at an average speed of 80 km/h.
- Coach A travels a distance of 420 km.
- Coach B travels 65 km further than Coach C but takes the same time.
- The time taken by Coach C is 120 minutes less than Coach A.

	Speed in km/h	Distance in km	Time taken in hours	Departure time	Arrival time
Coach A					
Coach B					
Coach C					

Resource 5.3.3a

More than, less than or equal

| 2400 ÷ 6 | 16 ÷ 4 | 80 ÷ 20 | 2400 ÷ 600 | 24 ÷ 6 |
| 1600 ÷ 40 | 1600 ÷ 4 | 8 ÷ 2 | 800 ÷ 200 | 240 ÷ 60 |

Use each division *only once* to make all the statements in the grid correct.

160 ÷ 40 > _____
24 ÷ 6 = _____
2400 ÷ 60 > _____
_____ = 160 ÷ 40
1600 ÷ 40 < _____
800 ÷ 20 < _____
80 ÷ 2 > _____
240 ÷ 6 > _____
_____ = 240 ÷ 60
800 ÷ 200 = _____

© HarperCollinsPublishers 2018

Resource 5.3.3b

Dividing by 24

First complete the multiplication facts.

1 × 24 = _____	2 × 24 = _____	3 × 24 = _____
4 × 24 = _____	5 × 24 = _____	6 × 24 = _____

Use the multiplication facts to help solve these divisions.

1) 33 ÷ 24 = _____

The quotient is _____

_____ × _____ = _____

The remainder is _____

The remainder is _____ the divisor.

2) 85 ÷ 24 = _____

The quotient is _____

_____ × _____ = _____

The remainder is _____

The remainder is _____ the divisor.

3) 107 ÷ 24 = _____

The quotient is _____

_____ × _____ = _____

The remainder is _____

The remainder is _____ the divisor.

4) 152 ÷ 24 =

The quotient is _____

_____ × _____ = _____

The remainder is _____

The remainder is _____ the divisor.

5) 63 ÷ 24 = _____

The quotient is _____

_____ × _____ = _____

The remainder is _____

The remainder is _____ the divisor.

6) _____ ÷ 24 = 3 r 1

The quotient is _____

_____ × _____ = _____

The remainder is _____

The remainder is _____ the divisor.

© HarperCollins*Publishers* 2018

Resource 5.3.3c

What division am I solving?

Alfie, Nisha and Ben have been solving division calculations. They each use multiplication to help them.

Can you find three different divisions that each child might have solved?

Complete each division to prove that you are correct.

'I used the multiplication 6 × 39 to help solve my division.' **Alfie**	'I used the multiplication 4 × 86 to help solve my division.' **Nisha**	'I used the multiplication 7 × 42 to help solve my division.' **Ben**
Alfie's division calculations might be: 1) 2) 3)	Nisha's division calculations might be: 1) 2) 3)	Ben's division calculations might be: 1) 2) 3)

© HarperCollins*Publishers* 2018

Resource 5.3.3d

Fastest and slowest

Write the names of the things in order from fastest to slowest each time.

1. Three boats sail a distance of 3 km. Boat A travels at a speed of 5 km/h, Boat B at a speed of 4.5 km/h and Boat C at a speed of 5.2 km/h.

   Fastest _____ Slowest

2. Three people run a 200 metre race. Ellie finishes the race in 28.1 seconds, Ahmed takes 35.6 seconds and Ben takes 27.9 seconds.

   Fastest _____ Slowest

3. Three trains each travel for 3 hours. Train A travels a distance of 285 km, Train B travels 301 km and Train C travels 292 km.

   Fastest _____ Slowest

4. Three children cycle the same distance to school. Bob cycles at 85 m/min, Carla cycles at 78.5 m/min and Luca at 80.7 m/min.

   Fastest _____ Slowest

5. Three animals each walk for 4.5 hours. The lion walks 45 km, the mouse 85 m and the dog walks 38 km.

   Fastest _____ Slowest

Now write a sentence about two of the things in Question 2 and Question 4.

_____ is faster because _____ than _____

_____ is faster because _____ than _____

© HarperCollins Publishers 2018

Resource 5.3.3e

Fastest first

Groups of three children are talking about the races they have run.

a) Find the fastest runner each time. Circle the name.

 **Jemma** I took $6\frac{1}{2}$ minutes to run 1200 metres.	 **Alf** I took 7.25 minutes to run the same distance.	 **Nina** I finished the same race in 420 seconds.
 **Marco** I ran 400 m in 2 minutes.	 **Anesha** I ran 0.5 km in 120 seconds.	 **Luca** I ran $\frac{1}{4}$ km in 70 seconds.
 **Jane** I ran at a speed of 9.5 m/s.	 **Pavlos** I ran at a speed of 60 m/min.	 **Helena** I ran at a speed of 4 km/h.

b) The winners of the three races will receive gold, silver or bronze, depending on who ran the fastest overall, who was second fastest and who was third fastest. Write the names of the three medal winners.

© HarperCollins*Publishers* 2018

Resource 5.3.4a

Guess the group

Match the groups of children to the questions. Answer each question about any remainders.

There are 175 seeds in a packet.
Each child plants 24 seeds.
How many children plant seeds?
How many seeds are left in the packet?

How many children can be given exactly 68p when £4.20 is shared between them?
How much money is remaining?

---

329 children are put in groups of equal size.
62 groups can be made in total.
How many children are in each group?
How many children are left without a group?

A jar of 399 marbles are divided into smaller bags of 42 marbles.
Each child in a group takes a small bag of marbles.
How many children are in the group?
How many marbles are left in the jar?

How many children can be given exactly 86p when £3.45 is shared between them?
How much money is remaining?

There are 380 stickers left in a packet.
Each child takes a sheet of 45 stickers.
How many children take a sheet?
How many stickers are remaining?

Resource 5.3.4b

The divisor is 32

1. Complete the number line to show the multiples of 32.

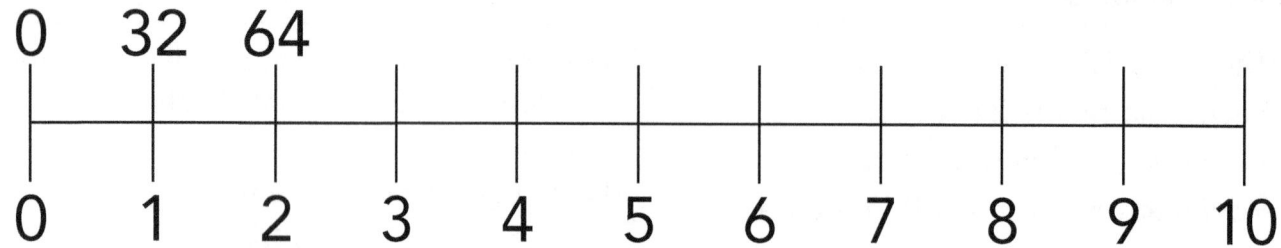

2. Use your number line to help solve these divisions. Use the column method.

a)

$32 \overline{)85}$

b)

$32 \overline{)210}$

c)

$32 \overline{)275}$

d)

$32 \overline{)149}$

e)

$32 \overline{)308}$

© HarperCollinsPublishers 2018

Resource 5.3.4c

Division errors

1. Check each division. Highlight any mistakes.

a)
```
      4 r 3
  73)295
      292
        3
```

b)
```
      8 r 6
  46)364
      358
        6
```

c)
```
      6 r 69
  58)417
      348
       69
```

d)
```
      6 r 7
  32)199
      192
        7
```

e)
```
      9 r 33
  61)572
      549
       33
```

f)
```
     12 r 5
  29)245
      240
        5
```

g)
```
      5 r 23
  84)443
      420
       23
```

h)
```
      6 r 7
  95)567
      570
        7
```

2. Use the column method to correct any divisions. Record them in your exercise book.

Resource 5.3.4d

Domino divisors

Work with a partner. Cut out the dominoes and share them out between you.

The first player lays any domino. Then take it in turns to look at the last calculation each time and lay a domino that gives the largest possible missing number.

Miss a turn if you have not got the domino needed.

The winner is the first to lay their last domino after both players have completed a turn.

6	275 ÷ 93 = _____	**2**	_____ × 45 < 215
1	49 × _____ < 362	**7**	387 ÷ 45 = _____
3	_____ × 52 < 296	**5**	412 ÷ _____ = 63
3	89 × _____ < 508	**5**	468 ÷ 73 = _____
2	_____ × 87 < 352	**9**	24 × _____ < 180
4	170 ÷ 89 = _____	**8**	67 × _____ < 210
7	235 ÷ _____ = 27	**8**	286 ÷ 74 = _____
6	_____ × 77 < 218	**4**	47 × _____ < 450

Writing division problems

Benji uses the calculation 38 × 5 + 12 to check his answers to these two different problems.

Problem A
A 202 cm length of ribbon is cut into pieces each with a length of 38 cm.
How many 38 cm pieces can be cut?
What length of ribbon is left over?

Problem B
Nisha has 202 marbles in a jar.
She gives 12 to her brother.
She divides the rest into bags of 38 marbles.
How many bags does she have?

1. Explain to your partner why Benji's checking calculation is correct for each problem. Talk about what the value '12' represents in each problem.

2. Now make up two problems for each of these checking calculations.
   Problem A should include a remainder.
   Problem B should include a value that is subtracted first before the division.

   i) 73 × 6 + 50

   Problem A

   Problem B

ii) 8 × 42 + 35

Problem A

Problem B

iii) 58 × 6 + 19

Problem A

Problem B

Resource 5.3.5a

Sorting quotients

1. Use what you know about the quotients for each of these divisions to help sort them.

   Write the divisions in the correct sets.

   | 356 ÷ 35 | 425 ÷ 45 | 290 ÷ 48 | 678 ÷ 83 | 609 ÷ 60 | 352 ÷ 89 |
   | 419 ÷ 54 | 521 ÷ 95 | 871 ÷ 86 | 233 ÷ 70 | 916 ÷ 99 | 94 ÷ 19 |

Quotient is less than 5	Quotient is between 5 and 10	Quotient is 10

2. Now write some more divisions of your own in each set. Explain to your partner how you know that each is in the correct set.

Resource 5.3.5b

Quotient spinner

1. Use the column method to help find the missing quotients on the spinner. Remember to use equivalent divisions to help estimate quotients.

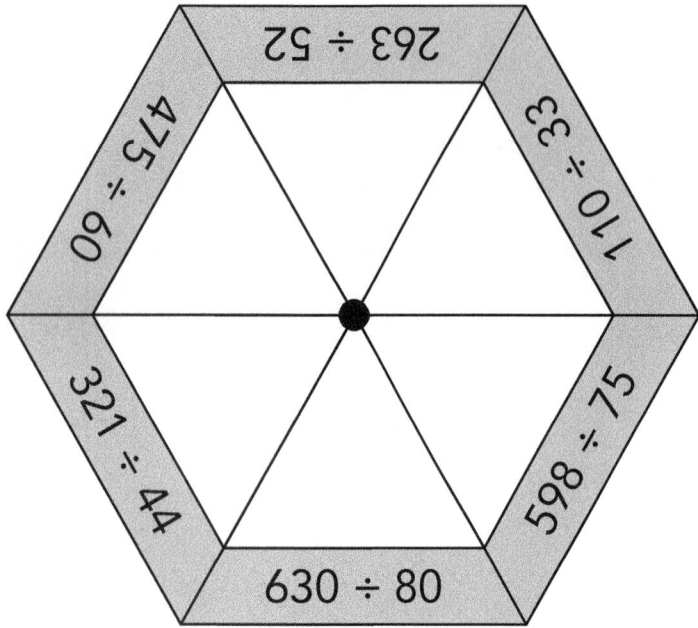

2. Choose one of the divisions from the spinner. Sketch an array to represent it.

Resource 5.3.5c

What number am I?

Use the clues to find the mystery number each time.
Decide how you will prove that your solution is correct.

1. What number am I?

   54 goes into me 7 times but there is a remainder.
   When 32 is subtracted from me I can be divided exactly by 9.
   When 19 is subtracted from me I can be divided exactly by 40.

2. What number am I?

   I am the remainder when 286 is divided by an odd number of tens.
   When you subtract me from 240, the number can be divided exactly by 28.
   9 times my number is less than 150.

Make up your own 'What number am I?' question.

3. What number am I?

   _____
   _____
   _____
   _____
   _____

Resource 5.3.5d

Bar models

Write the two calculations that are required to solve the problem each time.
Draw the bar model that represents 'how many times more' for each problem.

1. *In a school of 500 pupils, 80 are left-handed.*
   How many pupils are right-handed?
   Excluding any remainders, how many times more pupils are right-handed than left-handed?

   The two calculations are _____ and _____ .

2. *In a factory there are 1200 boxes.*
   350 boxes are filled with toys.
   The rest of the boxes are filled with clothes.
   Excluding any remainders, how many times more boxes of clothes are there than boxes of toys?

   The two calculations are _____ and _____ .

3. *In an aquarium there are 1150 fish.*
   240 fish are in a large tank in the entrance hall.
   The rest are in smaller tanks in the side rooms.
   Excluding any remainders, how many times more fish are in the side rooms than in the entrance hall?

   The two calculations are _____ and _____ .

Resource 5.3.6a

Squared paper

Resource 5.3.6b

Division errors

Check each division. Highlight any mistakes and correct them.

1. 384 ÷ 48 48 × 9 = 432 48 × 7 = 336 First 336 ÷ 48 = 7 Then 50 ÷ 48 = 1 r 2 Therefore, 384 ÷ 48 = 8 r 2	**2.** 261 ÷ 29 29 × 13 = 377 29 × 8 = 203 First 203 ÷ 29 = 8 Then 58 ÷ 29 = 2 Therefore, 261 ÷ 29 = 1	**3.** 3055 ÷ 65 65 × 50 = 3250 65 × 40 = 2600 First 2600 ÷ 65 = 50 Then 455 ÷ 65 = 7 Therefore, 3055 ÷ 65 = 57
4. 803 ÷ 73 73 × 11 = 810 73 × 10 = 730 First 730 ÷ 73 = 10 Then 83 ÷ 73 = 1 r 10 Therefore, 803 ÷ 73 = 11 r 10	**5.** 3528 ÷ 56 56 × 70 = 3920 56 × 60 = 3360 First 3360 ÷ 56 = 60 Then 168 ÷ 56 = 3 Therefore, 3528 ÷ 56 = 63	**6.** 1591 ÷ 37 37 × 50 = 1850 37 × 30 = 1147 First 1147 ÷ 37 = 30 Then 444 ÷ 37 = 12 Therefore, 1591 ÷ 37 = 42

Resource 5.3.6c

Quotient sort

1. Use what you know about the quotients for each of these divisions to help sort them.
   Write the divisions in the correct sets.

500 ÷ 40	509 ÷ 42	499 ÷ 45
300 ÷ 70	305 ÷ 73	298 ÷ 75
400 ÷ 60	408 ÷ 64	397 ÷ 68

Quotient is less than 5	Quotient is between 5 and 10	Quotient is 10 or more

2. Now write some more divisions of your own in each set. Explain to your partner how you know that each is in the correct set.

Resource 5.3.6d

Rolling digits

- Take it in turns to roll the 1–9 dice.
- Use the number to complete one of the calculations in a square on the grid.
- Explain to your partner whether the quotient will be a 1-digit or a 2-digit number.
- Your partner should check with a calculator.
- Cover the square with a counter if you are correct.
- The winner is the first player to get four counters in a row, column or on a diagonal.

_32 ÷ 53	461 ÷ _6	902 ÷ _0	_19 ÷ 41	702 ÷ 7_	_82 ÷ 38
575 ÷ _7	_88 ÷ 28	_61 ÷ 56	152 ÷ _5	4_3 ÷ 43	641 ÷ _4
_29 ÷ 22	185 ÷ _8	_14 ÷ 51	832 ÷ _3	416 ÷ _1	_39 ÷ 73
112 ÷ _1	5_2 ÷ 50	631 ÷ _3	_47 ÷ 34	299 ÷ _9	342 ÷ _4
_60 ÷ 16	278 ÷ _7	890 ÷ _0	_38 ÷ 93	8_2 ÷ 80	4_2 ÷ 49
5_2 ÷ 56	607 ÷ 6_	7_0 ÷ 78	691 ÷ _9	_28 ÷ 72	483 ÷ _8

Resource 5.3.7a

Comparing quotients

There are two sets of cards on this resource sheet. Give one set of cards to each group of pupils.

30 ÷ 6	300 ÷ 6
3000 ÷ 60	300 ÷ 60
3000 ÷ 6	300 ÷ 6
3000 ÷ 60	300 ÷ 60
30 ÷ 6	300 ÷ 6
3000 ÷ 60	300 ÷ 60
3000 ÷ 6	300 ÷ 6
3000 ÷ 60	300 ÷ 60

Quotient families

Find families of calculations that are related in some way.
For example, they are equivalent divisions or the quotient can be found by doubling or halving a known quotient.
One of the calculations is the odd one out. Can you start a family that it would be part of?

600 ÷ 12	490 ÷ 7	3600 ÷ 30	6000 ÷ 12
2700 ÷ 45	3000 ÷ 24	4900 ÷ 14	3000 ÷ 32
4900 ÷ 70	3600 ÷ 60	320 ÷ 40	6000 ÷ 24
360 ÷ 60	270 ÷ 9	3000 ÷ 16	2700 ÷ 90

Resource 5.3.7c

Larger or smaller?

1. Write the correct symbol >, < or = to show which quotient is larger or smaller.

3000 ÷ 47 ☐ 3000 ÷ 74	2400 ÷ 60 ☐ 2400 ÷ 61	7000 ÷ 99 ☐ 7000 ÷ 89
3500 ÷ 70 ☐ 3500 ÷ 7	5000 ÷ 24 ☐ 5000 ÷ 48	4800 ÷ 60 ☐ 4500 ÷ 50

2. Use the column method to find the actual quotients.

Quotient puzzle (1)

Choose calculations from the list and write them on the correct shapes so that the quotient in each hexagon is between the quotients in the pentagons on either side.

| 6000 ÷ 75 | 5000 ÷ 65 | 4000 ÷ 55 | 5600 ÷ 82 |
| 4200 ÷ 28 | 5200 ÷ 67 | 5300 ÷ 75 | 4200 ÷ 56 |

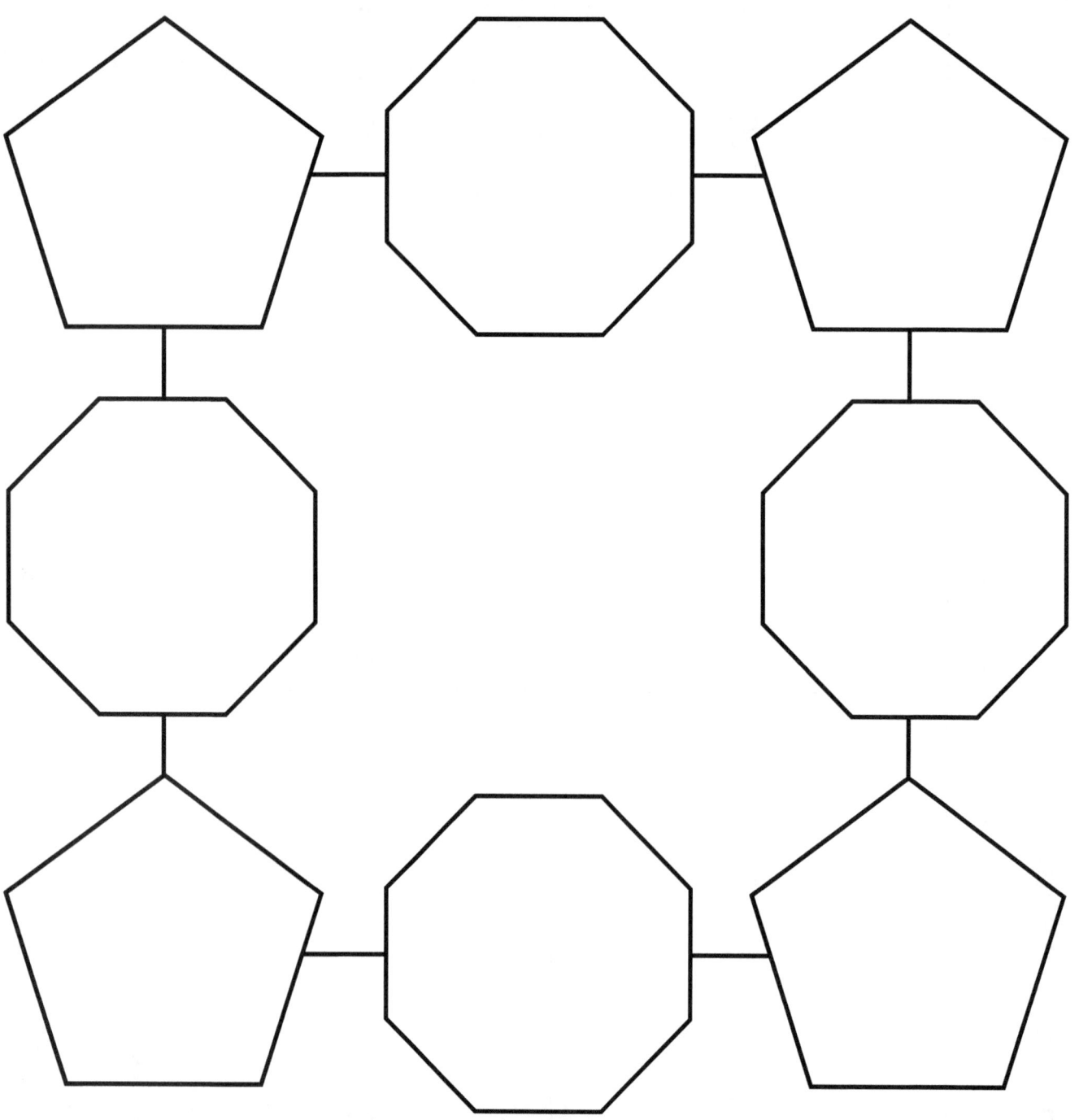

Picture problems

Write the calculation represented by each picture.
Find the answer each time.
Remember to calculate smartly, for example reordering, finding common factors and regrouping.

1. How many pencils in total?

   15 boxes of 25 pencils   25 pencils

2. How many pencils in total?

   25 pencils   22 boxes of 30 pencils

3. How many pencils in total?

   22 boxes of 30 pencils   30 boxes of 8 pencils

4. There are 2400 pencils in a box. Some more are added but some are taken away. How many pencils are left in the box?

   342 pencils → 2400 pencils → 142 pencils

5. How many pencils are in each pot?

   15 boxes of 30 pencils shared equally between 3 pots

6. There are 25 pencils in each pot. A box of 240 pencils is shared equally between them. How many pencils are in each pot now?

   240 pencils shared equally between 4 pots (25 pencils in each pot)

Calculation problems (1)

How do you know that the children are all talking about calculations that can be solved using division?

"45 times a number is 945. What is the number?"

"6300 is how many times bigger than 90?"

"400 is 25 times what number?"

"7200 is the product of two numbers. One of the numbers is 60. What is the other number?"

Resource 5.3.7g

Calculation problems (2)

Why has each child said that? What have they noticed?

I think that I should do the division first in the calculation 30 × 20 ÷ 15.

I will do the calculation 20 × 20 ÷ 50 in the order it is in. I will do the multiplication first.

Resource 5.3.7h

Missing numbers

1. Use eight of these number cards once each to make each of these problems correct.

   | 11 | 12 | 15 | 24 | 25 | 27 | 28 | 36 | 39 |

   a) The product of _____ and 44 is divided by 22. The quotient is 48.

   b) 975 is _____ times bigger than _____.

   c) The product of two 18s is divided by _____. The quotient is _____.

   d) The smallest 2-digit multiple of 7 is multiplied by 52.
   When the product is divided by _____, the quotient is 26.

   e) When the sum of _____ and 1452 is divided by 24, the quotient is 62.

   f) The largest 2-digit multiple of _____ is multiplied by the smallest 2-digit multiple of 9. When the product is divided by 54, the quotient is 33.

2. Use the leftover number card from the first activity.
   Write a problem so this is the missing number.

Resource 5.3.8a

Using known facts

$100 \div 25$	24×10	4×25	10×100
24×5	half of 48	double 16	50×0
5×50	16×20	$48 \div 24$	$100 \div 4$

Resource 5.3.8b

The answer is the same

Use each of the number cards once so that the answer to each calculation is the same two-digit even number.

| 3 | 4 | 5 | 12 | 15 | 25 | 27 | 44 | 60 | 200 |

___ + 4000 ÷ 250	480 × ___ ÷ 24
99 × 0 + ___ × 2	300 ÷ 20 × ___
6000 ÷ ___ ÷ 20	600 − ___ × 20
240 × ___ ÷ 200	___ + 900 ÷ 20
___ × 1000 ÷ 200	12 × 125 ÷ ___

Resource 5.3.8c

Quotient puzzle (2)

Choose calculations from the list and write them on the correct shapes so that the quotient in each hexagon is between the quotients in the pentagons on either side.

| 5600 ÷ 38 | 6200 ÷ 46 | 5000 ÷ 23 | 5300 ÷ 91 |
| 4000 ÷ 54 | 5200 ÷ 80 | 4300 ÷ 67 | 4500 ÷ 16 |

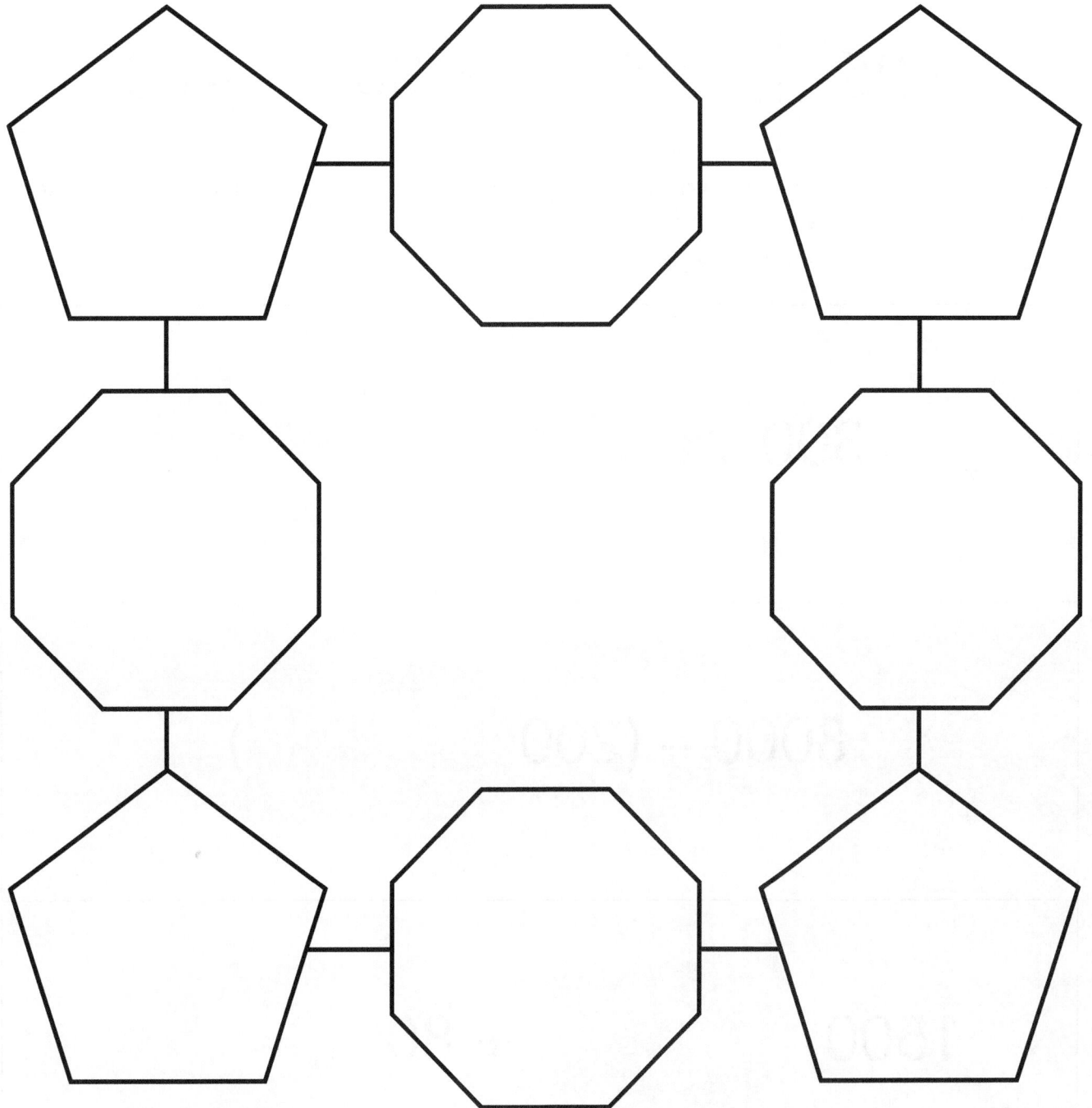

Resource 5.3.8d

Making calculations

Cut out the eight cards in the grid. Shuffle and place face down. Turn over the first five cards and place them in the calculations below.

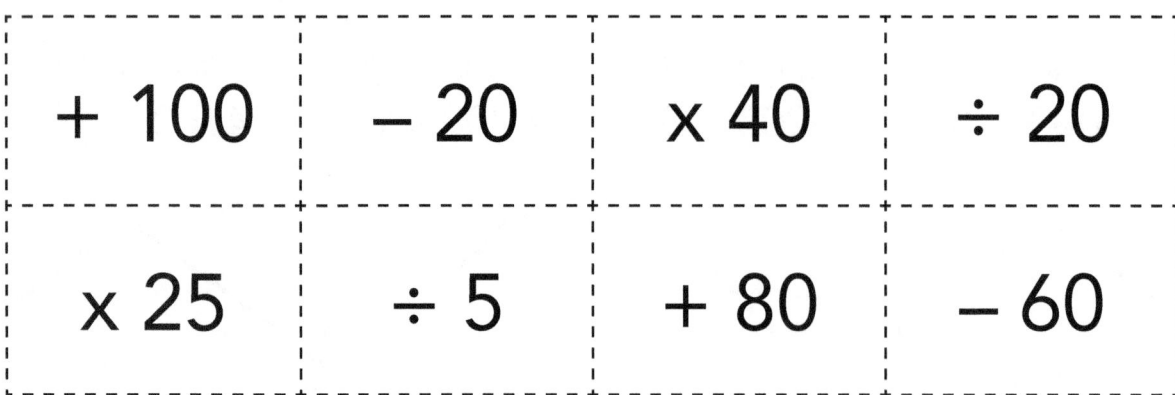

| + 100 | – 20 | x 40 | ÷ 20 |
| x 25 | ÷ 5 | + 80 | – 60 |

Describe to your partner how you will complete the calculations. Think about ways to make the calculation simpler and more efficient.

Put the five cards back into the pack, shuffle and repeat.

300 ☐ ☐

8000 – (200 ☐)

1500 ☐ + 80 ☐

Using bar models

Write the calculations that are required to solve each problem each time.
Draw the bar model that represents each problem.

1 a) 480 pupils in a school have a pet.
      This is 12 times the number of pupils who do not have a pet.

      How many pupils do not have a pet? _____

   b) What is the difference between the number of pupils with and without a pet?

      _____

2. In a factory there are 1500 large boxes and 750 small boxes.
   The total number of boxes are divided into 45 equal groups.

   How many boxes are in each group? _____

3. a) In an aquarium, fish are kept in large tanks and small tanks.
      There are 8400 fish in large tanks. This is 28 times the number of fish in the small tanks.

      How many fish are in the small tanks? _____

   b) What is the difference between the number of fish in the large tanks and the

      number of fish in the small tanks? _____

Division calculations

Discuss Ami and Luka's thinking and explain whether you agree or not.

> The quotient for 5462 ÷ 64 will be more than 100 because 64 is greater than 54.

> The quotient for 3720 ÷ 37 will be more than 100 because 3720 is more than 37 times 100.

Resource 5.3.8g

Quotient cruncher

a) Look at the divisions that are making their way into the 'Quotient cruncher'.
Decide whether the quotients will be 2-digit or 3-digit numbers.
Write the divisions in the correct Quotient cruncher collection box.

Remember
The first two digits in a 4-digit dividend must be equal to or greater than the divisor to give a 3-digit quotient.

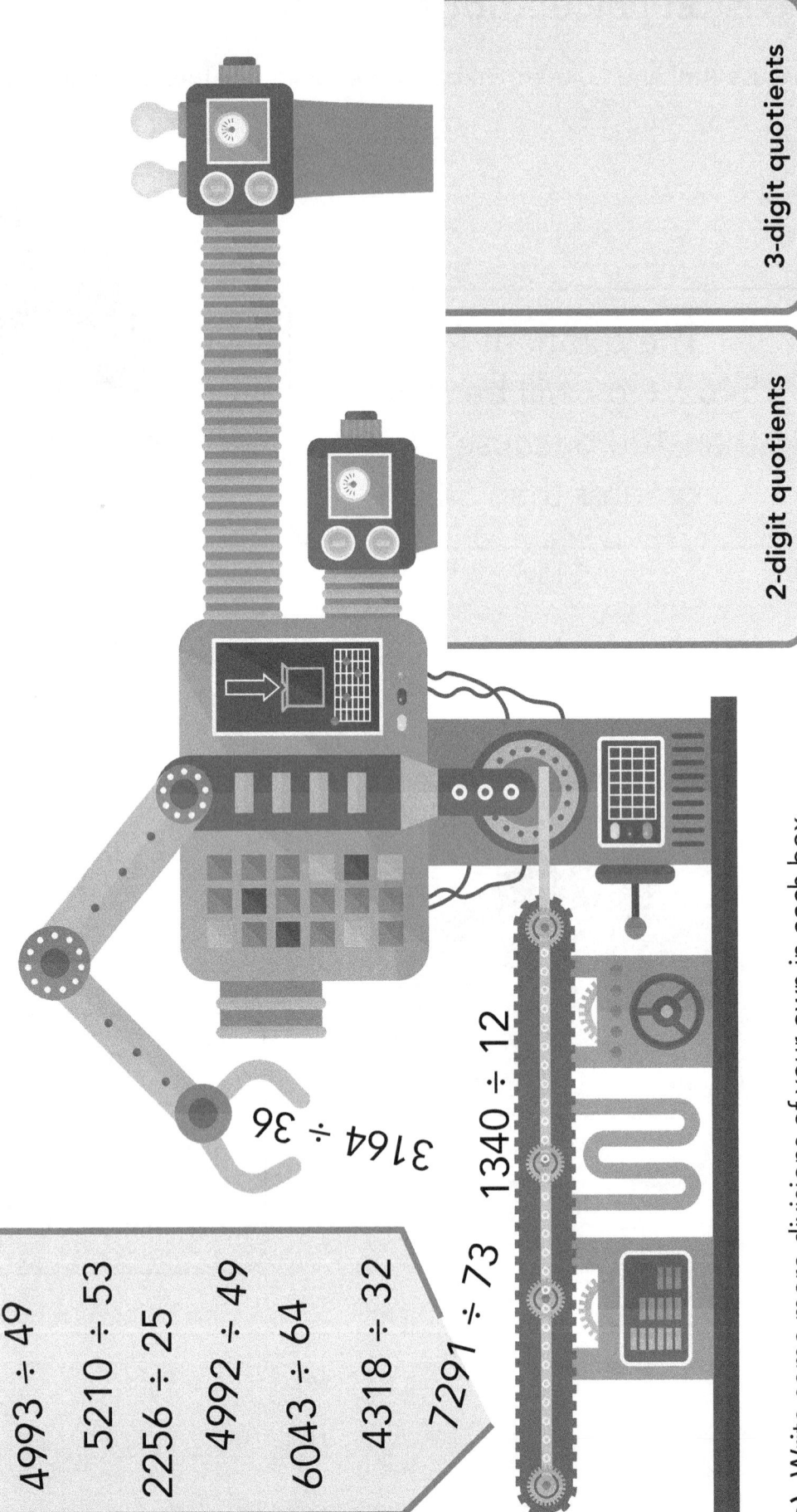

Divisions:
- 4993 ÷ 49
- 5210 ÷ 53
- 2256 ÷ 25
- 4992 ÷ 49
- 6043 ÷ 64
- 4318 ÷ 32
- 7291 ÷ 73
- 1340 ÷ 12
- 3164 ÷ 36

3-digit quotients

2-digit quotients

b) Write some more divisions of your own in each box.

Resource 5.4.1a

Comparing tenths

A game for two players.
- Cut out the 25 game cards and place the 22 tenth cards face down on the table.
- Take turns to each select a fraction card and place it in the left- or right-hand box on the game board. Choose <, > or = to place in the centre of the game board to make the statement correct.
- If it is correct, the player keeps the fraction cards; if not, the cards are put back face down on the table. The winner is the player with the greatest number of fraction cards at the end of the game.

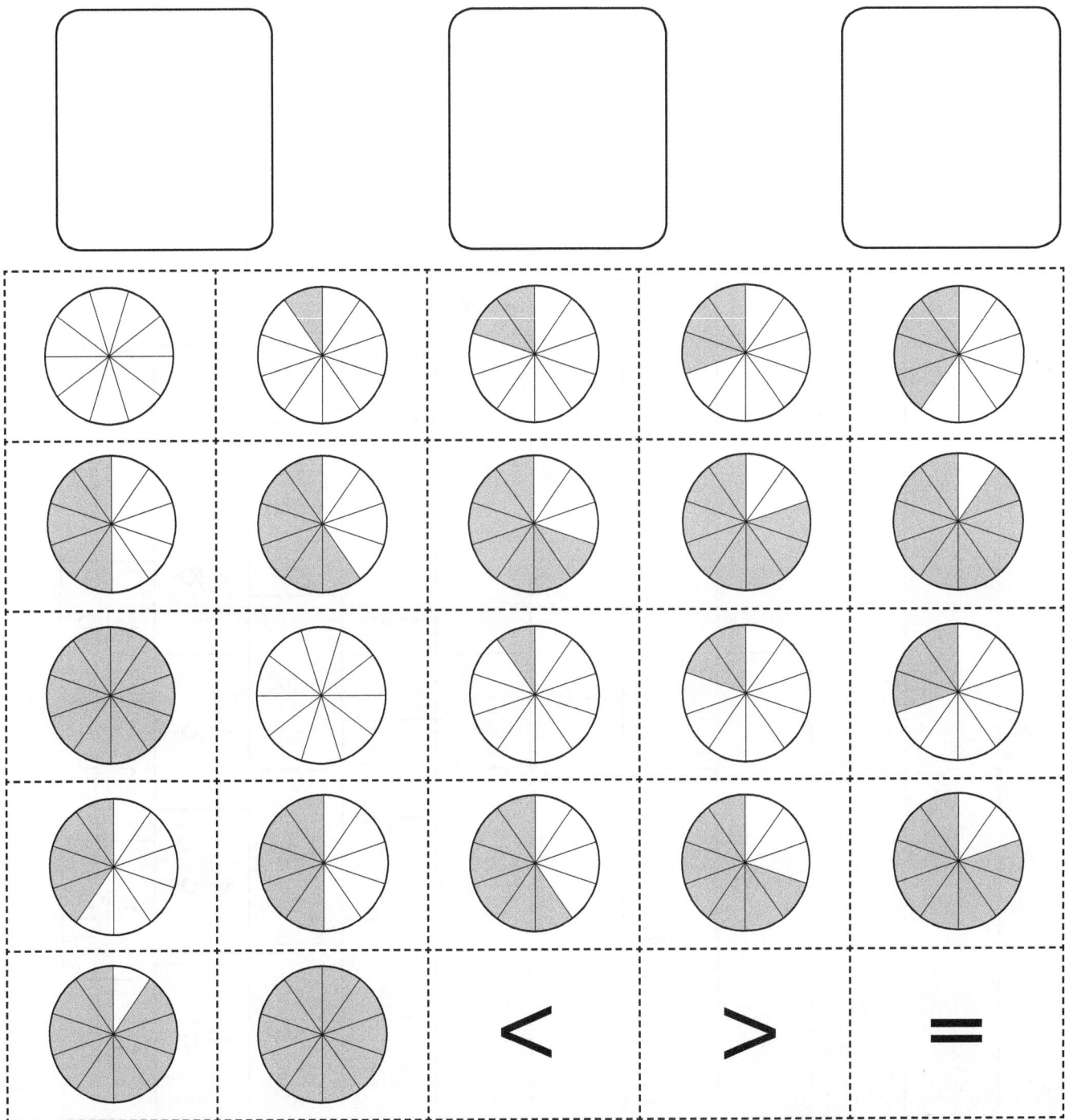

© HarperCollinsPublishers 2018

Fraction wall template

1									
$\frac{1}{2}$		$\frac{1}{3}$	$\frac{1}{4}$	$\frac{1}{5}$	$\frac{1}{6}$	$\frac{1}{7}$	$\frac{1}{8}$	$\frac{1}{9}$	$\frac{1}{10}$
									$\frac{1}{10}$
								$\frac{1}{9}$	
						$\frac{1}{7}$	$\frac{1}{8}$		$\frac{1}{10}$
					$\frac{1}{6}$			$\frac{1}{9}$	
			$\frac{1}{4}$	$\frac{1}{5}$			$\frac{1}{8}$		$\frac{1}{10}$
						$\frac{1}{7}$		$\frac{1}{9}$	
		$\frac{1}{3}$			$\frac{1}{6}$				$\frac{1}{10}$
				$\frac{1}{5}$			$\frac{1}{8}$	$\frac{1}{9}$	
						$\frac{1}{7}$			$\frac{1}{10}$
			$\frac{1}{4}$		$\frac{1}{6}$			$\frac{1}{9}$	
$\frac{1}{2}$							$\frac{1}{8}$		$\frac{1}{10}$
				$\frac{1}{5}$		$\frac{1}{7}$		$\frac{1}{9}$	
		$\frac{1}{3}$			$\frac{1}{6}$				$\frac{1}{10}$
			$\frac{1}{4}$				$\frac{1}{8}$	$\frac{1}{9}$	
				$\frac{1}{5}$	$\frac{1}{6}$	$\frac{1}{7}$			$\frac{1}{10}$

Resource 5.4.2b

Ordering shaded fractions

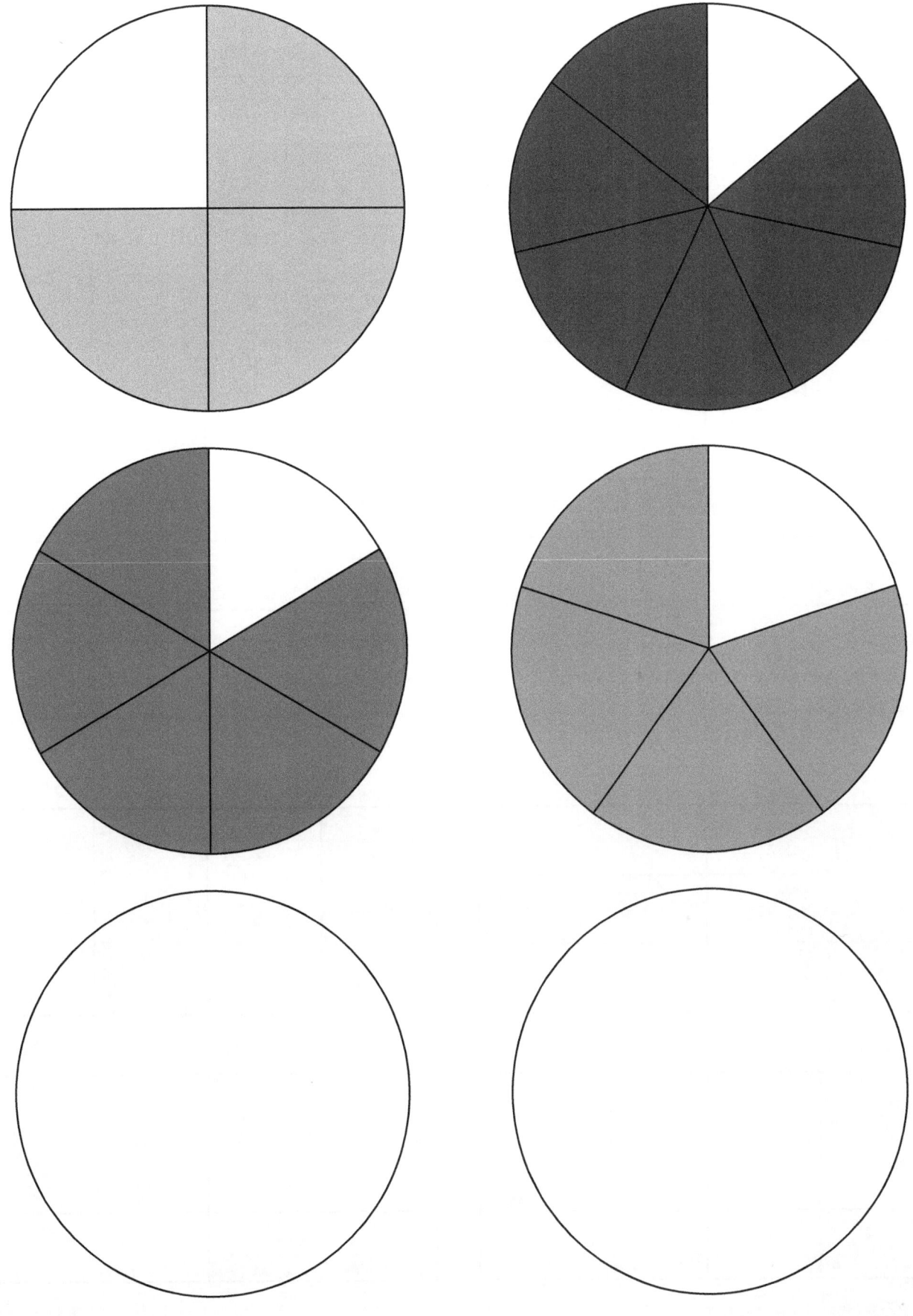

Resource 5.4.3a

Shaded rectangles

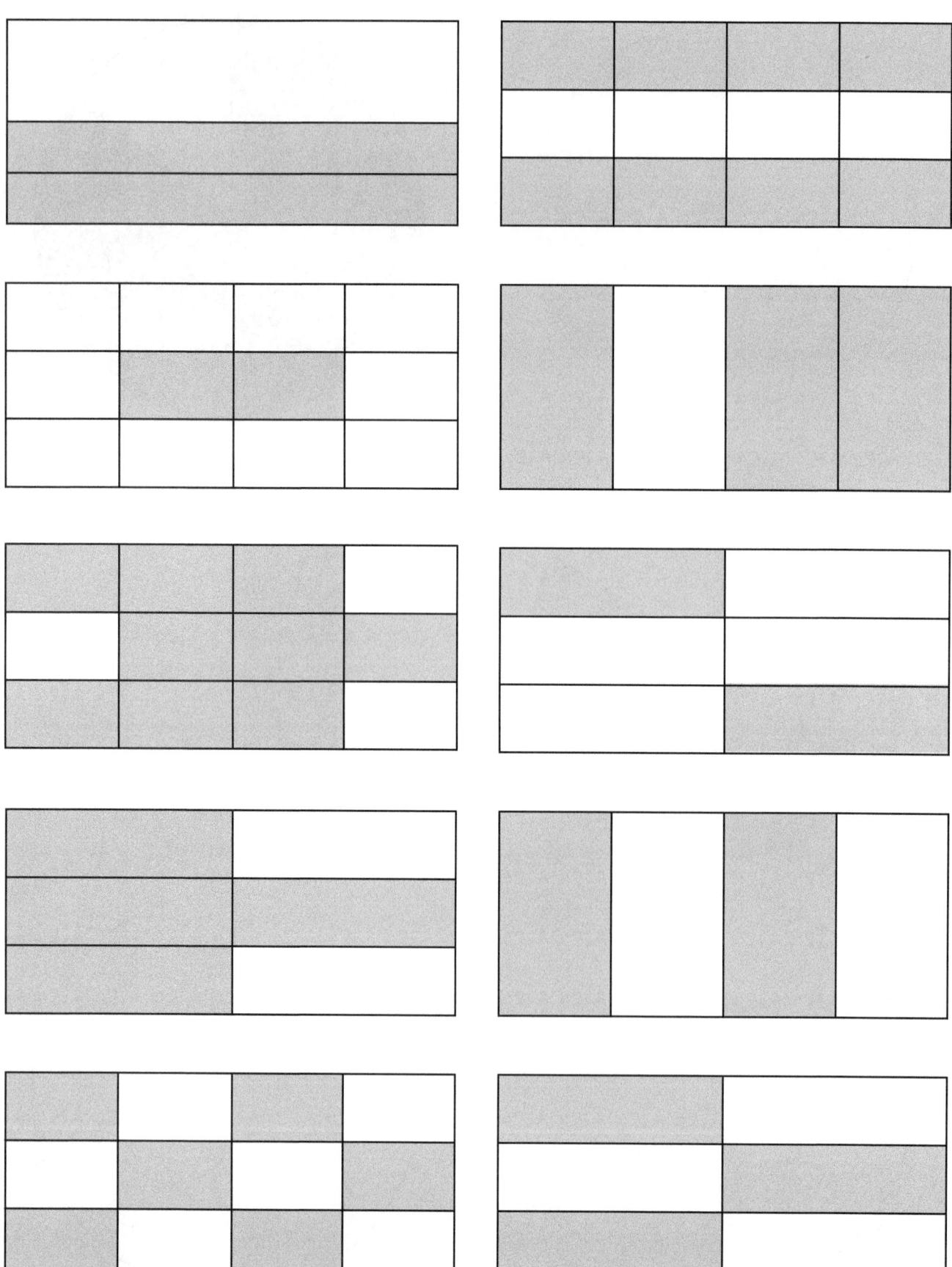

Sorting circles

Resource 5.4.3c

Comparing parts of a rectangle

Resource 5.4.3d

Fraction number lines

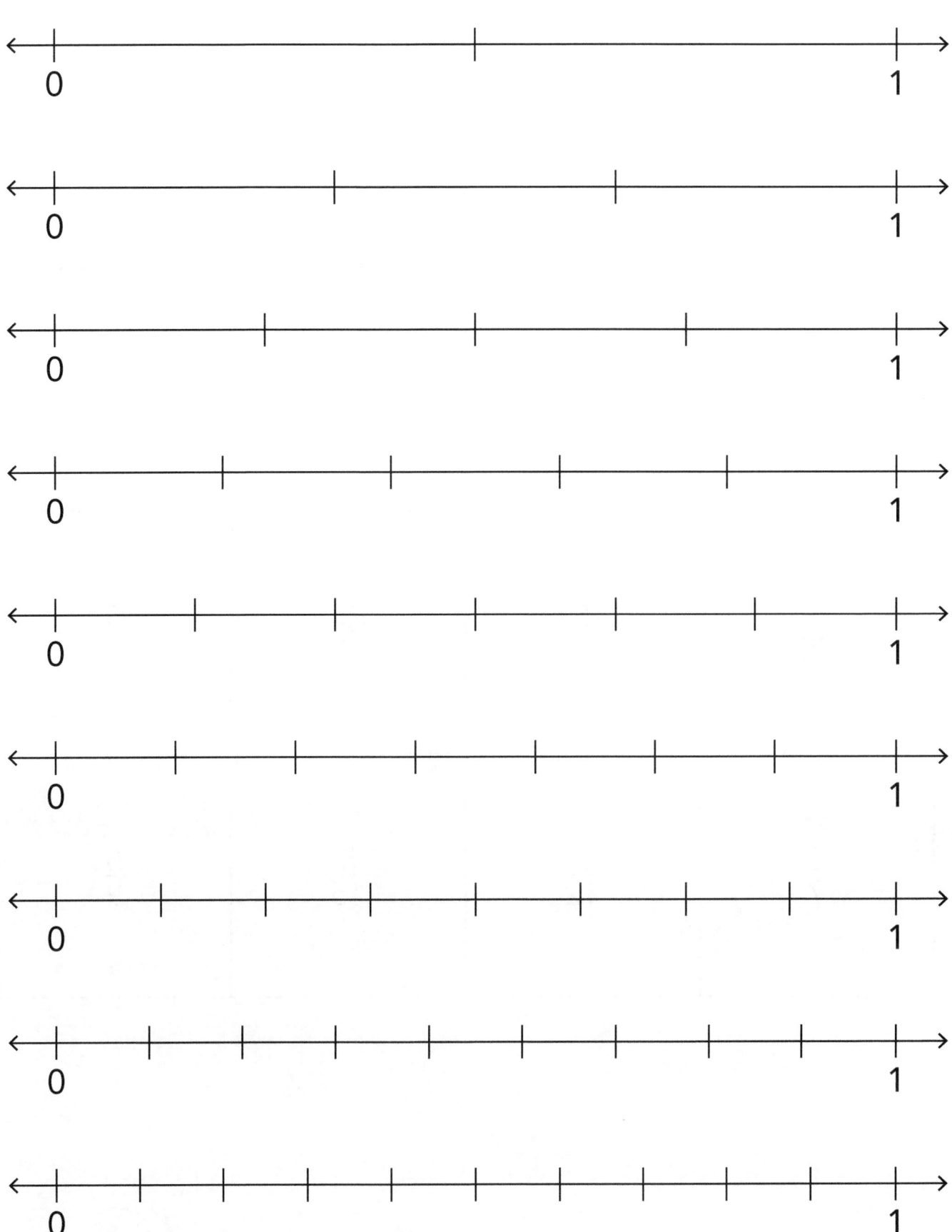

Resource 5.4.3e

Fractions to position on number lines

$\frac{5}{30}$	$\frac{5}{5}$	$\frac{5}{6}$	$\frac{5}{100}$
$\frac{5}{30}$	$\frac{5}{50}$	$\frac{5}{10}$	$\frac{5}{16}$
$\frac{5}{20}$	$\frac{5}{25}$	$\frac{5}{8}$	$\frac{5}{60}$
$\frac{5}{7}$	$\frac{5}{12}$	$\frac{5}{15}$	$\frac{5}{9}$

Resource 5.4.4a

Fractions of quantities

$\frac{1}{2}$ of 20	$\frac{1}{3}$ of 6	$\frac{1}{12}$ of 60	$\frac{1}{8}$ of 80
$\frac{1}{8}$ of 40	$\frac{1}{4}$ of 100	$\frac{1}{10}$ of 20	$\frac{1}{2}$ of 10
$\frac{1}{2}$ of 50	$\frac{1}{5}$ of 25	$\frac{1}{4}$ of 40	$\frac{1}{6}$ of 12
$\frac{1}{10}$ of 100	$\frac{1}{5}$ of 10	$\frac{1}{8}$ of 200	$\frac{1}{10}$ of 250

Resource 5.4.4b

Equivalent fraction puzzle

$\frac{2}{5}$	$\frac{3}{5}$
$\frac{6}{10}$	$\frac{10}{15}$
$\frac{2}{3}$	$\frac{4}{6}$
$\frac{6}{15}$	$\frac{8}{20}$
$\frac{9}{15}$	

Resource 5.4.5a

Fraction sort

$\frac{9}{16}$	$1\frac{5}{6}$	$\frac{5}{4}$
$3\frac{2}{3}$	$\frac{16}{9}$	$\frac{17}{20}$
$\frac{1}{100}$	$5\frac{1}{10}$	$\frac{10}{5}$
$\frac{13}{6}$	$\frac{2}{3}$	$4\frac{3}{5}$

Resource 5.4.5b

Improper fractions and mixed number pairs

$4\frac{8}{9}$	$\frac{47}{9}$	$\frac{29}{7}$
$\frac{32}{7}$	$\frac{44}{9}$	$5\frac{1}{7}$
$\frac{54}{9}$	$4\frac{1}{7}$	$5\frac{2}{9}$
$\frac{36}{7}$	6	$4\frac{4}{7}$

Resource 5.4.6a

Equivalent fractions – extending beyond 1

$\frac{2}{5}$	$\frac{24}{20}$	$\frac{8}{10}$
$\frac{12}{15}$	$\frac{6}{5}$	$\frac{4}{10}$
$\frac{6}{10}$	$\frac{12}{20}$	$\frac{6}{15}$
$\frac{4}{5}$	$\frac{18}{15}$	$\frac{12}{10}$
$\frac{16}{20}$	$\frac{3}{5}$	$\frac{8}{20}$

Resource 5.4.6b

Equivalent fractions – beyond 1

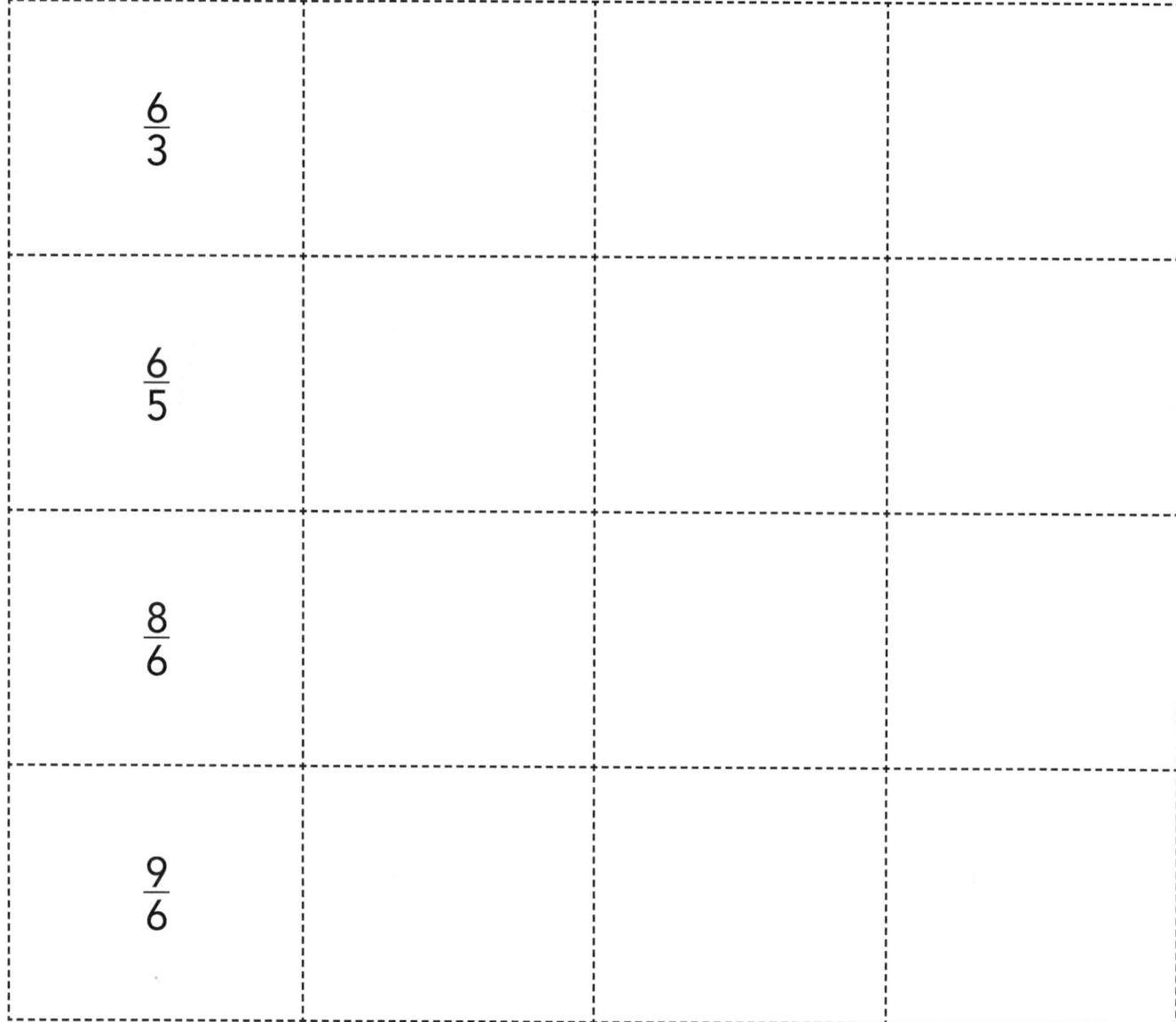

Resource 5.4.6c

Adding and subtracting fractions mentally

A game for two players.
- Print onto card and cut up the game cards. Divide the cards equally between two players.
- On a count of three, both players turn over their top card. Both players try to add or find the difference between the two cards. The first player to call out a correct answer wins the cards.
- Repeat until one player has won the entire deck.

$\frac{0}{25}$	$\frac{1}{25}$	$\frac{2}{25}$	$\frac{3}{25}$
$\frac{4}{25}$	$\frac{5}{25}$	$\frac{6}{25}$	$\frac{7}{25}$
$\frac{8}{25}$	$\frac{9}{25}$	$\frac{10}{25}$	$\frac{11}{25}$
$\frac{12}{25}$	$\frac{13}{25}$	$\frac{2}{25}$	$\frac{3}{25}$
$\frac{4}{25}$	$\frac{5}{25}$	$\frac{6}{25}$	$\frac{7}{25}$
$\frac{8}{25}$	$\frac{9}{25}$	$\frac{10}{25}$	$\frac{11}{25}$

Resource 5.4.8a

Calculation match

Draw lines to match each calculation on the top row to an equivalent calculation on the bottom row

| $3 \times \frac{4}{5}$ | $2 \times 3 + 2 \times \frac{1}{5}$ | $5 \times \frac{3}{5}$ | $4 \times 2\frac{2}{5}$ | $3 \times \frac{6}{5}$ |

| $\frac{5 \times 3}{5}$ | $3 \times 1\frac{1}{5}$ | $\frac{4}{5} + \frac{4}{5} + \frac{4}{5}$ | $2 \times 3\frac{1}{5}$ | $4 \times (2\frac{2}{5})$ |

Resource 5.5.1a

Counting in steps

The numbers in the grid can be sorted into three sequences, counting in steps of:
1. 1000
2. 10 000
3. 100 000.

Cut out the numbers and arrange the sequences in increasing order.

70 000	200 000	34 000	700 000	110 000
500 000	80 000	170 000	40 000	120 000
35 000	1 000 000	32 000	110 000	39 000
800 000	140 000	300 000	31 000	600 000
37 000	30 000	90 000	38 000	15 000
100 000	400 000	36 000	160 000	900 000

© HarperCollins*Publishers* 2018

Resource 5.5.1b

Find the number

Circle the numeral that correctly matches the number in words.

Number in words	Numerals		
1. fifty-four thousand six hundred	54 060	54 600	56 400
2. six million three hundred thousand	6 030 000	6 000 300	6 300 000
3. seven hundred and fifty thousand and twenty	750 020	750 200	752 000
4. forty-two billion	42 000 000	4 200 000 000	42 000 000
5. eighty-one million and eighty-one	8 100 081	810 081	81 000 081
6. thirty-five billion fifty-three million	3 553 000 000	35 530 000 000	35 053 000 000
7. nine million nine thousand nine hundred and nine	99 009 009	9 090 009	9 009 909
8. two million sixty thousand six hundred	2 060 600	2 600 060	26 000 600

Resource 5.5.1c

1, 2, 3 and zeros

All the numbers here contain one 1, one 2, one 3 and however many zero placeholders required.

Fill in the table. The first one has been done for you.

Number of digits	In words	In numerals
5 digits	Thirty-one thousand and twenty	31 020
☐ digits	Two hundred and thirty-one thousand	
☐ digits	One million two hundred thousand and three	
☐ digits	Three billion one hundred and two thousand	
☐ digits	Twenty billion and thirteen	

Complete the table. Remember one 1, one 2, one 3 and zeros only!

Number of digits	In words	In numerals
5 digits		
6 digits		
7 digits		
8 digits		
9 digits		
10 digits		

© HarperCollinsPublishers 2018

Resource 5.5.1d

Change the order

Put a < or > to make the number statement in the left-hand column true.

Underline *two adjacent* digits in the second number that, if they were swapped, would reverse the greater than or less than sign.

Write the new number statement in the right-hand column. The first one has been done for you.

< or >?	New number statement
45 765 342 < 45 7<u>82</u> 329	45 763 342 > 45 728 329
123 564 379 ☐ 123 564 378	
3 584 729 ☐ 5 267 896	
500 000 760 ☐ 500 000 704	
7 987 321 746 ☐ 7 899 456 543	
67 875 354 ☐ 67 098 325	
8 000 000 320 ☐ 8 000 000 149	
786 796 ☐ 786 797	
809 567 215 ☐ 809 534 215	
97 324 465 ☐ 97 327 532	

Is there more than one possible new solution for each question?

_____

Swap papers with another pair and check one another's answers.

Resource 5.5.2a

Five numbers

Look carefully at these numbers and answer the questions.

A	B	C	D	E
302 925 728	70 654 681	1 654 312 807	65 072 325	5 780 631

1. Write the letter of the number that has:

   a) 2 in the millions place _____

   b) 8 in the ten thousands place _____

   c) 6 in the hundred thousands place _____

   d) 1 in the billions place _____

   e) 6 in the ten millions place _____

2. Write the letter of the number that has a zero placeholder in the:

   a) thousands place _____

   b) ten millions place _____

   c) hundred thousands place _____

   d) millions place _____

   e) tens place _____

3. Round each number to the nearest million and then write the rounded number in words. The first one has been done for you.

   a) A 303 000 000   three hundred and three million

   b) B _____ _____

   c) C _____ _____

   d) D _____ _____

   e) E _____ _____

© HarperCollins*Publishers* 2018

Resource 5.5.2b

Number questions

Use these numbers to write and answer the following questions.

A	B	C	D	E
302 925 728	70 654 681	1 654 312 807	65 072 325	5 780 631

1. Write the letter of the number that has 2 in the millions place. [A]

   Write and answer four more similar questions so that the answers are:

2. C _____

3. E _____

4. D _____

5. B _____

6. Write the letter of the number that has a zero placeholder in the:

   a) thousands place _____

   b) ten millions place _____

   c) hundred thousands place _____

   d) millions place _____

   e) tens place _____

7. Round each number to the nearest million and then write the rounded number in words.

   a) A _____   _____

   b) B _____   _____

   c) C _____   _____

   d) D _____   _____

   e) E _____   _____

8. Put the numbers in order, starting from the smallest.

   _____

Resource 5.5.2c

Rounding 'to the nearest …' or 'up to the next …'

Are the following statements true or false?
Circle the correct answer.

1. 56 872 452 rounded to the nearest million is 57 000 000	True / False
2. 9 362 721 rounded up to the next million is 9 000 000	True / False
3. 78 173 245 rounded off to the nearest million is 78 000 000	True / False
4. 78 173 245 rounded up to the nearest million is 79 000 000	True / False
5. 56 872 452 rounded up to the nearest hundred thousand is 56 800 000	True / False
6. 7 394 765 rounded up to the next hundred thousand is 7 400 000	True / False
7. 453 851 rounded to the nearest thousand is 453 000	True / False
8. 91 987 869 rounded off to the nearest ten million is 90 000 000	True / False
9. 7 467 842 rounded up to the next million is 7 000 000	True / False
10. 86 432 537 rounded to the nearest ten million is 90 000 000	True / False

© HarperCollinsPublishers 2018

Resource 5.5.2d

Rounding statements

Complete these statements.
Insert 'to the nearest' or 'up to the next' to make the statement true.

1. 34 368 301 rounded _____ million is 34 000 000	
2. 5 432 678 210 rounded _____ billion is 5 000 000 000	
3. 836 332 rounded _____ thousand is 837 000	
4. 6 298 431 rounded _____ million is 6 000 000	
5. 45 464 rounded _____ ten thousand is 46 000	
6. 67 843 924 rounded _____ hundred thousand is 67 800 000	
7. 6 421 754 rounded _____ million is 7 000 000	
8. 345 980 rounded _____ hundred is 346 000	
9. 34 276 821 rounded _____ million is 34 000 000	
10. 709 453 231 rounded _____ million is 710 000 000	

Resource 5.5.3a

Order of operations

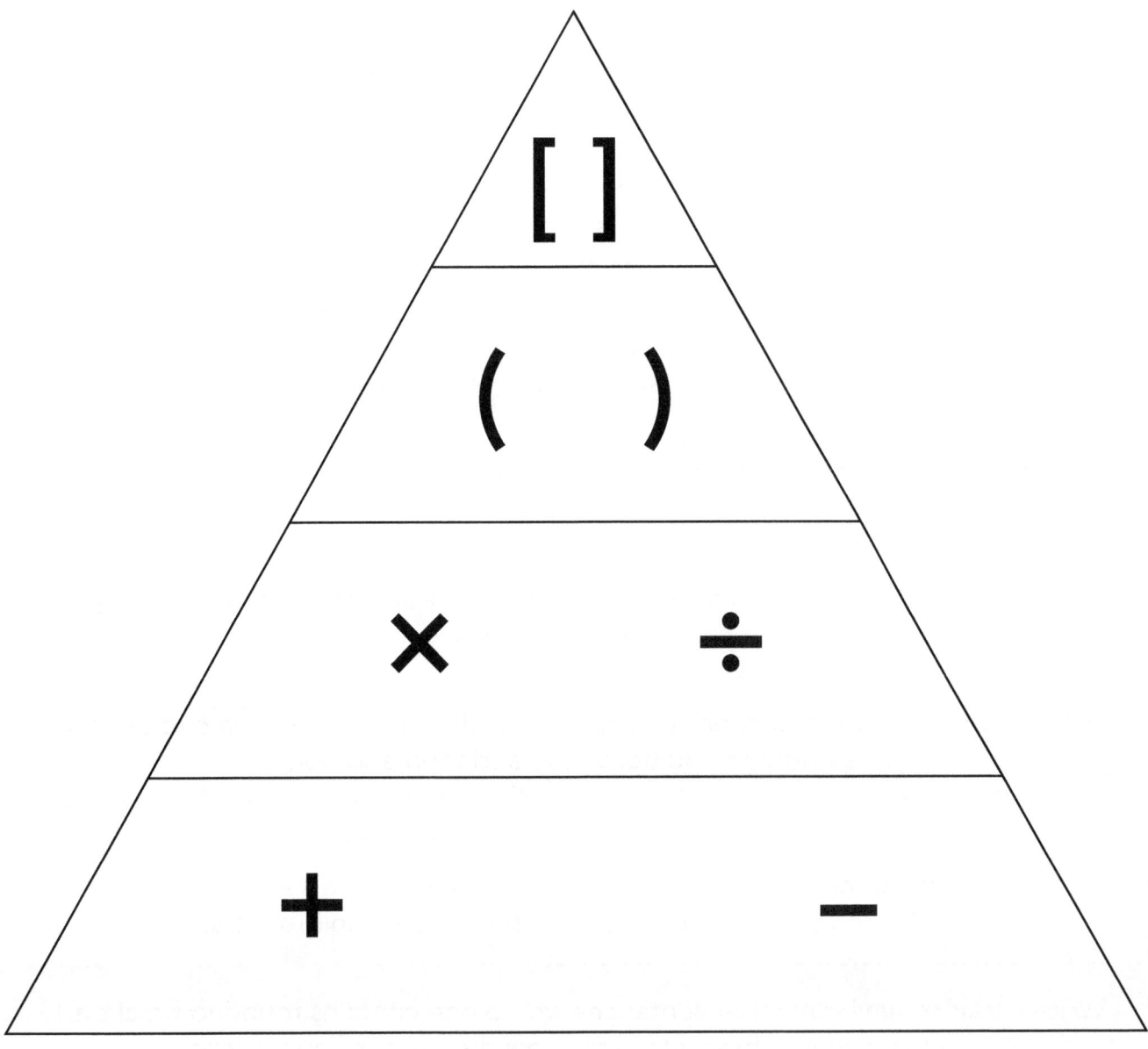

Resource 5.5.3b

Order of operations cards

Write a pair of number sentences containing the symbols +, x and then –.
One of your number sentences should contain brackets.

Write a pair of number sentences containing the symbols x, – and then ÷.
One of your number sentences should contain brackets.

Write a pair of number sentences that have the same numbers and contain only two steps.
One of your number sentences should contain brackets.

Write a pair of similar number sentences where both contain brackets, but in different places.

Write a pair of number sentences that look very similar but that give very different answers.

Write a pair of number sentences where the order of operations in one of them is addition, multiplication and then addition.
In the other one, the order should be multiplication, then addition, then addition.

Write a pair of number sentences containing the symbols –, x and then –.
One of your number sentences should contain brackets.

Write a pair of similar number sentences where one contains rounded brackets ( ) within squared brackets [ ] to show the order of operations.

Resource 5.5.5a

Blank 100 squares

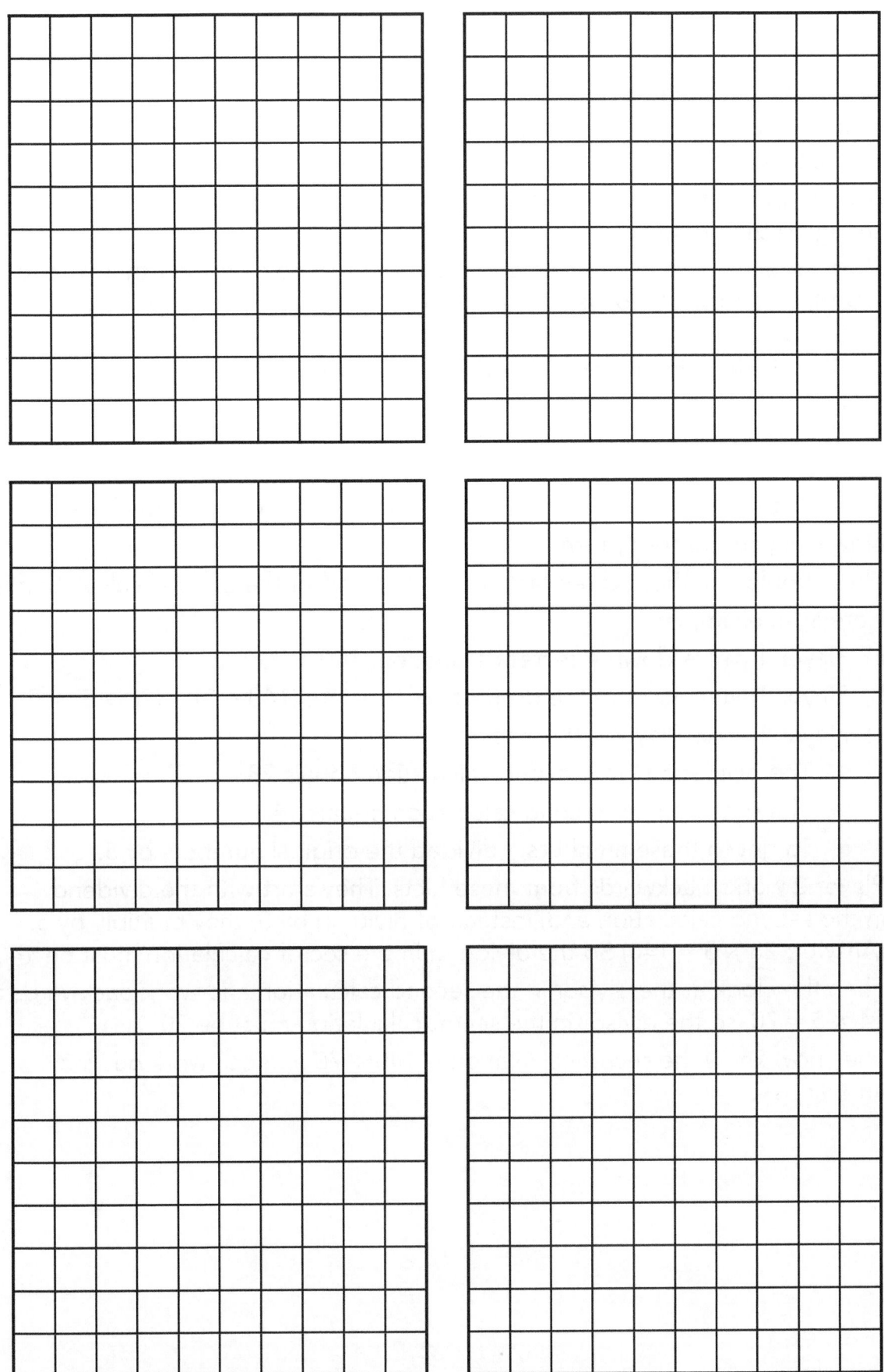

Resource 5.5.6a

Derive the division!

Work with a partner. The aim of the activity is to give your partner just enough clues about a calculation for them to work backwards and work out (or 'derive') the division calculation that it is based on.

1. Write down a secret division calculation of your choice. This is the calculation your partner will be trying to guess.
2. Use the property of division to alter the dividend and the divisor without changing the quotient.
3. Share three facts from your second calculation to help your partner work out what the first calculation is. Use these sentence starters to help you:

   - The dividend in my second calculation equals _____.

   - The divisor in my second calculation equals _____.

     - To get to these numbers, I multiplied/divided the original numbers by _____.
4. Now it is your partner's turn!
   They should use these three facts to work out what the original calculation is.
   Here is an example:
   a) Player 1 writes down a secret calculation: 140 ÷ 70 = 2
   b) Player 1 alters it using the property of division: (140 ÷ 5) ÷ (70 ÷ 5) = 2
   c) Player 1 gives Player 2 three facts:
      - The dividend in my second calculation equals 28.
      - The divisor in my second calculation equals 14.
      - To get to these numbers, I divided the original numbers by 5.
5. Player 2 works backwards from these facts. They start with the dividend in the second calculation and, instead of dividing by 5, they multiply by 5. (Answer: 28 × 5 = 140) So the dividend in the secret calculation must be 140.
   Then they look at the divisor in the second calculation and work backwards again. 14 × 5 = 70, so the divisor in the secret calculation must be 70.
   They now know the secret calculation is 140 ÷ 70 and can work out the answer as 2!

Resource 5.5.7a

Roman numerals

Cut out the cards.

I	1	V	5	X	10
X	10	L	50	C	100
D	500	M	1000	II	2
XV	15	XX	20	XXV	25
CC	200	CCC	300	MM	2000

Lay the cards face down. Player 1 turns over two cards and, if they match, wins the pair and has another turn.
If they are not a pair, turn the cards back over in the same place.
The winner is the player with the most pairs at the end of the game.

Resource 5.5.7b

Roman numeral sequences

Complete these Roman numeral sequences.

1. Count in ones to ten.

   __I__, _____, _____, _____, _____, _____, _____, _____, _____, __X__

2. Count in tens to a hundred.

   __X__, _____, _____, _____, _____, _____, __LXX__, _____, _____, _____

3. Count in hundreds to a thousand.

   __C__, _____, _____, _____, _____, _____, _____, _____, _____, __M__

4. Count in fifties to five hundred.

   __L__, _____, _____, _____, _____, _____, _____, _____, _____, __D__

Read these number sequences and work out the difference.

5. IX, XIX, XXIX, XXXIX, XLIX, LIX

   _____, _____, _____, _____, _____, _____

   The numbers are going up in _____.

6. III, V, VII, IX, XI, XIII, XV

   _____, _____, _____, _____, _____, _____, _____

   The numbers are going up in _____.

7. XXIV, XLIV, LXIV, LXXXIV, CIV, CXXIV

   _____, _____, _____, _____, _____, _____

   The numbers are going up in _____.

8. XCIX, XCIV, LXXXIX, LXXXIV, LXXIX, LXXIV, LXIX

   _____, _____, _____, _____, _____, _____

   The numbers are going down in _____.

Resource 5.5.7c

Famous dates

Write the sum of the symbols for each date in Roman numerals. Find the correct event and enter the matching letter in the final column.
The first one has been done for you.

Date in Roman numerals	Sum of the symbols	Correct event
MDCCCXXXVII	1000 + 500 + 300 + 30 + 7 = 1837	B
MM		
MLXVI		
MCCXV		
MCDXCII		
MDCLXVI		
MCMLII		
MDLXXXVIII		
MCMXIV		

Date and event in numerals
A. 1666, Great Fire of London
B. 1837, Victoria becomes Queen
C. 2000, Millennium
D. 1914, start of World War I
E. 1066, Battle of Hastings
F. 1588, defeat of the Spanish Armada
G. 1215, signing of the Magna Carta
H. 1952, coronation of Queen Elizabeth II
I. 1492, Columbus discovered America

© HarperCollinsPublishers 2018

Resource 5.5.7d

Before and after

Here are some dates. First determine the date and then try to work out the date for the year before and the year after in Roman numerals.

Before	Date	After
MMVII 2007	MMVIII 2008	MMIX 2009
	MDCCL	
	MCMXCIX	
	MCDXCIX	
	MXLVIII	
	MDCXC	

Compare your answers with a friend's answers.

Resource 5.5.8a

Favourite superheroes in Class 5A

Class 5A voted for their favourite superhero. Here is a pictogram showing how they voted.

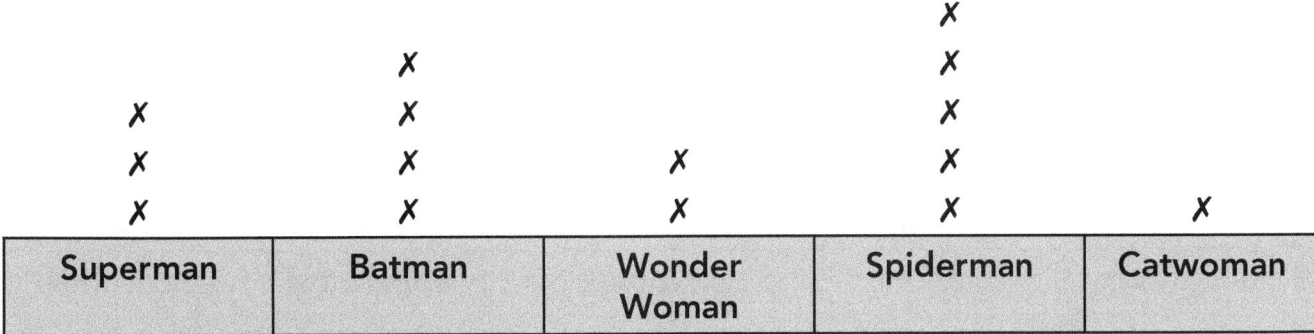

X represents 2 children.

1. Which superhero has the greatest number of votes? How many?

   _____

2. Which superhero has the least number of votes? How many?

   _____

3. How many more votes did Batman receive than Wonder Woman?

   _____

4. How many pupils are there in Class 5A?

   _____

5. Write and answer a question of your own from the data.

   _____

   _____

Year 5 favourite superheroes

There are two classes in Year 5, 5A and 5B.
Each class voted for their favourite superhero. Here are the results.

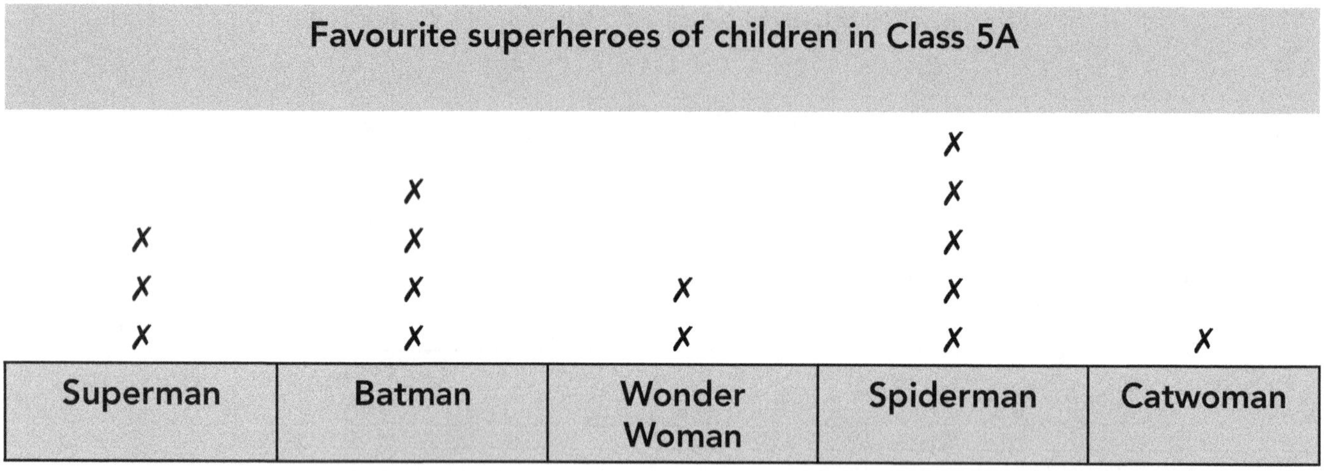

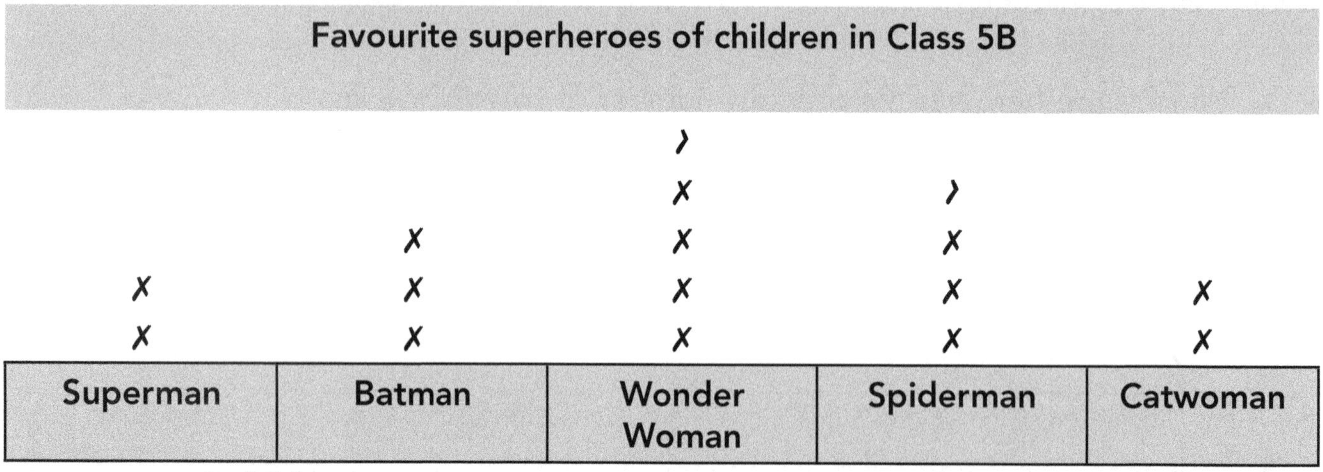

Favourite superheroes of children in Class 5A

Superman	Batman	Wonder Woman	Spiderman	Catwoman
X X X	X X X X	X X	X X X X X	X

Favourite superheroes of children in Class 5B

Superman	Batman	Wonder Woman	Spiderman	Catwoman
X X	X X X	X X X X X	X X X X	X X

X represents 2 children.

Answer these questions.

1. How many children are in each class? _____

2. In Class 5A, which superhero was most popular and which was least popular?

   _____

3. In Class 5B, which two superheroes received an odd number of votes?

   _____

4. How many more pupils voted for Wonder Woman in Class 5B than in Class 5A?

   _____

5. Use the data to complete a table showing the results for all Year 5 children (Classes 5A and 5B).

Superhero	Superman	Batman	Wonder Woman	Spiderman	Catwoman
Number of children					

6. How can you check that your numbers are correct?

   _____

Resource 5.5.8c

Javelin records

Peter is a talented javelin thrower.
His dad has kept records of his best throws every six months since he was aged 7.

Peter's age	7 years	$7\frac{1}{2}$ years	8 years	$8\frac{1}{2}$ years	9 years	$9\frac{1}{2}$ years
Javelin throw	14.9 m	17.5 m	19.4 m	21.8 m	23.3 m	

Answer the following questions

1. What was Peter's best throw aged $7\frac{1}{2}$? _____

2. How old was Peter when his best throw was 21.8 m? _____

3. What is the difference between Peter's throws aged 7 and aged 9? _____

4. How much did Peter's throw improve from $7\frac{1}{2}$ to 8 years? _____

5. In the next six months, Peter's best throw improved by 1.2 m. Fill in his record aged $9\frac{1}{2}$.

Resource 5.5.8d

High jump results

Linda, Alvin, Bob, Peter and May took part in a high jump competition. The results were very exciting. The difference between the first and last places was only 10 cm. Alvin achieved a jump of 122 cm, just 1 cm higher than Bob, and 3 cm higher than May. Linda's and Peter's jumps were just 2 cm apart, with Linda just taking 4th place.

Draw a table to show the results.

	Linda	Alvin	Bob	Peter	May
Height jumped					
Place					

Write and answer three questions from the data.

1. _____

2. _____

3. _____

Electric car sales

The line graph shows the sales of electric cars at a car salesroom.
Study the graph and answer the questions.

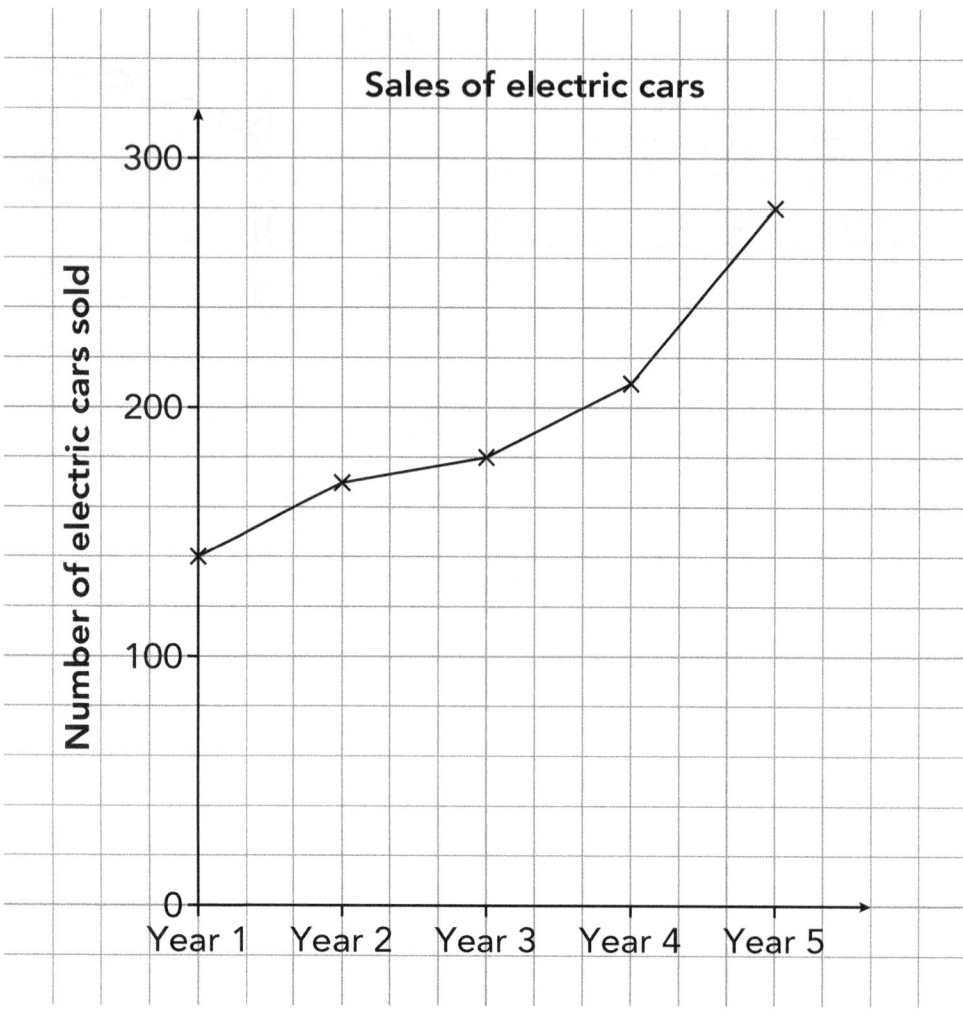

1. How many years does the graph cover? _____

2. Describe the scale on the vertical axis.

   _____

3. How many electric cars were sold in Year 4? _____

4. What is the increase in sales between Year 1 and Year 2? _____

5. Between which two years does the greatest annual increase occur? _____

6. Describe the trend shown by the graph.

_____

7. Use the data to complete the table.

Year	1	2	3	4	5
Number of electric cars sold					

Resource 5.5.8f

Electric bike sales

The table shows a shop's sales of electric bikes over five years.

Year	1	2	3	4	5
Number of electric bikes sold	200	230	270	310	390

Construct a line graph from the data. Make sure that the axes are labelled.

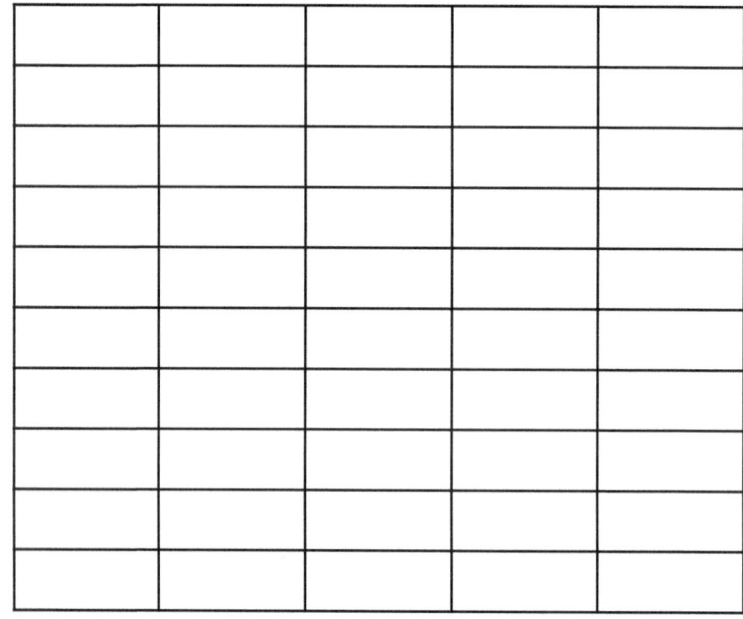

1. Describe the trend shown by the graph.

2. Write three questions of your own from the data.

   a) _____

   b) _____

   c) _____

3. Katy says, 'Sales have doubled over the five-year period'? Is she correct?

Answers

Chapter 1 Revising and improving

1.1 Multiplication and division

1. Column method used correctly.
   (a) 1080 (b) 1175
   (c) 14 732 (d) 302 600
   (e) 106 r 4 (Check: 106 × 9 + 4 = 958)
   (f) 130 (Check: 130 × 50 = 6500)
2. (a) 1494 (b) 3800 (c) 2563
   (d) 15 609 (e) 34 (f) 20 944
3. (a) 99 × 100 = 9900
   (b) 5 3
   (c) 8 116
   (d) 1, 2, 3 or 4   5, 6, 7, 8 or 9
4. (a) There are 12 possible multiplications: 23 × 45, 23 × 54, 24 × 35, 24 × 53, 25 × 43, 25 × 34, 32 × 45, 32 × 54, 34 × 52, 35 × 42, 42 × 53, 43 × 52
   The greatest product: 52 × 43 = 2236
   The smallest product: 24 × 35 = 840
   (b) 12 346 × 67 889 has the greatest product. Explanation should mention that this is because the second multiplication contains one more lot of a five-digit number that is only one less (12 346 lots of 67 889 compared to 12 345 lots of 67 890). So, the overall answer will be greater.

1.2 Addition and subtraction of fractions

1. $\frac{5}{6}$ $\frac{3}{8}$ $\frac{4}{12}$ or $\frac{1}{3}$
2. $\frac{6}{10}$ or $\frac{3}{5}$ $\frac{50}{100}$ or $\frac{5}{10}$ or $\frac{1}{2}$ $\frac{7}{7}$ or 1
3. (a) $\frac{4}{5}$ (b) $\frac{5}{9}$ (c) $\frac{39}{53}$ (d) $\frac{20}{143}$
   (e) $\frac{27}{87}$ (f) $\frac{151}{800}$ (g) $\frac{5}{19}$ (h) $\frac{2}{111}$
4. (a) $\frac{2}{5}$ (b) $\frac{3}{5} - \frac{2}{5} = \frac{1}{5}$ $\frac{1}{5}$ of 30 = 6 pupils
5. (a) $\frac{1}{5}$ or $\frac{2}{10}$
   (b) Most = storybooks, Least = fiction books;
   fiction books, mathematics books, science books, storybooks
6. (a) $\frac{3}{16}$ (b) $\frac{49}{100}$ (c) $\frac{16}{22}$ (d) $\frac{13}{100}$
7. $\frac{1}{8} + \frac{3}{8} + \frac{3}{8} = \frac{7}{8}$, so Joshua cannot complete his plan.
   $\frac{1}{8}$ of 96 = 12 (pages left)

1.3 Decimals (1)

1. (a) 2 5 7 9 2 (b) 200.304
   (c) 5 0.1 0.05 (d) 10 8 0.09
2. (b) 0.011 (c) 6.06 (d) 120
   (e) 80.03 (f) 16.2
3. (b) 0.560 (c) 3.000 (d) 10.200
   (e) 50.100 (f) 120.550
4. (a) 0.1 (b) 0.2 (c) 0.25
   (d) 0.7 (e) 0.29 (f) 0.237
5. (a) 0.01 (b) 0.15 (c) 2.20
   (d) 5.05 (e) 0.05 (f) 0.1
   (g) 5.5 (h) 3.18
6. 0 1 59 220
7. 45.79, 45.88 or 45.97

1.4 Decimals (2)

1. (a)
   0.5   5.5   8.5 10   14.5 16.5   19.5
   ↓   ↓   ↓   ↓   ↓   ↓   ↓
   0   2   4   6   8   10 12 14 16 18 20
   (b) (i) 19.5 (ii) 0.5
   (c) 0.5 5.5 8.5 10 14.5 16.5 19.5
2. (a) $\frac{1}{10}$ (b) $\frac{1}{100}$ (c) $\frac{23}{100}$
   (d) $\frac{1}{5}$ or $\frac{2}{10}$ (e) $\frac{1}{2}$ or $\frac{5}{10}$ (f) $\frac{99}{100}$
3. (a) > (b) = (c) >
   (d) > (e) > (f) >
4. (a) C (b) C (c) B (d) C
5. (a) 0.90 0.1 0.01 0.001
   (b) 10 m 0.91 km 1 km 1.1 km 1.50 km
6. (a) 0.12 0.13 0.21 0.23 0.31 0.32
   (b) 2.103 2.130 3.120 3.102
   (c) 0.123 0.321 1.023 1.320

1.5 Mathematics plaza — Which area is larger?

1. (a) 1 cm² (b) 4 cm²
   (c) 9 cm² (d) 16 cm² 25 cm²

(e) Answers may note that these are successive square numbers. They may also allude to the following fact: When the side length of a square is increased to n times its original length (n is a positive integer), its area is increased to n^2 times its original length.

2. (a) There are five possible shapes (with dimensions 9 × 1, 8 × 2, 7 × 3, 6 × 4 and 5 × 5)
   Example answer:

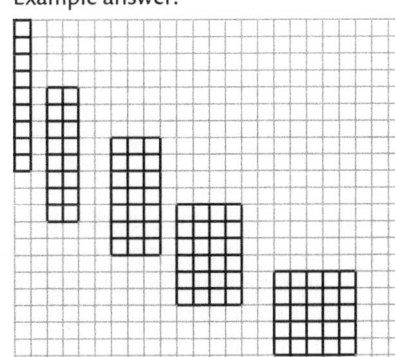

   (b) 1 × 9 = 9 (cm²)   2 × 8 = 16 (cm²)
   3 × 7 = 21 (cm²) 4 × 6 = 24 (cm²)
   5 × 5 = 25 (cm²)
   (c) the same   different   equal (or 'the same')

3. Table should be completed with pupils' working.
   The area will be the greatest when the length and width are both equal to 35 cm and the window is a square. Therefore, the length and width of a rectangular window should be 36 cm and 34 cm respectively (giving an area of 1224 cm²).

4. When the length is 16 m and the width is 8 m, the sheep pen has the maximum area. It is 128 m².

5. 288 m²

Chapter 1 test

1. (a) 813 (b) 80
   (c) 924 (d) 416
   (e) 700 (f) 14
   (g) 68   (h) 5

Answers

2 Column method used correctly.
   (a) 6068   (b) 262 300
   (c) 85 (Check: 85 × 40 = 3400)
3 (a) 100 000   (b) 6100
   (c) 7   (d) 531
4 (a) $\frac{5}{7}$ (b) $\frac{13}{15}$ (c) $\frac{6}{29}$
   (d) $\frac{156}{365}$ (e) $\frac{3}{49}$ (f) $\frac{43}{100}$
5 (a) $\frac{3}{10}$ (b) $\frac{3}{100}$ (c) $\frac{33}{100}$
   (d) $\frac{71}{100}$ (e) $\frac{7}{10}$ (f) $\frac{87}{100}$

6 (a) 2 3 3 5 3
   (b) 50 8 0.09
   (c) 1.05 0.6 365
   (d) 3
   (e) 8 112 7 99 4
   (f) 0.01 1 0.11 11
   (g) 36
   (h) 36
   (i) 25 51
7 $\frac{2}{4}$ or $\frac{1}{2}$ $\frac{9}{13}$ $\frac{70}{100}$ or $\frac{7}{10}$

8 (a) 46 kg (b) $\frac{1}{6}$ 10 (c) 225 m²
   (d) 196 m² (e) 42 cm

Chapter 2 Large numbers and measures

2.1 Knowing large numbers (1)

1 (a)

Group	Millions		Thousands		Ones
Place value	Hundred millions		Hundred thousands		Hundreds
	Ten millions		Ten thousands		Tens
	Millions		Thousands		Ones

   (b) 10
   (c) 378 28 867
   (d) thousands ones three hundred and seventy-eight million, twenty-eight thousand, eight hundred and sixty-seven
   (e) 21 001 036

2 (b)

Ten thousands	Thousands	Hundreds	Tens	Ones
2	5	1	9	8

   Twenty-five thousand, one hundred and ninety-eight
   2 × 10 000 + 5 × 1000 + 1 × 100 + 9 × 10 + 8 × 1
   20 000 + 5000 + 100 + 90 + 8

   (c)

Hundred thousands	Ten thousands	Thousands	Hundreds	Tens	Ones
4	1	2	7	0	8

   Four hundred and twelve thousand, seven hundred and eight
   4 × 100 000 + 1 × 10 000 + 2 × 1000 + 7 × 100 + 0 × 10 + 8 × 1
   400 000 + 10 000 + 2000 + 700 + 0 + 8

   (d)

Millions	Hundred thousands	Ten thousands	Thousands	Hundreds	Tens	Ones
2	3	9	5	1	9	8

   Two million, three hundred and ninety-five thousand, one hundred and ninety-eight
   2 × 1 000 000 + 3 × 100 000 + 9 × 10 000 + 5 × 1000 + 1 × 100 + 9 × 10 + 8 × 1
   2 000 000 + 300 000 + 90 000 + 5000 + 100 + 90 + 8

   (e)

Ten millions	Millions	Hundred thousands	Ten thousands	Thousands	Hundreds	Tens	Ones
7	6	2	0	3	0	0	0

   Seventy-six million, two hundred and three thousand
   7 × 10 000 000 + 6 × 1 000 000 + 2 × 100 000 + 0 × 10 000 + 3 × 1000 + 0 × 100 + 0 × 10 + 0 × 1
   70 000 000 + 6 000 000 + 200 000 + 0 + 3000 + 0 + 0 + 0

3 119 033 70 070 007 961 273 928 500 000 000
4 (a) ✗ (b) ✗ (c) ✓ (d) ✓
5 (a) 6 660 000
   (b) 6 606 000 6 066 000
   (c) 6 600 600 6 060 600 6 006 600
6 975 310 − 103 579 = 871 731

2.2 Knowing large numbers (2)

1 (a) hundred millions
   (b) ten thousands thousands millions
   (c) 2 3 500 709
   (d) ten billions 10 000 000 000
       hundred millions 500 000 000
       millions 6 000 000 tens 90
   (e) 913 4 913 004
   (f) 4000 4 40
   (g) 1 000 000 1000 1000
2 (a) C (b) B (c) C
3 (a) < (b) > (c) < (d) =
4 (a) 69 998 69 999 70 000 70 001 70 002
   (b)

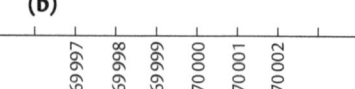

5 10 000 − 23 = 9977
   9977 + 999 = 10 976
6 (a) 808 000
   (b) 200 549
   (c) 698 055 (Check: 698 055 + 22 000 = 720 055)
   (d) 2494
   (e) 379 348
   (f) 5 087 988 (Check: 5 087 988 + 712 012 = 5 800 000)
7 50 600, 56 000, 60 500, 65 000, 500 006
   500 006, 65 000, 60 500, 56 000, 50 600
8 Answers will vary according to data used. For example: England: 53 012 456; Northern Ireland: 1 810 863; Scotland: 5 295 403: Wales: 3 063 456 Total: 63 182 178 (Source: 2011 UK census)

2.3 Knowing large numbers (3)

1 (a) 8 ten millions hundred thousands thousands ninety million, three hundred and one thousand

398

Answers

(b) 60 054 003
(c) 660 060 006 9
(d) 60 006 080 sixty million, six thousand and eighty
(e) 80 43
(f) 7

2 (a) eight million, two hundred and seventy-one thousand, two hundred and seventy
(b) twenty-three thousand, two hundred and fifty
(c) four million, seven hundred and ninety-one thousand
(d) five billion, nine hundred million

3 (a) ✗ (b) ✗ (c) ✓ (d) ✗
4 (a) D (b) B (c) A (d) E (e) C
(f) 4 050 000 800 > 400 050 008 > 40 050 008 > 40 000 080 > 405 008
5 (5976 − 1432) ÷ 8 = 568 (times)
6 100 000
7 790 212 450 212

2.4 Rounding large numbers (1)

1 The following numbers should be circled: 100 200 500 600
2 0   a 10 000 ✓
   20 000   b 30 000 ✓
   40 000 ✓   c 50 000
   70 000 ✓   d 80 000
   90 000 ✓   e 100 000
3 30 000 ✓   40 000
   100 000   110 000 ✓
   970 000 ✓ 980 000
   120 000 ✓ 130 000
   6 400 000 ✓ 6 410 000
   390 000   400 000 ✓
4 (a) 10 000   (b) 56 090 000
   (c) 440 000   (d) 1 100 000
   (e) 10 000   (f) 9 950 000
5 (a) 81 (b) 119 (c) 2 (d) 1
6 (a) One hundred and thirty-six thousand and ninety
   Fifty-nine thousand, four hundred
   Seventy thousand and twenty
   One million, sixty-four thousand, nine hundred and ninety-nine
   (b) 140 000 60 000 70 000 1 060 000
   (c) 1 064 999 > 136 090 > 70 020 > 59 400
7 (a) 7 777 000 Seven million, seven hundred and seventy-seven thousand 7 780 000
   (b) 0, 1, 2, 3 or 4 4
   (c) 5, 6, 7, 8 or 9 5
   (d) 10

8 7 000 070 7 000 007 The difference is 63

2.5 Rounding large numbers (2)

1 300 000 ✓   a 400 000
   700 000 ✓   b 800 000
   100 000 ✓   c 200 000
   900 000 ✓   d 1 000 000
   500 000   e 600 000 ✓
2 56 430 000 56 440 000
   56 400 000 56 500 000
   56 000 000 57 000 000
3 5 5
4

5 375 000	9 989 000	1 241 000	1 000 000
5 380 000	9 990 000	1 240 000	1 000 000
5 400 000	10 000 000	1 200 000	1 000 000
5 000 000	10 000 000	1 000 000	1 000 000

5 94 999 85 000
6 604 503 600 000 497

2.6 Converting kilograms and grams

1 1000
2 (a) kg (b) g (c) kg
   (d) g   (e) kg (f) g
3 (a) 307 000
   (b) 17 000
   (c) 6000
   (d) 72 025
   (e) 43 004
   (f) 46 798
4 (a) > (b) = (c) <
   (d) > (e) > (f) >
5 (a) B (b) B (c) A
6 (a) 2500 × 4 = 10 000 (g) = 10 (kg)
   (b) 8 × 620 = 4960 (kg) No.
   (c) 5000 ÷ 25 = 200 (boxes)
7 (a) ✗ (b) ✓ (c) ✗
8 46 − (46 − 26) × 2 = 6 (kg)

2.7 Litres and millilitres (1)

1 (a) large litres
   (b) 1000
2 Accept either of the following:
   A + B + C 400 + 500 + 100 = 1000 (ml)
   A + D 400 + 600 = 1000 (ml)
3 (a) litres   (b) litres
   (c) millilitres (d) millilitres
   (e) millilitres (f) millilitres
   (g) millilitres
4 (a) 2000   (b) 800 000
   (c) 82   (d) 50 000
   (e) 2.6   (f) 30 3
5 (a) 2000 − 400 = 1600 (ml)
   (b) 2000 ÷ 8 = 250 (ml)

6 (a) B (b) D (c) C (d) D
7 (375 + 11 000) ÷ 25 = 455 (ml)

2.8 Litres and millilitres (2)

1 (a) E (b) C (c) B (d) A (e) D
2 (a) millilitres litres
   (b) 1   (c) 4   (d) 13 000
   (e) 12   (f) 10   (g) 5500
   (h) 23   (i) 4567 (j) 56 10
   (k) 10 700
3 (a) 70 l > 7 l > 5970 ml > 5900 ml > 600 ml
   (b) 200 ml < 260 ml < 2 l < 2060 ml < 20 l
4 (a) 350 × 10 × 16 = 56 000 (ml) = 56 (litres)
   (b) 625 ÷ 5 × 8 = 1000 (ml) = 1 (litre)
5 (a) 1000
   (b) 500
   (c) 250 750 1500
   (d) 200 400 1200

Chapter 2 test

1 (a) 4   (b) 36   (c) 30
   (d) 910   (e) 200   (f) 210
   (g) 560   (h) 40   (i) 724
2 (a) 6448 (b) 7189
   (c) 17 012 (d) 26 r 40
3 (a) 4000 (b) 3295
   (c) 13 824 (d) 888
4 (a) third tens hundreds sixth ten thousands hundred thousands ninth millions ten millions hundred millions
   (b) nine million, twenty-five thousand 9 25
   (c) seventy million, seven hundred thousand 70 700
   (d) three million, eighty thousand, six hundred and four 3080 604
   (e) 300 003 three hundred thousand and three
   (f) 4 034 020
   (g) 1 020 000
   (h) 660 000 000
   (i) 90
   (j) 20 350
   (k) 8300
   (l) 3 litres 400 millilitres < 6 litres < 7080 millilitres < 10 litres 7 millilitres
   (m) 5000
   (n) 300 000
5 (a) C (b) A (c) A (d) B A B B
   (e) C (f) C

Answers

6 (a) 330 − 98 = 232
  (b) Divisor: 98 ÷ (6 + 1) = 14
      Dividend: 14 × 6 = 84
  (c) (78 − 31) × 4 = 188

(d) 23 × 105 ÷ 30 = 80 r 15
7 (a) 18 000 ÷ 300 = 60 (bottles)
  (b) (60 + 40) × 50 = 5000 (kg)
  (c) 74 000 × 3 + 12 000 = 234 000 (kg)

(d) 1 m = 100 cm so (30 000 × 600) ÷ (50 × 50) = 7200 (slates)
(e) (300 − 40) × 5 = 1300 (ml)
    40 × 5 = 200 (ml)

Chapter 3 Dividing by 2-digit numbers

3.1 Speed, time and distance (1)

1 (a) ✓ (b) ✗ (c) ✓ (d) ✓ (e) ✓
2 14 km/h 900 m/min 20 m/s
3 km/h km/min m/min m/min
4 100 m/min 120 m/min 125 m/min 130 m/min Tom
5 (a) 800 ÷ 8 = 100 (m/min)
  (b) 800 ÷ 5 = 160 (km/h)
6 Accept any approximation near to 5 m/s

3.2 Speed, time and distance (2)

1 Time = Distance ÷ Speed
  Speed = Distance ÷ Time
2 (a) Jim faster
  (b) Joanne faster
3

Speed	Time	Distance
84 m/min	6 min	504 m
7 km/h	**17 h**	119 km
118 m/min	8 min	**944 m**

4 (a) Samantha
  (b) Distance between office and home: 700 × 30 = 21 000 (m) = 21 (km)
      Distance between home and school: 16 ÷ 2 = 8 (km)
  (c) (18 + 27) × 8 = 360 (km)
  (d) (28 − 4 − 2) × 100 = 2200 (m)
5 Linda Appropriate working should be shown.

3.3 Dividing 2-digit or 3-digit numbers by a 2-digit number (1)

1 (a) 3   (b) 2   (c) 3   (d) 3
  (e) 30   (f) 20   (g) 30   (h) 30
  (i) 30   (j) 2   (k) 3   (l) 3
  (m) 3   (n) 2   (o) 3   (p) 3
2 (a) 23 s 4 23 s 4 4 92 7 less 4 remainder 7
  (b) 63 s 8 63 s 8 8 504 13 less 8 remainder 13
3 8 r 6 3 r 36 6 5 r 7 4 r 51 7 r 6
4 the sheep Its speed (13 m/s) is the fastest.
  the cat Its speed (12 m/s) is the second fastest.
  the hippo Its speed (10 m/s) is the slowest
5 (a) 4 coaches 4 × 480 = 1920 (pounds)
  (b) 11 minibuses 11 × 200 = 2200 (pounds)
  (c) 3 × 480 + 2 × 200 = 1840 (pounds) To hire 3 coaches and 2 minibuses. Also accept answers that suggest hiring 4 coaches as they are cheaper than 11 minibuses.

3.4 Dividing 2-digit or 3-digit numbers by a 2-digit number (2)

1 (b) 8 8 504 too big
      7 7 441 39 less 7
  (c) 4 4 372 too big
      3 3 279 81 less 3
  (d) 8 8 344 too big
      7 7 301 33 less 7
2 Column method used correctly.
  5 r 60 5 r 41 4 r 53
  3 r 18 8 r 2 7 r 54
3 6 6 7 8 8 9
4 (a) 192 ÷ 32 = 6
  (b) 344 ÷ 43 = 8
  (c) 100 000 ÷ 10 = 10 000
  (d) 100 000 ÷ 100 = 1000
5 (855 − 162) ÷ 63 = 11 (days)
6 (760 + 240) ÷ 25 = 40 (seconds)

3.5 Dividing 2-digit or 3-digit numbers by a 2-digit number (3)

1 (a) 4 4 112 too big 3 3 84 5 less 3
  (b) 4 4 112 too big 3 3 84 2 2 56 24 less 2
  (c) 9 6 7
  (d) 8 7 7
  (e) 7 6 7
  (f) 9 9 9
2 4 2 8 r 21 8 r 12 7 r 20 9 r 28

3 (a) 384 ÷ 48 = 8
  (b) 413 ÷ 59 = 7
  (c) 960 − 42 × 22 = 36
4 1000 − 130 = 870
  870 ÷ 130 = 6 (times) r 90
5 (a) 322 ÷ 63 = 5 r 7
  (b) 114 ÷ 16 = 7 r 2
  (c) 213 ÷ 22 = 9 r 15

3.6 Dividing multi-digit numbers by a 2-digit number (1)

1 (a) 120 240 120 10 7 17
  (b) 1900 2280 1900 50 228 6 56
2 25 16 r 20 12 r 20
3 Appropriate working shown.
  76 r 11 43 r 10 30 r 9
  23 r 10 18 r 45 12 r 3
4 (a) 3 r 30; 6 r 25; 9 r 20;
      12 r 15; 15 r 10; 18 r 5;
      21; 23 r 30; 26 r 25
  (b) 1, 2 or 3   4, 5, 6, 7, 8 or 9
5 (a) 2 tens 10
  (b) 1 7
  (c) 3
  (d) 3
6 516 ÷ 26 = 19 r 22
  990 ÷ 38 = 26 r 2

3.7 Dividing multi-digit numbers by a 2-digit number (2)

1 33 r 20 83 r 8
  166 r 8 125
2 Column method used correctly.
  51 r 53 64 r 8 92 r 32
  104 r 8 192 r 8 384 r 8
3 Appropriate working shown.
  3806 580 1000
  1212 1000 15 800
4 (a) 84 × 14 ÷ 49 = 24
  (b) (999 + 99) ÷ 18 = 61
  (c) 15 × 15 ÷ 225 = 1
5 (a) A (b) D
6 1215 ÷ 45 = 27
  1789 ÷ 38 = 47 r 3

Answers

3.8 Practice and exercise
1. (a) 700 (b) 10 (c) 0 (d) 200
   (e) 400 (f) 96 (g) 300 (h) 120
   (i) 4 (j) 4 (k) 3 (l) 100
2. (a) 266 200
   (b) 103 (Check: 32 × 103 = 3296)
   (c) 60 r 31 (Check: 42 × 60 + 31 = 2551)
3. Appropriate working shown.
   (a) 576 (b) 6400 (c) 24 427
   (d) 10 (e) 97 (f) 3
4. (a) 4736 − 4736 ÷ 16 = 4440
   (b) (565 + 191) ÷ 18 = 42
5. (a) 5 50 51
   (b) 4
   (c) 5 101 0 4 99 90
6. 44 hours
   11 hours
   5 hours and 30 minutes
   2 hours and 45 minutes
   2 hours
   48 minutes

Chapter 3 test
1. (a) 12 (b) 780 (c) 90 (d) 40
   (e) 1200 (f) 2970 (g) 31 (h) 50
   (i) 24 (j) 6 (k) 43 (l) 802
   (m) 4 (n) 1200 (o) 76 (p) 8
2. Column method used correctly
   (a) 46 828
   (b) 170 100
   (c) 205
   (d) 609 (Check: 609 × 28 = 17 052)
3. (a) 96 (b) 12 120 (c) 17 (d) 3026
4. (a) 2 610 000
   (b) 2 tens
   (c) 3 hundreds 2 48
   (d) 4, 5, 6, 7, 8 or 9
   (e) 3 1 or 2
5. (a) B (b) C (c) C (d) C (e) B
6. (a) 504 ÷ (84 ÷ 3) = 18 (days)
   (b) 3 × 60 + 310 = 490 (sets)
   (c) (10 + 5) × 3 = 45 (km)
   (d) 4500 − 125 × 24 = 1500 (bottles)
7. 140 km/h 251 km/h 805 km/h

Chapter 4 Comparing fractions, improper fractions and mixed numbers

4.1 Comparing fractions (1)
1. (a) 3 6 less (b) greater numerator
2. $\frac{3}{6} > \frac{2}{6}$ $\frac{5}{9} = \frac{5}{9}$ $\frac{7}{10} > \frac{3}{10}$
3. Any 3 blocks coloured, any 7 blocks coloured, any 1 block coloured
   $\frac{1}{8} < \frac{3}{8} < \frac{7}{8}$
4. (a) < (b) > (c) <
   (d) > (e) < (f) <
   (g) > > (h) < < (i) > <
5. $\frac{1}{9} < \frac{2}{9} < \frac{3}{9} < \frac{5}{9} < \frac{7}{9}$
6. $\frac{79}{80} > \frac{50}{80} > \frac{30}{80} > \frac{18}{80} > \frac{1}{80}$
7. $\frac{39}{39} - \frac{8}{39} - \frac{10}{39} - \frac{11}{39} = \frac{10}{39}$

4.2 Comparing fractions (2)
1. (a) less
   (b) less
   (c) smaller denominator
2. (a) $\frac{1}{3}$ $\frac{1}{4}$ $\frac{1}{5}$ $\frac{1}{8}$ (b) $\frac{1}{3} > \frac{1}{4} > \frac{1}{5} > \frac{1}{8}$
   (c) smaller smaller
3. (a) < (b) >
   (c) > (d) >
   (e) < (f) <
   (g) < < (h) > >
4. $\frac{1}{81} < \frac{1}{36} < \frac{1}{27} < \frac{1}{18} < \frac{1}{9}$
5. $\frac{1}{10} > \frac{1}{20} > \frac{1}{40} > \frac{1}{70} > \frac{1}{100}$
6. 30 ÷ 5 = 6 (pieces)
   20 ÷ 4 = 5 (pieces) Alex takes more

4.3 Comparing fractions (3)
1. (a) $\frac{3}{4}$ $\frac{6}{16}$ $\frac{2}{4}$ $\frac{2}{4}$ $\frac{3}{6}$ $\frac{2}{6}$ $\frac{4}{8}$ $\frac{5}{8}$
   (b) 4, 5 and 7
   (c) larger smaller
2. (a) < (b) > (c) < (d) <
   (e) > (f) > (g) > >
3. (a) 7 $\frac{4}{15}$
   (b) $\frac{5}{13}$ $\frac{4}{13}$ $\frac{1}{13}$
   (c) $\frac{1}{5}$ $\frac{2}{5}$ m $\frac{4}{5}$ $\frac{2}{5}$ m
   (d) 18
4. $\frac{5}{999} < \frac{5}{656} < \frac{5}{123} < \frac{5}{50} < \frac{5}{11}$
5. $\frac{4}{7} > \frac{2}{7} > \frac{2}{11}$
6. $\frac{9}{15}$m $> \frac{9}{20}$m
   The snail climbed higher.
7. Tom drank more. Hint:
   The amount Tom has left: $1 - \frac{3}{4} = \frac{1}{4}$.
   The amount Mary has left: $1 - \frac{2}{3} = \frac{1}{3}$
   $\frac{1}{3} > \frac{1}{4}$

4.4 Comparing fractions (4)
1. (a) Answer should mention that $\frac{1}{6}$ and $\frac{2}{12}$ of the same amount are the same.
   (b) Both Lee and Ming are correct. Lee is correct because one basket split into 6 equals $\frac{1}{6}$. If two baskets are shared between 12 monkeys, each basket can be considered to be split between 12 monkeys ($\frac{1}{12}$) and, as there are two baskets, each monkey has $\frac{2}{12}$.
   Ming is also correct because $\frac{1}{6}$ and $\frac{2}{12}$ are equal.
2. (a) 4 8 (b) 10 8
   (c) 2 10 (d) 4 99
   (e) 36 3 72 3 6
   (f) 33 300
3. (a) $\frac{1}{4}$ (b) $\frac{2}{6}$ $\frac{3}{9}$ $\frac{4}{12}$ (answer may vary)
   (c) 6 (d) $\frac{1}{4}$
4. (a) $\frac{4}{12} + \frac{6}{12} = \frac{10}{12}$ (m)
   (b) $1 - \frac{10}{12} = \frac{2}{12}$ (m)
5. $\frac{3}{7} = \frac{6}{14}$ $\frac{6}{14} > \frac{4}{14}$ Sam walked faster
6. $\frac{3}{4}$ of the pizzas Two methods of drawing:

Answers

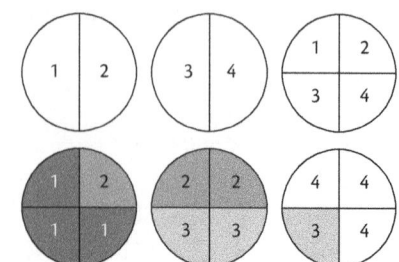

4.5 Improper fractions and mixed numbers

1. $\frac{3}{8}$ $\frac{8}{8}$ or 1 $\frac{9}{8}$ or $1\frac{1}{8}$

2. Proper fractions: $\frac{7}{12}$ $\frac{79}{100}$ $\frac{181}{365}$
   Improper fractions: $\frac{5}{3}$ $\frac{3}{2}$ $\frac{13}{12}$ $\frac{19}{6}$
   Mixed numbers: $7\frac{1}{18}$ $1\frac{4}{5}$ $30\frac{1}{2}$ $5\frac{1}{4}$

3.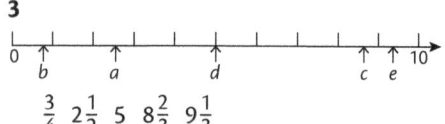
   $\frac{3}{4}$ $2\frac{1}{2}$ 5 $8\frac{2}{3}$ $9\frac{1}{3}$

4. (a) ✓ (b) ✓ (c) ✗ (d) ✓
   (e) ✗ (f) ✗ (g) ✓ (h) ✓

5. (a) $\frac{7}{3}$ (b) $\frac{13}{8}$ (c) $\frac{61}{9}$ (d) $\frac{2377}{39}$

6. (a) $4\frac{3}{7}$ (b) $6\frac{5}{8}$ (c) 9 (d) $3\frac{7}{30}$

7.

Quantity	As decimal	As mixed number	As improper fraction
2 m 10 cm	2.1 m	$2\frac{1}{10}$ m	$\frac{21}{10}$ m
90 minutes	1.5 h	$1\frac{1}{2}$ h	$\frac{3}{2}$ h
5 kg 200 g	5.2 kg	$5\frac{1}{5}$ kg	$\frac{26}{5}$ kg
1650 ml	1.65 l	$1\frac{65}{100}$ l	$\frac{165}{100}$ l
30 km 200 m	30.2 km	$30\frac{1}{5}$ km	$\frac{151}{5}$ km

8. (a) 0, 1, 2 or 3 (b) 5, 6, 7 or 8

4.6 Adding and subtracting fractions with related denominators (1)

1. $\frac{1}{2} = \frac{3}{6}$ $\frac{2}{5} = \frac{4}{10}$ $\frac{13}{18} = \frac{65}{90}$ $\frac{11}{10} = \frac{110}{100}$ $\frac{17}{20} = \frac{85}{100}$

2. (a) 2 (b) 4 (c) 20 (d) 26 (e) 75
   (f) Any equivalent fraction, for example $\frac{20}{34}$ or $\frac{30}{51}$

3. (a) $\frac{2}{5}$ (b) $\frac{2}{7}$ (c) 1
   (d) $\frac{4}{13}$ (e) $\frac{4}{9}$ (f) $\frac{18}{23}$

4. (b) $\frac{7}{10}$ (c) $\frac{25}{26}$ (d) $1\frac{3}{15}$ or $1\frac{1}{5}$
   (e) $1\frac{8}{35}$ (f) $2\frac{37}{77}$

5. (b) $\frac{1}{9}$ (c) $\frac{7}{22}$ (d) $\frac{5}{14}$ (e) $\frac{9}{150}$ (f) $\frac{19}{90}$

6. (a) $\frac{2}{3} = \frac{6}{9}$ $\frac{6}{9} > \frac{1}{9}$ Jason has more books.
   (b) $\frac{7}{9}$
   (c) $\frac{5}{9}$
   (d) 14 (books)
   Method 1: $\frac{2}{3} + \frac{1}{9} = \frac{6}{9} + \frac{1}{9} = \frac{7}{9}$
   $\frac{1}{9}$ of 18 = 2, so $\frac{7}{9}$ of 18 = 2 × 7 = 14
   Method 2: $\frac{2}{3}$ of 18 = 12, $\frac{1}{9}$ of 18 = 2 and 12 + 2 = 14

7. (a) $\frac{7}{8}$ (b) $\frac{3}{6}$ or $\frac{1}{2}$

8. D
   First express the fractions $\frac{1}{2}$ and $\frac{1}{3}$ with a common denominator, and then add the numerators, i.e., $\frac{1}{2} + \frac{1}{3} = \frac{3}{6} + \frac{2}{6} = \frac{5}{6}$.

4.7 Adding and subtracting fractions with related denominators (2)

1. (a) $\frac{5}{7}$ (b) 0 (c) $\frac{13}{8}$
   (d) $\frac{5}{9}$ (e) $\frac{47}{56}$ (f) $\frac{1}{10}$

2. (a) $1\frac{1}{2}$ (b) $15\frac{3}{7}$ (c) $58\frac{23}{100}$

3. (a) $\frac{2}{3}$ (b) $\frac{13}{15}$ (c) $4\frac{83}{100}$

4. (a) $4\frac{4}{7}$ (b) $2\frac{1}{6}$ (c) $\frac{4}{7}$
   (d) $\frac{25}{99}$ (e) $\frac{22}{25}$ (f) $1\frac{13}{18}$

5. (b) $5\frac{7}{13}$ (c) $\frac{3}{18}$ or $\frac{1}{6}$ (d) $2\frac{1}{12}$

6. $\frac{7}{6}$ or $1\frac{1}{6}$

7. Yes, it would be enough. He would use $7\frac{2}{5}$ m.

8. (a) $9\frac{17}{19}$ (b) $\frac{11}{3} - \frac{25}{9} = \frac{33}{9} - \frac{25}{9} = \frac{8}{9}$

4.8 Multiplying fractions by whole numbers

1. (a) 2 5 10 (b) 2 2 4
   (c) 3 3 9 (d) 1 1 1 1
   (e) 5 5 10 $1\frac{1}{9}$ (f) 4 4 4 $2\frac{2}{5}$

2. (b) $4\frac{1}{6}$ (c) $3\frac{3}{8}$

3. (a) false (b) false (c) true (d) true

4. (a) $\frac{5}{2}$ or $2\frac{1}{2}$ (b) $\frac{9}{10}$
   (c) $41\frac{9}{15}$ or $41\frac{3}{5}$ (d) $146\frac{2}{5}$
   (e) $8\frac{9}{12}$ or $8\frac{3}{4}$ (f) $\frac{13}{100}$

5. Perimeter = 2 × 9 + 2 × $5\frac{1}{2}$ = 18 + 11 = 29 m
   Area = 9 × $5\frac{1}{2}$ = $49\frac{1}{2}$ m²

6. (a) $8\frac{1}{4}$ (hours) (b) $5\frac{1}{2}$ (hours)
   (c) 11 (hours)

7. (a) $39\frac{2}{6}$ or $39\frac{1}{3}$ (b) $14\frac{17}{30}$

Chapter 4 test

1. (a) 120 (b) 30 (c) 307
   (d) $\frac{3}{5}$ (e) $\frac{7}{15}$ (f) $\frac{13}{14}$
   (g) $5\frac{3}{8}$ (h) $\frac{16}{17}$ (i) 21

2. (a) $1\frac{2}{15}$ (b) $\frac{4}{39}$
   (c) $3\frac{13}{48}$ (d) $4\frac{2}{3}$
   (e) $\frac{1}{2}$ (f) $3\frac{2}{9}$
   (g) $24\frac{5}{11}$ (h) $5\frac{13}{18}$

3. (a) 3 segments and 5 segments coloured respectively <
   (b) $\frac{3}{4} = \frac{6}{8} = \frac{9}{12} = \frac{12}{16}$
   (c) $3\frac{1}{4}$ $6\frac{1}{2}$
   (d) 3 $\frac{1}{4}$ $\frac{3}{4}$ $1\frac{1}{2}$

4. (a) > (b) < (c) >
   (d) = (e) < (f) >

5. (a) $\frac{8}{12}$ $\frac{4}{12}$ $\frac{4}{14}$ $\frac{1}{14}$ (b) 1 $\frac{3}{4}$ $\frac{1}{2}$ $\frac{2}{8}$

6. (a) A (b) C

7. (a) Ben
   (b) 7 kg
   (c) (i) $3\frac{9}{10}$ m
       (ii) $4\frac{7}{10}$ m
   (d) (i) $17\frac{7}{10}$ m
       (ii) $11\frac{8}{10}$ m or $11\frac{4}{5}$ m
       (iii) $47\frac{2}{10}$ m or $47\frac{1}{5}$ m

Answers

Chapter 5 Consolidation and enhancement

5.1 Large numbers and rounding (1)

1. (a) 411 000 511 000 900 000 700 000 600 000
   (b) 10 10
   (c) counting
   (d) 1 000 000 2 000 000
   (e) forty-three million, seven thousand and seventy 43 007 70
   (f) 587
2. (a) four million, two hundred and four thousand, three hundred and twenty-two
   (b) ten million, twenty-five thousand and ninety
   (c) twenty million, two hundred
   (d) one billion, ten million, one hundred and one thousand and ten
3. (a) 59 508 880 (b) 400 854 500
   (c) 2 616 329 (d) 110 409 011
4. (a) C (b) A D (c) B
5. (a) < (b) < (c) >
   (d) < (e) < (f) >
6. 36 890 000 36 900 000 40 000 000
   98 970 000 99 000 000 100 000 000
   109 830 000 109 800 000 110 000 000
7. (a) 853 000 850 000
   (b) 300 058 300 000
   (c) 853 000 835 000 583 000 538 000 385 000 358 000
   (d) 803 050 805 030 305 080 308 050 508 030 503 080
8. 5 499 999 4 500 000

5.2 Large numbers and rounding (2)

1. (a) hundred thousands eleventh
   (b) 4 000 444
   (c) 9
   (d) 305 002 001
   (e) 206 000 060
   (f) 1 000 008 003
   (g) 8 millions million
   (h) millions thousands 6 993 000
   (i) 258 499 999 257 500 000
2. (a) A (b) C (c) C (d) B (e) A
3. (a) 769 010 000 769 000 000 800 000 000
   (b) 5 210 180 000 5 211 000 000 5 300 000 000
   (c) 1 094 500 000 1 094 000 000 1 000 000 000
4. (a) any digit from 5 to 9
   (b) 4
   (c) 5
   (d) any digit from 0 to 9
   (e) 4
5. 555 321

5.3 Four operations of numbers

1. ✗ ✓
   When working on a number sentence involving four operations, perform all the multiplication and division first and then perform the addition and subtraction.
2. (b) 600 (c) 165 (d) 800
3. (a) 42 (b) 26 460
   (c) 301 (d) 671
4. (a) D (b) D (c) A
5. (a) (2000 ÷ 4 − 323) × 5 = 885
   (b) (600 ÷ 50 + 76) × 23 = 2024
6. (a) Any number except 0
   (b) 2
   (c) Any number except 0
   (d) 4

5.4 Properties of whole number operations (1)

1. (a) 88 (b) 330
   (c) 34 (d) 76
   (e) 80 (f) 89
   Property of subtraction used in (b) (d) (f)
2. (b) 132 32 − 21
   (c) 89
   (d) 19 + 919
   (e) a b c +
3. (a) 400 (b) 303
   (c) 245 (d) 4820
   (e) 461 (f) 530
4. Method 1: 1600 − 520 − 480 = 600 (bikes)
   Method 2: 1600 − (520 + 480) = 600 (bikes)
5. (a) 190 165 − (b) 42 − 27
6. (a) 200 (b) 3073 (c) 450
   (d) 590 (e) 144 (f) 4000
   (g) 790

5.5 Properties of whole number operations (2)

1. (a) 17 ÷ 25 (b) 25 × 4
   (c) 128 × (d) 17 ÷ ×
2. (a) 7 (b) 25 (c) 25
   (d) 10 (e) 10 (f) 120
3. (a) B (b) C (c) A
4. (a) Method 1: 240 ÷ 12 ÷ 2 = 10 (pupils)
   Method 2: 240 ÷ (12 × 2) = 10 (pupils)
   (b) 240 ÷ 4 ÷ 6 = 10 (pounds)
5. (a) 12 (b) 84

5.6 Properties of whole number operations (3)

1. 3 3 3 3 3 3
   multiplied divided quotient
   division × ÷
2. (b) ✓ (c) ✗ (d) ✗ (e) ✓
3. (a) divided by 8
   (b) unchanged / the same
   (c) 71
   (d) 1150 10 20
4. (a) 20
   (b) 16 r 100 (Check: 170 × 16 + 100 = 2820)
   (c) 70 r 20
   (d) 70 r 200 (Check: 900 × 70 + 200 = 63 200)
5. (a) 48 (b) 125 (c) 48
   (d) 80 (e) 13 (f) 10
6. (a) B (b) D (c) D
7. (a) It is increased by 40
   (b) It is decreased by 10
   (c) 4800
   (d) Yes, it remains unchanged.

5.7 Roman numerals including thousands

1.

Roman symbol	Value in digit
I	1
V	5
X	10
L	50
C	100
D	500
M	1000

2. 13 56
   95 104
   400 600
   1900 2007

3.

Roman numeral	Year
MM	2000
MD	1500
MDLII	1552
MCM	1900
MCMXCV	1995
MMXVI	2016

Answers

4

Year	Roman numeral
2010	MMX
2011	MMXI
2012	MMXII
2013	MMXIII
2014	MMXIV
2015	MMXV
2020	MMXX
2100	MMC

5.8 Solving problems in statistics

1 Choir   Science and ICT   10
No, because it is not clear if a pupil could participate in one or more than one school club.

2 (a) 42 cm
(b) 1st place: Bob, 2nd place: Alvin, 3rd place: Linda, 4th place: Peter, and 5th place: May.

3 (a) 5400
(b) Line graph drawn accurately. For example:

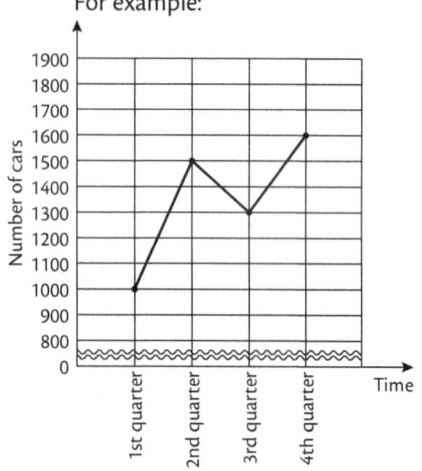

(c) (i) ✗   (ii) ✗   (iii) ✗   (iv) ✓

4 (a)

	Usage (m³)	Unit price	Charge
used	79	120p	9480p
Used water disposal	73	227p	16 571p
		Total charge	26 051p

(b) 79 m³ or 79 000 litres
(c) £260.51
(d) Answer will vary

Chapter 5 test

1 (a) 920   (b) 390   (c) 802
(d) 96   (e) 318   (f) 60
(g) 88   (h) 160   (i) 48
(j) $\frac{19}{30}$ (k) 32   (l) 9100

2 Column method used correctly.
(a) 80 r 400   (b) 37 620   (c) 30 r 2200

3 (a) 4   (b) 3240   (c) 2240
(d) 750   (e) 40 572   (f) 281 880
(g) $3\frac{8}{35}$ (h) $\frac{2}{9}$ (i) $1\frac{25}{28}$

4 (a) thousands   1000
(b) 120   4   5   6
(c) $\frac{5}{6}$
(d) 6   7
(e) 560 000
(f) 10 700 000   10 800 000
(g) $\frac{6}{100}$ or 0.06
(h) 16   2400 Answer may vary, for example 240 ÷ 8 or 120 ÷ 4
(i) 128
(j) 17 1000
(k) 409 999
(l) 15
(m) 6
(n) 3000

5 (a) ✓   (b) ✗   (c) ✗   (d) ✗   (e) ✗

6 (a) D   (b) C   (c) A   (d) A   (e) B

7 (a) 150 × 2 + 150 = 450
(b) (48 − 16) × 25 ÷ 8 = 100
(c) 125 × 8 + 12 = 1012

8 (a) 780 × 3 + 66 = 2406 (books)
(b) (i) (200 + 180) ÷ 4 = 95 (km per hour)
(ii) 315 ÷ (95 + 10) = 3 (hours)
(c) (12 × 2 + 12) × 3 + 7 = 115 (footballs)
(d) Red pens: (244 + 12) ÷ (7 + 1) = 32 (boxes)
Green pens: 32 × 7 − 12 = 212 (boxes)
(e) (i) 560
(ii) Line graph accurately drawn. For example:

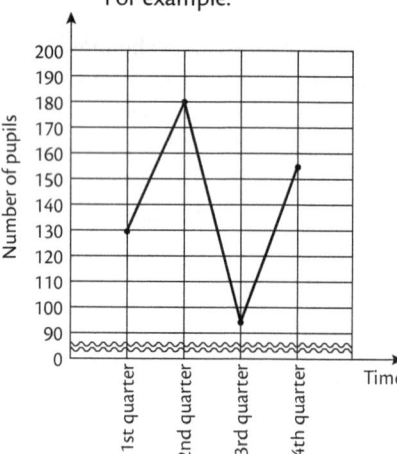

(iii) No. The total number of pupils divided by 6 year groups could be an estimate number of pupils for each year group, which is around or less than 100 pupils. (Answer may vary.)

Notes

Notes

Notes

Notes